CRITICAL PRAISE

"The author crams a wealth of anecdotes, stories and family history, all of which contributes to the picture of a consecrated religious woman, complex in her utter simplicity . . . an authoritative portrait, which considers criticism as well as praise." —*Publishers Weekly*

". . . offers the kind of glimpses that could come only from a co-worker who has had Mother Teresa's confidence for some 30 years . . . a story that holds up well." —The New York *Times Book Review*

"This totally enthralling book by Eileen Egan . . . makes unmistakably clear the impact one woman and her mission work have had on opening the world's eyes to the destitute situation created by overpopulation." —*Arkansas Democrat*

". . . an interesting biography . . ." —*National Review*

"It is the way Egan captures Mother Teresa's vision that makes this book so moving . . . [she] masterfully shows how the power of meekness works." —*Pleasure Hunt Magazine*

"The book is no simple biography. A thorough and exhaustive reference work written from a Catholic viewpoint . . . Egan treats the most horribly diseased indigent with as much dignity as she does world leaders, and this objectivity serves the book well." —Grand Rapids *Press*

". . . filled with insightful facts and interesting statements by people who came in contact with Mother Teresa." —UPI

"[Given] the author's firsthand knowledge and admiration of her subject and their 30 year friendship, which is a tremendous asset to the book, one might fear Egan's objectivity would be compromised. But that is not so . . . this outstanding 'vision' is highly recommended." —*Best Sellers*

". . . comprehensive, fact-filled, unemotional but compassionate biography . . . Egan skillfully weaves facts into the story in a natural way . . . [she] deserves the highest praise. Her book stands on its own factual record, on its details . . ." —*National Catholic Reporter*

"Here is a biography which deserves to be read by everyone." —Macon *Telegraph & News*

"The story will prove uplifting to many." —Charleston *Evening Post*

". . . the first genuine biography of this unusual woman." —Boston *Herald*

"Here at last is a first-rate look at the world-famous Yugoslavian nun and the religious community she founded in Calcutta . . . In these jam-packed pages marked by thorough research there is more than just the story of a life."
—Catholic New York

". . . excellent biography . . . luminous and exhaustive . . ."
—Commonweal

". . . revealing . . . in-depth . . . It is must reading."
—The Sunday Oklahoman

"A woman of great faith herself, Egan helps us get the sense of a whole life lived in the certainty of things not seen." *—The Review of Books*

"[a] thoughtful, intelligent, and straightforward account of the life and work of Mother Teresa . . . presented in a low key, neatly journalistic style . . . just enough facts to make the case and just enough anecdotal detail to expose the heart and soul of the vision and the visionary."
—Religion Teachers Journal

SUCH A VISION OF THE STREET

Mother Teresa-The Spirit and the Work

Eileen Egan

Complete and Unabridged

IMAGE BOOKS

A Division of Doubleday & Company, Inc.
Garden City, New York

Image Book edition published October 1986 by
special arrangement with Doubleday & Company, Inc.

Unless otherwise credited, photos courtesy of author
and/or Bojaxhiu family

For

Mary Agnes O'Sullivan-Bere

and

Jeremiah Egan

my parents

Library of Congress Cataloging in Publication Data

Egan, Eileen.
Such a vision of the street.

Includes index.
1. Teresa, Mother, 1910– . 2. Missionaries of
Charity—History. 3. Nuns—India—Calcutta—Biography.
4. Calcutta (India)—Biography. I. Title.
BX4406.5.Z8E38 1986 271'.97 [B] 86-4397
ISBN 0-385-17491-8

Printed in the United States of America

Contents

1

The Strands of a Life

At the shrine of the goddess Kali in Calcutta is a caravanserai. It is ivory in color and from its roof rise eight bulbous, fluted domes topped by delicate spires. The structure, in the shape of a quadrangle, is built around a large inner courtyard after the manner of the traditional *serai* or hostel for merchants and pilgrims. Such hostels marked the caravan routes of the Middle East as well as the silk route to Asia from ancient times and served the merchants with their spices, dyes, rare woods, and precious silks. In later centuries, the caravanserais served the pilgrims who journeyed from great distances to Mecca. This hostel was originally for pilgrims. It was built by a generous Hindu to shelter the poorest pilgrims who came to make their *puja,* their act of worship to Kali, goddess of death, destruction, and purification. Kali's black-visaged image with its extended tongue and necklace of skulls stands nearby under the squat silver dome of her temple.

Through the caravanserai doors, outlined with the fanciful scalloped tracery of the Moghul arch, cadaverous human beings were being carried at intervals. Nearby, on a tributary of the Hooghly River, through which flowed the holy waters of the Ganges, were the burning ghats where dead Hindus were placed for cremation on funeral pyres. It was the least likely place in which to find a Catholic nun, yet it was through those doors that Mother Teresa led me. The pilgrims' inn had become a hostel for pilgrims of the ultimate moment, men and women, barely alive, picked up from the alleyways and gutters of a scourged city. The year was 1955, eight years after the partition of the subcontinent of India along religious lines had given rise to an unstoppable cascade of refugees across newly made borders. Over four million of them had inundated truncated Bengal and one million had brought their destitution to its capital city, Calcutta.

The small unknown woman was in her midforties, vigorous and quick of movement. She was dressed in the rough cotton sari of the poor. It was white with three blue stripes and was also wrapped securely around her head. The only sign that she was a nun was a small black crucifix attached by a safety pin over her left shoulder. Her hands and feet were large for a woman little over five feet tall. Her eyes were brown with tawny lights, and her skin, after an uninterrupted stay of twenty-six years in India, was ochred by the sun. She could have been a woman from the Punjab or Kashmir. Actually, she had originated in a tiny country in southeastern Europe, little known and long isolated from the rest of the continent.

My keenest memory of my first visit to this house of the dying was a sari-clad woman leaning over the skeletonized remnant of a man. As I stood frozen with fear, knowing that every disease known to humankind was in that hall, she stroked his brown, sticklike arm and murmured consoling words in Bengali. The same woman, barely twenty-five years later, was the focus of all eyes as she mounted the platform of the Aula Magna of the University of Oslo in Norway. On December 10, 1979, before a king and a hall filled with academics, diplomats, politicians, members of the armed forces in full uniform, and an immense press corps, she received what has been termed the ultimate accolade, the Nobel Prize for Peace. Her white cotton sari shone under the spotlights as she took her place in front of the sunrise mural done by Edvard Munch. In the intervening time, the world had recognized the work of Mother Teresa, which had gone out from Calcutta to help the poorest of the poor, the suffering, the forsaken, the dying, and the disinherited of the earth.

The media of the world searched for their most telling encomiums on the announcement of the Nobel Award. The New York *Times* commented editorially that Mother Teresa was a "secular saint," undoubtedly considering it the very highest praise. The fact that Mother Teresa's concerns were not secular was indicated at Oslo when, on acceptance of the Nobel Prize, she asked everyone to join her in prayer. The prayer, already distributed to everyone in the Aula Magna, including the press, was the peace prayer attributed to everyone's saint, Francis, the poor man of Assisi. About eight hundred voices intoned in unison: "Lord, make me a channel of Your peace; where there is hatred, let me sow love; where there is injury, pardon; . . . where there is despair, hope . . . Grant that I may not so much seek to be consoled as to console, to be loved as to love, for it is in giving that we receive, it is in pardoning that we are pardoned, and it is in dying that we are born to eternal life."

Communal prayer was certainly a new departure for the Nobel ceremony. Another departure was the lack of a ceremonial banquet. Mother Teresa had accepted the Nobel Peace Prize because through it the poor of the world were being recognized. From the Aula Magna, we were directed to a simple reception where the Nobel Committee along with Mother Teresa could greet the guests in person. The funds set aside for the banquet, six thousand dollars, were donated to the poor in Calcutta. Mother

Teresa explained that this amount would allow her to feed hundreds of the poor for a year.

In the Aula Magna in Oslo, the various strands of Mother Teresa's life came together in the guests invited from Skopje, Yugoslavia, from Calcutta, India, from Palermo, Sicily, from various countries in Europe and from the United States.

Skopje, where Mother Teresa was born on August 26, 1910, was represented by its Catholic bishop, Nikola Prela. Though a citizen of Yugoslavia, Bishop Prela announced proudly, "I also am Albanian," identifying with Mother Teresa's ancestry and with the sizable Albanian minority in Yugoslavia particularly in the province of Kosovo. Besides Mother Teresa, there were two other sari-clad figures in the hall, invited by the Nobel Committee to be Mother Teresa's companions from Calcutta. They were Sister Agnes and Sister Gertrude, the first two young women to brave the streets of Calcutta with Mother Teresa in 1949. They thus became the forerunners of a new religious family in the Catholic Church, a family known as the Missionaries of Charity.

From Palermo, Sicily, came the only surviving member of Mother Teresa's immediate family, her brother, Lazar Bojaxhiu. Fleeing Albania after the defeat of the Albanian army in 1939 he made his way to Italy where he married an Italian woman. He had brought his only child, a daughter, also married to an Italian. From England came Mrs. Ann Blaikie, representing another important strand in Mother Teresa's life, that of the lay Co-Workers, who share the vision of Mother Teresa and the Missionaries of Charity, but adapt it to their life as lay persons. Ann Blaikie, for many years a resident of Calcutta while her late husband represented a business concern there, was in Oslo as head, or International Link, of the loosely organized International Association of Co-Workers. By her side was Jacqueline de Decker of Belgium, able to move about only with the help of complicated steel braces. Although already a lay missionary in India, she had wanted to join Mother Teresa in 1948, but her desire came to nothing when illness overtook her and forced her to return to her native country. The contact with Mother Teresa though had never been broken. Jacqueline de Decker became the link with Sick and Suffering Co-Workers around the world. Each suffering Co-Worker was given the name of a Missionary of Charity with whom the suffering person could be united in prayer and with whose work the housebound person could feel a daily spiritual involvement. Co-Workers were also invited from Sweden, Denmark, Finland, Holland, Germany, France, Switzerland, Italy, Malta, and this writer from the United States.

Even in the rush of events surrounding the Nobel Award, the evening Nobel Lecture, as distinct from the acceptance speech, the services at the Lutheran and Catholic cathedrals, the torchlight procession through the icy, starry Norwegian night, Mother Teresa found time to be sequestered with the Co-Workers. They met in prayer and thanksgiving for what Mother Teresa called the real Nobel gift, the recognition of the poor of the world. She discussed with the Co-Workers the "shared vision" of service to the poor and how it could be incarnated in places where there were no Missionaries of Charity in whose tasks they could have a part. The only absent strand was that of the Missionaries of Charity Brothers, the male branch of the Missionaries of Charity founded in 1963.

The Skopje from which Bishop Nikola Prela had journeyed was not the Skopje in which Mother Teresa was born in 1910. At her birth it was still in the Ottoman Empire, part of the tongue of land which represented the farthest thrust of that empire into Europe. Skopje then was a town of about twenty-five thousand persons. The bishop came from a city that had become part of Yugoslavia after the First World War. After the Second World War, it became the capital of Macedonia, one of the six federated republics of Yugoslavia. A hub of transport and industry, it was growing toward a population of half a million people and, though far behind Belgrade and Zagreb, was one of the leading cities of Yugoslavia, with its own university.

A devastating earthquake in 1963, in which one hundred fifty thousand people were left homeless, brought the little-known name of Skopje to world attention.

The marks of five centuries of Turkish rule and of Islamic presence were strong in the Skopje in which Mother Teresa spent her girlhood. A Turkish citadel marked it as an important center of Turkish rule. Towering minarets pierced the skyline and from the tiny balconies on the towers muezzins sent out calls to prayer to bring worshipers to scores of mosques on ancient streets. In one corner of the town was a busy oriental bazaar. There were signs, too, of a more ancient history. Skopje, earlier known as Liskub, or Uskub, was continuously inhabited from pre-Christian times. A bridge over the Vardar River was said to have been rebuilt in the fifteenth century on the foundations of a bridge constructed when the area was a Roman province. Byzantium left its impress with a large proportion of Orthodox believers grouped around richly ornamented churches. As Mother Teresa took her origins at a meeting place of diverse religions and cultures, it was undoubtedly easier for her to cross cultural boundaries and to view the externals of Western Christianity as no more than trappings.

The Catholic community in which Mother Teresa grew up was the smallest, hardly more than a tenth of the Albanian people. Catholic Albanians possessed a strong sense of identity that is forged by a tenacious resistance. To state that Mother Teresa is of Albanian origin might not seem to have much significance for a life lived away from her own people, a life in which she chose another citizenship, and eventually came to say,

"The people of the world are my people." There is, however, an ineradicable aspect of Albanian identity deeply imbedded in her character. It throws a vivid light on the reality of a rare woman.

It is called *besa* and will be illustrated later on.

The strength of Albanian identity can be seen as it lives on in enclaves of Albanians who fled before the Turkish occupation. One such enclave occupies the Piana degli Albanesi near Palermo in Sicily. When the Albanian hero Scanderbeg died in 1468, and with him a twenty-five year resistance to Ottoman rule, a stream of Albanians fled across the Adriatic to find refuge in Italy. They were committed to preserving their Christian faith. Many put down roots in Sicily. What is astonishing is not that a persecuted people has flourished in a hospitable setting, but that its members have preserved over time a distinctive cultural identity. In their churches and in their liturgy, their priests conserve an archaic form of Albanian celebrated in the Byzantine rite they brought with them. Among themselves, they communicate in a form of the Albanian tongue called Arbaresh. The people themselves are referred to as Arbaresh. On a visit to the Piana degli Albanesi, I met priests wearing the stovepipe headpieces with flowing veil as worn by Orthodox priests, though these Albanians were in union with Rome. They showed me their churches with bright icons memorializing saints from their own history, including St. Demetrius, the Great Martyr, as well as those commonly venerated in Italy. In visiting households, I found that the most beautiful possessions seemed to be women's costumes fashioned in the mode of dress of fifteenth-century Albania. While in the daily work life of their own communities and surrounding towns the inhabitants of Piana degli Albanesi were indistinguishable from their neighbors, in their homes they treasured a separate cultural existence. This culture bloomed on Sicilian streets on festival days when the women and girls appeared in dresses of the most exotically brilliant colors. Their embroidered bodices gave way to flaring skirts that touched the floor, and these were topped by fanciful aprons. In 1968, their festive costumes were seen in St. Peter's Basilica when Albanians of Piana degli Albanesi, with their bishops and priests, marked the five hundredth anniversary of the death of Scanderbeg. Gathered with them were men and women of Albanian origin from many countries, including the United States.

The priests of Piana degli Albanesi related that the origins of their people were in Illyria. This was the name of a whole area of the Balkan Peninsula in the times of ancient Rome. The Romans, who had captured the last Illyrian king, Gentius, in 167 B.C., subjugated the area and integrated it into their empire as the province of Illyria. Despite the division of Illyria between Byzantine and Rome, despite invasions by Slavs, Bulgars, and Serbs, despite the short life of the Albanian kingdom founded in the thirteenth century by Charles I, King of Naples, despite conquest by the Ottomans in 1385, under which the Albanian lords had to surrender their sons as hostage to guarantee fealty, despite the failures of risings against occupiers over the centuries, the one most undeniable sign of identity, the ancient name, is preserved. Illyr is still a surname among Albanian families.

Talking to Albanians and reading their literature, one realizes that here is a people almost lost to the history books but whose role in history has not been small. I was reminded of the Kurds, who enter the news of the twentieth century as a struggling and oppressed minority in Iran and Iraq, but who in the history books were the Medes, coupled with the great Persians. Albanians will tell you that Scanderbeg, given the title of Iskander Bey, Lord Alexander, by the Turks, was greeted as a great Christian leader by Pope Paul II. As a boy hostage of the Turkish Sultan, he was educated in the Muslim faith. His qualities gained the admiration of the Sultan Murad II who gave him an army command. When Iskander Bey learned that the Sultan planned an onslaught on the Albanians, he crossed over to his own people. He had belonged to the princely Castrioti and he returned to them and to their Catholic faith. The Turks might have seen his action in the light of the Koran which says that "There is no compelling men in their inner belief." He unified the quarreling Albanian princes under his command and in resisting the Ottoman armies never lost a battle. Following his death, however, the absorption of Albania into the Ottoman Empire was completed. This did not mean that his red banner with the black double-headed eagle was forgotten. It became the flag under which Albanians of all creeds struggled for freedom over the centuries.

Albanians will tell you that many great men have come from their stock; many, in fact, rose to power in the Turkish Empire, being named Pashas and Beys. One, Ali Pasha, was given charge of the territory of Albania in the nineteenth century and founded a dynasty that ruled Egypt until 1950. Catholic Albanians are proud of the fact that John Francis Albani, a descendant of Albanian refugees in Italy, became Pope Clement XI in 1700.

The Albani family also gave four cardinals to the Catholic Church. Albanian historians put forward proof that Christianity came to Albania in the Apostolic age. The Apostle Paul, in the Epistle to the Romans, Chapter 15, told of traveling "all the way from Jerusalem to Illyricum," to proclaim the Good News about Christ. The Epistle to Titus is believed to have been written from Nicopolis (now Preveza) in 66 A.D. Durrës, ancient Dyrrachium, is considered to be one of the most ancient bishoprics in the world, its bishop, St. Astio, having been martyred during the persecution of Caesar Troyanius, who lived from 98 to 117 A.D. St. Jerome, the great translator of the Bible, was of Illyrian origin. In the Council of Nicea, when the Apostles' Creed was accepted for the whole Catholic Church, five Albanian bishops participated. By the fourth century, there was a bishop in Uskub, ancient Skopje.

The fact that over the centuries all Christians did not join in the great sea of Islam owes much to the memory of age-old fidelity to the teachings of Jesus. There was also the crucial fact that Albanians living in mountainous and forested areas could jealously guard their traditions remote from centers of power and outside influences. There is no doubt that many, though not all, of the Christians of the cities and coastal areas, deprived of Christian teaching with the destruction of churches and monasteries, were eventually absorbed into the religion of the occupiers.

When I asked Mother Teresa if her people had been mountain people, she answered, "No, they were not. As far as we can know, they were city people. They say that we were peasants, but that is not true."

Then she laughed, "But that does not matter. We are all peasants before God."

"How did they preserve their faith?" I wanted to know. She answered in two words, "By prayer."

The ancestors of Mother Teresa prevailed in their faith and lived by a motto that was passed on as a demanding tradition from generation to generation, FE Y ATDHE (Faith and Fatherland).

Lazar Bojaxhiu, in describing his family, related that his mother was deeply and completely involved with her faith and the Church. He relished talking about his family, while Mother Teresa was always reticent about details of her personal life. Their family was a merchant family, with his grandfather and father engaged in business. His father, Lazar explained, while a faithful member of the Church, was a strong and ardent Albanian nationalist. The father, Nikola Bojaxhiu, provided well for his family, and when Mother Teresa was born, they were in extremely comfortable circumstances.

Bojaxhiu's business as a building contractor and wholesale importer of food prospered and called for him to do a great deal of traveling, even as far as Egypt. Besides his native Albanian and the Serbo-Croatian spoken around him, he spoke Turkish, Italian, and French. In Skopje, his firm was engaged in the construction of the first Skopje Theater. He became a member of the Skopje Town Council. The mother's maiden name was Dranafile Bernai, and her people came from the Venetian region. Lazar made it clear that this did not mean that she was not Albanian; in fact, her given name meant "rose" in Albanian. It was generally shortened to Drana.

Nikola Bojaxhiu married Dranafile Bernai in a Catholic ceremony in Prizren, later called Pristina. It was in Prizren that the movement for a free Albania had been revived in 1877, and Nikola was involved in the nationalistic cause there before he moved to Skopje. It was in the early nineteen hundreds that they moved to Skopje and soon owned two adjoining houses. The house they occupied was a spacious one, set in a pleasant garden with flowers and fruit trees. In 1904, a child was born to the couple, a girl, christened Age. Lazar was born in 1907, Agnes Gonxha was born in 1910, the date being August 26. The date usually given as that of her birth, August 27, was, Mother Teresa told me, the date of her baptism.

Lazar Bojaxhiu, a tall soldierly man of ramrod military carriage, told of his life in Skopje. "I was the middle one between Age and Gonxha. Agnes Gonxha was 'Mother's' full name, but we called her Gonxha." He had accepted the new identity of his sister and had caught the habit of calling her "Mother" from the Missionaries of Charity in Rome and Palermo.

" 'Gonxha' means a flower bud in Albanian, and we thought of her as a rosebud. When she was a child, she was plump, round and tidy. She was sensible and a little too serious for her age. Of the three of us, she was the one who did not steal the jam. However, being generous and kindhearted, she would help me in the dining room to pull open the drawer of the cupboard high up against the wall because I could not manage it myself."

Lazar's weakness for jam and desserts led him to get up during the night and help himself to whatever was in the cupboard. When he was somewhat older, Agnes Gonxha would hear him moving about and come after him, reminding him that he was not to touch any food after midnight if they were going to mass and communion with their mother in the morning. "But she never told on me," he said. Whenever possible, Drana attended morning mass in the Church of the Sacred Heart on the same street near their house. She took the children with her.

Lazar described his father as one who obviously relished life. "I was more like my father," he told me on one of our many meetings. "He was full of life and liked to be with people. Our house was full of visitors while he was alive. They talked a lot about politics. He told us never to forget whose children we were and from what background we came.

" 'Mother' was more like our own mother. When I see her with the Sisters in Palermo, I see our mother in her, so strong, so strict in religious practice."

Though in temperament Lazar resembled his father, he and Agnes Gonxha looked more like the mother, according to family photographs. They both inherited the oval and, in later life, elongated facial structure of Drana and her distinctive nose. Age exhibited the broader features of Nikola.

The household in which Agnes Gonxha grew up was one with a strong sense of values and strict commitment to them. The mother, whom the children began to refer to as "Nana Loke," "nana" meaning mother, and "loke" meaning soul, maintained order and strict discipline. "Nana Loke" can be translated as "mother of my soul." Drana was always busy, if not working in the home or helping others, she would be saying the rosary.

Mother Teresa told me a story that gave an insight into the mother's character. One evening, when the three young people were engaged in small talk that became sillier as the evening progressed, the mother sat listening but saying nothing. She left the room and turned off the main electric switch, plunging the house into darkness. "She told us," said Mother Teresa, "that there was no use wasting electricity so that such foolishness could go on." Mother Teresa reflected that quality in objecting to useless talk or waste of any kind.

When it was time to go to school, the three children attended an elementary school in the halls of Sacred Heart Church, where all their lessons were in the Albanian language. The course was only four years, and in the last year, Serbo-Croat was introduced as a second language. Following that, all education was in Serbo-Croat in state schools, and religious training was carried on in the family and in the parish. The mother's devotion to religion was expressed not only in attending mass and in other religious practices, but in works of mercy for those around her. She made it a part of her life never to turn away the needy, Lazar recalled, and Nikola supported her in this. He always left enough funds with her so that she would be ready to help anyone who came to her door. Often, they would be given a meal, and when the children asked who the people were, she would tell them that the needy were part of their family too. Poor people learned that they would not be turned away from the Bojaxhiu door.

When Drana found a woman alone and uncared for and agonizing with a painful tumor, she brought her into their home. "Our mother gave her shelter and looked after her. Then she saw that the woman was given care until she recovered," Lazar recounted. Admiration was in his voice, but I wondered how he had viewed the presence of an ailing woman among them in his boyhood days. Drana went regularly with food and money to visit the poor and Lazar remembered that even as a little girl it was Agnes Gonxha who accompanied her.

Lazar smiled when he related that every evening, the whole family would gather in the living room to recite the rosary. Mother Teresa would say again and again, "We were a very happy family." She described how, in preparation for her father's return in the evening, her mother would invariably arrange her hair and put on a fresh dress. Mother Teresa remarked that as children they were amused at their mother's careful preparation for her husband's appearance. It was as if each day Drana made the family reunion something of a festive occasion.

When Agnes Gonxha was nine years of age, in 1919, the family was visited by a sudden and bitter tragedy. Nikola's Albanian nationalism had led him into a movement to have the province of Kosovo, inhabited chiefly by Albanians, joined to a greater Albania after the First World War. He went to a political dinner in Belgrade with other national groups concerned with the future of the province. It must have been an important gathering to inspire him to journey one hundred sixty miles from his home. He left home a vigorous man of forty-five but came home a dying man. Drana sent the young Agnes Gonxha to the nearby parish for the priest, but he was not there. The young girl must have thought that the priest could be leaving or coming back from a trip; in any case, she directed her steps to the Skopje Railway Station. A priest she did not know was on the platform. She approached him and told him about her desperately ill father. The priest rushed with her to her home. After administering the rites of the dying to Nikola, he went back to the station. The family never saw him again. Nikola was taken, hemorrhaging, to the local hospital where no surgery could save him. The doctors and the family were convinced that poison had caused his death. Following Nikola's death, his business partner appropriated the assets of the business and the family was left with nothing but their shelter.

The mother was so broken by the suddenness of the loss that she was nearly paralyzed by grief. She leaned on the children and particularly on her eldest daughter, Age, to whom she temporarily confided the keys to the house. It took some time before she was again herself, and then she had to plan the next hard steps.

Drana Bojaxhiu had an enterprising spirit and it was only her enterprise that saved the family. She set up a business of handcrafted embroidery and was soon engaged in selling various types of cloth. The business expanded to include the locally crafted carpets for which Skopje was well known. Lazar accompanied his mother to the textile factories and recounted how impressed he was when the managers asked her to spend time with them so that they could get her advice on which designs and which materials to produce for increased sales.

The parish of the Sacred Heart was the other pivotal influence in the life of Agnes Gonxha. Its parishioners belonged chiefly to the minority group, since, as mentioned, Albanians of the Catholic faith were only a very small part of the population of Skopje. As it had been able to do for many minorities, the Church provided not only a religious function, but the means for the preservation of a culture and a sense of identity. One of the regular parish functions was an annual pilgrimage to the shrine of Our Lady of Cernagore in Letnica, not far from Skopje. Drana went on the regular pilgrimage and made another pilgrimage on foot. As Agnes Gonxha grew older, her mother grew concerned about her health. She tended to have a cough, and so on some occasions, Drana arranged for Agnes Gonxha to go to the shrine without the entire parish group, when there were apt to be less pilgrims about. Another matter that worried Drana was the fact that Agnes Gonxha spent so much of her time reading. "Like mother, like daughter" was particularly true in the question of not wasting time. When she was not studying, helping her friends with their studies, enjoying social affairs, or participating in parish activities, Agnes Gonxha was buried in a book. A Jesuit priest, Fr. Jambrenkovic, who became pastor of Sacred Heart in May 1925, established a parish library, where young people could find the classics of literature, including the novels of Dostoevski and those of Henryk Sienkiewicz. The Polish author was especially popular with young people, not only for *Quo Vadis,* concerning the heroism of Christians in the time of Nero, but his works on the struggle of Poland for national existence.

Much of Fr. Jambrenkovic's work was with young people, and he introduced a young people's society that was of crucial significance to the future of Agnes Gonxha—the Sodality of the Blessed Virgin Mary. The fact that Fr. Jambrenkovic was a member of the Society of Jesus accounted for the introduction of this rather than another young people's group in the parish. The Sodality, founded in 1563 among lay students in the Roman college of the Society of Jesus, had spread to Catholic communities all over the world. The words of St. Ignatius Loyola in his *Spiritual Exercises* were given to the young people as a challenge, "What have I done for Christ? What am I doing for Christ? What will I do for Christ?" The same Sodality was to enter Mother Teresa's life in Calcutta later on when the girls she was teaching in Entally went into the nearby slums as members of the same association. One of the aims of the Sodality was to involve young people in serving Christ in His poor.

Another activity of the Sodality consisted of learning about the lives of saints and missionaries. If Fr. Jambrenkovic had been a Franciscan priest, Agnes Gonxha and her friends would have learned about the far-flung missions of the sons of St. Francis. As it was, they learned in greater detail of the missions of the congregation founded by St. Ignatius Loyola and of the fact that priests of the Society of Jesus went on mission from Yugoslavia to Bengal in 1924. They went to join fellow Jesuits in the archdiocese of Calcutta which then comprised all of Bengal and neighboring areas. Their first stop was the seminary at Kurseong and they were later stationed in the district of 24-Parganas, on the outskirts of Calcutta, and the Sunderbans. In the Sunderbans, the Ganges reaches the Bay of Bengal and the waters of the bay creep into the land with inlets like so many long fingers. These were immensely difficult but exotic and fascinating missions and the Croatian priests wrote home telling of their adventures. Fr. Jambrenkovic, of Croatian origin himself, had great zeal for the missions and communicated it to the young people. His identification with the Albanian cause resulted in great sympathy between him and the Albanian young people.

Once, at a meeting of the young people, Agnes Gonxha cooperated with Fr. Jambrenkovic in describing mission activities from a world map of missions.

Along with their activity in the Sodality, Agnes Gonxha and Age were members of the church choir and also took part in the concerts of the Albanian Catholic Choir of Skopje. About twenty young men and women made up the choir. Both sisters had unusual singing voices and were known as the nightingales of the choir. There were plays at Christmas and other times when Agnes Gonxha was called upon to sing solos. There were social gatherings, outings, and nature walks in which the sisters took part with boys and girls of their own age. The young people's pilgrimages were times not only of prayer but of conviviality. They sang on the road in the horse-drawn carriages and at Cernagore.

In 1924, Lazar left home for military school in Graz, Austria, through a scholarship which his mother arranged with the Ministry of Education. He later transferred to a lycée frequented by other young Albanians and saw his family only on vacations.

During his times at home, the teenaged Bojaxhiu found he had different interests from those of his sisters. "I followed my sports hobbies," he related, "and I spent a lot of my time outside the house with young men of my age." Though Age shared the religious commitment of the family, it was his younger sister who was occupied with the mother in arranging parish festivals. Lazar recalled that Drana and Agnes Gonxha seemed to live in the church in those days. The two sisters were attending the Skopje Gymnasium, the state secondary school, and both were fine students. It was Lazar's impression that Age was the keener and more outstanding scholar. A photograph of Lazar, Age, and Agnes Gonxha shows the fourteen-year-old Mother Teresa as a plump young girl, already wearing grown-up shoes with medium high heels. Her hand is intertwined with that of her older brother. Other casual photographs from gymnasium days show the two sisters smiling among their friends, the family resemblance being sufficient to identify them. A more formal photograph of Mother Teresa taken at the age of seventeen or eighteen exhibits an immense change from the plump-faced girl of fourteen. The features are more clearly defined and already mature. The directness and intentness of her gaze are an earnest of the strength she was to reveal in later life.

Lazar remarked of those days, "Whenever I was home, she was very active and she became very good-looking." The Bojaxhiu home was open to the friends of Agnes Gonxha and Age. Some of her classmates came for extra tutoring by Agnes Gonxha. The "sensible and tidy" little girl grew into a teenager whose life was well organized. Her teaching gift must have asserted itself during those teenage years. She was later to say of her years in Loreto, "I love teaching most of all." Her teaching also extended to little children when she began to instruct them in the rudiments of the Catholic faith in the Albanian language.

Two of her cousins were in the same youth group and choir as Agnes Gonxha, File Babaci, whose married name was to become Cuni and who later emigrated to Australia, and Lorenc Antoni, a well-known musician and composer. Mrs. File Cuni renewed the relationship with Mother Teresa years later after she brought the Sisters to Australia. Lorenc Antoni was a second cousin of Agnes Gonxha, his grandmother, Maria Bojaxhiu Kajtazi, having been the sister of Nikola Bojaxhiu. In *Nëna Jone Tereze* (Our Mother Teresa), a vivid account of Mother Teresa in Albanian by the Reverend Dr. Lush Gjergji, Lorenc Antoni recalled that he and Mother Teresa grew up together, in school and in church. He described her as an excellent student, a fine organizer, and a person who could be counted on for fidelity in everything. She was a sociable young woman, Antoni remembered, and kind to all. He noted that she was open and friendly to those of other religions and groups.

Antoni, who directed a mandolin orchestra, gave mandolin lessons to three of the girls in the group and never thought of taking payment. Agnes Gonxha urged him to take a dinar from each of the girls for each lesson. "Take it," she told him, "and give it to me for the missions in India." This was in 1927, when she was seventeen years of age. She often carried a notebook with her and on occasion would read to her friends the poetry she had written. Two articles she wrote were published in the local newspaper, *Blagovest.* Antoni was convinced that his cousin had talent as a writer and could have gone on to become one. None of her early efforts have survived.

All the young people read the Sodality publications provided by Fr. Jambrenkovic, as well as a magazine devoted to the Catholic missions. At the priest's urging, they formed little prayer groups to say special prayers for missions around the world. At first, Agnes Gonxha did not want to become a nun and leave her family but as she approached her eighteenth birthday the call became so insistent that she assented to it. Agnes Gonxha's deepening interest in the missions in India was clear to Antoni and, though he was half expecting her to become a missionary, he reported that it was a shock when she confided her decision to him. She spent longer periods on retreat at the shrine of Cernagore in 1927 and 1928 and went there for the last time on August 15, 1928, the feast of the Assumption of the Virgin. Antoni related that Agnes Gonxha wondered how you could know if God was calling you and even if He was calling you. It was his recollection that Fr. Jambrenkovic talked of a vocation in terms of joy, explaining that when you think God is calling you, you should feel joy in the contemplation of serving God and your neighbor. A deep joy should be the compass which gives direction to the choice of a life's vocation.

With her spirit on fire to serve the Lord in Bengal, Agnes Gonxha asked about religious Sisters serving in the same area. "I wanted to be a missionary," she said later. "I wanted to go out and give the life of Christ to the people." The Yugoslav priests in Bengal wrote that the Sisters of the Institute of the Blessed Virgin Mary had long been active in the area. They were commonly called the Sisters of Loreto. Like the Jesuits, it was an international order and the mission in Bengal was served by the Irish province. Agnes Gonxha made the decision to apply for entry into this order. If she were to be accepted, it would mean lifetime separation from family and country, since in those days there were no vacations at home and little or no opportunity for family members to visit the far-off mission locales.

The route to Bengal for the Albanian girl from Skopje, in Yugoslav Macedonia, led through Ireland. The link of Ireland with India was of long duration, since generations of dispossessed young Catholic Irishmen "took the King's shilling" to serve the British Raj, colonizer of both Ireland and India. Many of them died in the plagues or in battles and considerable numbers married and fathered children. Church authorities reported that the surviving children of the poor Irish soldiers were being lost to the faith of their fathers. The state of the Catholic Church in Calcutta and Bengal was such that a group of Jesuits, including priests from Ireland, England, and France were sent in 1834 to minister to the area. The first result was the opening of St. Xavier's School which became so prestigious that Muslim and Hindu boys, as well as Christians, attended it. The need for a Catholic school for girls was urgent too, not only for the children of Irish fathers, but for the children of Calcutta's Portuguese, Dutch, Armenian, and British families.

An account of the Loreto Sisters in India, *First the Blade,* recounts how the Loreto Sisters first came to India. A German priest brought the invitation to the Sisters at their Motherhouse in Rathfarnham, in 1841, urging them to send a group of Sisters to serve as teachers and to care for the poor and orphaned in Calcutta. Mother Teresa Ball, who had founded the Irish province in 1822, received the priest at Loreto house, so named after the legendary home of Mary in Nazareth, said to have been transported to Dalmatia and from there to Loreto, Italy. The Sisters began to be called the "Loreto nuns" and the name clung to them after they left Ireland for missions overseas.

The invitation to India met with a positive but regretful "No" from Mother Teresa Ball who explained that the needs of the children in Ireland were urgent and that there had been many deaths in the ranks of the Sisters. Faced with the argument by the priest that she might be responsible for the souls of children to whom she was refusing a Christian education, Mother Teresa Ball allowed the priest to make his appeal directly to the community of Sisters.

The whole community showed an interest in India, and seven nuns were chosen for the mission. The priest was jubilant. "These were ladies," he wrote, "proficient in English, French, Italian, needlework, music—and excellent nuns. What can we wish for more?"

The seven professed nuns, accompanied by six postulants and shepherded by two priests, set out for India aboard the *Scotia* on August 23, 1841. It was not until December 30 of that year that the boat steamed up the Hooghly River, and the young women, all in their twenties except one who was nineteen, disembarked in Calcutta.

The Irish-born head of the diocese, Bishop Carew, held a service of gratitude in the historic Cathedral of Our Lady of the Rosary, the same cathedral in which just over a century later, Mother Teresa, having left Loreto, was to make her profession as a Missionary of Charity. The little band was then taken to a house at 5 Middleton Row that had been acquired for them—an "Arabian nights" setting with hangings, carpeting, and furniture left over from the former owner. The Sisters found ways to divest themselves of all lavishness and settled themselves into the simpler rooms. The remaining rooms were prepared for use as classrooms and rooms for boarders. The sixty-seven-foot dining room became the school hall. It was named Loreto House.

The Sisters were also taken to the orphanage at the cathedral called the Murgi Hatta church by the local people because of its location near a chicken market. When on January 10, 1842, the Loreto Sisters opened their doors to boarders and day pupils at Loreto House, they began classes for orphan girls at the Murgi Hatta church. The Loreto pattern was thus established: for every paid school, free education for the poor, an orphanage, or a widows' asylum. The reports of the Sisters in Calcutta to Mother Teresa Ball were so enthusiastic that there was a stream of volunteers from Rathfarnham to India. This stream did not abate when, in a period of twenty years, forty-two Loreto Sisters, all of them of younger years, died. Some succumbed to the rigors of the life and the climate, some from nursing the victims of cholera that periodically plagued Calcutta and its surroundings.

These were the Loreto Sisters, so intimately united with Calcutta and Bengal, to whom the young Agnes Gonxha Bojaxhiu would address herself as a candidate. These were her pioneering forerunners.

When Agnes Gonxha told her "Nana Loke" that she had decided to become a missionary, the mother knew that the parting would be forever.

"My little Gonxha (My little Rosebud)," as she called her, was barely eighteen. Mother Teresa told me that her mother went to her room and closed the door. She stayed there for twenty-four hours. Undoubtedly she prayed, and she might have wept uncontrollably. Mother Teresa never knew. When she came out, her personal feelings were under control. She was able to help and strengthen Agnes Gonxha in taking the steps to part from her. She gave her daughter advice that was forever carved on her heart. "Put your hand in His—in His hand—and walk all the way with Him."

The young people of the Sodality and choir held a concert, part of which was a farewell to Agnes Gonxha. On September 25, the day before her departure for Zagreb, she had a photograph taken, and that evening the young people gathered in the Bojaxhiu home, many bringing gifts. Antoni's gift must have meant much to him; he gave her his gold fountain pen. The next morning, the friends were at the Skopje Railroad Station to wave goodbye to Agnes Gonxha, who was accompanied by Drana and Age. As she waved her handkerchief to her friends while the train made its way out of the station, Agnes Gonxha was weeping.

The mother and the two daughters had little time in Zagreb, but without doubt savored each moment and fixed it in the memory as something they would treasure for the rest of their lives. In Zagreb, they met Betike Kanjc who also wished to join Loreto.

At the Zagreb Railroad Station, two bereft figures, Drana and Age, saw the train speed away, carrying "little Gonxha," the youngest of the family, out of their world. They returned to Skopje while the train rolled across Austria, eventually bringing Agnes Gonxha and Betike to Paris.

There the mother superior of the Loreto Sisters in Paris was ready to interview the two candidates. A Sister of Loreto described in a letter to me how the interview was arranged.

"In 1928, a member of the Society of Jesus, a native of Yugoslavia, came to Loreto House, Villa Molitor, Auteuil, Paris, to see Mother Eugene MacAvin, the Sister in charge. He told her that two young Yugoslavian girls whom he knew were anxious to become religious and to go on mission to India. He knew of no women religious from his country in India, but Yugoslavian Jesuits had been working in India and knew the Loreto Sisters and their work there. He inquired as to the possibility of his two protegées joining the Loreto Institute with a view to becoming members of the Indian province. Mother Eugene asked him to send the two girls to Paris where she would interview them and, should she consider this advisable, would recommend them to the Mother General, Mother M. Raphael Deasy. Mother Eugene was able to carry out this interview with the help of an interpreter from the Yugoslavian Embassy. Subsequently, the girls came to Loreto Abbey, Rathfarnham, Dublin, with the permission of

Mother Raphael. Having arrived in September, the two girls spent six weeks in the novitiate. They did not undergo any formal novitiate training at this stage as most of their time was spent studying English, their tutor being Mother M. Borgia Irwin, who had herself spent many years on the Indian mission. Because of the language barrier and because most of their time was spent in study, the girls had little opportunity of becoming known to, or knowing, the novices and postulants or the submistress of novices. They went to India about mid-November 1928."

It was understandable that the two young women left little impression. An old Irish Sister who was with them during the six weeks, when queried long afterward, could only recall them as quiet, self-effacing, obedient young women, intent on mastering the language in which their novitiate studies would be conducted.

On the ship with them for India were three young Franciscan Sisters. The five young women were able to order their prayer lives during the long voyage which took them through the Suez Canal, the Red Sea, the great expanse of the Indian Ocean, and finally into the Bay of Bengal. They celebrated Christmas aboard ship and marked it by putting together a little crèche. After seven weeks on the sea, they arrived in Calcutta in the first week of January 1929. Though long, Agnes Gonxha's voyage was only half as long as the voyage of her Loreto forerunners, whose ship eighty-eight years earlier in pre-Suez days had to round the Cape of Good Hope.

Like countless families who surrendered their sons and daughters to missions in far-off lands, the Bojaxhiu family would simply grieve, accept the grieving, and transcend it by sharing in prayer for the work of God in the world.

To Lazar, away from home, the news of his younger sister's decision was shocking and even incredible. In 1928, he was twenty-one and had been made a lieutenant. On September 1, 1928, Albania became a monarchy under King Zog I. The patriotic young man was to become an equerry of the king. In a letter sending him her good wishes on being made a lieutenant, Agnes Gonxha broke the news of her decision to become a nun and serve on the missions in India. His answer contained a question that expressed his anguish. How could a lovely young girl, he wanted to know, give up a good life and go so far away, probably never to see him or the family for the rest of her life. Agnes Gonxha wrote back explaining her decision, one sentence of which her brother quoted word for word, "You will serve a king of two million people. I shall serve the king of the whole world."

2

The Call Within a Call

It was on January 6, 1929, that Agnes Gonxha Bojaxhiu arrived in Calcutta, capital of Bengal. On that day, the church marks the feast of the Three Wise Men from the East who, guided by a star, came to Bethlehem and offered the newborn Jesus the gifts of gold, frankincense, and myrrh. In many cultures it is called "Little Christmas." The eighteen-year-old young woman was not to leave the province of Bengal for thirty-one years.

For her training as a novice in the Sisters of Loreto, Agnes Gonxha was sent four hundred and fifty miles northward, where Bengal borders on the kingdom of Sikkim. The town was Darjeeling, the City of the Thunderbolt, situated at an altitude of 7,000 feet. It was set on a massive curve of one of the foothills of the Himalayan range, the "abode of snow." Between dark clouds and surging fog, one could see the five peaks of Mt. Kanchenjunga, according to Hindus, the abode of Lord Siva. Farther off, there sometimes appeared the highest peak on the planet, Mt. Everest, known to the Tibetans as mother goddess of the land. Perhaps the views of far, everlasting snows compensated for the severely restricted life of the novitiate compound.

Darjeeling, with its cool, bracing air, served as a summer capital for the British during the period when Calcutta was the capital of India. Around the novices swirled the resort activities of the town, the life of Government House and of the tea plantations, but the young women were hermetically sealed from the life outside. They were immersed in preparing for a life lived in the spirit, a life centered in Jesus.

The novices studied the Scriptures, theology, and the implications of the evangelical counsels as embodied in the Holy Rule of the congregation. The rule was first prepared by Mary Ward who had founded the congregation in the seventeenth century. It owed much to the rule of the Society of Jesus. The Loreto Sisters had descended from the Institute of Mary through which its founder hoped to be able to teach poor and well-to-do alike. This meant dispensing with enclosure so as to have the freedom to go about and find the poorest women and girls. Mary Ward's dream was inscribed over her grave, "To love the poore, Persevere in the same, Live, die and rise with them Was all the ayme of Mary Ward." In that period, enclosure was imposed on religious Sisters and the Institute of Mary was suppressed by papal decree in 1690. The congregation was resuscitated in a few years. It became an international congregation devoted chiefly to teaching and received papal approval early in the eighteenth century. Because of its English origin, the Sisters belonging to the congregation were variously called Le Dame Inglese or Die Englischen Frauen. The Irish branch, founded in 1822, grew so quickly that, as mentioned, it was able to respond to the appeal from Calcutta in 1841. As in other parts of the world, the Sisters of Loreto taught girls and young women at all levels, beginning with grammar school and continuing through high school to university. The novices in Darjeeling pursued studies that would prepare them for the apostolate (they would never call it a career) of teaching. As all conversation and training was conducted in English Agnes Gonxha's immersion in the language was complete. In addition, the young women were introduced to Hindi and Bengali.

Sister M. Thérèse Breen, who was in the Darjeeling novitiate with Mother Teresa wrote me, "Life in the novitiate in the 1930s was very different from what we have today. The novice mistress trained us in everything, and this she did in great detail. We went weekly to our confessor. For two hours a day, from nine to eleven in the morning, we taught little boys and girls in St. Teresa's School. It was a one-roomed school and there were generally about twenty boys and girls from the families who lived around us on the hillside. I found Mother Teresa a very simple type of person. We never had any idea that she would ever leave Loreto. She was a sincere, religious type of novice."

Sister M. Thérèse went on to say that at dinner one of the Sisters would read aloud, sometimes from the rule of Loreto, and often from the lives of the saints.

One of the special attributes of Catholic education, whether it be that for intellectuals or for the smallest children, is the deep and studious attention paid to the holy ones of God. For each generation, the stories of those whose lives have been judged worthy of emulation by the faithful (by being declared saints) are preserved to give courage to those struggling for holiness. Regrettably the aim of encouraging those tempted to succumb to human weakness has too often been subverted by a certain type of hagiographical writing that removed the sainted one from ordinary life. Legends of levitations and bilocations, of visions and spectacular wonders so marked the accounts of saints that they practically filled a role similar to that of science fiction tales in modern times. St. John of Matera was said to have been led out of prison by an angel, a reminder of St. Peter. St. Elmo, patron of mariners, indicated his protection by the blue lights on the masts of ships—actually electrical discharges. The accounts of modern holy persons, however, became more sober and more nearly fulfilled the original purpose of moving the faithful to imitation. The story of a French Carmelite nun declared a saint in 1925 was one of utmost simplicity. She was St. Thérèse of the Child Jesus. The young Carmelite made her own the words of Jesus as recounted in the Gospel of Matthew. Seeing a small child in the midst of his followers, Jesus announced, "Unless you be converted and become like little children, you shall not enter the kingdom of heaven."

Holy persons, according to the almost infinite variety of temperaments, are set on fire by different teachings of Jesus. Yet each Gospel teaching can be an authentic path to Jesus since the Gospel is, in the end, unified by love. Yet personalities as different as Mother Teresa and Dorothy Day of the Catholic Worker have found special nourishment in the "little way." Both Mother Teresa and Dorothy Day were immersed in the daily, repetitive tasks of service to others and could echo St. Thérèse's words, "I prefer the monotony of obscure sacrifice to all ecstasies." Her autobiography, *The Story of a Soul*, translated into many languages, caught the imagination of millions. The narrative was filled, not with wonders, but texts from the holy Scriptures she loved.

Agnes Gonxha, between the ages of eighteen and twenty-one, was exposed to the thoughts and the example of Thérèse Martin, the young woman who was to become St. Thérèse of the Child Jesus. Often referred to as St. Thérèse of Lisieux, from her home place and the location of her convent, the young nun prayed to be sent to the missions, in particular, to the Carmelite convent of Hanoi in Indochina, then a colony of France. Tuberculosis ended her life at the age of twenty-four. Her love of the missions and her prayers for priests, especially missionaries, moved the Pope in 1927 to name her, along with St. Francis Xavier, patron of the missions of the world. Her story captured the Catholic world. Catholics, from priests to mothers of families, followed her in moving toward God by her "little way." "My little way," she wrote, "is the way of spiritual childhood, the way of trust and absolute self-surrender." When Agnes Gonxha made her first vows of poverty, chastity, and obedience as a Sister of Loreto on May 24, 1931, she took for her name in religious life, that of St. Thérèse. Her religious name was to be spelled in the Spanish way since Sister M. Thérèse Breen was already a novice in Loreto.

On many occasions she was asked if her patron saint was St. Teresa of Avila, the Carmelite nun of sixteenth-century Spain, often called the "great" St. Teresa. She was considered a doctor of the spiritual life, not only because of her reform of the Carmelite order and her writings for the spiritual growth of the Sisters, but for her *Interior Castle* which served for the instruction of the Church as a whole. "Not the big St. Teresa of Avila," Mother Teresa always explained, "but the little one." Many echoes of St. Thérèse are to be found in Mother Teresa's special vocation of love. St. Thérèse, after searching the gospels for her role in the Church, came to the realization that "Love contains all vocations." She wrote in her *Autobiography*, "Then, overcome by joy, I cried, 'Jesus, my love. At last I have found my vocation. My vocation is love. In the heart of the Church, my mother, I will be love, and then I will be all things.' "

Despite the difference between life in Yugoslavia and that in France, there were similarities in the early lives of Agnes Gonxha Bojaxhiu and Thérèse Martin. Both came from devout and close families, in which the mother was an enterprising woman. Thérèse Martin's mother conducted a business of making and selling Alençon lace. Both had happy childhoods, and each was the youngest child in the family. Thérèse Martin recalled that "My earliest memories are of smiles and tender caresses." Both experienced a clear moment of spiritual discernment. St. Thérèse of Lisieux underwent what she termed her "conversion" on Christmas Eve, 1886, when "On that blessed night the sweet Child Jesus, scarcely an hour old, filled the darkness of my soul with floods of light." As Jesus had become weak and little for love of her, the young woman, not yet fourteen years of age, felt that "He put His own weapons into my hands so that I went from strength to strength, beginning, if I may say so, 'to run as a giant.' " It was this strength that gave Thérèse Martin the audacity to break with accepted custom in an audience with the Holy Father. She asked Pope Leo XIII himself to waive the rules and give her permission to enter the Carmelite order at the age of fifteen.

Sister Teresa's time of spiritual discernment on September 10, 1946, gave her the courage to ask permission to break with an austere but protected life for a new and mysterious path in serving Jesus.

Sister Teresa now went down to Calcutta to take up the work of her order. She went down from crystal mountain air, fresh with the scent of flower-filled meadows, to a steaming city where all the problems of Asia had already met, problems which in the coming decades would become so agonizing that the world would be forced to turn a horrified eye upon them. The train ride between Darjeeling and Calcutta was to be, just fifteen years later, the locus of a decisive moment of spiritual discernment that catapulted her out of Loreto and into a new life.

Darjeeling, the terraced enclave of the British Empire with European-type buildings and imported luxuries, resembled another British enclave, Hong Kong. "The Peak" of Hong Kong was reserved for the British and the well-to-do, while the higher terraces of Darjeeling were similarly reserved. At the base lived the local people who served literally, the "higher-ups."

Descending to Calcutta, Sister Teresa came to a city bearing the inescapable signs of an imperial past, but where great riches coexisted with squalor and destitution of almost incredible proportions.

Sister Teresa was now equipped to teach, and she was placed in the school conducted by the Loreto Sisters in the eastern district of Calcutta. The school was situated in an extensive compound behind a solid wall, broken only by an impressive entrance erected in the classic style with two columns on each side. The entire compound, with its many buildings, was generally referred to as Loreto Entally.

There, Sister Teresa joined the other Loreto Sisters in the vocation of teaching. She was now fluent in English and became a teacher of geography and later of history. Loreto Entally was a large school, with about five hundred students, mostly boarders. They came from families able to afford the fees and were taught, as the Indians put it, "in the English medium."

In the same compound was another school, St. Mary's, attended at that time by about two hundred pupils. The girls came from a variety of backgrounds, some from middle-class families, some from poorer families, some half orphans, some full orphans. No distinction was made between those whose fees were paid and those cared for and supported by the Sisters. Classes were conducted in the Bengali tongue. Sister Teresa, after becoming fluent in English, soon learned to communicate, then teach, in Bengali. This became her fourth language, her fifth being Hindi.

The Loreto Sisters, from that memorable day of their arrival on December 30, 1841, had made a deep impact on Bengali society through the education of women and girls. Besides their six high schools in Calcutta, they conducted at Loreto House a University College for Women. This was the first of their Loreto colleges, others being opened in Lucknow and Darjeeling for later generations of Indian women. From their first foundation in Calcutta, the women of Loreto moved out to initiate centers of education for women and girls across the subcontinent from Dacca to Delhi to Bombay. The young women who received degrees from Loreto College were referred to admiringly as "Loreto Girls" and took responsible places in education and social welfare in the city, the province, and the nation. In free India, a Loreto graduate became the first woman judge of the Delhi High Court; another served as judge of the High Court of Calcutta. Others were elected to the Indian Parliament.

In those hard early days, Loreto Sisters of the Irish province could not depend on any support, other than new recruits, from their home country. In the 1840s Ireland endured one of history's most dreadful famines, with at least a million people dying when the potato crop failed. The Loreto mission had to be self-supporting. The Sisters established a set of fees which allowed them to use the funds provided by those of means to give free education to the poor.

The spirit of Loreto is reflected in a notice placed in the *Bengal Catholic Herald* of October 10, 1857, just sixteen years after their arrival.

Under "Prospectus of Loreto House," they announced that "The Loreto Sisters receive Young Ladies on the following terms." After listing the fields of study and the charges for boarders and day pupils, they added some key sentences indicating that the aim of the Sisters was to bring another dimension to the lives of their pupils, whether Christian or not.

"The moral conduct of the Young Ladies is watched over with the strictest attention, and while every effort is made to expand and adorn the mind, the heart is trained in virtue.

"The character of the pupils is carefully studied; they are taught by reasoning to correct their errors and are gradually formed to habits of regularity and order."

As the life of religious Sisters is the very model of "regularity and order," no better guides could be found for the inculcation of these qualities. The various European Christian groups in Calcutta, many of them critical of the Catholic Church as a whole, recognized this, as did many Hindu, Parsi, and Anglo-Indian families. They entrusted their daughters to the "Ladies of Loreto" in successive generations.

The 1857 notice in the *Bengal Catholic Herald,* made during the year of the Sepoy Rebellion, indicated that the "regularity and order" of the Sisters' mission endured despite troubles outside the walls. The Sepoy Rebellion, stemming from the uprising of the Bengal troops of the East India Company, was suppressed after atrocities on both sides. What it meant to the Loreto Sisters was a new flock of fatherless children to be cared for in the Entally compound. The fathers, many of them from Ireland, had lost their lives in the fray. What it meant to India was that rule over it passed from the British East India Company to the British Crown.

On May 14, 1937, Sister Teresa took lifetime vows of poverty, chastity, and obedience as a Loreto Sister in Darjeeling. She was now a professed nun.

The rigid, even rugged, schedule of the life of a Catholic nun is incomprehensible by worldly standards which set so much store by the outward marks of the successful life. Ease, possessions, recognition, the love of a husband and children, even privacy, are absent from the life of self-denial. What makes such a life possible, and even a source of happiness, is the fact that it is a chosen life, and that it is chosen out of love. Such burning spirits as that of Agnes Gonxha did not question a schedule that called for rising before dawn, to pray and to read the prescribed lessons in the breviary, the Psalms of David, other readings from the Hebrew Scriptures, selections from the New Testament and readings from the Fathers of the Church and the saints.

The central act of the day was attendance with the community at mass. The Eucharist, the body and blood of Jesus who chose the death of the cross to reconcile man to God, passed their lips before they entered upon the tasks of the day. The chapel at St. Mary's in Entally was a large one and students were free to attend mass. The day that began with the lifting of the heart and mind to God with private prayer and the mass, ended with the community prayer of Vespers and Benediction in which the Eucharistic host was raised in a monstrance for the devotion of the Sisters. The school day was a long one, with morning and afternoon classes, and in the early evenings the Sisters had tasks of supervising the young boarders.

Such a schedule, day after day, could only be lived by women whose hearts and souls were concentrated on one person, Jesus, and through Jesus, to the Creator of the universe. The infinite love of the Son of God who died for all of humankind was proof of the love of the Creator which streamed over all his creation, and the vocation of the Sister was therefore not to be seen simply in terms of self-denial. Rather it was an adventure in love, a sharing in the love that the Creator showered on His creation. With this love came a sharing in the cross of one who took up His cross out of love and told those who followed Him to take up the same cross.

The strength to live such a life with joy and serenity reaches into the greatest of mysteries, the mystery of grace, that abounding grace ready for all human creatures who call upon it.

For nineteen years, Sister Teresa, as novice and professed Sister, lived the life of a Loreto nun. She never looked back. "When I was eighteen, I decided to leave my home and become a nun. Since then, I never doubted even for a second that I did the right thing. It was the will of God, his choice." She followed the strict, unyielding schedule of a Sister-teacher, a schedule broken only by a yearly retreat for a deepening of religious commitment. Otherwise, there was little reason to break the strict enclosure of the convent and the compound. According to the rules of the order, no Sister ever went out unless it was a matter of urgency, such as a visit to a hospital. Even then, Sisters did not use public transportation. A car was sent and the Sister always had a companion.

Sister Teresa's chief subject was geography and, according to Magdalena Gomes, the pupil who later became Sister Gertrude and accompanied Mother Teresa to Oslo, she made the subject come alive for her students. In later years, these places were to come alive for Mother Teresa herself.

During a journey, she once remarked to me, "I taught geography for many years but I never thought I would visit so many of the places I taught about."

When she first came to teach at St. Mary's, the superior was Mother Cenacle, (shortened from Mary of the Cenacle, a title of the Blessed Virgin) a Loreto Sister whose origin was in Mauritius. The young Sister was guided by the older woman who was recognized as a person of great holiness. In time, Mother Teresa became the headmistress of St. Mary's. Side by side with the Loreto Sisters was a Sister order, the Daughters of St. Anne. The Sisters of Loreto had founded the affiliated order in 1898. It was a diocesan order composed of Bengali women who observed Indian dress, wearing a white sari in summer and a blue one in winter. They taught in the Bengali High School in their own tongue. The mother provincial of Loreto was mother superior of the Daughters of St. Anne. Sister Teresa was given charge of these Sisters in addition to her other duties. Many referred to her as the "Bengali Teresa" to distinguish her from Sister M. Thérèse Breen.

The Sodality of the Blessed Virgin, which had so influenced the life of Sister Teresa, was active in St. Mary's. Besides meetings and prayer and spiritual concerns, there was a study club. Hindu girls asked to join the study club and the director of the Sodality admitted them. The director was a priest of the Society of Jesus and the pastor of the Church of St. Teresa. He was Father Julien Henry, who was, like the archbishop of Calcutta, a member of the Belgian province of the Society. On the other side of the wall from St. Mary's, the teeming life of Calcutta was reflected in a *bustee*, or slum area, whose problems grew more acute each year. It was called Moti Jihl, Pearl Lake, from a discolored sump water pond at its center. Around it sprang the huts of the poor, mud-floored hovels, for which poor families had to struggle to meet the tiny monthly rental.

Father Henry helped the girls of the Sodality study club in their desire to touch the lives of these poor families. During the school week, Father Henry met with the class six through class eleven, in which the girls ranged from early teens to twenty, to discuss the ties that bind those who have and those who have less. These discussions led the girls to choose works of service. On Saturdays, they went out in groups and visited with families who lived in the huts and drew their water for drinking and washing from the dirty pond. Other groups went to visit the poor in the large Nilratan Sarkar Hospital. As Father Henry described their work, the girls could not do very much. They did bring needed items for the children of the *bustee* families and in Nilratan Sarkar sat and talked with patients, often trying to console them. They might bring some small gift and be called upon to write letters for them. The students became eager to belong to one of the groups moving from the compound into the world of need and suffering outside. They had learned from such teachers as Sister Teresa that there is joy in transcending self to serve others. Whatever her own feelings, Mother Teresa could not accompany them because of the rule of enclosure.

During the years that Sister Teresa taught behind the walls of the Entally compound, India went through the convulsions leading to freedom. Gandhi's nonviolent campaigns, including the historic Salt March, involved more and more of India's people in resistance. When Sister Teresa was in India only a year, the 1930 Salt March revealed the creative gift of Gandhi in choosing as a symbol for resistance the tax on salt. This had enormous impact in India where even the poorest of the poor needed salt as they worked the fields in India's furnace heat. The tax reached into the lives of India's millions to support the pomp of the British Raj. At the end of the twenty-four-day Salt March, in which many thousands joined him the world learned what Gandhi meant by nonviolence.

One of the women close to Gandhi was the poet Sarojini Naidu. Mother Teresa, who never met Gandhi and was separated by convent walls from the events leading to Indian freedom, was to have the cooperation of Sarojini's daughter, Padmaja Naidu. This was a close relationship since Naidu became governor of Bengal. Sarojini Naidu stood at Gandhi's side when he picked up a handful of salt at the seashore at Dandi, near Bombay. Later, she led Gandhi's followers in prayer before they moved nonviolently to occupy the Dharasana salt pans north of Bombay. "You will be beaten," she told them, "but you will not resist; you must not even raise a hand to ward off blows." When the nonviolent resisters were struck down with metal-tipped rods, they obeyed to the letter, though their skulls were cracked, their shoulder bones shattered, their bodies pierced and bleeding. Column after column advanced as their comrades were carried away, bloodied and writhing in pain. A press correspondent sent the story around the world, and people began to learn a word coined by Gandhi, "*satyagraha*" (holding on to truth), or Truth Force. He defined it as "the argument of suffering," in which the innocent person accepts suffering in order to move the heart of an oppressor.

Nonviolent resistance grew in the nineteen thirties and was intensified after 1939 when the Indian people were swept into the limitless violence of the Second World War. Britain, as it had done in the First World War, declared war on behalf of the Indian people without consulting them. Bengal suffered most disastrously. The dislocation brought about by the war, with its all-consuming priorities and the sequestering of river craft by which rice would have been delivered from Bengal's paddy land, contributed to one of history's most destructive famines. The Bengal famine of 1943 took the lives of at least two million people, perhaps as many as four million to five million, according to Indian figures. The fact that transportation took precedence over all other concerns is further attested to by the completion of the great Howrah Bridge over the Hooghly in 1943.

Sister Teresa was teaching in Calcutta when the streets of Mother Kali's city were filled with the starving who flocked to the city's soup kitchens. They perished in such numbers that the smoke from the burning ghats was continuous. The Bengal famine, like the Irish famine of a century earlier, has carved itself into folk memory so that it appears in the work of Bengali writers and artists. Satyajit Ray, the filmmaker who brought the life of Calcutta and Bengali villagers to the world, pictured the famine in the powerful film, *Distant Thunder.*

With Japanese armies in nearby Burma, Calcutta became a city on a war footing. There were occasional bombing raids. The entire Entally compound was requisitioned as a British military hospital, with dormitories serving as wards for the wounded. The Sisters of Loreto evacuated most of their pupils, including orphans, to convents and converted hotels in places as far away as Darjeeling, Shillong and Lucknow. Loreto House became a sort of "transit camp" for refugees from the war-ravaged Far East, including Maryknoll and Good Shepherd Sisters. Sister Teresa continued her tasks as headmistress, teacher, and Sister in charge of the Daughters of St. Anne from a building on Convent Road, Calcutta.

In 1946, another disaster struck Calcutta. In the Hindu-Muslim conflict that preceded partition and the freedom of the Indian subcontinent, a "Direct Action Day" was declared by the Muslim League for August 16. The day was declared a holiday by the Muslim leader of the Calcutta administration three days before Direct Action Day. The aim may have been to avert communal clashes, the term for violence between the two major religious groups. Bengal's population, like that of Calcutta, was divided between Muslims and Hindus. With people freed from their workplaces and Muslims at white heat over partitioning, a mass meeting was called by the Muslim League in the Maidan, Calcutta's great park. As the mass meeting broke up, Direct Action Day exploded into communal violence. Once unleashed, it raged in fiery frenzy for four days, bathing the streets of the city in blood. The roaring streets were brought to a complete standstill except for activities of human destruction. All deliveries of food and supplies were stopped. As headmistress of a school, Sister Teresa had to take action. She went outside the convent walls and thus came face to face with one of the apocalyptic events on the road to Indian freedom—and its unforeseen consequence, partition.

"I went out from St. Mary's, Entally," she related. "I had three hundred girls in the boarding school and we had nothing to eat.

"We were not supposed to go out into the streets, but I went anyway.

"Then I saw the bodies on the streets, stabbed, beaten, lying there in strange positions in their dried blood.

"We had been behind our safe walls. We knew that there had been rioting. People had been jumping over our walls, first a Hindu, then a Muslim.

"You see, our compound was between Moti Jihl, which was mainly Muslim then, and Tengra, with the potteries and the tanneries. That was Hindu. We took in each one and helped him to escape safely.

"When I went out on the street—only then I saw the death that was following them.

"A lorry full of soldiers stopped me and told me I should not be out on the street. No one should be out, they said.

"I told them I had to come out and take the risk. I had three hundred students who had nothing to eat. The soldiers had rice and they drove me back to the school and unloaded bags of rice."

Whenever Mother Teresa referred later to the Day of the Great Killing, as the Bengalis called it, and its aftermath, her face clouded over with indescribable sadness.

Accounts of those apocalyptic days describe how violence shook the city to its foundations. Shops were set afire with kerosene bombs while the owners were inside. Sewers were flooded with the crush of bodies tossed into them. In the open streets men and women, pierced with metal-tipped *lathis,* or with any variety of lethal blade, were left to bleed to death. Entrails spilled onto the sidewalks and half-dismembered bodies sprawled across gutters. Patches of encrusted blood were underfoot and a shapeless blotch on the wall might be a man's brain matted with hair. Some families barricaded themselves in their homes, while others fled for safety and crouched in terror in emergency hiding places. Vultures gathered to feast on exposed bodies. Eventually, when the bodies could be gathered for transport to the burning ghats, the smoke from human flesh filled the air. The Great Killing had possessed Kali's city. At least five thousand had died and another fifteen thousand Calcuttans were wounded.

Shortly after her foray into the streets of a city bloodied by massacre, Sister Teresa left Calcutta for Darjeeling for her annual retreat. I asked Mother Teresa early in our acquaintance if it was the Day of the Great Killing that had impelled her into breaking through the enclosure of convent walls to bring mercy to streets that knew such mercilessness. She said it was not. The impulsion had come from something that had occurred less than a month after the fury that had been unleashed around her on the dread day of August 16, 1946.

The constitutions of the Missionaries of Charity begin by referring to this occurrence. After two short quotations, one from John the Evangelist, "You have not chosen me but I have chosen you," and one from Mother

Teresa, "Let us make our Society Something Beautiful for God." The opening of the latest version reads:

> Our religious family started when our Foundress, Mother Teresa Bojaxhiu was inspired by the Holy Spirit with a special Charism on the 10th September, 1946. This inspiration . . . means that the Holy Spirit communicated God's will to Mother.

Mother Teresa has explained that the inspiration came to her while she was on the train to Darjeeling, the City of the Thunderbolt, in the Himalayas. What she heard was a call to give up all a second time, this time to follow Jesus to those who, like Him, "had not whereon to lay their heads," to those who were naked, despised, and forsaken. She was certain that the call was the will of God and that the work was to be His work. More she did not know.

"I was going to Darjeeling to make my retreat," she related. "It was on that train that I heard the call to give up all and follow Him into the slums—to serve Him in the poorest of the poor. I knew it was His will and that I had to follow Him. There was no doubt that it was to be His work."

"The message was quite clear," she explained, "I was to leave the convent and work with the poor while living among them. It was an order. I knew where I belonged, but I did not know how to get there."

When Sister Teresa came down from Darjeeling to Calcutta in May 1931, having made her first vows, and again in May 1937, having made her lifetime vows, she entered the city pledged to the obedience of faith, to be used by God's love in the Sisters of Loreto. When she came down from Darjeeling in October 1946, she was still pledged to the obedience of faith, but to be used by God in a way unknown to her. Here the words of her patron, St. Thérèse of the Child Jesus, took on reality. "My little way is the way of spiritual childhood, the way of trust and absolute self-surrender." The "little way" of absolute self-surrender becomes an enormous challenge when its direction must be found in a search through an impenetrable future on the streets of a scourged city.

Sister Teresa had already heard one clear call and had made her vows in response to it. The second call, no less clear, differed from the first in that there was no established route to follow, no acceptance at a Motherhouse, no period of novitiate training. It would take her away from the life of a teaching nun and, for this, releases and permissions had to be obtained. Passionately eager as she was to answer the new call, she would take no steps until these permissions had been accorded her. I am convinced that if these permissions had been slow in coming, or had taken the greater portion of her lifetime, she would have waited. A special legacy of Mother Teresa's Albanian heritage has been mentioned. It is a concept deep in the consciousness of Albanians that refers to the absolute sacredness of the word of honor, the inviolability of the pledged word in daily life. The concept, mentioned earlier, is contained in the word *besa.*

As Mother Teresa explained it to me, should a family promise hospitality to someone and he came to claim it, the family would provide it and protect that person at any cost. The cost might be heavy indeed if the person claiming hospitality were, as often happened, a hunted man stalked by seekers after retribution or vengeance. The pledge would be fulfilled even in the extreme situation that word came that the guest had been involved in the death of a member of the host family. As she was explaining *besa,* one could transport oneself back to the beleaguered people of Albania, engaged not only in resistance to occupation, but also in feuds among themselves. Their very lives depended on no document, no treaty, but hung by the slender thread of a simple word of honor.

The concept of *besa* was transferred, perhaps it might be said, transfigured, to apply to religious life. Sister Teresa was a vowed nun; these vows would continue to shape her life no matter where the new call led.

Entry into a religious order, when a young woman forswears the world for a lifetime of poverty, chastity, and obedience, is a dramatic event. In Loreto in those days, the Sisters on being professed, lay prone, according to Sister M. Thérèse Breen. The prostration, in which the face was to the floor, was a symbolic death. Leaving a religious order, especially before the Second Vatican Council, might be just as dramatic for the person concerned, but it would be a drama hidden in the heart—long drawn-out and painful.

❧

I was to meet in 1958, the persons who played out the hidden drama with Sister Teresa, first of all her spiritual director, Fr. Celeste Van Exem. I also came to know Archbishop Ferdinand Perier, Fr. Pierre Fallon, Fr. Julien Henry, and Fr. Robert Antoine. Uncommunicative regarding her personal life, Mother Teresa did not divulge the drama or pain in her struggle to leave one work for Jesus for a different one. Fr. Van Exem recounted some of the details. On her return to Calcutta in the fall of 1946, Sister Teresa revealed her momentous spiritual experience to her spiritual director. She conveyed it not in words but in a sheaf of papers in which she described the first inspiration, the call, and the continuation of that call that had come to her during the retreat.

In my presence, Mother Teresa stated that the call was not a vision, that in fact, she did not have visions. Fr. Van Exem also asserted that Sister Teresa told him that the call was no vision. He remarked that in those papers were all the marks of Mother Teresa's future work, starting with care for the poor in the streets and in their dwellings. The care would not be given behind the walls of institutions and those who joined in it would be bound to the poor by a special vow.

Fr. Van Exem, one of the team of Jesuit fathers in Calcutta, had arrived there during the Second World War. He began to celebrate mass and give sermons during the war period at St. Mary's School when it was evacuated to a building on Convent Road. Van Exem knew Arabic and the Arab world, being acquainted with such places as Cairo, Beirut, Damascus, and Amman. He had many contacts with the Muslims of Calcutta and joined with them in cultural events. His first memories of Sister Teresa were of a very active nun, who was everywhere at once. He remarked particularly on her penchant for moving furniture about. This was a penchant that did not leave her. I could not help noticing that when she visited the houses of her order around the world, she would decide that the chapel should be moved to a better location. That would mean moving all the furniture out of the refectory or dormitory to make place for the chapel. At a later date, the chapel might be moved again, or perhaps back to its original location, calling once more for furniture moving.

There was a time when Sister Teresa was suspected of having a lung weakness, according to Van Exem. She told him that on orders of Mother Dorothy, the mother provincial, she had to put aside her work and rest for several hours a day. The priest noted that when she told him this, her eyes were filled with tears. It was the only time that he ever saw her on the verge of weeping.

Having shared her clear call, Sister Teresa followed Van Exem's advice to the letter in taking the next steps. He explained to her that she could, if she wished, write direct to Rome to ask the Congregation for the Propagation of the Faith to release her from Loreto. Rome would then communicate with Loreto. Van Exem advised her against this however, and Mother Teresa, who loved her spiritual community, agreed. The alternative was to share the whole matter with the head of the Calcutta archdiocese and ask his cooperation. Van Exem told Mother Teresa that he would wait for a convenient time to take the question to Archbishop Perier and that in the meantime, neither he nor she was to tell anyone about it.

It was the end of 1946 before Van Exem brought the matter to Archbishop Perier, and the priest recalled that the archbishop became upset. He wondered about the effect on Loreto and did not relish the idea of a lone nun on Calcutta's streets. Perier decided that no steps should be taken for a year. Sister Teresa received the decision in the spirit of obedience despite her eagerness to respond to her call at the earliest possible moment.

The year 1947 was one of waiting.

It was the year when India entered into freedom, when, with the partition of the subcontinent into Pakistan and India, newly made borders were bathed in a sea of blood. The explosion of Hindu-Muslim violence cost at least a million lives. While there was enormous tragedy in the Punjab, when West Pakistan was severed from the body of the subcontinent, there was indescribable horror in Bengal, since the line of partition cut through its heart, even slicing through fields and communities. Of Bengal's total territory, twenty-eight thousand square miles went to India, and fifty-four thousand square miles went to the new Muslim state originally called East Pakistan. With partition, came one of the largest movements of population in history. As many as sixteen million men, women, and children were displaced, the Hindus and Sikhs fleeing into India and the Muslims into the two wings of the newly created Pakistan. At least four million Hindus streamed into West Bengal, India. Undoubtedly, relations between the two major religious communities had been exacerbated by the "divide-and-rule" policies of colonialism. In the first local elections permitted under British rule, Hindus could only vote for Hindus and Muslims for Muslim candidates. Attempts to have separate electoral lists for Christians failed because of the obdurate opposition of the Christians themselves. Gandhi went on a fast to oppose separate electoral lists for the so-called "untouchables," a policy which would have pitted them against other castes.

The Day of the Great Killing was a sign of the simmering violence in the two major communities. On January 1, 1947, the day Sister Teresa began her year of waiting, Gandhi was in Bengal, in a remote section crisscrossed by canals and watery inlets known as Noakhali. On that day he decided to start on a Pilgrimage of Penance through villages where Hindus had been killed, their homes set afire, their wives and daughters abducted and raped, and some of them forced to eat beef. With him Gandhi carried the Koran, the Bhagavad Gita, the *Practice and Precepts of Jesus* and a collection of *Jewish Thoughts.* Moved by fiery leaders, Muslims wanted to prove by violence that a free India embracing both Hindus and Muslims could not exist. The entry into freedom had to include states where Muslims would be the rulers. "Blood for blood" became the slogan, and the violence in Bengal provoked counterviolence in the neighboring state of Bihar, where the Hindu community took revenge; retaliatory violence spread across the continent.

During much of this time, Sister Teresa was not in Calcutta. She was sent by her superiors to the Loreto convent in Asansol, about three hours by train from the city. There she was put in charge of the kitchen as well as the garden, and she also taught geography. During that time, she corresponded regularly with her spiritual director, sending him letters which he described as very beautiful.

When India came into freedom on August 15, 1947, Gandhi was in Calcutta. The day that was supposed to bring unalloyed rejoicing was a time for mourning for many, and a time of agony for the millions who had been uprooted and denuded. Gandhi was housed in the Muslim quarter of Calcutta and was on a fast with the Bengali Muslim leader, H. S. Suhrawardy. Gandhi was greeted before dawn by groups of girls singing Tagore's songs of freedom. Throughout the day, thousands of men, women and children came to Beliaghata to "take *darshan.*" When Bengali officials appeared, Gandhi's words showed that he knew the sufferings of Bengal were not over. "From today," he told them, "you have to wear the crown of thorns. May God help you." India was now a secular republic, binding an incredible diversity of peoples into a federal, democratic system. Within its borders was a minority of over forty million Muslims.

During the year of waiting, Fr. Julien Henry, who was close to Sister Teresa through the Sodality and also as pastor of St. Teresa's Church near the Entally compound, was told by Archbishop Perier of a nun who wanted to leave her order to work among the slums he knew so well. The archbishop did not reveal her identity, but wanted Fr. Henry's reaction. Fr. Henry began to ask his parishioners to pray for a special intention, that a mother of the poor might come to their great, agonizing city. Privately, the priest thought that the nun in question was a Sister of Charity. He told Fr. Van Exem later that he never dreamed it could be Sister Teresa. Archbishop Perier on a visit to Europe asked advice from some people on the wisdom of having a Sister carry out the work outlined by the local teaching nun. He did not identify her. When he returned to Calcutta, he met once more with Fr. Van Exem on the subject of Sister Teresa. The archbishop stated that one of the persons he had consulted was Fr. John Jansens, the head of the Society of Jesus. What Perier wanted to search out was whether the whole plan was feasible, and even more, could it be a call from God. He told Van Exem that the response of Fr. Jansens was favorable to the whole idea.

At the end of the year, Archbishop Perier agreed that Sister Teresa could write to the Mother General of Loreto asking to be released from the congregation. The archbishop, however, insisted on seeing the letter first, otherwise he would take no part in the matter. Sister Teresa framed the letter to the Mother General of Loreto in Dublin, a letter then edited and typed by Fr. Van Exem. She asked simply for exclaustration, the freedom from strict enclosure and the life of Loreto, to take up work directly with the poor. Exclaustration meant that she wanted to continue to live by her vows but in a new setting. When the archbishop read the letter, he insisted on a crucial alteration. He wanted the word "exclaustration" changed to "secularization." This would mean that Sister Teresa would no longer be a vowed nun but would become a laywoman. To both Van Exem and Sister Teresa this was a severe blow, and Van Exem remonstrated with the archbishop, pointing out that if Sister Teresa were without vows, it would not be easy to have young women join her. The archbishop's reply was, "She must trust God fully." Sister Teresa rewrote the letter and requested secularization. The letter was sent through the archbishop early in January 1948, just nineteen years after her arrival in Calcutta.

My correspondence with the Loreto Motherhouse in Rathfarnham revealed that the Mother General at that time was Mother Gertrude M. Kennedy, but no copies of the letters exchanged would be released to me. The reply of Mother Gertrude also came through the intermediary of the archbishop, and Fr. Van Exem described it as "one of the nicest letters I have ever read in all my life." The letter was written by Mother Gertrude in her own hand. It was dated February 2, 1948, Van Exem remembered and he recalled its contents: "Since this is manifestly the will of God, I hereby give you permission to write to the Congregation in Rome. My consent is sufficient. Do not speak to your provincial or to your superiors in India. I did not speak to my Consultors on this. I can give you permission for this. Write to Rome and ask for the indult of exclaustration." The aim of breaking enclosure to reach the very poorest, denied to Mary Ward, the foundress of Sister Teresa's order, was on its way to becoming a reality two and a half centuries later.

Fr. Van Exem pointed out to the archbishop that in the opinion of the Mother General of the Loreto order Sister Teresa's course seemed to be accepted as the will of God. Sister Teresa, overjoyed, now had to write a letter to Rome. She recalled that she wrote to the Holy Father, Pope Pius XII. All such matters were then referred to the Congregation for the Propagation of the Faith. She asked and received the help of Fr. Van Exem. "I wrote that God was calling me to give up all and to surrender myself to him in the service of the poorest of the poor in the slums," she explained later.

Sister Teresa obeyed Mother Gertrude Kennedy of Loreto in asking for the indult of exclaustration. When the Archbishop read it, he came to the key word and stopped. He refused to forward the letter unless, once more, "exclaustration" was changed to "secularization." Perier was adamant. Sister Teresa rephrased the letter and it was delivered to Archbishop Perier, who sent it to the apostolic nuncio in Delhi for forwarding to Rome. Though he did not inform Fr. Van Exem, the archbishop wrote a covering letter giving details of Sister Teresa's life and service in Calcutta. After February 1948, when the second letter was sent, Sister Teresa frequently asked Fr. Van Exem if any reply had been received. March, April, May, June, and most of July went by with no sign from Rome.

At the end of July, Fr. Van Exem was called to the office of the archbishop, who announced to him, "She has it." What Sister Teresa had was not the "secularization" for which she had asked under obedience, but the "exclaustration" she had prayed for. She was still a religious Sister under vows. The decree was dated April 12, 1948, and Fr. Van Exem had no explanation for why "it got stuck in the nunciature."

The archbishop had tested her to the utmost, and her obedience had not faltered.

The indult of exclaustration was given for one year, at the will of the archbishop. If, at the end of the year, the archbishop was convinced that Sister Teresa should return to her community, she would reenter Loreto. The indult, or decree, was in Latin. The archbishop had had it translated and three copies had been prepared. The archbishop told Fr. Van Exem not to go to St. Mary's Entally with the decree during a school day, but to take it to Sister Teresa on the following Sunday. In the meantime, the priest placed the documents under an image representing the Immaculate Heart of Mary, a gift to him from Sister Teresa.

On Sunday, August 8, 1948, Fr. Van Exem went as usual to celebrate mass in the chapel at the Loreto compound in Entally. Following his custom, he gave the sermon during the mass in Bengali, and when the mass was finished, delivered a second sermon in Hindi. Afterward, he asked Sister Teresa to meet him in the convent parlor. When he told her that he had the reply to her letter in his hand, he recalled that she turned pale and said that she wanted to go to the chapel to pray. When she returned, he gave her the news that what she had been granted was the decree of exclaustration. He then had her sign the three copies of the decree, one for herself, one for the archbishop, and one for Rome.

"Can I go to the slums now?" Sister Teresa asked Van Exem. He explained that it was not so simple, since she was now under obedience to the archbishop of Calcutta.

At last she could inform her Loreto family of her decision, first Mother Dorothy Maher, provincial superior, then Mother Columba Ormiston, mistress of schools, and then the superior of Entally with whom she worked day in and day out, Sister Mary of the Cenacle. Mother Dorothy wrote a letter to the Loreto convents to tell the Sisters that Sister Teresa had received the decree of exclaustration which would mean that she would be leaving them. They were asked neither to criticize nor praise the action but to pray for their companion. The letter was posted in all the houses of Loreto in that part of India.

The emotional wrench of leaving Loreto must have been acute and Sister Teresa did not want to prolong it. She has asserted many times that to leave Loreto was the most difficult step of her whole life—and the greatest sacrifice. "It was much harder to leave Loreto than to leave my family and my country to enter religious life."

"Loreto," she said, "meant everything to me."

Sister Cenacle wept at the news, saying that losing Sister Teresa was like losing her right arm. Archbishop Perier was now willing to accept that the call to Sister Teresa was from God. She had accorded him the last full measure of obedience and she was now free to leave the enclosure of Loreto for whatever new life God had in store for her. The news of Sister Teresa's leaving caused a commotion at Entally. The parting from her students was short and informal—a few hymns and Bengali songs, the tribute of tears, and she was gone from among them.

Sister Teresa came to Fr. Van Exem in the sacristy of the convent chapel on August 8 or 9, most likely the eighth, the priest recalled. She asked him to bless something for her. It was a sari, the typical sari of a poor Bengali woman purchased, he thought, at the bazaar. With it was a small cross and a rosary. Sister Cenacle was with her, still weeping, but partially comforted by Fr. Van Exem who had explained that if this new work was not the will of God, Sister Teresa would be back with her at the end of the year.

At Fr. Van Exem's suggestion, and with the agreement of Archbishop Perier, Sister Teresa wrote to the Medical Mission Sisters at the Holy Family Hospital in Patna, capital of the neighboring state of Bihar. There she could learn the basic skills of caring for the sick among the city's poor. A reply came from the Medical Mission Sisters welcoming her to Holy Family Hospital. On the morning of August 16, Sister Teresa saw Fr. Van Exem briefly to tell him she was leaving. Fr. Julien Henry noted in his diary that Sister Teresa was leaving St. Mary's Entally for Patna on the sixteenth of August 1948. The European-type habit, with voluminous folds, a skirt reaching to the floor, a white coif around the head and a black veil reaching almost to the waist, was laid aside. It would hardly be practical in the fetid alleyways where the poor were living.

The Patna train left in the evening, departing from Howrah Station across the great Howrah Bridge over the Hooghly River. According to Fr. Van Exem, no one saw her slip out of Entally in her Indian garb.

August 16, 1948 was two years to the day after the Day of the Great Killing had bathed the streets of Calcutta in blood. In ten days, Sister Teresa would be thirty-eight years of age. She could hardly have dreamed that her life was to become so inextricably woven with the agonies of Calcutta that the very name of the city would become affixed to her own name.

A crucial and possibly decisive step in the process of exclaustration was known neither to Fr. Van Exem nor Mother Teresa. It came to light only in 1971 in Washington, D.C. The papal nuncio to Washington, Archbishop Luigi Raimondi received Mother Teresa in the nunciature and reminisced about the time that she had been preparing to respond to her second call.

"I was in the Delhi nunciature at the time," he recalled. "When we received your letter," he informed Mother Teresa, "we saw that the request covered only one year. We took into account the letter that Archbishop Perier sent with it. We knew about conditions in Calcutta and we made a decision. We granted the decree of exclaustraton in Delhi without forwarding it to Rome." Archbishop Raimondi made no mention of the momentous change of wording from "secularization" to "exclaustration," a change that had incalculable effects on Mother Teresa's entire future. It had in all likelihood faded entirely from his mind. The accompanying letter from the archbishop must have helped put everything in context, so that if the step were truly the will of God, he would not be the one to hinder it.

Mother Teresa made no comment and asked no questions. She evidently had no idea what Archbishop Perier had said in his letter. She had naively believed that the decree of exclaustration had come directly from Rome, from Pope Pius XII himself. It occurred to me that if her letter had been simply forwarded from the Delhi nunciature to Rome, it probably would have been dealt with in a routine manner. If the request had been granted, it would have been granted precisely as worded. Who, in far-off Rome, would have been minded to make a word change in such a matter? The action at the Delhi nunciature was a providential intervention when the future of a new congregation hung by a hair. The concept of prevenient grace might enter here. It is an anticipatory grace, often applied in reference to the Mother of Jesus. Catholics believe that she was preserved from original sin in anticipation of the fact that the Messiah was to be born of her. Perhaps by stretching the term somewhat, it was a sort of prevenient grace that prevented the request from an unknown nun in Calcutta from reaching the Vatican along with bagfuls of other mail from around the world.

Stories began at a later date to grow up around Mother Teresa, much as the *fioretti* became attached to Francis of Assisi. The *fioretti* (little flowers) were tales of near-miraculous events or extraordinary acts of providence mirroring the very special character of the poor man of Assisi. Already, some events in which I have participated with Mother Teresa have been retold in an embroidered form. As Mother Teresa was not in the habit of reading what was written about her, she did not correct or comment on such tales. Always aware of the role of the divine in daily life, what someone has called the "dailiness of grace," she often responded delightedly to some totally unexpected act of providence. "That's a first-class miracle," would be her response to the arrival of the right amount of money at the right moment, to the sudden availability of large stocks of bread as related in Chapter 13, "The Mango Showers of Calcutta," or to the finding of just the right medicine in a donation of a variety of medications. She was, of course, using "miracle" in the generally accepted sense rather than in its strict, scriptural meaning.

The change of wording from "secularization" to "exclaustration" was crucial to the very founding of the Missionaries of Charity. By comparison with that event, many of the *fioretti* clustering about the figure of Mother Teresa seemed pale.

Returning to 1948, it was on August 17 that a lonely nun, stripped of everything, stepped off the train at Patna, the ancient city on the Ganges that once housed an imperial court.

Sister Stephanie Ingendaa, the superior of the Medical Mission Sisters welcomed the sari-clad nun. Sister Stephanie from Germany, Sister-Doctor Elise Wynen from Holland, and Sister Cyril Jacko from the United States were happy to share their reminiscences with me. They told of days that formed a crucial link in the story of Mother Teresa. One person who did not enter their stories was a sari-clad European who came all the way from Madras to Patna for a private visit with Mother Teresa. She was a young Belgian Catholic anxious to give her life to India. This was Jacqueline de Decker, who in 1979 would be with Mother Teresa in Oslo, and whose own story is related in Chapter 19,"The Shared Vision," the account of the Co-Workers of Mother Teresa.

"In August 1948," recounted Sister Stephanie, "I received in Patna a letter from Sr. Teresa asking me whether it would be possible for her to stay with us at the hospital for a few months, live with the Indian Sisters who were in nurses' training and make contact with the people. She explained that she had received one year of exclaustration from Rome. She was going to work in future for the poor and destitute in Calcutta. Of course, I wrote her that she could come and stay as long as she would like. From that came my first known meeting with Mother Teresa, but we were often in contact after that."

The Holy Family Hospital was staffed by Sisters who were doctors with specialties in obstetrics and surgery, nurses, laboratory technicians, and nutritionists. At their nurses' training school, the Sisters prepared Indian girls in many branches of nursing skills.

Sister Elise Wynen, M.D., in recalling those days, wrote: "At the time of Mother Teresa's stay with us, we were living in a poor section of Patna City, called *Padri ki Haveli* (House of the Fathers). It was named after the first church built in that town, over a hundred years earlier. Our convent was put together from the former church. It was quite moderate in size, built of stone blocks, with a high ceiling, a worn stone floor, narrow gothic windows and whitewashed walls. The section of the sanctuary became our chapel, separated from the rest of the building by a half-brick wall. The main part of the church was the actual convent, divided into cubicles by bamboo rods and white cotton sheets. It was clean, cool and spartan. The cemetery, no longer in use, was our garden, and we often slept between the tombstones, the mosquito nets providing some privacy. We ate in the old servants' quarters, where our nurse-aides also lived and slept. All of us were fed from a small, dark kitchen with a coal stove. In charge of it was an old Hindu cook.

"The hospital was once a simple school building, two stories high, with a small, separate building which housed the operating and delivery room and the sterilizing equipment. Later, two more wards, a nurses' hostel and classrooms were added. We were much too busy to hold long discussions with Mother Teresa. She was just fitted into a cubicle, given a chair in the dining room and community room, and included into our day. Whenever there was a new admission, an emergency or an operation or delivery, Mother Teresa was called at the same time as the nurse called the doctor. She would come flying across the lawn and stay with the patient. She often needed help from the nurses for Hindi terms since she was more fluent in Bengali.

"In that way, she became acquainted with fatal accidents, mothers dying on the delivery room table, children sick from being abandoned by hopelessly torn and desperate families. She also attended cholera and smallpox patients. As I remember, nothing ever fazed her. She just wanted to know what was going on and what she could do to help. Soon, I would count on her to hold the patient's hand during painful procedures, to comfort a crying child, and to help the nurses whenever she could. We had many friends in the families living around us and were invited to weddings or feasts, to share in grief, or joy at recoveries, and Mother Teresa was always glad to go along. In her months in Patna, she did get to know the poor, especially the sick poor.

"During evening recreations, we would all talk together, and she would share her hopes and ideas with us. We did not spare her, and I think she welcomed our insights and criticisms. It soon became clear that if a group or community wanted to work for the poor, they would have to make up their minds to work *only* for the poor.

"Our recreation talks would go back and forth, from high ideas to practical proposals. From our own experience of hard work and poor conditions, we stressed strict rules of prayer, but no prayers after 9 P.M. We talked of our simple meals, but the absolute necessity of plenty of food, with adequate protein, and no exceptions, except for illness. We told of the need for a daily hour of rest, of one day a week off for those who worked on Sunday, and an annual time away from the place of work. Even clothes were discussed. We wore white cotton habits and veils which were changed daily or even twice a day. In the operating room, we wore gowns and caps.

Mother Teresa told us she wanted the sari. We said that for sake of health and hygiene that [it] should be washed daily, and the head covering kept to a minimum, no starch."

Sister-Doctor Elise concluded her reminiscences with the words:

"We all came to appreciate and admire Mother Teresa, and we visited her many times in Calcutta where her ideas were put into practice. While the city looked on in wonder, the poor came flocking. Nothing that has happened since then has ever surprised us. We knew her."

While Mother Teresa was still in Patna, Fr. Van Exem went to that city to make his retreat. Before beginning the retreat, he gave a talk to the Sisters and nurses at Holy Family Hospital and immediately afterward asked about Mother Teresa.

"I am here," came a voice from the group. He had failed to recognize Mother Teresa among the Indian and Anglo-Indian nurses. It was his first sight of her in the sari he had blessed.

Sister Cyril Jacko, an American Sister of Slovak origin, director of the nursing school, shared her experiences.

"When I, or others of our Patna Sisters, would pass through Calcutta, we always stayed with the Loreto nuns. They never failed to give us warm and generous hospitality.

"When Mother Teresa came to us at our hospital in August 1948, she was wearing an ordinary sari. It was nondescript cotton, like the sari of the poor, and white.

"It was a far cry from the long black habit and stiff white coif of Loreto. Some of our nurses, who had been her students in Calcutta, were shocked to see their Sister Teresa, their Headmistress, dressed this way, and they even cried. Later, they learned of her purpose and got used to her.

"We Sisters knew it was her period of transition for a future she was not sure of. In principle, yes, she was sure, but its shape was not clear to her. We welcomed her as a friend who needed help in preparing for a different life.

"Mother Teresa visited and lovingly attended patients in the wards. As she had never had any nursing before, and I was Director of the Nursing School, I was able to teach her many simple procedures, making a hospital bed, giving injections and medicines. As for obstetrics, Sister Stephanie, the Superior and instructor in midwifery, had her observe and eventually help with some deliveries. After one of her experiences, I remember her coming all blood-spattered, with a gleeful laugh into our convent, remarking, 'Our Loreto nuns should see this!'

"Mother Teresa emphasized the spirituality of her future life, the hours of prayer, penance and fasting. Her idea," Sister Cyril recalled, "was to eat as little as the poor. Our Sister Elise—Dr. Wynen—helped her understand how nutrition, good balanced food, adequate rest and personal hygiene were required of anyone out in the slums all day, working hard. A strong point of Mother Dengel's rule is 'Balance'—otherwise our Sister-doctors and Sister-nurses could not carry out their heavy tasks for long. Later, I learned that the young women who joined her had to eat a certain number of *chapatties* for breakfast—a good hearty breakfast. Also, after their work each day in the slums, it would be necessary to bathe and change their clothes. They washed their sari each day.

"I cannot forget how Mother Teresa helped a fifteen-year-old girl suffering from advanced tuberculosis—incurable as so many of the TB patients were then. From what I understood, the girl desired very much to join Mother Teresa in serving the poor. Toward the end of her stay, Mother Teresa somehow 'confirmed' her as an associate in her work. The young girl was able to say certain prayers for the work and also ministered to the other TB patients, talking with those unable to get out of bed. She died at Holy Family Hospital, a first follower of Mother Teresa.

"One remark I clearly recall making to her, as I recall her answer.

" 'Sister, it seems that with all you hope to do for the poor on the streets of Calcutta, you'll need help of all kinds. Someday you ought to visit the governor.'

"She replied, 'No, I could not do that, I couldn't approach a dignitary like that.'

"Her humble appearance and demeanor made the sentence ring with conviction.

"You can imagine my smile when we learned not too long afterward that there was an outing in the gardens of the governor's mansion for the slum children helped by Mother Teresa. I don't know how it came about.

"A few days before she left, Mother Teresa and I had a chat in the garden, our backyard cemetery among the tombstones. She remarked that she had no idea where or how she was going to proceed with the ideals she had. Her next step, she told me, was to go and live with the Little Sisters of the Poor in Calcutta, and from then on, God would direct her."

After her return to Calcutta, Mother Teresa kept in touch with the Medical Mission Sisters in Patna and could count on them as friends.

Sister Stephanie recalled, "In the course of the first year in Calcutta, she came to Patna to bring us three children she had picked up in the slums. All three were suffering from tuberculosis and badly in need of proper care. Two of them were cured, but for the third one, help came too late. She also brought with her six hundred rupees to defray some of the expenses.

"I was later to see how she worked with each person who is needy. She looks neither to the right nor the left, but only thinks, 'What can I do now?' I remember another time she needed our help. I received a letter from a man whose name, I think, was Gomez. He was a Catholic and was asking for the death certificate of his wife who had died at our hospital. It was some time before. We checked and found that he had never visited his wife, in fact no one had visited her. So I wrote to him that I was unable to comply with his wishes, since anybody could have written a letter like that.

"Some weeks went by and then a letter came from Mother Teresa. Was it true that Mrs. Gomez had died, and if so, would I please let her have the death certificate. She had come to know Mr. Gomez in the slums of Calcutta. He was living with another woman and was anxious to make his peace with God. If he had the certificate, the couple could get married properly. Of course, I saw that the document was sent to Mother Teresa. She got new clothes for both of them and they got married properly in church."

Mother Dengel, the Mother General of the Medical Mission Sisters, did not visit Patna during Mother Teresa's stay, but the generosity of her Sisters in housing and training the guest who was alone and poor was never forgotten. When Mother Teresa left them, the Sisters gave her a pair of sturdy sandals. Repeatedly repaired, they lasted a long time and were shared by various young women who came to join Mother Teresa. The "Patna sandals" were often referred to by the first members of the little band as a sign of the new life of carefree poverty.

In December 1948, Mother Teresa boarded the train for the three-hundred-mile journey to Calcutta. It was shortly after December 8, the feast of the Immaculate Conception of the Virgin Mary that she arrived on the streets where she knew she belonged. She took her place as an Indian among Indians. Her resources consisted of five rupees. As Sister Cyril Jacko pointed out, her garb was a "far cry" from that of a Loreto nun. The sari was arranged somewhat differently from that of a Bengali woman. It was wrapped around her head over a tiny cotton cap that approximated a nun's head covering. On her left shoulder a small black crucifix was attached with a safety pin.

Under her sandals, she wore no stockings, thus meriting the term "discalced" as applied to St. Teresa of Avila after she had led the Carmelite Sisters in dispensing with wearing stockings with their sandals.

Fr. Van Exem had raised the subject of shelter for Mother Teresa with the superior of the Little Sisters of the Poor. The Sisters conducted St. Joseph's Home for about two hundred aged people with little or no means. The superior wanted to know if Mother Teresa were over sixty, in which case she could be accepted as an inmate. When the priest explained that she was a former teaching Sister at Loreto, the superior asked if she were still a religious Sister under vows. Hearing that she was, that she had received a decree of exclaustration, and that she was under obedience to Archbishop Perier, the superior agreed to welcome her.

The Little Sisters of the Poor were founded in France by Jeanne Jugan, who was declared a saint in the twentieth century. They were vowed to the poverty and dependence on providence that Mother Teresa envisioned for her work, the difference being that they worked behind the walls of institutions. The Little Sisters of the Poor could have no regular income and they depended on donations for funds and supplies for their destitute inmates. They followed the pattern of complete surrender to providence in homes for the aged poor in twenty countries around the world.

At St. Joseph's Home, Mother Teresa began by making a short retreat under the direction of Fr. Van Exem. He was able to see her in the mornings and then she would pray alone. She spent some hours during her first days helping the Little Sisters in caring for the aged.

Then she stepped into the abyss of her new life, carrying her midday meal in a little packet as she left in the morning to visit the *bustees.* On December 21, 1948, she decided to start her work in Moti Jihl, the *bustee* where her students, members of the Sodality of the Blessed Virgin, had visited poor families under the leadership of Fr. Julien Henry. It was about an hour's walk from St. Joseph's Home. With the utter faith that she was answering a call, she gathered a few children around her and started an open-air school. She started it "right on the ground," a phrase that was to be a crucial one when the constitutions of the Missionaries of Charity came to be written.

When it came time to take her midday meal, she would find a quiet place to eat it, a place where she could find drinking water. Once, she told me, she knocked at the door of a convent to ask if she could come inside to take her meal. She was told to go around to the back and was left to eat her sparse food under the back stairs like a street beggar. She never mentioned the name of the convent. Such a reception was not too surprising, since she was a strange sight on Calcutta's streets, a lone nun who had become Indianized, and who spent her time in the alleyways of the poorest of the poor. Even one of her strongest supporters, Fr. Michael Gabric, a priest of the Yugoslav group in the Society of Jesus was nonplussed at the metamorphosis. It was the letters from the pioneer members of this group, reaching Skopje, that had first ignited Mother Teresa's imagination about coming to Bengal.

"We thought she was cracked," was his candid response.

Mother Teresa, at the request of Archbishop Perier, kept a record of those early days. Only a part of it remains. "God wants me to be a lonely nun," she wrote, "laden with the poverty of the cross. Today I learned a good lesson. The poverty of the poor is so hard. When I was going and going till my legs and arms were paining, I was thinking how they have to suffer to get food and shelter. Then the comfort of Loreto came to tempt me, but of my own free choice, my God, and out of love for you, I desire to remain and do whatever is your holy will in my regard, Give me courage now, this moment."

The loneliness of those first days, as she made her way across Calcutta to Moti Jihl, is unimaginable. For someone long accustomed to life lived with a beloved community, where every day had its preordained pattern, the uncharted day must have been dizzying. In addition, the conviction of being strange and unique must have been painful in the extreme. A sari-clad European woman was hardly a novelty, since many European women, married to Indians, adopted the graceful silk saris of the well-to-do. A European woman, swathed in rough cotton, with stockingless, sandaled feet was quite a different phenomenon on Calcutta's streets. The strength it took to face those streets, only occasionally accompanied by a poor Indian widow or a schoolgirl, was an indication of Mother Teresa's conviction. She was answering the call, cost what it may. The self-surrender of those days was absolute. The certainty of her own helplessness was so total that it buttressed her in her conviction, often asserted, "It was all God's work; none of it was mine."

Some accounts have mistakenly interpreted her words about the "comfort of Loreto" in material terms. Her sacrifice was that of leaving behind the certainty of a well-trod path to accept the risk of finding another path to the poor in a time of dislocation, violence, and death. Loreto Entally continued its indispensable work of educating those who could afford fees, as well as its task of giving the chance of a life of full dignity to orphans and to girls from the poorest families of the city. The picture of a nun leaving an easy, comfortable life serving the children of the well-to-do to pioneer among the poor does an immeasurable disservice to the truth and to all the women who long ago on January 10, 1842, on the very same morning, began classes both for pupils at Loreto House as well as for orphans at the Murgi Hatta church, the old cathedral church in the chicken market section of Calcutta.

The life work of the young woman who met Mother Teresa in Zagreb and accompanied her to Rathfarnham indicates that the Loreto Sisters never deserted the poor. Betike Kanjc became Sister Magdalena and remained in Loreto. Much of her life was spent in the village of Morapai in the Sunderbans, a delta village reachable only by a canal. She worked in the orphanage and widows' home of the Loreto Sisters and also in the free dispensary that served as many as three hundred patients a day. Sister Magdalena was later stationed in Asansol, from where she visited and cared for the sick and needy in the surrounding villages.

Fr. Van Exem's protective and guiding hand followed Mother Teresa when she needed a place of her own from which to start her work. He spoke to a member of a Bengali Catholic family, Alfred Gomes. The final word was to be that of his brother, Michael Gomes, a teacher, who lived at 14 Creek Lane with his family. A room on the second floor was offered to Mother Teresa, and in February 1949, she moved in, bringing with her a small suitcase. Soon the room was furnished to her taste, with a single chair, a packing case that served her as a desk, and some extra wooden boxes that could serve as seats. On the wall was the image of the Immaculate Heart of Mary, originally the gift of Mother Teresa to Fr. Van Exem. With her on her first visit came a widow who was the cook at St. Mary's Entally. After the Bengali custom, she was referred to by the name of her son as Charur Ma, the mother of Charu. Charur Ma, I discovered, was to live out her days in the Children's Home of the Missionaries of Charity.

Small gifts began to come to Mother Teresa and it was Charur Ma who accompanied her to shop for the supplies she needed for the *bustee* school. At other times, Mabel Gomes, the eight-year-old daughter of the Gomes family was Mother Teresa's companion. When he had time, Michael Gomes went with her to chemists' shops to ask for donations of medications for suffering people unable to buy them. The Gomes family were the earliest Co-Workers of Mother Teresa.

After waiting to hear of the whereabouts of their former headmistress and teacher, her students were relieved to learn that she was still in Calcutta. The initial amazement at seeing her in a cotton sari was expressed in various ways. Some, as Sister Cyril Jacko noted, actually burst into tears. After recovering from the shock of the transformation of Sister Teresa, who after all, had been referred to as "Bengali Teresa," it was easily accepted as a tribute to the culture that they loved. Now Sister Teresa had an address.

On March 19, 1949, on the feast of St. Joseph, honored in the Catholic Church as foster father of Jesus and protector of Mary, a young girl appeared at 14 Creek Lane. She was Subashini Das, who had been a boarder at St. Mary's School from the age of nine. She was in the last year of secondary school and had suffered a searing shock when parted suddenly from a teacher who had influenced her life and the lives of many others.

The short, earnest Bengali girl told her former headmistress that she had come to join her in the work in the Calcutta slums.

A few weeks later, Magdalena Gomes, not a member of the Gomes family, appeared at 14 Creek Lane. A former student at St. Mary's, she was also determined to share in the work. She recalled that when it came time to take her first meal, she was expected to sit on the same bench as her former headmistress. She was so diffident that she could not eat. Mother Teresa left the room until she had finished the meal.

By Easter 1949, there were three women sharing the hospitality of the Gomes home, and three women went together to Moti Jihl. They began to use the public buses and tram cars of the city, joining the masses who moved about to work or to beg. Subashini Das, who took Mother Teresa's first name as Sister Agnes, and Magdalena Gomes, who became Sister Gertrude, have been mentioned as representing at Oslo the strand of Mother Teresa's life so supremely important to her—the Missionaries of Charity.

Sister Agnes recalled that during the years of the Second World War, Mother Teresa had taken on much extra work. She helped in the running of St. Mary's in its temporary quarters on Convent Road. With many Sisters evacuated along with the pupils to safer places than Calcutta, Mother Teresa was called upon to teach many subjects besides geography, in particular English and religion.

"She taught religion in such a wonderful way," Sister Agnes told me, "that everything came alive for us. We felt in our souls the love of Jesus and His sacrifices for us. And we felt the beauty of sacrificing for Him. And also, she taught it in our own language. There were many religious vocations from our classes, to the Carmelites as well as to Loreto. I had wanted to become a nun and serve the poor. I came from a modest family and I did not see that I would be giving up anything if I entered one of the orders in Calcutta. It was not until Mother Teresa began to work that I knew what I wanted to do."

Sister Gertrude who was to complete her medical studies while a Missionary of Charity and eventually bring medical care to Yemen, recalled her high school days. "Mother Teresa took care of us personally. When we were ill, she stayed up to be our nurse. She did everything, even looking after our food. I often wondered how much sleep she could get. Once, when I was ill, it was Mother Teresa who took me to the hospital." It was also Mother Teresa who later helped Magdalena complete some work in mathematics so that her medical studies would not be interrupted.

"At Creek Lane, in the house of the Gomes family," Sister Agnes explained, "we lived as nuns, but without a rule at first. We felt our way would be recognized, maybe soon, maybe not so soon. But it would happen." The third young woman to present herself became Sister Dorothy, and the fourth, a young woman from Dacca, then East Pakistan, was Sister Margaret Mary.

Within a few months the number of young women who came to join "our way" was ten, almost all former students of Sister Teresa of St. Mary's in Entally. Four of them left school in their last year before they had taken their final examinations. This must have seemed strange behavior to parents looking forward to having a daughter with a secondary school diploma. Sister Gertrude's family was so shocked that it was two years before they were reconciled to her conduct.

Sister Teresa arranged their schedule so that they could spend time on the required courses and all passed their final tests. The first Sisters always remember the order of their coming and recall that two early candidates decided to leave after testing their vocation.

When her companions grew in number Mr. and Mrs. Gomes gave them a larger room. As the young women kept coming, the Gomes gave them the upper room, an extended space that resembled a loft such as artists use in New York, Paris, and other cities.

From the upper room, the young women, all garbed in saris, went out to the poorest areas and gave loving attention to two groups, the near-naked children condemned to lifetime illiteracy, and those others, many, but not all, aged, who were dying without care in the alleys and gutters of the crowded metropolis.

By August 16, 1949, the year of exclaustration was over. During that year, Mother Teresa had been under obedience to the archbishop, and it was now up to his good pleasure whether she was to remain outside the enclosure of Loreto. By that time, the reports of the work of the small band had reached Archbishop Ferdinand Perier. There was no question of having Mother Teresa return to enclosure, since in that case, the group of young women would have to be disbanded. They were considered just a group of pious women living in community and so could not have a chapel in their dwelling. They used to go to mass in St. Teresa's Church, their parish. A course that would allow the work to continue would be to have them accepted as a congregation for the diocese of Calcutta, directly under Perier himself. This course was now possible, since the band around Mother Teresa numbered more than ten members. Before taking any steps in this direction, the cautious hierarch made inquiries as to whether there were any adverse criticisms of Mother Teresa and the work of her group.

One day, Perier addressed himself to Van Exem and insisted that he tell him if he had heard any negative reports. In perfect candor, Van Exem reported that one of the old Jesuits was of the opinion that in leaving Loreto, Mother Teresa was responding "to the wiles of the devil." He could not understand leaving the fine work she was doing as a teacher for some uncertain effort in the slums. The old priest had expressed this opinion to one of Mother Teresa's former superiors in Loreto. The archbishop was so indignant that he insisted that the priest in question go to the superior and apologize for voicing such a criticism.

During 1949, Mother Teresa opted for Indian citizenship. Her identification with the people and the future of India was sealed. Toward the end of 1949, the archbishop showed himself completely in favor of Mother Teresa and of the young women who had joined her. At the beginning of 1950, the archbishop indicated his willingness to take steps to have Mother Teresa and her followers recognized as a congregation for his archdiocese. This recognition would have to come from Rome, from the office for the Propagation of the Faith. Perier was willing to take the constitution of the new congregation to Rome. He told Van Exem that he was planning to be in Rome in April 1950, and that if he had in his possession five copies of such a constitution, he would present them in person.

Mother Teresa wrote a first draft, expressing clearly the spiritual discernment she had received on the train to Darjeeling and during the ensuing retreat. What Sister Agnes described as "our way" was reflected in a fourth vow, added to the usual three vows of poverty, chastity, and obedience. The new congregation, to be called the Missionaries of Charity, was to have its members live by a fourth vow, "to give wholehearted and free service to the poorest of the poor."

Fr. Van Exem, from his knowledge of canon law and administration, put the first draft in better order and added some points that would complete it. The result was shown to a Fr. Sanders, who was the official canonist, the guardian of church law, of the diocese. The five copies were placed on the desk of Archbishop Perier who then presented them to Cardinal Pietro Fumosoni-Biondi, head of the office for the Propagation of the Faith for the Catholic Church. The constitution was accepted, fourth vow and all. It was that fourth vow lived out with such spectacular dedication that was to bring many young adherents and to attract the amazed attention of believers and nonbelievers alike. It was that same vow which was to bind the Missionaries of Charity forever to the very least of humanity.

The date of the acceptance of the Missionaries of Charity as a new congregation limited to the diocese of Calcutta was October 7, 1950, a feast dedicated to Our Lady of the Rosary.

A mass was held in the upper room of the Gomes house. One part of it had been arranged as a chapel. That first mass was celebrated by His Grace, Archbishop Perier himself, with Fr. Celeste Van Exem reading the decree of recognition of the new congregation.

The words of the decree read to the tiny band illuminated in a prophetic way the future of the Missionaries of Charity:

> To fulfill our mission of compassion and love to the poorest of the poor we go:
>
> — seeking out in towns and villages all over the world even amid squalid surroundings the poorest, the abandoned, the sick, the infirm, the leprosy patients, the dying, the desperate, the lost, the outcasts;
> — taking care of them,
> — rendering help to them,
> — visiting them assiduously,

— living Christ's love for them, and
— awakening their response to His great love.

Sister Teresa, teacher and headmistress in Loreto, became Mother Teresa, foundress of the Missionaries of Charity.

It was to be just Mother Teresa, not, as she pointed out on many occasions, "Reverend" Mother Teresa.

Mother Teresa did not forget her friends in Patna who had first given her hospitality. They were invited to the ceremony. Sister Cyril, American member of the team of Medical Mission Sisters who had helped with the speeded-up training course in nursing skills, was able to be present.

"I was there," recalled Sister Cyril, "for the mass and the breakfast afterwards. I climbed to the third floor of a multifamily house. The long room put into use as a chapel was extremely simple, with neither a chair nor a prie-dieu. At breakfast, I sat with Mother Teresa and the postulants. We occupied two benches alongside a table in that narrow room. I was favored with an egg, since I could not down the required number of *chapatties.* I realized that Mother Teresa was serious about taking care of the health of the young women. I felt very privileged to be there."

In the next two years, the number of young women choosing to join Mother Teresa grew to twenty-eight, one girl coming from as far away as Kerala in the southwest of the subcontinent. Though living dormitory style, it was not possible to continue in the upper room and in an annex next to it. Fr. Van Exem and Fr. Henry went about on their bicycles searching for a house. At that time, many Muslims were deciding to quit Calcutta to escape the sporadic violence still erupting between the religious communities. Among them was an ex-magistrate who had built a home on Lower Circular Road for his retirement years. It was with reluctance that he was making up his mind to leave the city where he had spent his life, to migrate to Dacca. The magistrate, Mr. Islam, was one of Fr. Van Exem's many Muslim friends. Just before finally deciding to part from his property, he stood in front of it with Van Exem. He asked the priest to wait for him while he went into the nearby mosque of Maula Ali to pray. When he returned, he said to the priest through tears, "I got that house from God. I give it back to Him."

The vicar-general of the diocese, Msgr. Eric Barber, with the approval of Archbishop Perier, acquired the house from Mr. Islam at a price representing hardly more than the value of the land. The advance of the 120,000 rupees by the diocese was an earnest of the confidence that Archbishop Perier now had in Mother Teresa and her plans.

Mother Teresa and the band of young women moved into the house at 54A Lower Circular Road in February 1953. The road had at first marked the boundary of Calcutta, but was now a main artery, loud with the cries of hawkers and the almost deafening clatter of jam-packed tramcars. This building became the nucleus of the Motherhouse of Missionaries of Charity. One of the rooms was immediately turned into a chapel in which was placed the image of the Immaculate Heart of Mary that had once belonged to Fr. Van Exem. It was from this house that Mother Teresa and a group of young women went one morning to the old Cathedral of Our Lady of the Rosary, the Murgi Hatta church. The young women were to make their first vows in the new congregation, and Mother Teresa was to pronounce her final vows as foundress of it. As she had already taken lifetime vows in Loreto, this was in the nature of a restatement of those vows in a new setting. This was in April 1953.

The Medical Mission Sisters were invited to be present and the superior, Sister-Doctor Stephanie came from Patna. She remembered the event. "My visit to Calcutta was on account of the ceremony of the congregation of the Missionaries of Charity. The ceremony took place in the cathedral. Mother Teresa pronounced her final vows before the others. According to the constitutions, she made them into the hands of the archbishop. After this, the first four Sisters made their first vows into the hands of Mother Teresa. I spent the day with them and went back to Patna in the evening."

From 54A Lower Circular Road, Calcutta, the work of the Missionaries of Charity was to move out across India and across the world. When, at a later date, I was asked to write an account of the Missionaries of Charity for the lay Co-Workers, another strand of Mother Teresa's life present at the Nobel Award ceremonies, Mother Teresa took me aside. In measured tones, reflecting their importance to her, she dictated the following words: "In the choice of works, there was neither planning nor preconceived ideas. We started our work as the suffering of the people called us. God showed us what to do."

3

The Distressing Disguise

The terrible anguish of Calcutta first directly assaulted my senses in 1955. I saw how Mother Teresa and the Missionaries of Charity went where the suffering of their people called them. Mother Teresa took me first to Sealdah Station, the terminus of the Eastern Railway. It was from that station on Lower Circular Road that she had set out on the momentous train journey to Darjeeling only nine years earlier. Could one ever be prepared for a refugee camp in the cavernous waiting room of a railway station, with uncounted thousands squatting on the stone floor, cooking, eating, suffering, and even dying while, nearby, trains regularly steamed in, coming to a raucous halt?

I had spent considerable time in Delhi and the region around it. In that city, I had visited a group of refugees who had fashioned shelter for themselves in the Red Fort, the Purana Kila. In the arcades and corners of the ancient, red brick, Mogul Fort, they had thrown up canvas, plank, and cardboard partitions behind which they could steal some privacy from a world that had cast them out, denuded and unprotected. But they had some advantages, including the bracing air of Delhi, and, it seemed to me, greater attention from government agencies. In addition, many American voluntary agencies like Church World Service and Catholic Relief Services, from whose headquarters staff I had come, were especially active in the capital where it was easy to reach enclaves of the needy.

In Sealdah, we picked our way over the prone bodies and possessions of the refugees, barely missing here the hand of a sleeping child, or there the belongings of an old woman crouching behind gunnysacks and staring out of sightless eyes. Among the massed brown bodies were men with chests like birdcages clad only in the *dhoti* around their loins and women in rough cotton saris like the one worn by Mother Teresa, except that theirs were dun-colored with dirt.

"There must be nearly ten thousand people here and around Sealdah,"

Mother Teresa told me. "They come in every day from the 'Dacca side.' " The "Dacca side" was the way many Calcuttans and West Bengalis referred to the area across the border, now a new nation.

A few feet from the ends of the railroad tracks converging on Calcutta from the foothills of the Himalayas rose an immense grill partition of heavy iron bars. Here began the halls and waiting rooms taken over by the refugees. The floor and outer walls of the cavernous station building were of gray-black stone, sectioned off by further partitions of iron bars. Sealdah had the look of a great, obscenely crowded jail.

"We bring them the food you send us. The bulgur is something they get used to, but it is the rice they like better."

Through the Food for Peace program of the United States Government, people-to-people agencies like Catholic Relief Services could channel American grains to needy groups overseas. The voluntary agencies, our own included, had persuaded the government to make the wheat available as bulgur, a form used since biblical times. Bulgur wheat comes in pearllike grains, similar to rice, and is parboiled. Thus it is possible to cook it over the tiny stoves of Asia where fuel is scarce. Wheat flour would be useless in such a situation as this since stoves for baking bread are unheard of, even in ordinary village life. I had a moment of satisfaction in remembering that I had helped to convince the Department of Agriculture to process some of the stored wheat into a form that could be used by the poorest of the poor in such centers of need as Calcutta and Hong Kong.

We walked by a woman who was leaning over a *chula,* a mud, bucketlike stove on which a small pot was boiling. The fuel was dried dung patties. In the pot was the bulgur and a soy mixture, high in protein, that the agency had shipped to India.

"We bring them the bulgur and the soy if they can fix them up themselves. But we have so many others. We bring the vats here and heat the mixture. We can only come a few days every week. The government brings supplies also. The rest of the time the people go begging. They go scavenging. If there is anything to find in our city, they will find it. Some of the men try to find little jobs like guarding a doorway or carrying loads. Each rupee is a godsend."

As we walked, children naked or near naked, began to follow us. There was soon a line of little starvelings. Small boys had dark scabs on their heads and some had the protruding bellies of hunger. Little girls in odd pieces of clothing joined them in holding out their hands. The one word I deciphered was "Ma" (Mother), a name they addressed to any female who might answer their appeals. One naked child lay on a piece of cloth, his eyes half open. Mother Teresa talked to the mother whose big black eyes began to fill with tears. The child was getting weaker every day. Mother

Teresa explained to me that she would have one of the Sisters bring the child to Shishu Bhavan. "That's our children's home," she told me.

Women in discolored saris stood listlessly on a queue holding brass and tin pots. Mother Teresa explained that the only water for drinking and for washing came from the Sealdah washrooms. Many faces brightened as we made our careful way, avoiding not only bodies but large beetles who scurried among the massed bodies. As I looked around, I saw it as a cavernous "Black Hole." Yawning before me was a steaming pit of misery. The mingled fumes of arriving steam engines, of diseased and sweating bodies, of cooking pots over the dung-burning stoves, of half-decayed foods guarded for future meals settled almost palpably over the teeming scene. I felt that the odor would cling to me until I left Calcutta. Mother Teresa seemed not to notice the stench.

The history texts of my Welsh school days gave us the impression that one of the most spectacular events in India's history was the night of the Black Hole of Calcutta. This was when the Nawab of Bengal, in 1756, during the struggle against the British, captured groups of British men, women, and children. They had taken refuge in the East India Company's Fort William. The Nawab's men did not kill their captives but herded 146 of them into a small British guardhouse called the Black Hole. It was probably done for safekeeping. During the suffocating heat of a Bengal June night, all but twenty-three of them perished. We were not taught that the Black Hole was only one small episode, leading to the long carnage that accompanied the subjugation of Bengal and the Indian subcontinent. It gave rise the next June to an armed attack, the Battle of Plassey. When Clive won the battle, he demanded millions of silver rupees in compensation and seized nine hundred square miles of land adjoining Calcutta, called to this day, 24-Parganas. While the East India Company collected the rent, most of the money was pocketed by Robert Clive. He was the first of a long line of Englishmen who became immensely rich from a rich province. The Indians looked upon the process as plundering or looting and point out that the word "loot" entered the English language through what transpired in Bengal.

Sealdah was only the visible tip of a spidery network of refugee camps that reached into the Bengal countryside. I learned that day after day, representatives of the refugee department of the West Bengal government came to Sealdah. They went through the masses of people, choosing fatherless families, or families in which the father was already incapacitated by tuberculosis or some other disease, for camps up country. But the tide of refugees was an inexorable one, beggaring the resources of Calcutta. Mother Teresa and the Sisters were a presence and a lifeline of help.

I had met Mother Teresa only that day, and so important was the American food that came through her hands to the starving, that she put other things aside to show me the needs of her people. I had been told in Delhi that I should not leave Calcutta without meeting a woman known as Mother Teresa who had formed a band of young women to work in the slums. At that time, she was unknown outside Calcutta and the horrifying conditions of the city had not yet captured the world press. I do not know what sort of woman I had expected to see after I had walked down the dirt lane that led from Lower Circular Road and pulled a rope at Number 54A. The sonorous clang of a bell brought an old woman who took me to a tiny spare parlor. It contained only a small table and four rickety unmatched chairs. Into it came a small woman with a resolute step. The firm step and the welcoming smile, along with a garb I had never before seen, are the first things that I remember from that first meeting. When I told her that I only had a short time in Calcutta on my way to Vietnam, she mentioned some places to which she would take me, Sealdah, pronounced Shealdah, and two others which I later recognized as Shishu Bhavan and Kalighat. My second impression was that her English was accented in a way I had not encountered before. It was not a simple Indian accent, nor a European accent that I could identify.

Mother Teresa walked with me from 54A Lower Circular Road, the Motherhouse of the Missionaries of Charity, to Shishu Bhavan, the children's home. That morning, I had been confronted by the bedraggled army of men, women, and children who lived on nearby streets. They had crept up to the entrance of the hotel and as I came out in the morning, they fastened entreating eyes on me. One of the chief tasks of the doormen seemed to be that of sweeping them away for the convenience of the guests. The women, some of them holding scrawny children, managed to smile, their shining, gazelle eyes alight with hope. The reality of the effort behind that smile, an effort that was meant to melt the hardest and most indifferent of hearts, I found excruciating.

My hotel was on Chowringhee Road, a wide thoroughfare facing the Maidan, Calcutta's great park referred to as its "lung." The vast, cleared space, a mile wide and two miles long, owed its existence to the "Black Hole" event, since the British forces vowed never to be cornered again. They cleared the entire area surrounding Fort William and this remained a parklike expanse in the heart of the city. I wondered how many shelterless people there might be if they were so visible in the center of the city. There were groups on Lower Circular Road, the long street which encircles the city from north to south. Some had erected tentlike coverings, supported by poles, over their heads, and squatted under them. I asked Mother Teresa if she knew how many street dwellers there were in the city. She did not know, nor was she sure of the population of the city itself.

What she knew was the number of children she and her sisters had snatched from almost certain death. That day there were sixty.

At the back of a courtyard which we entered through a metal gate was a large house whose main floor was occupied by a row of basketlike cribs. This was Shishu Bhavan, the children's home. Some of the infants were tiny wisps of creatures, being fed by young women dressed in saris that were completely white. Lacking were the three blue stripes, one broad and two narrow, that marked Mother Teresa's sari.

"The mother of this one died and a neighbor brought her to us," said Mother Teresa. "She must be six months old and we think we have saved her." The baby's wizened little face stretched into a smile as Mother Teresa picked her up and nestled her in her arms.

"This little boy we found in a rubbish heap. There was still life in him. Look at him now." His face was round and healthy.

"So many of our children have been abandoned. Many are premature and we do our best to nurse them back to life."

I watched the Sisters feeding the infants. Some of them had saris identical with that of Mother Teresa.

"Those are our novices," said Mother Teresa, pointing to the young women in white. "While they are preparing for final profession, they go out for part of the day to work with the people. That way they know the work."

In the next room, a dozen youngsters were playing on mats on the floor. I supposed they must be about two years of age.

The sister told me that some were three years of age, and some four or five years old.

"They come to us so weak so that even when they are three years of age, their legs can barely hold them up. They crawl for a while, like this one. He is three at least."

The older boys and girls were having a meal of rice and fish in a dining room. I supposed that if the boy we had seen in Sealdah survived, he would join this group.

That evening, as I talked with a Parsi engineer who had worked for many years in Calcutta, I learned that the number of street dwellers might be more than two hundred thousand and that the population of greater Calcutta might be somewhere between six million and eight million. I thought of the sixty children in Shishu Bhavan as contrasted with the numberless children in Sealdah and on streets and ghastly alleyways whose families scrounged to keep them alive from day to day. Mother Teresa seemed to follow an old maxim that the good that is possible is obligatory. She and her Sisters were obliged to do everything possible for the poorest and weakest; they were not paralyzed by the thought of what they could not do.

Mother Teresa saved Kalighat for the last. I have mentioned that first visit to the Hostel for the Dying and also the fear that held me frozen as Mother Teresa went from pallet to pallet, talking with and consoling men and women from whom life had taken everything but breath itself. Mother Teresa took me through the men's ward, telling me a little of the story of each one. There was a small card in a slot on the wall behind each one giving every bit of information that could be gleaned—the name, when and if he was able to give it, and often, the place where he had been picked up. The pilgrims' hostel, or *darmashalah,* was constructed like an ancient inn. In the middle of the long hall was a wide passageway. The pallets were ranged at right angles along the two sides and were raised about two feet from the floor. Lying side by side on the cement raised platforms were seventy men of all ages. There were Bengali, Oriya, Nepali, Madrasi, Anglo-Indians, Chinese, Hindus, Muslims, Christians—any attempt to classify them would be incomplete. Some were obviously wracked by pain. Some had the glazed eyes and labored breathing of death itself. Some were smiling as though amazed at their own recovery. I had expected to find old men, derelicts perhaps, at such a hostel. But many of the men were young, some only boys. Mother Teresa recalled the words of a man at Kalighat. Despite the care she gave him and the care given by the Sisters, nothing could save him. "I have lived like an animal on the street," he told her, "but I die like an angel, loved and cared for."

The women's ward presented the same picture of humanity in extremis. In front of me women were rotting with sores that had to be cleaned of maggots, others with growths on their faces and necks that were carefully dressed by the Sisters. Mother Teresa watched the young Sisters as they gave their whole attention to a hideous growth or cleaned bodily excretions.

Mother Teresa seated herself on the raised platform beside the patients. She spoke to them in Bengali, English, and what I assumed to be Hindustani. As she spoke, the patients would put a hand in hers. Even when the person was beyond speech, Mother Teresa would communicate by the consoling stroke of her strong fingers. She would caress the heads of men and women who were hardly more than skeletons. Their eyes were fixed in a haunted stare and their cheeks sunk so deep and the skin drawn so tight that the skull seemed struggling to burst through.

They seemed to me like Asian versions of the cadaverous survivors of Dachau or Auschwitz. Mother Teresa's merciful care for these barely alive human creatures brought me back to a Europe rising from the ashes, a Europe that had spawned a war which swept fifty million men, women, and children through the gates of death. I had reached Europe after the war's end to find that peace had not been achieved. This was proved by the fact that Europe was pockmarked with thousands of camps of Displaced Persons. Huddled in them were the survivors of the concentration camps and former slave laborers, imported for the Reich war machine. Among them were ordinary people fearful of returning to their home places in Eastern Europe. So careless had the world's nations become of human life that the victors of the Second World War had agreed to the expulsion of upward of seventeen million of the defeated from their homes in central Europe. These were the expellees and I had seen them scrounging for their very lives in destroyed Germany. The spirit of war which viewed human beings as "things," and which turned them into "things," lifeless bodies, did not vanish at war's end. People were still seen as "things" to be herded into camps or driven across frontiers.

Such merciless lack of care, such indiscriminate human destruction, along with the unspeakably discriminate extermination of Europe's Jewish population, were a world away, literally and in spirit, from Mother Teresa's passionate care in nurturing the tiniest spark of life. By her care, she was asserting that the spark was of infinite value, issuing from an infinite Creator. The person, no matter how disfigured, mattered.

Mother Teresa could not stop by every pallet. As I stayed close to her, many of them held out their hands to me. One of the sights that remained with me from my first visit to Calcutta was that of outstretched hands, waving feebly, using what infinitesimal strength was left in a search for human consolation.

Tremblingly aware of the diseases raging around me, I could not risk infection by touching the suffering human creatures even with one finger. I thought of the air flight already booked for Vietnam. I turned away from the wasted hands and closed my ears to the small ineffectual cries of the agonizing and dying.

I was filled with shame.

My shame was compounded when I talked with Mother Teresa.

"Our work," she said, "calls for us to see Jesus in everyone. He has told us that He is the hungry one. He is the naked one. He is the thirsty one. He is the one without a home. He is the one who is suffering. These are our treasures," she said, looking about at the rows of pallets in the caravanserai. "They are Jesus. Each one is Jesus in His distressing disguise."

"Jesus in His distressing disguise." It was that phrase that rang in my brain. Jesus, covered with spittle in the gutter, Jesus assaulted by maggots, Jesus crying out for being forsaken. It was that conviction of Jesus in the other person, no matter how distressing the disguise, that brought me back to Calcutta just three years later.

4

Between the Idea and the Reality

When next I accompanied Mother Teresa to Sealdah Station, there was not the same press of bodies. By 1958, Sealdah had become a sort of refugee "village," the squatters having staked out their living spaces with carefully laid stones. Between my first and second visits, representatives of the state of West Bengal had continued to come regularly to sweep the refugees out of the station, sending them to resettlement projects in the countryside. As the families were moved out of the camps, other trekkers moved in, having managed a one-way ticket into West Bengal, or having simply walked across the Indo-Pakistan border. The number of border crossers must have dwindled somewhat. When Mother Teresa and her Sisters made the rounds, there were pathways between the staked-out squares. Besides those who needed food and clothing, there were some who could be helped only at a clinic. A few could be moved from the station precincts and given full care by the Missionaries of Charity. A child could be rescued from slow death through care at the children's home; a man or woman could be taken to the Home for the Dying where sometimes death could be outwitted.

When as children we played house in a Welsh village we often gathered stones and arranged them in squares in the garden or in nearby meadows. Once inside our square, we were "at home," and our playmate neighbors, in similarly marked-off squares could only enter after knocking on invisible walls. In Sealdah, the gathered stones and pieces of brick delineated a six-foot, or at most, an eight-foot square—a "no trespass" area for neighbor or passerby. Within the square, families of three or four, sometimes more, played, in a sort of fantastic and desperate way, at keeping house. The walls and roofs were as completely imaginary as those of our childhood days, yet even Sealdah's children seemed to respect the invisible walls. Either they squatted inside, or they ran around in the passageways and open spaces of the station precincts.

As I accompanied Mother Teresa, I saw how many of the improvised living spaces were in effect "dying spaces." In one home base set against a soot-darkened wall, we found a man sitting on his haunches. Around him were arranged a few brass pots and some jute sacks, gathered for flight, from some thatched village of what had been East Bengal. As Mother Teresa spoke to him, he moved his position and stretched out a fleshless arm to help balance himself. He had left East Pakistan with his wife and child. His home village had been in the Dacca region and he had worked on the land. His wife and child, he told her, were out begging on the streets of the city. He had no strength to go out anymore. He was wearing only a discolored muslin *dhoti* over his loins and his chest was caved in. His oval, finely formed face was drawn tight over the skeletal bones.

"Advanced TB," said Mother Teresa. "There is no place for him anywhere right now."

About fifteen feet away, in a little domain marked off against the high iron grill fence, a slight young woman was washing a baby's face with a piece of rag. He was totally naked, as were most of the smaller children. He might have been two years of age. She dipped the rag into the water pan that she had filled at the station washroom. We watched her as she squeezed the rag and concentrated on the task of washing the child, down to the soles of his dirt-caked feet. When she looked up, we could see that she was scarcely more than eighteen years old.

"We came here with nothing but our baby," she told Mother Teresa. "We have never left Sealdah since we came."

"Is your husband out working?" she was asked.

"I don't know what he is doing now," the girl replied with a strange look, puzzled or stricken, it was hard to tell.

"Perhaps he has to beg for you," Mother Teresa said.

"No," the girl said. "He ran away. He went mad here."

She looked down and resumed rubbing the child's body, possibly to regain control of her features. When she looked up again, she had assumed a winning smile. She dropped the rag and the smile was accompanied by the suggestion of an open hand. I marveled, as I often did, at the acting talents of the Bengalis. They could be starving, or in pain, or sick at heart, but when they saw a likely prospect, they managed to produce their stock-in trade, a smile melting in its warmth and sweetness. I did something dangerous in that setting, I slipped her some rupees, but surreptitiously to avoid being mobbed. I knew that sooner or later she would be moved to a Permanent Liability Camp. She might be settled in what I called a "purdah" camp, a camp without men, for women and children. Even Sealdah, bleak and dreadful as it was, might be preferred to such a camp that I soon saw sequestered in a lonely part of the Bengal countryside.

In many respects, the activities of village life proceeded almost normally inside Sealdah's bleak walls. Bathing out of aluminum pans and tins went on continuously. There was cooking over the tiny bucketlike stoves of baked mud. Here and there round-bellied brass pots gleamed through the murk like pale suns. Many were engaged in the engrossing task of searching each other's heads for lice. A few knots of people gathered around radios, listening as though entranced. The only activity I did not see was any kind of productive work, the work that would have made their lives meaningful. I could picture the men at the various stages of rice culture in rich paddy land, or preparing jute fibers for the factory by setting them in water and then spreading them to dry like coarse strands of hair. The women would be husking rice with a foot pedal or, in the afternoons, bathing in the village "tank" with their saris wrapped around them. Around the village there would be mango trees and plantains with their wide fronds and an occasional banyan with writhing exposed roots.

Here in Sealdah was a conglomeration of people thrown into a common existence of bleak ugliness by the flux of history. They had been thrust willy-nilly into a village of anguish and despair. The myriad ties of village life had been severed, and the immemorial skills of daily life, handed down from generation to generation, were falling into desuetude.

Sealdah was only one of the artificial "villages" of Calcutta with which Mother Teresa and her young congregation were concerned. In Calcutta's poorest *bustees,* destitute refugees squatted in any open space, constructing or renting desolate approximations of their mud and thatch shelters in *mofussils,* or villages that now belonged to others. Their new gathering places were near filthy canals and slaughterhouses. The ill, the most famished, the least aggressive lived in holes and crannies or in the open street. It was the refugee cascade of misery, along with the splitting of Calcutta from its hinterland, that increased to a piercing intensity the already dread problems of Calcutta, a city with a density of population well over one hundred thousand per square mile. Long a magnet for the poor of the whole region of India, Calcutta became after 1947, hideously swollen, like a hydrocephalic head on the hinterland of a body shrunken disastrously to a fraction of its size.

It was in this setting that the work of Mother Teresa had its birth. Just as Mother Teresa had explained, there had been "neither planning nor preconceived ideas," and each work was started "as the sufferings of the people called us." She relied on the Spirit for discernment as to what was to be done. The way in which she responded to the Spirit reveals in a special way her utter trust in the providence of the Creator. The experience of those early days revealed the pattern of the work as it expanded to other cities and, in time, to other continents. The arrowlike movement to

Calcutta's poorest, the most helpless and most rejected, the refugees in Sealdah, the school-less and abandoned children, the lepers and dying destitutes, had its counterpart later on as Mother Teresa led her Missionaries of Charity into Latin America, Africa, the Middle East, Asia, Australia, Europe, and even into the inner cities of the United States.

Toward the end of 1957 and into the early months of 1958, I was present at a crucial time in the growth of a work of mercy that was later to become known throughout India and the world. I had time to gather facts so that more American help might try to relieve the agony of Calcutta and Bengal, and in the evenings I recorded my day's experiences. Before leaving I asked a Calcutta photographer to accompany me to some of the places where I had spent my time.

The sufferings of Sealdah called Mother Teresa and the Missionaries of Charity to bring food to that "village" of the homeless and to pluck some of them from the station floor for care in the Home for the Dying or at Shishu Bhavan. Earlier, when she had been all alone, she had answered the call to go to the *bustees.*

As a teacher she had been drawn to the school-less children of the Moti Jihl *bustee* where her students had met the poor through the program of the Sodality of Mary. She had looked at those children over the wall of the large compound that enclosed St. Mary's School. During her well-ordered day as a Sister of Loreto, she could glimpse the chaos of the life of the poor as their huts crept up to lean against the very walls of the compound. Her vowed life was bounded by a wall. Having been permitted to breach that wall, she presented herself at the doors of the huts to ask the parents of the children if they wanted their children to have some schooling. She could not offer a school, as such, since none existed. I accompanied Mother Teresa to Moti Jihl and saw the scum-covered pond which gave the *bustee* its name of Pearl Lake. If it resembled a pearl, it was surely a black pearl. Naked children were playing around the pond. Their eyes, edged with coal blacking, were enormous. This was put on as a protection against the sun's glare. A number of them had stomachs that protruded like shining brown balloons under pathetically thin rib cages.

"There was the first of our schools," Mother Teresa said. "You see that plum tree over there?"

On the far side of the pond was a single tree, thinly leaved and no taller than a man. There was no telling if it could be the original tree or one that burgeoned later. I chose to believe it was the tree that stood there a few years earlier when Mother Teresa first presented herself at the entrances of the huts of the poor.

"After I had talked with the mothers and fathers and asked if they wanted their children to learn, they sent them to me. The first day I had just a few children, perhaps five. I sat on a chair under the tree and the children gathered round me on the ground."

"You mean," I asked, "that one day there was no school, and the very next day, there was a school?"

"Yes, that was the only way. I had no money for slates or chalk or a blackboard, so when it came time to write something, I took a stick to mark it on the ground where the children were sitting.

"They were such good children. They wanted to learn. Soon more than forty came every day. Then we got a few benches and we could have managed very nicely until monsoon time."

I realized that the day on which Mother Teresa had started the open-air school in Moti Jihl was December 21, 1948. It was less than two weeks after she had stepped off the train from Patna into the abyss of a new life with utter faith that she was answering a call. One could picture the children sitting around her, their high voices echoing hers in the singsong of the Bengali alphabet. Their voices must have traveled round the *bustee* with an entirely new and hopeful sound, the sound of the shackles of illiteracy being broken. The mothers accepted the woman who was garbed as they were except that her head as well as her body was swathed in the sari.

The loneliness of those days must have been excruciating to someone accustomed to a protected classroom and the security of a loving religious community at the close of the day. Yet the new solitude was accepted in the spirit of the patron she had chosen, the "little" Saint Thérèse whose "way" emphasized the acceptance of the monotony of obscure sacrifices. St. Thérèse had written that the great way of heroic martyrdom was not open to many, while slow, secret, "death by pin stabs" was the "little way" open to the generality of folk. Yet it demands its own special type of courage. The courage that sustained Mother Teresa was of the transcendent sort that issues from a spiritual conviction. As a person, she had a firm sense of self. One has to have a true sense of self in order to transcend it. Mother Teresa's character was centered in the merciful love of an all-powerful Creator and the confidence that this engendered. She was not a victim of an education that was guilt- and fear-producing. She was able to stand alone.

After Subashini Das joined her on March 19, 1949, and shortly thereafter, at Easter, Magdalena Gomes, the way to Moti Jihl was not so lonely. By that time, Mother Teresa was sheltered in the Gomes home, and they could start out together from Creek Lane, attend mass together at St. Teresa's Church, and divide up the pupils into manageable groups. The school had been moved indoors.

"When some of my students joined me," Mother Teresa explained, "we were given a little money. We rented a room nearest the tree. Then we rented two rooms and we did not need to worry about the monsoon after that." The rent of each room was eight rupees a month, the rupees coming as providential gifts to the tiny band.

I saw the location of the two dirt-floored huts, now occupied by families.

Mother Teresa taught not only the elements of reading and writing and practical figuring, but also basic cleanliness. She obtained cakes of soap and gave them out as prizes for attendance and cleanliness. She taught the children the importance of washing and combing their hair and of keeping as clean as possible in conditions where there was no regular water supply and only a community privy. In each privy shed was a large container. When it was filled with human excrement, it was supposed to be emptied by employees of the Corporation of Calcutta. This did not happen as regularly as needed, and the inhabitants often shunned the shed, with its overpowering stench to relieve themselves against walls or in gulleys. Yet, with a cake of soap, hands, heads and bodies could be cleaned and the natural immunities of the children could be buttressed by the germ-killing power of soap.

Mother Teresa did in Moti Jihl what Gandhi had done when he settled in Delhi. He lived in a cell near a cluster of huts constructed under his direction to shelter homeless "untouchables." He spent time with them, hearing their problems from their own lips. His often repeated advice to them was to learn to read and to make every effort to keep clean. Like the people of Moti Jihl, who lived in the utmost squalor, the sweepers in the Delhi colony whose daily work dealt with the refuse left by others could at least hold out cleanliness as an ideal.

As I entered the one-story brick building in 1958, I heard the singsong of children in the first class reciting the alphabet. There were benches and colorful letter charts on oil cloth. There was a blackboard and each child had a slate and chalk. I walked through six classrooms filled with nearly two hundred boys and girls who turned smiling, plum-dark eyes on Mother Teresa.

I thought of the obscene congestion in which they lived, lying down at night jammed into a tiny space and wrapped in the darkness of the Bengal night or cowering from the monsoon downpour. In the school, they seemed to relish the order of the simple classroom. No one slid an inch along the shiny bench or nudged a seatmate.

"After there are a hundred regular pupils, the Corporation of Calcutta puts up a school building. These children would be out on the street hawking all day for a few *annas.* They would be learning all sorts of bad things. Here they can begin to have a better life."

Besides the school, there was a new and proud feature of the *bustee,* a community pump. It stood in squat dignity between the solitary plum tree and the school building. It was Mother Teresa who had championed before Dr. B. C. Roy and the Corporation of Calcutta the urgency of bringing a water supply to this section of Moti Jihl. When I had first glimpsed Moti Jihl three years earlier, the people had only the brackish water of the pond for all their needs. It was hardly surprising that Calcutta had its annual outbreak of cholera. Many *bustee* areas still did not have piped-in water. In 1958 there were five thousand cases of cholera with close to eighteen hundred deaths.

As we walked round the *bustee,* everybody seemed to know Mother Teresa. We went into closed, dusty courtyards around which a dozen or more one-room dirt-floored houses were grouped. Greetings came to her from all sides. A lot of deep bowing went on, grown men and women suddenly moving toward the ground. She tried to lift them up and give and receive from them the *Namaskar* greeting with folded hands; but a few succeeded, and insisted on finishing the gesture by placing a hand on the sandaled foot. *Namaskar,* though used as "good morning" or "good day," has the connotation of saluting the divinity in the other. The people of Moti Jihl insisted on showing the ultimate mark of respect to a poor woman who had sat among them to share with their children as a free gift the indispensable tools of the intellect, children whose only sure legacy would otherwise have been illiteracy.

I made it a point to visit the other free schools that by now had been set up by Mother Teresa in many parts of Calcutta.

A school with a special history was that in the Bechbagan district, crowded with refugees from East Bengal as well as the poor who had migrated to the city from Bihar and Orissa. Children roamed about, devising games and caring for younger brothers and sisters while their parents struggled from day to day to keep alive. When Mother Teresa visited with the families, underemployed, underfed and badly sheltered, they told her that what they wanted most was a chance for their children. She talked with the poor and less poor. On Ahiriputera Street she had a conversation with a man who had done well. He was an electrician and his four sons worked with him in the same trade. His home was arranged as it would have been in any traditional Indian village, with his married sons and their wives and children around him. They lived decently and securely as a joint family in a large courtyard protected from the outside world by a wall. Mother Teresa told him her story and of how she was looking for a place to open a school for the neighborhood. The school would be completely free and she had a team of young teachers ready to start.

Hearing her story, the man told one of his own. As a boy he had prayed for the chance to learn to read and write, but there had been none. He had gone to work with his hands and had developed skill as an electrician. His five children were grown and married, the four sons and their wives and children occupying the compound with him, and his married daughter and her seven children living with her husband's family. He hoped that there might be a chance to help others, trapped as he had been, to escape from such a prison. He thought this might be the chance. His compound was large, and even though he had ten grandchildren, he felt that some order could be maintained during school hours. He talked it over with his entire family and they agreed to the plan.

He came to Mother Teresa to offer the Ahiriputera Street compound for a school and Mother Teresa accepted.

When I entered the Ahiriputera Street compound through a roughly fashioned gate one morning I found that the earth-floored court was pleasantly tree-shaded. At one end of the court was a large shed, probably designed for storage of tools. Cooking, washing, and all the chores of five families took place in the courtyard, but at that time, all family activities were held in abeyance, except for a few cooking pots on the porches of the separate dwellings.

Two hundred and sixty children were sitting on low benches and grouped into six classes. The Bengali patriarch was there to meet us, a strong-featured man with a shock of iron-gray hair. He had a typical Bengali name—and he will be referred to here as Charan Bannerjee. We talked quietly while three Bengali Sisters held the attention of their pupils in the main open courtyard. They were writing, on portable blackboards, letters of an alphabet that looked impossibly complex to me. Just inside the gate, a smaller group was being introduced to school life in another tongue; I supposed it might have been Oriya or Bihari. In the storage shed, two more classes were in session. In a corner of the compound, a large vat of rice, to which a soybean concentrate had been added, was simmering. This was watched over by a few mothers whose children were in school. Another mother was guarding several jars of milk, mixed earlier from milk powder. Each child received a bowl of food and a glass of milk before leaving school. Even into this busy compound came the food channeled from the United States to India in the Food for Peace Program. Besides sending food shipments to the Indian Government, the American Government utilized people-to-people agencies like Catholic Relief Services, Church World Service, and CARE to reach the hungry. A free glass of milk, carefully mixed with time allowed for dissolving the milk powder, was no small item in Calcutta. Milk as sold in the city was often a health hazard. Milkmen, bringing in their milk cans down the Hooghly, sold milk on the way, but the liquid contents of the cans did not diminish. What a poor family paid for was milk liberally diluted with Hooghly water.

Charan Bannerjee's expressive eyes glistened as he held out his hands as though in a benediction over the scene. We met his wife and daughter-in-law and the smallest children. The older ones were in the classes. Life had been good to him and his seed, he seemed to be saying, and he was saying thanks. When he talked of Mother Teresa and the young Sisters he shook his head as though in disbelief that they had separated themselves from their own families. Here were young women working for the children of others instead of having children of their own.

The children rose to say good-bye to Mother Teresa and, as we left, it occurred to me that Mother Teresa had among her gifts a special one that in social work courses is referred to as community organizing.

In visiting the schools conducted by the Sisters, I was to see other evidences of this gift, a gift of which Mother Teresa was unaware. Already fourteen free schools had come into being, each one revealing the fascinating diversity of Calcutta life. One was the Murgi Hatta, or chicken market school, adjacent to the ancient Catholic cathedral of Calcutta. Now the quarter was a small Chinatown, and the Missionaries of Charity taught the girls. I saw rows of Calcutta Chinese children lined up waiting for their classes, impressive in their uniformity and neatness, all with short haircuts and straight black bangs.

The boys were taught by the priests and brothers of the order of Don Bosco, called Salesians. The Italian branch of the order had been given charge of the cathedral parish after it had been served by the Jesuit priests from Belgium. They in turn had taken over the church from the Portuguese, who in accordance with the *"Padroado* of the East," exercised the privilege of evangelizing the lands reached by Portugal's navigators. As I wandered through the dark and shadowy interior of the church, I realized anew why Mother Teresa's route to India came through Ireland. There were memorials to the soldiers who had served and died in the British armies of occupation. Yet the words *"Patria Hibernia"* (Fatherland Ireland) were etched under their names on the plaques. They were the Irishmen, who, as the saying goes, occupied Calcutta for the British so that the Scotch businessmen could run it. As a person whose ancestors had left Limerick to serve in that army, I noted that a wing of that very school had been erected in 1849 to perpetuate the memory of Daniel O'Connell, known as "the Liberator." The metal plaque was hidden at the end of a passageway. In those days when both Ireland and India lived under colonialism sentiments favoring freedom were not for public display. The plaque memorialized the services rendered by "O'Connell to his native country Ireland but also to the cause of religious and rational liberty throughout the universe." O'Connell, who died in 1847, anticipated Gan-

Drana Bojaxhiu (mother) with son, Lazar, and two young cousins.

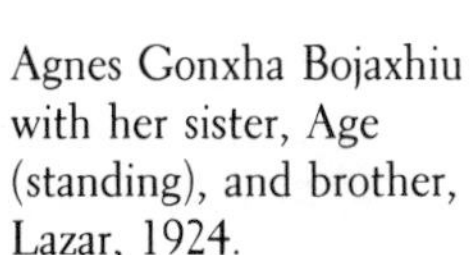

Agnes Gonxha Bojaxhiu with her sister, Age (standing), and brother, Lazar, 1924.

As a young woman in Skopje, 1928.

As Sister Teresa in Loreto, c. 1930.

Mother Teresa at door of Shishu Bhavan, 1958. *(Homer Page)*

Home for the Dying.

Mother Teresa and author at the side entrance of the Home for the Dying.

Arrival at the Home for the Dying.

dhi in insisting on struggling for freedom by nonviolent means; regrettably, he could not inspire his followers to be faithful to such means.

In another school, the Fatima School, we entered yet another facet of Calcutta life. Located on the New Improvement Trust, it was housed in a large metal-roofed shed with a raised concrete floor. There were eight classes, and the Sisters took it for granted that the first four grades had to be taught in two tongues; half in English, since the children were of Anglo-Indian stock and spoke English at home, the other half in Hindi, since they were not of Bengali stock. In a separate shed, older boys were enrolled in an industrial course, turning out chairs, as well as desks and benches that were destined for the *bustee* schools. Girls were sitting before five sewing machines, adding another skill besides their achievement of literacy. In all the schools, a daily glass of milk was given to each child. Only to the very poorest was there a meal of rice, with soy concentrate or beans added.

The fifteenth school was opened while I was in Calcutta. I saw it as the most daring project of all, since it was for children who shared the living death of a cluster of leper families. Mother Teresa told me of her plan and I walked around the *bustee* with her. It was in Dhappa, a section enveloped in gray dust and reeking with the miasma of the filth canal that ran through it. It was the slaughterhouse district and overhead the vultures turned in endless, meaningless circles, waiting for nightfall before settling in quiet rows on the slaughterhouse roofs.

Children stopped in their play to watch us as we searched up and down lanes and alleyways for an open space for a school. We found one at the edge of the *bustee* facing a paved road. There was a wide expanse of sidewalk with one store. Mother Teresa walked back and forth on the pavement, making calculations. She decided that even with several rows of benches, there would be enough room for people to reach the shop. It was a three-sided stall, with the front completely open to the street.

Mother Teresa explained her school scheme to the proprietor. I had no idea how she phrased her request. She might have used the same phrase she had used a few mornings before to the assembly of a Hindu high school. "I am going to give you the chance to do something beautiful for God." He did not take long to make up his mind. The school could begin.

Sister Angela, a round-faced Bengali girl who hardly ever spoke without a warm smile, was put in charge. Two Sisters would help her, Sister Marcella and Sister Francisca. Both young women were members of India's tribal people, belonging to the Oraon group. An empty room in the area was rented for eight rupees a month. It happened to be in a Muslim court. Benches made by the boys at the Fatima School were carted over. In one afternoon, all the equipment for a grammar school was placed in storage in the room—blackboards, chalk, erasers, slates, and the magnificent picture charts of the alphabet on durable oil cloth.

Sister Angela went to the families already being treated for leprosy from a mobile clinic. She told them that a school for their children would begin on the following Monday. It was to be out in the open. Hours would be from 8:30 to 11 A.M.

On Monday morning, the benches were set up on the pavement. As the children arrived, their names were taken and a check was made of the language used by the child's family. Only a third of the children said that Bengali was their own tongue. This did not surprise Sister Angela. Even though Calcutta is a magnet for the poor of the area, it is even more of a magnet for the victims of leprosy. It is common practice for them to leave their home communities and migrate to the nearest city. There, they are not known and besides they can beg more profitably in a metropolis.

Eighty-five children were counted. Uncounted, but present during the first days were a number of parents who watched every move with wary eyes. They noticed that the Sisters came in the mobile clinic, familiar to them since they received antileprosy treatment during its rounds. Some of the parents, I found out, began to argue among themselves, some saying that the Sisters would carry the children away to a hospital. They stood on guard. Others insisted that the Sisters could be trusted. The Muslims approached the Sisters to find out if they were going to make their children Christian.

It took about a week for the wary observers to believe that the Sisters were doing exactly what they had promised, giving their children a free, elementary school education. Yet the school continued to have difficulties. The traffic of cars and carts on the road, the comings and goings on the sidewalk, the noise of occasional street arguments made learning difficult. The unflagging discipline and attention of the children despite the intrusions were an incredible sight.

It was decided to move the school. A second spot was found under a jutting roof at the end of an alleyway. At least there would be no traffic noises. The school went well, with Sister Angela and Sister Marcella teaching the two Hindi groups and Sister Francisca leading the Bengali class. Mother Teresa came to see how the school was progressing and to study the children.

The classes were nearly over, and the children were waiting for the dismissal signal. Mother Teresa was talking in a low tone to Sister Angela.

"This boy has white spots on his face. Be sure, Sister, that he comes to the clinic. That little girl in the first row, too.

"This one we already treat," she went on. "He has the lesion on his face.

"The hands of that little boy—there are sores on his fingers. The tips are already blunted. He is tainted.

"This little boy has got the sores on his feet."

The children were studying me intently, and I kept smiling at them as I heard the words in Mother Teresa's low voice. As each phrase fell into the air, I felt as though a sentence was being passed over each little head, a sentence on the unknowing. The sentence was to one of the most dread diseases ever to afflict mankind, leprosy, whose depredations might take years to scale these smooth skins and deform these young bodies. It was a nightmare in broad daylight. The cruelty of their fate possessed my imagination.

And yet, I thought, here where life was at its cruelest, mercy was nearest. Mother Teresa looked on the faces of these scourged children and saw the face of God. Compassion shone from her eyes. She and the three young Sisters were gathering to themselves the most rejected of all the children of God. As the class was dismissed and the children moved away, I heard their words of farewell. One word I understood, "Sisterji." The suffix "-ji" is one of love and respect as used in Gandhiji.

It was nearly noon, but Mother Teresa and the Sisters stood in the glaring light to discuss the site of the school. The smell of the cow-dung fuel cakes drying by the walls of the houses and the clouds of flies that left them to assail us did not seem to concern the Sisters. The number of children was nearing a hundred and when that number was reached, the Calcutta Corporation would allot a square of land and erect a school building on it. Meantime, even the space at the end of the alleyway was no real solution as a place for real concentration. The children had to be taken indoors.

Mother Teresa led us to where the benches and other equipment were being stored. The room was located in a court of twelve dwellings owned by a Muslim woman. She had refused Sister Angela's request to hold a class in one of the rooms that was empty. Mother Teresa asked for a chance to discuss the matter in person. A middle-aged woman came out to her.

They greeted each other with "Salaam," "Peace," and confronted each other. The woman had an air of self-confidence and her gray and black flowered sari hung well on her ample figure. Mother Teresa, much shorter and compact in her plain cotton sari, faced her with an utter lack of self-consciousness that was its own assurance. The encounter of a Muslim matriarch and a Mother Superior had its own fascination.

Mother Teresa explained the short history of the school and of how the children were so anxious to learn that they struggled to pay attention above the noise of traffic and in the open air at the end of an alley. If these children could study inside, in a classroom like the one in the court, they would learn more easily. She explained that many of the children would be coming from Muslim courts nearby, and they would not have to cross a paved road where cars dashed by. Besides, the school should be indoors by monsoon time.

The woman said little, but took us to see another room that had just been vacated by a family. She introduced us to her daughter, a tall young woman in a red and blue sari. A baby was balanced on her right hip. Faithful to the Bengali Indian custom of establishing a familial relationship, Mother Teresa addressed the woman as "Ma." A knot of near-naked children stood at a distance, their eager eyes taking in the scene. The woman spoke decisively. The Sisters, she told Mother Teresa, could have their classes in the two rooms in the courtyard. The rent would be eight rupees a month for each room. Then came her own contribution, which as proprietor only she could promise. With a proud shake of her head, she announced that during the morning school hours she would clear the court of smoking *chula* stoves and of the clothes drying on clotheslines.

The school came into existence, as with all the projects of Mother Teresa, quietly and naturally. Like the school under the plum tree nine years earlier, one day it was not there and the next day it was there. There was no campaign for funds, no public appeal. In a few weeks one wondered how such a service could *not* have existed. For Mother Teresa, there was no break between the apprehension of a need and an action to meet that need, however small that action might be.

For the generality of people, there is a hiatus, a time of pause and calculation between the apprehension of a truth and its embodiment in their lives. The poet called this hiatus "the Shadow." "Between the idea and the reality . . ." wrote T. S. Eliot in "The Hollow Men," "Between the conception/And the creation/Between the emotion/And the response/Falls the Shadow."

For Mother Teresa, no "Shadow" fell as she faced an abyss of need. She chose the simple, humble action of gathering children around her under a plum tree, or of lifting a dying human creature from the gutter to provide a human death. The fact that she might be considered "cracked" or left to eat under the backstairs as a beggar did not hold her back.

One point she made over and over again, especially later when confronted by batteries of press interviewers, whether in New York, Rome, Beirut, or Melbourne:

"If I had not picked up that first person dying on the street, I would not have picked up the thousands later on."

5

Such a Vision of the Street—Kalighat

It was the caravanserai at Kalighat that first focused outside attention on the needs of Calcutta and the work of Mother Teresa. I often saw it as growing out of a lone wheelbarrow.

Though at first, Mother Teresa turned her energies to the children, she found that as she crossed Calcutta she could not ignore those who lay down to sleep on the street and could not rise for want of strength or because of raging sickness. Many were long-term street dwellers who had used up all their strength in begging and were now breathing their last from exposure and starvation. Even those who had shelter and work were perilously close to the street. Prolonged illness, or arrears in paying for a rented room, would result in their being thrust outdoors for their final hours. The threat of the shelterlessness of the street hovered over countless inhabitants of Calcutta, in particular over the refugees whose hold on the economy was precarious and whose family ties had often been broken.

To orthodox Hindus, death, like birth, has elements of impurity and pollution. The only time when *harijan* women (formerly referred to as untouchables) are allowed to come near a woman of higher caste is at the time of birth. Those who handle corpses come from the lowest of the subcastes. If a destitute man were to die in a rented room, the owner, who might also be poor, would be forced to paint it to remove the pollution. The poor man might be unceremoniously moved out of doors at the sign of approaching death. Countless people were left piteously alone in their death agony until the twitching limbs quieted and the stertorous breathing faded utterly.

These Mother Teresa and the Sisters found in the gutters at their feet, left there or placed there to pass out of life lingeringly of some dread disease or mercifully quickly of a destroying fever. Maggots had often infested the untended flesh and would be feeding on the bodies of the helpless living, not waiting for death as the customary invitation to the feast. The only way to be sure of rescue from the streets was to die. Only then would the body be picked up for speedy consignment to the funeral pyre.

Mother Teresa has related how she picked up a woman who had been half eaten by rats and ants and took her to the nearest hospital. The hospital refused to admit her. Mother Teresa stood her ground and would not leave until the woman was admitted. Anyone who has dealt with hospitals knows how intimidating professional staff can be, especially toward those bereft of funds, as Mother Teresa and her patient were. To understand Mother Teresa, one must take into account her resistance to intimidation and her fearlessness in defending the helpless and voiceless.

Mother Teresa told me that she began to use a taxi when she found a human body drained of strength lying on the open street. She would wrap the person in a sheet or blanket for the trip to the nearest hospital. After a cursory examination, the suffering person was more often than not turned away. Sometimes she went from hospital to hospital with her helpless burdens. Though she planted herself in the waiting rooms, hospital staffs were often adamant in their refusal. There were times when the taxi driver refused to take her and her patient away when admittance was refused. Then she had to bargain with rickshaw men who also hesitated to transport a near corpse. The hospitals had their reasons. The person might obviously be dying and beyond help. For a person suffering from a lingeringly fatal disease such as tuberculosis, there was simply no possibility for long-term care. As it was, the usually crowded hospitals of Calcutta had patients jam-packed in the corridors, on the floors, and in every corner.

When all else failed, Mother Teresa told me, she would borrow a workman's wheelbarrow to trundle a scrap of humanity covered with filthy rags to a hospital.

The man or woman turned away from hospital after hospital could not be tossed once more into the open street. There was nothing for it but to accept responsibility for the rejected human being. "We cannot let a child of God die like an animal in the gutter," was Mother Teresa's decision.

Mother Teresa rented a room in the Moti Jihl *bustee* and personally tended a man rejected by all. Soon, a second pathetic bundle was brought to the same room. She acted to assert the inviolable and infinite dignity of each human being, even the most repulsive-looking. If she could do no more, she would invest their last hours with something of that human dignity. And if she could do no more than allow them a human death rather than let them die like animals in the gutter, she would do that. For those cast off by all, she and the Sisters would mirror by their loving care the love of the Creator for all the human creatures who came forth from His hand. Soon two stifling rooms in Moti Jihl were filled with the dying.

The Missionaries of Charity began to pray for a building, for any place where they could care for their people. The urgency was great.

There were cases when a person perished while Mother Teresa was trying to rescue him or her. She knew that pet dogs would not be left to die untended and said so. She made an appeal to the Commissioner of Police and the Health Officer of the Calcutta Corporation. Calcutta already had a center where the dying were brought by the police and by city ambulances, but it was pitifully inadequate in the face of the agony on the streets. The offer of a group of educated young Indian women of good family to devote themselves without recompense to society's rejects—and above all to the dying—must have seemed to Dr. Ahmed, the Health Officer, hardly credible. Yet Mother Teresa's utter seriousness was unmistakable. Here was a woman who had signified her identification with India by renouncing old ties and becoming an Indian citizen. There was a space, located next to Calcutta's most ancient and most revered shrine that might be put to this use.

The Health Officer asked Mother Teresa to come and inspect the building that had been used as a *darmashalah,* a pilgrim's hostel, near the Temple of Kali. It seemed the answer to the needs of the people, since it had two sleeping wards, electricity, gas connections for cooking and a large enclosed courtyard where patients could take the air and where clothes and bedding could be hung up to dry. Mother Teresa was satisfied with it. She had about twenty young women ready to work and more were joining her every day. It must have been from necessity, as well as from the need to have the novices know at firsthand the taxing nature of the work, that the young girls began immediately to participate in the work even in their period of apprenticeship as religious Sisters. The Health Officer announced that Mother Teresa could have the hostel provisionally. As it had been recently used by squatters, there was filth everywhere. A squad of Sisters took over and in a week it was clean enough to move the patients from Moti Jihl. The caravanserai for pilgrims had now become the caravanserai for other pilgrims abandoned by all.

Mother Teresa called the pilgrim's hostel Nirmal Hriday, Bengali for Pure or Immaculate Heart. It was named in honor of the Virgin Mary since it was opened in 1952 on the feast day dedicated to Mary's Immaculate Heart, August 22. Mother Teresa made a solemn commitment that no leprosy patient would be admitted to the hostel. It was also decided that only those patients would be taken in who had been refused by the city hospitals. The ambulances of the municipality began to deliver to Nirmal Hriday the street cases rejected elsewhere. It was an abode of last resort.

By the late fall of 1957, the Nirmal Hriday was an accepted part of Calcutta's underside, not the Calcutta of Chowringhee, with its hotels and shops, nor the Calcutta of the private clubs and the affluent suburbs like Alipore, nor even the Calcutta of the arts, of the gifted Bengali writers, painters, and filmmakers. The Home for the Dying was known to the police and health services of the city and to the growing number of people of many castes and creeds who came to volunteer at Kalighat. It was never called anything but Kalighat, the name coming from the cremation place near the Kali Temple. Here the ashes of dead Hindus were cast into a tributary of the Ganges.

In the Calcutta of Kalighat, in steaming, dusty south Calcutta, I found myself light-years away from Europeanized Calcutta. It was a strongly Hindu section in perhaps the most Hindu city of all India. The entrance to the Kalighat Home for the Dying fronted two of the most thronged streets of the area. As I stood on the sidewalk, cows arrogantly edged men and women into the filth of the gutter. Beggars smiled with bloody teeth after spitting out red betel nut juice on the pavement. I would have to get used to stepping on the bloodlike splotches without wincing and to turning away from at least some of the begging hands. Vendors of colored images of Kali, wheedling and importuning, left their stalls to pursue likely customers. Pilgrims, squatting to rest on the sidewalk or eating a quick meal, took over any unused space. The men were covered, or partially covered, by all manner of dress, from the loincloth or *dhoti* to shirts and trousers. The women seemed to come from all groups, being enveloped in white cotton saris and silk ones in shiningly brilliant colors. I learned that through the action of Gandhi, the Kali temple had been thrown open to the so-called "untouchables" in 1936, so I assumed that they were among the pilgrims.

Mother Teresa brought me up to date. She told me that in a period of just over five years, more than eight thousand of the dying had been received. Of them, more than thirty-five hundred had perished, the Hindus being taken to the burning ghats nearby, and the Christians and Muslims to their separate burial grounds. "At first," Mother Teresa said, "most died, no matter what we did. Then in 1955 and 1956 about half lived. And now, more live than die.

"The foods from the American people have helped to bring these people back to life. America will be blessed for doing this thing. You must tell that to them and bring our thanks. We get food from here, but I don't know what we would do without the rice and bulgur and *ghee* from your side." (Ghee was surplus butter, melted and shipped in large cans.)

The dropped walkways between the raised platforms, which on my earlier visit were open passageways, were now filled with a third row of patients. I read the chalk notations on the small blackboard at the entrance,

"Men 72, Women 69." That morning Mother Teresa herself gave calcium injections. A volunteer medical man was dispensing other medicaments. Four Sisters were washing and changing the women, going methodically up and down the line of pallets. If the stench from some was heavy and clinging, the Sisters did not heed it. They were joking and laughing with those who could respond, smiling and coaxing those who were in pain. Then they cleaned up the men and with buckets and mops swept through the wards. A staff of eight paid workers, some snatched from death at Kalighat, were cooking the meal in great vats. Soon the food was handed out on tin plates, and the hall became quiet. It was about eleven o'clock in the morning and from the high windows on one side of the hall came beams of light like so many streamers of filmy voile. There were minutes of unutterable beauty. The Sisters sat down to feed those too weak to hold a spoon. It was a laborious task and I asked one of them, Sister Vijaya, if she were not getting tired. "How can I get tired?" she asked. "It is Jesus I am feeding." The gaunt-faced woman patient was dribbling much of the food and her face had to be wiped again and again. Sister Vijaya's name meant "victory" and I felt that she had achieved a victory over her natural feeling.

My own fear had disappeared. I took the precautions ordered by the doctor. My shame at turning away from the dying on my earlier visit was being lessened by the practical work I was taking on at portside. Catholic Relief Services was making regular shipments of food and medicaments from Food for Peace stocks and these had to be warehoused and marked for distribution for Mother Teresa's centers and for centers in Krishnagar and other parts of Bengal as well as Bihar and Orissa. We needed a fuller port staff and more administrative staff in Calcutta and I had determined that the increase of staff would be my special task. I became acquainted with the port area where incredible arrays of goods were unloaded and where exports were placed on ships destined for the down river voyage to the Bay of Bengal. Soon the staff of Catholic Relief Services was increased and the feeding program expanded.

The closeness to the shrine of Kali had great meaning for Mother Teresa since it was a holy place for her people, but that very closeness brought trouble. There was thought to be defilement in having dying people brought there, for the Home for the Dying stood on sacred temple precincts. Several times, when the Sisters arrived with Mother Teresa to tend the patients, they were met by groups of Hindus demonstrating against their presence. They were even threatened with violence. One man shouted that he would kill them as he approached Mother Teresa. She did not move, but said with a smile, "If you kill us, we would only hope to reach God sooner." No one was hurt. This was not the only time that

Mother Teresa was threatened with death. Her reply was always the same: "I would only go to God sooner."

The Brahmins serving as hereditary temple priests were aghast that Catholic Sisters should be given the right to work so near their shrine. Over the years they sent regular notices asking for their eviction and petitioned the Calcutta Corporation to see that they were removed. The agreement by the Health Officer had only been a provisional one and they wanted it discontinued. The matter was certainly on the list of items for discussion at the meetings of the Corporation, but somehow was never acted upon.

One event helped somewhat with the temple priests. One of the Kali priests developed tuberculosis and was so obviously in the last stages of the disease that he was turned away by several Calcutta hospitals. Mother Teresa accepted him at Nirmal Hriday and gave him a corner to himself. He was only twenty-eight years of age with a great yearning for life. He loathed Nirmal Hriday and raged against the sickness that was destroying him. Karma, the concept of an ultimate justice which explains all inequalities, is supposed to "free the mind from resentment against God and man." But the wasted young Brahmin, lying on his pallet, found no cure for his devouring resentment in the underlying teaching of Hinduism, just as some Christians fail to derive consolation in times of trouble from the teaching of the resurrection repeated serenely in happier periods.

Mother Teresa and the Sisters gave him the tender care they gave to other sufferers. Mother Teresa began to notice a change in the young man, the rage subsiding and something of resignation replacing it. Before he died, a sweetness shone from him that was a living memory to Mother Teresa and the Missionaries of Charity. After they realized that one of their fellow priests had been bathed and fed and comforted by every available medical aid, the priests of Kali became less hostile. They knew that someone close to them had been cared for with a wholehearted love that asked nothing in return.

There were other expressions of hostility. Once a group of young people, chiefly students, who feared that the Catholic Sisters would convert people to Christianity in a place sacred to Hinduism, went to Kalighat. Their leader entered the *darmashalah* intent on getting Mother Teresa out of it. When he saw the helpless, emaciated examples of humanity being cleaned and washed and their sores being dressed by the Sisters, he had a change of heart. He came out to the protesters stating that he would get Mother Teresa and the Sisters out of Kalighat only on one condition: they would have to get their mothers and sisters to come day in and day out to do the same work. The group left and did not return.

I was not a witness to the metamorphosis of the priest of Kali in the Home for the Dying, but as I came to the Home day after day, I was witness to similar cases. For many, Kalighat was a haven of such peace and acceptance as they had never known. Charubala was one example. On the card in the metal slot on the wall above her pallet was the word by which she described herself, "widow." Charubala was that phenomenon known as a "child widow." Her head of gray hair was shorn like a man's. She knew a little English as well as Bengali and explained that her parents had arranged a marriage for her before she was ten years of age. It was in Maldah in the northern part of Bengal. When she was ten, the man to whom she was "married" died before the arrangement had been consummated. Charubala became a child widow. A woman whose husband dies is assumed to have a very bad karma to have helped bring this dreadful fate upon herself. Charubala's life must have been like that of many child widows; she remained in the homes of relatives, working for them for her keep.

Her fate must have been unbearable because she simply walked out and left Maldah behind her. Migrating to Calcutta, she scrounged for a living washing dishes and doing housework. When a paralysis of the spine bound her legs, she was of use to no one and was left on the street to die. At Kalighat, Charubala found Mother Teresa who had time to have a little chat with her in Bengali. She had young women to wash and comb her hair and keep her helpless body clean. Charubala could use her hands and she would help feed Mary the woman next to her too weak to feed herself. Mary, an Anglo-Indian, was too advanced with starvation to survive. While she lived, she held a large black rosary in her wasted hands, moving her lips in constant silent prayer. As her eyes dimmed, she slipped almost imperceptibly out of life.

The unutterable surprise of being cared for, lovingly and gently, for the first time in her life, brought a joy to Charubala that shone out of her eyes.

Her most regular visitor was a Jesuit priest steeped in Bengali culture and a professor of the epic in one of Calcutta's secular universities. Father Robert Antoine was the closest thing to a chaplain at Kalighat, and he came regularly to chat with the people and serve them in small ways. He lived and dressed as a Bengali and was indistinguishable from the lay volunteers. For the occasional Catholic, he was ready with priestly aid. Paralyzed Charubala had all the verve and humor native to the Bengalis. She knew that Father Antoine loved Bengali music, and she would spend her time making up songs for his visits. She told everyone that she, who had never had a son, now had one, Father Antoine, for her own. She saw many die in the months that she lay in Kalighat and she sang of this to Father Antoine. He learned to sing one of her songs with her and translated it for me. "The evening has come. Those who came after me have gone before me. I who came here months before them must stay after they have gone. God, when will you take me away. Those who came after me have gone before me." The softly sung chorus, with its acceptance of the passage from life, brought a sort of peace to many in the ward—at that moment numbering sixty-eight women. Charubala made up little songs for anyone who visited her and for the women placed on the pallet beside her. She loved to talk and I could always find someone to translate when her tiny supply of English ran out. It became clear that it was not the care alone that brought her contentment. What brought the brilliant light into her eyes was the fact that probably for the first time in her life, people took time to listen to her, to respond to her, to praise her little songs, and even to sing with her.

One old man who was always glad to see me was Mr. Daniels, an ancient Anglo-Indian who must have had a comfortable life while the Anglo-Indians served as a buffer between the British colonials and the Indian people. Certain jobs, like those on India's railways and in the police force, were their sinecure. Mr. Daniels, who was extremely tall, had a long, fine face, an aquiline nose, and a courtly manner. He talked in that special Anglo-Indian accent that sounds somewhat like an Irish or Welsh accent. If his descent into destitution brought him grief, one would never know it. We talked of the weather and of how he felt each day as though we were in a neat parlor. He had one of the corners in the hall and, even though he was weak, he would manage to sit up against the wall to eat his meal out of the tin plate with care and dignity. He was simply fading out of life and he symbolized to me many other Anglo-Indians who had fallen on days of need and who as a group were fading out of Indian society as a separate and recognizable force.

On holidays like Dewali and Christmas, gifts were brought for the men and women in Kalighat. At Christmas time, I asked Mother Teresa what I could bring that would give a little pleasure to the patients.

"I will tell you something interesting," she replied. "When our people are surely near death, I ask if there is any food they would like us to get for them. So often the request is the same—grapes. I don't know why, but it is almost always so. Grapes are very expensive here in Calcutta and we cannot always get them."

This somehow struck me as natural, since in Britain, grapes were the specially prized fruits offered to the person confined to a sickbed. In highly Anglicized Calcutta, the ill looked for the same gift as a sign of care and affection. In Calcutta's New Market, a Victorian redbrick monstrosity housing endless rows of booths and stores, from handicrafts and clothing to foods and garden produce, I found dark plump grapes brought down from Kashmir. Even those closest to death enjoyed them, if not by actually eating many, by smiling when they tasted one or two.

"A few of our people beg for fresh oranges, or Indian sweets like Rosho Gulla. And the men beg for cigarettes. This is not a hospital," she reminded me, "but a home for the destitute dying. If a case is hopeless, all we can do is give them the few things that bring comfort. A cigarette brings great comfort to some of our people."

At Christmas, as I went from pallet to pallet, I realized how many of the people in Kalighat, especially the men, were young. One had to gaze long enough to see that the gouged-out cheeks, the dropped and salivating jaws, were those of starved young men. One young man had just been carried in from Howrah Station. Howrah was across the Hooghly River and was the rail terminus for central India. Like Sealdah, it had its village of destitute squatters who were served as often as possible by the Sisters. Mother Teresa knew him.

"Joseph," she told me, "used to be a first-class rascal." She did not give any further details, but I assumed he must have been at least a pilferer and petty thief. He was able to sit up and talk. His full name was Joseph da Cruz and he was from the "Dacca side." He was very dark-skinned and his high cheekbones were so fleshless that the tightly stretched skin seemed ready to burst asunder. He took the grapes in spidery fingers and his smile seemed a prefiguration of the skull beneath the skin. By New Year's Day, Joseph was clearly dying. He began to whimper and made pitifully unintelligible attempts at words. Father Antoine placed a hand on the almost fleshless head and whispered words of comfort close to his ear. The eyes that had been alive and full of expression receded into their sockets and he seemed to be receding out of life. I did not expect to see him again.

As we made our way down the crowded middle passageway, we passed a man whose clasped palms were extended in the Hindu greeting. I returned the greeting, and realized that he kept his hands aloft in a rigid, catatonic position. Suddenly, he prostrated himself, then raised himself several times. Finally, he fell backward in what seemed to be a trance.

"He was brought in last night," said Mother Teresa. "He tells us nothing. He is mad."

I had not known that the insane gathered up from the streets were also brought to Kalighat. As we went through the little hallway to the women's ward, we saw a woman tied with thick rags to a post. Another patient was sitting near, guarding her.

"She is mad, too," said Mother Teresa. "I must find a place for her. She tears the beds apart and beats the other women."

Hanging around the neck of the bound woman was an enormous goiter and her gray-streaked long hair was matted wildly.

For Joseph, all was over but the long dying. As I came to Kalighat, I found that he would rally in some mysterious way, continuing his precarious hold on breath for days lengthening into weeks. He came to know and greet me. One day he mentioned that he would like some cigarettes and tea. By that time he could eat no solid food, so along with the tea and cigarettes I brought a concentrated food drink that is given to children. He did satisfy his desire to draw on a cigarette but then found it too strong for him. One morning he beckoned Mother Teresa to come close to him.

"I will ask God to bless you, Mother, and to bless the lady," he whispered. There was no whimpering; he was perfectly intelligible. Forty-seven days after he had seemed to be sinking into death, he took his ultimate breath. He was one of those taken into the enclosure of Calcutta's new cemetery where all Christians, Protestant and Catholic, were received.

Mother Teresa had found Co-Workers among the various religious communities to take care of those who died at Kalighat. Christian and Muslim burial societies took care of their co-religionists. The many Hindus were taken by local people to the nearby burning ghat. For Hindus, to die near the shrine to the goddess Kali and to be cremated near that holy place was a desirable and blessed passage from one life to another. They were able to receive on their lips at Nirmal Hriday the waters of the holy Ganges. Muslims on the other hand could read or hear readings from the Koran. Fr. Antoine and other Christian volunteers consoled the Christians.

There were many with whom there could be no communication whatsoever. In the card in the slot attached to the wall, or to the pillow if they were placed in the passageway, was a single word, "Unknown." There was no date of birth, only the date of being found.

One boy was carried in and placed with special care on a pallet since his frail body was already skeletonized. On his card were the words, "Age about 14." His jaw lay open and his lips parched as though in a grotesque and perpetual grin. He was fed liquids with a spoon and several people spoke gently to him in various languages. Most agreed that he looked like a Madrasi, and someone spoke to him in Madrasi. There was a flicker of the eyes but no response. After less than twenty-four hours, he passed out of life. I was reminded of the Negro spiritual: "He said not a murmurin' word."

Every day hidden behind the heavy burlap curtain in a section of the hall between the two wards were several of the dead. The number of dead was chalked on a blackboard. I would often stand in meditation before that blackboard.

As I made my way through the halls of the dying, I was struck by the distinctive attitude toward death and dying when it is seen as a transmigration, as one of many such transmigrations. The Christian view that each person's life and death are unique was related always to the life and death of the person of Jesus the Christ. The dignity with which Christians surround death is absent when dying is seen as a passage, such as when a snake sheds its skin. The snake is the living spirit moving on to inhabit another form of life, while the discarded skin is the body that is being vacated. *Samsara,* the continual transmigration from body to body, is compared to an ever-rolling wheel. The living being is often likened to the rim, being crushed and again coming to life. As said before, in a poor *bustee,* a dying person would be carried outside to expire in order to prevent the pollution of a room. A translation of the Bhagavad Gita refers to the body as simply the "casing" of the spirit. The course of the living spirit from "casing" to "casing," or sheath to sheath, continues each time bearing with it the weight of character, or *gunas* from its previous casing or sheath. When the spirit is released from its passage to another body, it achieves *moksha* or liberation.

The care with which Mother Teresa gathered up scraps of humanity from Calcutta's streets was a startling sight. The love lavished on men and women abandoned by all, covered with loathsome sores and unable to take care even of their bodily functions, was evidence of another view, not only of dying but of life itself.

In fact, over the heads of men and women fighting for their every breath on these streets and in death-filled Kalighat, two different world views were in collision.

One view held that the melancholy events which had overtaken the destitute dying persons on their pallets arose out of a system of justice related to their evil deeds. This was the concept of karma, the law of cause and effect in the moral world. Such presumption of moral responsibility, of guilt, a guilt incurred in the current or in an earlier incarnation, would seem to those raised in the Christian tradition, to have the effect of robbing the suffering itself and the sufferers of their dignity. The putrefying sores, the maggots were only the visible marks of invisible moral evils. As karma was explained to me, I began to see it as justice made visible. The person cannot escape the law of karma. He is bound by it as he is bound by the law of gravity. Karma is an all-pervading element of Indian spiritual life, entering also into the Buddhist tradition.

The other view of life was much more mysterious. No judgment could be made on the sufferers nor guilt imputed to them. Yet there was the possibility that the sufferers were reaping what they had sown. Their anguish, however, might not be the result of evildoing and might ennoble them to the dignity of the Incarnate God-man.

The age-old dilemma of innocent suffering is the drama of one of the most beautiful books of Hebrew Scriptures, the story of Job. Here the just man, Job, is visited with dreadful afflictions, including tormenting sores all over his body. Job's "comforters" argue about the reason for his sufferings and one of the deepest questions of life is broached. Is the justice of God always exhibited in visible blessings for the good and punishment for the wicked? The death of Christ on the cross answered this question for believing Christians. Jesus' innocent suffering was redemptive, and all innocent suffering could be joined with this great redemptive act. Though sinless, Jesus' willing acceptance of death was for sinners. Remission of punishment due to sin was always possible. Forgiveness was always available through repentance. Yet for traditional Hindus, the figure of Christ on the crucifix evoked a question. Father Pierre Fallon, a priest with long residence in Calcutta repeated it for me. "What awful thing is He guilty of," his Hindu friends asked him glancing at the pierced body on the cross, "to deserve that degree of suffering?"

Thus the man or woman perishing in the gutter was viewed as working out his or her karma. Those who passed by did not need to stop to pick up a matchstick figure out of the gutter or give a drink of water to one gasping with thirst. Merciful help is certainly not absent in Hindu society; helping the sufferer has a relation to one's own karma in that it improves the karma of the one giving aid. Thus the belief in karma need not imply a simple fatalism though it may lead to it. The impulsion to extend mercy could hardly be the same imperative that it is in Christianity where the works of mercy are linked ineluctably to eternal salvation.

Those who saw Mother Teresa lavish love on the most repulsive-looking of human creatures were startled because they saw the scene as part of the reincarnational pattern. Resignation on the part of the sufferer might mean that he or she would soon shed that outworn "casing" and enter a better one. Mother Teresa saw the same human being, exuding pus from sores, unable to remove the maggots already attacking the body, in the light of the Incarnation which pointed to the Resurrection into eternal life. The castoff, the least of humankind at her feet was Jesus in His "distressing disguise." He or she was at the climactic point of the only life that was given by the Creator. Her vision was that brought by the Incarnation, that of Jesus, the Universal Brother, the heart of whose Good News was love that overleapt all barriers and united those able to extend mercy and those perishing for want of it.

T. S. Eliot wrote in "Preludes" of someone who "had such a vision of the street as the street hardly understands."

How often it came back to me as Mother Teresa went about serving the forsaken and abandoned in the light of the Incarnation that those, like Charubala, who were bathed in that reflected light had no idea of its source. Enough for Charubala that she had encountered love, that she was no longer unwanted; enough for those lying in the streets that mercy had appeared in their lives and had made a difference. Day after day, year after year, the vision of Mother Teresa lit up some of the darkest streets of the world. People might have wondered at the broken body on the crucifix that Mother Teresa wore on her shoulder. They did not know that in Mother Teresa's heart there was a connection between the broken body she cherished and their own brokenness. To her, the broken body on the crucifix was a constant reminder of One whose love was so great, so indiscriminate, that He exchanged His life for the saving of all, even of the worst evildoers. The conviction grew that Mother Teresa by her every act was expressing a particular vision—"such a vision of the street as the street hardly understands."

6

Lepers

If Mother Teresa's love of the abandoned and dying was a mysterious and startling sight to onlookers, her love of the lepers rotting away in *bustees* around Calcutta was even more startling. Of the nearly three thousand clusters of *bustee* shacks that went to make up the great expanse of slums around Calcutta, some of them were inhabited by clusters of lepers. The leper is the classic reject, the immemorially shunned human creature. For many of us, leprosy was the first disease we dreaded from the biblical stories that came to us in our early impressionable years.

Use of the medical term, Hansen's disease, which does not conjure up quite the same dread and aversion, is replacing "leprosy." Yet the old name was current in Calcutta. While afflicted persons no longer have to warn of their unclean presence by ringing a bell, the stigma of leprosy falls cruelly on its victims in twentieth-century India. It falls also on their families.

Families of any stature would not admit that one of their members had contracted leprosy. There were stories of a boy or girl being hidden in closetlike rooms from the time the disease was discovered. For the poor, the marks of leprosy often meant migration. The stigma was lifted from the family by the absence of the afflicted person who would be expected to earn a living by begging in the nearest town or city. The lepers of Calcutta had converged on the city from the whole region.

Mother Teresa had committed herself to keeping lepers out of Kalighat. She found a way to go to them in their *bustees* no matter how distant from the heart of the city.

This was made possible by a mobile medical unit.

When I made my brief visit to Calcutta in 1955, the head of the Catholic Relief Services office in Delhi, the Reverend Alfred Schneider, in directing me to Mother Teresa for the first time, gave me the task of finding out what single item she needed most for her work.

"I need a mobile clinic," she told me, "to carry help to the poorest of our poor, the ones who cannot get to the hospital at all."

Schneider himself, who had chosen to live with the poor in a tiny house that had been servants' quarters, had saved about twenty-five hundred dollars and wanted to give it all to Mother Teresa. When I returned to New York, Bishop Edward Swanstrom, Director of Catholic Relief Services, offered to cover the remaining cost of a mobile medical van. We informed Mother Teresa and she decided to obtain the van through a local dealer. With the aid of Fali Manekshaw, a Parsi engineer, a van was converted for medical work at a total cost of about five thousand dollars.

The mobile clinic was ready in 1956 and was used in the setting up of Mother and Child Clinics in six poor quarters around the city. Calcutta doctors, many of them volunteers, examined mothers and children whose diseases might otherwise have gone unchecked.

Many of the women came in time for healing to be accomplished; some came when disease had so wracked the human frame that only palliatives could be given. One of the clinics was in the Kidderpore dock district. I remember in particular a woman who was brought to the clinic in a rickshaw from which she had to be lifted bodily, helpless and moaning. Accompanying her was a rheumy-eyed old woman, fantastically matted and dirty, who explained to Mother Teresa that she was the patient's mother. Mother Teresa helped bring in the sick woman, saying a reassuring "*Accha, accha*" (Good, good), as the woman was finally placed in the doctor's consulting room. She was a young woman, the mother of four children. Her face was a mask of suffering. Her sticklike legs were bloated at the ankles. Her heart and kidneys were seriously weakened. She needed a whole series of medical aids, but in addition, food and vitamins. One could only wonder how long she could be kept alive.

Most of the women who came to the Kidderpore clinic wore the *burqa*, the all-enveloping garment of the Muslim woman. A small crocheted slit at eye level allowed her some contact with the outside world. The clinic was held every Tuesday.

"No matter what else I have to do, I come here on Tuesday," Mother Teresa told me. "In this part we have many Muslim families and the men won't let the women leave the house unless they can be sure that there will be no men here. When I started the clinic, I promised them that. They have trusted me. The doctor is a woman and, of course, they know our Sisters."

A succession of *burqa*-clad women came, lifting the tentlike covering to reveal not only a tragic variety of untreated diseases but jewels shining brightly on the left nostril. Many brought their children, an alarming number of them suffering from eye diseases. From the dust of the dock area, from the smoke of fires fueled by dung patties and twigs, the eyes of the children were suppurating and often closed by infection. For some, medication and a little improvement in hygiene would halt the ailment, but others were headed for permanent blindness. One would hear the words of the doctor, "The left eye is finished, Sister." The doctor and Sisters were busy washing out and cleaning infections, giving instructions on hygiene for eyes and body, and supplying eye medications.

Many of the children were found to have signs of tuberculosis and arrangements were made for them to have X rays at Shishu Bhavan. Sleeping on earthen floors and coping with Calcutta's monsoon rains caused lung and throat ailments to soar. But there was another affliction among the poor of the city. I learned about it at Kidderpore from Mother Teresa. She asked me to note especially a healthy-looking little boy who had joined the line with his mother and a baby sister. He had been one of the many children afflicted by worms, she told me, not tapeworms, but what were called in Calcutta, red worms. Brought to Shishu Bhavan, he had passed forty worms before the treatment was over. Smaller children in the *bustees* had been known to die of suffocation when the red worms rose up in the gullet and blocked the throat passage. Worm medicines, administered with constant care, were effective in banishing the scourge, but the chances of reinvasion of the body were great.

Often there was need for translation from one language to another since the busy Kidderpore docks and warehouse district had long been a mecca for workers from eastern India, including Bihar, Orissa, and Madras, as well as from Nepal to the north. Dozens of other languages could be heard in Calcutta; some say as many as sixty. The Muslims were almost all Bengali speakers whose ancestors had lived in the province from time immemorial, handing on the legacy of brutally hard work and poverty from generation to generation. One could only note how well Mother Teresa knew her city in preparing for the special needs of women who would be the least likely to travel a distance to a Calcutta hospital to be examined by a male physician. Each of the clinics was located in a corner of the city where the free medical services were pathetically inadequate.

One day in 1957, five lepers appeared at the Motherhouse of the Missionaries of Charity. Their dread secret had been discovered and they had been thrown out of their jobs. No one would take them in, not even their own families. Cast off by everyone, they knocked on Mother Teresa's door. This was a sign for her that she must do something for the lepers. The mobile clinic became the vehicle, literally and figuratively, for a new service to those who, more than all others, deserved the description "poorest of the poor."

A clipping from the *Calcutta Statesman* for September 27, 1957, was sent to me and illustrated the next step in the story. By now the work of Mother Teresa was being noticed in the local press. Under a photograph of

Archbishop Perier of Calcutta and Mother Teresa standing beside the mobile van, a staff reporter wrote:

> Mother Teresa's Mobile Leprosy Clinic was opened by the Archbishop of Calcutta, His Grace, the Most Rev. Dr. Ferdinand Perier, at Sishu Bhavan on Lower Circular Road, on Wednesday. A mobile van with medicines and equipment will visit four centres weekly in the bustee areas of Howrah, Tiljala, Dhappa and Moti Jihl, from where Mother Teresa and her Sisters of Charity have received requests for leprosy treatment. The services of a doctor who has received training for this work in the School for Tropical Medicine has been retained. Three nuns who have received training in nursing patients suffering from leprosy will assist him. A small laboratory has been set up at Sishu Bhavan. There are about 30,000 leprosy patients in Calcutta.

By the time I arrived in Calcutta in 1958, the number of leper stations had doubled to eight. I found that the mobile clinic was a bright blue vehicle, impressively narrow and compact in design. It could easily transport six persons along with medicines, disinfectants, records, and large supplies of food.

"We used to have a leper hospital right in Calcutta, Gobra Hospital," Mother Teresa said, "but they closed it down. That's why we have to go to them. There were places for them to report but many did not. The poor spread the disease and their children are finished. Then there are the ones who are not poor. When their secret is found out, their life is impossible. Men have told me that they have had to leave home and just disappear. Their daughters would never get husbands if they stayed home. Their sons would not get jobs."

Mother Teresa did not relate to me that she had put up a fight for the lepers, urging the Chief Minister of Bengal, Dr. B.C. Roy, to keep Gobra Hospital open. But the institution stood in the way of a building project and the neighborhood was anxious to have the lepers sent elsewhere, anywhere but in their midst. Roy bowed to the needs of the city and Mother Teresa lost the fight.

I was soon traveling in the mobile clinic. In front with the driver was Dr. Salil Bhor, the specialist in Hansen's disease from the Institute for Tropical Medicine. Sitting on the wooden seats in the ambulance and storage section were Mother Teresa and two nursing sisters. We left greater Calcutta and drove over the vaulting Howrah Bridge to the left bank of the Hooghly River into Howrah. Howrah is actually a separate city facing Calcutta. Looking backward or forward from the height of the bridge, the two municipalities seemed to shimmer in the sunlight but it was their human misery that seemed to rise before me.

Even during British days, Howrah was known for its gangs of *goondas* or thugs, who operated in the Hooghlyside businesses of jute, textiles, glass, and steel. Some were paid by rival business concerns and the Hooghly was a convenient dumping ground for victims. Now, with thousands of homeless vagrants, *goonda*-ism was rampant and gangs were busy stealing and murdering at a rate that alarmed and frustrated the commissioners of the Howrah municipality.

Descending from the bridge, our route led through the oldest part of Howrah, past an impressive Catholic church built in 1830, dedicated to Our Lady of Happy Voyage. At the back of the church were former army barracks still used as a refugee camp for some two hundred families of Hindu refugees from Pakistan. It was guarded by soldiers so that as these families were resettled, their places would not be seized by other squatters. Hundreds making their home in and around the Howrah Railway Station were watching, ready to dart inside the vacated quarters.

Then came a section that earlier had been a Muslim quarter. Emptied in the riots following the creation of Pakistan, Hindu families had expropriated row upon row of houses. We passed the apartment houses and palaces of businessmen, mostly Marwari, I was told. The Marwari, originally from another part of India, were known for their adeptness in financial matters. We then entered sections that were more and more decrepit. These were the spawning grounds of gangs and general lawlessness.

Finally, we reached a *maidan* or open meadow. This was our first leper treatment station. Patches of dry stubble grass gave a little color to the dun-colored *maidan*. It was about two o'clock in the afternoon, and though it was January, usually the cooler season, the sun was blazing down. All over the *maidan*, men, women, and children were squatting in the pitiless glare, eating, holding infants, just staring vacantly. They had no other home than this. Some had put up as shelter some pieces of canvas on sticks. Two tents of the type that American children would use as backyard playhouses gave some privacy to the aristocracy of the *maidan* society. As soon as the mobile clinic was parked on the roadside, a table was set up for Dr. Bhor. Groups of lepers converged upon us almost immediately, most of them smiling, many of them grasping sticks with stubs of hands to keep themselves upright. By the roadside, in full view of the *maidan* dwellers, they received their examination, treatment, medications, and supply of powdered milk. A regular stop had been scheduled there because these destitute people, handicapped for the most part, could not manage the journey to the station farther out in the Howrah municipality.

One of the last patients was a woman with a thin, ravaged face. Mother Teresa greeted her and the woman's eyes softened and smiled like dark soft plums in the rough worn face. Mother Teresa turned to me. "Mary," she said, "is the saddest case I have ever heard." Coming from a woman who walked daily in the steps of tragedy, this statement startled me. I asked for details. Mary was a poor Christian from the South of India. She married a non-Christian and had a little girl by him. After that he took three other wives. The man had used her as an instrument to beg, and after that, to sell her body for money. She was covered with sores. When she found out she was a leper, he threw her out on the open *maidan.* "What that man does is against all religion," said Mother Teresa. Her eyes were filled with sorrow as they gazed on the poor festering body. Medical help was the only service that she could bring to the misused creature.

The chief leprosy station in Howrah was in the Pilkhana section where almost all the one hundred and thirty-five listed patients were waiting in quiet clusters that quickly formed into an orderly line. The background was a dusty, squared clearing behind which stood the large government rice *godowns* or warehouses. Railway sidings served this busy supply depot, and many in the community filled the menial jobs on the railroad. Others of the mixed Muslim and Hindu group were employed in some type of domestic service in Calcutta. On three sides of the clearing were massed thousands of brick and mud dwelling places, some with only a lattice screen as a front door.

There were several men with deformed bulbous faces in the line and some children between eight and twelve. A few men and women crouched in wooden boxes because they could not walk at all. One man had no hand, just a stump ending at the wrist. Several of the women were dressed in clean and colorful silk saris, mothers from hardworking families who found that the plague had struck their homes. What was encouraging to Mother Teresa and the doctor was the willingness of these mothers to admit the disease. They came regularly for treatment knowing that only in this way could they eliminate the dread possibility that through them the scourge would touch and take hold of the ones they loved.

As we drove out of Pilkhana Square, we had to stop and wait on one of the crowded streets. A truck was parked, and there was hardly room for another car to pass without having the tires lodge in the open drain that ran alongside the squalid homes. The drain was an old one, constructed of stone, and as we waited, children used it as a toilet. The houses were very much like stalls, having only one solid wall at the back, while the side walls were made of bamboo lattice. There was a small latticed section in some of these homes where a cow lay tethered. Children shouted and men got up from their burlap-covered *charpoys* to look on as the driver, helped by the truck crew, put down some slats of tin and wood over the drain. The vehicle made the short distance past the truck safely and we rejoined the traffic that converged on the long Howrah Bridge back to the center of the city.

As I accompanied the team to the leper stations (my minimal participation was to give out the packages of food, chiefly powdered milk) I realized the almost insuperable difficulties in reaching Calcutta's lepers. When the Calcutta leprosarium, the Gobra Hospital, which had served the city for generations, was closed, it was replaced by a modern institution at Gouripur. This was situated outside the metropolis and the ambulatory cases were told to report for treatment at the Hospital for Tropical Diseases. For fear of being carted away to a leprosarium, or of being separated from their begging stations, large numbers of lepers did not report for treatment. The figure of thirty thousand lepers was much too low in Mother Teresa's estimation. These were only the registered leprosy patients. From the work of the Missionaries of Charity in the *bustees,* it was clear that there were at least double that number, possibly triple the registered figure.

The worst cases of leprosy, those whose fingers and toes had already rotted away, were trundled in makeshift carts for begging excursions into the center of Calcutta. They were taken by a member of the family or by a companion to the doors of the city's varied houses of worship. On Friday evenings, they presented themselves before the mosques and were sure to receive alms from even the poorest Muslims. They came without fail on Sunday to the Christian churches. At the Church of St. Thomas on Middleton Street, they regularly formed a little knot, many bringing their children. Those who left the church would be followed down Middleton Street, almost to Park Street, with beseeching cries and outstretched, claw-like hands. Somehow, what remains in my memory is the call of a resolute child who chose to follow me, repeating in her piping voice, *"Salaam, Mami, salaam."* (Peace, Mother, peace.)

Mother Teresa sent Sister Shanti, already trained in medicine, to specialize in antileprosy work in the Hospital for Tropical Diseases. If the lepers could be reached for treatment, they could be rendered noninfectious. With the latest antileprosy medications and food supplements, they could at least be brought to the state where they would not pass on the disease to others.

Moti Jihl, the site of Mother Teresa's plunge into the service of the poor, was also the site of a leper station. As usual, we started out from Shishu Bhavan and traversed the central section of Calcutta, avoiding the occasional loitering cow, or the small herds of cows or sheep being led into the Maidan. On the sidewalks, street vendors and sometimes families were cooking their meals on little fires. Men, women, and children stood in front of large faucets to fill their pots with water or to give themselves a quick wash. Holy men in yellow robes, smeared with ashes or marked with the lines of Vishnu or Siva on their foreheads, walked with special dignity among the crowds. Occasionally, a man who had surrendered everything, even clothing, went by. His nakedness was described as *digambara*, open to the sky.

From the side streets, loud with the traffic and with the sounds of life lived in the open, we passed through streets that became narrower and narrower until we reached lanes where it was only with great care that the mobile clinic could be safely steered. It was then that I realized why such a narrow vehicle had been chosen. Now the lanes were no longer paved and a fine dust joined with the all-pervasive smells to assault the traveler.

Entering the open space, not far from the brackish pond and the Sisters' school, the mobile clinic, blue and shining bright, stopped before a large storage shed with a corrugated metal roof.

A short Bengali who was waiting there unlocked the door and the files were brought out. Dr. Bhor put on his gloves and mask and began to examine the line of people who had formed in front of the shed. They were covered, or partially covered, by the colorless, dust-laden garments of the poor. All were barefoot and the unmistakable marks of the leper were visible—the stumps where toes had been and the poor remnants of fingers. The disease itself, I discovered, could not be blamed for the loss of extremities. After the nerves had been attacked by the disease, the patient would not feel a cut, a blow, or the onset of infection.

Each patient brought a small wooden plaque with his name and address pasted on it. As he received the plaque, Dr. Bhor studied the case in the loose-leaf card file. For each leper there was a large stiff card with places for various entries. On one side was a schematic representation of the human body, and on this the doctor marked the body areas of the patient that were already affected by the disease. The two nursing Sisters did all the dressings and cleaning of affected parts. I saw one of the Sisters work long and hard on a swollen and disintegrating foot while the patient, an old man, sat motionless on the floor. There were some patients with the bulbous excrescences on their faces that marked them unmistakably as lepers even if their extremities were whole.

One of the patients on the line was a sixteen-year-old boy. He was thin, but looked as healthy as others in the neighborhood. "He is all alone," Mother Teresa told me. "A few months ago he looked very, very bad, but every week he improves. He had the bulbous face, but look at him now. Because the improvement showed, many others are coming."

I wondered where he lived if he had no family. "A poor family took him in. The man who opened up the shed for us is the one who had taken him into his house. He is only a *durwan* (guard) and earns sixty rupees a month, but he can still help someone else. The boy is negative now." This boy and many others were far from a cure, but at least the first steps of combating infection had been accomplished.

The patients received dosages of antileprosy sulfones in a little tin box and in addition, a supply of American powdered milk and whatever foods were available. Then they trekked back to their windowless shacks.

Dhappa, where I had witnessed the founding of a school for the children of lepers, was probably the area of Calcutta most heavily infested with the disease. Our destination was a section lying between two canals, the South Canal, a wide waterway, and the Dhappa Canal, a sewer channel that gave off a killing stench. Along the banks of the Dhappa Canal was the slaughterhouse district which could be recognized from a distance by the flocks of vultures wheeling incessantly over it, their circling designs rising and falling in the air in rhythm with some mysterious *Totentanz* (dance of death). They seemed small for vultures and I thought the flocks of dark whirlers were kites, birds which were everywhere in the air above Calcutta. At an open-air lunch in a "proper" suburban garden in Alipore, a kite had swooped down to pick off a piece of food from a guest's plate. But Calcutta residents claim that over the slaughterhouse, there are only vultures because these birds devour pieces of dead animals, while kites only feast on smaller prey they have themselves killed.

In the slaughterhouses, only the Muslims would slaughter and dress the beef while only a small group among the *harijans* (formerly referred to as untouchables) would kill the pigs and prepare the pork for serving—chiefly to non-Indians. We passed a new dispensary in Dhappa, a gift to the slaughterhouse district from a member of the small caste of pig killers, who by thrift, grew rich at his calling. As so few Hindus could engage in such work because of their beliefs, the small caste group with a monopoly on pig slaughter had become, because of steady employment and frugal habits, comfortably situated by local standards.

The leprosy clinic was held out-of-doors at the end of a dead-end alleyway. Treatment began at two o'clock in the afternoon, and by three o'clock, Mother Teresa began counting the number of patients who had presented themselves. Because their dossiers were in a numbered file, she could tell that many were not on the line for treatment. We went searching the neighborhood for the missing lepers. Some we found laboriously making their way to the mobile clinic, bringing their boys and girls, already positive cases, with them. An old Muslim whose hands and feet were wasted, and whose legs could no longer support him, was being pulled slowly by his wife in a wooden cart, the size of a youngster's go-cart.

We reached the sequestered spot where the leper families were congregated and here we found the people for whom Mother Teresa was searching.

The leper station was scheduled for the same hour at the same spot on the same day of each week. The older patients were accustomed to the routine and presented themselves with regularity. Here in this corner of Dhappa, Mother Teresa had encountered what might be called a nest of lepers, a nucleus of infected families living off by themselves in several rows of low houses around an open space muddy with swamp water. They were cut off from normal living as the marks of the disease were on almost all of them. We went from hut to hut and Mother Teresa talked with them, telling them to make their way to the van clinic. The dwellings were whitewashed mud, each with a little mud porch raised above the unpaved road of grayish-brown earth.

We looked inside one of the houses. It was windowless like a cave. Since there was no *charpoy* or bed of any kind, the family must have huddled on the earthen floor at night. Most of the men and women were sitting or lying on the tiny porches in the afternoon sun. Some were somnolent from hunger or from the debilitation of the disease; a few grimaced as though in pain.

A prone woman in a red sari, grayed with dust, twisted in pain as Mother Teresa came over to her. She tried to sit up and then huddled down once more on the bed of sackcloth. Scantily dressed men drew pieces of cloth over them as Mother Teresa approached. A glazed orange sun lit up the still afternoon scene, the mud houses, and the scourged human forms lying or sitting on sackcloth on the verandas; and not far away the dark flocks of vultures wheeled and turned in incessant search for the rejected pieces of dead flesh. The fine grayish dust raised by our feet and by the children playing on the pathway seemed to glisten with a baleful light.

I became aware of a whitewashed patch of wall opposite one of the rows of mud houses. A few steps had been carefully fashioned out of mud, so as to lead to a tablelike space. Its unexpected clean whiteness was impressive. Over the patch sprouted a small tree whose slender leaves were coated with the dust so that they looked hoary and old. It was a pipal tree and under its shade in the center of the mud table stood a flat, whitened stone on which, daubed in bright red paint, was the figure of Hanuman, the monkey god. In mythic times Hanuman and his tribe had earned the gratitude of the Hindus by making a bridge of stones so that the God Rama could cross the Straits of Comorin to rescue Sita, his abducted bride. Here, before the freshly painted form of the monkey, the unclean could make their *puja* or worship under a tree that was considered holy. We asked the families about the shrine and were told that the owner of their row of houses had set up the altar.

The monkey god appears in the shrines of village India as a protecting spirit and because of him, monkeys are treated as sacred. The Hindu sense of a general holiness, extending to man, animal, and nature, could be felt even in this desolate scene.

I asked Mother Teresa how all these leper families managed to live. She said that no one really knew. Some did quite well begging and they seemed to share with each other. A few had relatives who helped them or members of the family as yet untouched by the disease who shared their earnings with them. As we walked back to the mobile clinic, a little group was forming behind us, persuaded by Mother Teresa to come for examination and treatment.

We made a detour to visit a Muslim quarter, encountering an old lady propelling herself with a stick grasped in both hands. Her hair was matted and she peered with dim eyes out of a face marred by bulbous excrescences. Her nose was hideously bloated. Mother Teresa went over to her.

"Anna," she said and waited. The old woman stopped and squinted her dim eyes. She recognized Mother Teresa and they began to talk in Bengali. Mother Teresa took down her address. "I didn't know what had happened to Anna," she told me later. "She and her sister lived in a room in this area years ago when we first came here. They are Catholics. Poor Anna. She is a beggar. There is no place for her. Not even a leprosarium will take a hopeless case like her. She was at Gobra Hospital years ago."

Anna was given a card to come on clinic days. Anna walked back to her little room, using her stick like a punt before her and shuffling her feet forward with immense effort. I could not see how she could make her way to beg. The next time I saw Anna she was bedridden. Her little room was almost completely dark inside—the only spot of light being the reflection from the low doorway on her one piece of brass cookware. Her sister was caring for her, but without the money from begging, they had no way to buy food. We left some rupees so that they could buy food and Mother Teresa planned to send Sisters to visit and help them.

When we returned to the mobile clinic later that afternoon, there was still a long lineup in the alley. The doctor and the two nursing Sisters, with Mother Teresa plunging in to help, were occupied until the short twilight was over at about six o'clock. Wearing the same surgical gloves as the doctor and nurses, I handed out the supplementary food in amounts that would help the patient's entire family.

The Sisters who went to help Anna the beggar did not have to make many visits. I never saw her again since the Sisters told us that her spirit left her leprous body a few days after we saw her. One was led to wonder how many other unknown afflicted people expired in those cavelike hovels without human consolation or care.

A leper station set up at Titagarh, just outside Calcutta, became in time a leper community, largely self-supporting. A full-time doctor from the Missionaries of Charity Brothers was part of the community. What was important in 1957 and 1958 was the fact that the community of Calcutta got caught up in the fire of a crusade. Various societies, following the lead of such women's groups as the Marian Society, joined to support a citywide collection for the lepers. The emblem of the collection was a bell, the ancient symbol of the unclean, but now used as a sign of compassion. The theme of the collection, carried on posters, in newspapers, and on the mobile van itself, was "Touch the Leper with Your Compassion." The involvement of the wider community made it possible to treat many more leprosy patients, and when the results of the treatment could become visible, more clusters of lepers were uncovered. Eventually, a whole town of leper families, Shanti Nagar, the Town of Peace, was established by Mother Teresa with a Sister-Doctor of the Missionaries of Charity in charge. It was situated on a green and pleasant plot of thirty-five acres donated by the government and located two hundred miles from Calcutta. The Calcutta collection, as well as help from abroad, would make it possible for hundreds of families to live an existence approaching that of normal families. Each family inhabited a simple home while receiving the medical help that would either arrest the disease or cure it altogether. As I saw the collection in progress all over the city, with men and women ringing a bell and accepting donations on street corners, I marveled again at the formidable gift for communication and community organization of Mother Teresa, a gift of which its possessor was completely unaware. While ascribing everything to the providence of God, Mother Teresa was willing to say that she had put herself totally at His disposal. She was simply an instrument. This, she kept pointing out, was true of anyone who put himself or herself totally at the disposal of the Creator. Instruments, however, do have distinctive and often astounding gifts.

7

Home for the Destitute Living

The caravanserai for the destitute dying inexorably led Mother Teresa to the work of rescue for children. This gave rise to Shishu Bhavan, the children's home which I briefly visited in 1955. Tiny scraps of humanity like Usha were the reason for Shishu Bhavan. When I saw her, she was three years old. There were marks of healed and dried scabs on her body and on her shaved skull. When her mother, an emaciated girl, had been picked up from the street, she was clutching a tiny body that was one continuous sore. The young mother, ravaged by fever and starvation, could not be saved and she breathed her last at Kalighat. The home for the destitute dying called forth a home for the destitute living, for waifs like Usha. Mother Teresa made it known that she needed a home for them. An old Muslim came to the door of the Motherhouse and told a Sister that a big house was for rent a few minutes away. The old man left and was never seen again, but the Sisters immediately investigated the address he gave. Mother Teresa rented it for homeless children and called it Nirmala Shishu Bhavan, the Children's Home of the Immaculate. There Usha received hourly care that brought her through the first weeks after her mother's death. Then came the slow care that closed the unhealed sore of her body.

By 1958, there were ninety children at Shishu Bhavan and I came to know them as their stark stories etched themselves in my mind. Kanak had been in Shishu Bhavan nearly two years when I saw him. At four, he was a strong personality and would exercise his initiative by going down the line after a meal to wipe the noses of the younger children. He and his mother were street cases. The mother was in the last stages of tuberculosis and died shortly after being carried into Kalighat. She seemed to be in her early twenties.

Shadona Mukherjee had been found on the street with her mother and a younger brother about a year before I saw her. She was seven years old, a thin, light-skinned child with cropped hair. She was old enough to feel the loss of her mother who was at the point of death when picked up on the street. Shadona must have realized what was happening as her mother grew weaker. She used to weep for her brother who had been sent from Shishu Bhavan for treatment at a hospital. I had met children in every situation of need and bereavement, whether bereft of parents, brothers and sisters, home or home places. The children I had seen could always be brought to the point of smiling. If necessary, they could be provoked into a smile. Until I met Shadona, I could never give credence to the stories of children who had forgotten how to smile and who could not be provoked into smiling. Shadona ate her meals and obediently joined the other children at playtime, but her face always preserved the same withdrawn expression of reticence and fear. I began to wonder if she would be a victim of a lifelong emotional disorder. After a while, on my regular visits to Shishu Bhavan, she would approach me and hesitantly cling to my dress. She would accept the candy I brought and would eat it with her grave expression unchanged. After a while, she joined the other children in calling me "Auntie 'Ello" from my habit of greeting each one with a "Hello." There was a change when her brother Pachu was brought back to Shishu Bhavan. She hovered over him and pushed him toward me so that he would receive his share of candy before she did. I began to notice the shy shadow of a smile when she called me "Auntie 'Ello" and again when she came over to enunciate a careful "Bye-bye" as I left. One day, I tied a bright blue satin ribbon around her almost bald little head. The wan face and great eyes lit up with a smile of real pleasure. The Sisters assured me it was Shadona's first known smile since her mother's death.

Mary Ann, probably six or seven years old, was a street case in her own right, if there can be said to be such a right. She was a throwaway child. She had been cast into the street at one of the busiest street crossings in Calcutta, the junction of Lower Circular Road and Bow Bazaar Street, near the Sealdah Station. It was quite obvious why that spot had been chosen, but she had been picked up from the trolley tracks before her scrawny little body could be crushed. Mary Ann could neither walk nor talk. She responded with a throaty gurgling sound when people petted or spoke to her. Her little face with its open dribbling mouth seemed to be set in a perpetual smile. Her legs were bent and withered, and her right wrist was permanently crooked, giving her hand a clawlike appearance. Her fingers were long and thin like those of an old woman. Mary Ann had to be fed with a spoon. Her only physical disease was rickets, the result of long starvation, and possibly close confinement of movement. The other children at Shishu Bhavan rocked her in a little rocking chair and played with her when she was in her crib, as older children play with a baby. In this case, it was mites of three or four who played with a girl twice their age.

She snuggled peacefully in Mother Teresa's arms and often made a guttural whimpering sound when she had to be put down.

The limited floor space at Shishu Bhavan was divided into a sick children's ward, a well children's dormitory, and a large screened porch where the smaller children played and ate. Besides the rocking chair, the community toys consisted of a large rocking horse and a low baby carriage. Two or three active youngsters were almost always on the rocking horse, but the favorite game was to play train with the baby carriage with three or four children being pulled from one end of the porch to the other.

The waifs at Shishu Bhavan were an uninhibited group, doting on visitors and often suggesting that the children should be given "*misti*" or candy. They wore a variety of costumes depending on the haphazard donations of garments and the ingenuity in remaking them. Perhaps the most striking innovation during my stay was a new set of dress pants for all the boys. The color was midnight blue, of an unusual iridescent sheen, and the material a rich plush velvet of the upholstery type. The donated bolt was enough for all the boys and the effect of the new outfit was nothing short of dazzling. The little boys seemed proud of their outfits.

At the far end of the porch were three beds for children recovering from tuberculosis of the bone. Rashid Sekandar, a Muslim boy of ten had his leg in a cast and his face often was drawn with pain. Rashid's father, an unemployed factory sweeper, could find no hospital which could accept the child for the lengthy recovery period. He and his wife and nine children occupied a single room in a slum section of the Kidderpore suburb. In such areas lived the poorest of the Muslim community who, even after the riots, slayings, and abductions which rent the Muslim and Hindu communities apart from 1946 onward, still did not leave Calcutta for Pakistan. Mother Teresa, during her visit to the Kidderpore clinic was asked by Rashid's father for some help with the boy. Not only was Rashid brought for convalescence to Shishu Bhavan, but another brother, a victim of rickets, was placed in the newly opened children's home at Jamshedpur, an initiative of English Group-Captain Leonard Cheshire and his Indian committee. Still others among the Sekandar children were suffering from prolonged hunger and for these Mother Teresa supplied regular food allotments of American surplus foods.

❧

Shishu Bhavan became the center for two other services to the hungry and ill. One was the supplying of food to the most destitute of families. By this time, the shipments of Food for Peace stocks, along with foods purchased by Catholic Relief Services, were flowing into Calcutta with regularity. Portside warehousing and distribution were well organized. Shishu Bhavan, with its large courtyard, became an important distribution center.

Great vats of rice were cooked in the morning so that families could present themselves with containers for "take-out" meals. Sometimes the gruel contained a soy protein and powdered milk, at other times, beans. Though the people seemed to prefer rice, they learned to like bulgur wheat, the product known from ancient times which can then be boiled like rice. The bulgur, to which beans and soy were added, came to be much prized by the hungry families.

Mother Teresa knew her city. One day, only Muslim families like the Sekandars would be waiting when the metal gates of Shishu Bhavan were opened. Another day, only Hindu families were served. The Christians, mostly Anglo-Indians, received their portions on another day. The families were given cards of different colors by the Sisters during their days in the slum schools and in family visiting. Soon the number of people receiving food at Shishu Bhavan rose from four thousand to seven thousand. When I saw the size of the groups, mostly near-starving women holding babies at their breasts and leading toddlers, I realized how easy it would have been for a communal riot to be stirred up.

Shishu Bhavan soon housed a clinic in a room cut off from the children's center and reached by a separate entrance. Every Saturday afternoon, an Anglo-Indian doctor, Ivy Cecil, volunteered her time to examine and treat the women of the surrounding area. Dr. Cecil told me that the four free clinics of the Calcutta Corporation for poor women and children, even when they worked overtime, could only reach a fraction of the destitute.

I sat in Dr. Cecil's consulting room one afternoon as her patients, many of them regular patients with chronic diseases, were treated. One was a new patient, an old woman with a face corrugated like ancient leather. I was interested to know her age since her dessicated, furrowed cheeks brought the word "crone" to mind.

"She probably won't know how old she is," Dr. Cecil said. "Our people hardly ever do. But we make the attempt to work it out."

In reply to the question about her age, the old woman gave the expected reply that as for the number of years, she could not say. The next question was the age of her oldest child. Her first son, she explained, had two children. He had been married about five years, perhaps more.

"The only way we can estimate the age of the women who come to us," explained Dr. Cecil, "is by getting the approximate age of the children, and even grandchildren. We count that they are sixteen or seventeen when the first child is born. Her son may be about twenty-five. She is most likely in her early forties."

She was one of the countless women I encountered in the *bustees* of Calcutta whose wasted bodies, hung with loose, discolored garments, gave them the appearance of ninety year olds though they had not reached the half-century mark. A woman like this one was blessed since she still had family ties, even though she lived in a hovel. She undoubtedly saw herself as more fortunate than widows, so often left to scrounge for themselves. Widows I encountered everywhere in the slums, their bad karma expressed by the loss of their husbands. By custom, their hair was cut short. Their shorn heads erased any distinction between the sexes and seemed to turn the unfortunate women into withered neuters.

There were many well children for whom Shishu Bhavan was the only haven. Among them were five-year old Biren and Kanak, his brother of two, who like many others in the refugee-packed city, were born on the street. When their mother, a beggar, became ill, Mother Teresa and her Sisters accepted her and her children at Shishu Bhavan. The mother's illness did not prove serious and as soon as she was well, she disappeared, leaving her children at the home.

Douglas, about eight years of age, was a healthy child, aside from a severely cleft lip and palate. An Anglo-Indian child, whose family had abandoned him to settle in England, Douglas spoke fluent English and was learning Bengali with his companions. After Mother Teresa had brought his case to the attention of the American Women's Club of Calcutta, she was given the funds to arrange for an operation to close the cleft palate and mitigate the harelip.

Also counted among the well children were a group of teenaged girls who were placed in serious danger when one or both of their parents died, or when, due to illness or desertion of the father, the family broke up. If such girls were not married by fifteen or sixteen years of age, they became targets for rape and then prostitution.

"These girls," said Mother Teresa, "are defenseless when the men around them see that they have no strong family. Sometimes, they are taken by force by one of the men. They are put out on the street when the man moves away, or is finished with them. Others are used by men and are given eight *annas* (about ten cents) as payment. Of course they become diseased. The nine girls here were rescued from such a life." A few girls charged with vagrancy were rescued from jail when Mother Teresa accepted responsibility for them.

The girls seemed happy and serene at their tasks of caring for the children and washing the linens and clothes. I watched them as they laundered their saris in the courtyard. They were singing Bengali songs and looked plump and healthy.

"I am sorry for Jyoti," Mother Teresa said, indicating one of the girls in the courtyard in the act of wringing out a sari. Jyoti Biswas was a sturdy girl with a fine face and aquiline nose. Her hair hung down her back in two thick braids.

"She is eighteen, and it is going to be hard for her to get married at her age. Anyway, men would avoid her because of her family. Her father was a leper. He was killed on the 'Day of the Great Killing.' Her mother got TB.

"They lived in Moti Jihl when we first started our work. She was such a good little girl. She and her sister took care of the mother until she died. Jyoti is free from leprosy and so is her sister. They were tested and examined. Her sister was lucky. She found a good husband when she was sixteen. The two younger brothers are lepers. They beg for their food and we give them treatment and some food when we go to Moti Jihl.

"Jyoti gave me a surprise the other day. She asked me if she could stay with our Sisters for good." It was very rare that Mother Teresa showed emotion, but her strong face tightened and her eyes were glinting with tears as she looked at the girl who was tossing her long braids over her shoulder as she hung the cotton sari on a line to dry. "Then she wanted to know if she could make to me all the promises—the vows, she means—that the regular Sisters make for life. That was not possible."

Jyoti and I became friends and before I returned to the United States, I left a sari as a parting memento. I followed her progress, first from the accounts of Mother Teresa and later on my return to Calcutta.

In point of fact, Jyoti did remain with the Sisters and she did get married. She moved from Shishu Bhavan to help run the leper community in Titagarh. When an eligible man proposed, the Missionaries of Charity provided household necessities and the couple lived in a small home at Titagarh. The other teenaged girls at Shishu Bhavan were being introduced to skills they could never have acquired in the foul slums. They became acquainted, through the daily training of the Sisters, with the simplest tasks of cleanliness, including the careful washing of their hands before touching food or dishes. They gained confidence in the warm atmosphere of Shishu Bhavan and were ready when jobs became available. There was an activity in one corner of Shishu Bhavan for intelligent girls who lacked particular skills. They applied themselves to the study of English and typing under volunteer teachers. Their classroom was a crowded one with thirty girls absorbed in an exercise on thirty clacking typewriters. The young people barely looked up when visitors entered the room but continued to bend over the machines with an unbroken intensity of concentration. It was plain that for them everything depended on making this skill their own. It would mean a life of self-respect rather than a life of dread uncertainty and hunger. As with Jyoti, some of the girls were able to embark on married life with the basic necessities supplied by Mother Teresa and the Sisters. For the poorest of the poor, when the prospective groom had no resources other than perhaps a job as *durwan,* or guard, the girl would bring as her dowry a few towels, a *charpoy* (the simplest of beds), and a few cooking utensils. It occurred to me that Mother Teresa brought mercy into every phase of life from birth, to giving in marriage, to dying.

8

Walls and Patterns

As I went about the streets of Calcutta with Mother Teresa in 1958, I noticed how often the conversation returned to the word "walls."

"Our Sisters must go out on the street," Mother Teresa said. "They must take the tram like our people, or walk to where they are going. That is why we must not start institutions and stay inside. We must not stay behind walls and have our people come to us."

"What if you were asked to take charge of an orphanage where the Sisters would live full time and staff the institution?" I asked her one day.

"We would say that some other congregation could do that work better than we could. We would say that our work is outside, outside the walls where the other congregations do not go. Our people cannot come to us from Dhappa or Howrah, so we must go to them." Her voice was firm.

Mother Teresa did not minimize the irreplaceable work all around us that was carried on behind walls, not only the walls of the buildings themselves, the walls of the compounds, sometimes part of an acre, sometimes many acres, surrounding the buildings. One could not be long in Calcutta without realizing that many Christian organizations, both Protestant and Catholic, had long been present to mitigate the sufferings of the city's poor. In the city and in Bengal were outstanding examples of institutions staffed by Christians from overseas working side by side with Indian Christians. The Christian presence reflected the various European presences starting with that of the Portuguese. The Portuguese had left not only the Calcutta Cathedral of Our Lady of the Rosary, but such shrines as Our Lady of Happy Voyage in Bandel. The French had established a center on the Hooghly before Job Charnock of the British East India Company but had been displaced by the British. Charity, especially for orphans, was a mark of the Christian enterprise, as well as educational programs. The so-called "Carey Christians" were evangelized by William Carey, founder of the Baptist Missionary Society. A prodigious linguist, Carey translated the Bible into Bengali and other Indian tongues.

An Indian enterprise rivaling Christian social service was the network established by the Ramakrishna Mission. The centers for social uplift were conducted by a monastic order founded by Swami Vivekananda, a follower of the Bengali mystic known as Ramakrishna Paramahamsa. As monks, those who conducted the centers of the Ramakrishna Mission grounded their work for the needy in a life of contemplation. Many find it a strange providence that Mother Teresa's simple work of rescuing the dying attracted attention when it was housed near Kali's temple, and that Ramakrishna's work arose out of his devotion to the goddess Kali. He lived out his life in the temple of Kali at Dakshineswar, near Calcutta, and opened his spiritual consciousness also to Jesus, the Mother of Jesus, and to the teachings of Mohammed. Swami Vivekananda gained great numbers of adherents preaching that the highest form of devotion to the Great Mother Kali was social service.

Mother Teresa saw the urgent need for the institutions that had grown out of the Christian presence, in particular, the educational institutions for women, the hospitals and leprosariums. Lay Christian women and Sisters formed the heart of the Indian nursing corps. Mother Teresa herself had first been part of the work of education and then had profited from the hospitality and training at the Holy Family Hospital in Patna. She revered the work of the Little Sisters of the Poor who in the beginning had given her shelter among the aged poor in their care. She was in frequent contact with the Franciscan Missionaries of Mary who had a home for girls not far from Shishu Bhavan. They accepted older girls, and I saw the girls, many orphaned or abandoned, who were being introduced to an ordered life of education and practical training. The Sisters, many of them Indian, were leading the girls in an embroidery class. The saris being worked on were wedding garments destined for the well-to-do women of Calcutta. It was a day of festival when I visited, so shortly afterward the young women dropped their needlework and presented a program from their repertory of Indian dances and songs. For many generations this necessary training had been quietly conducted behind a small compound, secure from the wretchedness of the streets. As I became more and more conscious of the necessity of walls and the compounds behind which good works could be achieved, I also realized the necessity to leap over them in the face of the human need rarely before so concentrated in one city.

Older boys were often given into the care of the Christian Brothers of Ireland at their large institution in Dum Dum, the site of Calcutta's airport. The name came from the arsenal there producing lead-nosed dum-dum bullets that spread on impact, inflicting a tearing wound on the human body. They were so frightful that they were banned after the Boer

War. The Christian Brothers were another reminder of the link between Ireland and India, when young Irishmen, fleeing in the last century the greatest destitution of the Western World, fed the ranks of the British garrisons in India, chiefly the lower ranks, as any reader of Kipling cannot fail to note. Scattered about the city were their schools for boys where Brothers, teaching without salary, provided a rounded education for modest fees or no fees at all. In time, the Irish Christian Brothers were internationalized, becoming the Congregation of Christian Brothers, their number being increased by Indian members.

The renowned vocational training offered by the Brothers and Fathers of Don Bosco, known popularly as Salesians, was expanded by an unusual event. Father Doro, an ebullient Salesian priest, won the first prize in the Calcutta lottery. Someone had given him a ticket and the prize was so enormous that it enabled his congregation to erect a strikingly modern school for technical training at Park Circus. I could not help but notice that many automotive repair workers throughout Bengal had come from one of the network of Salesian schools. Most of the teachers originated in Italy's northern provinces.

Mother Teresa still maintained family ties with the Loreto Sisters. One day, returning from Moti Jihl, we went through the wide gates of the Loreto compound in Entally. Entering St. Mary's School, we were greeted by an old Sister on duty who remembered Mother Teresa from the days just over a decade earlier when she was headmistress of the school. There were no students about since it was holiday time.

The old Sister said she still thought about Mother Teresa and what made her happy was that Mother Teresa still thought about Entally and took time to pay a visit. As we walked along the corridor and into the office that had been Mother Teresa's as headmistress of St. Mary's, I marveled at the brightness of the polished floors, a special brightness achieved only in floors in convents. In those classrooms, Mother Teresa had inspired young women with a love of goodness and compassion for the poor, in addition to imparting knowledge that would be called for on examination papers. In the sacristy of the impressive chapel, she had brought her first cheap sari to be blessed. Always purposeful, Mother Teresa soon hurried me out of the compound. As we went through the gates, I thought of the unprecedented courage it took for Sister Teresa to walk through those gates one evening in August a decade ago, after having laid aside a garb that had been part of her life for nineteen years.

One day, in talking about the days at St. Mary's, she made a casual remark, "The love the students had for me and the influence I had over them for good—it was nothing I could take pride in. It was God using me." That remark stayed with me, illuminating the special charism of Mother Teresa as a teacher and later as founder of an order. Her great gifts were there for all to see and experience, but with them went an utter unself-consciousness, the sense of being an instrument through which a higher purpose could be accomplished.

Even by 1958, the Missionaries of Charity, few as they were, had become an accepted feature of Calcutta's streets. It was a time when Mother Teresa's dream was to reach a total of one hundred Sisters to initiate new works for which the sufferings of the people cried out. I asked Mother Teresa if she worried about the safety of the Sisters as they left, two by two in the early mornings to go to the *bustees*. She replied that they were in the hands of the Lord.

"They pray their way, even on the trams. When they walk, they recite the rosary." I thought of the low voices of the young women, repeating the "Our Father" and including in "Father" all the children of the human family, all the people around them who had their own name and concept of the Creator.

"Now, they tell me," said Mother Teresa with a smile that brought a quick brightness to her eyes, "the time that it takes to reach different places by the number of rosaries they can say. 'It took us three rosaries, or four rosaries, to get there, Mother,' they tell me. When they pray as they go along, the people see it and respect them. In India there is a great respect for holiness, even among the rascals. The Sisters are all young. They walk so fast that many people call them the 'running Sisters.'"

Another term for the Sisters I heard from a Bengali who said many ordinary Bengalis called from *"prem prochariko,"* the "preachers of love" —who do not preach in words.

Michael Gomes greeted us when Mother Teresa and I visited 14 Creek Lane, first home of the Missionaries of Charity. We went to the second-floor room where the then Sister Teresa had been given a room after she had broken through the barriers that separated the enclosed, walled-in life of a religious woman under vows from what was referred to as "the world." This was "world" in its most pejorative sense, joined with "the flesh and the devil" in an unholy triad as the enemies of holiness and salvation.

It was a rambling house of three stories of no particular character, where a joint family of several families could coexist. I could not linger on the second floor in the room that the Gomes family had given the then Sister Teresa for it was now in use by the family.

"Let us go upstairs," said Mother Teresa. Michael Gomes, the gentle Bengali teacher, led us to a large upper room that ran the length of the house. It was to this space that the group around Mother Teresa climbed as their number grew. They had needed an extra room for a sick bay when one of them became ill, but even at the end of 1949, when there were ten young women, there was no problem of space.

Gomes explained to me that two of his brothers had chosen East Pakistan at the time of partition in 1947. This choice had meant remaining with the ancient Catholic community of East Bengal whose ancestors had been evangelized by early Portuguese missioners. There still exists in what is now Bangladesh a complex of villages called the "Bengal Rome" whose inhabitants even to this day bear such names as Gomes, Rozario, and da Silva.

The generosity of Michael Gomes and his wife had expanded, along with the increasing number of young women, as they opened the upper room and released the entire floor. Mother Teresa laughed as we made our way up the narrow, winding stairs. She described the busy traffic on those stairs when twenty, twenty-five, twenty-eight young women ran up and down, bringing their water buckets for cooking and washing. They always seemed to be rushing in those days, she recalled, rushing to get their saris washed, to get the meals cooked, to scrub the floors, to reach the washing cubicle on the roof. They always had to be careful not to spill the precious water as they passed each other on the stairs. They sounded like happy days, days of discovery, of a new community coming to life.

"An American cardinal came to visit us here at Creek Lane," Mother Teresa told me. "It was Cardinal Spellman, and Archbishop Perier sent him, I think. It must have been in 1952. We were very crowded but I brought him here to this room. He asked me where we lived. I told him, 'Here in this room, Your Eminence. This is our refectory. We move the tables and benches to the side.' He wanted to know where the rest of our convent was, where we could study. 'We study here, too, Your Eminence,' I said. Then I added, 'And this is also our dormitory.' When the cardinal asked if we had a chapel, I brought him to this end of the room.

" 'It is also our chapel, Your Eminence,' I told him and I showed him the altar behind the partition. I don't know what he was thinking, but he began to smile. He said mass for us."

Francis Cardinal Spellman must have been returning from visiting the troops at the height of the conflict in Korea. I, too, wondered what he might have thought of the little band in the upper room, willingly divested of all, even privacy, so that they could serve those involuntarily divested of all, and most obscenely of all, of privacy.

Michael Gomes and his wife took no money from Mother Teresa and the Missionaries of Charity. Gomes himself was a devout man and an active member of an association called the Legion of Mary, founded in Dublin by Frank Duff. Its purpose is to express by whatever means possible Christian concern for one's neighbors and it is grounded in a regular program of prayer. The Gomes family considered that Mother Teresa had been sent from God and that to receive her was a blessing. "We received. We did not give," was the way he put it.

Not only at Creek Lane did I feel close to the beginnings of the ten-year-old Missionaries of Charity. Still alive and active in 1958 was the person who, besides testing to the utmost the second "call" of Mother Teresa, was, in a historical sense, responsible for her presence in Bengal. It was he who had originally invited Jesuit priests of Yugoslav origin to join him in serving the archdiocese of Calcutta. He was, of course, the head of the archdiocese, the Most Reverend Ferdinand Perier.

Straight-backed and slender, he was at eighty-three, fully alive and energetic and in complete charge of a diocese whose agonies he had lived with for thirty-seven years. A native of Antwerp, Belgium, he was sent by the Society of Jesus to the Bengal Mission in 1906 and completed his seminary training in Kurseong.

Dioceses in the mission field were often entrusted to the Society of Jesus, originally known as the Company of Jesus, the largest order in the Catholic Church. Known for their scholarship, the priests of the Society became conversant with the languages, history, and spiritual traditions of the people among whom they found themselves. They were commonly called Jesuits, a term that originally betokened a hostility that still adheres to the adjective "jesuitical," connoting crafty, cunning, or underhanded. This was traced to their struggle for the Church during the bitter days of the Reformation and Counterreformation.

No one could have filled the common meaning of jesuitical less than Dr. Ferdinand Perier. His manner was keen, but marked by a spontaneous openness. The expression in his bright blue eyes was one of alertness and expectancy. His facial features were topped by a fringe of fine white hair. His white beard was neatly trimmed.

When he was consecrated as bishop in 1921, he was given the title Episcopus Plataearum, which he translated as "Bishop of the Streets." In 1924, when he succeeded to the diocese of Calcutta he realized that he needed to reach the neglected Catholics in the innumerable marshes and backwaters of the district of 24-Parganas. It was due to Perier's persuasive powers that the Yugoslav Jesuits agreed to come to a difficult mission. At that time, Mother Teresa was a fourteen year old in the Skopje Gymnasium and soon the letters came back to Skopje from Bengal with the results that have been described.

On many occasions, I was a guest with His Grace, as he was called in Calcutta, at the Calcutta Club, an old club which from the beginning admitted both Indians and English, with an Indian and an Englishman alternating as presidents. It had been established in opposition to those clubs that would not allow Indians past their doors unless they came as servants through the back entrance. The old archbishop knew this and his white cassock with wide red band at the waist was occasionally seen at the club. At public functions a red cape was draped over the cassock. As with other members of the Society of Jesus, Archbishop Perier's intellectual training had been rigorous, and he could relate to Bengali intellectuals in such associations as the Oriental Institute. But a bishop's first duty is as a shepherd, a father, and it was as a father that the people of Bengal knew the archbishop, his own flock and the ordinary villagers with whom he came in contact on his visitations. In 1924, his diocese extended into rural areas, including Ranchi, and numbered close to three hundred thousand Catholics. He was known as a strenuous walker and his regular visits to isolated villages were made on foot, as well as by bicycle or on horseback. One of his priests remarked, "The archbishop! He is as tough as a nut, if I may say so reverently." In 1927, new dioceses were carved out of Calcutta by the Holy See and Dr. Perier was left with less than forty thousand Catholics in the Calcutta area, half of them in the city of Calcutta itself. His title as "Bishop of the Streets" had proved prophetic.

At the Calcutta Club we talked of old days in Bengal and I asked him about Mother Teresa. I wondered if just over ten years earlier he had thought that a Loreto Sister could possibly persevere in a city so riven with agitation and need.

"In my mind, I gave her a year," he replied. "When her own Mother General agreed, I decided to send on her request to the nuncio in Delhi. If she attempted such a work and came back to her congregation after a year, nothing would be lost. If the hand of God was in the work, then it would go on."

There had been another nun in Calcutta who had asked the archbishop for leave to request exclaustration. He had insisted on delay as a way of testing her new vocation. In the end, the nun expressed deep gratitude to the archbishop for giving her time to realize that the step would have been unwise.

The archbishop smiled, his blue eyes alight with joy. "None of us can foretell what will come from the hand of God. No one could predict that in this diocese, with all its needs, a new society would spring up so quietly and that people from overseas would come to bring more help to the poor because of it."

He did not elaborate, but it was clear that he had been among those who had not predicted the developments with regard to the Missionaries of Charity. Yet when it became clear to him that the hand of God was in Mother Teresa's work, his generosity was unstinting, including giving the power to his vicar-general to lay out the money for the Motherhouse on Lower Circular Road.

His Grace was a stern taskmaster as long as the Missionaries of Charity was a congregation under his care. Already in 1958, Mother Teresa mentioned to me her ardent wish to send Sisters to other parts of India. Invitations had come to her from bishops in many parts of the country. Some had arisen because young women from their dioceses had already entered the order. She was wondering where the first foundation outside of Calcutta would be, and she mentioned in particular, Ranchi and Delhi. Perier was adamant in observing to the letter the rule that a diocesan congregation would confine its works to that diocese for the first decade of its existence. However, he relented a little and in 1959, just before the ten years were completed, a team of Sisters sped off to Ranchi in response to a long-standing invitation. From Ranchi had come many Missionaries of Charity, chiefly from the ranks of the tribal people of the region.

His Grace, Dr. Ferdinand Perier, had been the instrument in the protection of a small green shoot during its earliest years. In 1960, in his eighty-fifth year, he resigned from the archdiocese of Calcutta, which then passed, as did other dioceses of India under European bishops, to Indian leadership.

Meeting the members of the Society of Jesus in Calcutta, men of vastly differing gifts and temperaments, one realized how they all responded in their own ways to the discipline of an exacting life. St. Ignatius, a former soldier, had left them a spirituality undergirded by his Spiritual Exercises. He had taken the term "exercises" from the training exercises that are an integral part of the military life. Each priest filled a role in the diocese in line with the ideas and wishes of His Grace, the archbishop, and as in the case of Mother Teresa's communications in preparation for leaving Loreto, the word of His Grace was the final word.

Fr. Julien Henry was a large-boned man, impressive in his long white cassock. His eyes were compassionate, set deep in a countenance of strong features, especially a prominent nose. Like His Grace, he had a mustache and a short beard, already streaked with gray. While His Grace had the mien of a city man and had, in fact, embarked on a financial career in Antwerp before finding his vocation as a priest, Fr. Henry had come from Belgian crafts people, from a family of glassblowers. He had arrived in Calcutta one year before the outbreak of the Second World War, and the fact that he had lived through times of war, famine, and communal violence was etched in the deep lines of his face. He knew Mother Teresa as headmistress of St. Mary's Entally. As Entally was in St. Teresa's parish, he went there regularly to celebrate mass and to give instructions to the Catholic students. His work with the Sodality of the Blessed Virgin Mary had lasted from 1941 to 1947. It was to his parish, St. Teresa's, that

Mother Teresa's little band trooped for morning mass before they were given permission for their own chapel at 14 Creek Lane.

St. Teresa's was a church I frequented and I felt the fatherly presence of its pastor. We talked about increasing the flow of food from the United States to help stem the tide of starvation among Calcutta's neediest. This was of intense concern to him. Fr. Henry was proud of the way that various Catholic orders of priests, Sisters, and religious Brothers were turning their energies to healing the wounds of the people around them, but proudest of new works of mercy of the Missionaries of Charity. One of the first clinics for mothers and children had been opened by Mother Teresa in an old building behind St. Teresa's Church. One could see why Mother Teresa would address herself to this gentle priest for help in the training of the Sisters, a training that was no less thorough and rigorous for being accompanied by ground-breaking work with the abandoned and dying. Between October 1950 and April 1953 when the first Sisters were professed, Fr. Henry's role in their spiritual preparation was of fundamental importance. He was also reputed to be something of an inventor and had devised a plan for draining the great Salt Lake swamp outside Calcutta to provide a housing and industrial center.

Father Celesta Van Exem in 1958 was pastor of a parish in Howrah across the Hooghly River. When Mother Teresa introduced me to him on one of our visits to Howrah, it was evident in what reverence she held him. The few who knew of his key role between late 1946 and October 7, 1950, termed him the "Co-Founder" of the Missionaries of Charity. He was an imposing presence, careful of speech and about fifty years of age. His beard was neatly trimmed.

Mother Teresa, who rarely made comments about people and never about the Sisters, except in praise, said, as we left the parish, "He is a very holy man."

It occurred to me that men like Fr. Van Exem and Fr. Henry would have been especially receptive to Mother Teresa's addition of a fourth vow to achieve a special purpose. As members of the Society of Jesus, they themselves had taken a fourth vow, that of obedience to the Pope. This meant going wherever the Pope should send them for the salvation of souls. The places where the Jesuit priests were ordered to go, as something like spiritual "shock troops," included areas where souls were in danger through persecution. As one example, in Elizabethan times during Penal Laws, they obeyed the order to enter England and Wales as missionaries. Twenty-six of them fell victim to the hangman's noose (their bodies being then drawn and quartered) or the headsman's axe. Their maxim was "For the Greater Glory of God" which sustained them in both life and death.

Fr. Van Exem, a respected scholar whose knowledge of the Koran endeared him to his Muslim friends, had served as director of the Oriental

Institute. Yet, he took time to perform the simplest acts to help Mother Teresa in her efforts to serve the poor.

When the little group of young women was beginning the work without resources, he placed an advertisement in the *Calcutta Statesman* describing what was being done in the Calcutta *bustees.* To his surprise, the first gift of a hundred rupees came from the Chief Minister of Bengal. The *Statesman* carried regular news stories on the work of Mother Teresa after that notice, undoubtedly the first time her name had appeared in the public press. Successive articles brought continual help from the Calcutta community. It was a sick and destitute man from Howrah, he remembered later, who was sheltered by Mother Teresa and the Sisters at Moti Jihl before the hostel at the Kali Temple was opened to them. His name was Mendez, and he recovered from his illness.

Van Exem's close association with the new congregation, cemented when he read the decree of recognition of October 7, 1950, brought him new responsibilities. The training in work and prayer under Mother Teresa became a regular, intensive spiritual formation in April 1951. Fr. Van Exem, along with Fr. Julien Henry, adjusted their parish work so that they could give the young women the rigorous preparation they needed before they could take vows as nuns. The enthusiasm of Mother Teresa and that first band was of such burning intensity that they were simultaneously able to work in the slums and throw themselves into spiritual studies. It was because of the devotion of Celeste Van Exem and Julien Henry that the young women were ready to pronounce their first vows in two years, in April 1953. Van Exem remembered that Archbishop Perier had asked Mother Teresa to write a history of the congregation from the beginning and, at night, she would address herself to this task, describing the events of the day. She could not continue this for long because at night she had to answer the letters that came to her from young women interested in the new congregation. The notebook she kept in the early months was one of the items in Van Exem's keeping for a long time. Mother Teresa eventually persuaded Van Exem to return it to her, and she told him that she intended to destroy it. There may have been revelations of her own reactions and emotions that she preferred not to share.

The other members of the Society of Jesus supporting Mother Teresa at the beginning were in direct contrast to Fr. Van Exem and Fr. Henry. Fr. Robert Antoine has already been mentioned as a sort of chaplain at Kalighat. Fr. Antoine and Fr. Pierre Fallon lived in a students' hostel and seemed themselves members of a more youthful generation. They darted about the city on small motorcycles. Both had been professors at St. Xavier's College. When I went to visit them in their hostel, Shanti Bhavan, the House of Peace, I had to journey to a section inhabited by few Europeans. I found Fr. Antoine sitting on the floor surrounded by snowy layers of papers, a number of *tablas* (Indian drums), and a profusion of other musical instruments. He explained the disorder by stating that he was in the process of composing the words and music of a hymn in Bengali.

I expressed my astonishment and told him that I was glad to have arrived at such a fantastic moment.

"If I had known you were coming," Father Antoine said laughingly, "I would have been doing something even more fantastic."

As I came to know him, I found it rather easy to give credence to his joke. A small, wiry, effervescent man, he shared the outgoing, exuberant quality of many Bengalis. Much of Father Antoine's time was spent in preparing his lectures for a course on the epic for Jadavpore University. Through his course, his students were led from their own epics, the *Mahabharata* and *Ramayana,* to such epics as the *Gilgamesh* of the ancient Middle East to those of Europe, including the *Song of Roland* and Dante's *Divine Comedy.* He was later made head of the University's Department of Comparative Literature. One of his tasks was that of translating the Psalms of David into Sanskrit. He and Fr. Fallon were very much a part of Bengali cultural life. They were very different in appearance as well as in temperament. Fr. Antoine was clean-shaven, while Fr. Fallon had a small beard. Fallon's face was pale and ascetic and he looked at the world with clear, luminous eyes. In contrast to Antoine's outgoing manner, Fallon's was one of gentle, almost shy friendliness.

Fr. Fallon discussed the deep importance of karma in the lives of those around him, how the sense of inevitable retribution without the chance for forgiveness or remission influenced their reactions. It made for a greater acceptance of one's lot, even the most bitter lot. There was always the chance to improve one's karma by acceptance of one's fate and by acceptable conduct—and hope for better in the next incarnation. *Maya* I had thought of as roughly equivalent to the Christian concept of the transitoriness of life, but Fallon stressed that it went much deeper, leading the serious Hindu into viewing the world of sense as an illusion.

It was Fr. Fallon who had conducted the retreat in Darjeeling which Mother Teresa attended after her time of spiritual discernment on the train. When asked about that retreat at a later date, his only comment was that Mother Teresa seemed unusually quiet and withdrawn, as though lost in meditation.

Robert Antoine and Pierre Fallon, immersed as they were in Bengali culture, welcomed Mother Teresa's step in adopting Indian garb. Their fervent support of the new work inspired their students who soon began to volunteer for the most demanding part of it, service in the Home for the Dying. One of the student volunteers was Rama Coomaraswamy, son of the philosopher and art historian, Ananda Coomaraswamy. Rama was in

Calcutta to study philosophy and possibly follow in the footsteps of his father who built up the collection of Indian and Islamic Arts in the Museum of Fine Arts in Boston. Rama, who had been received into the Catholic Church in Boston, was in Calcutta with his American wife, Bernadette Martocchio Coomaraswamy. Bernadette had become ill in Calcutta and they had lost a child through miscarriage. Rama began to go to Kalighat as soon as it opened in 1952 and continued going through 1953.

"We did what needed to be done to help the Sisters," Rama recalled. "Sometimes we bathed the men as they were brought in from the streets, washing off the filth and the spittle—and maybe the maggots. I remember shaving them and giving them haircuts, even cutting their fingernails and toenails. We often had to sit down and feed a starving man slowly and patiently so that he would not die. But they did die—at that time we lost about a third of the people who were picked up. Then it was our job to carry them from the hall into the side space where the corpses were kept. We had nothing to do with the burial or with the burning ghat.

"The ones who survived found that they mattered. They seemed surprised to be treated as human beings, that someone took time to serve them and feed them. It only took a few days for them to look human again."

Mother Teresa smilingly referred to Rama as "one of my first volunteers." When Rama and Bernadette returned to the United States, he changed the course of his life, choosing to study medicine, and arranging for his internship at New York City's immense city hospital, Bellevue, a hospital that always had its doors open to the city's poorest, its injured, and its homeless.

Mother Teresa's confidence in Fr. Antoine was shown later. When the Missionaries of Charity Brothers were founded in 1963, she asked that he be freed to help train the young postulants. The Society of Jesus could not release him though since his duties at Jadavpore were too demanding and his relationships with the students too important to interrupt.

Another member of the Society of Jesus working in Bengal was Father Michael Gabric of Croatian origin from Yugoslavia. He gave himself completely to his duties as parish priest in Basanti in 24-Parganas. He was tall and spare with shining dark eyes and a fine hawk nose. The asceticism of his appearance was softened by a frequent smile. I suppose he was aware that it was because of the prior arrival of his own group of priests in Bengal that resulted years later in Mother Teresa's coming to the province, but it was never mentioned. Though initially surprised at Mother Teresa's transformation, he soon gave her unconditional support and joined in prayers for her new work. When he journeyed into Calcutta from his parish, he visited the Missionaries of Charity and we would meet to talk of his work in Basanti, the Bengali word for the spring of the year. In his area he was invaluable with the operation of a modern dispensary, a school for the basic tools of the intellect, and a technical school. Mother Teresa urged me to see his work and I accepted his invitation to take a trip that would involve at some point taking a boat. The day I was scheduled to make the journey, a flood occurred, and the visit was never made.

Father Gabric shared a language with Mother Teresa and they habitually conversed in the Serbo-Croat tongue. She had unlimited admiration for men like Father Gabric whose lives were spent among isolated rural groups. They brought to Christians and those around them not only schools and technical training, but dispensaries and hospitals. They were doing for the hidden poor in their mud and thatch villages, so often devastated by flood and typhoon, what Mother Teresa was doing for those on the streets of a devastated city.

At a critical time, Mother Teresa found support and understanding among five priests vastly different in temperament but one in an abnegation that allowed them to implant themselves in an alien culture and an alien soil. Fulfilling the aim of "becoming all things to all men," they in time became one with that culture and that soil.

One of the qualities that marked Mother Teresa was the absolute equality with which she treated everyone with whom she came in contact. There was an unself-conscious openness to the person, whether that person was of the highest or lowest estate, whether in authority or helpless and powerless, whether belonging to the rich of the city or to its most destitute.

Examples at the opposite ends of the scale would be that of an official of the Bengali or the Calcutta Government and that of a family which depended for part of its income on Moti Jihl mud.

To reach a government official in Calcutta, one entered a building on Dalhousie Square whose graceful porticos were reflected in an enormous artificial pool or tank. On the way to a poor family in Moti Jihl—or Dhappa or Howrah—one often had to straddle the path because at its center was the only runoff for filth and excrement. Even in places where the sewers, many over a hundred years old, still operated, there was often an overpowering stench. I was warned to be careful of a special breed of local rats, unusually large and voracious. In the reeking parts of Howrah where I accompanied the Missionaries of Charity, one hardly needed to be told that there had never been any sewers. It is only fair to say that after a month or six weeks, there was a merciful change of perception, and one was hardly aware of the miasmal vapors in which one might be enveloped.

To return to Dalhousie Square, it was the symbol of Calcutta's wealth when the East India Company brought in teams of clerks or "writers" to take charge of its accounts. Built in 1780, it was a massive construction, designed to house and feed the young accountants as well as provide office space for the voluminous records of the lucrative trade between the colonial child and the mother country. Though the buildings housed the government offices of West Bengal, they continued to be called the "Writers' Buildings."

Until 1912, Calcutta was actually an imperial city, capital of British India. It was only in that year that the British moved the capital to Delhi. Angered at the 1905 partition of Bengal, resisters, including terrorists, made ruling from Calcutta too dangerous. In that period, Bengal became known as the "suburb of dissent." By the middle of the twentieth century, when I knew it, it had become for countless, helpless victims of history, a "suburb of despair."

In 1958 Calcutta still had many of the marks of a world-girdling empire that had receded just a decade earlier. There were still signs of what had once been termed a "city of palaces," though from the beginning, the palaces of the merchant princes of the East India Company stood amid huts of incredible squalor. "Palace, byre and hovel—poverty and pride—side by side," in the words of Kipling. The Calcutta of the alien merchant princes has been likened to colonized Dublin which could present a cultured, gracious face while "beyond the pale," slum dwellers and evicted peasants, huddled in smoky huts along with their animals, were existing in the worst destitution in the Western World. In fact, the Bengalis, artistic and voluble, constantly resisting the "established disorder," have often been compared to the Irish.

Not only British wealth marked Calcutta. Renowned Bengali families, the Tagores being one example, laid the foundations of their fortunes in colonial days. There grew up also the palaces of the new leaders of finance and industry, including the incredible Marble Palace of the Mullicks set in the very congested heart of the city. Birla Park, a private, guarded family park in Alipore at the city's outskirts was the refuge of the Birla family. The Birla brothers, in their almost limitless wealth dispersed in a multiplicity of holdings, have been compared to the Rockefeller brothers. Though the family had originated in western India, their schools and technical institutes were a feature of Calcutta life. G. D. Birla, a financial supporter of Gandhi and mandated by the Mahatma to head the first national organization on behalf of "untouchables," continued the work through the Birla Education Trust. Granted the unparalleled Birla wealth, one wondered if, by pouring all of it into Calcutta, the deep wounds of the city could even be stanched. At a later date, Mrs. Sarala Birla, a young member of the extended family, became actively involved with Mother Teresa's work.

Our route to the caravanserai of the dying often gave me pause. As we turned off from Lower Circular Road on the way to Kalighat, we could see from the mobile clinic the shining white domes of a building of grandiose proportions. It was the Victoria Memorial, begun in that fateful year of 1905, and under it was the idealized statue of Victoria at the age of eighteen at her accession to the British throne. She was actually a matronly fifty-seven when she was declared Empress of India.

The carved letters, VRI, Victoria Regina Imperatrix, were placed on the building honoring the Empress in 1921. I wondered if any of those present at the dedication could have imagined that in little more than a quarter of a century, VRI would be an absurd anachronism. Even more absurd was the erection of so lordly a pile on the soft alluvial soil of Calcutta. Into that soggy soil it was slowly sinking, kept in place by a complicated contraption of pontoons.

The Memorial, for which the Indian people had been taxed more than ten million rupees, was an art gallery and museum and a resting place for variegated relics of British rule. Other vestiges of empire served as centers of government. The Raj Bhavan, formerly Government House, with its cupola and graceful pillars, had been built after the style of a British manor house in the Derbyshire countryside. Occasionally I went with Mother Teresa to Dalhousie Square where our destination was the sprawling Writers' Buildings already described.

Among the government officials with whom Mother Teresa had dealings on behalf of the poor was Dr. B. C. Roy, a physician, an old campaigner with Gandhi for the independence of India and the uplift of its poor. Even after entering government service and eventually becoming Chief Minister of Bengal, he took time in the early morning to give free medical service to the needy. When Mother Teresa needed to see him, she would ask for an appointment, but he soon advised her that she could see him at any time. To him Mother Teresa brought her requests and suggestions, such as the need for piped-in water for a forgotten *bustee.* Roy would initial the request and pass it along for action. When I went with her, she had some small matters to clear up, but she also wanted to let him know about the increased food supplies, especially rice and bulgur wheat that would be coming from the United States for Calcutta's poor through American people-to-people agencies.

The dignified man behind the desk was a member of Brahmo Samaj, the Society of God, a reformist Hindu association which, while honoring the highest in Indian culture and Hindu tradition, established an opening to Islam and to the ethics of Christianity. Founded in the early nineteenth century by a Bengali Brahmin, Ram Mohan Roy, the Brahmo Samaj campaigned against the burning of widows with their husbands' corpses. This act of religious custom was common in Calcutta at the time, with close to five hundred widows placing themselves on funeral pyres in the city in a given year. The renowned Tagore family, also Bengali Brahmins, were members of Brahmo Samaj and part of the intellectual ferment that continually arose in and flowed out of Bengal. Dr. B. C. Roy was one with Mother Teresa in all work to relieve the agony around them. Their mutual respect was evident, and I felt I was in the presence of two beings who responded literally to Gandhi's advice. This was engraved on the black marble slab marking the spot of his cremation. "Recall the face of the poorest and most helpless man whom you may have seen and ask yourself if the step you contemplate is going to be of any use to him. Will he be able to gain anything from it?"

Mother Teresa gave the same courteous attention to each person, whether it was B. C. Roy, P. C. Sen, who also became Chief Minister, Padmaja Naidu, Governor of Bengal, or the poorest *bustee* dweller. I could not forget the visit to a tiny home in Moti Jihl, where the father, an unemployed laborer supported his family by making wall brackets, shelves, picture frames, and statues of the Virgin Mary with the Child Jesus. Mother Teresa admired the man for his industry and for the fact that he and his wife had sent all their children to the Moti Jihl school. The four younger children were still pupils.

"They are a very good family," she told me as we entered their tiny home. "They work and they help each other." After school, we found out, the children searched the *bustee* area for scraps of wood and discarded packing boxes. Two older boys, about eleven and twelve, went into downtown Calcutta in search of discarded packing cases. Later they went back to hawk the finished objects on the streets. A small boy was outside the home carefully sawing the frail wood of a crate. We asked him his age. He was nine years old.

The home was, by *bustee* standards, a good one. It was built of brick and cement, called *pukka* construction. It was large enough for two beds, a number of boxes, a small stove, and some cooking utensils. The mother explained that the rent was just over seven rupees a month, a sum they managed to earn each month. Their rent had to be paid first, she explained, or they would have no place to live. It was the food that was uncertain. One could imagine the choice that had to be made as the rent came due between food and shelter. The *bustee* landlords were not known to be merciful. In most cases, they had constructed the *pukka* homes or huts and had to pay rent themselves on the land which was in the hands of others. The many people whom I had considered squatters, free of rent, were actually paying rent on their mud huts. The hut owner collected his rupees, keeping his portion and passing on the remainder to the landowner.

The daily glass of milk and other foods given out at school helped this family and many other families to survive.

The brightest spot in any *bustee* hut was usually the image of Durga, or perhaps of black-visaged Kali, but here, on a tiny shelf, was a statue of the Virgin Mary. Mary was clad in a sari and squatting like an Indian woman with the Infant Jesus lying across her knees. I asked the maker how he had fashioned the little statue and he pointed outside to the mud surrounding Moti Jihl pond. He had managed to bake the figure and paint it in striking colors, the sari of the Virgin being bright red. The makers of clay figures of gods and goddesses could do very well among the millions of the devout, especially during the festivals of Durga and Saraswati, goddess of learning and therefore of students. With less than fifty thousand Catholics in the city, the father could not market too many statues.

His eldest daughter, Chand, meaning "moon," a teenager, earned some money as cook and dishwasher for some affluent families. The other daughters had similar Bengali names, Shandha, Evening, Tara, Star, and Shurji Sun, the youngest. As Christians, they also had baptismal names, Chand being Agnes. The mother had sent for Mother Teresa because of Shurji, huddled in a blanket, her face to the wall. Mother Teresa put her arm around the girl and found that the girl was not physically ill, but inundated by the pain around her. Soon the sensitive fourteen year old, who seemed to have reached the age where she could see the bars of the cage entrapping her, was in Shishu Bhavan. She was to study and help with the smaller children.

Before we left, Mother Teresa had expressed our admiration to the father for his sculpture of the Virgin and I had ordered a similar figure to bring back to the United States. He said it would be ready in a week. He explained that he had to wait first for the mud to dry and then for the paint to dry. I offered to pay him, but in the expansive Bengali way, he refused payment. There was no argument; I merely slipped into his wife's hand some rupee notes that would pay their rent for the next two months. In just a week, Chand brought my statue to Shishu Bhavan. In deference, I suppose, to my color, this Virgin had chalk white skin. Instead of the red sari, she was robed in the traditional blue. For good measure, he sent at the same time the original statue that we had admired. I brought them both back to the United States as examples of what could be fashioned out of Moti Jihl mud.

Shurji I used to see at Shishu Bhavan, busy and smiling. It was perhaps the only way in which she could have been rescued. In those days of 1957 and 1958, Mother Teresa was able herself to take action for individuals. As her order grew, she never retreated into administration, though there was an increasing amount of it. She continued to go as often as possible to Shishu Bhavan and Kalighat, the schools, the clinics, and the leper stations. The Sisters, catching her spirit, carried out in their daily work her attitude of personal attention to human needs, emotional and spiritual as well as physical. Without perhaps being conscious of it, they followed Mother Teresa in giving the same respect to the poor and powerless as they gave to those with riches and worldly power.

The frequent mention of the word "walls" by Mother Teresa has already been referred to. When she left the walls of Loreto behind her, she began to evolve new patterns in order to reach the goals which she had set for herself, serving the poor while living close to them. These patterns were not analyzed and worked out, to be imposed on reality like a schema. Instead, they grew to meet needs and situations. Again and again it was clear that Mother Teresa proceeded without "preconceived ideas." Once the basic Jesus-centered goal was established, the means were only to be found as the Spirit of God showed the way. There was a parallel in the life of Gandhi who saw his progress in terms of "experiments with truth," in day-to-day dependence on enlightenment from God whom he identified as Truth.

First, there were the practical solutions for Sisters who had to go out on the streets to reach the people. Sisters within institutions just presented themselves at the convent refectory and a drink of water was as close as the nearest faucet.

"You see that each Sister carries a bag like mine," Mother Teresa said. It was a homemade bag, the material being khaki cloth with the handles crafted from wood by the boys in the vocational school. Some of the same cloth covered the pallets in Kalighat. It had been part of a shipment of surplus cloth obtained by Catholic Relief Services for relief and aid programs.

"She always carries a bottle of water in it, so that if she is out in the heat, she can take a drink of water without asking our people for anything."

I could see that a young woman, teaching in an open-air school in a *bustee,* would have to have a source of liquid, especially in the dry months when the dust and furnace heat enveloped everyone. The children would stop off at the community faucet on their way home, but the Sisters would take out their own supply. One might have hoped that it would be cool water out of a thermos, but that would not have matched the poverty around them. The bottles were old glass bottles recycled from other uses, mostly containers for cooking oil.

"Our people always want to say 'Thank you' to the Sisters," Mother

Teresa told me, "and they will offer them a cup of tea, or something to eat, maybe the last thing they have. Or perhaps they will buy a sweet to be ready for the Sisters. Then we began to have invitations from the other side. Better-off families would invite the Sisters for tea. The simple answer is that the Sisters cannot accept anything—from the richest or the poorest. That way nobody feels hurt."

The outward pattern of the Sisters' lives was an expression of the special poverty called for by the fourth vow linking them with the very poorest. The Sisters always looked like fresh white flowers in the murky streets, their saris gleaming in the sunlight. The courtyard of the Motherhouse often resembled a lake over which billowed rows of white sails. So porous was the material of the sari that it dried quickly indoors during the monsoon. Later, the number of saris grew from "one to wash and one to wear," to "one to wash, one to wear, and one to mend." The saris were made of the same rough cotton as those worn by the city's poor women and I saw many women with identical saris except that the bands were red rather than blue. At the beginning of the work, the sari cost less than an American dollar, actually the equivalent of about seventy cents. Later, the sari did not change but the price rose somewhat. I once innocently asked if the Sisters could not have saris made of *khadi,* the homespun cotton so important to the Gandhian thrust for Indian self-reliance. It was still produced in millions of yards in communities all over India. I was told that they would like nothing better, but that *khadi,* involving handwork and a fair price to the producer, was simply too high in price. Besides the saris, each Sister had a change of undergarments, often made out of flour sacks, washed and washed again to soften the material, a pair of sandals, a small crucifix, and a rosary. The Sisters demonstrated a life stripped down and simplified to such a point that all nonessentials were sheared away. Besides the saris, each Sister had a metal spoon and rimmed plate like those given to children. Such a plate was the only kind that could hold without spilling the stew-type dishes that constituted the main meal. Often the Indian gravy, *dall,* was part of the meal. With so little time needed for the details of living, it was not surprising that the Sisters could achieve prodigies of work. And along with these achievements went a program of prayer and meditation that made it possible to persevere in works that might otherwise seem beyond human endurance.

The day for the Sisters began at twenty to five in the morning. It is a day at the far end of the spectrum from that lived in a consumer society, one filled with getting and spending and turned to goals of self-fulfillment and success. Yet, paradoxically and perhaps incomprehensibly, it is a pattern that brings an almost palpable peace and joy to those who live it. As she dressed, the Sister kissed her sari and prayed that the habit would be a reminder of "my separation from the world and its vanities. Let the world be nothing to me and I nothing to the world. Let it remind me of my baptismal robe and help me to keep my heart pure from sin just for today."

While putting on her sandals, her prayer continued, "Of my own free will, dear Jesus, I shall follow You wherever You shall go in search of souls, at any cost to myself and out of pure love of You."

Following Indian custom, the Sisters shed their sandals at the chapel entrance and padded their way barefoot into the chapel for a half hour of prayer and meditation. In the chapel were neither pews nor seats as in Indian holy places. After meditation, the Sisters recited from their prayer book a prayer of stark and total abandonment to the Lord by St. Ignatius, founder of the Company of Jesus. "Take, O Lord, and receive all our liberty, our memory, our understanding and our whole will, whatever we have and possess. You have given us all these; to you, O Lord, we restore them; all are yours, dispose of them in any way according to your Will. Give us your love and your grace, for this is enough for us."

Mass was at six o'clock in the morning. I thought of the blackboard with the day's numbers at the entrance to Kalighat as I saw the blackboard at the door of the chapel. On it were various messages, including the saint to be commemorated and the hymn to be sung. Always on the blackboard were the names of those who had asked for special prayers. Anyone, of any spiritual tradition, who had asked Mother Teresa or the Sisters for remembrance in prayers, was commended to the Creator.

As Mother Teresa was to say repeatedly, the lives of the Sisters were "woven about the Eucharist," the commemoration of the Last Supper when Jesus offered Himself as the victim for the sin of the world. The central act of the liturgy of the Catholic Church, so often attended listlessly as a Sunday duty by church members, becomes on Lower Circular Road the fulcrum about which the whole day turns. Priest after priest stood at the altar table in the chapel, facing the Sisters, to deliver the prescribed readings from the Scriptures. Then came the words of the New Covenant, words of awesome import, repeated millions of times since that day preceding the Crucifixion, "This is my body. This is my blood which shall be shed for you and for many for the remission of sins." The Sisters relived the spiritual reality. Each time the bread was broken by a priest, it was the body of the Lord that was wounded, and each time the wine was poured it was His blood that was being shed. Each time it was the Resurrected Lord who was shared as the Sisters went forward to take communion. The great mystery of the bread and wine becoming the body and blood of the Savior extended into the coming day for Mother Teresa and for every Sister. One of the questions in their prayer book is "Do I live the mass during the day?" The Sisters relied on the transcendent life brought by Jesus.

Behind the priest at the altar of the Motherhouse chapel was a large crucifix with two words, I THIRST. These words recalled not only the words of Jesus on the cross, but a symbolic thirst, his thirst for the love of humankind. The words also recalled the sixty-ninth Psalm in the Hebrew Scriptures, in which the suffering one cries out prophetically, "In my thirst they gave me vinegar to drink." The other spiritual nourishment, which brought renewal for each day, were the Scriptures, selections from both the New Testament and Hebrew Scriptures being read every day of the year.

As the Sisters went out every morning, they lived the mass in seeing the most rejected person, the most horribly disfigured person, the person receiving life's bitterest drafts of sorrow, as the Lord who had shared with them His body and blood. I could not have foreseen, even in my wildest imaginings, that from here as heart and center, hundreds of chapels would be founded in an ever-widening circle. In less than two decades, I would see I THIRST in chapels planted in poor and sequestered corners of the world, from an aboriginal settlement in the outback of Australia to a gathering place for the sick and helpless in Tanzania on the African continent. One of the prayers recited after Communion was "Radiating Christ," composed by John Henry Newman, the English cardinal.

> Dear Jesus, help us to spread your fragrance everywhere we go . . .
> Let us preach you without preaching, not by words, but by our example . . .

This prayer always reminded me of Gandhi's words to a Christian, "A rose does not need to preach. It simply spreads its fragrance. The fragrance is its sermon."

I occasionally joined the Sisters for the early morning mass. Already, Calcutta had sprung to life and the noise of Lower Circular Road was building up. However, the almost palpable atmosphere of recollection enveloped me during the most sacred moments of the mass, and I was shocked back into reality when I heard once more the street clamor entering through the open windows. I had been deaf to it during the service.

There was an occasional hymn from a mimeographed hymnbook mostly in English. Hearing the Sisters sing, one might wonder if one of the tests to enter the congregation had been that of possessing a fine voice. They would raise their voices in exquisite harmony to sing, "From many grapes and grains of wheat/One host we bring to Thee our God./Transform, we pray, this humble gift/To Jesus' precious flesh and blood . . . And may we all one body be/In Christ's unbounded peace and love."

Only after receiving nourishment for the soul through meditation and the reception of the Communion did the Sisters take their breakfast, generally tea and a few *chapatties.* Then there were the joyful sounds of many young voices as they gathered their supplies to set out for Shishu Bhavan, the schools, the dispensaries, the leper stations, and the Home for the Dying.

Some walked to Shishu Bhavan, some piled into the van for the journey to Kalighat or a leper station, others rushed to get a place in the tramcars that clanged along Lower Circular Road.

A little after noon, they were back at the Motherhouse, ready for a stew with rice or bulgur wheat and often another *chapatti.* The house was again filled with the sound of many voices and the clatter of metal spoons on metal plates. After the washing of dishes, there was a period of somnolent silence. The Sisters had been up and about for over seven hours and had done what many would consider a hard day's work. At one o'clock, the Sisters lay down for a short rest. This custom was taken over from the Medical Mission Sisters. Some immediately fell into a deep sleep, only to be awakened in half an hour for prayers and a return to work. The second part of the day was almost like a second full day of work. The Sisters became so accustomed to the pattern that it was difficult to break it. Once I had to see a Sister right after lunch when she should have been taking her rest. Her eyelids kept drooping, and I soon found I was talking to someone who was sitting up but in a dead sleep.

At two o'clock, the Sisters were out on the streets again, some changing their work, now going to a dispensary after teaching at morning school, or to a leper station after a morning at Kalighat. At six o'clock, they were back at the Motherhouse for fifteen minutes of adoration in the chapel. Some years later, the chapel adoration was changed to a full hour. Supper followed. Then came time for reading and for recreation. Perhaps the Sisters were not as boisterous as the Brothers, who were described as going wild at recreation time, working off the strains and tensions of the day. Without doubt, however, there was fun and teasing and tales by voluble young women about the strange and unexpected occurrences that came their way daily in Calcutta.

It is only possible to give a glancing description of the prayers that helped form the Sisters' day. One prayer in the little prayer book was to be said before the crucifix and made it clear that each Sister was to see her life as a "living sacrifice," even to the point of praying for martyrdom. A regular feature consisted of reciting the traditional litanies of the Church, the litany of the Lord's passion for the season of Lent, the special litanies for the seasons of Christmas and Easter, and the litany of Mary, mother of Jesus. This litany, recited in Catholic households and parishes the world over, resonates with ancient poetry, ". . . Cause of our joy/Spiritual vessel/Vessel of honor/Vessel of singular devotion/Mystical rose/Tower of David/Tower of ivory/House of gold/Ark of the Covenant/Gate of heaven/Morning star/Health of the sick/Refuge of sinners/Comforter of the afflicted." "Cause of our joy" was often on the lips of the Missionaries of Charity. Mary was viewed as the gate through whom Jesus had entered the human family with the Good News of the gospel.

In addition, there was a special litany for every day of the week. Monday's litany was that of the Holy Spirit. Tuesday's litany was of particular interest, since it was the litany of humility, attributed to Cardinal Merry del Val of Spain. The repeated response to each petition was, "Jesus grant me the grace to desire it." The petitions were many, including, "That others may be loved more than I . . ." "That others may be chosen and I set aside . . ." "That others may be praised and I go unnoticed . . ." "That others may become holier than I provided that I may become as holy as I should . . ."

Mother Teresa's insistence on community prayer and community recreation was absolute. Not only were the Sisters to be a community of prayer and work, but they were also a family which took joy in each other's company. At the Motherhouse, this sense of close community developed naturally, but when the Sisters moved out of Calcutta and eventually overseas, Mother Teresa's emphasis on it was so strong that it was never lost. While other orders of Sisters, becoming involved in taxing programs demanding travel and extended absence from their communities, deemphasized the role of community, Mother Teresa saw this as a dangerous threat to the underpinnings of religious life and even to its continuance.

There was no need for the Sisters to be away from the Motherhouse at night since the schools, dispensaries, and leper stations needed no night watch. At Shishu Bhavan, Sisters took turns staying overnight, along with a woman who served as a permanent housemother and several young women as aides. From the beginning, the Sisters needed workers at Kalighat to help lift and carry the patients and to manage the large cooking vats. These workers, trained by the Sisters, watched over the wards until the Sisters arrived in the early morning. As time went on, a few married couples stayed in Kalighat at night, receiving pay and board as well as shelter in homes that were part of the roof of the caravanserai.

Before lying down to sleep, the Sister who had prayed over her habit and sandals while dressing, for the day to be lived in the presence of God, examined her conscience, basing her questions on the four vows.

"Do I realize that I am really rich when I possess the Kingdom, and am I really happy to be poor? Do I make myself available precisely because I am poor and am available for Christ? Is my obedience active and responsible and the expression of my love for God? Do I pray the work? Do I meet Christ in the distressing disguise of the poor I serve?"

The Sister recited an act of contrition, asking pardon of the Creator for anything done during the day that might have been an offense. Then it was time to sleep, generally by ten o'clock at night.

That hour did not apply to Mother Teresa. As the congregation kept growing, more and more letters had to be answered. She chose the night hours to write out her replies in longhand at the table in her room. Whether she remained at work to midnight or beyond, she arose at the appointed time. In a way unknown to most mortals, she kept to this schedule year after year, never adverting to fatigue, never losing her recollection, or her composure in dealing with the multitudes who entered her life. Once, when I asked her how she could manage with so little sleep and had embarked on a little lecture about the body's need for sleep, she gave a sort of mischievous smile and said, "I sleep fast." The next morning, at the bell at 4:40 A.M., one of the Sisters calls out "Let us bless the Lord," and the Sisters in the dormitory respond, "Thanks be to God." The round begins again, a round in which the transcendent aspect of life suffuses every other aspect.

Though a regular time schedule was kept by the Sisters, the work was so varied and the urgencies presented by the people so unpredictable that the work did not become tedious or boring. Also, Mother Teresa knew how to vary the schedule. Every Thursday, the Sisters stayed at the Motherhouse. They cleaned and scrubbed it, they had time to study, and they attended to such tasks as mending their saris. The shining white garment that looked so fresh on the street might, in fact, be mended in half a dozen places, with larger holes actually replaced by weaving with heavy white thread. On Thursdays, too, there were picnics, with volunteers taking the Sisters to some quiet spot where they could play like the young people they were. Sometimes unheard-of food came their way when friends like Mrs. Katherine Bracken, a volunteer from the American Consulate, would send enough ice cream so that each Sister could have a portion. Each Sister had a patron saint and the feast day was marked in some special way, if only by songs and cards, homemade with crayon and glue. The annual feast of the society, on August 22, the feast of the Immaculate Heart of Mary, was always an exciting time, with many priests and even bishops coming to the Motherhouse to celebrate mass and give special homilies. When the name of the feast day was changed to the Queenship of Mary, and the date was changed for the rest of the Church, the Missionaries of Charity were permitted to retain the former name and date.

The Sisters made special Bengali sweets when they had the makings; they sang, and they danced Indian dances including the dance of the lighted candles, that expressed sacred traditions. While much of the singing was in English, the Sisters, coming from different parts of India began teaching each other the hymns of their own regions in their ancient tongues. From Kerala in the south came age-old hymns, many to Mary, in Malayalam. From Bombay in the west came hymns in Konkani, and even from Nepal to the north of India came sacred songs of Christian groups. These were added to the Bengali and Hindi hymns and to the occasional Latin anthem.

As in other convents, gifts were circulated, the same gift going from one person to another on different occasions. On one festival occasion, I received a tall, carved crucifix in a box. I was delighted with it. At the bottom of the box was a small note that had been overlooked. It said, "To our dear Durwan with love and prayers from all." It had already served its purpose as a gift from the Sisters to Sister Nirmala, a Nepali. In Calcutta, many Nepalis work as *durwans,* or gatekeepers or guards. It was a way of lovingly teasing Sister Nirmala.

One would often see Sisters garbed in all-white saris, lacking the three blue stripes, accompanying the other Sisters to Kalighat and the other centers around Calcutta. These were the novices, still to make their first profession in the Missionaries of Charity. In most congregations, the novitiate was customarily the time to be secluded away from the "world" in its pejorative sense. While the novices in the Missionaries of Charity were immersed in the Scriptures, in theology and church history, as well as in close study of the constitutions of the congregation, they joined in the work. When it came time to take the vows of profession, they would know fully to what they were giving themselves. On Thursdays, when the professed Sisters were at the Motherhouse, it was the novices who took their places.

It was not only the novices who confronted the difficult work. Young women who may have come with the sweet illusion of leaning lovingly over a suffering child or a noble-faced old man, were taken matter-of-factly to Kalighat to help wash and feed a woman still expelling worms. No one called it a test, but test it was.

Mother Teresa had established a fairly reasonable schedule of preparation comparable to that of other congregations. On arriving, the young candidates were called aspirants. Following a period of six months, they became postulants. Postulant comes from the Latin word to ask, and the first year was a time of asking for acceptance. Once accepted, the young women were admitted as novices and were now officially in training for the commitment in vows. The novitiate took two years, ending in the first profession of vows. At any time during the first three years, the young women were free to leave the society. Only after the first profession was it necessary to have permission from Mother Teresa to leave. Following renewal of vows in the fourth and fifth year, lifetime vows were taken after six years in the Missionaries of Charity. Before final vows there was a year of intensive spiritual preparation called the tertianship, taken either in Calcutta or Rome.

The pattern of the day of the Missionaries of Charity was carried over to other cities of India and, in time, to many countries of the world. When possible, there was a day of rest and recreation on Thursdays. When novitiates were opened overseas, candidates were introduced immediately to the actual work.

Not only was the pattern of a day girded with prayer worked out in Calcutta, but also the general pattern of the works to which the congregation would dedicate itself.

This pattern was made explicit in the constitutions of the congregation. After the first paragraph of the constitutions, already cited, in which the Missionaries of Charity represent the answer to the special call given to Mother Teresa on September 10, 1946, there follows paragraph two, on the aim.

> Our aim is to quench the infinite thirst of Jesus Christ on the cross for love of souls by the profession of the evangelical counsels and wholehearted free service to the poorest of the poor.

The third paragraph is specific in its description of the ways to serve:

> Our particular mission is to labor at the salvation and sanctification of the poorest of the poor by:
>
> — nursing the sick and the dying destitutes
> — gathering and teaching little street children
> — visiting and caring for beggars and their children
> — giving shelter to the abandoned
> — caring for the unwanted, the unloved, and lonely
> — proclaiming the word of God by our presence and spiritual works of mercy
> — adoration of Jesus in and by the Blessed Sacrament.
>
> In so doing we prove our love for Jesus
>
> — under the appearance of bread and
> — under the distressing disguise of the poorest of the poor.

The constitutions stress two points of bedrock importance for the future of the Missionaries of Charity. First "our particular mission," as described, is the very essence of the work of the Missionaries of Charity, and "shall not be changed without leave by the Holy See." Secondly, say the constitutions, the Missionaries of Charity will "remain right on the ground by living Christ's concern for the poorest and lowliest" only until there may be "others who can help them better and in a more lasting way."

The humility and concreteness of the constitutions came clearly from the heart and hands of a woman dealing humbly and concretely with the wounds and agonies of humankind. The pattern of working "right on the ground" manifested itself first in a city tormented by every form of suffering, every agony. It seemed to bring to life the prescription Gandhi had given to Christians in 1927. "Let them start at the bottom, let them enter into what is best in their life and offer nothing inconsistent with it. That will make their work more efficacious, and what they will say and offer to the people will be appreciated without suspicion and hostility. In a word, let them go to the people not as patrons, but as one of them, not to oblige them but to serve them and to work among them."

9

The Age of Kali?

Watching the stream of pilgrims to the shrine of Kali from the Home for the Dying, one wondered what went on under her wide silver dome. Father Robert Antoine, respected by the Brahmin priests for his immersion in Bengali culture and his respected post, mentioned earlier, as professor of the epic at Jadavpore University, brought me inside the temple of the goddess. We took our places in the long line of pilgrims who were propitiating Kali with orange-bright marigolds on flat banana leaves and food offerings on pottery shards. The offerings were placed on the receptacles with tongs and were touched neither by vendor nor pilgrim. By special permission, we were permitted to join the pilgrims without the customary offering.

Father Antoine pointed out that the pilgrims were taking care not to breathe in the scent of the flowers because that scent, the essence, was considered to belong to the goddess. Into that statue, the divinity itself is seen as having in some sense taken up her abode. From an anteroom, we were conducted into a passageway that led into the temple proper. There, through a slit in a thick stone wall, we got our glimpse of Kali the Terrible, "haunter of the burning ghats." It is a glimpse that lasts a lifetime.

The image is of black stone, all but the coal-black face and arms painted over. Kali's red eyes glare fiercely and her tongue is ever extended as a reminder that she has licked the blood of those she has slain. The garland around her neck consists of skulls. Her four arms hold high a severed head, dripping red drops of blood, a knife and handfuls of clotted blood. As I took in these details, I realized that Mother Kali's figure was poised in the steps of a dance. I was trying to unite the disparate elements of dance and death when I had to move away from the aperture and out of range of Kali's blood-red eyes to make way for pilgrims ready to place their gentle flower offerings on stands.

We had arrived in the early morning when everything seemed wrapped in a miasma. It was just after a ritual killing had taken place in the temple courtyard. A male goat, pinioned between two posts, had been beheaded with one stroke. On the mound where the animal's head had fallen, a host of flies scurried, feasting on the surface darkened by spurting blood. We had seen that the pilgrims, squatting in the anterooms and walking with us along the passageway, had a red mark on their foreheads. While we waited, we viewed the stone shaft or *lingam* representing the organ of generation in which form the god Siva is honored.

"To make that mark, they have dipped a finger in the blood of the goat," Father Antoine explained. Many Hindus turn away from the bloody sacrifice of goats and sheep at Kali's temple. Geoffrey Ashe, biographer of Gandhi, noted that on Gandhi's return to India from his nonviolent campaigns in South Africa, he visited Calcutta. Looking in at Kali's temple, Ashe recounts, "he was revolted by the blood of sacrificed sheep." Indians know, too, that the band of robber-murderers from whom we get the word "thug," were devotees of Kali.

Yet, to one conversant with the Judaeo-Christian concept of sacrifice, the sacrifice at the Kali shrine would call to mind a long tradition. In the Temple at Jerusalem, the goat was dispatched with a single stroke and was offered as propitiation for sin. We read in the Hebrew Scriptures, in the sixteenth chapter of Leviticus, "The goat that is determined by lot for the Lord, Aaron shall bring in and offer up as a sin offering." The primordial element of sacrifice, the cleansing power of blood offered in expiation, seems to have been retained in this survival from an earlier religious phase. It has been established that the basic rule of India's Vedic religion included both animal and human sacrifice. Some say that ritual animal slaughter was assimilated into Hinduism long after Vedic times from India's aboriginal tribes. There is so much that is uncertain here that one might come to a tentative conclusion that the root concept of the expiatory power of the blood of the sacrificed victim may be surviving in Hinduism as an undercurrent in a changed setting.

Those who follow the New Covenant see in Jesus the "Lamb of God," whose blood, willingly shed, bought remission, once and for all, for the sins of the human family. Could it not be that it was the concept of remission, so alien to the iron rule of karma, that was living on here? Could it not be a survival from an age before the iron law of karma had taken hold?

Despite the fact that a collision of values, of world views, exploded over the domes of the caravanserai and the Kali temple, the presence of blood sacrifice hinted at a deep concordance, unrecognized by either side.

Not far away on a tributary of the Hooghly into which flowed the waters of the sacred Ganges, was Kalighat, the busy cremation place. We saw the piles of wood and twigs stocked for future pyres and some arranged for immediate cremation. There were sheet-wrapped bodies, one of which was about to be placed on the pyre. Some jars of *ghee*, clarified butter, were at hand. The workers around these scenes of death would be from the group in the Hindu system marked for such defiling work, the so-called "untouchables."

If a family member were present, that person would ignite the pyre by placing the burning brand in the mouth of the corpse. I supposed an attendant would perform the necessary rite if the corpse had come from the Home for the Dying. Soon would come the crackling of twigs and the cracking of bones. The acrid smoke from the burning ghat followed us as we returned to the Home for the Dying. I realized one compelling reason behind the Health Officer's provision of Kali's Pilgrim Hostel to Mother Teresa for the care of the dying might well have been its location so close to the burning ghat. As expected, most of those brought to the hostel died. The Health Officer could not have foreseen that soon more than half of those brought to the Home for the Dying would be saved from the Kalighat cremation place.

The conjunction of Mother Kali and Mother Teresa, Kali Ma and Teresa Ma, was either a strange turn of fate or of providence, according to one's inclination. It was Kali who had given her name to Calcutta in the first place. Job Charnock of the East India Company had chosen to settle in a spot on the Hooghly River where there had existed from time immemorial a shrine to Kali. The village that grew around the shrine (closer to the site of Sealdah Station than Kalighat) was named Kalikata because at that point, in mythic times, the little toe of the right foot of the dismembered goddess had fallen. Kali was the wife of Siva, the Destroyer, who formed with Brahma, the Creator, and Vishnu, the Preserver, the trinity at the apex of the Hindu pantheon of gods and goddesses. When Kali died, Siva, enraged, carried her body about the world on his shoulders in a mourning dance. Wherever he stopped, he brought destruction. Vishnu halted the destructive dance before the whole world was consumed by the rage of the god. He threw a knife at Kali's body and sliced it into fifty-two pieces which were scattered about the earth.

Kalikata along with two neighboring villages were legally occupied by a *firman*, or license, from the Moghul Emperor Aurangzeb. This allowed Job Charnock and the East India Company trading privileges. With Charnock's band were a group of Portuguese, the survivors of a decimated settlement of 1632. History records that he allotted them a small parcel of land on which the first Catholic chapel of Calcutta was built.

After Charnock's death, the three villages were officially purchased by the East India Company. The names of the other two villages have faded from history, but little Kalikata with its temple became the seed of Calcutta and of an empire. Trading privileges gave rise to political privilege and later hegemony. It was here that the aims of the East India Company were realized. They were enunciated in its charter, signed by Queen Elizabeth in 1599, namely, "For the honour of this our realm of England as for the increase of our navigation and advancement of trade merchandise." Charnock had chosen the marshy spot to pitch tents for himself and the British sailors because he was attracted by a large shade tree there. The sailors were less attracted by the spot and by some strange prescience referred to it as Golgotha, which is, of course, Hebrew for Calvary, the place of the crucifixion of Jesus. It was a name given to a place that was to become a Calvary for countless members of the human family, and also a place where women with a crucifix on their saris called each scourged human being Jesus.

In Hindu cosmology, time is divided into cycles of *mahayugas,* or aeons, and four *yugas,* or ages. The fourth of these yugas is the *Kaliyuga,* an age of irreligion and cruelty which leads to destruction by flood and fire. According to A. E. Basham in *The Wonder That Was India,* "We are at present in the Kali-Yuga." Many Hindus concur with him. Certainly the age of Kali seems to have possessed Kali's city with its famine, its Day of the Great Killing, its mass homelessness, and its continuing agony.

Many wondered if other agonies were in store, predicting that the smaller incidents of violence might burst forth into massive, revolutionary violence. When two Soviet leaders made their 1958 stopover in Calcutta, a solid crush of people lined the entire twelve-mile route from Dum Dum Airport to the Raj Bhavan. When Nikolai Bulganin and Nikita Khrushchev appeared in the Maidan Park, more than two million people, one of the most massive assemblages of people ever held in India, greeted them with frenetic enthusiasm. Bengal was still a "suburb of dissent," the focus of upheaval and sporadic violence.

As I glanced back from Kali's shrine and her burning ghat to the ivory, bulbous domes of the caravanserai sheltering the dying, I would hardly have found it credible to consider that a score of years later, Mother Teresa, Teresa Ma, would be, in the minds of millions, more tied to Calcutta and Bengal than Kali Ma, Mother Kali. I could not have fantasized that when Mother Teresa received the Nobel Peace Prize, she would be called by Bengal's Chief Minister, a Communist, the "Mother of Bengal."

10

Indian Passport to Rome

"I asked His Grace and he told me that I should go—therefore if all goes well and it is really the will of God I will come for the convention.

"Thank God I have plenty to do—otherwise I would be terrified of that big public. Being an Indian citizen, I will have to get an Indian passport.

"On the way back, could you come with me to Rome—for I want to get the pontifical recognition for our society. All the houses are doing well. We have grown to 119 Sisters. I am glad that I will have the chance to thank personally the greathearted Americans for their love of God's poor."

In this letter written to me from Calcutta on August 9, 1960, Mother Teresa agreed to leave India for the first time following her arrival there in January 1929. His Grace, of course, was Archbishop Ferdinand Perier of Calcutta, episcopal shepherd of the Missionaries of Charity.

On a bracing, sunlit October day, just two months later, I was at the airport in Las Vegas, Nevada, to meet one of the most incongruous figures ever to visit that city, known for its gambling and for quick marriages after speedy divorces in nearby Reno.

The convention was the national convention of the National Council of Catholic Women, with over three thousand delegates representing some ten million Catholic women nationwide. Las Vegas, an unlikely place for such a gathering, was chosen since the city fathers had offered the National Council of Catholic Women free use of a great horseshoe-shaped convention hall for their meetings and exhibits. Armed with her first Indian passport, Mother Teresa traveled alone from Calcutta to Los Angeles where she was met by Katherine Bracken, one of Mother Teresa's volunteers while serving as U. S. Consul in Calcutta. The enveloping cotton sari and stockingless feet in rough sandals must have occasioned interest on the journey from Asia. Mother Teresa told me she had been mystified at the ripple of laughter that arose as she responded to questions about her destination with the words "Las Vegas."

The invitation had come from Catholic Relief Services, headed by Bishop Edward Swanstrom, since the Catholic women worked closely with Catholic Relief Services in a program entitled "The Works of Peace." This program supplied funds and other aids for women's health and development programs around the world. As consultant to the women's program, I had introduced them to the work of Mother Teresa upon returning from Calcutta in 1958. My suggestion to have her address the convention was eagerly accepted, particularly as the convention theme was "These Works of Love." The phrase was drawn from a blessing sent to the women by Pope John XXIII who had commended them for their generosity on behalf of needy women and children faraway, from whom they would never receive a word of thanks. "You have the consolation," Pope John wrote, "of knowing that these works of love performed on behalf of those united to you only by the bond of charity, will last beyond the other good works of your lifetime. These works of love will go with you into eternity and help you to unite with the source of all love, God."

Among the first to greet Mother Teresa in Las Vegas was Cardinal Cushing, Archbishop of Boston, who smilingly dubbed her "Mahatma Gandhi," and never called her anything else for the four days of the meeting.

I had accompanied Mother Teresa when she had addressed some groups in Calcutta but she had evidently not considered such groups in her own city in public.

Just before she faced this new, unknown public, I took out for her a photograph of Sister Shanti. She later told me that it was Sister Shanti's calm face that had brought her courage and peace, *shanti* being Hindi for peace.

An audience of over three thousand women stared with curiosity at the sari-wrapped figure standing before them. Mother Teresa placed her hands together, palm to palm, in the traditional Indian greeting and bowed her head. "This is the way we greet the people in India," she said.

Then she continued, "I have never spoken in public before. This is the first time, and to be here with you and to be able to tell you the love story of God's mercy for the poorest of the poor—it is a grace of God." She brought the women a greeting from the woman Governor of West Bengal Province, Padmaja Naidu.

Mother Teresa cited as examples of India's contemporary women the girls who had joined her congregation. They represented the varied languages and castes of the Indian subcontinent. Their heroism in serving the dying, the lepers, the homeless, the hungry, the ill of an afflicted city, she told them, was strengthened by the help and understanding they received from the women of the United States. Of the 119 Missionaries of Charity, she told them, all but three were Indian girls.

There was rapt attention from the audience and Mother Teresa seemed to have lost all consciousness of self as she told of her people.

"Two or three weeks back, before I came here, a woman suffering in the last stages of TB came with her little son, Jamal. Jamal is a Mohammedan name. When we met she only asked: 'Mother, as I have got a terrible disease and my days are counted, take my child, give him a home, love him.' I took the child and I told her: 'Well, as long as you are alive, come twice or three times a day, if you like, and see the child. I will keep the child with me as long as you are alive.' And there was this woman walking at least two or three miles every day, and she loved the child in such a heroic way. She would not touch him and begged me: 'Mother, take my child in your arms; you love him and by seeing you love him, that will give me pleasure. Because if I touch the child I may give him the disease.' This is what your help has done for Indian mothers. It has helped to draw out of those good mothers the best in them."

Mother Teresa continued: "We in India love our children. The mothers, as poor as they may be, as sick as they may be—cling to their children. A leper woman, living far away from Titagarh, one of our leper centers, had heard that the Sisters were taking care of leper patients. She had it herself, and she had a little child of two. Bhakti was her name. Bhakti means love. She walked miles to the clinic just to make sure that her little Bhakti didn't have the disease. She thought that she saw on her body a white spot, the sign of the disease. And though her own feet were partly eaten away, and her hands were without fingers, still this brave woman, this loving woman, carried the child all the way for several miles to the Sisters to make sure that her child did not have leprosy. And when the Sisters examined her and found that the child was safe, she was so happy she was not afraid to walk back all the way . . . And examples such as these happen daily, and the joy and the happiness these people feel—it is you who share in it."

Mother Teresa told the women that she was not going to ask them for further aid. She explained her complete dependence on the providence of God. People only needed to know the needs of their fellow human beings, she pointed out. "I don't beg. I have not begged from the time we started the work. But I go to the people—the Hindus, the Mohammedans, and the Christians—and I tell them: 'I have come to give you a chance to do something beautiful for God.' And the people, they want to do something beautiful for God and they come forward."

In the convention exhibit hall, one of the booths featured "The Works of Peace," illustrating the involvement of American Catholic women with the needy overseas, with photographs of the needy in Seoul, Santiago, Saigon, as well as Calcutta. Mother Teresa sat at the booth, replying to incessant questions about the white, blue-bordered sari, about the vow of free service to the poorest of the poor, about her own origins, her missionary commitment, about the Home for the Dying, about helping leprosy patients. She was carrying her order's customary canvas bag, fashioned from a piece of surplus army cloth and a wooden handle made in a *bustee.* Quietly, people slipped money into the bag until it had to be emptied again and again. Repeatedly women came to tell me that the money they had set aside for a festive dinner was being put into Mother Teresa's bag to feed the hungry. There were many telling talks given during those four days by a succession of well-known speakers. I wondered if any message was carried back by the women to thousands of parishes throughout the nation more graphically than the message of Mother Teresa, not simply the message of words delivered by a reluctant public speaker, but the message of her presence.

While the convention was taking place, the pleasure and gambling empire carved out of the desert was in swinging activity night and day. On the wide highway known as the Strip, hotels offered unparalleled luxuries around the clock, tables laden with food, swimming pools, lobbies filled with clunking slot machines and spinning roulette wheels. In downtown Las Vegas, the main street was so festooned with thousands of electric lights that it was referred to as Glitter Gulch. There, nightclubs and gambling palaces seemed never to close. Every so often, on the Strip as on Glitter Gulch one passed a series of small wooden chapels, so tiny they looked like toy churches for a miniature play village. Bright signs hung from their neon-lit dwarf steeples, WEDDINGS—COMPLETE WITH CORSAGE —ANY TIME OF DAY OR NIGHT.

The Christian is supposed to be in the world but not of it. Mother Teresa's presence at Las Vegas illustrated this in a dramatic way. On her way from the convent to the convention hall, Mother Teresa saw the signs of the gaiety, the dedication to pleasure, the gambling, the great clusters of lights. I asked her what she thought of the city.

She looked around, smiled, and said one word, "Dewali."

Dewali is the yearly Hindu festival of lights, a time of joy to commemorate the return of the god Rama from Sri Lanka with his beloved Sita who had been abducted. Towns and villages blossom with candles and strings of electric bulbs. Mother Teresa made no moral pronouncement, but the very idea of a perpetual "Dewali" would be as unthinkable to her as to any Indian.

Mother Teresa did carry one souvenir from Las Vegas. To give her time to meditate before her talk, we drove to the Nevada desert. We sat silently in the sunlight. She settled by herself near a cactus plant for contemplation. At last, she picked up a few of the long cactus spines which were easily twined into a crown of thorns. This she took back to Calcutta as a tangible memento of Las Vegas. It was placed on the head of the crucified Christ hanging behind the altar in the novitiate chapel.

❧

One of the places Mother Teresa wanted to visit was Peoria, Illinois, since the Catholic women of that diocese had been sending funds for the support of the Mother and Child Clinics such as the one at Kidderpore. The link between Peoria and Calcutta had been initiated in 1958. Mrs. Robert Hugh Mahoney, president of the National Council of Catholic Women, who was to be the main speaker, had become sick with an illness that was to be fatal. She suggested that I take her place. I had just returned from India and filled with what I had experienced in Calcutta, I told the story of Mother Teresa and the Missionaries of Charity. Struck by the vast abyss separating their lives from the lives of the women of Bengal, the Catholic women voted to sponsor the Mother and Child Clinics of Mother Teresa. In addition to their support of Catholic Relief Services and other local programs of Catholic Charities, they conducted an annual appeal for Mother Teresa's work.

The meeting with Mother Teresa took place in the auditorium of the high school of Henry, a small town in the flat corn belt of Illinois. No greater contrast with Las Vegas could have been imagined. Here was Middle America in many senses, the families of small farmers of the Midwest, of small businessmen, of production workers, families who were faithful members of their local parishes. It was a Sunday afternoon, and buses had been chartered from communities all throughout the diocese to bring families to meet Mother Teresa. At that time, her work was probably better known in Peoria than in other parts of the United States since in preparation for the special collection the women had made a study of postpartition India and its problems.

After thanking those present, Mother Teresa told a little story that illustrated something that happened often in her work, the providential coming together of the different gifts and people to meet the needs of the poor.

"For many years," she said, "I have been praying with the Sisters that we may be able to do something more for the mother and child in the slums. As you know, we work only for the poorest of the poor. The amount of things that we got was just enough to meet the needs of the day. Now we have three Sisters who will soon be finished as doctors and we will soon be able to go further in—into the heart of the slums that up to now we have not been able to go to because of the want of Sisters who could do the work.

"Last year, ending December 31, we had treated seventy-four thousand people that passed through the six dispensaries. It is your charity that helped keep our work for the mother and child going. But we needed another clinic.

Inside the Home for the Dying—Kalighat. *(Pierre André Pittet—Geneva)*

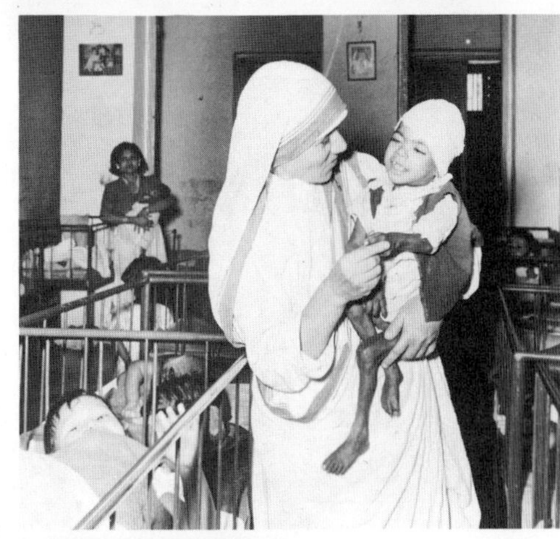

Mary Ann—a "street case" in her own right.

Comforting a dying man.

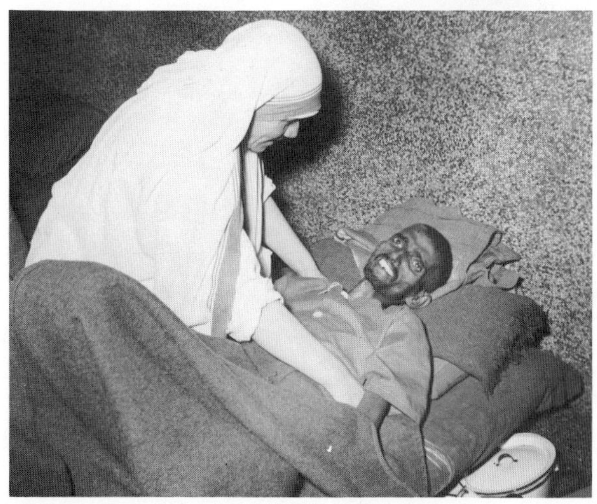

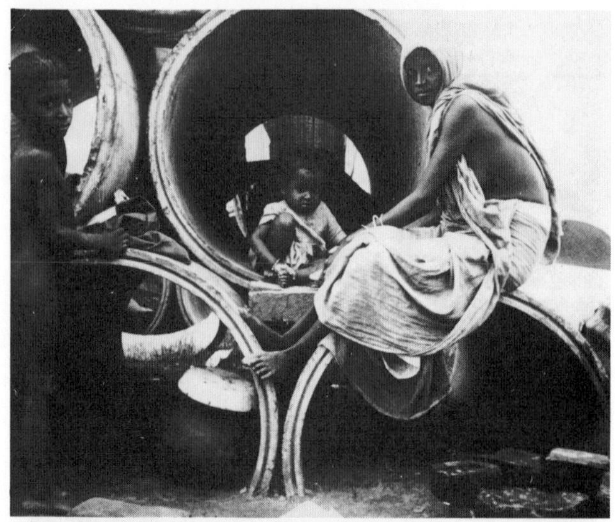

Refugees at Calcutta's outskirts.

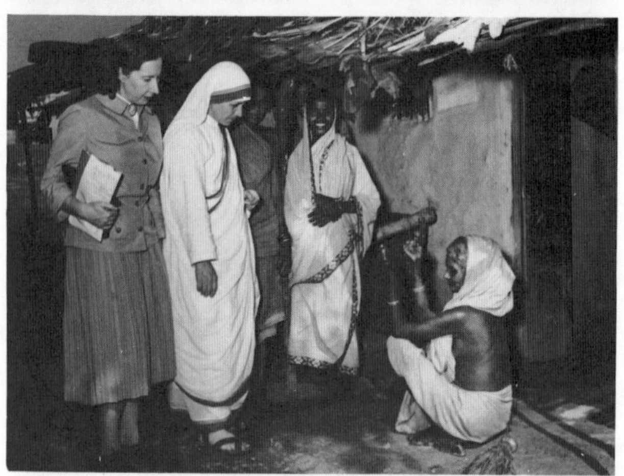

Mother Teresa and author visit Dhappa lepers, 1958.

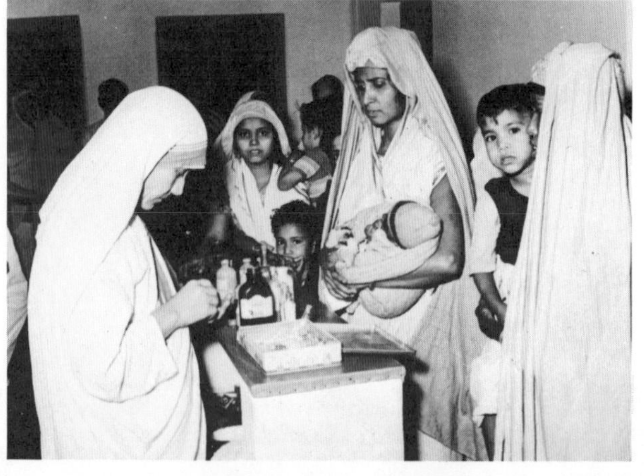

Muslim women and children receive medical aid at Kidderpore Clinic.

Sister Pauline and Sister Nirmala hanging laundry, Venezuela, 1969.

Sisters at work in Cocorote, Venezuela.

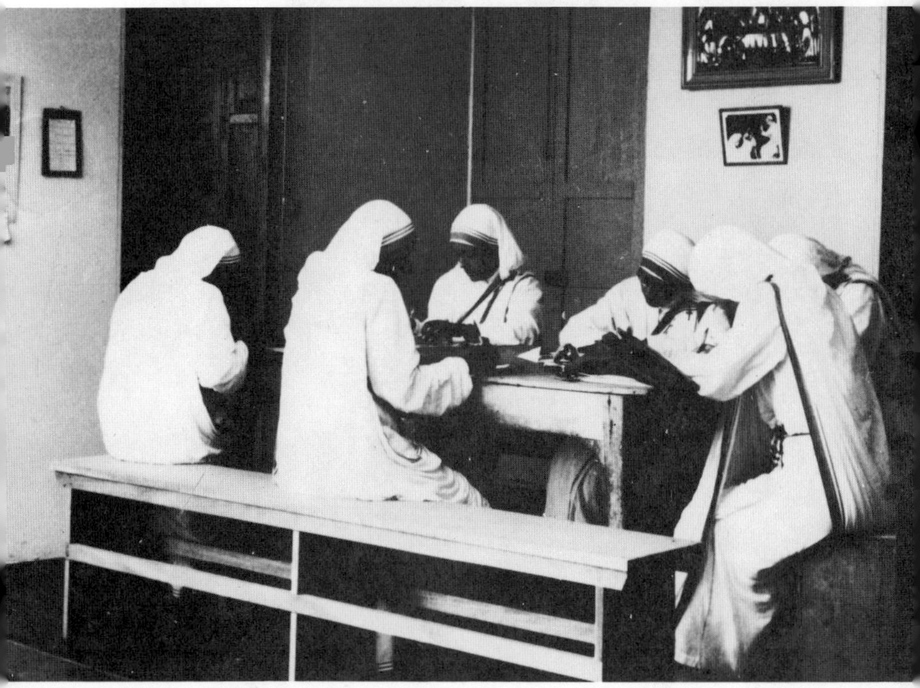

Missionaries of Charity outside South Bronx convent. *(Stephen LaSala)*

A Missionary of Charity novice on a picnic with East Harlem children. *(Chris Sheridan)*

Sister Andrea with young friend in East Harlem. *(Chris Sheridan)*

"The whole convent and the children in the slums prayed, and it was very strange that in the same week, so to say in the same day, we got the answer. By the morning mail, I got the letter from Mrs. Lamet that your group had vowed to help the work in India for the mother and child through your Madonna Plan.

"In the afternoon, I had a letter from a lady doctor, an English lady doctor who had seen the work, and she wanted to help the congregation and do the work for the mother and child. Next day, I got a letter to say that the land that I had been looking for, for a seventh clinic, can be ours. So the place, the money, and the persons to do the work came as an answer to prayer, and today we have seven such clinic where the Sisters, with the lady doctors, Hindu and Mohammedan, work for the same idea, with the same love, with the same devotion for their own people—the people of the slums.

"A high government official said once: 'You and we do the same social work. But the difference between you and us is one we cannot pass over. You work for somebody and we work for something.' He knew that Somebody is Jesus. But it is Jesus in the disguise of the people suffering in the streets and slums of our cities."

After the meeting, we went by car to Chicago. It was a golden October day as we drove through Illinois, with cornfields stretching endlessly on both sides of the road. Every now and then the flat landscape was broken by aluminum bins in which surplus corn was stored. From storage places such as these, the "Food for Peace" program fanned out to feed the famished in distressed areas of the world. We stopped before a cluster of twenty grain bins and got out of the car. Mother Teresa gazed for a long time at the grain growing in the fields and at the grain stored from earlier harvests. Her eyes were held by the fields bursting with the richness of yet another bumper crop.

She spoke meditatively, addressing our companions, but also, it seemed, Americans in general. "May God bless you for what you are doing for our poor mothers, our children, our sick and dying, our lepers. I am glad I came here to see this sight and to meet the good people."

In Washington D.C., Mother Teresa was greeted warmly by Patrick Cardinal O'Boyle, formerly director of Catholic Relief Services. He accompanied her on a visit to the Cathedral of St. Matthew and sped her on her way with a gift of funds. A friend of the family of the presidential candidate Senator John F. Kennedy wanted to arrange a meeting with Mrs. Jacqueline Kennedy, but the future First Lady was expecting her second child and was not well enough for a meeting.

Mother Teresa was to stay with the Franciscan Missionaries of Mary in New York City, but our plane arrived so late that I engaged rooms instead at Leo House, a plain hospice founded originally for Catholic immigrants. With its chapel and quiet dining room, it was a convenient stopping-off place for members of religious orders in transit through the city.

Mother Teresa had often mentioned her gratitude to the Medical Mission Sisters. The morning after our arrival at Leo House, we went to the chapel for an early mass. A woman in a quiet gray uniform with white-banded black headdress was in the pew directly in front of us. The trim habit, I recognized, could only be that of the Medical Mission Sisters. She got up to leave as we did. Astonishment gripped me when I realized that it was Mother Anna Dengel, foundress of the order. I looked at the two small women, neither one over five feet tall, as they walked out of the chapel. I could not help ponder on the mighty spiritual force incarnated by these two twentieth century Mother Foundresses.

Mother Dengel explained that she had just flown in from Rome where the congregation maintained its generalate. She had been invited to New York City to take part in a meeting. We discovered in the press that she had been named "Woman of the Year" by a nonsectarian federation of women's organizations.

We took breakfast together in the Leo House dining room where Mother Teresa reiterated her lifelong gratitude for the hospitality and training she had received at Holy Family Hospital in Patna. The two women were concerned with the growth of each other's mission to humankind. Mother Dengel knew a great deal about the work of Mother Teresa and the Missionaries of Charity. She wanted to know how many centers the young Indian Sisters were conducting in Calcutta and where they would be working next. She was especially interested in the courses of study they would be following. In turn, she replied to Mother Teresa's questions about the hospitals and clinics of the Medical Mission Sisters in Pakistan, India, Africa, Latin America, and the United States, where they had opened a Midwifery Institute to train midwives to deliver babies in the Indian villages of New Mexico.

Other than in the matter of height, the two women presented some contrast in appearance. Mother Teresa, vibrant and untiring, was at fifty just entering middle age. She seemed to be a poet of the poor and lowly after the manner of St. Francis. She was not a specialist, but a woman who found new and creative ways to express the compassion and love of the Creator in the upheavals of the twentieth century. Mother Dengel was at sixty-eight just past middle age, ample and still vigorous, with a rich voice and a trace of accent from her native Austrian Tyrol. Her compassion was expressed in putting the highest of medical and nursing skills at the service of the lowliest and most obscure of suffering humankind. Even her eminently practical habit spoke clearly of her mission of scientific skill.

As they talked, I thought of some strange similarities that had marked their lives and careers. Both had been moved to lives of special and even revolutionary service by the needs of India. Though both had come from southern Europe, both had launched their future lives by way of Ireland. Mother Dengel had taken her medical studies at the University of Cork. As she was there during the First World War, her Austrian nationality made her an "enemy alien" to the British and her movements were severely restricted. In 1919, she journeyed to India to take over the direction of St. Catherine's Hospital in Rawal Pindi, then part of India. The hospital had been founded by Dr. Agnes McLaren, a Scotchwoman working for the Presbyterian missions. It was she who had arranged for Mother Dengel's scholarship at Cork University. Her death occurred before Anna Dengel received her degree in medicine.

During four years of work at St. Catherine's and in its crowded outpatient clinic, Dr. Dengel came into contact with the work of the Franciscan Missionaries of Mary. Drawn to the religious life, she made a decision to join that order, even though her yearning was to bring modern obstetrics and surgery to deprived women. In that period, professed nuns were forbidden by the Church to practice either obstetrics or surgery.

Just as Mother Teresa had had a moment of overwhelmingly clear discernment on the train to Darjeeling, Mother Dengel had her moment of discernment after reading Dr. Agnes McLaren's report of her work among sick and poor Moslem women. Anna Dengel's consciousness was seized with the certainty that among these women in purdah, tragically cut off from medical care, was a need that only women could fill. "The decision to offer myself," she wrote, "was so simple and clear to me that I did not feel the need to seek advice. I was determined to become a mission doctor."

Just as Mother Teresa eventually founded a new order to reach the poorest of the poor, Mother Dengel had to establish an entirely new foundation so that she could come to the suffering as both a nun and as a mission doctor. During a retreat, she had a second time of discernment when the retreat master, an Austrian Jesuit, helped strengthen her spirit when she was tempted to relinquish her dream. He urged her to step out into the unknown and attempt to open a pathway for nuns to give full medical service in the mission field. By 1925, Dr. Anna Dengel, with three companions, had launched the Medical Mission Sisters with the blessing of the church. It was not until 1936, after she had made several visits to Rome that the Holy See lifted its ban and allowed nuns, in "the holy experiment" of the Medical Mission Sisters, to give full medical service. The lifting of the ban had application to all religious Sisters.

The work of Mother Dengel and that of Mother Teresa became further intertwined at a later date. When the Patna Holy Family Hospital moved to new quarters, the old building was turned over to the Missionaries of Charity. Mother Teresa's first haven of refuge after leaving Loreto became a Home for the Destitute Dying, another Kalighat. By that time, the largest single group in the Medical Mission Sisters were Indian women.

The similarity between the two women was grounded in their tenderness toward all their fellow human beings and their championship of the most rejected of the earth. Mother Dengel, who lost her mother at the age of nine, attributed "the compassion I have for the women and children of India to this great sorrow." At the same age, Mother Teresa had also suffered, in a sudden and searing tragedy, the loss of a parent, her father.

Beyond all other similarities, it seemed to me, was their identity with that strong woman who called out in joy at being chosen by the Creator to bear in her flesh the incarnate God: "He has shown might with his arm, he has scattered the proud in the conceit of their heart. He has put down the mighty from their thrones and has exalted the lowly. He has filled the hungry with good things, and the rich he has sent away empty."

While in New York City, Mother Teresa presented herself at the chancery office of the archdiocese, but Cardinal Spellman was not in the city. She paid a visit to the headquarters office of Catholic Relief Services to thank in person Bishop Edward Swanstrom for the aid being channeled to the world and in particular to India. The entire staff of the agency, by then a world-girdling agency serving the needy and refugees in sixty countries and areas of the globe, gathered to hear her. She told them that she spoke for the hungry, the homeless, the abandoned, the lepers, in bringing gratitude from India. Her next visit was to the office of Bishop Fulton J. Sheen, at that time nationally known for his television program on ethics and religion in daily living. He was head of the American section of the foreign mission organization called the Propagation of the Faith. A man of powerful presence and singular dramatic gifts, he summoned his entire staff to pray together with a woman who stood for the poor of the earth.

Mother Teresa wanted to get all possible help for leprosy patients, and we went on to the headquarters of the United Nations to talk with a representative of the World Health Organization. The director himself, Dr. Marcolino Candau, received us in his office overlooking the East River. He listened intently as Mother Teresa told of her efforts to reach leprosy patients in the *bustees* of Calcutta. I mentioned that I had been present at the opening of a school for the children of leprosy patients. Mother Teresa recounted simply that the aim of the Missionaries of Charity was to bring help and healing to the poorest of the poor and that their wholehearted service was to be without any recompense. The poorest of the poor are our lepers, she told him. They are rejected by all. Suddenly, I saw tears glistening in the eyes of the international officer. He took notes and told her that on her return to India, she should make the same appeal through the Indian Government which could then obtain supplies from the World Health Organization.

Mother Teresa gave two talks in New York City, one to the Walter Farrell Guild, a group of lay Catholics concerned with the implications of the gospel in their personal and working lives; the other talk was at the regular Friday evening meeting of the Catholic Worker movement. This was held in the Hospitality House then on Chrystie Street on New York's Lower East Side. The lay volunteers, those who were given hospitality, and those persons interested in the movement attended the meetings which were held regularly from its founding in 1933. Dorothy Day, who had cofounded the movement with Peter Maurin, was a witness and focus for several generations of a lay style of life modeled on a threefold theme of "Cult, Culture, and Cultivation." It called for "the daily practice of the works of mercy" and living among the poor in houses of hospitality in the cities. There were also voluntary communities on the land. The Catholic Worker aroused the most controversy by its position on gospel nonviolence, in which Jesus' command to "love one's enemy" was accepted in its literal sense. The position of conscientious objection to war arising out of this position, while originally a minority one among Catholics, became more general when it was validated by the Second Vatican Council in its document "The Church in the Modern World." The monthly paper, *The Catholic Worker,* spread these ideas around the world.

Before the meeting, Dorothy Day took Mother Teresa on a tour of the Lower East Side, the area in which the New York Catholic Worker had always worked. We walked through the Bowery and came upon a man slumped on the sidewalk and leaning against a building. His eyes were half open. Mother Teresa went over to him. "What can we do for him? Where can we take him?" she asked. Dorothy Day explained that the man was not dying but drunk. He opened his eyes and waved to us as we passed. His wave seemed to mean that he wanted us to keep on going. We passed the cheap hotels for the down-and-out where those who were broken on the wheel of life took refuge after they had dropped out of the world of work and responsibility. Every now and then, men in filthy sweaters or raggedy overcoats would lurch toward us. Their faces were lined with tiredness and with the unutterable hurts that they had absorbed from life. Mother Teresa wondered how we could pass by a man sitting on the sidewalk clearly oblivious to the world about him. We had to explain that the burden fell on the New York police. When someone became ill or totally unconscious, the police were called. The "street cases" were then often taken by police ambulance to Bellevue Hospital, if, as often happened, they had pneumonia, or to a drying-out center for alcoholics maintained by public funds.

At a small gathering in my home, Mother Teresa talked with a group of women, chiefly from the diocese of Brooklyn, who had been strong supporters of "The Works of Peace" programs on behalf of women overseas. I had timed the meeting so that Mother Teresa could receive a long-distance call from a woman in Minneapolis, Mrs. Patricia Kump. She had been so moved by a feature on Mother Teresa as to wish to be associated with her in some way. The feature had appeared in a brilliantly edited publication, *Jubilee,* subtitled "A Magazine for the Church and Her People," and consisted chiefly of striking photographs by Homer Page. On my return from my round-the-world trip of 1955, I had described for editor Edward Rice my response to the work of Mother Teresa. He asked a photographer to go and take pictures of the places I had described, Kalighat, Shishu Bhavan, the desolate streets of Calcutta. The magazine, with Mother Teresa on its cover, appeared in February 1958 and, in actuality, introduced Mother Teresa to the American Catholic community. The subscribers of *Jubilee* at that time numbered about sixty thousand. Patricia Kump, the wife of Dr. Warren Kump, an anesthesiologist, told Mother Teresa that she was busy with four young children, all adopted, since the couple found that they would have no children of their own. In her prayers and meditations, Patricia Kump related how the story and picture of the faraway nun had strengthened her in her own spiritual life and consoled her in her weariness. Mother Teresa thanked her for her prayers which brought them closer together. Patricia and Warren Kump were later to work closely with Mother Teresa as national and international leaders in the Association of Co-Workers of Mother Teresa.

Mother Teresa became acquainted with a few examples of the work of Sisters on behalf of the poor and needy in New York. She was glad to be a guest of the Franciscan Missionaries of Mary in the Divine Providence Shelter on Forty-fifth Street on Manhattan's East Side. The Franciscan Missionaries of Mary were well known to her in India where they had a nationwide network of eighty communities conducting leper centers, hospitals, dispensaries, orphanages, and shelters.

The Divine Providence Shelter took in children who could not be cared for by their families. In some cases, the mother was ill, physically or mentally. There were always children whose parents were in prison, sometimes the father, sometimes the mother, sometimes both. In many cases, the father was absent and the mother had been abandoned and had to go out to work. The shelter was known to many generations of young people and students who gave regular volunteer service under the direction of the Sisters.

We also visited the St. Charles Orthopedic Hospital in Brooklyn, conducted by the Daughters of Wisdom for severely handicapped youngsters. A photographer from *Jubilee* Magazine accompanied us and this gave rise to the second photographic presentation on Mother Teresa by the magazine. It was the issue of December 1960, and Mother Teresa's face again appeared on the cover. To *Jubilee*'s editor, Edward Rice, Mother Teresa said that she had found America "a big change" saying that "the people have taken me by surprise. I have always been too busy to think what America would be like, but what I've seen I'll never forget . . . only affection, kindness and love." She explained to Rice that she hoped by the end of the year to build a shelter for the homeless and ill in Delhi and that the Indian Government had already set aside an acre of land for that purpose. Asked about funds, she explained that she had none, but added that she was not worried about raising them. She told Rice that she went to those who could help and used a phrase that was becoming familiar, "When I ask them, 'Will you do something beautiful for God,' how can they refuse?"

❧

Before leaving New York, Mother Teresa asked me how to get to Greenwich, Connecticut. She wanted to visit the home of Rama Coomaraswamy, already mentioned as one of her first volunteers. Rama and Bernadette had informed Mother Teresa that their daughter was seriously ill. We went by car and had our dinner of tuna fish sandwiches and tea while we parked by the side of the road. Mother Teresa shrank from eating in public and would miss or postpone a meal to avoid relaxing her rule of not eating in private homes. Rama Coomaraswamy and his wife Bernadette made their home in an old coach house, hardly living up to the image of Greenwich as one of the most affluent of suburbs. The young parents told Mother Teresa that their five-year-old Francesca had leukemia. It was Rama who had made the diagnosis. A brilliant child, Francesca had been enrolled in a Montessori school from the age of three. Francesca delighted Mother Teresa by reciting prayers and by telling her how she loved to go to church where Jesus was on the altar.

Mother Teresa held Francesca tenderly throughout the evening. Before leaving, she asked Rama and Bernadette to return Jesus' love even when the sign of His love was the cross He was giving them.

I was to see Francesca dying on a hospital bed just a year later. Her hands and feet were pierced with tubes and I thought again of the cross.

The child died on December 8, 1961, the day celebrated in the Catholic Church as the feast of the Immaculate Conception of Mary.

Bernadette Coomaraswamy, who later became a lawyer, was one of the founding members of the Co-Workers of Mother Teresa in the United States and provided them with free legal services. Rama, whose first experience with disease and death came through volunteering at Kalighat, specialized in thoracic surgery after interning at New York's city hospital. He became widely known for his many papers on the subject. When their family of three boys became four with the arrival of a girl, she was given the name of Teresa.

It was arranged that my work at Catholic Relief Services could be handled while I accompanied Mother Teresa to Rome. On the way, we stopped off in London, where the Catholic Relief Services office provided a car so that during a week of continuous rain, we could make many calls. First to welcome Mother Teresa to London was Ann Blaikie who had helped her in the Marian Society in Calcutta. Her husband John's company had transferred him to England in September 1960, and the family, including three children, were settling near London.

Mrs. Vijaya Lakshmi Pandit, India's High Commissioner to the United Kingdom, received Mother Teresa at her home during the evening hours. Mother Teresa, adhering to her rule of not accepting food in private homes (unless circumstances made it strictly necessary), refused even tea. We talked about the refugee problem, particularly in the province of Bengal, and the burdens it placed on governmental resources. Mrs. Pandit, who along with her brother Prime Minister Nehru, had served several prison terms during the years of the Gandhi movement, was happy at the news of Mother Teresa's work in the voluntary sector. She hoped that such work in the Gandhi spirit would keep growing. Mrs. Pandit made a promise to visit Mother Teresa's work on her return to India, a promise she kept later on by visiting the Home in Delhi.

Mother Teresa stayed in a little convent hostel on Cavendish Street run by nuns dressed in secular garb, one of the first congregations to do so. A message came that she was to present herself at the BBC studios for a televised interview. It had been set up by Lady Hamilton. The interview, conducted by Derek Hart, was part of the evening news service. It was a short one and it seemed to me that the interviewer, accustomed to more obviously newsworthy prospects, was a little abashed by having an unknown nun in strange garb ushered into his studio.

A meeting was arranged with Anglican canon, John Milford, a representative of OXFAM, a voluntary overseas aid and development agency. Milford was fascinated by Mother Teresa's brief description of her work. He asked question after question, wanting her to expatiate on how she came to start this or that work. When she came to the subject of the lepers, he said that he thought that some of the latest medications could be released to her in Calcutta through ICI, the Imperial Chemical Industries. He would write ahead for her and she was to be in touch with them.

Mother Teresa was never one for sightseeing, but the gentle Canon told her she could not leave London without visiting the Great Hall of the Guildhall. It was closed but he had it opened for Mother Teresa. Our footsteps echoed in the venerable building, part of it erected before the fourteenth century and now repaired after much damage in the Second World War. We stood before the strangely commanding statues of Gog and Magog. Gog and Magog were named in Revelation as the two nations which followed Satan in fighting against the kingdom of God at the climactic battle of Armageddon. These, we learned, were wooden copies of the originals which had been burned in 1940 during the bombing of London.

The next stop was in Germany, where the office of the Catholic Relief Services had informed both Caritas, the Catholic Charities agency, and Misereor, the recently founded Catholic overseas aid agency, as well as the press of Mother Teresa's arrival. As she got down from the plane in Frankfurt, wrapped in a rough woolen blanket against the icy cold, she was surprised by a squad of photographers.

Mother Teresa was better known in Germany, at least among the Catholic community, than she had been in the United States or England. The year before, in its first appeal publication, *Weltelend* (World Misery), Misereor had brought to readers throughout West Germany the plight of the needy and starving of the world. Misereor, Latin for "I have compassion," recalled Jesus' words over the hungry multitude before he performed the miracle of the loaves and fishes. Scenes of the starving of Calcutta leapt from the pages of *Weltelend,* as did scenes from *der Todeshalle von Kalkutta,* the Home for the Dying at Kalighat. Starvation to the Germans was not simply a far-off specter. At war's end, a destroyed and defeated country was divided into sealed-off zones and upward of seventeen million ethnic Germans were expelled into a destroyed landscape. The scenes of hunger evoked a deep visceral response, and their reaction to the work of Mother Teresa was immediate. *Erdkreis,* a photomagazine similar to *Jubilee* had also published photographs of *der Todeshalle von Kalkutta* and its director, the Reverend Jakob Holl, was on hand to interview Mother Teresa and to take photographs.

The question asked by Edward Rice in New York regarding funds for the construction of a home for the destitute in Delhi was answered in Aachen.

The trip to Aachen led to the headquarters of Misereor where Mother Teresa was welcomed by the director, Monsignor Gottfried Dossing and his staff. Misereor was ready to help Mother Teresa in any way she wished, up to and including funds for a needed institution.

Mother Teresa was ready with a project, a new building for the Home for the Dying in Delhi. She described the acre of ground already set aside for it. In general, Misereor sponsored self-help projects, particularly agricultural projects where able-bodied but poor people in the developing world could unite to meet their food needs. Mother Teresa's project was far from meeting such a criterion. There was no guarantee that helpless people rescued from the streets would ever be completely self-supporting. Nevertheless, Msgr. Dossing and the Misereor committee agreed to fund the construction of the Nirmal Hriday for Delhi.

The question of accounting procedures arose. Would the Missionaries of Charity be able to send financial reports on the project to Misereor? Mother Teresa explained that every rupee would go into the Home for the Dying, but that the Sisters would not have the time to spend with complicated financial forms. Misereor agreed to two important steps: a staff member would study the situation in Delhi and estimate the total cost, and after the completion of the building, Misereor accountants would submit the financial report.

Afterward, Mother Teresa explained there were groups anxious to "adopt" a work of the Sisters and then receive special reports on "our project." As the number of Shishu Bhavans, schools, and clinics grew in India, she realized that separate reports to numerous sponsors would be so time-consuming that the poor would suffer. Every donation was scrupulously recorded and acknowledged and put into the stream of resources to support centers already in operation or to start new ones.

As we had a stopover in Munich, Mother Teresa accepted my suggestion that we take a few hours to visit nearby Dachau, the forerunner of all the concentration camps that pockmarked occupied Europe. We were soon standing before a gas chamber disguised as a shower room. The building, in fact the whole camp, had been preserved as a memorial to the victims who had been enslaved and killed there. Missing was a word that had still endured on the door of the chamber when I had first seen it in 1947, a word intended not for those herded into the chamber, but for the superintendents of death, *Lebensgefährlich* (Mortal Danger). I reviewed for Mother Teresa the enormous network of camps, some of them slave labor camps, others extermination camps like Auschwitz, where eleven million human beings, six million of them Jews, had gone to their deaths. What Mother Teresa saw gave a hint of the larger gas chambers into which Cyclon B gas was spewed to bring death to people for whom the crematorium ovens had already been stoked. She paused before the small crematorium ovens, just body size. We moved away to walk between rows of blockhouses left standing as a reminder of what had occurred on the blood-soaked acres of hundreds of concentration camps.

We were told that the person who fought for Dachau as a memorial was a Father Leonard Roth, a former priest-inmate who had survived, but that 2,579 other priest-inmates, many of them Polish, had perished there. At the end of the blockhouses was a round tower constructed of crude stones. There was no door or roof, but above the tower, supported by fine wires as though suspended in air, was a jagged crown of thorns. It was constructed of shining copper. The tower, topped by its reminder of all innocent suffering, was called the Chapel of the Agony of Christ. It had been dedicated to all those who had perished in Dachau and in the satanic concentration camp world.

Mother Teresa was speechless before the details of mass persecution and murder conjured up by Dachau. After a long while, she said one word, "Colosseum."

"This stands for the Colosseum of our day. But then it was the pagans who threw innocent people to their death. It was not idolators of those pagan gods who threw these lives away—and how many millions of them. We are getting worse, not better."

A separate part of the camp still had its inmates, four hundred of them. I knew Mother Teresa would not want to leave without seeing a special example of post-World War II poverty, the German ethnic peoples expelled from Eastern Europe. We visited blockhouses that had been converted into dismal habitations. Some of the women gathered around Mother Teresa as we walked along the strange streets. As I was telling Mother Teresa of the seventeen million people of German ethnic origin turned out of their homes by Allied agreement at war's end, an old woman approached us. Her head was wrapped in a black babushka and her eyes were fixed with hungry curiosity on Mother Teresa's figure. I told her and a small group of women that Mother Teresa was a Catholic Sister and that she cared for the dying and the poor in India. The old woman smiled. Her name was Theresia, the same name, and she was also Catholic. She had lost her home in Hungary. One son was with her, a war invalid, and another son had been killed in the war. We accepted her invitation to make a brief visit to the home she had confected out of a bare barracks.

As Mother Teresa made her way out of Dachau, her usually quick walk was slowed down, and her face was a mask of suffering.

"To think," she said quietly, "that human beings could do these things to other human beings."

Mother Teresa had promised to visit the parents of a young German woman who had entered the Missionaries of Charity, one of the first three women from outside India to do so. In Freiburg im Breisgau, she found the parents of Sister Andrea longing for news of their daughter. Bernhard and Anna Bonk remembered the time when Barbara read about Mother Teresa's work in a mission magazine and had made up her mind to join the order. What had moved her heart more than anything else, her mother, Anna Bonk, explained, was Mother Teresa's love of the lepers.

"Barbara wanted to be a doctor and also to work among the lepers," her mother explained.

Mother Teresa told the parents that their daughter was doing beautifully at medical school, but whether she would work among lepers or among other people who needed help would not be known until later.

Bernhard Bonk, not yet resigned to the loss of his daughter, was silent. A dignified and cultured man, who had served as the mayor of a town in Silesia, he had undergone the physical and emotional deprivation of being expelled from his home at the end of the Second World War. He and his family, like Theresia in her blockhouse quarters, were among those who suffered in the mass expulsions sanctioned by the Potsdam Agreement of 1945. After living with his family in an expellee camp, he had found a job in Freiburg im Breisgau where he had brought his family. They were living in a tiny spare apartment, the other daughter married to an American soldier and the son at university.

"Barbara was the one closest to my husband," Mrs. Bonk told us. "So much has happened to him and to us all. Of course, I miss her, but he misses her in a very deep way." The man's face was lined with tragedy and Mother Teresa did her best to tell him of the joy of the work in Calcutta.

The parish church of Freiburg held a special evening service at which Mother Teresa was invited inside the altar rail to talk to the congregation. She told the simple story of the beginnings of the work in Calcutta and of her happiness that one of the first girls outside of India who had come to join the Missionaries of Charity had come from their community. Her talk was translated sentence by sentence. The church was almost dark, and a spotlight shone on the short, white-garbed figure. The congregation was completely absorbed in her words. Such attention was hardly surprising from those who could identify with what she was describing, hunger and loss, and in many cases like that of the Bonks, enforced homelessness.

A morning was spent at the Werthmannhaus, the headquarters of Caritas, the German Catholic Charities agency and the first Catholic welfare agency to be organized on a nationwide basis anywhere in the world. Martin Vorgrimmler, who had dealt with Catholic Relief Services in the massive postwar relief program, received us. Vorgrimmler along with others of the headquarters staff like Dr. Gertrud Luckner were heroic figures, having been persecuted for aiding the persecuted. Luckner had spent over two years in Ravensbruck concentration camp for being part of a secret

Caritas operation to help German Jews and, whenever possible, spirit them out of the country. Vorgrimmler, when he realized that their secret operation had been infiltrated, escaped questioning by the Gestapo by joining the German army, though he was overage. Caritas, like other religion-related welfare organizations, was gutted during the Hitler period when the totalitarian state's welfare system was imposed on German society. Caritas had sprung back to life after the war was over and Germany refashioned its traditional Christian institutions.

Vorgrimmler told Mother Teresa that the people of Germany had been given a lifeline of help from Catholics overseas, especially from the Catholics of America. Caritas could not let Mother Teresa return to Calcutta without an expression of their gratitude in the form of a gift for her poor. We were taken into the office of the Caritas director who had prepared for Mother Teresa a check for one hundred thousand deutsche marks, about twenty-five thousand dollars.

We then learned that Mother Teresa's meeting with the archbishop was to take place in an hour. We decided to walk to his residence. We made our way along a scrupulously clean sidewalk, beside which was a concave gutter through which flowed a stream of water. I knew that this was one of the last cities in Western Europe to preserve alongside some of its ancient streets the open drains from which horses could drink and by means of which, I supposed, refuse could be carried away. I was so fascinated in studying this medieval vestige, that I lost my footing and fell into the stream. I was flat on my back, struggling to get up, when Mother Teresa reached down and lifted me up.

"Now that you have picked me up out of the gutter," I said, "you are responsible for me."

We both laughed. We decided that we would continue on our way to the archbishop. (I was dry in front but dripping wet in back.) When His Excellency asked us to sit down, I hesitated, but Mother Teresa motioned me into a chair. It was of pale green velvet.

The archbishop was delighted to meet the Mother Teresa who had become known to German Catholics through *Weltelend* and he hoped that their charity was reaching as far as Calcutta. He was glad to learn that the poor of India would be sharing in the funds collected. On making an exit, I backed out before Mother Teresa, leaving the velvet chair in a sorry state.

After Germany, there was a short stopover in Geneva, Switzerland. Through Mr. Jean Chenard, head of the Geneva office of Catholic Relief Services, Mother Teresa was invited to meet with Swiss Caritas and the organization of the Swiss people for overseas aid, Don Suisse, or Schweize Spende. She was invited to address the representatives of the international Catholic agencies involved in a consultative status with the United Nations. Her evocation of the gospel elicited a warm response from a group of lay and Catholic intellectuals representing such organizations as the International Catholic Migration Commission, Pax Romana, the international federation of Catholic university graduates and students, and the International Catholic Child Bureau.

Mother Teresa's heart and eyes were turned toward Rome as they had been throughout the journey. She had written to her Sisters on the First Friday of October, just before she took the plane for her first journey away from them:

"On the twenty-fifth at 5.45 A.M. I am leaving by P.A.A. and will be in America—God willing, on the twenty-sixth, 6.30 A.M. I go but my heart and my mind and the whole of me is with you. It is the will of God that I should go. Therefore, let us be happy, in spite of our feelings.

"During my absence, Sr. M. Agnes—the assistant general and the council general will take all responsibility. God will take care of you all, my children, if you remain one; if you love each other as God has loved you—with an intense love—as Mother loves you with an undivided love. Cling round the Society because in the center is Jesus. Be fervent and loving with Jesus and you are sure to reach great sanctity. Let Jesus' love for you be the cause of your love for your Sisters and the Poor.

"I am not afraid to leave you, for I know the great gift God has given me—in giving you to me. On my way back—that will be about the fifteenth of November—I shall go to Rome. Begin a novena to the Sacred Heart, from our book from the 11th November. I am going to try and see our Holy Father and beg of him to take our little Society under his special care and grant us a pontifical recognition. As you know, we are not worthy of this great gift, but if it is God's Holy Will, we will get it. You pray and make many sacrifices.

"During this time it would make me very happy if the seniors make sacrifices in obedience; juniors in charity; novices in poverty; postulants in chastity.

Seniors—Obedience: Prompt, simple, blind, cheerful, for Jesus was obedient unto death.

Juniors—Charity: words, deeds, thoughts, desires, feelings—for Jesus went about doing good.

Novices—Poverty: in desires and attachments, in likes and dislikes—for Jesus being rich made Himself poor for me.

Postulants—Chastity: in thoughts and affections, in desires and attachments, in not listening to idle conversations—for Jesus is a jealous lover.

"Be faithful in little things, for in them our strength lies. To the good God nothing is little because He is great and we so small—that is why He stoops down and takes the trouble to make those little things for us—to give us a chance to prove our love for Him. Because he makes them, they are very great. He cannot make anything small; they are infinite. Yes, my dear children, be faithful in little practices of love, of little sacrifices—of the little interior mortifications—of little fidelities to rule, which will build in you the life of holiness—make you Christlike.

"To the feet of Christ's Vicar on earth I will carry each one of you—just as you are—and I am sure with his fatherly love [he] will bless each one of you and obtain for you the graces you need to become Saints."

A wintry sun pervaded Rome as Mother Teresa arrived in the Holy City. For people like the Albanians, Poles, or Irish, who have known deprivation for their defense of the Roman Catholic faith, the city of the Seven Hills, the city of Peter's crucifixion, has an almost mystical significance. For Mother Teresa, coming to Rome to ask that the "little Society" in Calcutta be placed directly under the See of Peter was a climactic event in her religious life.

The constitutions having been written, Mother Teresa would now make personal and formal application for recognition of the Missionaries of Charity as a society of pontifical right. If the Holy See agreed, the Society would then no longer be under the protection of the archbishop of Calcutta but directly under Rome. Only with this recognition could the Sisters begin to move out from India to other countries.

While waiting for this momentous appointment, Mother Teresa met with Lazar Bojaxhiu, the brother whom she had not seen in over thirty years. Lazar was now a man of fifty-three and an exile. He and his family came up from Palermo and were staying in a tiny pensione. Knowing that Mother Teresa could not entertain the family in the convent where she was a guest, the Christian Brothers of Ireland opened the parlor of their school on Via Marcantonio Colonna. Mother Teresa knew the Brothers from their houses in Calcutta. The Brothers arranged for Mother Teresa and the Bojaxhiu family to take a meal together. The sister and brother had time to talk of the intervening time, of Lazar's escape from death when a band of partisans had decided to shoot him during the days of chaos at war's end in Italy. Mother Teresa finally met Lazar's courageous Italian wife, Maria, who had thrown herself across her husband's body so that she would have to be shot first. The would-be executioners changed their minds.

With Lazar and Maria was their daughter Agi, ten years old. Sister and brother, like any members of a family reunited after long separation, talked about their mother, Drana. There was sadness in being completely cut off from her and from their sister, Age. There was no way to come into direct contact with them or to bring them out of Albania. Lazar, in Palermo, was starting life anew as the representative of a pharmaceutical firm. The refugee division of Catholic Relief Services aided Lazar and refugees of over a dozen other nationalities to find some small niche in the Italian economy in the years following the Second World War. Mother Teresa was soon the guest of the Albanian refugee colony of Rome. The Rev. Joseph J. Oroshi and Professor Ernest Koligi were clearly proud of an Albanian Catholic who was becoming a recognized figure in the Church.

One afternoon, at the invitation of Archbishop Franjo Seper, we presented ourselves at an imposing building on Borgo Santo Spirito, just behind the Via della Conciliazione and close to the Basilica of St. Peter. The Yugoslav-born archbishop, later to become a cardinal and head of the Holy Office, began the conversation in English. With a hearty laugh, he greeted Mother Teresa with the words, "So this is the little person I have been hearing so much about."

Mother Teresa was not to present her petition directly to "Christ's Vicar on earth," Pope John XXIII, but to a cardinal deputed by him. She was, however, invited to a mass celebrated by the Holy Father. It took place in the Sistine Chapel and was a mass in memory of prelates who had died during the previous year. A number of cardinals, archbishops, and bishops surrounded the Holy Father on the altar. Under Michelangelo's mighty depiction of the creation of man and the final judgment by his Creator, the *missa pro defunctis* was a rite to force one's mind to contemplate the "four last things."

As Pope John was leaving the chapel, Mother Teresa was the only one to step forward to kiss his ring. He paused in the procession to gaze at her and to give her his blessing.

On the morning that Mother Teresa was to meet with the cardinal, she knocked on the door of my convent room before dawn. She had a short document she wanted me to type. I was carrying a portable typewriter requested by Father Michael Gabric, the Jesuit working in Basanti in the Ganges Delta. The first exercise on that typewriter consisted of two, single-spaced pages outlining in broad terms the special mission of the Missionaries of Charity. It was a sort of précis highlighting particular aspects of the constitutions.

For a person whose typing is marked by frequent errors, and who tends to be hopelessly inept in the early morning hours, the result was an intense surprise. I found I had reached the last line with speed and utter accuracy. At the point of questioning how this could be, I made the first error—at almost the last word.

Carrying the statement, Mother Teresa made her way to Piazza di

Spagna, past the statue of the Immaculate Conception, to the Sacred Congregation for the Propagation of the Faith. I accompanied her. The fact that I had some command of Italian was of service to her. Mother Teresa's visit had been announced and the words *Madre fondatrice,* repeated many times in a sort of reverential whisper, speeded us on through many corridors. Finally, we were in the presence of Gregory Cardinal Agagianian. With him was Archbishop Pietro Sigismondi. They placed us both on a red plush settee raised above the room in a sort of alcove. Cardinal Agagianian perused with great attention the document that had been typed that morning. There was much discussion in Italian with his fellow prelate.

Cardinal Agagianian posed many questions to Mother Teresa, asking about the varied types of work of the Sisters, their training, and in particular about the fourth vow of "wholehearted and free service to the poorest of the poor." Mother Teresa told them of their total dependence on the providence of God and of a life "woven about the Eucharist." The cardinal seemed to wonder how in a mission land the Sisters could exist and work without dependence on a regular outside source of funds. Mother Teresa kept insisting that dependence on God's providence had seen them through thus far, even before sporadic help had begun to spring up from overseas sources. She stressed how little the Sisters themselves needed because of their literal insistence on poverty of life, including dress and housing.

The two ecclesiastics pored over the Sisters' prayer book, a little manual printed on the cheapest of paper. It was printed in English as the common language of the Society. They went over their daily prayers and the prayers for various times of the day, traditional prayers such as the *Anima Christi* (Soul of Christ) and the peace prayer attributed to St. Francis of Assisi. They looked into the section of devotions with its novenas and litanies. After the ecclesiastics had studied the poor little manual and had seemingly found it acceptable, Archbishop Sigismondi turned to Cardinal Agagianian and remarked in Italian, "The prayer book has no permission." With a look of impish humor, Cardinal Agagianian retorted, *"Sono povere."* (They are poor.)

Remembering this, I took note of a later edition of the prayer book. On its front page were two names of key importance to the Missionaries of Charity:

Nihil Obstat
C. Van Exem, S.J.
14. 8 - '62
Imprimatur
✠Ferdinandus, S.J.
Archbishop of Calcutta

With her main mission completed, Mother Teresa was consumed with eagerness to return to the Sisters at the Motherhouse in Calcutta. She was carrying for them a gift she prized, a supply of black crucifixes marked ROME for those to be professed as Missionaries of Charity. They were a gift from Msgr. Andrew P. Landi, director of the Catholic Relief Services program for Italy.

When Mother Teresa parted from her brother for a second time, she did not know if they would meet again. Lazar returned with Maria and Agi to Palermo.

When we arrived at the Rome airport, an Indian woman in a striking cream and purple silk sari sought her out. A conversation went on for several minutes, and then the woman's expression changed and she suddenly walked away. I noticed the abruptness of her leaving.

"What happened, Mother?" I inquired.

"We had a good conversation about India and the Sisters," Mother Teresa told me. "She asked me about the work of the Sisters. I told her about Shishu Bhavan and the other work and then I began to tell her about the work for the lepers. She asked me if I worked with lepers myself. I said 'Yes,' and she left me. You must expect that when you work with lepers."

"Did she say goodbye?" I asked.

Mother Teresa smiled a bit ruefully and shook her head in the negative.

In later years, it became clear how this first trip out of India for an obscure nun of Indian citizenship was a foreshadowing, in the profound designs of God, of much in her future life. A few examples are significant. Mother Teresa described in 1960 how she would be terrified of that big public. In the course of the next quarter century, she would be called upon to address groups that dwarfed the "big public" of Las Vegas. Mother Teresa's name alone would fill civic auditoriums from Vancouver, Canada, to Dallas, Texas, and other Catholic gatherings around the world. At the Eucharistic Congress in Philadelphia in 1976, eight thousand persons packed a hall at which two champions of the poor, Mother Teresa and Dom Helder Camara of Brazil, told of their life commitment. At the Eucharistic Congress in Melbourne, Australia, she faced, in the open air, a "big public" of fifty thousand people.

The 1960 visit to Catholic Relief Services headquarters in New York City cemented the relationship with the agency and there was a steady increase in the flow of life-giving foods, including Food for Peace supplies as well as medicines and funds to Calcutta, to Bengal, and to all India. In most of the areas of need outside India where the Missionaries of Charity eventually worked, they counted on help from Catholic Relief Services.

Mother Teresa's first contact with the United Nations through her meeting with Dr. Marcolino Candau was the beginning of a concern for her work by United Nations agencies. In 1975, her image was struck on a medal by the United Nations Food and Agriculture Organization. The Ceres Medal, named for the Roman goddess of agriculture, honored Mother Teresa for reaching out to feed the poorest of the poor and presented her as an example for others to follow in a hungry world.

The contact with Dorothy Day of the Catholic Worker was maintained over the years and was strengthened by Dorothy Day's visit to Calcutta in 1970. The friendship was broken only by Dorothy Day's death in 1980.

The quiet visit to London's Guildhall was a foreshadowing of another visit by Mother Teresa in 1973 when she was the central figure of the occasion. The Great Hall of the Guildhall was filled to pay honor to her as the first recipient of the Templeton Prize for Progress in Religion from the hand of Prince Philip. Canon John Milford's suggestion in 1960 that Mother Teresa receive help through ICI (Imperial Chemical Industries) of Calcutta moved to an almost incredible climax. The ICI made over to Mother Teresa, just fifteen years later in 1975, its enormous compound at Tiljala, Calcutta, complete with buildings. Rechristened "Prem Dan" (Gift of Love), the compound soon served many purposes, including housing for volunteers from overseas, shelter for the emotionally disturbed poor, tailoring courses for women from the slums, and a self-help program that made use of the thousands of coconut shells thrown away daily in Calcutta. Collected and brought to Prem Dan, the shells were stripped of their rough fibers by the poor who then manufactured them, in the literal sense of the term, into coconut matting and rugs. The shells were then used to meet Prem Dan's fuel needs. Food for the army of mat makers came from American Food for Peace stocks through Catholic Relief Services.

The meeting with Misereor bore fruit when the sum of 150,000 marks went into the construction of the Home for the Dying in Delhi.

Though Mother Teresa's contact with Pope John XXIII had been fleeting, it could be said that the old pope touched her life at a later date. When the Pope John XXIII Peace Prize was inaugurated, she was called to receive it in Rome from the hands of Pope Paul VI. It came to her on January 6, 1971, the forty-second anniversary to the day of her arrival in Calcutta.

Finally, the visit to Rome and the audience with two prelates was the first step in a decision of crucial significance for the future of Mother Teresa and the Missionaries of Charity. This decision was the acceptance of the congregation as a new family in the universal church. When it became a Society of pontifical right, it was empowered to carry its works of mercy outside India and around the world.

11

The New World

The woman's fine-featured face was wasted but still beautiful. She lay on a low pallet, while two Missionaries of Charity washed and fed her. With her dusky skin, the patient might have been in the Home for the Dying in the caravanserai of Kali's Temple. It was clear, however, that she was at the other end of the world when the two young Sisters stepped outside. Their saris shone blindingly bright against the near tropical greenery of a remote village in Venezuela. It was midsummer in 1966.

"Blessed be those who come to help me," said Asunción from her pallet. "May the Lord and the Blessed Virgin help them."

Asunción's pallet lay in a dark corner of a tiny cottage standing at the end of a lane. For an hour and a half, Sister Nirmala and Sister Pauline had been working, putting clean clothes on the thin form and replacing the grimy bed coverings with clean sheets. Drawing water from the open-air pump, they had washed all the pitiful clothing, including bedclothes, now drying in the brilliant July sun. They blew up a cooking fire on the porch and prepared a meal. They arranged some food and vitamins and explained to Asunción that they would be back in three days. Neighbors would come by in the meantime.

Asunción, a widow, had two sons, she told the Sisters. One had gone away; she did not know where. Just "*fuera,*" and he never came back to visit. The other son lived in the city but came to see her rarely. When she became ill, the neighbors did what they could. They did not let her die. Asunción was the poorest woman in a poor village in the state of Lara. It was the summer of 1966 and the Missionaries of Charity were carrying out in a new setting the mission of their Society to remain right on the ground by living Christ's concern for the poorest and the lowliest.

The Missionaries of Charity's entry into Venezuela arose out of one of the great councils of the Catholic Church, the Second Vatican Council. The Council, called by Pope John XXIII, brought the bishops of the entire world to Rome for four sessions beginning in the fall of 1962. Prelates discussed their problems among themselves at the coffee bar underneath St. Peter's and in their quarters. One conversation held by two Council fathers brought the Missionaries of Charity to the New World.

Bishop Benitez of Barquisimeto, Venezuela, described problems that troubled his heart but for which he could find no solution. He was talking with the papal internuncio to New Delhi, Archbishop James Robert Knox. Though not the poorest of countries, there were areas in his diocese, explained the Latin American bishop, where the poor received little medical care and a special section where lived the descendants of Africans brought in to work the copper mines. The people who lived on the land lacked education and the bishop feared many things, including the exploitation of potentially rich land at the expense of poor cultivators. The women, especially, had been neglected and the bishop told of a crying need for religious Sisters who would be willing to live with great simplicity in order to work with them.

Archbishop Knox described to Bishop Benitez the work of the Missionaries of Charity, in particular, their ability to live simply and to help the very poorest.

The invitation to send a team of Sisters was relayed to Mother Teresa through Archbishop Knox. There could be no response since the Missionaries of Charity were still limited to India. The next step was the recognition of the Missionaries of Charity as a Society of pontifical right, able to work anywhere in the world. That this recognition came speedily owed much to the enthusiasm of Archbishop Knox for the work he had seen in India.

After Mother Teresa's informal presentation of the matter during the Rome visit of 1960, much had happened in the congregation, and reports on the Sisters' work had reached the Holy See. These reports had come not only from Archbishop Knox, but from many sources, including the bishops in whose dioceses the Sisters were caring for the poor, the schoolless, the homeless, and the leprous.

After bringing the very first team of Sisters to Ranchi, in Bihar, from which area many young women of India's tribal groups had entered the congregation, Mother Teresa took the second team to Delhi. During 1960, Mother Teresa started foundations in Jhansi and Agra in Uttar Pradesh. In the Asansol district of Bengal, the work for lepers was begun in 1961, with a mobile clinic leprosy service. This inspired the founding of a town for lepers, Shanti Nagar, the Town of Peace. Also in 1961, Mother Teresa brought teams to Ambala in the Punjab and to Bhagalpur in Bihar. Amravati in Maharashtra came next, in 1962.

In April 1963, just fifteen years after she had made the crucial journey to the Medical Mission Sisters in Patna, Bihar, Mother Teresa returned to the city with a team of her own Sisters. The same year, she opened a house in Raigarh in Madhya Pradesh. Four teams left Calcutta in 1964, to work in Darjeeling, Bengal, site of Mother Teresa's novitiate, to Jamshedpur, the Pittsburgh of India, to Goa, on the west coast, a relic of Portugal's colony, and to Trivandrum, in Kerala, southern India. In Goa, the chapel of St. Francis Xavier was given to the care of the Missionaries of Charity.

The Sisters, schooled in Calcutta, were prepared for the worst they could find in other parts of India. They followed the pattern established in Calcutta and adapted it to local needs, in particular, in Trivandrum, where they worked among the poor families of fishermen.

As Fr. Celeste Van Exem had shepherded Mother Teresa's efforts in obtaining recognition for the Sisters as a diocesan congregation, so now, Archbishop Knox became a spiritual shepherd. Besides his strong support, and the support of many others with direct experience of the Sisters' work, the expanded constitutions were sent to the Holy See, to the Sacred Congregation for the Propagation of the Faith, later renamed the Sacred Congregation for the Evangelization of Peoples. Mother Teresa had wanted to stipulate in the original constitution that the Missionaries of Charity would not own the buildings from which they carried out their works. These buildings were to be the property of the Church so that the Sisters could maintain the poverty on which their congregation was based. This was not practical in India because of the situation of the Catholic Church there. It was omitted in the earlier draft on the advice of Fr. Van Exem and was also omitted from the expanded document.

The prefect of the Congregation for the Propagation of the Faith was Gregory Cardinal Agagianian, whom Mother Teresa had approached on her first visit to Rome in 1960. On February 1, 1965, the Holy See announced its decision and issued what is called the *Decretum Laudis* (Decree of Praise). This meant that the Holy See applauded the work of the Missionaries of Charity and accepted the congregation as one of pontifical right. There were over three hundred Sisters, including novices. Only now could Mother Teresa send the Sisters outside of India's borders. The first overseas mission of the Missionaries of Charity was a mission to the New World. Mother Teresa brought the Sisters to Cocorote, in the diocese of Barquisimeto, Venezuela, on July 26, 1965.

Many joys and some difficulties and tragedies came with the new foundations across India, but one stood out in Mother Teresa's memory. She told us about it one evening during those first weeks in Venezuela. Sister-Doctor Leonia was in charge of the foundation in Raigarh. Coming to Calcutta for a meeting of the Sisters, she developed alarming symptoms. When she started brushing her teeth, she experienced spasms and began to make the dry barking sounds that portend a fateful disease. She was taken to the hospital and tests proved that she was a victim of rabies. Months before she had rescued a puppy from a pack of dogs and had suffered a dog bite. She had cauterized the wound, but evidently the procedure was not effective.

The hospital doctor, thinking Sister Leonia was unconscious, announced the sad news to Mother Teresa, "She will be dead within forty-eight hours." Sister Leonia overheard him and took it very hard.

Mother Teresa sat by her holding her hand, and told the agonizing Sister, "I have received you into this work for Jesus; I will be with you to help you go from us to Him." Sister Leonia became calm. The doctors were amazed that she could show such superhuman control in the terrible spasms that overcame her body. She did not shout or scream. Within the forty-eight hours, she had passed out of life.

Mother Teresa did not entrust the Sisters to new locations without first visiting them and studying them herself. She had done this in India, and she followed the same course in the New World. In the fall of 1964, she paid a short visit to Venezuela at the invitation of Bishop Benitez. I accompanied her and at the same time looked into the Catholic Relief Services programs there. In a way, it seemed to me, Mother Teresa resembled the Apostles who had been ready to move out into the known world with the Good News even before all of Jerusalem had accepted the word. The needs of Calcutta were still there, as were the problems of India.

Waiting for Mother Teresa at Barquisimeto Airport were the priest who was vicar for religious of the diocese, Sister Teresita, the Sister-Director of Mary Help of Christians School with three Salesian Sisters, two Sisters of St. Joseph of Tarbes, and three Sisters of the Society of St. Anne. Almost all of them were from Italy.

The bishop arranged for us to be the guests at the boarding school of the Salesian Sisters. We were given rooms on the courtyard. From our windows we looked out on flowering shrubs and trees. Towering over them were the jacarandas, whose blooms moved in the breeze like spreading flames. I noticed that Mother Teresa, contrary to her usual custom, sometimes took a short nap between meetings. She explained that she had been given a medication by the doctors. The doctors, it turned out, were those who had treated her in a nursing home after a road mishap.

"It was on the road near Darjeeling," she told me. "There was a car coming toward us and we had to stop suddenly. My head struck an iron bar. They had to put nineteen stitches in my head in a nursing home in Darjeeling. When I saw the bill for each day, I ran to our Shishu Bhavan in Darjeeling. Mrs. Gandhi came to me there. If we had not stopped, we would have toppled down the hill road." Indira Gandhi was of course India's Prime Minister.

One afternoon I had to call her for a meeting in Barquisimeto and she was sound asleep. It was the effect of the medication. She decided she would take no more of it.

Two priests from Spain, Father Tomas and Father Manuel became our guides. They, with a third member, served over thirty-five remote communities, some of them in a section called "Zona Negra" (Black Belt). This area was inhabited by Afro-Venezuelans. Spanish priests, they explained, offered themselves to Venezuelan dioceses for a period of five years. Following that, some returned to Spain, but a number committed themselves to work in Venezuela for life. All were from the Murcia region of Spain. They drove us first to the village of Chino, a sleepy, primitive, jungle community.

Lush vegetation surrounded the dwellings constructed of mud striped with horizontal rows of bamboo twigs. These the priests told us were replicas of dwellings in African villages. Other dwellings were built of plain mud bricks and a few stood out since they were made of cement and painted bright blue. We got out of the car to look at a half-built chapel. Green creepers and thick grass were already growing on the unfinished floor and over the half-erected walls. Two large brass bells intended for the chapel were lying on the grass. The metal had turned a soft gray-green from exposure.

In a short time, a half dozen children came silently out of the dwellings and stood staring at us. The boys were naked from the waist up, the girls in worn cotton dresses. None had shoes. At first, they were too shy to respond to our greetings but soon they told us their names and ages. Several men finally came out and saluted the priests. No women came out to greet us.

In the next village, with such conveniences as electricity, tap water, and a police station, there was much excitement at the appearance of a group of visitors, especially a visitor from faraway in sandals and an enveloping white garment. Father Tomas explained that the small woman was a nun and that she hoped to come back into the area with young Sisters to work especially with the women. Mother Teresa was soon surrounded by about fifty women, some holding infants in their arms. The church was opened up and the church bell rang in jubilee.

The villagers trooped in to fill the benches. Father Tomas gave a brief homily, telling them that while he did not see them very often, he always enjoyed being with them. He would be soon with them for holy mass, but in the meantime, he had brought them a visitor who wanted to meet them and work alongside them. He led the people in prayer, asking them to remember especially Madre Teresa and her Sisters.

During the rest of our drive through the Zona Negra, we were accompanied by two handsome black women. They showed us their own fields of tall corn, plantains, and mango trees. As we drove over the rough dirt roads we came to fields of sugar cane and grove after grove of sweet limes. The limes were as large as oranges and a delicate light green in color. The people who lived here, the priests told us, could live fairly well if they had skills in managing their own affairs. Misery was a compelling and bitter presence though amid these groves of sweet limes. There was a beginning of exploitation as outsiders offered seemingly generous prices for the holdings of the local people. Once the money was spent, the people became dependent upon a daily wage. Instead of growing basic foodstuffs, they would find themselves completely in a money economy.

The priests took us to San Felipe in the nearby state of Yaracuy, where they were proud of the impressive modern church from which they conducted their mission. Then they brought us to a smaller town, Cocorote, about five miles away where there was a church dedicated to St. Jerónimo. It was a modest church in the Spanish colonial style. Next to the church was a simple house that would have served as a rectory if there had been a priest in residence.

"One of us says mass regularly in Cocorote," Father Tomas told Mother Teresa.

"Then our Sisters will come here," said Mother Teresa. She entrusted them to the spiritual care of Father Tomas and Father Manuel.

It was a dramatic moment when the Indian citizens presented themselves to the Indian Government for passports and exit visas for a mission overseas. India had been on the receiving side of missionaries from Spain, Portugal, Germany, Italy, Ireland, England, the United States, and other Western countries. Now this situation was reversed. The reason now was not for Sisters to leave India to learn the ways of the West, for study or for training, but to bring their own skills to people of another society. The Indian Government responded with alacrity. The problem was that rupees could not be taken out of India. This problem was met by the Catholic women of Brooklyn. On her return from Venezuela, Mother Teresa had spoken about her plans to a meeting of the Diocesan Council of Catholic Women. Immediately, the women had pledged funds and were ready to sponsor the venture, not only at its beginning, but for many years afterward.

Within a year after her visit to Venezuela, Mother Teresa sent a team of four Sisters to make their headquarters in Cocorote and, within months, sent three more Sisters. The pioneer group first to leave India was an all-Indian team.

Sister Nirmala and Sister Pauline, who had been nurses for the helpless Asunción, were as different as two Indian girls could be. Sister Nirmala had originated in Nepal, a country to the north of India. She had the high cheekbones and elongated eyes of the Nepali. She came from an army family, her father having been an officer in the Indian army. A convert to the Catholic Church, she was completing her course for a B.A. degree at Patna Women's College when a priest showed her the first article in *Jubilee* magazine on Mother Teresa and her work. She went to Calcutta to investigate and stayed to become a Missionary of Charity. She was, she told me, number seventy-six in the Missionaries of Charity.

Sister Pauline had the round facial contours of a Bengali. Her family had originated in Dacca, but she was brought up in Calcutta. She was one of the early Missionaries of Charity, having entered the Society in 1952. While she served as superior of the Missionaries of Charity in Goa, she had learned Konkani, her fourth language after Bengali, Hindi, and English. She was doing very well in Spanish, her fifth tongue. Two Sisters, Sister Justin and Sister Rosario, were from India's tribal people, the Oraons, in north-central India. Both girls carried the black dot of the tribal people between their eyes.

"Our language is Oraon," Sister Justin told me. "I could not speak Hindi or Bengali and I sounded so strange when I first tried to. Now we can manage."

Sister Paul came from Mangalore, farther south and Sister Dolores came from the southernmost state of Kerala. Sister Dolores told Mother Teresa that she felt quite at home in Venezuela, with the palm trees and mangos of her home state. She had attended a girls' secondary school "in the English medium," as the Indians put it, though her own language was Malayalam.

One day, Bishop Picachy, then the auxiliary bishop of Calcutta, gave a talk to the girls and described the work of the Missionaries of Charity. The future Sr. Dolores was immediately drawn to the work and made her way to Calcutta to present her petition to Mother Teresa.

With Mother Teresa, I saw this exotic team in action as they traveled to meet the needs of the very poorest like Asunción in villages all over the countryside. The rectory of the church of San Jerónimo, a building deserted for many years, became their convent. Between the house and the street was a garden dominated by a mango tree heavy with young green fruit. The parlor struck me by its similarity to the parlor of the Motherhouse in Calcutta. There was a bare wooden table and several simple chairs.

When the Sisters arrived to take up residence in Cocorote, the bishop and the local people had prepared a cozy home for them. There was a large stuffed couch in the parlor, the Sisters told me, and comfortable lounge chairs. Attractive drapes had been hung on the windows of all the rooms. In the kitchen was a refrigerator. All these things though intended for the Missionaries of Charity were given away by them to poor families and replaced with more spartan items. The drapes were welcomed by the poor who could make them into bed coverings and even dresses. The plain furniture was more practical since the parlor was utilized as a training center. Here the Sisters began their work with sewing and typing classes for the neighborhood girls. The sewing machines, cloth, and typewriters were supplied by the Catholic women of Brooklyn.

Some of the girls asked for lessons in simple English, and the Sisters responded with regular classes. For lack of space, the English classes were held in the belfry room of the church. In return, local women drilled the Sisters in Venezuelan Spanish.

Another skill the Sisters needed was the ability to drive a car. With help, they learned to operate a donated station wagon which they painted bright blue, like the mobile van used in Calcutta to visit the leper stations. Soon they were maneuvering the station wagon over every sort of road, chiefly unpaved, to reach the *campos,* the isolated villages around them. Often the last part of the journey had to be made on foot.

The Sisters did not have to look far for poor people. In an abandoned building to the side of San Jerónimo were two families who had migrated from the mountain areas. They were living as squatters, hoping that life in Cocorote would be better than in their isolated hamlet. In one family were five children, in the other four. Each family lived in one stone-floored room. Although there was water in the backyard pump, there was no money to buy soap. The pay the men received for occasional day labor was hardly enough for food. All the children had some sort of skin rash and the babies had eye infections. The Sisters were the only regular visitors to these new arrivals. Soap and clean clothes were part of the help that would make them more acceptable members of the Cocorote community.

The stratification of life in Venezuelan towns, and to a degree in towns the world over, is such that people above a certain income and level of education rarely have close and continuing contact with people below their level. The Sisters became a bridge between those who had what they needed for a decent life and those, like the migrants, who lacked everything. The Cocorote community became involved in the work of the Sisters and in their welfare. A butcher began sending donations of meat, most often a stewing chicken; a poor man with a business of selling a sort of tortilla, brought a few every morning. They resembled the *chapatties* that were the Sisters' regular breakfast in India, so they enjoyed them. The community respected the poverty of the Sisters and supplied only basic needs. The community also began bringing to the Sisters what they could distribute in the *campos* and started to take part in the Sisters' work for the neediest of the region.

After the Spanish priests had introduced the Sisters to the people they served, the Sisters helped out with the classes of religious instruction, classes that were preparation for the sacraments of the Church. These classes earned for the Sisters the trust of the people. They would ask the Sisters to visit their poor homes and listen to their troubles. Mother Teresa joined the Sisters on a trip to Taria for a regular family visit. The living room was empty of furniture, as was the case in most of the village homes, despite the availability of many types of wood in the area.

"My husband still can't go to work," the mother explained. "His leg is still giving him pain." The man sat up and displayed a badly swollen knee and a large sore on the calf of the leg.

"We have three hectares of land, but it is far from here," the woman told us. "We grow corn and *plátanos.*" The baby continued to nurse at her breast.

We went into the back room and as we entered, a donkey stalked out. In the corner crouched a child on all fours. "I have four children," the woman said. "You have not seen Rosameli before."

The child had been hidden from the Sisters, but now Sister Nirmala picked her up, a girl with a lovely face and shy, brown eyes. Her legs hung down like dry, wasted sticks. Sister carried her out into the sunny backyard, noisy with the comings and goings of the donkey, some pigs, chickens, and a dog. The Sisters wanted to know if the child had ever walked.

"Oh yes," the mother replied. "She walked like the other children. Then she got the asthma and she went to the hospital. When she came back, she could not walk. She is six now." The child was a victim of poliomyelitis.

"Why don't you bring her to classes at the church? She is a lovely little girl," asked Sister Nirmala, cuddling the child.

"We have no clothes to go anywhere. Perhaps when my husband feels better . . ."

"We can bring you some clothes the next time, Mrs. Rumbo," the Sister said after she had given her a supply of soap and vitamins.

"Rumbo is my own name," the woman volunteered. "The children are all Rumbitos. We have not been married so they have my name."

Rosameli was looking less shy and was beginning to smile. Her back, we noted, had already become arched, curving inward, from her habit of crawling. The Sisters were going to look into physical therapy for her. A woman living nearby came to meet the Sisters. She was surrounded by children. Speaking to Mother Teresa, she said, "I have nine children in all," adding, "my husband was killed by a truck many years ago."

Sensing perhaps our surprise at so many small children in the absence of a husband, she patted the fat young baby boy at her feet.

"This is the last. The last—no more."

It sounded like a commitment.

A nearby village was Palmerejo, and a sign, *Bar Palmerejo,* announced the beginning of the community, as a sign on another bar, *La Salida* (The Exit), marked its boundary a few hundred feet farther on. A section of dirt road marked Palmerejo's main street.

Mother Teresa, led by Sister Nirmala, greeted children who must have reminded her of the children who clustered around her in Calcutta's Moti Jihl. Many of the littlest boys were totally naked, while the girls always had some covering. The children greeted the *Hermanitas,* the "little Sisters" as they called the Indian Sisters, and followed them. They had accepted the nuns easily, saying, "These are *our* Sisters." They were referring to the fact that the Sisters were dark-skinned.

The main street was busy with athletic long-snouted pigs nosing in garbage, slender goats staring curiously from behind bushes, cocks and hens scurrying to the side as an occasional truck or car sped by, and burros, lumbering along the roadside with enormous piles of firewood, bananas, or limes. It was often necessary to step aside to avoid a discarded mango pit, feasted on by myriads of black ants.

One of the homes Mother Teresa wanted to visit was a palm-thatched dwelling, with the usual walls of mud and slatted sticks. It was inhabited by an old woman she had visited before. The inside of the dwelling was mercifully dark and the air moved through the slats in a slight breeze. The old woman lifted herself from a pallet raised about a foot from the dirt floor and smiled broadly to greet *Madre Teresa* and the *Hermanitas.* She smoothed her matted hair from her face and extended her hand to me, saying "Florencia Antonia Perez."

Florencia told Mother Teresa that she was feeling much better. As she moved toward the door opening, I could see that her ankles were puffed up like rising dough. She told Mother Teresa that she was taking her medicines and was using the soap of the *Hermanitas* to keep everything clean. Sister Nirmala and I translated for Mother Teresa who wanted to know whether her son still took care of her.

"Surely, he is still with me. He won't go away. Now he is working in the fields."

We paid a visit to the village chapel dedicated to Saint Rosalia, a holy woman of Sicily. A group of people gathered quietly in the chapel and Mother Teresa spoke to them of love for one another, while Sister Nirmala and I translated. She told them of the need to love and help each other and to remember those who suffered. Mother Teresa told them to pray to the one God who hears our prayers no matter from what part of the world they come. One of the images on the wall of the chapel attracted Mother Teresa. It seemed to be a painting by a local artist and represented three identical seated figures with bright red beards. Mother Teresa wondered if there were any reason to represent Christ three times. As we examined it more closely, we saw that on the beard of one was a large open eye, on the breast of the second a dove, and on the third, a lamb. We could only conclude that the eye must be the all-seeing eye of the Father; the dove, the Holy Spirit; and the lamb, Jesus.

"This must be the Trinity," Mother Teresa said, "but I have never seen anything like this before."

Outside the chapel, there were questions about our home places. They did not know where India was, but they knew that it was the country of *La Madre* and the *Hermanitas.* There were bright smiles when I mentioned that I was from New York City. A girl of fourteen told us proudly that she had finished the six grades of primary school in Farriar. She was wearing a white cotton dress, clean and ironed.

"A Brooklyn dress," said Sister Nirmala.

When we asked her what she was going to do now that she had finished school, she looked surprised, as though such an idea had never occurred to her.

"I stay home and watch the house. I have a brother and four sisters and my father is dead. My mother works in the *caña* [the sugar cane]."

We found out that the mother received six bolivares a day, whereas a man would receive ten bolivares for the same work. At that time, a bolivar was not quite five to the American dollar.

Before leaving, we paid a visit to the Palmerejo school. Mother Teresa told the teachers how impressed she was by the quiet concentration of the pupils. They were all leaning over their desks. The teachers explained that it was examination time. The school was a well-constructed cement building of one floor, with windows along the entire wall. Standing outside, and looking through venetian blinds into the quiet classrooms, were a number of children of various ages.

"These are the one who do not go to school—perhaps they come for one year, and then drop out. We have only three grades here in Palmerejo. Less than half of the children finish the course here. For the next grade, the children have to go to the next village, to Farriar."

"But don't the parents insist that their children go to school?" we wanted to know.

The woman teacher answered, "There is not much discipline over the children. We have more than a hundred family groups here, but less than ten percent are formally married. One man can have two wives at one time and he will boast that his women live together as friendly sisters. Another man will live in turn with several women who cluster in the same section. That is the man's way of proving himself."

"And think of the size of the families," the male teacher put in. "A family of five or six children is a small one. It is hard to have order or discipline. The fathers do not enforce it. The mother is all. The children usually give us the name of the mother. They often do not know which is their father. One of the problems is the housing. These are new houses, around the school, but most of them have only three rooms. No matter how large the family, they crowd into that small space."

Mother Teresa sighed. These problems were different from those of Calcutta. She was learning at firsthand that the Sisters would be meeting new challenges. She did not lay down rules. The Sisters knew they had to express the commitment of the order—to reach the poorest—in new ways.

Someone gave us a report on "The Disintegration of the Family Nucleus," a report that applied not only to this part of Latin America but to the Caribbean where the Sisters would be working in later years. In their daily work, the Sisters attempted to shore up disintegrating families by training the young women, by helping families in trouble, and by aiding couples with large numbers of children to enter into formal marriage.

Back in India, the family had remained more stable, even among the pavement dwellers of Calcutta. Those who conducted a study of Calcutta's homeless for the World Health Organization were surprised to find that beggars and those who kept alive by scrap-picking maintained a remarkable family stability against incredible odds. This reality contradicted the impression held by many that the street dwellers of Calcutta were derelicts.

Here in Venezuela Father Tomas had been working on the marriage problem for some time. Like Bishop Benitez, he saw the women as the key to the problem.

"They are not able to take care of themselves in life," he explained. "They cannot earn money except for the few who go out to the fields. They can only cook the simplest foods. They submit to men out of hunger, out of a low sense of themselves, out of a sort of passivity. In Spain, when women submit to men outside of marriage, it is out of passion, a giving in to temptation. Here it is a sort of fatalism. They bear children by one or a succession of men just to stay alive. If the women had some skills, they would have a better sense of themselves and would see that there are other choices."

Before leaving Cocorote, Mother Teresa learned that the Sisters had been offered a site for a center. It was a block of ruins that had once been a hotel. Long abandoned, it had been serving as a garbage dump for the town. It was overrun with bushes and green creepers. As we went through the ruined gate, a few men came by and warned us not to take more than a few steps because the site was a haunt of snakes. Mother Teresa tried to pierce the gloom under the overhanging creepers.

"The space is good," she decided. "Let us get the people to help us clean it up and then we can see what we can do with it."

Local people cleared out the garbage dump and in a few years there was a center which served for training as well as a refuge for the helpless and abandoned of the region. In the meantime, the Sisters found their way into communities which had had little contact with the outside world, Agua Negra, La Haya, Buena Vista Guayago, Tulipan, Las Peñas, Crucito, Marroquiña, and Las Flores, to name a few. Mother Teresa told of receiving reports that the Missionaries of Charity were needed to do almost everything in addition to the works of mercy.

"They preach," she said. "They lead the prayers; they even give out Communion. All they cannot do," she said smiling, "is to celebrate the mass."

"What about confessions?" I asked. "They cannot hear confessions yet, can they?"

"Oh, yes; they hear confessions all the time." She burst out laughing. "They just cannot give absolution."

Sister Nirmala related that men had come to her to tell her that if they could go to confession to her, or to one of the Sisters, it would be like telling their sins to their mothers. "You are like our mother," one said, "I could come and tell my faults to you. But not to a man like myself."

Before leaving Venezuela for Paris, Mother Teresa took time to see the poor of the capital, Caracas. She talked with priests and social workers in the crowded *ranchos* growing up outside the central city. Rural people, finding that such heavy work as road-building was open to them, flocked to the city and never returned to their home places. Throngs moved in after them, settling in huts and rough dwellings built up and down the hilly outskirts of the city. Two American priests staffed a parish among the newcomers. One of them brought Mother Teresa to his parishioners, mostly dark-skinned. He explained, "Only the worst jobs are open to them. Even when they get some training, they can't seem to rise to office-type jobs. White collars are usually on white necks."

He took Mother Teresa to a community faucet where a line of women of various skin colors, the majority with darker skins, and other clearly Afro-Venezuelans, were waiting to fill up their water cans. Many placed the large cans on their heads and with regal balance were able to make their way along uneven and winding lanes to their homes.

"Some have built themselves homes and what they want most is piped-in water. Things haven't been standing still. There has been a lot of building."

He pointed to the bottom of the hill where there were six multistory buildings. "These are called *'bloques'*; they call sixteen-story buildings *'superbloques.'* "

"Who are those buildings for?" Mother Teresa wanted to know.

"They are for our poor people, but the families are rushed into them without preparation. They have piped-in water and there is elevator service, but only to the fifth, eighth, and sixteenth floors. But everything seems to break down, the water system and the elevators."

When we walked down to the *bloques,* we saw mounds of rubbish on the pavements and dozens of children playing in and around them.

"Be on your guard," the priest warned us. "Keep looking up. Garbage is tossed out of the windows here. It is too much effort to cart it down, especially when the elevators are stuck.

"We say mass in a hall in each of the *superbloques.* Some good things are happening. The people begin to form committees and cooperate with each other. But there is a long way to go. This area must have the highest birth rate in the world, as well as the highest rate of illegitimacy. It is the young people who need help. We have been told that close to forty-five percent of the population in Venezuela is under fifteen. The new parishes have sprung up everywhere and we are trying to help these people bring some order and even some justice into their lives."

Mother Teresa thanked the priests who were, she felt, "truly doing God's work for the people." She added, "How much work must still be done." It was clear that in her mind she was looking toward the future. It was not long before an invitation came to her to send Missionaries of Charity to work in the crowded *ranchos,* as the people called their new communities, and she was ready with teams of Sisters.

In Barrio Unión, we were told that over seventy thousand people lived in makeshift shacks. A large cement gully snaked down the hillside carrying waste water and sewage. A boy followed us and asked us to visit his family. We agreed. His name, he told us, was Joséito Guevara. He pointed out his home near the bottom of the hill, where his mother and grandmother greeted us. The mother told us she had eleven children, from two months to seventeen years in age, all living in four rooms. Her husband was a taxi driver and earned enough for all of them.

"Thank God," she said. "Seven of our children are in school, in *Fe y Alegría.*" In the *Fe y Alegría* building was a school bringing hundreds of barrio children to the sixth grade, and a medical clinic. Everyone paid a token amount so that they had the dignity of a feeling of self-reliance. It was run by a group of Catholic lay volunteers.

I translated Mother Teresa's "You are a fortunate woman. May God bless you all."

"Amen," said the woman.

While governmental monies had been expended in the *ranchos,* it was Catholic groups like *Fe y Alegría* (Faith and Joy) that were leading the government in providing free education and training for the young people.

In driving across the city, we saw the affluent sections of Caracas. We were caught in traffic snarls when thousands of cars choked the roads. The suburban sections, *urbanizaciones,* spoke of plenty, with their villas, lovely gardens, and swimming pools. We had occasion to meet some of the residents, good parishioners in their own well-appointed parishes. They inhabited a world apart from the people in the *ranchos.* They regretted the deprivation of the other world, but their regret seemed to remain in the realm of the emotions, rather than moving them to involve themselves with groups like *Fe y Alegría.*

"I am thinking," said Mother Teresa, "that maybe we should have a special mission to the rich, not just to the poor."

The destination after Caracas was Frankfurt, Germany, but we broke our journey for a few hours in Paris. Mother Teresa's resilience after a tiring flight was always remarkable, but in the Paris airport it was especially noticeable. The two French Brothers who met us told us that a mass would be celebrated momentarily in the airport.

"The holy mass? Here?" she asked, her face lighting up with a smile. The Brothers led us quickly to a corner where a priest was beginning the celebration of mass for the benefit of a large group of young vacationers. There was time for a homily on how a vacation may give new strength for studies and work, and Mother Teresa joined them in the reception of Holy Communion.

Mother Teresa sat down to talk with the two men, Brother Marquisette and Brother Jacques of the Little Brothers of Notre Dame. Their mission was to the homebound poor, bringing them not only meals, but gifts to brighten their lives, in particular plants and flowers. They talked of Brother Marquisette's visit to Kalighat, where he astounded the patients by presenting them with roses. They smiled at the remark of a visitor from Germany who arrived as the roses were placed behind the pallets. "That is the French touch; flowers before bread."

At the Frankfurt Airport on July 24, 1966, a woman long involved with Mother Teresa's work, Josepha Gosselke, was on hand. She was a teacher in the Edith Stein Secondary School and was accompanied by Karl Sadura, a school administrator. He had taken days of leave to drive Mother Teresa around West Germany. There was time for Mother Teresa to talk before the assembled students of the school named for the Carmelite nun, born to Jewish parents, who died as a victim at Auschwitz extermination camp.

Mother Teresa asked Sadura if he would take her first to Wattenscheid, to visit the parents of Sister Anand, a Sister-Doctor from Germany who was working in Calcutta. The meeting was in a home for the aged, airy, cheerful, and perfectly appointed. Josepha Gosselke translated as Mother Teresa thanked Mr. and Mrs. Johannes Hegemann for the gift of their daughter to a beautiful work among the poor and suffering. They were a dignified couple, she with fair skin and pure white silky hair; he a tall distinguished man who gave us his card. He had been a teacher but added to his name were the letters, I.R. He explained, *"Das meint 'Im Ruhestand.'"* (That means I am 'In Retirement.')

Tragedy looked out of Hegemann's eyes as he told Mother Teresa that his son, who had been finishing medical school was killed in the Second World War. The old woman said nothing and Mother Teresa took her hand in her own. She gave them details of the work in Calcutta and shared with them her joy at being able to work in Venezuela. Another visit was to Sister Stephanie Ingendaa, the hardy German missioner who in 1948 had been superior of the Patna community of the Medical Mission Sisters. The two women embraced and Mother Teresa said, "I have come to thank you once more for the love you showed me and the work."

They talked about their common work as Sister Stephanie showed us the Center of her congregation in Ludwigsburg. The Medical Mission Sisters were already involved in hospital work, nurses' training, and health care in the Caribbean and Latin America. Nodding toward Mother Teresa, Sister Stephanie said to me, "I am not at all surprised that her work has grown like this. She had the spirit then. I could feel it. We were glad to help her a little on her way."

She wrote me later, "I have had a great love and admiration for M. Teresa since our lives became connected. She and I always understood each other and were happy that our lives could fill each other up and that God used our different talents for His people."

Mother Teresa spent a few days in Rome before taking the plane for Calcutta. She spent most of the time in efforts to see her dear mother, "Nana Loke," whom she had not seen since that far-off day on the Zagreb station. As an exile, her brother, Lazar, could not take direct steps with Albanian authorities, since he was on the "blacklist" of the Albanian regime, then the bastion of Maoism in Europe. If Drana and Age could come to Italy, he could give them a home. Drana had written to Mother

Teresa and Lazar, "I want to see you before I die. This is the only grace I ask of God."

In 1932, Lazar had arranged for Age to join him in Tirana where the young woman, trained in economics, eventually worked as a translator and broadcaster for Radio Tirana. In 1934, they persuaded their mother to give up the house in Skopje to make her home with them in Tirana. Mother Teresa had not only the love of a sister for Age, but deep admiration. She always admired self-sacrifice and devotion to duty, and it was these qualities that Age showed in turning down several offers of marriage so that she could care for Nana Loke.

Both Mother Teresa and Lazar had kept in communication through letters, though even these had been interrupted for a time after the imposition of the Marxist regime following the Second World War. Mother Teresa had retained her fluency in written Albanian only through writing to her mother. Lazar never lost his fluency in spoken Albanian which was the Gheg form of the tongue rather than the Tosk. He spoke of the torture of knowing that his mother and sisters were "buried alive" away from family members and from the world at large. He contacted friends and officials, in particular those in French diplomatic circles, for aid in having Drana and Age leave Tirana. Only one response was ever received by French authorities from Albanian officials. "Mrs. Drana Bojaxhiu and Miss Age Bojaxhiu are not physically fit to travel abroad."

"This was not true," said Lazar. "My mother and sister were not ill or confined to bed. Their only illness was that of solitude and hopelessness."

Mother Teresa made a desperate attempt to have Drana and Age come to Italy by going in person to see the Albanians. We made our way to the Albanian Embassy and found it a building shuttered and silent as a tomb. There was no sign of life even after we had rung a loud bell three times. At last, a man with a broad face and surprised blue eyes open the door. He was evidently not accustomed to visitors. He said nothing as though trying to puzzle out what idiom at his command could reach us.

Mother Teresa fastened her tawny eyes on him and said simply in her native tongue, *"Sou de Schipteru."* (I am from Albania.) This was literally correct since she could no longer say she was Albanian, having acquired Indian citizenship.

The Embassy employee looked from Mother Teresa to me as though unable to credit his senses and then said a few brusque words which we took to be an invitation to enter the building. He preceded us into a dark, shuttered parlor. Instead of opening the shutters to admit the midmorning sun, he turned on the electric lights. The overstuffed chairs were shrouded in muslin coverings and the floor was bare wood. A fantasy came to me that the parlor was in mourning for that terrible day, Good Friday 1939, when Mussolini had invaded tiny Albania.

The three of us settled into the large chairs around a low coffee table and Mother Teresa said once more, *"Sou de Schipteru."*

The man replied with a burst of speech while Mother Teresa struggled to form a few words. A blush rose and covered her face; she turned to me smiling ruefully. "I can't find the words in my mother tongue. It's too far back."

At that point, I thought I had better explain our presence, since the Albanian was looking uneasy.

"I am an American," I started in Italian.

"Si, signora?" he said, clearly making it a question.

I explained that the woman who had come to see him was from an Albanian family. Many years earlier, nearly forty years before, she had gone to India to become a Catholic nun. In all that time she had not seen her mother and sister who were now living in Tirana. I told him how she decided to serve the poor on the streets of Calcutta and how many young women had joined her. Her group was called the Missionaries of Charity. While her name had been Agnes Gonxha Bojaxhiu, she was now known to everyone as Mother Teresa. I pointed out that though she had become an Indian citizen, her origin was known and she had brought great honor to Albania.

The Albanian's face lit up at my rather shameless appeal to nationalism. Mother Teresa asked him if he spoke Serbo-Croatian. He did and, from then on, Mother Teresa told her own tale.

All suspicion had been dissolved. The man listened eagerly and, at one point, raised his large hand to his face and wiped away tears that streamed from his eyes.

He offered us coffee and I explained the rule of Mother Teresa's order not to accept food or drink outside the convent. He asked for more details of the work in Calcutta and I told him of the Home for the Dying and of how many human beings had been snatched from death and how the Sisters gave free education in schools for the poor.

"You say, signora, that this small woman has started all this work?"

I saw him glance at her questioningly. His eyes moved from her sari-wrapped head to her bare feet in squat sandals.

I added, "Now a group of men have started to do the same work. I consider that she is one of the best-known Albanians outside of your country."

"I will do my best for her. I will explain to the attaché, and you must come back tomorrow at the same hour." He talked with Mother Teresa in Serbo-Croatian as he walked us to the door.

I asked Mother Teresa what she had said to the man that moved him to tears.

"I only told him the truth, that I came as a child seeking for its mother.

"Then I explained that my mother is old and ill. She is eighty-one and longs to see me as I long to see her after so many years. I told him that I was helpless to do anything and that only the Albanians could give her the permission to come to Rome."

The following day the attaché was waiting for us. He spoke some words in Albanian with Mother Teresa, seemingly just to test her as a fellow Albanian. She replied, but haltingly, and one could almost see her reach down into the layers of Serbo-Croat, English, Bengali, and Hindi that lay atop the language of her childhood. He seemed satisfied that she was the person that she claimed to be and asked me to describe her work. He promised to get in contact with the government in Tirana.

Meanwhile, we found a temporary home for Mrs. Drana Bojaxhiu and Age Bojaxhiu in Rome and we sent them a cable to tell them that if they received exit visas we would be there to meet them. The Rome office of Catholic Relief Services was ready to cooperate with Lazar Bojaxhiu in resettling the mother and daughter. Mother Teresa planned to leave for India Friday evening and wanted to do everything possible to help her mother come to Rome even though she might not be there to see her.

On Friday morning we went again to the Albanian Embassy and this time were met by another staff member. The attaché, he explained, was "*fuori Roma.*" He told Mother Teresa that he had no news for her about the exit visas.

"Where did he go?" I asked.

"Bari," he replied.

I stressed to him that as soon as there was word, I could be called. Monsignor Andrew Landi would follow through after I had left Rome.

The Albanian agreed and indicated that the interview was over. There was no move to invite us into the parlor.

When Mother Teresa studied the map and saw the location of Bari, her hopes rose. She was sure that the attaché was on his way to Albania across the Adriatic and would help her mother and her sister to come to Rome. Mother Teresa's temperament, despite the sufferings that she met daily, was always radiantly hopeful and trusting. She left for the plane expressing her trust in the Albanian officials.

Though there were more calls to the Albanian Embassy, no exit visas were ever issued. In two years, Drana Bojaxhiu was dead. A few years later, Age followed her in death.

The woman who was able to cross continents to assuage the sufferings of others was not able to help the one to whom she owed her life.

12

Three Continents

When a religious superior of women told Pope Pius XI of her concern that vocations to her congregation were diminishing, she explained that her Sisters were responding by praying for increased vocations. The reply of the Holy Father must have come to her as a surprise.

"Sister," the pope is reported to have said, "There is a Hindu expression which is, 'When you pray, you must move your feet.' "

Though there had been some decline in the entrance to the vowed life before the Second World War (Pope Pius XI died in 1939) the decline became precipitous, even catastrophic for many women's congregations, after the Second Vatican Council. The last session of the Council ended in December 1965.

The Sisters around Mother Teresa, increasing in numbers each year from the Society's foundation in 1950, had become known as "the running Sisters," in Calcutta as they moved swiftly and unerringly to find and serve the poor, the rejected, the diseased, and the dying.

From 1965 through 1970, they moved their feet in reaching the neediest members of society in nine foundations in three continents outside of India. One foundation was established in the Middle East, bridge between continents and civilizations. Because I was able to see at firsthand an example of the work in Europe, Australia, and Africa, it seems well to give details of the development of those foundations. In Rome, the Sisters moved straight to Italy's urban poor; in Bourke, Australia, to the continent's first and, for a long time, maltreated inhabitants, the aborigines; and in Tabora, Tanzania, Africa, to those human beings who fell between the cracks of a new social order.

The overseas foundations were in addition to thirteen new houses opened during the same period in towns and cities all over India. This brought to over thirty the total of Indian foundations outside Calcutta. The sixty centers, including schools and leper centers, in Calcutta were not counted as separate foundations since they all emanated from the Motherhouse at 54A Lower Circular Road.

The work for lepers, begun in 1961 in the Asansol district of Bengal, came to fruition with the inauguration in 1969 of a town for the people nobody wanted. It was named Shanti Nagar, Town of Peace. The thirty-four acre plot in the countryside provided real homes as well as treatment for leper families and lone victims of leprosy. Sr. Frances Xavier was in overall charge of Shanti Nagar, aided in daily tasks by the residents.

Once having crossed the seas with a team of sari-clad young women, Mother Teresa paused. The work of the Sisters in the parish of San Jerónimo, Cocorote, Yaracuy, went well, with the Sisters going about their work quietly. Mother Teresa had brought the Venezuelan team to the Vatican on their way from India. They were greeted by Pope Paul VI and by Gregory Cardinal Agagianian. They were photographed with Cardinal Agagianian to whom they were grateful for the Decree of Praise for the congregation. These meetings may have had something to do with the fact that Pope Paul VI had asked Mother Teresa to bring the work of the Sisters to Rome itself.

A call to Rome for someone like Mother Teresa, raised in a special reverence for the Eternal City, had to be heeded. On August 22, 1968, the feast of the Immaculate Heart of Mary, she shepherded a team of Indian Sisters to Rome. August 22, the anniversary of the opening of the Home for the Dying sixteen years earlier in 1952 was an important date in the history of the congregation.

Questions were raised about bringing Sisters from far-off India, where needs were so agonizing, to the center of Catholic Christianity where literally scores of women's congregations were working and studying. The list of Italian women's congregations active in Rome was a long and impressive one. In addition, women belonging to international orders were in evidence everywhere, including the Vatican itself. The two charitable services for the poor operating in the heart of Vatican City were conducted by such orders: the papal storerooms, supplying clothing, mostly new, to the poor, were staffed by the Franciscan Missionaries of Mary, and the St. Marta Clinic, for the poor mothers of Rome's ancient slums and newer *borgate,* was in the charge of members of the largest order of women religious in the Church, the Daughters of Charity of St. Vincent de Paul.

The *borgate,* the outlying sections of Rome, are rarely visited by tourists. Their residents are the poorest families of Rome who could not pay the rents of Rome's central city and, above all, the immigrants from Italy's depressed southern provinces. Urban sprawl took a particular form in Rome, with resourceful Italians constructing their own shelters, called *baracche,* and making them as livable as possible. Acres of these barracks spread throughout the suburbs around Rome, with municipal services such as water, sewage, and street lights, following later, if at all. Tiles of burnt-orange terra-cotta formed the flat roofs, often secured by heavy stones. The families showed that they did not expect to be moved by planting tiny gardens and vines. While the winter months were grim in the extreme, the spring and summer months displayed the ebullience of nature and of the Italian character. A few of the famous pines and cypresses of Rome grew undisturbed.

The "right on the ground" work to which the Missionaries of Charity were committed by their constitutions was exactly what was needed in the peripheries of the ancient city. Mother Teresa brought the Sisters to the parish of San Stefano. After living for a short time in a small house nearby, they moved one day into a *baracca* no different from that of their neighbors. They were only one row of barracks away from the Acquedotto Felice, an aqueduct of rich, red-brown stones that centuries earlier had brought drinking water to the fountain of Acqua Felice for the citizens of Rome. At first the authorities looked askance at the strange newcomers to the shantytown, but decided to let them be when it was clear that they could bring order and help to a neglected and often anarchic community. The Sisters arranged for the installation of electricity, with a meter so that they could pay for current. Many of the *baracche* dwellers had found ways to "tap into" electric sources and paid nothing. The authorities began a system of putting the word out to paying customers that at a certain time in the evening they were to turn off all lights. They would then sweep down on the illegal users of current whose bulbs were brightly shining.

The Sisters received their mail at an address in Tor Fiscale, named for the thirteenth-century tower which loomed above them. It had served as a tollgate in times past.

By the time I visited the Sisters with Mother Teresa in late April of 1973, they were a part of the Tor Fiscale community, their barracks-convent an almost incredible hub of activity. The Sisters had built a trellis which was already covered with vines and pink climbing roses clung to the fence and convent wall. Here and there, tiny flowers and feathery green plants sprouted from old oil cans. An ailanthus tree was growing tall, its leaves just showing the first light green tufts. Pale yellow butterflies glinted in the sun. The Sisters even had a dog which joined the battalion of Tor Fiscale dogs in barking whenever a car drove by.

Sister Stella, painfully thin but gifted with febrile energy, looked after the whole activity, speaking Italian with easy perfection. From what I knew of Malayalam, her native tongue, any other language would be child's play. She was superior of a community gradually becoming international with Sister Columkille from County Tyrone, Ireland, and an Italian Sister in addition to the eight Indian Sisters. The convent was one long barracks, with dormitory, washroom, kitchen, and refectory leading into one another. At one end was the parlor, painted white, with a rough table and a few unmatched chairs, a facsimile of the Calcutta parlor. The chapel was also painted white, but color rose up from the odd strips of red, blue, and brown carpet on the floor. Behind the altar and above a large crucifix were the words, HO SETE (I Thirst).

It was here that a priest in a wheelchair often said mass for the Sisters. Father Mario was preparing to join the Xaverian Missions in India or Burma when an automobile accident paralyzed him and killed his three companions. With his dream of an Eastern mission ended, he found joy in serving Sisters from the East.

Attached to the barracks-convent was a small fenced-off yard where the Sisters, hidden from public gaze, could hang their saris and grain-sack tunics to dry.

Mother Teresa was pleased with the large shedlike construction across the yard from the Sisters' quarters. Beginning in 1970, a group of English students had spent their summer holidays enlarging the convent and building the large shed with corrugated metal roof which was actually a community center.

"The students worked very hard," said Sister Stella. "They even dug foundations under the direction of old Alfredo. Then they learned from our people how to be bricklayers. The young people of Tor Fiscale joined in with them after a while and they became friends. Whatever they didn't finish, we did ourselves, painting and fixing."

Sister Stella laughed. "We had to learn how to do a lot of things. The Sisters are good carpenters."

"Our Sisters have become first-class builders," said Mother Teresa admiringly.

We saw the community in action: it was, in the Italian social work term, a *"polivalente"* center, one put to many uses. One room was an *asilo,* a day-care center for over sixty children of women who went into town to work, mostly domestic work. A woman who might have been in her late thirties brought her plump young son in a stroller and moved away, calling out, *"Ciao,* Gino." Mother Teresa put her hand on the hand of the child and smiled at him. The mother turned back. *"Sono io bestiola, ma vado alla messa,"* she said.

Then, unaccountably, she blessed herself in a self-conscious way and looked down. I was wondering if the equivalent of *bestiola* would be "lowlife" or "beastly" as the woman and her sister went out the metal gate. Their destination was the city where they jointly plied what has been referred to as the oldest of professions.

Young girls and women came to a sewing class, both hand sewing and practicing on fine machines. Some brushed up on reading since their literacy, a frail acquisition, often faded through disuse. At five o'clock in the afternoon, the benches in the largest room were filled as youngsters came for *dopo-scuola,* the afterschool program of study and recreation. Reading and study were next to impossible in the *baracche* where families of eight and more were packed into two or three rooms. An amazing transformation occurred when the rambunctious shining-eyed children were called in from the tiny playground. The Sisters were waiting for them and signaled them to slide into places on the benches. Books were taken out quietly and the Sisters were there to answer questions and provide help.

One or two Sisters went out during the morning hours to visit the homes of their neighbors. A mother might be ill and need someone to clean the barracks or prepare a meal. There were also the old people, living alone. Even in Italy, where the family is bound by bands of steel, there were old people, from the south, who were completely alone. I went with a Sister to an ancient survivor, sitting on a low stool and taking the sun in front of his whitewashed shanty.

"*Eccomi* (Here I am), Sister, waiting for you," he said, his gnarled face breaking into a smile so that his eyes could hardly be seen. With a bucket filled with water and a supply of soap, the Sister washed his dishes and then cleaned the *baracca.* She placed a bowl of cooked rice with dots of some kind of meat in it on his clean wooden table. Looking at the grimy, torn curtains, she told the old man, "Next time I'll bring new curtains; then your *baracca* will be nicer than ever." The old man got up off his stool to thank the Sister. He was a bent little man who did his best to kiss the Sister's hand with full dignity. She waved him goodbye and told him she would be back soon.

Another old gentleman of ninety-three, barely able to leave his cot in the mornings, was faithful to the anticlericalism rife among Latin European men. The Sister came regularly to make his life more comfortable and refused to take the few lire he offered her. Her explanation as to why she was caring for him freely and cheerfully brought mention of Jesus and His teachings of love for one another. Mother Teresa often recounted what happened one day. The old man said to the Sister, "You have brought me God. Now bring me the priest." He went to confession and returned to the sacraments of his early years in the dim past. He died soon afterward.

Another old man became so ill that he was taken to the hospital. He was known to all as someone who loved his wine, a friendly drunk. His cross toward the end of his life was that his stomach would no longer accept alcohol.

"We went to see Emilio in the hospital," said Sister Sylvia. "He was our friend. He did not live long once he left here. That drawing of an old man in our parlor is Emilio. One of our people did it. Nobody wants to forget Emilio."

On May 4, the parish of San Stefano was filled for a service of profession in which Mother Teresa received four young girls into the Missionaries of Charity. They exchanged the all-white sari of the novice for the blue-bordered habit of the full-fledged Missionary of Charity. Not only the residents of Tor Fiscale filled San Stefano, but friends and Co-Workers from every part of Rome. Hymns in Italian filled the air. Later, the largest room of the community center was the scene of a reception, with a cardinal in his red robes, several monsignori, and priests mingling with a great variety of guests, including Mother Teresa's brother, Lazar Bojaxhiu from Palermo. The Rome foundation had become a novitiate, with novices spending part of their time as usual in the actual work as preparation for their life commitment.

Lazar Bojaxhiu was profoundly impressed by the ceremony. "Those young girls so full of happiness as they give their lives away, so to speak. You see how they live here."

He turned to Mother Teresa. "I did not know you before. It is now that I come to know you."

Mother Teresa laughed. "You are always a boy."

We chatted after the reception.

"When I read about my sister," said Bojaxhiu, "I ask myself, 'is it *my* sister saying these things?' I finally put the question to her, 'How do you know what you will say at these meetings?'

"And she said, 'It will come to me at the time.' What faith! What confidence! Frankly, I had little of religion after I left home. When I was given a scholarship to study in Vienna and then at the Lycée, one of my colleagues was Enver Hoxha, now head of Albania. Russian representatives came to the Albanian students and picked out a few for special attention. Enver was one of them. He was taken to Moscow where he became a firm Communist. None of the boys in the Lycée had any interest in religion. Most of them were atheists. I was supposed to go from there to Saint-Cyr, but I had seen Italy and I had such a passion for it that I went to the military academy in Turin."

Bojaxhiu brought out a clipping from an Italian newspaper. "This is what is happening in Albania. A priest has been shot for baptizing a baby. His name was Father Stephan Kurti, and he was a distant relative of ours. The sister of our grandmother married a Kurti. He was imprisoned after the war as an anti-Communist and then freed for good conduct. In 1965 over two thousand mosques, churches, and religious buildings, Orthodox and Catholic, were demolished or used as warehouses or museums. For protesting the demolition of Catholic churches, he was imprisoned again. A woman in the prison camp, who had given birth to a child, asked him to baptize it in secret. He agreed, even though by the law of 1967, this could be dangerous to his life. He was tried by a 'people's tribune' in a desecrated Catholic church.

"The Albanian or Italian partisans would have killed me except for my wife. When the Americans liberated Italy, I went to an American colonel and said, 'I am a colonel of a surrendered army. I can work for you. I can drive a car. He made me his jeep driver and I earned 250,000 lire (about $350) a month."

Bojaxhiu was cast down by the state of Albania, the country for which his father had died, and in which his mother and sister had passed away, despite all efforts to bring them out. He was a man of open and sunny disposition and he soon recovered his equanimity.

"Just think, I did not see my sister for all those years until you came with her to Rome in 1960. After a few visits, I feel I know her."

Mother Teresa for a long time nursed a very special project for a team of Missionaries of Charity. She told me that she wanted them to work in Vatican City.

"But there are the Franciscan Missionaries of Mary and the St. Vincent de Paul Sisters there already," I pointed out.

"I don't mean that," Mother Teresa replied. "I mean a refuge for old men who would live and be cared for right in the heart of Vatican City."

She visualized it. "Perhaps there could be twelve of them, rejected by all. The Sisters would care for them and on Holy Thursday, when the Holy Father would wash the feet of the poor, he would have his own poor right there. Wouldn't that be beautiful?"

On a visit to the 108-acre State of Vatican City, I had seen a round tower, beautifully constructed and empty. I wondered if the tower could be the refuge Mother was dreaming of. When we asked about it, we discovered that the tower was just being converted by a squad of Vatican workers, the *Sampietrini.* It was to serve as a proper and private dwelling place for the Orthodox Patriarch Athenagoras who was journeying to Rome to talk with the pope after centuries of silence between the separated churches.

One afternoon, a cardinal dropped in at Tor Fiscale for an informal visit. Mother Teresa and the Sisters gathered round him as if he were their father. He was James Robert Knox and had been named a cardinal earlier that year. He had kept in constant touch with the Sisters after his crucial role in supporting the Missionaries of Charity in their effort to be recognized as a society of pontifical right.

The Archbishop Knox High School in Calcutta memorialized his ten-year stay in India. The school was opened by Mother Teresa for youngsters deprived of secondary school, who could only make it up by attending school in the evening hours.

It was Knox who had organized the visit of Pope Paul VI to Bombay for the Eucharistic Congress in 1964, when millions of non-Catholic Indians lined the papal route for *darshan,* the blessing accompanying the sight of a holy person. Knox was delighted when his friend Mother Teresa received as a gift from the Holy Father, the white Cadillac automobile which had been a gift to the Pope from Notre Dame University in South Bend. If the vehicle could have been converted to be used as an ambulance, or even as a hearse, Mother Teresa might have retained it. After all, it was a papal gift. She talked over the matter, and finally decided to raffle what to her was a "white elephant." She realized the sum of 460,000 rupees from the selling of the tickets. In a conversation with a Parsi woman who shared an Indian railway carriage with me, I learned that her nephew had won the automobile. As it was for him also a "white elephant," he sold it and sent a significant part of the proceeds to Mother Teresa.

As mentioned, the then Archbishop Knox had been the effective instrument of Mother Teresa's first overseas mission in Venezuela. If it seemed surprising that Mother Teresa would bring her work to Europe, a developed area, how much more surprising that she would bring it to Australia, a country without great extremes of riches or poverty. Yet, in September 1969, a team of Missionaries of Charity had arrived to start work in Australia. It was once more the quiet influence of James Robert Knox, who served as Melbourne's Archbishop from 1967 until called to Rome in 1974.

The cardinal, a mild man with a kind and deferential manner, displayed unaccustomed passion when he discussed racism. His antiracism increased during his time as apostolic delegate to British East Africa in the 1950s. He told of that period when the Kikiyu people, desperate at the sequestration of their ancestral lands under colonialism, and seeing no hope for their situation, took to resistance and violence. Hundreds were condemned to death. Knox was opposed to the executions and often stayed with the condemned men right up to the moment of execution.

Knox had an abiding concern for the native people of his own Australia. It was to serve them, Australia's dark people, the aborigines, that Mother Teresa was invited to Australia. After visiting them in their "reserve" or "camp" in Bourke, New South Wales, she accepted the call. She related in Rome an occurrence that almost prevented her trip.

"Whenever I go on a long trip, something happens to me," she said smiling.

A few days before she left for Australia, she fell out of bed. She hit her arm.

"The bone was out here," she said, pointing to a spot on her forearm above the left elbow. The doctor told her she could not travel.

"I will have to go," she told him, so the doctor bound up the arm and the whole body.

"In traveling the binding was worse than the trouble with the arm. I asked the Sister to take it off. Later the bone came out again. But I could manage. Remember," she smiled, "before I left for Venezuela, I had the accident to my head."

Just a year after their arrival, I saw the Missionaries of Charity among the aborigines. It was in August 1970. The occasion presented itself when I was asked with Dorothy Day to participate in a series of meetings on poverty and peacemaking in Sydney and Melbourne. When I mentioned that I would be leaving Sydney for Bourke, the response came in two expressions: "Back of Bourke?" and then, "What for?"

"Back of Bourke" came from an old poem and meant "back of beyond." Beyond Bourke was the outback, the dry heartland of the Australian continent with its millions of square miles of desert, an expanse almost equaling the area of the United States. The Sisters were informed that I was coming. To reach them I flew over the Blue Mountains flanking Sydney. These gave way to a red clay expanse and finally to a flat expanse the color of faded khaki.

In Bourke, the sun shone blindingly on the long, off-white structure, looking something like a hangar for a small plane. It was the Sisters' convent. A Sister with a dark, round face and broad nose appeared behind the screen door in answer to my knock. I climbed the three wooden steps to enter the building and realized that though I am of medium height, I towered over her. She was no more than four feet ten in height and unmistakably a tribal Indian.

"I am Sister Scholastica," she said with a smile. She sat me down in a little parlor before a table covered with a white cloth. A piece of muslin served as a curtain over the one window. Two other Sisters came in, Sister Shushuma and Sister Christopher. I recognized with what exquisite charity Mother Teresa had chosen the team. These three Sisters were all from the Ranchi area, all members of India's tribal community. They were not too different from Australia's aboriginal community. They were outside the Indian caste system and were apt to be considered on a par with the outcastes or *harijans,* just as the aborigines were outside the accepted classes in Australian society.

The superior soon returned, Sister Laetitia, a Bengali. Soon afterward,

Sister Celine, a member of the so-called St. Thomas Christians of Kerala, a proud minority among India's Christians, appeared. The Sisters' "hangar" was at the edge of Bourke. Near them was a project of new houses, about a dozen of which had been completed and the foundations of others already laid.

"Our people are moving into the new homes. It will be quite a change from the camp, where they have been living," said Sister Laetitia. "We will take you there tomorrow."

As I ate a meal of lamb curry and an apple, I saw a group of women with dark and not-so-dark faces enter another section of the building. They were coming for a sewing class, preparing to make curtains and bedcovers and other supplies needed in their new houses. The building, I realized, was not only a convent. Half of it was a center for activities for the aborigines.

There were cooking classes where the mothers practiced planning meals and preparing foods that could be stored. For schoolchildren, there was help with their lessons and a room with children's books and art supplies for drawing and painting.

We started out early the next day to visit the camp.

"They need patient help to set up housekeeping and care for their homes. Over at the camp we are working very slowly and simply. The families let us know what they want and need, and then we can work together."

We were driving along in the Sisters' small bus. An occasional gum tree was so dust-laden that it scarcely broke the monotony of the landscape. It was a windy day and the sun though bright did not bring much warmth.

A dirt road led into the camp which turned out to be an acre of dun-colored earth around which, in a semicircle, were huts of corrugated iron, called "humpies." Some had patches of rust. Others were painted bright green or yellow.

"There are thirty-three families in the camp," said Sister Laetitia. "The related families live close to one another."

At the left as we entered was a hole in the earth filled with garbage. This was the "rubbish tip" for the camp, but strewn over the camp were cans and many bottles that gave back spurts of light.

A large building set apart from the others was also of corrugated iron, but of a silvery newness.

"That is the 'ablution block,'" explained Sister Laetitia. "They can all do their laundry here. The water can be heated."

Our first visit was to Mrs. Violet Willow Taylor, a youngish woman sitting in a wheelchair, her wasted legs and feet bare. She was a victim of polio. Her skin was fairly light and her wavy hair was pitch-black and hung about her shoulders. Cradled in her arms was a baby wrapped in a thick woolen shawl against the wind. The shawl slipped from the baby's head and a round tearful face looked up at us. The child was pale.

"Baby has pain in his ear again," said Mrs. Taylor as the child started crying uncontrollably.

"We'll have to get the doctor again," said Sister. "How is the rest of the family?"

"They're all fine but baby," said the mother.

"There are so many ear infections and bronchial troubles among our families," said Sister. "They have so little room that the infections pass from one to the other."

Mrs. Taylor, I found, was one of four Willow sisters living in the camp with their families.

"Mr. Taylor has been wonderful since his wife got polio," explained Sister Laetitia. "What a thoughtful husband. He carries her everywhere and helps her and the children in every way. They have five children. He works on the roads."

We met Violet's sisters, the three other women in the Willow family, Ruby with seven children, Patsy with four, and Evelyn, the youngest, with two.

In another house was a woman whose father at ninety-seven was now taking his ease after working most of his life making and repairing fences on the stations, the great farms for sheep and cattle. Mrs. Rita McKillop, a placid woman, had eleven children.

"Three of my boys are married," she told me. "My married daughter's moved into one of the new houses near the Sisters. That should be nice for 'er."

The children were in school.

"Nearly half of the children in the Bourke school are part-aborigine," Sister Laetitia told me. "As you can see, there are very few pure aborigines here. The trouble is that the children are easily discouraged from going to school; a cold day, any slight excuse will keep them home. That's why we bought the bus. We come early in the morning and pick up the children for school. Attendance is much better and they are doing better at school."

"You're the bus drivers of the school bus," I remarked, "as well as everything else."

"That's what they needed from us," the Sister replied.

"What is hard is to see them leave school at fifteen, no matter what we do. The boys and young men take seasonal jobs, shearing sheep, driving cattle, or picking fruit or cotton. They sometimes come back with a lot of money since they have no expenses. One young aborigine came back here with three thousand dollars. For about three months he took everybody to the pictures and bought drinks for his mates and presents for the women. At the end of that time he had nothing. Sharing is a beautiful part of their culture and when they lived off the land, it was how they had to live. But now, it means that they think little of tomorrow.

"It is the same with everything. When they have money, they eat well. They like stews which they can make on their own little iron stoves. But after they spend their money, they live on bread and syrup or bread and jam. Another reason to get the children to school is that they get a good lunch there.

"Of course, they get pensions from the government and the children who continue secondary school get a monthly grant. So few take advantage. Drinking is a scourge and they start so young."

The Sister visited from house to house and chatted with each family. It was like a friend visiting other friends and introducing another friend from faraway.

There was time to talk with Sister Scholastica who told me she had come from the village of Phulwartoli in the Ranchi area. It was a village of twenty-five families, all Catholic.

"In our part of the country," she explained, "the whole village will be Catholic, or it will be Protestant or the people's religion."

Her father had died when she was five years of age, and her mother could not work their plot of four acres, so she went half-shares with the men who cultivated the rice and vegetables.

"We have much paddy land around the village," she said. "My mother sent us all to school on the money we got from the field. I went to a boarding school in Ranchi. After leaving school, I helped my mother and I also helped with the marriages of my two brothers. I was reading about the work of Mother Teresa in our Catholic paper. Then I decided to become a Sister."

One morning I went to the camp with Sister Christopher. Our longest visit was with Lucy, the only full-blooded aborigine in the camp. Her color was a rich black while the rest of the camp residents varied from walnut color to fair. Lucy thought she might be ninety years of age and seemed to be the only one who had any remembrance of the old language. She was teaching some words to Sister.

She held out her hand. *"Maya."* She pointed to her eyes, *"pubroo,"* and to her ear, *manga.* These were the sounds I heard. The old woman was pleased that she merited such close and loving attention. We had a wonderful morning. It was hard to say who enjoyed it more, Lucy, Sister Christopher, or me.

A local Bourke man conversant with aboriginal history confirmed what the Missionaries of Charity had told me about the strong sense of community among the aboriginal people.

"Yes, the Sisters have it right. The 'abos,' that is how we term them, have a communal culture. They are in a transitional state, a 'no-man's land' culturally. They have not yet crossed over into the culture of individual earning and accumulation. Employers in a hurry to get a job finished can never get used to having their 'abo' workmen just take off and disappear into the outback. They turn up weeks or months later—ready for work again. But the job's done."

That was the "walkabout" I had been hearing about, a slipping away into an earlier freedom.

The experience of the Missionaries of Charity in Bourke gave rise to an invitation to open a house in Katherine, in the Northern Territory. There, two thousand miles away, the Sisters settled among others of Australia's first inhabitants. These lived closer to their original culture.

While the Sisters' initial foundations in Australia were for the continent's first inhabitants, they were soon involved in working others of society's marginal groups, alcoholics and isolated people, ill and aged. So successful were they in Melbourne, that they were given a farm in Greenvale to help alcoholics toward complete rehabilitation. In typical fashion, as soon as another agency could take over the farm, the Missionaries of Charity surrendered it. They were following their constitutions in giving a service only until they could find others who could do the work better and in a more lasting way.

Mother Teresa told a story of the simple task with which the Melbourne work began. Mother Teresa went to the room of an old man living alone and gave it a thorough cleaning. He sat in the dark while a beautiful lamp, covered with dust, was never used. She asked him why he did not light the lamp and his answer was that there was no one to light it for.

"If the Sisters come to visit you, will you light it?" she asked.

"Yes," he replied, "I will light it if I hear the sound of a human voice."

When Mother Teresa returned to Melbourne, the old man greeted her as his friend.

Beautiful things grew out of the Sisters' presence in Bourke. I wondered how significant it must have been to the aborigines to see that the shelter of the Sisters was much less commodious than their homes in the new housing project. The Sisters succeeded in intertwining the lives of the aborigines with that of "white" Australians as a sequel to having intertwined their own lives with the aborigines. A Christmas letter from Bourke described a Christmas party with "white" Australians in which a group of aborigine women played guitars and sang carols to hearty applause.

"Our ladies," wrote the Sister, "were surprised at the gifts they have. All these years they could never guess that their gifts and their lives could be meaningful to others."

She told how groups of aboriginal children were flown to Melbourne to spend holidays with Australian families. During these holidays, the children were invited to Raheen, the home of Mother Teresa's friend, Archbishop Knox, whose joy it was to be host at parties for them. The women in the sewing classes became so adept that they not only met the needs of their homes and families but were able to take orders for children's school uniforms from various schools.

Movements for aboriginal rights had germinated in many parts of Australia, with the support of religious groups and, in particular, youth groups. There were speeches, marches, and fasts supporting the return of large tracts of land to their original owners. In the meantime, aborigines and part-aborigines responded to those who told them through daily cooperation that they were children of God. The Sisters were not doing great things, but simply the "things that no one else had time for." That included listening with love and care to words that had survived out of a dim and often murderously cruel past, *maya, pubroo, manga.*

How to work for the "poorest of the poor" in a country where the word "poor" is not to be mentioned? That was the challenge put to Mother Teresa when she answered a call to Tanzania. During her second visit to Venezuela, she mentioned that the Bishop of Tabora had sent an invitation to bring Sisters to his diocese. Mother Teresa said that she was going to visit Tabora as soon as possible. I asked her where it was and she smiled. "I believe it is near the middle of Africa, but I am not sure." Her trust in the bishops, the official "teaching church," was so absolute that she would have made her way there if it had been on the equator.

The Tabora foundation, like that of Venezuela, was also a child of the Second Vatican Council. Dr. Ferdinand Perier of Calcutta, as well as Archbishop Knox, described the work of Mother Teresa and the Sisters to other Council fathers. The Bishop of Tabora needed the work of such women and sent an invitation to Mother Teresa.

After her visit to Tabora, she told me how she dealt with the matter of not talking about the poor.

"In Dar-es-Salaam, when I was explaining the work of our Sisters so that they could get visas, a man in the ministry said, 'Here, we do not single out poor people. We do not want to use that word "poor" for some of our people.' "

He told Mother Teresa that Tanzania was not a rich country, but a country in which everyone had to struggle together for a better future.

Mother Teresa's vocabulary was flexible.

"I simply told him that we would come to Tanzania to work for 'our people.' "

She must have made it clear that what she meant by "our people" was not the Indian community of Tanzania, which was sometimes resented because of their prominence in trade, but rather people who had special needs that could be cared for with free service.

The Missionaries of Charity arrived in September 1968 and were able to start their work immediately because Archbishop Mark Mihayo of Tabora had arranged for the White Sisters of Africa to turn over a large compound to them.

It was a morning of brilliant clarity when I arrived in Tabora in a Fokker Friendship plane that brought me direct from Dar es Salaam, Harbor of Peace, on the Indian Ocean. It was in the fall of 1970, following the visit to Australia. The city was not equatorial, but temperate, situated at an altitude of nearly four thousand feet. As Mother Teresa had said, it was situated near the middle of Africa. It was also nearly in the center of Tanzania and had once been a meeting place for caravans. Much of the trading had been in ivory and enslaved human beings. The plane flew quite low and I was told to watch out for small groves of mango trees. The African men and women being carried off for the slave trade a few centuries earlier would be allowed to stop every twenty miles or so at a watering place. There they would eat mangos and throw the pits away; hence the small thick groves that grew up. I did see such clumps of trees and I was willing to accept the explanation.

Sister Shanti, the tall fair-skinned superior, met me at the heavy wooden gate of the compound. She had been in Tabora only a year. Her face was luminous with a beauty that was deeper than physical. The compound was in the outskirts of a city marked by the gleaming white minarets of mosques, a Catholic cathedral, an Anglican church, other Christian churches, many shops, and an impressive, newly built produce market. Along the streets were jacaranda trees forty feet high. The flame trees that I had known in Latin America here flaunted flowers of brilliant purple.

The compound was like a little village constructed on a square and surrounded by its own wall. While in India the Sisters lived at some distance from their people and thus could be seen walking on the streets of such cities as Calcutta, here they only had to walk across a dirt courtyard to reach their charges. I was soon standing in front of the old people's home which stretched about a hundred feet along the entire back wall of the compound.

"Our buildings are at least seventy-five years old," said Sister Shanti. "They were constructed of mud bricks held together by timber and then plastered. We've already had one accident. The back wall crumbled after a heavy rain. We were grateful to the White Sisters of Africa for giving us this place, but we will soon have to have new buildings."

She explained that they were constantly having the buildings repaired and shored up and that more work would have to be done before the rains came in October.

There were thirty-nine old people, most of them women. On seeing me, a few of the women put a hand over their mouths. They moved it rapidly back and forth, delivering an unearthly, high-pitched yodeling sound. This was their way of welcoming me.

One of the most ancient of the women was Catherine, blind and disfigured, most likely by smallpox. She remembered when the Germans had administered their East Africa territories from Tabora. She sat in the sun with a group of women with various handicaps, some sightless, some almost sightless, some bent nearly double. Two blind men, Samuel and Joseph, sat talking together at the end of the row near piles of firewood. All were waiting for the meal the Sisters were preparing in two vats over a wood fire in the kitchen. Food supplies from Catholic Relief Services, including corn, oil, and powdered milk, were reaching the Sisters as part of the Food for Peace program distributed to many Tanzanian welfare centers. The Sisters were making a stew of corn, which they called maize, with some meat. The meal would be rounded out with spinach and oil. The quadrangle was well-arranged. To the right of the entrance was the convent, a dormitory, refectory, and chapel. Behind these mud-dried walls, it seemed to me, was the ultimate simplicity in religious life. To the left was the parlor, a medical supply center, and a large kitchen, all cement-floored. Along the left wall were three nurseries for about twenty-five or thirty children. The facing right wall had no buildings. Just behind it was a luxuriant mango tree that gave some shade to the compound. A large section of the compound was given to a garden of dark green spinach called *chicha.* In among the spinach were bunches of orange-colored chilios, pepperlike plants, which gave flavor to the cooked spinach.

These and some papaw trees had been planted by the Sisters. Three tall coconut palms had been there when the Sisters came, as had been a climbing plant with white flowers. The scent of minty spice from these flowers was a blessing in the crowded quadrangle where odors could at times be overpowering.

Sister Shanti explained that several of the children in the nurseries were only given to the Sisters until a relative could care for them.

"This baby girl was born in the Tabora Hospital. She was a first child and the mother died giving birth. The father brought her here. He asked us to care for her until he can arrange his life. I know he will come back for her."

The people had soon learned that Sister Shanti was a medical doctor. The police van would draw up to the door to put an abandoned child into the hands of the Sisters.

Dark heads looked up from mats on the floor.

"These little boys will be left here, I think. They are twins. We call them Cosmas and Damian. Their mother was walking toward Tabora, probably to the hospital, when the babies were born on the roadside. She died there. The grandfather brought them to us. They are Catholic." (Cosmas and Damian were twin brothers from Arabia martyred for their faith.)

About a quarter of all Tanzanians are said to be Catholic, I learned, and about thirty percent Muslim, while the remainder are of various Christian groups or traditional beliefs.

"We are in touch with the social welfare people about Cosmas and Damian," Sister Shanti said. "They may locate other relatives.

"Asmani is a Muslim child. He is six now and reminds us that he is not to eat pork. We are very careful of the diet here. Mzee came here from the hospital. He was paralyzed a few years ago by a blow to the head. No one seems to want him. He must be about five."

Mzee put out his left hand and took mine. His right hand was withered as was his right leg. His black eyes were shining as he gave me a happy smile. In cribs nearby were Pili, whose head was nearly as large as his torso, and Edisi, whose legs were wasted. Both had been deserted, Sister explained.

The Sisters were soon busy feeding the infants and children amid much teasing and laughter. Helping them were African girls who had finished schooling in Tabora schools. Sisters Amrita, Gregory, Bertrilla, Regina, and Carmen had originated in different parts of the Indian subcontinent, from Bengal to Kerala and the Karnataka state, bordering on the Arabian Sea. They blended easily with the young Africans, all communicating in Swahili. When it came time for their meal, the old people attacked it with relish, spooning it up from enamel soup plates and holding them out for more. Then came the great washing up with water from the one large faucet in the compound.

I sat in the parlor while the Sisters took their midday rest. I had been learning about *Ujamaa,* the concept under which Tanzania was mobilizing the people to work together to become self-supporting. *Ujamaa* meant familyhood, togetherness for self-reliance, or even socialism. Julius Nyerere, the President, spent time working in an *Ujamaa* village, and young people who took advantage of higher education, which was free, had to give in return some years of national service. *Ujamaa* called for outlying villages to be grouped together so that the needs of an agricultural country could be better planned and distributed. The aim was that in the new villages, schooling, as well as medical and social services and safe drinking water, could be made available to all. At that time, over a thousand *Ujamaa* villages had been organized, some as small as thirty families.

As I looked at the activity of the Tabora compound, I meditated on the fact that in the best of welfare systems, even in the developed societies, there were those who fell between the cracks. Here in a corner of Tabora was an *Ujamaa* village expressly for those who could not contribute to the new society. Catherine, Samuel, Pili, and Edisi needed an *Ujamaa* village based solely on love. Sister Shanti and five Sisters had created it and were living in it.

I wondered aloud to Sister Shanti how the six Sisters, even helped by the African girls, three of whom assisted them with night duty, could manage a community of so many helpless people day after day, caring for the sick among them, growing food for them, building fires, washing and cleaning endlessly.

Sister Shanti smiled. "Our work does not end at the gate of the compound. We have to help those who come to the gate, and we work in the country around here."

In a little while, she opened the gate and there, waiting, was a knot of men. Among them were two figures who carved themselves in my memory. One held a bowl between the palms of his hands. The fingers had been eaten away long before by leprosy. "*Chakula*—food, food—" he said, and the stew was ladled into his receptacle. Another man, tall and well-built, took a few active steps toward the gate. He said nothing. His bowl was under his arm. He balanced it in the crook of his right elbow. His right arm ended in a rough stump. The other hand had seemingly been hacked away, leaving only the thumb. He ate hungrily, scooping up the stew directly into his open mouth with his thumb.

"Sizia comes regularly," said Sister Shanti. "He was a thief who repeated his crime." The strict Muslim code, I discovered, was enforced in the countryside during the various European occupations. Theft brought the punishment of the amputation of a hand. A repeater lost all but the thumb of the other hand. Generally it was enough to lose one hand.

"Sizia's only way of life is begging. He is completely alone. His family must have deserted him," Sister Shanti explained.

The man stared at us even as he scooped up the food. I had a desire to communicate with him, to talk with this injured creature. Sister Shanti recounted that he talked little, but he did tell her that he was not like the other men who came to the gate; he was the one with no religion.

One morning, I accompanied Sister Amrita and Sister Gregory along a sandy road to Malebi, some miles out of Tabora. The Sisters drove slowly and carefully in the aged station wagon over a route they took three times a week. How to describe Malebi. Briefly, it was referred to as a Paupers' Camp, and camp it was. Two large sheds had been built in a cleared field and in them were gathered the local beggars, along with the indigent, the helpless, the old without families or whose families could not care for them.

As we drove up, the women sitting in the sun began a welcoming yodel such as I had first heard in the Tabora compound, only here it was louder and more piercing and echoed throughout the countryside.

"They are always glad to see us," said Sister Amrita. "That is the greeting from women and girls."

Sister Amrita and Sister Gregory went to work, bathing the women crippled with arthritis, combing their hair, washing their clothes, sweeping the various rooms in the women's shed. It was a time of recreation for the women, who talked volubly with the Sisters. One expression came over and over again, *"Mungu aku Bariki, Mama."* Sister Gregory spelled it and translated it. "God bless you, lady."

All was done under the watchful eyes of the director of Malebi who saw to it that the old people were fed and cared for in a general way. His aides were a number of young men, sent to him by the courts, first offenders, or sentenced for a petty crime. One of their tasks was caring for a large garden where much of the food for the camp was grown.

The director took us into the men's shed, where the Sisters went straight to the bed of Salum, totally crippled by arthritis. Despite obvious pain, the old man smiled when the Sisters had bathed him and made his bed. Over in the corner was Paul, formerly a town beggar, who showed me his thirteen books. He pointed to the pictures while he studiously pored over a printed book. He held it upside down. He found out that I was Christian and informed me that Jesus was born in Mwanza but died in Tabora.

In workmanlike fashion, the Sisters went from room to room sweeping out dust and rubbish and depositing it in a bin. The place was swept at other times, but the Sisters found it helped to do the rooms thoroughly on Monday, Wednesday, and Friday.

Sister Amrita (meaning immortal or deathless in Hindi) and Sister Gregory seemed to enjoy their visit to this out-of-the-way center of need. It came to me that the Paupers' Camp was nothing but the "workhouse" of an earlier stage of history, when the indigent of English towns were gathered into one place so that they would not assail the sensibilities of respectable citizens by public begging. The Sisters referred to the Paupers' Camp as the Village of Peace.

"Sister Shanti only comes when someone has become ill," explained Sister Gregory. "The director comes for her in emergencies."

Sister Shanti, in fact, was a person on demand in villages in a wide radius around Tabora. She asked me to accompany her to Ipuli, Upuge, and Cheyo. Cheyo was a community of no more than seventy people, but around it were tiny communities with perhaps a thousand people scattered among the *shamba.* It was in Cheyo that Sister Shanti sat on a bench under a mango tree to see the patients that came to her. After a while, the people constructed a two-room mud and twig hut, the first room, a waiting room with roughhewn benches, and the second an examination room for Sister.

"We find so many of our people have red worms, hookworm anemia, bilharzia, and rheumatoid arthritis. Many of the pregnant mothers need special care. I do what I can and then send them to Tabora Hospital."

Another name for bilharzia, I discovered, was the common work, "flukes," or intestinal parasites.

We saw women carrying water for their families from an unprotected water hole in old kerosene cans. I wondered how they could be as strong and healthy as they seemed.

At Upuge, a village of Catholics, we went to morning mass, the people having been called by striking an impressive drum standing at the church door. The mass was celebrated in Swahili and the responses from the whole congregation were in the same tongue. The hymns sung with gusto to African tunes were accompanied by enthusiastic clapping.

The next village was Ipuli, where Sister Shanti went to visit a woman whose husband had just died. On the way, she coached me on how to behave. We found the middle-aged woman sitting disconsolately before her hut. Her head was wrapped in a gray bandanna. Sister bent over her, talking softly and leaving a gift. When it was my turn, I said the required words of sorrow, only one of which I remembered later, *opole.* The widow replied gently in Swahili. Then I quietly left the expected gift of money. This was added to many such money gifts. I supposed the custom grew out of the hard life that a widow could expect.

As we left the village, Sister stopped the car and began picking the small orange chilios from the bushes near the road. Like Mother Teresa, the Sisters wasted nothing and saved everything.

Returning to Tabora, Sister Shanti told me of the Goan origin of her family. It had been four hundred years since her family had left Goa for Mangalore. They then settled in Bombay where she had done her university studies. After four years working in a Bombay pharmaceutical house, she learned about the work of Mother Teresa through an article. It was in 1959, and she decided that she wanted to be a Missionary of Charity and was accepted by Mother Teresa. After her novitiate, she began her medical studies at Nilratan Medical College of Calcutta University, specializing in Hansen's disease, or leprosy.

Sister Shanti introduced me to the White Sisters and White Fathers of Tabora. The well-constructed convent of the White Sisters was on the far side of the compound wall. In fact, the towering mango tree giving shade to the compound was in their garden. There now were only three or four White Sisters where once there must have been dozens, since the cool, high-roofed chapel had obviously been built for a large group. As I knelt in the chapel with its gray marble floor, I thought of the contributions of the White Sisters and Fathers of Africa, actually called the Society of Missions of Africa. They had pioneered in education and reconciliation between Christianity and the Muslim culture of Africa in particular. Founded in Algiers in 1868 by Cardinal Charles Lavigerie, they had moved into the interior of Africa as their numbers grew. The term "White Father" came from their wearing white garments like the Arab people of North Africa. The Sisters followed in also wearing white habits.

At the house of the White Fathers in Tabora were the archives of decades of work by men who gave their lives to the African peoples of the region. One file set my imagination on fire—the file on *Freibriefe.* These were documents announcing that a slave had been purchased and set free. Tabora, earlier called Kaseh, was an important center for the slave trade.

"There is a ruined building at the edge of town that used to be the slave mart," the White Father informed me. "When the Fathers had enough money, they would go down and redeem as many of the captured Africans as they could."

I held in my hands the *Freibriefe* for Mbambo, aged twenty-four, and for Misalu and Kalekua, both aged about thirty. Acting against slavery, one of the greatest crimes of history, Cardinal Lavigerie had denounced it far and wide. In 1888, he joined with leaders of other Christian churches at a London meeting which brought to public attention existing situations of enslavement. Along with his passionate denunciations went the work of his followers who defended the dignity and brotherhood of man in the only way they could. Like Mother Teresa, the priest who redeemed a slave must have been convinced that when one could not change a system, one could still give witness by serving the person hurt or victimized by it.

I wondered how the Missionaries of Charity would continue to manage with the crumbling compound and what would happen during the rainy seasons to come. The answer came in time.

The large, solidly constructed convent and grounds of the White Sisters became theirs. They moved the children and old people into the more commodious quarters. It was a juxtaposition of the older and newer Church that was occurring similarly around the world. The White Sisters, after a glorious history in areas like Tanzania, were declining in numbers and their work diminishing. The church, renewing itself, had placed near them the instruments of renewal, young sisters from Asia. One thought of little Francis, the poor man, who was the instrument of renewing the Church over seven hundred years earlier.

Mother Teresa arrived in Amman, Jordan, on July 16, 1970. She came from Rome with five Sisters, Sisters Damien, Pascal, Susan, Christine, and Clarence. This signaled the entry of the Missionaries of Charity into the Middle East, the troubled bridge between Europe and Asia. It was not surprising that their first experience was a "baptism of fire." The next team of Sisters for the Middle East settled in Gaza, Israel, in 1973, and in 1979, Mother Teresa brought Sisters to Beirut, Lebanon.

Mother Teresa decided to stay with the Sisters in Amman for six weeks, and it was well that she did. It was August 30 when Mother Teresa left the little team with her blessing, to return to India. On the day that she left them, the Sisters heard the first shots of what was to escalate into a ten-day civil war in September.

The Sisters' first home was with a community of Arab Sisters, but with Mother Teresa's help, they were soon settled in a flat that served as a convent. Besides learning Arabic, to which they applied themselves immediately, they began to learn how to respond to the culture and living habits of the people around them.

The noise of the shooting on the evening of August 30 did not unduly disturb the Sisters. Sister Damien described the noise of the shooting as "heavy Dewali," referring to the joyfully noisy festival of lights in India. "Of course, we did not know much," she related, "so we went to sleep."

The next day, the girl who taught them Arabic asked them if they had slept. They told her they had.

"She congratulated us on our art of sleeping," Sister Damien recounted, "but gave us many a good advice regarding bombing and shooting. Thanks to her, when the civil war began, we knew what to do."

The art or gift of sleep was something one noted in the Missionaries of Charity, from Mother Teresa on to the Sisters who settled in the noisy hearts of the world's great cities.

On September 13, their house shook with bombing that came so close that a house on a nearby hill was completely blown up.

Sister Damien commented, "We did not know why this Dewali was going on." The Sisters ventured out to cross the road to attend church, but stopped to try to understand the words of a man who was shouting at them. They did not know enough Arabic but realized that he was also shooting in their direction. He missed them, so they were able to attend church and return safely.

One night a group of armed men knocked at the door and demanded entry. The men, to the Sisters' eyes, looked fierce and frightening, but they merely looked over the flat and went away.

Soon the rain of bombs and mortar shells prevented all unnecessary movement and destroyed the art of sleeping. The immediate area of the convent suffered no direct hits, but all the glass in the outer rooms was shattered by the heavy artillery. The Sisters, with a small group of children, prayed, ate, and slept in the corridor of the house. Once two Sisters left the protection of the four walls to dash out to bring medicine to the housekeeper of the priest across the road. The priest himself had braved the firing to get help. The woman later recovered.

One night, while they were awake praying, a light pierced the darkness. It crept under the door and moved about the room. It took some time for the fearful Sisters to realize that the light came from low-flying helicopters searching for enemies. At midnight, a few nights later, the Sisters heard the crying of hundreds of voices, "*Allah akbar.*" (God is great.) At the same time, church bells began to ring. One of the Sisters ran to the Arab Sisters to find out if peace had come. She was told that it was not peace, but the people, fearing that the war was coming closer to them, were calling out to God to spare their lives. The Arab Sister advised the Missionaries of Charity to try to sleep.

"But," remarked Sister Damien, "can anyone imagine going to sleep hearing the people's cry echoing in the mountains?"

The violence was closing in on their quarter when the fighting stopped and the people could go out to find and bury their dead.

Mother Teresa told a story of those days. The Sisters got to a telephone and as she put it, "They made a trunk call to me. They told me about the violence, and they wanted to know if they should stay. I listened to them and we talked it over. They were willing to stay there. Before hanging up, I said, 'Call me up when you are dead.' They laughed and went back to praying."

Only a Mother whose love had been proved could have evoked laughter by such joking about life and death.

The Sisters spent the days after peace had been restored bringing food and medicines to children, to the ill, and to the wounded. The "baptism of fire" had served to bring them close to the suffering people. Within two years, the Sisters were accepted in the entire area and had worked out a schedule that took them to many centers of need. To their clinic in a Bedouin village came two hundred people, many of them children. In Karamah, on the banks of the River Jordan, Sisters Damien, Pascal, and Christine also had a clinic for people who were still rebuilding their destroyed homes. At a home for beggars, the handicapped, and those they called "mental people," the three Sisters not only gave medical aid, but regularly bathed and cleaned the residents. The old men always begged for cigarettes from the Sisters. In Misdar, one of the poorest quarters of Amman, the Sisters brought medical help to the infants and children. In the Hashmi refugee camp, the Mother and Child Clinic was a center not only for medical help but for supplementary feeding of bread and milk to malnourished children.

On January 1, 1977, the Sisters, now fluent in Arabic, opened their own home for the destitute. They called it the "Home of Peace." It was situated on the outskirts of Amman in the midst of wheat fields, vines, and olive trees. Besides the aged and homeless, there were multihandicapped persons and those who were deaf and dumb. For the few blind persons, the Sisters were given free places in the local hospital if surgery could help them. The home started with forty-two men and twenty-four women, mostly Muslim.

"Their faith is deep," wrote the Sisters, "and they often talk about God. Once a week, a Sheik comes to pray with the Mohammedans and a mass is held for the Christians. Before and after meals, the Christians and Mohammedans say prayers. Those who die here, die in peace."

The reports from the Sisters were revealing in what they omitted, or passed over casually, as well as in what they included. It is hard to imagine how, in the Home of Peace, some dozens of people, many handicapped and helpless, could be fed, bathed, and fully cared for when water had to be carried from a well. Even after water was piped in, the Sisters were still managing without electric lights.

In three continents, Europe, Australia, and Africa, and in the troubled bridge between East and West, the Missionaries of Charity were putting flesh on a vision, a vision caught from the charism of Mother Teresa. It was articulated in the constitutions which they studied regularly and nourished by Mother Teresa's visits and letters. In addition, a communication on rough mimeographed paper was regularly circulated among the Sisters all around the world. It was a sharing of their experiences among the world's poorest and was called *Ek Dil,* an expression describing the unity among the Sisters in their far-flung houses.

Ek Dil in Hindi, stands for "One Heart."

13

The Mango Showers of Calcutta

Dorothy Day and I arrived in Calcutta on the last day of August 1970. After a visit to Australia, we arrived just in time for a *hartal*, a one-day general strike.

It was close to midnight when our plane put down at Dum Dum Airport. We did not expect Mother Teresa to be there to meet us; yet, as we emerged into the blinding light of the waiting room, there she was. A garland of white flowers hung over her arms. First, she put her hands together in the Indian greeting, and then, gravely put the wreath over the head of Dorothy Day. "Welcome to Calcutta and India." It was Dorothy Day's one and only visit to India.

Sister Gertrude put the garland around my neck with the same welcoming words. Not even the Swami-founder of the Krishna Consciousness Movement, who was on the same plane with us and was similarly garlanded by his waiting followers, received a more Indian welcome than we did.

We were introduced to Chloe Wing of the American Consulate who offered us the hospitality of her home. Then we emerged from the air-conditioned terminal into the steamy Bengal night for a ride into the heart of the city.

"It is better not to go out on the streets at all on Martyrs' Day," Mother Teresa said. "The West Bengal Government has called in the Indian Army," added Sister Gertrude. "It is not just the strike, but there may be quite a bit of violence."

Calcutta was still scourged not only by want and suffering that constricted the heart, but still in the throes of seemingly endless violence. We listened to the radio during the one-day strike for Martyrs' Day and heard how a van carrying prisoners had been attacked by acid bombs. Three policemen were blinded. Five policemen were injured in another attack. The Day of the Martyrs seemed to provide chiefly an excuse for violence.

Some told us that it commemorated all Indians who had suffered and died under colonialism, while others insisted that the martyrs were a group of Bengali peasants shot in the act of "liberating" large stocks of rice. I wondered how the city managed to survive at all, with its precarious life and order threatened from so many sources.

Then another threat presented itself. It revealed, as little else could, the way Mother Teresa and the Missionaries of Charity were woven into the very life of Calcutta. It disclosed how people spontaneously approached Mother Teresa in their need, no matter what form that need would take, even that of flood.

By September 1970, the monsoon rains were already over. When a light but steady rain began, we were told, "We call these the mango showers. They will not last long."

But the showers became heavier and heavier and beat down on the city for more than a week. Water collected in the main streets and stopped all traffic, including the buses and tramcars that brought people to work. Unnumbered clusters of huts made of bamboo matting, perched against the protection of the walls of railway stations and the British cemetery, or upright and leaning crazily against each other in the *bustees,* were mercilessly battered.

The only people of Calcutta who gained from the disaster of the mango showers were the rickshaw *wallahs.* I had not believed that I would allow myself to be carried along by another human being, but I set aside feelings of guilt and did allow myself to be pulled along through streets where sometimes muddy water stood a good foot high. Even walking in that part of town was dangerous since one could easily fall into an open drain hole. The rickshaw *wallahs* seemed to know their locations.

My refuge from guilt was to pay the man far more than he asked, and the asking price had been raised enormously during the mango showers. From behind the piece of tarpaulin that partly protected me, I could see that the hutments of bamboo matting were now undifferentiated mounds of slimy mud.

An army of desperate people made their way to Shishu Bhavan on Lower Circular Road where normally some thousands received one meal a day. Now the numbers swelled and something happened that Mother Teresa and the Sisters always called the miracle of the bread. "It's a first-class miracle," said Mother Teresa in amazement. All the schools were closed, and there were masses of school bread, thousands upon thousands of loaves, ready for distribution. CARE, which operated a school-feeding program in Calcutta, offered all the bread to Mother Teresa. Enriched with vitamins and protein, the bread came in wrapped loaves, each divided into six two-inch thick chunks. When I reached Shishu Bhavan, a large truck loaded with bread was already parked at the gate. The cases were being unloaded. Each case was marked "CARE People-to-People Gift—Not to be sold or exchanged."

The rice and grains supplied by Catholic Relief Services were distributed as usual in cooked form from vats in the courtyard of Shishu Bhavan. The recipients were identified as described earlier by variously colored tickets. Newcomers received bread and cans of evaporated milk.

The bread also helped another group affected by the flood. Among the new people who came for food was a man who insisted on seeing Mother Teresa personally.

He was a well-built handsome Bengali dressed only in a *dhoti.* He wore sandals and around his neck was a piece of cotton called a *gamcha.* He said his name was Sarkar. He was from Panchonagram 55 Colony in 24-Parganas. His village was underwater and the people were sitting on the roof of the school, he explained to the Sisters. One baby had just been born in the next village which was also flooded and two other mothers were ready to give birth. No one had come to them, he said. Mother Teresa helped them before and he had come to talk with her personally.

Mother Teresa came out and immediately recognized the man. They spoke in Bengali and a smile broke over his tired face.

"This is Deben Sarkar, the teacher," Mother Teresa told me. "He has been a leader of his people, all refugees from the Dacca side. The hardest workers I know. And now they are rained out. Two whole villages. We must go to them. We must be in time to save those young mothers."

A Sister told me that Sarkar's people, all Hindus, had come from Dacca, and some from Noakhali in East Pakistan in 1967. He said that he trusted Mother Teresa not only because she gave help but because she did not try to convert his people.

Another truck loaded with bread and the mobile clinic of the Missionaries of Charity started off from Shishu Bhavan with Sister Agnes in the lead truck. The rain had stopped temporarily.

We drove through Dhappa and on my left I glimpsed the *bustee* of lepers with its temple to Hanuman, the monkey god. After going through a dank area known as "the Potteries"—where the pottery itself had been on strike for nearly a year—we passed a rubber factory and landed in a quarter that looked like a corner of crowded Hong Kong. Every face was Chinese.

"Where can we put your people when we get them to shore?" Mother Teresa asked Sarkar.

"Most of the flooded people are in that school," he pointed ahead to the larger building in the area.

We stopped in front of a dark, gray stucco building that looked like a rundown barracks but was, in fact, the elementary school known as the Chinese School.

"Let us look in here," Mother Teresa said.

We climbed down and found that the school was surrounded by a grisly moat of floodwater with a few drowned animals floating in it. The water was of a sulfurous color and the stench was one I had never experienced before.

"That must come from the rubber factory," said Mother Teresa as she took off her sandals and put them in the lorry. She was going to wade through the filth-filled moat to reach the door of the school. I took off my shoes and followed her. The water was up to our knees and I felt it stab at the skin of my feet and legs. We had about forty feet of wading to do and Mother Teresa held her sari above her knees as we brushed by the dead animals, including a bloated black and white pig.

We entered a large hall, which was dark except for a few paraffin lamps and some carefully guarded candles. Nobody seemed surprised to see Mother Teresa and they answered her questions eagerly. Opening off the assembly hall were ten classrooms. All were filled with people, sitting on benches or on the damp stone floor. Mothers were feeding infants from elongated breasts.

Mother Teresa talked with two men who were spokesmen for the flood victims. They told her that there were more than a thousand of the homeless in the Chinese School. They had come from the community farther to the south where the land was lower than in this area.

"Yes, we have got some food but the people are still hungry. For days no one could get to us."

When Mother Teresa asked if the villages from Colonies 55 and 56 could be brought in after they were rescued, the men refused absolutely. They could not take a chance with any more children or any more diseases.

Mother Teresa did not argue but told the men they could have some of the supply of the proteinized bread. We made a quick calculation. Six hundred loaves would be thirty-six hundred thick chunks of bread. There were also vitamins in the van for nursing mothers and the children.

The men made quick work of wading through the water with the food supplies on their heads and then we were on our way. We came to the edge of Calcutta, where a marshy land area had been filled in with the city's garbage. As Calcutta ends, there begins the area known as 24-Parganas.

Here Sarkar stepped down and pointed to a cluster of people who seemed to be poised on a large raft in the midst of a glassy lake. Sarkar waved his *gamcha* at them and many small pieces of cloth began moving as though a flock of gulls was trying to take off.

We stood a couple of feet from where the land ended and the filled-in marshland began. At that point, the marsh was only slightly lower than the solid earth. Inundated by continuous rain, it had turned into a mud bath as dangerous as quicksand.

"The water was up to here," said Sarkar, pointing to a spot midway on his bare chest. "We stood in our homes, holding our children up like this." He held his arms before him. "We were waiting for the water to go down. Then we carried everything to the roof of the school. We thought someone would come to get us and bring us out, but nobody came. Colony 56 is the same."

In the distance, we saw a large dark blotch on the gray water that must have been the second refugee village. As we were talking, a small raftlike boat came ashore and five men stepped from it. They were the leaders of Colony 55 and they said that two large country boats had been sent out to them. They would soon bring everyone from Colony 55 to shore.

Sarkar explained that the whole group wanted to stay together except these five men, who would remain on the roof of the sunken village to protect their belongings.

"What are those white balloons on the rooftop?" I wanted to know.

Through Sister Agnes, Sarkar explained that some of the villagers were *dhobi wallahs,* washermen and washerwomen, and these were the white sacks of clean clothes that had been ready for delivery when the rains struck. We saw the large country boats circling Colony 55. Children and the precious sacks of clothing began to be handed down to the boatmen. The pale gray sky became darker and everything seemed the same colorless expanse, water below and sky above. Suddenly, as though the clouds could not support them any longer, heavy drops began to fall. I watched them strike the shiny water hyacinth leaves and the water lily pads that stretched out like empty plates at the edge of the shore. We could do nothing but stand and hope that everyone could be led safely into the rescue boats. The big drops made the leaves shiver. I remembered reading "Water drips; leaf quivers," in Tagore's account of his childhood. The words were the famous words of an old Bengali primer, "*Jal padey; pata nadey.*"

I felt that I was watching the most typical Bengali scene of all—the rain disturbing a leaf poised over water. Mother Teresa suggested we join in prayer. We stood still in the rain and prayed without a break. At last the boats came to shore and we helped the mothers and children onto the wet but fairly firm land. The mother and tiny infant were immediately transferred to the van.

"We must take all the women and children to Shishu Bhavan," said Mother Teresa. "Then I will find a place for everyone else and I will come back and pick you up." The small convoy left.

Sister Agnes and I stayed with about fifty villagers. All we had in the way of food were the remaining cases of bread. These we had decided to earmark for the five men who would guard the village. A shivering old man came to us and pointed to a sickly boy with him.

"He has not had anything to eat today. Could you give him something?"

Sister Agnes talked with the village guards. They decided to distribute one case of bread among their fellow villagers, who were gathered helplessly around the single big tree. They gave each person a chunk of bread and all stood around gravely munching the soggy bread under the leaves that seemed to give them a sense of protection from the raindrops.

Some of the older children were with us and they stood watching me. Sometimes I felt the light touch of a soft hand brushing my arm.

I asked each one if he was in school. The answer was always a smiling "Yes." One of the men explained to Sister Agnes, "All of our children go to school and they all finish the classes. Deben Sarkar is a good leader for our children. They can all read and write. No matter what happens, we will repair the school first."

He looked out at the almost submerged village. Sister Agnes translated a brokenhearted monologue: "All our work. The mats we made, could anyone count them? And the days that we walked to Calcutta to sell them. Who will help us to start again?"

Sister Agnes was telling me that most of the men made their living by weaving mats from the *hogla* reeds. They were so industrious that they supplied a steady market in Calcutta. They had done better for themselves than many colonized refugees. Now the disaster of the mango showers had dented the hopes of two of the hardest-working refugee colonies. Homes, workrooms, and school—representing years of day in, day out labor—would have to be excavated in God-knows-what state from a bed of mud.

I looked at the man who had been speaking. He turned his head away but I could see that the muscles of his face and jaw were working. The palm of his right hand was busy wiping away the drops that were not only from the rain.

When the truck returned, Mother Teresa brought the good news that everyone from Colony 55 and Chatchanatolla Colony 56 would be sheltered in the Taltala High School not far from Shishu Bhavan. By the end of the day, after a series of trips by truck and van, all the three hundred stranded were flood victims under shelter. I spent the next day at the Taltala School. We had stocks of *gamchas,* small, all-purpose cotton squares, saris, and children's clothing to give out. We found that leading the volunteers who had converged on the school was a team of Loreto Sisters from Loreto College, Mother Teresa's companions during her years of teaching. By 1970, the old voluminous habit had been trimmed down and simplified.

There were groups of students from various high schools and colleges, including Xavier and Taltala schools. On the blackboard of one of the larger classrooms was scrawled in foot-high letters: MAKE THE 70s THE

DECADE OF LIBERATION—Mao. One of the volunteers asked me what I thought of it. He eyed me intently from enormous, intelligent eyes poised above a prominent beak nose. He was about twenty, tall, and very angular. I did not know which group he belonged to. I had heard that in addition to the Christian and Hindu students there was unexpectedly a group of Naxalite students. The Naxalites proper were Maoists who took their name from Naxal Bari, a Bengal town where the peasants had "liberated" the land and held it against all comers.

Many Calcutta students had been attracted to the Naxalites in the hope of quick revolution, Chinese style. They had formed commandolike squads to invade the Bengal countryside on weekends. Their revolutionary acts included beheading the local landowners. Others put their chemistry to practical use in fashioning the acid and pipebombs used against Calcutta policemen. It was the violence and riots of Calcutta life in the late sixties, a time of leftist rule, that drove away or bankrupted a number of job-producing industries.

"Did Mao Tse-tung really say that?" I casually asked him as I went on counting a pile of red-bordered saris.

"Oh yes, he did," he replied. "He meant that other places can take example from China. What do you think? You are American, aren't you?"

I could sense a confrontation a sentence or two away and decided to avoid it.

"Yes, I'm American. But I am also Gandhian. I am for liberation that does not call for violence. How do you feel about that outlook?"

"I myself think the Naxalites are right. Many of us do. Gandhi might have been all right against the British, but not now. We see things getting worse every year. That's why students at Jadvapore got rid of the Gandhi library. Those books were destroyed because the ideas are useless. In China things get better. There is no hunger like we have here in Bengal." His voice was getting higher and two others, in the white shirts of middle class students, came to stand by him. It seemed to me that the faith of these students in violence was complete, their hatred of nonviolence virulent.

"Do you go out to the countryside on the weekends?" I asked. It was a probe. I was trying to find out if he was an active Naxalite or a student sympathizer.

"I am a student. I am busy with my studies. I want to be an engineer, but I also want a better life for people," he said. The eyes of the two other boys were fixed on me, quite balefully I thought.

"You *are* American," said one of them in a tone of accusation.

I continued to be busily sorting out the clothing and making piles for the list of families in my hand.

"She says she's a Gandhian," said the young man with the beak nose.

The other two moved away reluctantly. Perhaps they had thought they were on the trail of a Central Intelligence agent.

When I told Mother Teresa about it, she did not seem surprised that far-left Naxalite students were working side by side with nuns from a prominent Roman Catholic women's college. It occurred to me that only Mother Teresa could have brought such extremes of Calcutta society together, and probably only Mother Teresa could have persuaded the authorities to give over a central city high school to the flood refugees. Meanwhile, she was busy checking on the mothers and children in Shishu Bhavan. Savitri, one of the pregnant women, had already given birth to a tiny, perfect baby attended by Sister Gertrude and some other Sisters. The other expectant mother was not yet in labor and I saw her sitting serenely with her three small children in a corner of a room in Shishu Bhavan.

Mother Teresa was already thinking ahead to what would have to be done when the waters receded.

"We will need tarpaulins and heavy poles. Then the men can start repairing the school and the houses. We'll find the food for the time being. We've got to give them work until they go back to making mats. We can help them to make *gamchas.* Everybody uses those."

I learned that after the waters had receded and the village was made livable again, the concern of Mother Teresa continued. The Sisters opened a village dispensary in Panchonagram Colony 55 to serve both 55 and Colony 56.

During the rains, Dorothy Day remained in the apartment of Chloe Wing in a block of apartments occupied by consular staff. She was praying, reading the Psalms of David, and writing reports for *The Catholic Worker.* Afterward, she told me how intensely she had longed to take part in Mother Teresa's rescue of the flood victims. She was forced to accept the fact that at seventy-two, such activity was ruled out.

One day, we received a message that Brother Andrew, head of the Missionaries of Charity Brothers would come from Mansatala Row to visit us. The Brothers had been founded by Mother Teresa just seven years earlier, in 1963, and were almost unknown. Their story is related in Chapter 8 of this book.

We looked out of the window to see a tall thin man opening the gate of the small courtyard. He was carrying his shoes in his hands and his trousers were rolled above his knees as he waded up to the door of the apartment house. Brother Andrew was drenched; his dark hair dangling limply down his thin face. Over hot cups of tea he told Dorothy Day that he had always wanted to meet her. The Catholic Worker movement, he related in an unmistakably Australian accent, had played a pivotal role in his spiritual life. During his time in the Jesuit Seminary at Poona, his concern was with an intense spiritual life—as he described it, a sort of disembodied spiritual life. He had been sent to India for training since he was to serve in the Indian missions of the Society.

Immersion in the sorrows and struggles of the poor as a direct expression of the gospel of Jesus had not occurred to him as a seminarian. *The Catholic Worker* newspaper arrived regularly, addressed to some priest who had long since moved to another part of India.

Dorothy Day smiled. A *Catholic Worker* subscription, once entered into, is hardly ever discontinued, even though no renewal funds are received. Not even the death of the subscriber halts its arrival.

Dorothy remarked that it was the hope of the movement that the paper would bring benefit to whoever might read it.

Brother Andrew went on to become ordained as a Jesuit priest for the Church in India.

We found Brother Andrew a person of striking appearance, with his long fine face and thin aquiline nose. His bright blue eyes, rimmed by dark lashes, gave his face a Byzantine, or perhaps an El Greco look. This was heightened by a spare beard.

The conversation made the dark afternoon, with raindrops beating steadily on the windows, pass speedily and raised Dorothy Day's spirits.

"I have been reading *The Catholic Worker* now for twenty years," he said. "I owe so much to the Catholic Worker movement. Reading about the Houses of Hospitality in America, I always wanted to do something like that. I was so impressed by the idea of a community where the poor and lonely could come in. I read your books, too, Dorothy," he added.

"In 1963," he said with a laugh, "Mother Teresa was buttonholing priests to start a Brothers' branch and she finally kidnaped me from the Jesuits."

He invited Dorothy Day to come to the Brothers' house on Mansatala Row as soon as the rains stopped.

"We are seventy-seven now, professed, novices, and young men looking into the life. You will find us very simple people," he told Dorothy Day. "Nearly three quarters are from the tribal groups near Ranchi, the Oraons. Calcutta is new to them. They come from simple villages. It is the first time they have locked a door or turned on a light."

Brother Andrew wondered about the necessity for the extreme rigidity of religious training. Some of the young men knew Hindi, but now all of them had to learn English. There was no way of escaping it since it was the common language in which religious literature was available. But he regretted the enormous energy that had to be spent in learning to speak and read it.

"A thing I learned from you," Brother Andrew told Dorothy Day, "is to give hospitality to the visitor. We can put people up, since young people just sleep on the floor, in the refectory, or anywhere. Meeting young men from so many places, from the United States, from France, and from Germany, gives tremendous confidence to our young brothers."

Dorothy Day and Brother Andrew were kindred spirits and found much to talk about, one topic being the role of providence and the danger of quietism if one simply awaited events. Dorothy Day said, "Yes, everything is providential, but I would not consider it providential to remain if I were in the backseat of a car with a maniac driver. I would jump out."

She mentioned how often people, especially her former friends who were atheists, asked her if she really believed in Jesus Christ as the Son of God.

"I tell them," Dorothy Day said, "that I believe that he is the Son of God just as the Creed teaches."

Then she added, "Sometimes I believe more strongly than others."

They both laughed.

When Dorothy Day went to meet the community of Brothers, she found a house not so different from one of the Catholic Worker houses on New York's Lower East Side. The Brothers gathered around her, sitting on coconut matting on the floor of a long narrow room. Young faces, many reminding me of Sister Christopher and Sister Scholastica in the aborigines' camp in Australia, looked up expectantly at Dorothy Day. They wore no kind of habit, merely a cotton shirt and cheap duck trousers. They were barefoot, having placed their sandals outside the door. Their one distinguishing mark was a cross pinned to the shirt.

Dorothy Day told of a lay Catholic movement devoted, as they were, to poverty, in order to share the poverty of the poor and to serve them. Even in New York, there were poor people, people not able to manage, who could not hold a job. They would come and stay in a house something like this one and help the Catholic Worker community, all volunteers, prepare the meals and the food for the soup line.

One Brother asked a question, and the others were emboldened to follow suit. "How long did the lay people stay? Did the poor ones get better and get jobs? Did anybody sleep in the streets?"

Brother Andrew told us that the Brothers were just starting to work in Kalighat, taking over the men's ward, and putting in night duty. They were already working in Calcutta's two railway stations and had picked up homeless boys found scrounging in the stations and on the streets. Many were ill, crippled, or mentally retarded. The professed Brothers lived in two homes, one for the youngsters and one for homeless men. A team of Brothers had reached marooned flood victims in villages around Bomandanga.

At the Motherhouse of the Missionaries of Charity, Mother Teresa

Profession Day in Tondo, Philippines, 1980.

India—a community at prayer. *(Holl)*

Original chapel in Calcutta (every chapel in the world has the words "I Thirst" above the crucifix).

The squat, silvered dome of Kali's temple (far right) and the bulbous towers of Kalighat.

Arrival in the New World, Venezuela.

Missionaries of Charity visiting with residents of the Zona Negra.

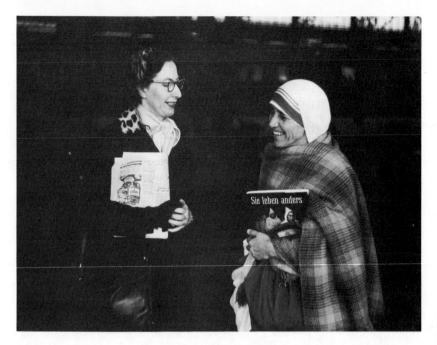

Arrival in Germany, 1960—Mother Teresa's first overseas trip from Calcutta. *(Holl)*

Pope Paul VI presenting the Pope John XXIII Peace Award to Mother Teresa in Rome, 1971. *(Felici)*

remembered her visit to New York's Bowery with Dorothy Day. It was a Thursday afternoon and nearly a hundred Sisters were at home. Along with the Indian Sisters there were Sisters and novices from six European countries. Mother Teresa told them that she had talked at the Catholic Worker center in New York and now Dorothy Day was at the Motherhouse to talk to the Missionaries of Charity community. I told them something of the founding of the Catholic Worker by Dorothy Day, a convert to the Catholic Church. She had found inspiration in a mentor, Peter Maurin, a man who lived the life of poverty of the poor man of Assisi. It was he who had opened to her the riches of Church teaching.

Dorothy Day was given a chair while Mother Teresa and the Sisters settled themselves on the floor. There was a motherliness about Dorothy Day with her braided white hair crowning her head and her ample body covered by a nondescript cotton dress.

She was indeed a mother and a grandmother of nine, but she was also something else, the founding mother of a lay movement that deeply affected the Church of the twentieth century in the United States and throughout the world. The banked fire of her championship of the poor and voiceless charged her talk now as always with irresistible intensity. She told of the "daily practice of the works of mercy," at a personal sacrifice. The work started in the New York house and then in houses that sprang up in the poorer sections of over forty American cities. The monthly paper published by the movement went around the world in close to one hundred thousand copies.

"We keep repeating the message of Gospel nonviolence and the importance of voluntary poverty in serving the poor. For us," she said, "everything depends on seeing the poor as ambassadors of Christ, and of keeping open our Houses of Hospitality for those against whom other doors are shut."

She told of her refusal and the refusal of other Catholic Workers to interrupt the works of mercy even in wartime, when Jesus' command to "love the enemy" was replaced by the command of the state to kill, starve, and maim the enemy. She explained that her manifesto when the Second World War was declared was the Sermon on the Mount. The Catholic Worker movement, she went on, took Jesus at His word when He told His followers to do good in return for evil, thus overcoming evil by good not by violence. She mentioned her arrests when she and many others refused to go to civil defense shelters at the order of New York authorities. They felt that civil defense drills were preparing people's minds for war. Going to prison had given her the chance to perform another work of mercy, visiting those in prison. This created a stir and occasioned questions on the number of times she had been in jail. The Indian Sisters were acquainted with the number of Indian women who had gone to jail in Gandhi's nonviolent campaigns, but for a Catholic woman to go to jail for the Sermon on the Mount was a different matter. Dorothy Day explained that she must have gone to jail about half a dozen times for peace and human rights.

When young people are free to come and go, Dorothy Day explained, there is a constant turnover in the Catholic Worker community, but it is surprising how many stay on for years—without salary and without security. In doing the work, she explained, there was always a sense of community—and a dependence on God's providence to replace those who leave.

Mother Teresa and the Sisters closed the meeting with a hymn which included, "When in prison, you came to my cell . . . . Now enter into the home of my Father."

The hymn echoed Jesus' description of the Last Judgment:

> Whatsoever you do to the least of my brothers,
> That you do unto me.
>
> When I was hungry, you gave me to eat;
> When I was thirsty, you gave me to drink.
> NOW ENTER INTO THE HOME OF MY FATHER.
>
> When I was homeless, you opened your door;
> When I was naked, you gave me your coat;
> NOW ENTER INTO THE HOME OF MY FATHER.
>
> You saw me covered with spittle and blood;
> You knew my features though grimy with sweat;
> NOW ENTER INTO THE HOME OF MY FATHER.

We sat moved as Mother Teresa's clear voice, along with nearly a hundred young voices, brought to life the works of mercy in eleven verses, mentioning finding a job for a stranger and carrying the cross with blacks or Chinese.

Mother Teresa then led us up to the chapel of the Motherhouse on the fourth and top floor so that we could join with the Sisters in an hour of meditation. It flanked Lower Circular Road and the clanging of streetcars, the honking of aged taxis, the cries of street hawkers, and the voices of an unending army of pedestrians crashed through the louvered windows. Fixing one's attention on the altar, with its roughly carved crucifix and the stark letters I THIRST, helped blunt the attack of sound.

The two women founders kneeling in front of me in the Calcutta chapel were visionaries who brought people to them and their work by their unique vision, not by argument. For each one, the mass was the central act of the day. Despite her schedule of travel, Dorothy Day hardly ever missed daily mass.

Each blazed forth a special genius. With an unerring precision, coupled with the wild abandon of faith in providence, each had gone straight to the least wanted, the poorest, in her society—one to the poor of the megalopolis of New York, the other to the poor of the megalopolis of Calcutta. Each had insisted on face-to-face contact with those who might seem unlovable, but who were lovable in the all-embracing love of the Universal Brother, Jesus.

Each had made a banquet to which had been called the lame, the halt, and the blind. Before we left the Motherhouse, Dorothy Day remarked on the simple crucifix worn by each Sister over her left shoulder. Mother Teresa asked Dorothy Day if she would be willing to wear one. Dorothy Day said she would like to.

Mother Teresa took out a big safety pin and attached the black cross with the corpus of Christ on the left shoulder of Dorothy Day's blue and white cotton dress.

"I will wear it as you do," Dorothy Day promised.

"You are now a spiritual Missionary of Charity," Mother Teresa said. "There are nearly six hundred of us in the world, including professed Sisters, novices, and aspirants. You are one of us."

On our visit to Shishu Bhavan, we found that there was one section solely for premature babies, tiny mites brought in by midwives who knew that otherwise they would be destroyed or thrown into dustbins. Many were born to unwed mothers. There were one hundred and twenty children in all, a half a dozen being mentally retarded.

Kathu, a blind boy of about six, heard our voices and came to Mother Teresa to be hugged. Then Mother Teresa showed us the courtyard with the large storage of foodstuffs from Catholic Relief Services.

"We now feed about seven thousand from our poorest families every day," she said. "How they suffer if they do not get the food. We could not give it out on Martyrs' Day because of Section 144, but we tried to make it up."

Section 144 was the law prohibiting public gatherings that might be used for incendiary purposes. The only gathering allowed on that day of the *hartal*, or enforced holiday, was a large political meeting in Mullick Square fronting the Maidan. Without that venting of emotions, there might have been rioting.

A Mother and Child Clinic had been opened in one part of Shishu Bhavan and a group of young women were learning and helping out. We met Tara, meaning Star, a girl in her early teens with a spirited gaze. She had just received a new sari and told us through a Sister how proud she was of it.

Mother Teresa took me aside.

"Tara's mother has a cancerous growth and she is suffering. Tara fought with her mother and struck her. I asked the child to come to me. I told her, 'In forty-two years, I have never touched anyone but I shall do to you what you did to your mother.' So, I did. She was surprised. She's been an angel ever since."

I wanted to know about friends of earlier days. Shadona Mukherjee, the little girl who took so long to smile and who used to push her sick little brother toward me to get his candy, had known another tragedy. The boy had died. Shadona was now in high school in Jamshedpur and learning to type. It was time for her to be married the Sisters thought.

Another death was that of Douglas, the Anglo-Indian boy with the cleft lip, abandoned by his parents when they chose to go to England. Douglas, Mother Teresa told me, had undergone a fairly successful operation to cure his harelip. A European family had taken him into their home and were planning to adopt him. Their marriage did not last, and so they returned Douglas to Shishu Bhavan.

Accustomed to Mother Teresa, he had said, "Mother, you want me, don't you?" She assured him that she would always want him. In a couple of years, the boy contracted pneumonia and died. Speechless Mary Ann of the wasted limbs must have been nearly twenty and was no longer at Shishu Bhavan. I did not have a chance to see her, but I learned that she responded to certain words as though she understood them and would say the word "Yes" when she wanted something. Jyoti, the daughter of a leper father, was helping to manage the leper center at Titagarh, but there was not time enough to drive there.

We met Sister Lourdes, who finished giving a bottle to a tiny infant and began to tell us an adoption story. She said that there were more and more people showing interest in adopting babies from Shishu Bhavan. Hindu families had adopted over forty of the children—something very rare in Indian society. Already, families in Sweden, Switzerland, Germany, Ireland, France, and the United States and Canada had adopted children from the Home. The Indian Government had quietly granted the exit visas.

Sister Audrey told us of the sponsoring of schoolchildren by young people in England, Germany, and Holland. Already eight hundred and fifty children were adopted, their school fees, clothing, and medical needs being met with a monthly donation of funds. I had a chance to talk with Sister Dorothy, M.C. number three after Sisters Agnes and Gertrude. She told me that she had known Mother Teresa from the time she was a little girl. When she was in high school, she learned from Mother Teresa of a Belgian woman who wanted to give her life to the poor of India. Mother Teresa told the story to the entire class. "Then," said Sister Dorothy, "she asked us how many of us would consider such work with the poor. Almost all of us put up our hands. I realized later that Mother might have been thinking of what to do on the streets."

At the Kalighat Home for the Dying, Mother Teresa introduced us to Sister Jaya, a Bengali Sister-Nurse with a strong voice and a bouncing manner. Nothing had changed around Kalighat; the streets were still thronged with pilgrims and hawkers, and we had to step carefully to avoid the blood-red clots from the spit of betel chewers.

We went into the women's ward where Mother Teresa told them that we had come a long way to pay a visit. A thin old woman, hair shorn like a man's, took Mother Teresa's hand in hers and kissed it. Then she smiled a happy smile at the three of us. A few were sitting on their haunches. Clasping their hands, they returned the *"Namaskar"* greeting I gave them. Sister Jaya teasingly patted the head of an old crone who tilted up her head and gave her a red, gummy grin. Some lay curled up like shriveled infants, their eyes closed. One could only wonder how soon their eyes would close forever.

As we approached the men's ward, we found that they were just having their dinner. Dorothy Day and I sat on a stone slab in a small corridor between the wards. Some of the men, able to feed themselves, meticulously dipped the fingers of their right hand into the plastic water glass and flicked the water into the center passageway. Then they ate the food from clean fingers.

A Sister was feeding the most recent arrival, lying on a pallet near us, giving him tiny spoonfuls so that he would not die from the effects of a sudden heavy meal.

Sister Jaya pointed to the blackboard near us. The figures were: WOMEN —79; MEN—59. September 10, 1970. Dead: WOMEN—3; MEN—5.

The name Jaya means victory. Standing in that corridor, with those stark figures, I pondered on the numbers who were surviving. Few of them might still be alive without the care of the Sisters at Kalighat. Each survivor meant a victory.

Turning to Dorothy Day, I said something about being forced to think of the ultimate things in such a setting and she commented, "At my time in life, one thinks of death every day."

Mother Teresa was out on the street meeting an ambulance. In the back of the vehicle resting on a wicker chair and held by a young Sister was a cadaverous woman. She was whimpering, trying to say something but unable to form the words. A terrible throaty sound was forcing itself out of her mouth as though she would die in the attempt to tell us something. We lowered her from the ambulance in the chair and I supported her wasted legs as we brought her into the women's ward.

She was the only patient I helped bring into the Home for the Dying. She was an Anglo-Indian widow, Mrs. John, the Sister told me, and one of the helpless people visited by the Sisters. They had not been able to visit her in recent days and upon returning, they found her near death from a stroke. Her rented room had to be vacated. As we placed her on a pallet to be washed and fed, I saw the agony in her large dark eyes.

Not long ago, Mrs. John must have been a beautiful woman, belonging to a special and even privileged group. But that group, the lower-echelon corps of Anglo-Indians who formed a network of skilled and reliable workers in colonial India, had lost privileged access to certain categories of work. She was one among many others who had sunk into penury in the new India.

"Our Sisters don't go to Sealdah Station anymore," Mother Teresa told me. "That is the Brothers' work now."

I went back to the station, remembering what a dreadful "Black Hole" it had been in 1955 and the improvement when the refugee ranks had thinned out in 1958. I somehow thought that as the number of refugees had dwindled, Sealdah would probably present a more controlled situation.

Events do not proceed predictably or logically in Calcutta. Sealdah in 1970 was more of a "Black Hole" than in 1955. The Brothers, moving about among five thousand people, picked out those near death, children who needed medical attention, or boys who needed shelter. They were indistinguishable from other Indian men if one missed the small crucifix pinned to their shirt. Not only refugees from across the border were clinging to Sealdah's inhospitable walls, but people fleeing from the isolation of resettlement camps and, now, people who crept in when their huts had collapsed in the rains. All were being fed a *kidgeree* from enormous vats set up in the station. Some of the food came from U.S. Food For Peace stocks through Catholic Relief Services. The feeding program was an effort of local volunteers who operated under a large cotton banner lettered with the words, "Marwari Welfare Association."

I paid a quick visit to Moti Jihl where the school for slum children was large and flourishing. The houses of *pukka* construction had stood up well. I sought out the home of the statue-maker to tell him that I still enjoyed the two statues of the Virgin Mary that came from his hand. His wife was there and gave me the news that he had died, as had two of their sons. She was dandling a little grandson on her lap. The rest of the family was surviving, and I supposed that Evening and Star were also married. Sun had married an Anglo-Indian and Moon (Agnes), who had brought me the statue with the chalk-white skin, was no longer an occasional cook and dishwasher. She had taken training in nursing under Sister Gertrude and

Sister Frances Xavier and was now the supervisor of the leper center in Dhappa.

With Mother Teresa, I returned to Dhappa to find that the very worst cases in that cluster of lepers were housed in a large, shedlike building. The Sisters had opened it when they found that there were many lepers completely alone and unable even to beg or feed themselves. Agnes was in charge, dressed in a simple sari and displaying an assured manner. She was in her late twenties and had never married, an unheard-of choice for a Hindu girl, but one accepted in the Christian community. She took care of the cooking and the physical aspects of the center. For this, she was paid a monthly salary, the funds coming from donations for leper care. The center was impressively clean and the bedding on the cots, where a few of the patients lay inert, was fresh.

Mother Teresa pointed out a man who spoke English. He stood up, a tall man, clearly Indian, but when he told me his name was Thomas Williams, I realized he was Anglo-Indian.

"I went to New York twice," he told me. "I used to travel a lot because I used to be second steward on a ship. But now," he held out clawed stumps for hands, "I am here."

It was as though he had said, "This is the absolute end."

The Sisters came with the doctor to the center to dress the sores and to have the patients checked. The open-air leper station was still held regularly at Dhappa, and the rows of one-room houses with raised verandas was still there. People with fingers or feet half eaten away or with gutted eye sockets sat on the verandas, some with their precious wooden carts beside them. They were still ready for forays into Calcutta streets especially to mosques and churches at the proper times. The smell from the canals and the slaughterhouses still lay heavily on the air, and there was an abundance of gray dust.

I looked for the pipal tree and the open-air shrine to the monkey god Hanuman, whose image had been painted on a whitewashed stone. It was no longer there, but was replaced by a neat little *mandir,* a temple with a roof of tiles.

The reunion with Father Robert Antoine revealed that he was still a professor at Jadavpore University. Always close to the work of Mother Teresa and in the thick of Bengali culture and student life, he still lived in the hostel for poor students. He knew that they managed to raise their board by untold sacrifices on their part and on the part of their families. He told me of visiting the home of one of his students to find that it consisted of one room. The student's parents and seven younger children lived there. The faith of young people in education as a way to better their lot was almost mystical, despite all evidence to the contrary.

There was that other faith, the faith in revolution, and I told him about my meeting with the Naxalite students in Taltala High School. Father Antoine said that many of the seven thousand students in Jadavpore expressed their disgust at the claims of politicians. They saw them as using Gandhi to cloak their own ambitions. The students not only destroyed Gandhian books in libraries, he said, but went about shooting at photographs and images of Gandhi.

A few days earlier, there had been an incident showing the power of the Maoist students. The university had arranged with the student union, led by one Communist faction, to hold postponed examinations on September 3. The Maoist group had not been consulted. They burst into the room where the examinations were kept, drew their guns, and destroyed all the examinations.

The university had started faculties of engineering and science, he related, and there was little doubt that the bombs sporadically exploded around Calcutta were manufactured by students. So many of them, especially those belonging to refugee families, saw before them an abyss of absolute poverty into which they could sink like stones forever. Agitators gave them hope in announcing that Lenin's revolution having moved from Moscow to Peking was now, through Mao, reaching Calcutta. Father Antoine's deep sympathy for young people facing a black future in a city with unfathomable need showed on his expressive features. Yet he had not lost his ardent manner. No matter what the depth of crisis in Calcutta, he would not be deflected from whatever good he could do as a priest and a teacher.

He told us that the precautions that had to be taken to protect Gandhi's statue at the edge of the Maidan revealed much about Kali's city. It had to be surrounded by a wire fence and sandbags and guarded by a twenty-four-hour patrol of soldiers. By night, floodlights threw their beams continuously on the statue to circumvent those bent on destroying it.

Before leaving Calcutta, we saw the statue, protected just as Father Antoine had described it. The figure of Gandhi stood on a fifteen-foot-high pedestal. The father of his country was carved holding a staff, as if walking along a road as a pilgrim. It had been in Bengal that he had actually walked from village to village as a pilgrim for peace between Muslim and Hindu.

On the pedestal were Gandhi's words:

In the midst of death,
life persists.
In the midst of untruth,

truth persists.
In the midst of darkness,
light persists.
Hence, I gather that God is
Life, Truth and Light.

I wondered if there could be a more tragic commentary on life in a scourged city than the necessity to defend such sentiments with a platoon of soldiers. It was in this setting that Mother Teresa's work of compassion persisted.

When it was time to leave Calcutta, Dum Dum Airport was so sodden from the rain that our plane could not take off. We decided to leave from Howrah Station by the Kalka mail train to Delhi. At dusk we crossed the Howrah Bridge in the van with Mother Teresa. We moved slowly in a great wave of vehicular traffic yet it was insignificant in comparison with the tide of people making their way on foot.

As we got out of the van, Mother Teresa motioned to a porter to pick up our bags. She knew his name and introduced him to us.

"This is Ashok, a good man. He is from Chapra."

Ashok wore a dark red overblouse like the other porters and he braced our suitcases on a scarf wrapped around his head. He spoke English and told us that he had his secondary school matriculation, the equivalent of a high school education. He supported his wife and children on his porter's earnings—about two hundred rupees a month, he told us.

"I cannot find any other work," he said, but there was no complaint in his voice. Around us, huddled into every corner of the Howrah Station were squatters who had nothing at all.

Mother Teresa, after finding out that there was no dining car on the train, went off looking for some food. She came back with a parting gift of a bag of apples—brown-flecked and small. A dining car was to meet the Kalka mail train in time for breakfast the next morning, and we looked forward to that.

To Mother Teresa's "God bless you" we took off. The dining car never did meet the Kalka mail train. We washed the small brown apples in the washroom and were glad to have them.

14

The Eyes of the World

Two more disparate characters could hardly be dreamed up. He was an urbane Englishman, an international journalist and author, so extraordinarily gifted with words and iconoclastic wit that he became editor of *Punch.* His war service was in intelligence and he won military decorations. His memoirs, self-deprecatingly entitled *Chronicles of Wasted Time,* were compared by *The Times* of London to those of Carlyle or Rousseau. At one time he was on the verge of suicide.

She was a woman who had "left the world" at eighteen, and whose mind and heart were concentrated on God, her Society of Sisters, and the least members of the human family. Her faith was rocklike in its absolute certainty.

It was a momentous encounter when Malcolm Muggeridge met Mother Teresa to interview her on television for the British Broadcasting Company. The London meeting seemed to be nothing extraordinary to the participants at the time. To Muggeridge it was part of his BBC work and he dutifully read up on his subject as he came up to London on the train. To Mother Teresa it was one of the countless times that she answered the call, always difficult, to meet the media. As she explained to me, "They asked me to talk to Malcolm Muggeridge. I didn't know who he was."

The interview was arranged at the initiative of Oliver Hunkin of the BBC and was conducted in the Holy Child Convent in Cavendish Square. John Southworth, first chairman of the Co-Workers of Mother Teresa in England and a leader in voluntary efforts against leprosy, was awaiting her. "Mother Teresa was late," he recalled, "and Malcolm Muggeridge was getting impatient waiting for her. When she did arrive, she came over to talk to us. Muggeridge literally swept her off to the room where the camera had been set up with a brisk, "Come along, Mother Teresa!"

Muggeridge did not feel that anything memorable had occurred during the interview. The result was so technically poor that the BBC planned a late night showing, but was persuaded instead to run it on a Sunday evening. The response was so unprecedented with a storm of letters following, including gifts for Mother Teresa's work, that a second showing was scheduled. A second storm of letters surprised the studio and Muggeridge himself, to whom many of the letters were directed.

From that first television interview came a second one, a film released in 1970, and later a book all by Muggeridge. These helped turn the eyes of the world to Mother Teresa and the work of the Missionaries of Charity.

"When they first wanted to make a film, I said 'No,' " Mother Teresa told me. "But His Grace, the archbishop, said it would help the people to understand the work, so I agreed. Malcolm Muggeridge came to mass each day while they were making the film."

How greatly the TV interviews, the film and book increased the momentum of young women entering the Missionaries of Charity is a matter of conjecture. The momentum was already in process.

Within religious circles, and particularly in the Catholic Church, Mother Teresa and her work had already made a powerful impact. Young women were already flocking to the Missionaries of Charity. In 1970 alone, 139 new candidates had been received into the Society and 36 novices had pronounced their first vows. In all, the Society comprised 585 Sisters, of whom 332 were fully professed nuns, 175 novices, and 78 were postulants. Already young women had come to Calcutta from many places outside India, from Pakistan, Ceylon, Nepal, Malaysia, Yugoslavia, Germany, Malta, France, Mauritania, Ireland, Venezuela, and Italy. The various regions of India were well represented: West Bengal, Bihar, Orissa, Chota Nagpur, Madhya Pradesh, Punjab, Goa, Madras, Maharashtra, Gujarat, and Kerala.

So powerful a witness as that of Mother Teresa to the inviolable sacredness of human life in an age of mass destruction of human beings in war and in planned extermination could not escape attention. The Church itself was certainly paying attention. On January 6, 1971, before the appearance of the Muggeridge book, the Pope John XXIII Peace Award was presented to Mother Teresa in Rome by Pope Paul VI. Roman cardinals heading the various congregations of the Church were present at the ceremony.

"Humble Mother Teresa," said the Pope, "in whom we like to see the thousands and thousands of people dedicated full time to the personal service of the most needy, becomes an example and symbol of the discovery, in which lies the secret of world peace, which we are all seeking. It is the discovery, ever so up-to-date, that man is our brother and she who comes to us as a Missionary of Charity is the apostle of brotherhood and the messenger of peace."

In giving a blessing, the Pope included all who shared Mother Teresa's aspirations and labors.

Muggeridge, an inspired wordsmith, took a favorite expression of Mother Teresa's as both the title of his book and of the film he made with the BBC, *Something Beautiful for God.*

I happened to be passing through London in April 1971, when the book was officially launched. Mrs. Ann Blaikie, whom Mother Teresa had chosen to head her International Co-Workers, was invited and asked me to accompany her.

Muggeridge, introduced by the publisher, Lady Collins, was his usual witty self, contrasting Mother Teresa's motivation of seeing Christ in the sufferer, with that of a humanist, so shrill in defense of the downtrodden. "In all my travels around the world," he said mischievously, "I have never seen one leprosarium conducted by humanists."

Talking to us afterwards, he explained a sort of prescience in including in the book a sheaf of nine pages of Mother Teresa's own words.

"Mother Teresa will never write about herself or her work," said Muggeridge. "When she is considered for the Nobel Prize, there should be something in print in her own words."

At the time, I thought his enthusiasm was carrying him away, since I could hardly imagine the Nobel Prize for Peace being given to a nun, no matter how extraordinary her contribution. Peace Prize recipients tended to be chosen from the world of politics or humanistic welfare.

The book confronted the central issue of human suffering. The film showed heart-stopping scenes of this suffering in the Home for the Dying, in Shishu Bhavan, and in the leper center. It depicted the work of the Sisters and Brothers in assuaging such suffering, as Mother Teresa had insisted. During the scene with the lepers, Muggeridge himself walked off camera, his eyes streaming with tears. Above all, the screen revealed Mother Teresa herself, luminously loving and unaware of the camera, surrounded by the people so dear to her.

There was a line of connection between Mother Teresa and Malcolm Muggeridge in that he had a firsthand acquaintance with Calcutta and had recently been drawn to Jesus as described in his book, *Jesus Rediscovered.* He made no secret of his lack of interest in institutionalized religion and, in particular, an opposition to the religious institution to which Mother Teresa owed her allegiance. His championship of Mother Teresa was a personal crusade and he dismissed as "preposterous" the idea that seemed to have entered Mother Teresa's mind that he might join her Church.

Yet, by fate or providence, as one chooses to see it, the book and film by Malcolm Muggeridge became the means of turning the eyes of the world on the work of compassion that had begun so obscurely in Calcutta. I was witness again and again to the outpourings of love and compassion inspired by Mother Teresa's story as related by Muggeridge.

Mother Teresa was in New York in the fall of 1971 at the time of the American publication of the book, since the Missionaries of Charity were just then starting work in the city. The invitation of Terence Cardinal Cooke to bring the Missionaries of Charity to the archdiocese of New York was made in 1970 when the cardinal asked Mother Teresa to visit the chancery office just behind St. Patrick's Cathedral on Fifth Avenue at Fiftieth Street. Mother Teresa was passing through New York after addressing the National Council of Catholic Women in Minneapolis, Minnesota. The October meeting was the sixtieth anniversary of the organization which had first brought Mother Teresa from India to address their convention in Las Vegas ten years earlier.

The invitation was to provide a team of Sisters to work with migrant workers and their families. The destination first mentioned by the cardinal was Newburgh, an old town on the banks of the Hudson River and the Sisters were to arrive in April 1971. Mother Teresa, in the meantime, had been hearing about Harlem. She was drawn to the area where New York's black population had long been concentrated, and the South Bronx, where the majority of the people were black and Hispanic, meaning of Puerto Rican origin. Shortly after the interview with the cardinal, Father William McPeake, a priest of the New York archdiocese, drove us through the streets of Harlem and the South Bronx. We could not miss the lordly churches of Harlem—the Baptist and Methodist churches and such Catholic churches as the grandiose St. Augustine's. We saw a few new schools, standing bright and new among the older tenements, and 125th Street crowded with shoppers and with large numbers of people simply lounging about. We spent more time in the South Bronx, moving slowly through Willis Avenue reading the signs *Gallinas Vivas* (Live Chickens), *Supermercado* for supermarket, and *Bodegas* everywhere from 138th to 149th Street. We turned in at various side streets, such as Kelly Street and Fox Street. There were still some of the old solid tenements left, built at the turn of the century by immigrant laborers from Ireland and Italy. They were built with fine small bricks and still housed hardworking families. Yet many blocks conjured up scenes of postwar Germany, of bombed out Frankfurt or Berlin. There were streets with almost all the houses completely battered. Streets were littered with empty bottles and cans and with great piles of garbage lying loose or bursting out of green plastic bags. On one street where most of the houses were empty hulks, men were sitting on the stoops, their eyes drooping, their hands limp on their laps.

"Are they hungry?" Mother Teresa asked. "Is this Calcutta Number Two?"

Father McPeake explained that it was not hunger but drugs.

"Why do they go into drugs?" Mother Teresa wanted to know.

"There are so many reasons," the priest replied. "These people were poor and unskilled to begin with. And with all the prejudice, they have little self-esteem. They escape from it all this way. And then they need money for the drug habit. And so we have the crime that ravages the neighborhoods."

Suddenly Fr. McPeake turned to Mother Teresa and said, "With all the need in India, why would you have to come here?"

"Only to serve," she replied.

"But how do you think you can serve?"

"We can be a bridge between those who have and those who have less. We can also be a bridge because our Sisters being dark may come much closer to dark people."

It was in the midst of the South Bronx that Mother Teresa finally placed her Sisters. The arrival of the team was delayed six months by the emergency arising in an area soon to be called Bangladesh. The long-simmering differences between the Pakistanis of West and East Pakistan, deeply divided by culture, ethnic origin, and language, broke through the one uniting feature, that of Islam. East Pakistan wanted greater, even complete autonomy. The scourged province of East Pakistan, inundated in 1970 by a cyclone and by tidal waves that swept away more than 300,000 lives, endured in the spring of 1971 the man-made scourge of war with the onslaught of West Pakistani troops. It was the Hindu minority of East Pakistan which suffered most atrociously and Mother Teresa plunged in with energy and compassion to help deal with the monstrous happenings at Calcutta's door. About 250,000 refugees from East Pakistan pressed at the gates of Calcutta, the luckiest of them finding shelter in enormous sewer pipes in Salt Lake. In all, close to ten million people, in an incredible cascade, tumbled out of East Pakistan into India. They found themselves along the border of one of the world's poorest provinces, Bengal, and brought their burdens to already overburdened communities.

Mother Teresa moved into the sea of helpless people to serve the most helpless of all, the children and the dying. Her charismatic leadership became evident during the emergency. At a meeting of Mother Generals of many congregations in Rome shortly after the storm broke, she described the agony of the people. Massive help was needed to keep a dread cholera epidemic at bay. Fifteen Sisters from various congregations offered themselves as volunteers. Mother Teresa rushed with their passports to

Indian authorities, who waived all regulations regarding missionaries to admit the Sisters for emergency service. All the Sisters from overseas, including four Americans, lived in the Calcutta Motherhouse, sleeping dormitory-style like the Missionaries of Charity. They ate the same food and kept the same hours. Mother Teresa often related how deeply moved she had been when she wanted to thank the volunteer Sisters as they prepared to leave for their home convents. They reversed the procedure, thanking her, and insisting that they had received much more than they gave.

Mother Teresa took over a center in Green Park, near Dum Dum Airport, for child refugees near death from starvation and disease. It was part of Operation Lifeline and brought together child refugees with little chance for survival. The Sisters had to care for the children day and night and improvised a dormitory for themselves at the center.

In Salt Lake, a swampy expanse once a lake, the Calcutta Corporation had planned a housing development to relieve the congestion of Calcutta. Enormous sewer pipes were part of the preparation and into them crept the homeless for protection against the monsoon rains. Another housing development grew up in the spring of 1971. Rows of huts three miles long were thrown together to shelter men, women, and children who had made their way by walking, by riding bullock carts, by fording streams and rivers in fishing craft. No one knew the number of those who perished on their way, their corpses left to become bloated and black by the roadside or in the open fields. Many reached Salt Lake in a dying condition.

Prime Minister Indira Gandhi did not turn the refugees back, but stated in Parliament: "We will go through hell to meet this situation."

An impressive appeal booklet was published and distributed around the world, which featured an appeal by Mother Teresa.

"Let us remember this," she stated, "the people of Pakistan, the people of India, the people of Vietnam, all people wherever they may be, are the children of God, all created by the same hand. Today the Pakistan refugees belong especially to us. They are a part of God's family in this world. The problem is not only India's problem; it is the world's problem. We have millions of children suffering from malnutrition and starvation. Unless the world comes in with food and proteins, these children will die—and the world will have to answer for their death."

Mother Teresa paid a compliment to her country and to the Prime Minister in terms characteristic of her. "India has been wonderful in accepting and taking care of the millions of Pakistan refugees and we in India will take care of them. In opening the door to them, the Indian Prime Minister, Mrs. Gandhi, has done a wonderful Christlike thing."

The world did respond through governments, intergovernmental and voluntary agencies, with food, medicine, tarpaulins, building materials, trucks, and workers. Catholic Relief Services sent shiploads of food that reached over two of the ten million people in Salt Lake and all along the refugee-packed border area.

Mother Teresa and her Sisters took the worst work in Salt Lake, the cleaning of reeking hospital tents for those attacked by dysentery, cholera, smallpox, and other diseases made more lethal by privation.

Agencies such as the Office of the UN High Commissioner for Refugees and voluntary people-to-people agencies from all over the world had joined in. Expertise from overseas was exemplified by engineers from Germany who installed ten miles of pipelines for a water system and built a series of septic tanks. The cholera epidemic that threatened Calcutta from the refugee encampment was miraculously avoided.

One of the Sisters told me, "We went out by lorry early every morning and started our work. It was so hard to clean up those terrible places and make the people a bit clean. We have taken care of the sick and of the dying, but we could not get used to so many dying, especially the children. When I picked up the dead children, I could hardly feel their weight."

It was not long before the most tragic cases, those who had no family members with them, old people who had seen children and grandchildren die and were themselves not expected to live, were offered to Mother Teresa. No one in the world wanted them. Would she take them into the Home for the Dying in Kalighat? She accepted them and those who had come from across a border were nursed with the same tenderness as those brought in from a nearby street.

Senator Edward Kennedy, as chairman of the Committee on Refugees of the United States Senate, met with Mother Teresa and went with her to Salt Lake and to the Center near Dum Dum Airport.

"You see infants," he related, "with their skin hanging loosely in folds from their bones, lacking the strength to lift their heads. You see children with legs and feet swollen with edema and malnutrition, limp in the arms of their mothers. You see babies going blind for lack of vitamins, or covered with sores that will not heal. You see in the eyes of their parents, the despair of ever having their children well again. And, most difficult of all, you see the corpse of the child who died just the night before. I have a collection of personal observations that have really burned my soul."

A photograph taken in Salt Lake showed Mother Teresa hugging a refugee child to her breast. The expression on her face is one of agony and, as she explained later, anger. The child had simply been abandoned. The work in Dum Dum for suffering and dying child refugees and in the reeking sick bays of the Salt Lake encampment consumed her strength. Mother Teresa paid what she thought was to be a quick visit to the Sisters in Benares (Varanasi) and fell ill from utter exhaustion. I received a cable that she would not be able to come to New York in August.

When informed of this, Cardinal Cooke found that another group of Sisters was willing to serve the migrant workers. He made a decision to have the Missionaries of Charity work with the people in New York City's most troubled areas. This was the work that had been closest to Mother Teresa's heart from the beginning. A flurry of cables followed and Mother Teresa agreed to place the team in New York City. She was not accustomed to American phraseology and queried as to what section of New York was the "Inner City." This was explained and the matter was settled.

Another problem presented itself, since Mother Teresa had promised to be present at three meetings in September. Whenever a date was set for her arrival in the United States, a spate of invitations was generated. They were sent to me as the link with Mother Teresa. I made copies and sent the originals to Calcutta. Mother Teresa would inform me by letter or cable through the Calcutta office of Catholic Relief Services which engagements she would accept. I would then inform the group and make the necessary travel arrangements for her.

This method, begun in 1960, worked smoothly for seventeen years, especially after the Calcutta office of Catholic Relief Services installed a telex machine for almost instant communication with New York. When the Sisters were well established in New York, the superior took on the task of scheduling Mother Teresa's visits—though thereafter the Calcutta telex still continued to be useful.

Early in September Mother Teresa was to speak at the Conference of Major Superiors of Religious Congregations in Atlanta, Georgia. She was also scheduled to receive the Good Samaritan Award of the National Catholic Development Conference in Boston, Massachusetts, and to be awarded an honorary doctorate of Humane Letters at the Catholic University of America in Washington, D.C.

When I telephoned to cancel the Atlanta appearance, there was deep disappointment. At a time when Mother Teresa's congregation was going against all the signs of decline in religious orders, they wanted to hear directly from her. Yet Mother Teresa in her simplicity wanted to learn from them. She wrote:

> "Dear Major Superiors,
>
> I am very sorry to have to disappoint you. I have been looking forward to meeting you and learning from you, but as you know, I have been working very hard with the refugee problem, and so I find myself physically unable to come to the meeting."

When I telephoned to cancel Mother Teresa's appearance at the Boston meeting, the organizers stated that there was an open space in the program for a talk by Mother Teresa. It was too late for them to arrange for anyone else to fill it, so they insisted that I relate my experiences with the Missionaries of Charity. In Mother Teresa's name, I accepted the Good Samaritan Award from Fr. Edward J. Gorry, president of the National Catholic Development Conference and a priest of the Passionist Congregation. Citing Mother Teresa as an "apostle of love," he stated, "In honoring Mother Teresa, we honor her selfless efforts to alleviate the misery and suffering of the poor and needy of the world, which are an inspiration to mankind, and a splendid example of the concern for humanity which the Good Samaritan Award is intended to recognize."

The third engagement, involving a special convocation at the Catholic University of America in Washington, D.C., was canceled. In writing to Patrick Cardinal O'Boyle, Archbishop of Washington, Mother Teresa added a note, "Maybe Our Lord does not want honor for the Society." Catholic University persisted and when I informed them that Mother Teresa would be with the Sisters in New York during the month of October, they rescheduled the convocation for October 29. Mother Teresa's presence inspired a large attendance at the convocation. Before the president of the university conferred the degree, I was asked to describe the beginning of Mother Teresa's work, as well as its meaning and expansion. It was the first of many honorary degrees conferred on Mother Teresa in the coming decade.

One of the cables I sent to Mother Teresa in September contained this message: "Malcolm Muggeridge counts on you to be in New York October 21 and 22 for a few programs. Please confirm."

Mother Teresa would not confirm her presence for October but told us to expect the team of Missionaries of Charity in September—without her. She wrote asking for help for the Sisters in their first days, and Cardinal Cooke arranged for them to live temporarily with the Handmaids of Mary, a congregation of black Sisters in their Harlem convent.

In September 1971, I received a letter from the Calcutta Motherhouse announcing the coming of the Missionaries of Charity to New York. The writer was the German girl who had studied medicine and wanted to take up leprosy work. It was in her hometown, Freiburg, that I had fallen into the drain gutter to be picked up by Mother Teresa.

She wrote:

Dear Miss Egan,

This is Sr. Andrea, whose home you visited with Mother Teresa in Freiburg, Germany—so I think I won't have to introduce myself all over again.

Mother has just asked me to give you the list of names of the Sisters who will be coming to New York—so here they are:

Sr. M. Rosemary, a Bengali Sister
Sr. M. Sophia, } both from Kerala
Sr. M. Gilbert, }
and Sr. M. Paul, a Mangalorian, at present in London.
She will join us in Rome.

Now, as for the preparation of our new home. I know you and everybody would like to do it as beautifully as you can think of. But Mother and I would like to ask you urgently not to prepare anything lest it be not in keeping with our poverty. If it is possible to get for us six simple iron beds and some simple furniture—preferably second-hand and even not varnished, that would do perfectly (e.g., a table, two simple benches and a plain stool, a cupboard and some shelves for books, etc.) Old boxes of all sizes will come in handy. I'm sure you understand and will help us to keep up our spirit.

Looking forward to meeting you. Please do not forget to help us with your prayers, too. And may God be ever in your heart.

Sr. M. Andrea, M.C.

P.S. We are bringing our own Indian kitchen utensils and our mattresses.

The letter reflected as nothing else Mother Teresa's insistence on the strictest adherence to poverty of life, an adherence that could easily be weakened in a consumer society.

I could not see the expressions on the faces of the customs officers at Kennedy Airport as the five Sisters presented their bizarre baggage, but when the line of Sisters approached me, hugging their bedrolls, I thought of the poorest immigrants of the nineteenth century who brought their bulging bedding and pillows to the New World. I felt I knew Sister Andrea already and soon knew the other Sisters. Sister Gilbert was the youngest and we soon referred to her as "the baby" of the team.

At the convent of the Handmaids of Mary in Harlem, the superior of the congregation, Sister Miriam Cecelia looked surprised. She had arranged sleeping quarters for the Missionaries of Charity. Her hospitality and the warmth of her Sisters, especially Sister Jacqueline Banks, made the first weeks of the Missionaries of Charity in New York a time of joy.

When one of the Handmaids of Mary, Sister Mary Bernard, celebrated her silver jubilee as a Sister, the Missionaries of Charity were invited to join in the festivity. It began with a mass at 5:30 P.M. in St. Aloysius, one of Harlem's black parishes. The mass was concelebrated by fourteen priests. As Sister Andrea described it, "Relations and friends came from all parts of the compass, wearing their best clothes and flowers to rejoice with Sister . . . After the jubilee mass, there was a feast in the parish school, with a jazz band. Owing to the noise, it was hardly possible to hear oneself speak. Physically handicapped people in wheelchairs came to the party.

"One girl, by name Barbara, twenty-seven years old, had been suffering from multiple sclerosis for nine years. She looked unhappy and wanted nothing to do with me. When I told her that my own given name had also been Barbara, and that as a doctor I had been working with many physically handicapped people in India, she relaxed a bit. Her withdrawn demeanor changed in that rather noisy atmosphere quite amicably. We parted like old friends and I thank God that I was able to open a door to her heart."

There were weeks of learning, of meeting people, of descending into the depths of New York through its subways. The convent of the Handmaids of Mary was at 15 West 124th Street, a block away from jam-packed 125th Street, one of the main arteries of Harlem's ebullient life. Black Muslims smiled and greeted the Sisters evidently considering them visitors from some overseas Islamic country. Women members of the Black Muslims often wore white, including white head coverings.

I had remembered the need for six simple iron beds, the sixth being for Mother Teresa herself. These could not be found even in secondhand furniture stores. I decided the best place to forage for such metal bedsteads would be in the warehouse of Catholic Relief Services. The agency often received donations from hospitals that were being renovated or from institutions that were closing down. I found some metal bedsteads, very low, with the head of the bed curved and supported by upright bars. I took Sister Andrea to see them. She was amazed.

"They are exactly what we need. That's the M.C. bed we have in Calcutta."

We delivered the bedsteads to the convent. The shiny metal springs were just right for the mattresses brought from India.

Often such happy coincidences occurred with Mother Teresa and the Sisters. Again and again I was to experience with them that "things come down right." These beds, for example, were certainly in place at the right time. Mother Teresa would attribute it to providence, in the sense that *Provisor providebit* (The Provider will provide). God, as the Provider of all, has and will provide for His creatures. I often thought of the distinction between ordinary providence by which our daily needs are met, and extraordinary providence in which an unusual and totally unexpected or even wildly improbable answer materializes to meet a need. Mother Teresa seemed to make no distinction between ordinary and extraordinary providence. Almost every time she spoke, she called attention to the loving delicacy with which God reached down to meet human needs, beginning with His coming to human beings in human form.

Besides the message from Malcolm Muggeridge, mentioned before, there were two other pressing calls that had to be answered.

One call had been from Washington, D.C., where Mother Teresa was to receive an award from the Joseph P. Kennedy Jr. Foundation, on October 15, 1971. The other call had been from Toronto, Canada, where Mother Teresa was to join Jean Vanier in addressing a youth rally on the "Secret of Peace" on October 18, 1971.

We finally heard that Mother Teresa's usual resilience had asserted itself. She was to arrive in New York on October 14 and would visit Rome and Belfast, Northern Ireland, on the way. For the first time, as she stepped out of customs at Kennedy Airport, Mother Teresa found her own Sisters waiting to greet her.

They rushed under the restraining ropes and greeted her in the Indian manner, wreathing her in a garland of white flowers. These were not real flowers as Indian custom would have it, to envelop the visitor in a sea of scent, but crepe paper facsimiles, intricately fashioned by the Sisters. Mother Teresa placed her right hand in blessing on the head of each Sister.

On arrival in Harlem, Sister Miriam Cecelia embraced her as a sister as well as a Sister-Religious and made her feel at home among her own family of Sisters.

The reunion was brief since Mother Teresa had to hurry to Washington, D.C. The Joseph P. Kennedy Jr. Foundation had as its purpose to study the causes and treatment of mental retardation. The foundation was named for Joseph P. Kennedy, Jr., the eldest of the four Kennedy brothers, who had been killed in the Second World War. The sole surviving son, following the deaths by assassination of President John F. Kennedy and Senator Robert Kennedy, Senator Edward M. Kennedy, was the foundation's president.

One of the Kennedy daughters, Rosemary, was mentally retarded and the foundation seemed a clear example of how a seeming tragedy could be turned to compassionate service to others. Already forty-two million dollars had been spent by the foundation in research into the prevention and amelioration of mental retardation, in awards, and in programs for retarded and handicapped children. The 1971 awards totaling $120,000 were made at a symposium entitled "Choices on Our Consciences." Mother Teresa found herself in a unique and ground-breaking conference which attracted dozens of speakers, including Nobel laureates, scientists, moralists, and medical personnel as well as hundreds of participants. It aired questions of life and death too seldom brought to public notice.

Mother Teresa attended a general session on "Who Should Survive: Is Survival a Right?" which included a film taken at a hospital dealing with a newborn baby permitted to die of starvation. Johns Hopkins Hospital in Baltimore had allowed a filming of the case because it highlighted a dilemma of hospital authorities. The parents of an infant had refused to sign the permission for lifesaving surgery. The newborn was seen in his crib, while the parents, their identities concealed and their backs to the camera, were told that their baby had been diagnosed as a mongoloid, afflicted with Down's syndrome, and therefore subject to severe retardation. They were informed that he also needed an operation to relieve a blockage of the intestines. Without that operation, the child could not be fed and would die. The mother, a nurse, said that among other things, she did not want a mongoloid child to affect the lives of their two normal children. The father said he would go along with his wife since she knew more about such things than he did. They categorically refused permission for the surgery.

The film showed the child in a separate room with a dread notice attached to its crib, NOTHING BY MOUTH. The doctors had nothing further to do with the child, but the nurses had to give daily care to an infant sentenced to death. One nurse said she would hold him and rock him and found it easy to love him. For fifteen days, the child put up a fight for life and finally expired.

In the panel discussion afterward, the question was raised as to whether the doctors should have obtained a court order allowing them to countermand the parents' decision. It was pointed out that such a court order would probably have been obtained despite the choice of the parents if it had been a normal child. The certainty that mongoloids would be severely retarded was disputed by such evidence as the fact that two victims of Down's syndrome had received doctorates at Harvard.

I asked Mother Teresa what she would have done if she had been in Johns Hopkins Hospital in the face of the parents' refusal to permit the lifesaving operation.

"Court order or no court order, I would have snatched up that baby and run with him to where he could be saved. I wouldn't care if the police came after me. I wouldn't give up that baby."

Mother Teresa served as the respondent on a panel on "Why Should People Care?" One of the panelists was Elie Wiesel, who as a child survived the extermination camp of Auschwitz, scene of the murder of over four million human beings. He pointed to indifference and forgetfulness of great crimes like the Holocaust as a reason why more of mankind—even mankind itself—might fall victim to mass destruction. "The tale of what was done to my people," said Wiesel, "can save mankind from a similar fate. Which means: we must care—lest we fall victims to our own indifference."

Mother Teresa talked of the discarded people she found on the streets of Calcutta where she started her work and referred to the millions of refugees from East Pakistan suffering at that moment in Bengal. Each of them, she said, must be recognized as having the divine spirit and, therefore, must be loved and helped.

Wiesel's presence as a witness to man's death-dealing powers, in the same room with Mother Teresa's witness to life's inviolable sacredness and the duty to nurture it, formed the most poignantly dramatic conjunction of the symposium.

In the same panel and hovering over the compassionate presence of Elie Wiesel and Mother Teresa was the dispassionate spirit of science itself in the person of Jacques Monod, Nobel laureate in genetics. The expression on his classic face was unchanging as he recited from the conclusion of his book, *Chance and Necessity,* the last chapter of which had been distributed to the participants. To Monod, man had to come to terms with the fact that he is alone in an unfeeling universe from which he has emerged by chance.

Monod questioned the effect on society's future when the natural weeding out of the unfit (as has heretofore happened in history) is suspended and genetic cripples live long enough to reproduce.

By chance (to use Monod's term), Monod was sitting at the same table as Mother Teresa at a reception at the home of Sargent and Eunice Kennedy Shriver. Nodding in the direction of Mother Teresa, Monod asked me what she did. I explained her work for the poorest of the poor, including the rescue of the dying, and mentioned that she had founded a new religious society in Calcutta to carry out the work.

Monod trained his cool blue eyes on Mother Teresa and looked aghast: "You cannot mean a new religious group in India?"

The theater at the John F. Kennedy Center for the Performing Arts was filled on the evening of October 16, for the presentation of the awards. Each award amounted to twelve thousand dollars and carried with it a silver-based Waterford crystal vase and a crystal plate with an image of St. Raphael the Archangel. A note explained that the Kennedy Foundation had chosen the "Seraph Raphael, chief of the guardian angels who protect and guide mankind," as a symbol in order to "honor knowledge as the servant of compassion and love."

Various members of the Kennedy family presented the eight awards. Most of the award recipients gave a brief response of appreciation. The briefest of all came from the behaviorist, B. F. Skinner, whose experiments with reinforcing acceptable behavior through rewards had been successful with many retarded persons. Accepting the check inside the large vase, he turned to the audience which exploded with appreciative laughter when he said two words: "Very reinforcing."

When it came time to present the award to Mother Teresa, Senator Kennedy himself mounted the stage. As an introduction, he had a section of the film *Something Beautiful for God* shown on the screen. It was the scene in which Mother Teresa looks into the eyes of one of the discarded scraps of humanity at Shishu Bhavan, a wisp of an infant. "There's life in her," says Mother Teresa with delight in her voice.

Senator Kennedy stated that his mother, Mrs. Rose Kennedy, had wished to make the presentation but was not well enough to be with them. Said Senator Kennedy, "In her unique geography of compassion, Mother Teresa knows where the need is and in her unique faith never doubts that the means to meet it, in help and material resources, will be forthcoming. It is our privilege to ensure that her faith is ever more abundantly fulfilled."

Mother Teresa merely said, "Thank you. God bless you."

In the report of the award ceremony in *Christian Century*, J. Robert Nelson wrote, "For Dr. Skinner, for the scientists and the social leaders, they had clapped their hands. For this tiny woman from Calcutta, they rise to their feet . . . In all the magic ceremony at Camelot there are no religious trappings, no churchmen to 'give the invocation,' no facile reference to God. But for *that* audience, there could have been no more authentic witness to the power of Christ in human affairs."

Andrew Young, then chairman of the Atlanta Community Relations Committee, was a fellow respondent with Mother Teresa at the panel on "Why Should People Care?" In introducing him to Mother Teresa, I told her of his work with Martin Luther King, a work much influenced by the nonviolent campaigns of Gandhi with the specific inspiration of the suffering Christ. She enthusiastically invited Young to visit with her and the Sisters in Harlem. Young accepted, explaining that he had to go to New York in any case.

On the evening of October 17, Andrew Young was at the door of the Harlem convent of the Handmaids of Mary. Soon he was sitting with Mother Teresa and the Sisters in the convent parlor and hearing Mother Teresa explain that she wanted to know about the beautiful things in the lives of American blacks. What she had heard up to then was mostly a recital of problems. I was one of those who had stressed the problems and how different they were from those of India. Young told her something of his association with Martin Luther King and of his own life. He described the strong role of religion in the life of black people in the South. The Sisters were eagerly drinking in his words. Perhaps it was Young who mentioned the hymns and gospel singing are so much a part of black religious life. In any case, Mother Teresa asked him to sing a hymn.

Young's rich baritone was soon raised in "Lead, Kindly Light." Mother Teresa's clear soprano joined in. We all sat transfixed; it was something we wanted to remember. Young took out photographs of his wife and daughter and Mother Teresa told him of the places where her family of Sisters were working.

"Lead, Kindly Light," the hymn written by Cardinal Newman, was a favorite hymn of Mahatma Gandhi. It seemed a good beginning for religious Sisters from India. Young was soon to become the first black congressman from Georgia and later the U.S. Ambassador to the UN before returning to become the elected mayor of Atlanta. Mother Teresa found that the twelve-thousand-dollar award had been increased to fifteen thousand dollars through a personal gift from Mrs. Rose Kennedy. She turned the Waterford crystal vase over to Sister Andrea, saying, "This will be for the chapel in your New York house." The funds, she told us, would go toward making the Dum Dum center for near dying refugee children a permanent center for retarded and handicapped children. It would be called, she told us, the Nirmala Kennedy Center. I wondered if any other new centers arose from the symposium on "Choices on Our Consciences."

Massey Hall in Toronto was packed on the evening of October 18, 1971, to hear Mother Teresa and Jean Vanier address themselves to the "Secret of Peace."

The audience was chiefly young people, united in a youth corps of worship and service, led by Father Tom McKillop. McKillop was young himself, with a cool manner that was the very opposite of the "hyped-up" approach that was supposed to arouse young people. This authentic reserve seemed to be his special charism in a culture where young people were bombarded with excited appeals to buy this or consume that in order to experience instant happiness.

An afternoon mass was celebrated by Fr. McKillop in a small inner-city house where the Sisters of St. Joseph made their home. Sister Sue Mosteller, who as Canadian representative of Jean Vanier's L'Arche movement, had helped set up the meeting, was a Sister of St. Joseph. We all sat on the floor as if we had been at mass in India. Learning that Massey Hall would be crowded with three thousand people, Mother Teresa turned to Vanier and told him of her hesitancy in speaking before large audiences. Vanier told her not to be disturbed, that he would be sitting near her on the stage. Unmentioned was the support of his prayers.

The immensely tall Jean Vanier, with a Mother Teresa who never looked so tiny, came out on the stage of Massey Hall to the rousing and boisterous sounds of folk music. Not only was every seat taken, but youngsters were sitting in the aisles and the overflow squatted on every inch of the stage. As the spotlight beamed on them and Jean Vanier rose to introduce Mother Teresa, a stillness fell on the hall. Vanier was one of their own, already a well-known author and son of a former governor-general of Canada. In every way he was the opposite of Mother Teresa, an intellectual who had completed doctoral studies in philosophy and theology. Yet as he introduced his friend Mother Teresa, it was clear that despite their difference, they were embodiments of the same quality, merciful love. His phrasing differed little from that of Mother Teresa, since his work for disfigured and disabled people came out of his belief in the Disfigured One.

Mother Teresa described the work of the Sisters in Calcutta in showing love to the abandoned and dying, to the lepers, to children deprived of schooling, to children discarded in dustbins. Then she concretized her message, telling them that peace began right in their own homes. It was so easy, she said, to think of how one would work in Calcutta, and to miss the very person we are living with, a person near to us, who needs a loving word, who needs our loving help. It has to start right where people find themselves.

"Children," she said, "ask your parents to teach you how to pray. That is the beginning."

While she spoke, Vanier squatted on the crowded stage, not much shorter in this position than Mother Teresa on her feet. In his turn, Vanier emphasized her message, pointing out those who joined peace demonstrations should first be reconciled with those around them, starting with their own families. The young people should search out in their own city where there were pockets of suffering and need. There are such places of need in every city, he told them, "little Calcuttas," in the homes for the retarded and institutions for the mentally ill. The burden of his message was that peace must start with reconciliation and service. The secret to peace must first be found in the heart of each person.

The message, or perhaps the persons in whom the message was incarnated, captured the young people. They seemed to hunger for a key to peace that could start exactly where they were, and then spread to those around them. There were questions from the audience, and the spotlight beamed mercilessly on the speakers all evening since the event was being filmed. It emphasized the weary lines on Mother Teresa's face and the tiredness of her red-rimmed eyes. With a last "God bless you," she was able to leave the stage after a meeting lasting three hours.

Returning to the little convent of the Sisters of St. Joseph, we met, near St. Michael's Cathedral, a woman coworker of Father McKillop's, Tia Durkin. Mother Teresa sought her out in the dark street and took her hand saying, "I want to thank you very, very much for tonight." Tia

Durkin's voice showed her surprise. She said she had done nothing meriting the thanks of Mother Teresa.

"Oh yes, you did," Mother Teresa said. "When I started to speak, I saw your eyes looking at me with such love. I thought to myself, I'll be all right: so then I looked at you and talked to you this evening. I want to thank you for what you did."

With Mother Teresa, at all times and in all places, it was the person who mattered. The next morning, Mother Teresa was up before dawn for meditation and prayers to face a day that included a television interview in which she and Jean Vanier faced challenging and perceptive questions from Patrick Watson.

Watson adverted to the fact that both Mother Teresa and Jean Vanier were considered to be saints. He asked them whether they had any fear of dying. Vanier broke in with the response that he hoped that Mother Teresa would be holding his hand when he was dying. Watson asked Mother Teresa about her notion of love. She always talked of loving people in Jesus, he said, because they represented Jesus. What if he, Patrick Watson, for example, felt that that was not enough. Supposing he wanted to be loved for his own sake, what would she say to that?

Mother Teresa smiled and said that Jesus comes in so many forms, even so many disguises, that there was no difficulty in loving each person as a person. The words of the priest-poet, Gerard Manley Hopkins, ran through my mind. He came close to catching the limitless fascination of Christ for those whose lives were bound up with His, saying, "for Christ plays in ten thousand places, lovely in limbs and lovely in eyes not His . . ."

Further in the interview, Watson probed for the reason that Mother Teresa had granted it. Did she want people to give money? Did she want greater support for her work? Mother Teresa made it clear that she did not make appeals for her work, that the only support was providence. Then, pressed on Watson, why did she agree to this interview? Mother Teresa explained that she agreed because interviewing was his work, his job, and she wanted to cooperate.

At that point, Watson, obviously moved, said, "This is too much." He asked the cameras to go off and thanked Mother Teresa and Jean Vanier.

Malcolm Muggeridge was awaiting Mother Teresa in New York, with more television and press appearances scheduled in connection with *Something Beautiful for God,* which had been published in New York, October 6, 1971. Before making public appearances, Mother Teresa stopped off, as she always did, at the Consulate of India to greet the consul general.

One of the first television appearances was a joint one, with David Frost putting the questions to Mother Teresa and to Malcolm Muggeridge. The question of the contrast between suffering humanity and a loving God seemed the point about which Frost, a minister's son, hovered in his talk with Muggeridge. It was clear that he found it hard to digest Muggeridge's reference to suffering as part of the everlasting drama between Creator and creature, a drama that enriches life and makes it more fascinating. Mother Teresa talked simply about her work with the poor and with those cast off by society. Her summing up drew the program together.

"You must know the poor in order to love them. You must love the poor in order to serve them."

Sitting in the studio and watching the interview while awaiting his own interview was the novelist Norman Mailer. On being introduced to Mother Teresa, Mailer volunteered the comment: "I have not been in favor of religious programming on TV. This has turned me around. I can see its place now."

An appearance on the *Today Show,* a program viewed by millions across the country, was moved up from eight o'clock in the morning to seven o'clock so that a harpist could take the later time. At six o'clock we left the South Bronx for the television studio where Mother Teresa was introduced to Barbara Walters. The latter was not at her best, describing Mother Teresa as a "humanitarian" and filling in six minutes with flat, workmanlike questions that elicited straight answers from Mother Teresa.

On our way to television and press interviews, we drove through the theater district. A theater was showing *Oh! Calcutta!* one of the most avante-garde theater pieces ever to reach New York, from the point of view of nudity. Mother Teresa looked up at the marquee, looked away, and sighed a deep sigh. She made no query about it.

Muggeridge had purchased the New York *Times* and was glancing through it for a notice about his book. Mother Teresa caught sight of a large advertisement for *Something Beautiful for God,* featuring her photograph as it appeared on the cover.

"There she is," she remarked.

We laughed, but it was a spontaneously revealing remark. All this publicity was outside of her, had nothing to do with her personally. She was simply an instrument.

For the next few days, we made a joke of this attitude. I would say deferentially, "Would *she* be ready to leave for the visit with Cardinal Cooke? *Her* is ready to go." Or, "Will *she* please come to the telephone?" Mother Teresa went along with the joke. When I picked up the copy of the book she had autographed for me, I found "One for her from—She—God love you and keep you always in His own Heart. God bless you.—M. Teresa M.C."

Before leaving, Malcolm Muggeridge came to the convent of the Missionaries of Charity in the South Bronx. They had just moved from Harlem, from the hospitality of the black Sisters.

The convent was a sturdy, three-story building vacated sometime previously by Sisters who had taught in the parish school of St. Pius X. Mother Teresa was happy with its simplicity. One room had already been chosen for the chapel and Mother Teresa was planning to put up I THIRST on the wall behind the altar. It had to be a temporary shelter for the Sisters, Mother Teresa was told, since along with the few remaining houses on the block, it was already condemned and scheduled for demolition.

The Sisters were cooking their first meal, rejoicing to have their Mother with them. Their dining room was ready, a narrow table, alongside of which were two wooden benches. They were freshly painted in bright green and had probably served as garden benches. One of the sisters had neatly sawed off the backs. Malcolm, a vegetarian, made a meal of a cheese sandwich which I believe he brought in his pocket.

Muggeridge brought up a practical question. He was being paid for the David Frost interview. Could he put it to some special use? The royalties from *Something Beautiful for God* had already been committed by Muggeridge to Mother Teresa's work. I remembered Shadona, the sad youngster whose little brother had died. The Sisters thought it time for her to get married. Muggeridge was pleased with the idea of a dowry.

He later sent a note: "Enclosed is the David Frost check duly endorsed, and I hope that it will help Shadona to get a good husband." He added that while he felt that things went fairly well in New York, "One has an uneasy feeling that a great many Americans do not know what Mother Teresa is all about."

We left Mother Teresa and the Sisters settling into a new home and made our way from the South Bronx into Manhattan. Looking about us, we could not help but be reminded of wartime. Immediately outside the convent was a field of rubble, and just beyond, a row of gutted houses, ruined as if by a fire bomb. Something beautiful had quietly alighted in the midst of a troubled neighborhood in a landscape marked with signs of destruction.

Malcolm Muggeridge's book had been launched in the United States and would carry Mother Teresa's story into country after country, with translations ranging from the Scandinavian to the Hungarian. It was also printed in Braille and issued on cassettes as a "Talking Book." The film spoke its own language of compassion on television screens and in innumerable private showings for Co-Worker groups around the world from the United States to Australia. For the first time in history, a living nun had emerged as a screen personality.

The interest of the press and the media in general, already aroused by the poignance and drama of Mother Teresa's work, was now intensified.

Squads of pressmen met her at airports and batteries of cameras were turned on her as she came to address meetings. She could have refused, but she was convinced that the world needed the Good News as never before. It needed to be reminded that all creation, and the crown of creation, humankind, came forth from the loving hand of the Creator, and that the lives of his creatures should reflect that love. She was a small instrument for carrying the Good News, no more "than a pencil in His hands." It was an unutterable sacrifice for her, but one she accepted patiently and good-humoredly, even when she was at the point of exhaustion.

An interviewer once reminded Mother Teresa that she asked people to make sacrifices, to share in the sufferings of the cross. What, he wondered, was her own share in the sufferings of the cross? She looked around at the newspapermen who blocked her way out of the airport, at the cameras trained on her every move, and with a rueful smile, answered him in one word, "This."

15

To Give a Reason

From an ever-widening circle, calls came to Mother Teresa as the work was reported by the media and as people saw for themselves how the Missionaries of Charity incarnated fidelity to the least of humankind around the world.

The calls came from expected sources, like the Vatican, which invited her to join the delegation to the International Women's Year Conference of the United Nations in Mexico City. They also came from national hierarchies which asked for her presence at Eucharistic Congresses and from ecumenical gatherings. They came from the church in Africa, taking the Sisters to Tanzania, but also to Ethiopia. They came from bishops in islands in the Indian Ocean and in the Southwest Pacific, taking Sisters to Mauritius and Papua New Guinea. Most unexpected of all came the call from Yemen where there were needs to be met, but not a single native Christian.

Mother Teresa felt impelled to answer these calls, sometimes to address great crowds, sometimes to take teams of Sisters to remote corners of the planet. One of the qualities of the followers of Jesus, as described by St. Paul, was that of being "ready always to give everyone a reason for that hope which is in you."

That Mother Teresa communicated hope, even to those of other traditions, was made clear in a statement by the President of India, V. V. Giri. In presenting the Nehru Award, decided upon earlier but delayed until 1972 because of her extensive journeyings, Giri stated: "Mother Teresa is among those emancipated souls who have transcended all barriers of race, religion, creed, and nation. In this troubled world of today, embittered by numerous conflicts and hatred, the life and work of Mother Teresa bring new hope for the future of mankind."

In a world of vanishing values and at a time when hope for justice and peace became dim in many parts of the globe, people wanted to hear in person from Mother Teresa the reason for the hope that shone from her face and lit up her words.

While she answered these calls, she always did her best to spend time between journeys with the young Sisters still in training. For the first fifteen years of the life of the congregation, she had personally focused her mind and heart on forming them; in a sense, she had hand-tooled the early Missionaries of Charity, so that when she began to be called away, they could transmit what they had received to the postulants and novices. She attempted always to give special attention to the tertians, those about to take final vows. She attempted to visit every house in every country once a year or, at least, once in every two years.

She also considered the needs of Bengal as having a special call on her heart and her energies, as was indicated in the delay in coming to New York because of the refugee crisis in West Bengal.

The same crisis claimed the attention of Mother Teresa and the Missionaries of Charity at the end of 1971.

The stream of nearly ten million refugees who had survived in Salt Lake and in a thousand camps along the entire border with East Pakistan was turned back after the events in December 1971. Those events consisted of an armed offensive on East Pakistan by the Indian Army and the surrender on December 16, of the troops of West Pakistan. The burden of the refugee presence was lifted from a province and a city ready to sink under it.

Cholera, a yearly visitor to Calcutta, threatened to break out at Salt Lake and to engulf the city in an especially virulent epidemic. It was only stemmed by an incredibly effective convergence of compassion from overseas joined with local and voluntary agencies. The United Nations agencies, representatives of various governments, international voluntary agencies, like Caritas, Catholic Relief Services, and Church World Service, channeled literally mountains of medical supplies and tent materials in an unprecedented lifesaving campaign. The Indian Red Cross, as overall coordinator, was able to reach not only Salt Lake but the farthest camps where refugees were competing with local people for scarce resources, especially firewood. The initial compassion of local people was giving way to fear for their own survival in the face of diminishing resources.

At the end of the two-week war in December, refugees recrossed the border by every means possible, many of them reluctantly because of the terror they had known. They entered a country with a new name, Bangla Desh (Bengal Nation), which had declared its complete autonomy from West Pakistan. While the resistance fighters and the people freed from occupation sang the Tagore song, *Sonar Bangla* (Golden Bengal), they soon faced the fact that their nation was considered to be an "international basket case."

On one of the first truck convoys to enter Bangladesh on December 17 was Mother Teresa. With her were Sister Gertrude and several other Sisters ready to bind up the wounds of war.

"We first had to bury some of the dead," Mother Teresa told me. We were sitting in a little parlor in the Calcutta Motherhouse. It was early in March 1972 and I was on my way to Dacca. The agony of a people seemed to capture her face, more deeply lined with every passing year.

"We saw the most terrible sufferings and need in Bangladesh, and we must do all we can. Our Sisters started right away to help. But the greatest need in Bangladesh," she said slowly, "is for forgiveness. You have no idea how these people have suffered. There is so much bitterness and hatred left. Perhaps if they believed that people cared about them, if they felt loved, they could find it in their hearts to forgive what was done to them. I think this is the only thing that can bring peace.

"We went to Khulna, Pabna, and Rajshahi, as well as Dacca," she related. "In Pabna, the authorities wanted to give us a large building, a regular palace, but I did not accept. There were not many girls coming to ask for help, and I think also that it is better for the Missionaries of Charity to work in more simple houses. I talked with the people and I decided that we could work in Dacca and Khulna. One thing I told them was that we would take all the babies and find homes for them. Killing, I said, is killing; even if the child is not yet born."

Mother Teresa's concern for young girls and their infants arose from the fact that besides the enormous loss of life and the visible devastation of the occupation, the burnt villages, the mounds of corpses, the looted schools and institutions, there was a hidden devastation. It was a trail of rape reaching from one corner of the country to the other. Some estimated the number of violated women at two hundred thousand. The occupying army had earned the hatred of the people because of the number of misused girls, including thousands abducted from schools and homes and kept in army cantonments. An untold number of young women were pregnant.

There was immeasurable gratitude to those who saved young women from rape, notably the Sisters of a convent near Mymensingh. This convent suddenly acquired nearly a hundred new "novices" and kept them hidden behind convent walls. A complex of Christian villages around Nagari sheltered hunted girls and threatened families. The pastor of Nagari, an American Holy Cross priest, Fr. Ed Goedert, turned school buildings into emergency homes. Eventually, the wrath of the occupiers was turned against Goedert's flock.

To enter Bangladesh, it was necessary for me to obtain a travel pass in Calcutta. It was in the parlor of the Calcutta Motherhouse that I spent the next two days while arranging for it. The nights were spent on a thin mattress placed on raised boards. The first night, the noises of Lower Circular Road were so insistent that there was no question of sleep. Toward morning, when drowsiness began to take over, the bells and rumble of tramcars became louder, as did the croaking of crows and the loud calls of food vendors. I lay there thinking of old London where the streets had also been loud with the cries of vendors of the fast foods of the day.

When I got up to clean my teeth, I opened a bottle of Fanta, an orange drink, as a substitute for water to which I was not yet immunized. On the following night, sleep came immediately and was uninterrupted. Even Calcutta's night sounds cannot penetrate after one has spent the daytime hours moving about the streets.

Heavy-eyed and relieved that that first night was over, I went to mass with the Sisters. Sister Benedict served me the Sisters' breakfast of tea and *chapatties,* with the addition of eggs for the guest. She told me she was a native of what was now Bangladesh.

"My family is from Noakhali," she told me. "When Gandhi came in the time of partition, I was a little girl. I was the one they chose from our village to put the *mala* around his neck. I have never forgotten that."

I wondered if the fact that her family was Christian and, therefore, outside the communal strife had been the reason for the choice. Gandhi's pilgrimage through the violence-torn Noakhali district was an attempt at reconciliation between Muslims and Hindus. It was attacks against Hindus in Noakhali that motivated the Hindu communities in Bihar to drive out Bihari Muslims, who then took refuge in newly demarcated East Pakistan. I was to see the dread effects of that expulsion in a short time.

Before leaving for Dacca, I went with Mother Teresa to visit one of the few good things that sprouted during the refugee influx—and remained. It was the Nirmala Kennedy Center at Green Park near Dum Dum Airport. The buildings constructed to shelter the most famished of the refugee children during 1971 were turned over to Mother Teresa. With funds from the Kennedy Award, the buildings were renovated to provide shelter for mentally retarded and physically handicapped children. Already over a hundred children, some so grossly handicapped that they could not feed themselves, some so retarded that they could be taught very little, were cared for in cheerful, well-lighted rooms. A squad of Sisters and helpers were continually busy with the little ones, changing, feeding, hugging, laughing, talking, and singing. I stopped at the crib of a child with spidery legs and useless arms. The Sister had just changed the sheet and washed off the rubber sheet underneath. She was a little girl of about six who gave me so melting a smile that it evoked love and at the same time returned the love already given. It occurred to me that elsewhere she would have been a candidate for extinction. I could hardly credit my senses which told me that the place was sweet-smelling and spotless. As the number of helpless little ones rose to four hundred, I felt sure that the Sisters would continue to perform the same daily miracle.

One little girl with a bright blue ribbon in her hair bounded about, greeting us, and taking Mother Teresa's hand. She must have been about three years of age.

"This is Indira," said Mother Teresa. "She was left behind when the people went back to Bangladesh. No one knows who she is. Her parents may have died. We'll keep her here in case someone comes for her. Later, she can come to Shishu Bhavan."

I saw little Indira as the last of the millions of the displaced, a tiny human relic of massive misery.

On the "Dacca side," as it was referred to, a native of Dacca, Sister Margaret Mary, met me. She had been named by Mother Teresa to head a house for violated and pregnant women. Sister Margaret Mary was one of the first group of twelve pioneers in the Missionaries of Charity.

Bishop Ganguly of Dacca gave the Missionaries of Charity a three-hundred-year-old convent in old Dacca. It was said to have anciently served as a convent of the Poor Clares, the companion order of the Friars of St. Francis. It was one of the vestiges of the Portuguese presence and their *Padroado* of the East. It stood on Islampur Road, behind a thick gray wall which could not keep out the noises of the market stalls where everything from textiles to hot foods were sold. Punctuating the human sounds was the incessant honking of a steady stream of bicycle rickshaws. Overlooking the side wall were the beautiful white cupolas of an old Moghul mosque.

Sister Margaret Mary showed me the rabbit warren of individual cells where the nuns had been housed and the larger rooms which had been converted into dormitories and a spotless labor room. Some few dozen girls came to live in seclusion with the Sisters while waiting for their infants to be born. The large numbers expected to fill the old building never appeared. Sister Margaret Mary had traveled to many communities offering the security of the convent and the possibility of adoption for the unwanted infants.

"People have taken seriously what Mother Teresa said about adoptions. We have received 111 offers of adoption, many from people in France, Belgium, and Germany. The other day, we found a tiny baby at our door, probably injured in an abortion attempt. We did all we could and took it to Holy Family Hospital, but it died."

Sister Margaret Mary asked the girls if any would like to meet and talk with me. Only one of them agreed. I understood the reluctance of the others. Despite the call from Sheik Mujibur Rahman, leader of the new nation, that the sacrifices of the violated women should be recognized and that they should be considered heroines of the nation, the girls feared that they would have no future. A religious Muslim told me, "One of the greatest crimes in Islam is rape, worse than theft or evils like that."

The young girl who sat with me in the convent parlor was a beautiful nineteen year old with enormous liquid eyes and a fine, straight nose. In her arms was a perfect seven-and-a-half-pound baby, just ten days old.

She told me her story through Sister Margaret Mary. She is referred to here as Yasmin, not by her true name.

An officer of the West Pakistan engineer corps came to her home and demanded that her family deliver her up to them. He told them that if they did so, the family would escape injury. If they did not, he would shoot her father and brothers and take her in any case. The father refused to give her up and was shot twice in the shoulder. He was carried off and she thought he had died. The officer then took her and forced her to stay with him in the barracks until almost the time of surrender. She was never put in a cantonment for the use of other soldiers.

"What are you planning to do now?" I wanted to know.

"I will take my exams in April and finish my studies. My parents are taking me back." She explained that her father had been thrown on a heap of bodies but was able to crawl away on returning to consciousness.

Yasmin's attitude was that of the "new woman" of Bangladesh. She was taking up her life just where she had left it and she had decided to keep her baby. She said that she would insist that any man who wanted to marry her would have to accept the child.

Yasmin was far from the broken-spirited Muslim women we had been led to expect. She was exceptional, but the Yasmins did exist, only, however, in the cities among educated girls coming from families with some education.

The visit with the Missionaries of Charity in Khulna told a different story. Sister Josephine told me that no Khulna or rural women had appeared for help. The Sisters had thrown themselves into other urgent work, providing medical aid for mothers and children in the Khulna transit camp for returning refugees and then for the villages in the area. In a country with less than a thousand nurses for its 1972 population of about 75 million their help was crucial.

The girls who were pregnant were kept in the women's quarters of their homes. I discovered that violated women tried to keep it a secret if they did not become pregnant. Whole villages kept it a secret if a mass rape had occurred there, or otherwise the marriageable girls would be shunned. Instead of women, it was fathers, brothers, uncles, who came to talk to those opening their doors to violated girls, including several government establishments. The men explained that they knew someone who might need help at a later date. The word "might" was predicated on the fact that the village method of inducing miscarriage, the eating of the papaw fruit, might be successful. If that failed, then there was another method. In the sequestered women's quarters, when a birth had occurred, no one knew what happened to an unwelcome child.

During my time in Khulna, I planned to visit nearby Khalispur, home of a large Bihari colony. As the Bihari minority, caught in the middle of the struggle, had identified with West Pakistan, they were now the target of reprisals after the surrender of West Pakistan. In my naiveté, I was going to look into their need for emergency aid. Several people told me to stay away from Khalispur, and when I insisted, someone said, "You will be killed."

Sister Josephine and the other Sisters kept me in their house in Khulna and I soon realized why. The day was March 10, 1972. Rioting had broken out in Khalispur with vengeance being taken on the Biharis. A jute mill where they worked and where many had taken refuge was besieged. No one could count how many Biharis lost their lives, mostly by being hacked to death. Truckloads of bodies were carted away. One person told me that the number of truckloads was forty-eight.

I began to understand Mother Teresa's insistence on the prime importance of forgiveness. Was it too soon to expect a forgiveness? Too recent were terrible atrocities like the shallow graves which villagers uncovered, with the long black hair of the women threaded through the earth, or the villages in which most of the men had perished?

On my return to Dacca, Sister Margaret Mary suggested I accompany Sister Vincentia to a village adopted by the Sisters, one of the villages within a twenty-mile radius of the city to which the Sisters brought medical and food aid. The adopted village, Modhomgram, was a village of widows. Sister Vincentia was a round-faced Bengali with a warm, outgoing manner. We were driven by car to the edge of the town. Then Sister led me along a narrow winding road for a mile and a half. We crossed a river in a tiny ferry and made our way on a lane through paddy land and fields planted with onions. Sister Vincentia came regularly along this route with another Sister. She recounted that on the morning of November 25, 1971, seventeen heads of families were lined up and shot to death. Only six heads of families escaped. A dozen village homes were set on fire.

Ten of the village widows rose to meet Sister Vincentia. Some of them seemed to emerge out of a torpor as she greeted them. Chopola stood out, her dark eyes tragically large above sunken cheeks. She was wrapped in a ragged red-bordered cotton sari that had once been white. Chopola was the mother of nine children. With her was one of her daughters,

Nobadurga, and her small children. Both husbands had been shot together.

Some of the families were still living in tenting or under charred trees nearly four months after the event. They needed better shelter before the start of the monsoon in late May or early June.

Women like Chopola and Nobadurga in this Hindu village had no marketable skills of any kind. A program of training in sewing was considered, but only as a long-term plan. Some of them were making their way into Dacca to beg, Sister Vincentia said, and she was working out a program to prevent more of this. The one thing that all Bengali village women knew how to make was puffed rice, a food used at breakfast and other meals. Provided with the rice or the money to buy it, the women had the time to undertake the intricate process of preparing puffed rice in their little mud bucket stoves. They could then sell the prepared rice in the Dacca market. The puffed rice could also go into the making of a popular sweet called muri kadu by adding brown sugar or date juice. For small outlays, which came to the Sisters from many sources, the widows could prepare the puffed rice candies and sell them from a rented market stall. For another small outlay, a widow could have her destroyed home reconstructed, pressed mud floor, bamboo frame, and all. Sister Vincentia and the Missionaries of Charity in Dacca were fashioning projects of self-reliance that were "right on the ground."

The Bangladesh authorities often took the Sisters to islands of misery on the delta country islands (in the literal and figurative sense), so that the Sisters could work out particularized responses overlooked in larger programs.

Sister Vincentia, who brought life into a nearly dead community, died a few years later in Calcutta. She was killed instantly, crushed to death when a truck rammed into the van in which she was riding.

Countless small projects, as well as larger programs of self-reliance and rehabilitation converged on Bangladesh, a crucible of suffering. Forgiveness was slow in coming. The people's pent-up rage and unrelieved grief found expression in more attacks on Bihari civilians. The surrendered soldiers of West Pakistan, still in the country, were protected until they could be evacuated. Many Biharis eventually chose evacuation to West Pakistan, but quietly the Missionaries of Charity included them in their medical, feeding, and rehabilitation programs. The old convent on Islampur Road was renovated and became a Shishu Bhavan, not only for orphaned and abandoned children, but for malnourished youngsters who appeared for care at the mobile clinic stops in the villages.

"As soon as the Sisters reach the village in the mobile clinic, there are patients from everywhere," wrote Sister Margaret Mary. "Since it is a Mother and Child Clinic, women without children try to grab children from right and left and come for medicine. Sometimes five hundred women and children crowd about us." Often the mobile clinic had to be parked while the Sisters went by other means to reach the people. "Some of our dispensary stops," she continued, "are an adventure for the Sisters, especially the ones that are not used to the water and ignorant about swimming. With their bags and boxes, they jump onto the boat and have the pleasure of a dip into the dirty water. But the Sisters are brave and the next day, they are ready for the jump."

Infants barely able to survive, and three and four year olds barely able to walk were brought to Shishu Bhavan for a stay of several months and then returned to their families. Many young girls made Shishu Bhavan their temporary home until, as the Sisters put it, they had "some trade in hand." Many became expert tailors and dressmakers and found paid work.

In the villages of the Khulna district, the mobile clinic arrival was an equally popular event, with hundreds appearing for simple medications, vitamins, and baby foods that they could obtain nowhere else. Mobile clinic stops were made where Bihari children were in need and the same help was given to them.

Dacca had its homeless and its destitute and a Home of Compassion was opened for them in the Tezgaon district. It was not far from the cemetery of the American and Canadian priests who had died while serving as missionaries in the Dacca area. The Home of Compassion was run exactly like Nirmal Hriday in Calcutta, with the Sisters being mindful of the special religious duties of Muslim patients. When Sister-Doctor Gertrude left, another doctor who had been associated with Holy Family Hospital came to work full time with the Sisters. The help for Mother Teresa's centers in Bangladesh poured in from many sources; one, however, stands out. The monks of the Cistercian Abbey of Holy Trinity in the desert of Utah, had a fund of twenty thousand dollars to renovate the monastery. The entire amount went instead to Mother Teresa.

The work of Mother Teresa expanded to five centers, including Sylhet and Hausaid, with funds and resources reaching them in an uninterrupted stream. Early in 1983 after the Sisters had given over ten years of service, an interruption was threatened. The government considered a law that would sequester all donations from overseas, even for nongovernmental groups, and distribute them through government agencies. Mother Teresa went to Dacca to talk things over with the President of the Council of Ministers, General Hussain M. Ershad. She explained that the Sisters had to have a regular flow of funds, medications, and food to continue their work. Without this assurance, she explained, the Sisters could not work in the country. She asked General Ershad to come with her to the Home of Compassion. It was his first visit and he saw face to face the destitute of Dacca who had nowhere else to turn. "He changed," Mother Teresa related. There was no interruption and the Sisters continued to receive directly the aid and resources sent from outside Bangladesh.

With the announcement in April 1973 of a new prize in the field of religion came word that the first recipient was to be Mother Teresa of Calcutta. The awarding of the Templeton Prize for Progress in Religion was a powerful sign that Mother Teresa's message of love crossing all frontiers had pierced frontiers that were often the most intractable of all, the frontiers of religion. Mr. and Mrs. John Templeton decided to use their considerable fortune to inaugurate an annual award whose purpose would be "to stimulate the knowledge of God on the part of mankind everywhere." A hoped-for result would be a "better understanding of the meaning of life and a greater emphasis on the kind of dedication that brings human life more into concert with the divine will."

Nine judges were drawn from the major religious traditions of the world, and included Professor S. Chatterji, Hindu; Sir Mohammad Zafrulla Khan, Muslim; Sir Alan Mocatta, Jewish; Abbot Kosho Ohtani, Buddhist; and the Reverend Dr. Eugene Carson Blake, former General Secretary of the World Council of Churches, as well as representatives of other Christian groups. To them came over two thousand nominations for a prize that would exceed in value the Noble Prize; their choice fell on Mother Teresa. The citation stated that "she has been instrumental in widening and deepening man's knowledge and love of God, and thereby furthering the quest for the quality of life that mirrors the divine."

It seemed as though Mother Teresa had come to personify love of God as expressed in works of mercy, another name for love, among God's creatures. Through making the works of mercy for her brothers and sisters of every race and creed the central work of her life, she had struck a chord common to the great religious traditions of the world. Not only Christianity, which relates final salvation to the performance of the works of mercy, taught the bedrock importance of mercy. In Islam, almsgiving is a duty imposed by Allah, the All-Merciful. The Hebrew Scriptures enjoin merciful care for the stranger, the orphaned, and the poor. In Buddhism, the concept of mercy has become actualized in a goddess of mercy. In Hinduism, an act of mercy for a person in need, though not called for by any merit in that person, improves the karma of the merciful person. The filial piety of Confucius is a system of mercy reaching to the least member in an extended family. The life of one woman seemed to remind the great spiritualities that mercy is a quality imprinted by the Creator on the fleshy tablets of the hearts of His creatures.

Mother Teresa was in London to accept the prize on April 25, 1973, in the same ancient Guildhall that Canon John Milford had shown her in

1960. I could not help contrasting this visit with that of thirteen years earlier when Mother Teresa was an unknown nun and, in abundant kindness, an Anglican minister insisted not only in taking steps to help her work but on showing her something beautiful from history. Not only representatives of various religious groups including the former Catholic archbishop of Bombay, Archbishop T. D. Roberts, were invited, but also Malcolm Muggeridge and his wife Kitty and Mother Teresa's Co-Workers, Mrs. Ann Blaikie and myself. The hall was filled with people from the arts and London society in general. Large numbers of the audience were in full evening dress. Mother Teresa never seemed so small as she did looking up to Prince Philip and the towering Dr. Eugene Blake on the platform of the Guildhall. Prince Philip made the presentation with a cogent and extended speech, in which he stated, "Mother Teresa has shown by her life what people can do when the faith is strong. By any standard what she has done is good and the world today is desperately in need of this sort of goodness, this sort of practical compassion."

We waited for the response of Mother Teresa, given as usual without any notes and after a barely perceptible sign of the cross upon her lips with her thumb. Some of us wondered whether an ecumenical note would be struck on this very rare occasion. The response she gave came from the very depths of her consciousness, and in those depths was the only reason for her hope, Jesus.

Mother Teresa began by saying, "We are here today to thank God for giving grace to Mr. Templeton to give of his best, to be spent for the glory of God. In giving this award to me, it is given to the people, to all those who share with me throughout the world in the work of love, in spreading God's love among men . . .

"Today, as before, when Jesus comes amongst His own, His own don't know Him. He comes in the rotting bodies of the poor. He comes even in the rich who are being suffocated by their riches, in the loneliness of their hearts, and there is no one to love them. Jesus comes to you and to me. And often, very often, we pass Him by. Here in England, and in many other places such as Calcutta, we find lonely people who are known only by their addresses, by the number of their room. Where are we, then? Do we really know that there are such people? . . .

"These are the people we must know. This is Jesus yesterday and today and tomorrow, and you and I must know who they are. That knowledge will lead us to love them. And that love, to service. Let us not be satisfied with just paying money. Money is not enough. Money can be got. They need your hand to serve them. They need your hearts to love them."

She talked about touching the body of Christ in the poor, the unwanted, the unemployed, the uncared for, the hungry, the naked, and the homeless. "They are there for the finding," she told the men and women who filled the Guildhall.

Mother Teresa concluded with the words, "It is written in the Scriptures, 'I looked for one to care for me and I could not find him.' How terrible it would be if Jesus had to say that to us today, after dying for us on the cross."

After the ceremony, Mother Teresa told me how impressed she had been by the simplicity of the meal preceding the award. Out of deference to her, a plain one-course meal of fish had been served. Her dining companion had been Prince Philip and they had talked of many things. He wanted to know more about the work of the congregation and Mother Teresa had an opportunity to expand on the reasons that led the Sisters to such work. The conversation turned to the education given to women in particular.

They seemed to have agreed on the fact that women and men should not have identical educations and that the education devised for men might not meet all the needs of women. I wondered if Prince Philip felt this applied to the Queen as well as to the ordinary woman, since Queen Elizabeth as head of the Church of England had very special duties to her subjects.

I wondered also if it had occurred to Mother Teresa that she was talking to the only man in the world whose wife was the head of a Church.

❧

By 1973, the Missionaries of Charity were also in London, with a house in Southall, a few miles outside of London among Indian immigrants and with another in Bravington Road, in a working class district. Sister Frederick, of Maltese origin, who had come to the Missionaries of Charity after nineteen years as a Sister of St. Joseph, was the superior. She told us of the aged living in isolated and depressing small rooms, and of the vagrant women sheltered by the Sisters.

While I was in London, the St. Mungo Society, a group of Catholics of Scotch origin, told us of the unsolved problem of homeless men, not vagrants, not shiftless, but young men who had come to London to work. Mostly unskilled, they got jobs in hotels and restaurants as cleaners and dishwashers. Finding a room within their means was very difficult and, often as not, they were forced to pay night-to-night rates. If their jobs were terminated or their pay delayed, they found themselves out on the street. This is where we found them on a chilly April night as Sister Frederick and I joined the St. Mungo group on their nightly round. They knew exactly where to go, since the men always chose spots in alleyways or on pavements where the heating systems of hotels and other large buildings were vented through gratings. We would find six or more men huddled over these gratings. Talking with them, we discovered that they were mostly poor young men from Glasgow or Dublin, or even rural Scotland or Ireland, who thought they would find easy money in the great city.

It was a vivid introduction to the underside of London nightlife. The Missionaries of Charity were able to expand their work to include a night shelter for men.

Just four months after the Guildhall ceremony, on August 22, 1973, Mother Teresa with five Sisters landed in a seaport on the Red Sea to work in a country where there were no native Christians. The port was Hodeida and the country, the Yemen Arab Republic.

They were there at the invitation of a Yemeni sheik, the Governor of Hodeida, Sheik Sinaan Abou Luhoom. Headed by Sister-Doctor Gertrude, the team of Missionaries of Charity was prepared to bring aid and medical care to the poor. No convent awaited them. For the first weeks, the Sisters were given the apartment of William Keane, the director of the Catholic Relief Services program in North Yemen. It might be questioned how the Missionaries of Charity came to a completely Muslim country, one living by ancient tribal ways, where the muezzin's call to prayer was the only sound of religion echoing throughout the land. In the early years of Christianity, there had been Christian communities in the land, which was part of the biblical kingdom of Sheba, whose queen had journeyed to meet King Solomon. For over a millennium, there had been no Christian presence in Yemen, whose name stemmed from Al-Yaman, the right hand, referring to the country's position, if one is facing east, to the right of the Kaaba, the most venerated Muslim sanctuary.

The arrival of Mother Teresa with Christian nuns on the soil of Yemen arose out of a famine relief program conducted by Catholic Relief Services when Yemeni people were dying in the wake of a six-year drought and famine. Food supplies from various sources including Europe proved to be insufficient. There was no lifeline to the United States since it was during a period of broken relations between the two countries. In 1970, Catholic Relief Services began to bring in emergency relief supplies of wheat, sorghum, and medications. The relief effort was conducted with such dispatch that many lives were saved. The U.S. Government gave Catholic Relief Services permission to utilize some American Food for Peace stocks to meet the emergency.

Governmental agencies in Yemen, starting in the 1960s, made brave attempts to have their country speed through the advances of centuries in a period of a few years. One example was the medical facility constructed in Hodeida, Al-Olofi. An international staff had to be gathered in support of Yemen's limited core of medically trained personnel. Asked to help in finding medical personnel, Msgr. Joseph J. Harnett, Middle East director of Catholic Relief Services, found volunteers from many countries, including doctors and nurses from a voluntary agency of Ireland called Irish Concern. Too few were willing to accept long-term assignments.

Sheik Sinaan Abou Luhoom, grateful for the aid of Catholic Relief Services, came to the offices of the agency in Rome with what he considered to be a solution to the problem of staffing the hospital. The sheik was accompanied by a Lebanese businessman, also a Muslim. They had an unusual proposal to make to Msgr. Joseph Harnett. The sheik related that his Lebanese friend had pointed to a new way of providing more permanent medical help. The sheik had learned that many hospitals were staffed by Catholic nuns who gave steady and devoted service. Could Msgr. Harnett find a group of nuns who would be willing to come to Yemen to carry out a mission of healing? They would be protected, and while they could not work at conversions, they would be free to practice their own faith.

Harnett told the sheik he thought he knew such a group of nuns, nuns with much experience in compassionate care for even the very poorest people. They came from India, where they were acquainted with the Muslim as well as the Hindu community. When Harnett related the hopes of the sheik to Mother Teresa, he found no response at all.

Mother Teresa stated categorically that the Missionaries of Charity could not staff an institution, no matter how worthy. Their special mission was to go out in search of whoever was poorest and to work out a program in terms of their own vows. If there were poor to be served in Yemen, the Missionaries of Charity would consider working there. When this was conveyed to the sheik, his disappointment at not finding long-term staff for his hospital was mitigated by the fact that the nuns might be willing to serve the needy in other ways.

Mother Teresa was invited to visit Yemen. Msgr. Harnett arranged the trip and she went to Hodeida. The Sisters could do much in Yemen; of that there was no doubt.

A formal request then came to Mother Teresa to bring her Missionaries of Charity to Yemen. She indicated her willingness to serve but made it clear that there must be a priest in Hodeida who could celebrate daily mass for the Sisters. The sheik understood this and agreed that there would be no difficulty in having a priest reside in Hodeida. There was no question of building a church, and the priest would have to obtain a work permit that would involve a full-time occupation while in Yemen. The first priest to volunteer for Yemen came from Harnett's own diocese of Philadelphia, Father John Kiniry. He was given a relief task in the office of Catholic Relief Services. When Mother Teresa was asked about the matter of evangelism, she said that the work of the Sisters would show the people God's love. The people might love God more and become better Muslims.

On August 12, Mother Teresa along with Msgr. Harnett and the Yemen team of Sisters were received by Pope Paul VI at Castel Gondolfo. The Holy Father asked Msgr. Harnett to join him in giving a blessing to the team.

The day chosen for the arrival in Hodeida was August 22, the church feast dear to the Missionaries of Charity. Church authorities agreed to the new foundation. In fact, Archbishop Pio Laghi as apostolic delegate had paved the way for Mother Teresa to send Sisters to such places in the Middle East as Gaza and Jordan, as well as to such African countries as Ethiopia.

It was not long before Sister Gertrude, as superior, was heading Dar Al-Agaza, a home for the destitute, providing for them clean quarters and daily food, much of it shipped in by Catholic Relief Services. The large gray stone building had been constructed by the governorate of Hodeida on the city's outskirts. The building soon housed a Mother and Child Clinic. Muslim mothers, as in the Kidderpore district of Calcutta, were unafraid to throw off their veils before another woman. At the clinic, Sister Gertrude reported dealing with tropical diseases, tuberculosis, blindness, and an occasional case of leprosy. Soon a mobile clinic allowed her and the other Sisters to visit the surrounding villages. It was donated by Irish Co-Workers, and a letter from Sister Gertrude described the use to which it had been put.

"I'm sure," she wrote, "you would like to know something about this place. To start with, our people are very poor. They live in straw huts in which one cannot stand up straight, but one has to bend in two. They have had no medical facilities, so when they get really sick, they just wait for the end to take place. Sometimes they burn with a red hot iron the place where they have the pain, so that they may die of burns, rather than of the disease itself."

With the Hodeida clinic and the mobile clinic, between four hundred and five hundred patients were seen on a given day. It was not long before another building was added to the Dar Al-Agaza for the destitute, and the Sisters found themselves running a mental asylum called Dar Al-Salem (Home of Peace). Sister Gertrude described the various activities.

"We have sewing classes for girls and married women, adult education for older children who did not get the chance for early schooling, and preschool education for local slum children. We have food distribution, giving out uncooked grain to beggar and poor families, and Food-for-Work programs—which means gardening in desertlike sandy soil. It is a very big compound, but easy for us to manage the crowds and the many activities with the help of local poor girls, women, and boys who are really so good to take part in the work. Government people also cooperate and help to do things for their own people. There is much sharing from all sides, including Co-Workers and material help. Though educationally deprived, in religion the people are so true and convinced. They practice their belief. Prayer is regularly called out in all the mosques many times during the day to remind man what is due to God, to pay Him homage, praise, and thanksgiving."

Anyone who knew Yemen would wonder why there was no mention in her letter of the furnace heat of the hot months or of the difficulty of getting enough food from the market where eggs, for example, were bird-size and already half rotten. A Catholic Relief Service staff member wrote: "Sister Gertrude was a visionary who saw needs and dreamed dreams of answering those needs with hard work, the charity of the gospel, and trust in the providence of God. Besides everything else, she has led her Sisters and the people in planting a huge garden which is nothing less than a bit of paradise."

Within a year, the Sisters were in Ta'izz, perched in the interior highlands. Mother Teresa had visited the city and found that the lepers there were a heartbreaking spectacle. Always seeing suffering in terms of Christ on the cross, she called the leper settlement an "open Calvary." The Sisters, with the cooperation of Dr. Ahmed Al-Ramy of the Ministry of Health, soon opened a leper city called Midinat al-Noor (City of Light). With daily care and medical and food supplies, the new city began to justify its name.

A Sister wrote from Ta'izz, "It is not possible to imagine how things are here. But it is wonderful to have such joyful acceptance from these poor lepers of our Sisters' efforts to bring love and care into their lives. The people are so good, so simple and loving, and so poor. You can look at them and just think of the Old Testament, the psalms. Loving, poor people, so God-oriented.

"Everything is God, 'Allah' for them, and God's will is everything, in their every event."

With the opening of a home for the destitute in San'a, the capital and cultural center, the Missionaries of Charity were present in the three chief cities of Yemen. Unassumingly, they had entered Yemen society, faithful to their own religious practices of daily mass and prayer and honoring the religious practices of the people they served. When Father John Kiniry had to return to the United States, a Canadian priest belonging to the White Fathers of Africa, came to Hodeida. His job was to serve as administrator of the Al-Alofi medical center. Father Michel Gagnon was at home in Arabic after long experience in Algeria. Gagnon was later named bishop of Djbouti.

Mother Teresa related the experience of Yemen on a visit to Missionhurst Seminary in Washington, D.C.

I remember when we went to Yemen, a completely Muslim country. I told the Prime Minister: "I am ready to give you the Sisters under one condition, that you allow a priest to come also. Without Jesus, we won't go." Then they consulted with each other and they decided that if they wanted Sisters, they must allow them priests. So the priest was allowed to come. And after eight hundred years, there was this missionary, a White Father, who brought the burning light of the tabernacle into the country. And then I was told, "Don't wear the cross." I went straight to the Governor and said to him, "What we are wearing, this is our sign. It is an external sign of our dedication. We belong to Him." They did not want us to pray the rosary on the street. We pray the rosary on the street and it doesn't matter what street we are on. "This is our strength," I said, "We pray." Then he said, "You must remain. We have accepted you as you are, not as somebody else wants you to be." And today, the Sisters are there with the cross and praying the rosary in the streets.

One wondered if the example of humble and effective work by Catholic nuns in Jordan and Yemen could have contributed to an unprecedented statement of Colonel Muammar Qaddafi speaking at a public meeting in Benghazi. The statement was carried by the official Libyan press agency in February 1981 as follows:

"We need a revolutionary nuns' movement because we consider that the Christian nuns' movement is a challenge to Moslem women."

In any case, the Missionaries of Charity contributed a Christian presence in a country where such a presence had been absent for nearly a millennium. Their presence was without evangelization, without even a church building, but rather, it was a presence of love and compassionate service to brothers and sisters in the same human family who suffered and were in need.

The continuous journeyings of Mother Teresa would make for overly extensive reading, even though each account would have its interest and drama. Three meetings during 1974 not recounted elsewhere need to be recorded. It was during that year that Mother Teresa became greatly disturbed by the drastic reduction in the flow of foods from the United States to the poor of Calcutta and other Indian cities. The foods, supplied from Food for Peace stocks, arrived regularly in millions of pounds through American people-to-people agencies such as CARE, Church World Service, and Catholic Relief Services.

A new policy aimed to channel food chiefly, if not only, to food-for-work projects. Such projects had helped bring new life to drought- and famine-ravaged Bihar, where the people-to-people agencies provided food to the builders of hygienic wells, sanitary facilities, and new rural roads. The aim of limiting food supplies to such projects was laudable in itself, but resulted in penalizing many hungry people including those served by the Missionaries of Charity. Meals in the Home for the Dying, and in similar hostels in other Indian cities, began to be diminished. People receiving rations in health programs, including thousands of leper patients, received no more American foods. Children in slum schools were threatened with the loss of the free tiffin that gave them energy to learn. All supplies of powdered milk had been cut off. Families who depended on an extra ration from U.S. food stocks in their desperate fight for survival had to manage without it.

Mother Teresa happened to be visiting the Sisters in New York in July 1974 when the twentieth anniversary of the Food for Peace program was being marked in Washington, D.C. At a hearing called by the Senate Committee on Foreign Relations, Senator Hubert H. Humphrey invited witnesses to testify on the accomplishments and challenges of the program. Mother Teresa was asked to appear as a "surprise witness" to open the hearing.

Mother Teresa thanked Senator Humphrey for the chance to stand in the hearing room for the poor and hungry of the world.

"The poor are the hope of mankind," she told the committee. "They are also the hope of the people of America, for in them we see the hungry Christ looking up at us. Will we refuse Him?

"When the 'health cases' are cut off, and we have almost no food to give them, then we find that people stop coming for treatment. I mean, for example, the forty-six thousand lepers we are taking care of."

She did not need to elaborate on the results when the program of arresting the dread disease was interrupted. Other witnesses from voluntary agencies stated that in the preceding three years the overseas beneficiaries from American food abundance had been cut by forty percent.

In thanking Mother Teresa, Senator Humphrey stated that her opening words were an invocation for the meeting.

"I wanted very much," he said, "to hear from someone who employs in her life the virtues of compassion, love, and kindness, because governments sometimes become dehumanized." Long a spokesman on world food problems in the U.S. Government, Humphrey had just been named world food adviser to the American delegation to the UN World Food Conference.

Senator Mark Hatfield brought Mother Teresa to his office, where Mrs. Hatfield had prepared a buffet luncheon. Senator and Mrs. Hatfield had visited Calcutta not long before and discussed its continuing needs. Among the guests were Senator Edward M. Kennedy and Daniel Parker, Director of the Agency for International Development (AID), under which the Food for Peace program was administered. Parker was placed between Mother Teresa and me to learn of the importance of the Food for Peace program in relieving tragic human need as well as in providing self-help assistance. During her conversation with Senator Hatfield, Mother Teresa made a statement that the senator was to quote publicly more than once. "I am not called to be successful," she told him, "but to be faithful."

As a sequel to the meeting, I was asked to summarize the situation in a memorandum. After some weeks, during which there were discussions in Washington and Delhi, changes were made in the Food for Peace program. I received a reply through Catholic Relief Services from the coordinator of the Food for Peace office announcing that the feeding programs for "health cases," for needy families, and for hungry children would be reinstated. Mother Teresa's gratitude to everyone who had reinstated the "poorest of the poor" was great. She never forgot the goodness of Senator Humphrey who had helped inspire the Food for Peace program. When she heard later of his illness, which proved fatal, she wrote to him as his friend and as a friend of the poor. She assured the senator of her prayers on his behalf.

While in Washington, Mother Teresa was asked by Sargent and Eunice Kennedy Shriver to accompany them to meet Robert S. McNamara, head of the World Bank. Few entrances in the world are more imposing than that of the World Bank. Mother Teresa did not even look up as she slipped in under the great shield of the International Monetary Fund. McNamara had told Sargent Shriver that he had met Mother Teresa during the 1960s with his late wife who had been deeply impressed by her. He had also been at the Kennedy Award ceremony in 1971. He informed Shriver that he found Mother Teresa a unique human being.

McNamara was accustomed to dealing with governments, from the richest superpowers to the poorest ministates and to calculating in terms of millions and billions of dollars. McNamara had come to the World Bank straight from dealing with military matters as U.S. Secretary of Defense. He now gave full attention to the small works of peace of the Missionaries of Charity, not only in India but in Tanzania and Yemen, and in other pockets of hunger around the world. McNamara wondered if Mother Teresa's Sisters could receive any of the enormous supplies of foods and dairy products exported by the United States in the Food for Peace program. He was aware of how these supplies were channeled to governments, he said, but could not a way be found to channel them to programs for the hungry run by Mother Teresa and other groups close to the poor. I was able to explain that a way had been found, and that Mother Teresa's programs, as well as other voluntary programs, had been utilizing American abundance in serving the poor. While the bulk of the foods had entered government-to-government programs under Title I of the Food for Peace legislation, there was another section, Title II. Under this title, recognized American voluntary agencies, including church-related agencies, had been able to draw on American food stocks to feed the poor overseas on the basis of need, without reference to race or creed or any other factor. It was the cutback in Title II programs that Mother Teresa had addressed at Senator Humphrey's hearing as a voice for the hungry. McNamara, involved as he was with "macro" projects among governments, was glad to learn of the "micro" programs that reached directly into the lives of the poor.

When the President of the Nobel Peace Award Committee quoted Robert S. McNamara in Oslo in 1979, it became clear that he had played a decisive, if not the decisive, role in bringing the Nobel Prize to Mother Teresa.

An evening ecumenical service at Washington's National Presbyterian Church was Mother Teresa's next engagement. Frank Collins, who during diplomatic service in Calcutta had helped Mother Teresa, was asked to relate his experiences. The ambassador from Bangladesh spoke movingly of the help of her Sisters to his people, both while they were refugees and after the lifting of the occupation in 1972. Dr. Louis H. Evans, the eloquent pastor of the church, called for the leading of the Holy Spirit on all believers and announced to the packed congregation that this was the first time Mother Teresa had spoken from the sanctuary of a Protestant church. Dr. Evans prepared for Mother Teresa's talk by asking the congregation to recite antiphonally with him from that part of Chapter Twenty-five of the Gospel of St. Matthew in which Jesus identifies himself with "the least," the hungry, naked, homeless one. Mother Teresa's talk, as always, showed how that gospel was translated from abstract words into concrete application to the least and the most shunned among the human family. The service was recorded and a taped cassette prepared by the Co-Workers had wide distribution.

In June 1975, Mother Teresa found herself in Mexico City. She had not come by invitation of the local hierarchy to study the needs of the poor, nor did she stay in some sequestered convent while she looked into the realities of life in slum alleyways. She was booked into a hotel in the center of the city and took part in a historic meeting, the first international gathering focusing on the state of the world's women. The Vatican had asked her to be a member of its delegation to the World Conference of the International Women's Year, held on the thirtieth anniversary of the United Nations. With her on the delegation were several women, including Rosemary Goldie from Australia, a member of the Vatican Commission for the Laity; and Mrs. Bernadette Kunambi, president of the Tanzanian branch of the International Union of Catholic Women's Organizations. The delegation, led by Bishop Ramon Torrella Cascante of the

Vatican Commission on Justice and Peace, enjoyed observer status for the Vatican. It was an unforeseen trip for Mother Teresa and it constituted for her a wrenching parting from her Sisters at the time. It yielded, however, a totally unexpected harvest.

The blue-bordered white sari was scarcely noticeable among the incredible variety of dress worn by women from a hundred and twenty-five nations of the world. Many of the women from Africa and Asia wore indigenous costumes that were nothing less than spectacular. Bright silk saris mingled with the brilliant cottons and headdresses of Africa and the butterfly sleeves of the Philippines. These merely provided the backdrop for two weeks of serious discussions under the themes of "Equality, Development, and Peace."

Mother Teresa blended in with thousands of delegates who heard the United Nations Secretary-General, Kurt Waldheim, President Luis Echeverría Álvarez of Mexico, and Mrs. Helvi Sipila, secretary-general of the conference address themselves to the themes at an impressive opening session. I had flown to Mexico with Mother Teresa and attended as a representative of Pax Christi, the international Catholic movement for peace.

We were given programs in various languages and many were surprised to find that Mexico, as host country, used the image of a nun with pen in hand on the program cover. Mexico's fairly recent history has included bouts of persecution of the Catholic Church and severe restrictions on religious orders, even a ban on the wearing of religious habits in public. For this reason, some wondered at the use of an image of a seventeenth-century nun in connection with a discussion on the equality of women. The Mexicans were making a point. President Luis Echeverría, at the opening meeting, stated: "This meeting is an act of justice toward one half of the human race." The use of the image of Sor Juana Inez de la Cruz was, in a way, an act of justice toward a Sister of the Convent of St. Jerome in Mexico City. Recognized by many in her time, and in later history, as a true genius, Sister Juana Inez de la Cruz besides being the greatest lyric poet of her era had studied, on her own, theology, the Bible, history, mathematics, and law. She was fluent in self-taught Latin. When she put forward a criticisim of a priestly sermon, she was severely reprimanded by the bishop, who asserted that she should engage in "more suitable pursuits than those of the mind." Her reply was a twenty-thousand word defense of woman as person and of her right to education. In obedience to the bishop, Sister Juana Inez de la Cruz gave up her library. She spent her time in religious pursuits and died soon afterward while caring for people during a plague.

The presence of a Vatican delegation at the World Conference indicated that while in history, the place of women in the church had often been obscured by local customs and traditions alien to Christianity, the liberation of women bought by Christ was becoming a reality. That reality was rooted in the same baptism for man and woman. Mother Teresa was free to speak, to move about, to respond to the media in ways unthinkable in earlier generations.

Mother Teresa faithfully attended all the plenary meetings at which government after government made formal speeches, some heavily larded with attacks on imperialism, exploitation, and hegemonism. She participated actively in workshop sessions on development.

The setting was Tlatelolco, the Plaza de las Tres Culturas (Plaza of the Three Cultures), where one could not escape from its powerful symbolism. Facing an open square was an excavated pyramid, representing the first culture, that of pre-Spanish Mexico in which human sacrifice was not unknown. Mother Teresa made several visits to an example of the second culture, a much-treasured colonial church with the baptismal font where the Indian, Juan Diego, was baptized. Here in Tlatelolco in 1531, the Virgin appeared to Juan Diego and, as the Virgin of Guadalupe, became the patroness of the Mexican people. Her church became a sanctuary attracting the biggest pilgrimages in the Western Hemisphere. The third culture was that of contemporary Mexico, exemplified by the modern tower, part of the Ministry of Foreign Affairs, in which the meetings were held.

We studied the moving words emblazoned on a large plaque in the center of the Plaza of the Three Cultures. It memorialized the fact that there the Aztec Emperor Cuauhtémoc had surrendered to Hernán Cortés. It was neither a victory nor a defeat, the plaque pointed out irenically, but the painful birth of a new people, the mixed peoples of today's Mexico.

Many women pointed out that without peace there could not be equality nor development and others that their developing countries needed a new world economic order. An American journalist reported, "The Holy See delegation is trying to put some spiritual input into the World Plan of Action for Women but the going is rough at best."

The Holy See's resolution was presented by Mother Teresa. The general subject was "The Integration of Women in the Development Process as Equal Partners with Men." The title of the resolution was "Women in Poverty." It began by pointing to poverty as a "debilitating force that limits the enjoyment of basic human rights," and as a state that "creates powerlessness and lack of hope." It urged "all women to have a special concern for poor and disadvantaged women on whom poverty places particularly crushing burdens." It ended by urging "women who have at least some material comforts to become co-workers with the very poor and disadvantaged women by sharing with them in the day-to-day struggle to improve their living conditions." Mother Teresa had made a mark on the resolution in inserting one of her favorite words, "co-worker," found in the works of Gandhi.

Probably no woman from any of the 125 countries had more credibility than this one woman in talking of women in poverty. The resolution was accepted and appeared in the final report of the Mexico Conference.

As soon as there was a break, Mother Teresa wanted to scour the city to visit the poor. The Hotel Geneva, where the delegation stayed, was in the Zona Rosa, the pleasant tourist quarter of Mexico City. Since mass was said in the hotel in the early morning hours before the group set out for meetings, Mother Teresa had seen nothing of the city.

We found someone to take Mother Teresa to a sprawling slum among the many growing slums that were catapulting Mexico City into one of the most populous cities of the globe. The place was called Nezahualcóyotl, Neza for short. We walked along paths that were unpaved but clear of rubbish. As far as we could see were houses constructed of a marvelous variety of materials, from heavy stones to corrugated metal. Many had tiny gardens and climbing plants that softened the harsh outlines of homes that were little more than huts. We began to talk to a woman who was hanging out children's clothes. She told us that her family had migrated from Oaxaca. Her husband worked for a bus company in Mexico City, and the family had enough to eat. She emphasized that it was much better in Neza than in the village where they had lived. Responding to her question about Mother Teresa, I told her that she was a Sister. I had to stress that she was a regular Catholic Sister, but from India. The woman then called to a woman in the next dwelling (also of solid stone construction), and we found ourselves talking to another newcomer from an Oaxacan village. It was simple to go from house to house and talk with whichever member of the family was present. Some families had eight or nine children, and despite the dreadful crowding in which they existed, the children seemed decently clean. What struck us was the fact that with these newcomers to the city, the family unit had survived. Mother Teresa felt there was great hope in Neza.

One day the press sought out Mother Teresa and published her photograph as well as a vivid account of the work among the poorest of the poor in Asia, Africa, and Latin America. She was also cited on the Voice of America morning broadcast regarding the international conference.

One person Mother Teresa mentioned was Father Augustin Pro, a Jesuit priest who had been executed during the persecution of Plutarco Eliás Calles. While she was in the novitiate in Darjeeling, the reading of the Sisters had included the life and death of Father Pro. "It was called *God's Jester,*" Mother Teresa recalled. "It told us about the ways he escaped from the persecutors and was able to give the last rites and say mass secretly. I have never forgotten it."

A professor in the Social Service School of the University of Mexico came to greet us and asked Mother Teresa what she would like to see of Mexico City.

"Can you tell us where Father Pro is buried?" Mother Teresa wanted to know.

The professor, a patriotic Mexican, led us to the spot at the National Lottery Building, where the priest fell before a firing squad. Calles had the execution photographed as a warning to others flouting the antireligious laws, and the gruesome photographs went around the world. The metal marker was small and could hardly be seen behind a post. It merely said that at the wall opposite *"cayó muerto"* (fell dead) the Rev. Miguel Augustin Pro, S.J., shot on November 23, 1927.

The professor accompanied us to the vast cemetery where the tomb of Augustin Pro was clearly a place of pilgrimage. There were fresh flowers around it and holy cards from people who had asked for his intercession for special needs. For Mother Teresa, it was a chance to kneel in silence in a quiet and blessed place. It was our last day in Mexico City. Mother Teresa was breathing easier after the almost endless meetings. As with many other people, the altitude of Mexico City had had its effect on her and on the first night, she had slept not at all. Despite this, she never lost her calm, her ability to pay attention, to give a smile that radiated serenity. Somehow, the visit to the tomb of the fugitive priest, who had risked and then offered up his life, seemed to bring the Mexican visit to a meaningful close.

We returned to the hotel to pick up our bags and make our way to the airport. José Chavez, editor of *El Signo,* a Catholic monthly magazine, had arranged for Mother Teresa to stop at his home on the way. She was to meet a group of active Catholics anxious to know more about her work.

I went to Mother Teresa's room so that we could start out together, and she handed me the telephone. A man's voice wanted to know if I spoke Spanish. When I replied in Spanish, he introduced himself as Señor Gomes del Campo and said that President Echeverría wanted to see Mother Teresa before she left. He would send the car for her to come to Los Pinos, the President's residence. I relayed the message to Mother Teresa who said she would be happy to meet the President, but she wanted to be sure she would not miss the promised meeting with Mr. and Mrs. Chavez. We were soon driven through the guarded gates of Los Pinos and along a pine-bordered path at the end of which in a well-lighted mansion, President and Mrs. Echeverría were awaiting Mother Teresa. With them were Mr. Gomes del Campo and his wife who was fluent in English. The President posed many searching questions to Mother Teresa about the work of the Sisters. He had evidently read the newspaper accounts. She began with the account of reaching out to the poorest of the poor in

Calcutta and went on to tell of the work in other cities of India and in other countries. Interest was expressed in the sari as worn by Mother Teresa. She explained it had become the religious habit of the Sisters wherever they worked.

Besides describing the work of the Sisters among the homeless, the poor, the orphaned, and the leprous, Mother Teresa told of their daily schedule, beginning with their rising at twenty to five in the morning and their daily mass in preparation for the day's work. She took pains to make clear that the Missionaries of Charity were Catholic Sisters in the traditional sense.

The point of the meeting then occurred. President Echeverría asked if Mother Teresa would send her Sisters to work in Mexico. I suddenly thought of Father Pro who had witnessed by his death for the Catholic faith in Mexico and of the strange fact that this invitation was coming so soon after the visit to his tomb. One wondered about the community of saints, the teaching that there is a bond between holy people that links them indissolubly, even across the border of death.

Mother Teresa replied that as hers was a religious society, the invitation to come to Mexico would have to come from the head of the local Church. President Echeverría seemed optimistic that that could be arranged. He turned to Mr. Gomes del Campo, who nodded. It developed that Gomes del Campo was a Catholic whom Echeverría called on for advice in such matters.

The President stressed his humanistic concerns for the poorest of his country and of the world and presented us with booklets on the "New International Economic Order," a prime concern of countries belonging to the Third World. Mr. Gomes del Campo told me that the President had been impressed by newspaper reports of the Missionaries of Charity, in particular, their ability to work in and to adjust to different cultures in the less developed world.

Echeverría reiterated his desire to have Mother Teresa come back to Mexico with Sisters to work among his people. He went further and said that he personally would see that they got any help they needed to begin their work. Mrs. Echeverría brought some of their eight children to meet Mother Teresa and then accompanied her down the long hall to the door of the mansion. At the door she presented Mother Teresa with a small lacquered cross, not a crucifix, since it lacked the corpus of Christ. With infinite delicacy, since like her husband, she could not be counted as a believer, she said, "I would like you to have this as an example of the fine work done by our poor people."

There was time for Mother Teresa to spend at the simple home of Mr. and Mrs. José Chavez in the company of some Catholics who numbered among them professors, writers, and members of the local parish.

The invitation from the cardinal of Mexico City to come there arrived in Calcutta sometime later, and in the following year, a team of Sisters arrived in the capital. President Luis Echeverría fulfilled his promise to help them start their work, one gift being a vehicle. Mother Teresa and the Sisters decided on their place of work—near the mountains of garbage of a great city and among the men, women, and children who made their living there as garbage pickers.

Immediately after the International Women's Year Conference, Mother Teresa decided to visit her Sisters in Peru and Venezuela and pay a preparatory visit to Haiti. The house in Peru offered another proof of the far-reaching effects of Malcolm Muggerridge's *Something Beautiful for God.* At the request of the editor of the *National Catholic Reporter,* a weekly published in Kansas City, I wrote a review of the book for a special Christmas book issue. One who read the review was the Rev. Richard Mulroy, an American Norbertine Father serving on mission in Lima, Peru. He had come from the Norbertine Abbey of De Pere, Wisconsin. The extended review gave a description of the beginnings of the Missionaries of Charity in Calcutta and the way in which they searched out the poor in other cities of India and overseas. Don Ricardo, as he was called in Lima, felt that these were the Sisters needed in Lima, the city where St. Rose of Lima and St. Martin de Porres, both Dominicans, and their friends, had followed Jesus with holy lives.

On a short visit, Mother Teresa surveyed the situation of Lima, a city that in little more than a decade had grown from a population of 1.5 million to over 4 million and was still growing, with the poor migrating daily from the Peruvian hinterland. The cardinal of Lima asked the auxiliary bishop, Luis Bamburen, and Father Mulroy to help Mother Teresa. They found a modest house on a huge hill called "El Augustino," covered by the dwellings and shacks of the poor. It was one of the almost endless *barriadas* that stretched around Lima.

On a later visit, Mulroy took Mother Teresa to a deserted convent, a former Motherhouse, already unoccupied for two years.

"This is where we must be; here we can open a home for the abandoned," Mother Teresa decided.

When the Motherhouse had been built, a few generations earlier, the neighborhood was a quiet suburban setting. With the onrush of newcomers, it was now in the heart of a jam-packed and turbulent sector of the city, a sector known as La Parada, or stopping place. The building was purchased and opened in May 1974.

It was to La Parada that we now made our way, threading through the innumerable stands and stalls of an enormous market that reached up to the very wall surrounding the convent.

"This is *'Hogar de la Paz,'* our 'Home of Peace,'" said Sister Pauline, the superior, opening the door of the dirty pink convent. The Sisters were ecstatic at the unexpected visit of Mother Teresa and took her about the building, arranged Spanish style around a large enclosed patio. The Sisters had planted a practical vegetable garden alongside the peach and lemon trees.

The abandoned of every age and affliction were in the Home of Peace. On one side, next to the kitchens and washrooms, were the children; on another side, sick and elderly women, and on a third side, destitute and homeless men. Standing on the fourth side of the rectangle was a large chapel which had once served the large community of Sisters as well as the surrounding district. Mother Teresa walked about the dusty, unused chapel, surveying the cracks in the wall. It needed structural repairs before it could serve as a sanctuary for the Missionaries of Charity and for the crowded *barriada.* It could accommodate at least four hundred persons. The convent of the Missionaries of Charity, along with a tiny chapel, occupied rooms on the second floor of the spacious building.

Mother Teresa was pleased that the doorkeeper for the Sisters' compound was named Jesús. We talked with the residents, some very old, some nearly blind, some hardly able to move because of arthritis.

We found that one of them bore the name of Messias. He was an articulate young man with classic features, a newspaperman and writer. A wasting disease had attacked his muscles so that he could only move about in a wheelchair. Messias told me that once he had had so many friends he could not count them, but when he could no longer earn and was confined to his room, he could not count on them. They did not want to see his affliction and left him alone. He still had hopes he would improve and that some of his friends would rescue him. He asked me for some books, so that he could become proficient in English. I found an English grammar and Spanish-English dictionary in downtown Lima. When I presented them to Messias, his incapacitated neighbor, Theophane, told me that he, too, wanted to study English. Messias offered to help him. This was not merely a gesture. A letter from Sister Pauline informed me that Messias practiced so that he spoke English quite well and helped Theophane. Both, she wrote, had caught the spirit of the Hogar.

Old men, who had drunk their health away, and were picked up dying from the streets, were beginning to eat regular meals at the Hogar. Old women, discharged from the public hospitals with no home or family to receive them, found a loving reception and clean beds.

Among the children were orphans, crippled, retarded, mongoloid, and abandoned infants and youngsters. Among the children between six and ten years of age, were two small boys who had large heads and who walked with difficulty like a pair of old men. They measured their steps and pushed one foot hesitantly in front of the other as if to test whether the ground would hold them. They had bright eyes and were not megalocephalic, but merely had larger heads than one would find on six or seven year olds. I asked Sister Pauline about them.

"They are Absalom and Ezechiel, brothers," she told me. "Their ages are twelve and fourteen and they just came to us a few months ago."

A Sister-Nurse working in a mountain village found two hungry little boys in a tiny, dark dwelling. Their father was out working in the fields. When he returned, he related that the mother of the boys had died some years before and that he was never able to care for the boys. The Sister noticed that the boys did not talk at all and, often as not, moved about on all fours. Only occasionally did they raise their stunted bodies to walk upright and needed then to hold on to some support.

Horrified at what she saw, the Sister talked with the neighbors and learned that the father drank and simply neglected the children. Sometimes the neighbors, poor themselves, fed the starvelings. She asked the father if he would allow her to take the boys to Lima where they could be cared for. The man agreed with obvious relief and the Sister arranged for the legal papers and got permission to put them in the care of the Sisters at the Home of Peace.

Because of hunger, year in and year out, the bones of the boys had not developed. They were already beginning to walk a little more easily now on their short legs and the other children were urged to be kind to them. A voluble young man of ten, Carlos, told me that he sat next to them on the bench for meals. They soon learned how to use a spoon. He told the other children not to laugh at Absalom and Ezechiel but to teach them to talk. As yet, only indistinguishable sounds issued from their throats. Carlos imitated the strange babbling sounds with gusto. It was not clear whether or not the boys were deaf.

Both boys were delighted to have someone take their hand and go walking and they would return a bright smile for a smile. The older boys and girls were given tasks to perform, such as folding towels and bed sheets. Absalom and Ezechiel soon joined the group and imitated the actions of the other children. They caught me standing near them and studying them. Absalom looked up and turned his head away shyly, but there was a pleased smile on his face. It was a smile that seemed to mingle shyness at realizing someone was watching him, with pride in the fact that he could do something worth watching. The boys were given extra food and special calcium for their poor weak bones.

When Sister Pauline left Lima for another house, she was replaced by Sister Anand, the German Sister-Doctor, with whom I continued a correspondence. Absalom and Ezechiel did grow, she informed me, but even many medical tests could not devise ways to overcome the long years of lack of food and almost total neglect.

Her report brought me up to date, relating that a young Peruvian doctor was helping her, coming twice a week to visit the patients and prescribe medicine. More and more people were coming to help, including students, people from local parishes, from the Legion of Mary, and from other congregations of Sisters. The restored chapel was already serving as a parish, with about two hundred people coming for morning and evening mass. Sister Anand visited the *barriadas,* sometimes having to bring back a sick baby in her arms.

One of the problems around the Home of Peace was that of garbage. "So much is left lying to rot," she wrote, "unsold vegetables, fruit that has gone bad, all sorts of refuse. There are gangs of young thieves who steal wristwatches, purses, and carrier bags. Spectacles are torn off noses and the thieves quickly disappear. Most visitors know this. So far, the Sisters have been left in peace."

She continued, "The stands for shoes, iron, and wood tools lean against our walls. The secondhand stalls sell everything from the smallest screw to furniture, fridges, records, etc. On the other side are the fruit and vegetable stalls, as well as stalls for fish, flowers, and all sorts of clothing. One can get all kinds of things to eat, not to mention the stands where alcohol can be bought, and where one or two drunks lie about. We have pulled several out of the mire. One poor man died the next day. Once we found a corpse outside our door. So, even here, the work is not so different from the work in India. Only the faces, the speech, and the customs are different."

The people of El Augustino were enthusiastic to have the Sisters among them. As Sister Anand reported, with the work of the Home of Peace, the Sisters found time to visit needy and sick families in the *barriadas,* where, during the drizzle, the pathways became treacherously slimy. The scourge of the poor of Lima was tuberculosis. Lima's factories had reached the point of demanding a chest examination before considering a person for a job. A group of Co-Workers including men and women from many professions, doctors, teachers, and housewives, were soon helping the Sisters. One of the most faithful was a teacher, Judith Ramos, who belonged to a Catholic lay organization called the Legion of Mary.

There was one small group, however, who did not welcome the Sisters and who stunned them by suggesting that it would be better if they left. A certain group of priests told the Sisters that the problems of Peru demanded more than they could give. It was time to change the very structures that were giving rise to the poverty with which they were surrounded. The Missionaries of Charity were doing nothing to change these structures, they were told, and were thus prolonging the misery of the people.

The Sisters did not argue but carried on with their own ministry, the backbreaking task of feeding an old woman discharged from a government hospital, washing a rheumy-eyed old drunk left to die on the street, or rescuing little boys abandoned to darkness and hunger.

Father Richard Mulroy came early every morning to celebrate mass. As the cardinal of Lima had put the Sisters specifically in Fr. Mulroy's spiritual charge, the Sisters liked to call him their "cardinal protector." He told me that something inexplicable had happened to his health since he had been given charge of the Sisters. As the victim of a series of heart attacks, he had been advised to return to a less active life at his monastery in Wisconsin to save his life. After he decided to remain in Lima, he had suffered no more heart attacks and found himself able to work harder than ever before.

On our return to Venezuela, the Missionaries of Charity were well-established in a section called Catía la Mar, outside Caracas. The convent was perched on a steep hill at the apex of which was an enormous water tank, hence the name of the street. Calle el Tanque.

Sister Gilbert, who had been the youngest of the team to come to New York, was now an assured young Sister, heading a free day care center for the mothers of the district. By caring for and feeding over fifty tiny preschoolers, the Sisters liberated poor mothers to earn the money their families needed to survive.

The Sisters took Mother Teresa to visit the huts of sick people living alone, men and women who had migrated to the city and whose families had died or drifted away. The local priest and one of the Sisters accompanied Mother Teresa as she made her way up and down the steep streets to meet the people who were aided by the Sisters. She came upon a level space on which a storage shed had been constructed. It was for sale. She asked the Sisters what they thought of it and they found it good. That was the big decision of the visit, the opening of a Home for the Destitute.

The first candidate lived nearby, an aged black man with grizzled hair and a benign expression. His wife had died and his sight was failing. The Sisters had to bring him food. He peered at the Sister until he was sure of her identity. Then he took her hand to kiss it, thanking her over and over again for her goodness and asking God to repay her.

At that time, there were three houses of the Missionaries of Charity in Venezuela. It was Mother Teresa's plan to have more than one group of Sisters in any given country so as not to allow a house of the Sisters to remain isolated for long. Even though they were distant from each other, the Sisters could unite for retreats and strengthen each other in their spiritual commitment. During a short visit to Cocorote, Mother Teresa saw how Sister Dolores led the rosary and afternoon devotions in the churches of Cocorote and San Felipe.

The Sister was totally accepted by the congregations, and her Venezuelan Spanish was their tongue. They joined her in singing:

"Como granas que han hecho el mismo pan,
Como notas que tejen un cantar,
Como gutas de agua que se funden in el mar,
Los Cristianos un cuerpo formaran.

"Like the grains of the same loaf of bread,
Like the notes which one song blends,
Like drops of water that melt into the sea,
Christians will form one body."

In a few years, there was a network of five houses of Sisters in Venezuela, not only in Cocorote and Catía la Mar, but Marin, Cuidad Guyana, and finally, in a slum near the center of Caracas. Though Venezuela was hardly the neediest country in Latin America and with the advent of oil revenues, hardly a poor country at all, there were islands of need where people found themselves cut off from human contact and human aid. The Sisters were crucial not only for what they did, but for the creative energy they drew forth on behalf of the poor from the surrounding community.

Haiti, in contrast with Venezuela, was a place of spectacular poverty, the single poorest nation of the Western Hemisphere. It met Mother Teresa's category of the "poorest of the poor." A French-Canadian priest, at the airport to meet someone who actually did not arrive, offered Mother Teresa a place to stay. A telegram sent the day before announcing our arrival failed to arrive. We were soon careening up a corkscrew path to the peak of a hill on the outskirts of Port-au-Prince. There we found the Communauté de Sainte Marie, a Catholic center serving the poor clustered in shacks at the base of the hill. We were given comfortable rooms whose walls, like the building itself, were of rough boards. A team of Canadian Catholics helped the priest in reaching his parishioners. At mass, besides the singing of hymns in Haitian French, there was an interlude of tom-toms, a custom of their African ancestors that the Haitians had never relinquished. Very much at home, Mother Teresa spoke at the mass, her words being translated by the Canadian priest.

With the help of the priest and a car from Catholic Relief Services, Mother Teresa was able to become acquainted with the slums so often compared to those of Calcutta. The center of the city had been cleared of all hovels and of the obvious signs of poverty, and new hotels and villas spoke of another level of life. The ebullient artistic gifts of the Haitian people found expression in the paintings that enlivened the *camionnettes,* the miniature buses that darted everywhere about the streets. Each *camionnette,* bright with figures and scenes in reds, greens, yellows, and purples, seemed to have its own dedication—to St. Paul, St. Pierre, St. Marie Mère de Dieu, to St. Antoine, and even to the Saint Esprit.

We spent much time in a massive slum with the improbable name of Brooklyn. We walked along dirt alleyways with groups of scantily clad children at our heels. Many of them sucked on mango pits. As the pits were discarded, hosts of flies descended on them in hungry platoons. The boys and girls reached out their hands to touch Mother Teresa when she smiled at them and patted their heads. They smiled back, their teeth dazzlingly white against beautiful black faces. We walked by tin-roofed shacks, barely ten feet square, housing entire families. Some were no more than chicken coops, others almost miraculously shored up with bricks and heavy boards to resemble solid homes. The smell of burnt garbage and human waste in open drainage ditches hung over everything. Here, without plumbing, piped-in water, or electric light, families kept alive human values and a measure of dignity and even gaiety.

Every now and then, a shedlike structure stood apart; this was a slum school, one of the hundreds run by priests and religious Sisters which brought the tools of the intellect to the children of the swarming slums. It was clear that Mother Teresa felt that she belonged with the loving, lovable people around her. When Mother Teresa presented herself at the home of Archbishop François Ligonde, he told her she had come at the right time. He was meeting with the priests of Haiti who were gathered for prayer and for discussions of their spiritual and social tasks. Mother Teresa was soon on the podium before the priests, telling them of the spirit of her work and encouraging them in their work for the people of Haiti. Besides the Haitian priests, there were missionaries from various countries, from the United States, Canada, Holland, and France.

Sister Carmeline, one of the Sisters from New York, was sent as superior of a team to open a house in Port-au-Prince, a house that received the cast-off and dying, as in Calcutta.

The gleaming white building, Coeur Immaculé de Marie (Immaculate Heart of Mary), gave dignity and care to the very least of the least in Port-au-Prince. The ill and incapacitated too often had to wait for a bed in the overcrowded general hospital. The waiting place was termed the "Depot," and sometimes death came before a bed became available. Sister Carmeline wrote that it was from the Depot that the Sisters received many of their patients. Just as funds from the United States helped in the construction of the building, so, willing volunteers journeyed every summer from the United States. Sister Carmeline wrote: "Monsignor Feiten brings a medical team, and a construction team to work in our home for the dying. They also help us in our dispensaries. They built another building which serves as a clinic in the morning and a school in the afternoon. There is also a dentist for our people. Isn't it beautiful?"

Monsignor Richard Feiten, a Catholic Charities director from Minnesota, was one of the founders of the Co-Workers in the United States.

A school and feeding center for hundreds of children followed as well as four dispensaries. A house was eventually opened in Jacmel, Jeremie. Here, the Sisters settled among some of the most isolated and needy rural people of the hemisphere.

From Port-au-Prince, Haiti, to New York City constituted a leap in time as well as a transfer of place. In Haiti, low on the scale of economic development, human need was a naked reality. In New York City where over a million of its people drew some sort of welfare in an advanced, computerized system, human need was less obvious and not so simple to address.

It was the end of July 1975 when Mother Teresa reached the Missionaries of Charity in the South Bronx. July and August in New York City can be suffocatingly tropical, but instead of tropical forests, there are the forests of buildings, with heat, often reaching over ninety degrees for days on end, rising in steamy waves from the sidewalks. It is the time when disturbances and riots simmer and break out. Mother Teresa found Sister Andrea and the Sisters conducting what they called a summer camp. Sister Andrea, the young woman who had wanted to work among the lepers of India, and who had completed her medical studies in Calcutta with honors, had been given a vastly different post. Just as at Mother Teresa's suggestion, she had willingly given back the gold medal awarded her at the end of the medical course in Calcutta, she had accepted the assignment to New York City. Her English was perfect, and during her years in Calcutta, she had mastered Bengali and Hindi. These tongues were in addition to her native German and the Polish she had learned when her home place became Polish territory after the Second World War.

Sister Andrea with the Sisters had surveyed the terrain of the South Bronx and decided that one of the chief concerns of the Sisters would be young people, the young blacks and Hispanics who suffered most from being at the bottom rung on the economic ladder. After four years in the city, the Caucasian Sister with the classic features, accompanied by dark Sisters, all dressed alike in enveloping garments, were part of the landscape of the South Bronx and Harlem.

The camp was one of the responses of the Sisters. Camping brings up images of cool lakes, shady trees, and sports in the fresh country air. The summer day camp of the Missionaries of Charity in the South Bronx gathered over a hundred young people who would otherwise spend their days on the sidewalks. Too many were children of broken homes, children without a childhood, left to spend their time on the streets without discipline or protection. The Bronx, a borough of about 1.5 million people, held streets which were hotbeds of violence, crime, and trafficking in drugs. These were concentrated in the part of the borough called the South Bronx.

Mother Teresa saw how the boys and girls assembled at nine in the morning at St. Rita's School for community singing and prayer. Then they were divided into various groups, the boys being the Great Eagles, Junior Eagles, and Fledglings. The girls were all Butterflies, Yellow, Blue, or Pink, according to their ages. Joining their groups, the youngsters started the scheduled activities, workshops for woodworking and carpentry, the arts and crafts center, a reading center and groups for music, drama, and sports.

Sister Andrea knew not only the needs of the people among whom she worked and how to combine their talents in the various programs, but also how to go outside the community for volunteers and aid. Every year, the Co-Workers, headed by Mrs. Helen Sartan, and including local women, helped serve the midday meal for the campers. The food was supplied by the City of New York. Group leaders with special skills joined the Sisters, among them, Maryknoll Brothers, several novices in the Jesuit order, and lay volunteers.

Each year, the program varied somewhat depending on the possibilities of the volunteers. When I took a group of teenage boys to the United Nations, I found their curiosity enormously aroused. They sat quietly to hear answers to their questions about the problems of peace and the work of UN agencies around the world.

The young people, both boys and girls, took eagerly to the woodworking courses, proudly taking home their handiwork in the form of animals, fish, and wall crucifixes. They also fashioned clay vases and surprised themselves with their proficiency in painting.

Every week, these youngsters were lifted out of the South Bronx and transported to the countryside. One haven opened to them was Maryknoll, the central house of the Maryknoll order, the Catholic Foreign Mission Society of America. There, on a bluff overlooking the wide Hudson River, there was a picnic, games on the grounds, and swimming at a nearby pool.

On Saturdays, the Sisters made regular visits to the women's prison on Riker's Island in New York's East River. Some of the young women were relatives of the boys and girls in the summer camp. Mother Teresa went to the prison with the Sisters. Fifty women prisoners heard her tell them how much God loved them and how precious they were in God's sight.

Rampant crime, especially by young people, kept older citizens locked inside their homes. The prison population was heavily drawn from the area covered by the local police precincts, the 40th Precinct, in which the convent was located, as well as the next precinct, the 41st.

The 41st Precinct, Fort Apache, so-called because it was like a besieged fortress in the midst of dangerous enemies, attained national fame in films and books. The police were seen by many as targets. They were armed, but so were the criminals for whom the purchase of guns was well within their means.

Visiting the homes of many shut-ins, the Sisters found not only fear, but decay and dirt and went to work scrubbing and cleaning. The men and women they visited did not lack an income of sorts, a welfare check that was too often stolen from the mailbox or a Social Security check that would barely meet basic needs.

Mother Teresa often repeated the story told her by one of the Sisters in the Bronx.

"They came to a room from which a bad odor was coming. When the room was broken into, they found a woman who had been dead four or five days. No one had come to see her. They did not even know her name. Many of the people are known only by the numbers of their rooms or apartments."

Mother Teresa commented that she felt in the South Bronx a tremendous hunger for love and respect, a feeling of unwantedness and of being unloved among so many people. "One of the greatest of diseases is to be nobody to no one," she remarked.

The spartan simplicity of the lives of Sister Andrea and the team of Sisters was greater than that of the people among whom they lived. Visiters to the convent found in the bathroom, not rolls of toilet paper purchased from the store, but scraps of newspaper such as are utilized by the poorest people the world over. Some of us thought this a bit excessive until Sister Carmeline was suddenly sent from New York to start the work in Haiti. We realized that since the Sisters never became accustomed to the easy living of the developed world, there was no need for adjustment when they were dispatched to less developed areas.

The Spanish the Sisters spoke was the Spanish of Americans from Puerto Rico, far removed from classic Castilian. Their English became markedly colloquial. One day when a visitor began mouthing simplistic and prettified religious maxims in the midst of the South Bronx, Sister Andrea turned to me and remarked, "I don't want to hear anymore of that crap."

When the Sisters arrived in New York, Terence Cardinal Cooke informed Mother Teresa that the archdiocese was ready to supply a grant for their support. Mother Teresa explained, "I refused the offer from Cardinal

Cooke of five hundred dollars a month for each Sister working in New York. I said to him, 'Do you think, Your Eminence, that God is going to become bankrupt in New York?' "

There was never any difficulty in meeting the meager needs of the Sisters who daily brought to the poor the personal services that the rich could only command by money. A poor parish became rich in activities and in services—and poor it was. St. Rita's parish, a basement church which had never been completed, mirrored the changes that came to the Church following the Second Vatican Council.

Four priests had joined in the experiment of a team ministry for St. Rita's. First, the parochial school had to be closed for lack of Sisters as teachers. Then, the team split apart, two of the priests leaving the priestly ministry and the two remaining priests deciding to work in Central America. Priests were recruited from Spain to fill in the breach for the largely Hispanic parishioners. The Missionaries of Charity from India were helping rebuild the parish and the community.

Mother Teresa arrived back in Calcutta in August 1975, in time to send out invitations asking Calcuttans of all groups to join with the Missionaries of Charity in thanksgiving for the twenty-five years of work they had been permitted to carry out among the poor.

The Silver Jubilee was to be October 7, 1975. What transpired was an expression of thanksgiving across religious lines almost without parallel in history.

To Mother Teresa came a response not only from Armenian, Protestant, Methodist, Assembly of God, and Mar Thoma churches on the Christian side, but also from Hindus, Buddhists, Jains, Jews, Parsis, and Muslims.

16

To Give Thanks

In the Moghen David Synagogue of Calcutta, Mother Teresa recited the *Magnificat*, the prayer of a Jewish maiden, "My soul doth magnify the Lord, and my spirit hath rejoiced in God, my Savior . . .

"For He that is mighty hath done great things to me;
And holy is His name . . .
He hath filled the hungry with good things;
And the rich he hath sent empty away.
He hath received Israel, His servant,
Being mindful of His Mercy;
As he spoke to our fathers,
to Abraham and to his seed forever."

A Sister accompanying Mother Teresa told also of the readings from the Psalms and how the chief rabbi took Mother Teresa and the Sisters into the Holy of Holies after the service to show them the scrolls of the prophets, "very old and precious." The afternoon service on October 6, wrote one of the Sisters, "took us back to the days of Our Lord."

The service was in response to the letter from Mother Teresa regarding the Silver Jubilee of the congregation. The letter went out in September to ask for a common religious thanksgiving to mark the twenty-fifth anniversary of the foundation of the Missionaries of Charity on October 7, 1950. The invitations went to every religious group in Calcutta, not requesting them to come to a religious service with the Sisters, but to hold their own services.

Every group responded and the program of thanksgiving services was published in the *Calcutta Statesman* and in the *Calcutta Herald*, the local Catholic weekly. Desmond Dorg of the *Calcutta Statesman*, who had early followed the work of Mother Teresa in his newspaper accounts, wrote a feature article about the Silver Jubilee. A page of photographs accompanied the article, as well as the streamer headline: CALCUTTA THANKS MOTHER AND THE MISSIONARIES OF CHARITY FOR 25 YEARS OF SERVICE. The outpouring of gratitude revealed not only Mother Teresa's stamp on Calcutta, but Calcutta's stamp on Mother Teresa.

"Simplicity. No expenses, no concerts, no decorations, only thank you to God," was the way Mother Teresa envisioned the thanksgiving celebration. "I want God to be the central figure in our celebration so that everybody's attention may be drawn to God and all may acknowledge that it is His work and not ours."

Mrs. Ann Blaikie, an international link of the Co-Workers, was in Calcutta. Others of us shared the description of the events as sent in the mimeographed pages of *Ek Dil* (One Heart) to the closely knit family of Sisters around the world.

Beginning with Sunday, September 28, 1975, a service was held in the Armenian Holy Church of Nazareth on Calcutta's Armenian Street. Between that day and October 7, eighteen religious communities offered thanks in their own manner, asking Mother Teresa and a group of her Sisters to take part with them.

Mother Teresa took a different group of professed Sisters and third-year novices to each religious celebration. Sometimes she took six, sometimes ten, sometimes a dozen, since the Sisters had all their work to do throughout the celebrations.

On October 7, during Id, the Muslim month of fasting, five thousand Muslim men, garbed in white, gathered in the open Maidan, around the Shahid Minar monument, like a human sea. After their own prayers, they said prayers of thanks for the merciful work of the Sisters. Respectful of Muslim custom, Mother Teresa and the Sisters were at some distance on the edge of the throng. Some remained in a car Sister Nirmala told me, while a tiny group stood outside with heads bowed.

It might have been the first time in history that eighteen spiritual paths had united in a single act of thanksgiving at one time. Perhaps only in Calcutta could the unique and dramatic series of events have taken place. Perhaps only Mother Teresa could have inspired it.

The expressions of thanks at the religious functions give a picture found nowhere else of the impact of Mother Teresa and the Missionaries of Charity on the city where the work was born. In sending out the call, a short account of the Missionaries of Charity to date was prepared.

"From a first group that numbered 12, the Missionaries of Charity now count 1,133 members spread across the world.

"In India, the Missionaries of Charity have the following houses statewise: Andhra Pradesh, 3; Bihar, 7; Gujarat, 1; Haryana, 1; Kerala, 5; Meghalaya, 2; Madhya Pradesh, 3; Maharashtra, 5; Mysore, 3; Orissa, 3;

Tamil Nadu, 6; Uttar Pradesh, 7; Union Territories, 2; and West Bengal, 13.

"Outside India, the Congregation is at work as follows: Africa, 2 houses; Australia, 4; Bangladesh, 3; Europe, 6; Mauritius, 1; Middle East, 4; Papua New Guinea, 2; the U.S.A., 1; and South America, 4."

In the synagogue on Canning Street, verses from Psalms 117 and 118 were intoned in Hebrew and English. "Almighty God," said the rabbi, "it is with a heart full of joy that we have assembled here to give expression to our great joy and render thanksgiving on the occasion of the Silver Jubilee of the Society of the Missionaries of Charity for their humanitarian and selfless work, and through them for the poor of the world."

And now, Psalm 118, verse 24:

"This is the day that the Lord hath made; we will be glad and rejoice therein."

He went on, "And now, the day Mother Teresa has hoped for has come . . . We, the Jews of Calcutta, join in thanksgiving unto the Lord and pray that the Heavenly Father in His mercy preserve Mother Teresa and her band of workers, guard and deliver them from all trouble and sorrow. Hasten the days when the children of men understand that they have one Father, that one God created us all. Then shall the light of universal justice flood the world, and the knowledge of God cover the earth, as the waters cover the sea. Amen."

The Armenian church was a reminder of how ancient was the presence of this persecuted people in India. A Sister with Mother Teresa wrote that "the morning service was extremely solemn and rich, with all its ancient grandeur and splendor." The priest, pointing out that "The crown of God's work is man," commended Mother Teresa for reaching out to "innocent, condemned people," especially children. "The past twenty-five years have been hard and difficult," said the priest. He called to mind that Mother Teresa's Sisters, "in fighting a heroic battle against disease and famine, giving the orphans and the hungry food, work, education, and medical treatment were engaged in "God-pleasing work."

Three other services of thanksgiving took place on September 28, one in the Methodist church on Dharamtala Street in the center of Calcutta, one in St. James Church on Lower Circular Road, and one in the Jain Temple belonging to the more ascetic of the strains of Jain spirituality.

In the Methodist church, the Sister reported, "The people sang their hearts out, nearly bringing down the roof of the church. At the end of the service, the people flocked to Mother for blessing."

At St. James Church, the minister welcomed Mother Teresa and the Sisters to the brightly lit and spacious church. "He called all to worship," recalled the Sister, "stressing the presence of God among His children and His loving concern for each one of His creatures, especially the suffering ones, the lowly, the hungry, the uncared for, the unwanted, and the homeless. He thanked God for showing His loving concern for each of His children through Mother and her order." There were readings from the New Testament and hymns, with the children singing, "Seek ye first the Kingdom of God." The service ended with a collection for the Missionaries of Charity and a solemn blessing by the minister.

At the Digambara Jain Temple, Mother Teresa and the Sisters were greeted by the sound of cymbals and drums, all played by young girls. The Jains, of whom there are about three million in India, carry to the furthest extreme the teaching of noninjury, applying nonviolence to insect, bird, man, or beast. The monks often wear masks over their faces to avoid the possibility of swallowing even the tiniest mite in the air. Mother Teresa's care for human life appealed to them. The Jains picked up abandoned and decrepit animals as Mother Teresa picked up dying human beings, providing care and healing. Jain men were known to spend their years of retirement caring for hungry and sick pigeons in the cities of India. The word "Digambara" means absolutely nude, "sky-clad," and refers to the monks who are the most ascetic among this ascetic sect. They wear no clothes, practice celibacy, nonpossession, fasting, and mortification. For the Jains, an early offshoot from Hinduism, liberation from the cycle of rebirth comes from rigid asceticism and solicitude for all living beings.

When Mother Teresa and the Missionaries of Charity arrived for the *puja* in the Jain Temple, four of the totally nude monks were seated at the left of the worship stand. At the right were Jain nuns in white saris.

A Sister wrote, "Five young girls sang the *'Meri, Bhawana'* ('My Contemplation') while the whole congregation chanted after them. This was followed by the procession and enthronement of the statue of Mahavira. Five worshipers dressed in fine loincloths bathed the statue, pouring water with silver cups, while the congregation cheered and clapped with reverence. After the *puja,* Mother spoke on 'Service to one's neighbor.' The main Digambar monk spoke very beautifully, saying a few words on the teaching of Mahavira. 'Live and let others live.' "

Mahavira (Great Hero) was the last of the twenty-four Tirthankaras, the saint-founders of Jainism and is considered to be a historical figure. "My Contemplation," cited here in part, indicates the high moral teaching of the Jains.

May I never cause pain to any living being,

May I never utter untruth,

And may I never covet the wealth or wife of another.

May I never drink the nectar of contentment . . .

May there be mutual love in the world,

May delusion dwell at a distance . . .

May all understand the Laws of Truth and joyfully sorrow and sufferings endure.

Om,
Peace,
Shanti,
Shanti,
Shanti.

Something that went on without interruption throughout the *puja* made so deep an impression on Mother Teresa that she talked about it with awe. A Jain nun, as an act of penance, began to pull out each hair in her head. One by one, she tugged at the hairs with her fingers until they came loose. The Sisters said that this act of penance, of willingly accepting suffering, was known as *keshlocha.* They reported that "During the whole process, there was not even a wrinkle of pain on her face."

Mother Teresa told me that this affected her so much that she felt she ought to do likewise. So, she reached up under her head covering and drew out a few hairs from her own head.

"It was very painful, but I wanted to do it," said Mother Teresa. "I can never forget that Jain nun, with blood all over her scalp, calmly continuing to pull out the hairs and accepting the pain."

October 2 was Gandhi's birthday, a hundred and six years after his birth in 1869. As an adopted daughter of India, Mother Teresa would not allow the Jubilee week to pass without remembering the father of the nation. The Leprosy Rehabilitation Center at Titagarh was inaugurated as the Gandhiji Prem Nivas (Gandhi Center of Love) on being turned over to the Missionaries of Charity Brothers. At one stroke, three effects were achieved. Attention was paid to Gandhi, apostle of nonviolence, who had asked that missionaries should live the Sermon on the Mount rather than talk about it; attention was focused on the Brothers, already twelve years old, but whose work was little known though they lived and worked with the poorest and had taken over the men's halls in the Home for the Dying. It also brought into the Jubilee the very least of the community, shunned even by their own families, the lepers. To the inauguration of Gandhiji Prem Nivas came the highest political officer of the state, the Governor of Bengal, Mr. A. L. Dias, with his wife.

The same evening found Mother Teresa at the Assembly of God church, at a thanksgiving presided over by the pastor, the Rev. Buntain. The Sister, in describing the service, said,

"The Rev. Buntain met Mother Teresa and the Sisters at the door and escorted them into the church where a huge assembly of people had gathered. Over the altar a banner hung with the words, 'Missionaries of Charity—25 years—love lives on.' The Rev. Buntain opened the prayer service with a sermon on the works of the Society and how we help each other to bring Christ's love to the destitute of Calcutta. A number of hymns were sung by the youth choirs, the Hindi and Bengali choirs. Throughout the service, the Rev. Buntain, assisted by another pastor, prayed, praising God for all He had done through us. The people sang wholeheartedly, clapping their hands and raising their voices with 'Alleluia,' 'Amen,' and 'Bless Mother Teresa.' "

The Brahmo Samaj, the Calcutta-born reformist Hindu Society of God, held a simple service on October 3. Dr. B. C. Roy, Bengal's Chief Minister, was one of the members of Brahmo Samaj who honored and supported Mother Teresa's work.

"The morning of the fourth of October," wrote a Sister, "found us right inside the Hindu Temple of Shree Lakshmi Narayan. As we got down from the bus sent by Mrs. Sarala Birla to take us there, all the people touched Mother's feet and led her near the sanctuary. All of us followed Mother. Mrs. Birla herself offered the *puja* in thanksgiving and asked for a long life for Mother and blessing on the Society. The priest and all present there invoked the thousand names of God with great devotion. All was in Sanskrit and very solemn."

After the morning *puja* in the Hindu *mandir,* Mother Teresa took her band in the afternoon to the Parsis, those descendants of seventh-century Persian refugees who preserved their ancient Zoroastrian faith by fleeing into India at the coming of Islam. Their small number, about 150,000, heavily concentrated in Bombay, gives no hint of their enormous impact on the economic modernization of India and even on its liberation. Known for their Fire Temples, actually places of worship where fire is reverenced, and for their Towers of Silence where their dead are left as food for vultures to avoid contamination of the earth, their faith embodies a strict moral code. The Parsi belief in a final judgment is similar to that of Jews and Christians.

Dr. Anklesaria, speaking for the Parsis, stated that Jesus had influenced history more than any other being and then asked a question, "How did this come about? It was because this Man gave to the world a message of love—a message very similar to that given us by our own prophet, Zarathustra, four thousand years earlier—a message that spelt out: Love thy fellowmen for thou art thy brother's keeper; love him with good thoughts, good words, and good deeds; love little children for they are the innocent of the earth; care for all those that are sick, suffering, and in need.

"Today, here in our midst, is a daughter of Christ, who has based her whole life on her Master's teaching."

Then, Dr. Anklesaria asked on behalf of his community that Mother Teresa address them.

Mother Teresa began, "I am very grateful to God to have given me this wonderful opportunity to be with you and together with you to thank God for what He has done in us and through us for the poor of the world. It was you together with us who made it possible to accept to do and to continue doing and putting the love of God into a living action."

She thanked all those who had the courage to say "Yes" to the service of the poor, to the parents who gave their children to the service of God, and to the poor "who have accepted our love with such blind trust, accepted our compassion, accepted our service . . . . Also let us thank the thousands and thousands of people who have helped us to help these people, the rich and the poor. The rich who have opened their hearts to give until it hurts; the poor who have shared the little they have and have had the courage to share all."

Mother Teresa ended by asking for their prayers. "You pray for us that we may not spoil God's work, for the work is His work." It was exactly the same request for prayer that she was to put later to Pope John Paul II.

Sunday, October 5, began with a morning mass at the Cathedral of Our Lady of the Rosary. Immediately after the mass, Mother Teresa took the Sisters to another address on the same street, Portuguese Church Street, to a separate group of Jains. In contrast to the Digambaras, the "sky-clad" or "space-clad" monks, the Swetambaras are known as the "white-clothed." Like the address given by Dr. Anklesaria, the address of Muni Sri Roopchandra illuminated the extensive interaction of religions that has marked and still marks the life of Bengal.

Muni Sri's sermon on prayer as the source of infinite power was filled with references to Christian sources, as well as to Lord Mahavira, and with the concordances he found between the two religious traditions.

"The tremendous power of prayer lies not in the words we utter but in the heart that we conceive it in," he said. "If you say, 'Lord, Lord' and do nothing, sayeth Jesus of Nazareth, 'it will avail you nothing.' "

After citing Lord Mahavira's path to perfection through right knowledge, right vision, and right conduct, as the three crown jewels of spirituality, Muni Sri referred to the Christian gospels, "If you do not love your brother whom you see, how can you love God whom you do not see?" He ended by saying "Words are flesh, ideas are the spirit which is ever one and the same in all nations and periods of history. Let our prayer be born of the spirit and not of mere flesh and blood."

At the Sikh Gurudwara, Mother Teresa sat between two bearded and turbaned Sikhs for the act of thanksgiving which filled a large hall. The

Sikhs, founded by Guru Nanak, in the early sixteenth century, eliminated the caste system of Hinduism but adopted some elements of Hinduism as well as of Islam. Celebrated for their martial prowess, the Sikhs are known to the poor of India, as well as to hungry strangers, even young Americans, for the free food kitchens attached to many Gurudwaras.

A beautiful litany, composed for the occasion, greeted Mother Teresa at the Syrian Mar Thoma Church, the church which claims St. Thomas the Apostle as its founder in southern India.

"O God of love and pity, we thank thee for all those who are engaged in the missionary task of thy Church. At this hour, we especially thank thee for thy guidance in the founding of the Society of the Missionaries of Charity," began the priest.

The congregation responded, "We thank thee, O God."

The ten verses of the litany ended with the prayer:

"For the spiritual growth, for the strength to serve, for the increase of love and wisdom, and for all the blessings the Sisters have received, through their service to the poor and the unwanted, we thank thee, O God."

An impressive order of service was printed at the cathedral handicapped training center for the service of thanksgiving at St. Paul's Cathedral. Much preparation had gone into the Silver Jubilee celebration on Sunday evening, October 5, and every step in the service was lovingly planned.

The constitutions of the Missionaries of Charity had been studied so that selections could be chosen for the appropriate responsive readings.

Bishop R. W. Bryan presided over the service in the spacious cathedral which was filled to capacity. It began with a procession of the clergy from different denominations behind a banner which read, CHURCH OF NORTH INDIA—UNITY—WITNESS—SERVICE. "After the bishop," wrote a Sister, "walked our Mother, and after her, our Governor, Mr. Dias, and Mrs. Dias. A priest read out from the constitutions: 'God is love. A Missionary of Charity must be a missionary of love.' The congregation responded, 'We must spread God's love on earth.'

"The priest leader read extensively from the constitutions, concluding with, 'The spirit of our society is one of love and total surrender, loving trust and cheerfulness as lived by Jesus and His Mother in the gospel.'

"The entire congregation, from the printed programs, responded:

"Christ was entirely at the disposal of His Father for the ransom of many. 'Though He was God, He did not count equality with God a thing to be grasped, but emptied Himself, taking the form of a servant, being born in the likeness of man.'

"It was a really wonderful experience," commented the Sister, "to hear such a huge congregation of such a variety of people from all walks of life reading and meditating on the words of the gospels and our constitutions which our Mother has given us. It became somewhat a universal gift for them all!

"In 'Poverty Is Our Dowry,' Mother Teresa talked of the special calling of the Sisters.

"She thanked all who had helped with the work over the years and paid special tribute to Archbishop Perier. Then she thanked all the Sisters and Brothers and all the Co-Workers. Her final words of gratitude were for 'the poor who have accepted us all these years.'

"The Governor, Sri A. L. Dias, told us that the inauguration of Gandhiji Prem Nivas, the Leprosy Rehabilitation Center in Titagarh, on Gandhi's birthday, had been for him a real spiritual experience.

"Bishop Bryan had included the Brothers, who led some prayers, and he also had brought the girls' choir from Prem Dan, the former Chemical Industries complex at Tiljala. Many of the girls had grown up in Shishu Bhavan. Gifts of handiwork fashioned by children of the *bustees* were presented to Mother as a sign of solidarity with the poorest of Calcutta. Gifts were also brought to her by a handicapped child and a leprosy patient."

Sister concluded her description, "The end of the beautiful service came with the singing of the hymn, 'Now Thank We All Our God.' The blessing was imparted on us present and also on the absent Missionaries of Charity and our Co-Workers and our poor people all over the world by his lordship, the bishop."

Only two non-Catholic events remained for Monday, October 7; the first, already described—when Mother Teresa and the Sisters sat in a car or stood with bowed heads at the edge of the Maidan—and a service in the Buddhist temple. "The monks," wrote the Sister, "solemnly chanted their prayer of thanksgiving and then the people prayed together with the monks."

At the end of the service, the head monk of the Mahabodhi Society gave Mother Teresa two electric candles, one of which was placed with the sanctuary lamp in the convent chapel. Though Buddhists do not share the Christian belief in a personal God, they share the Christian commitment to mercy for one's fellow human beings. A Buddhist leader told me that he saw Mother Teresa in the light of the *Bodhisattva*, the enlightened being, called "regarder of the cries of the world." She was also likened to a *Bodhisattva* because of her "joyful participation in the sorrows of humanity."

A Sister commented on the series of thanksgiving services so unique in religious history. "We all feel that this kind of celebrating the Silver Jubilee was really a gift of the Holy Spirit who gave Mother the idea to hold it in this unique way. We ourselves had very little to prepare. With our work, all went on as usual."

The church feast of St. Thérèse, Mother Teresa's patron, fell during the Jubilee week on October 1. This called for a family affair for the Sisters. Father Celeste Van Exem, who, as Mother Teresa's spiritual director, had played so crucial a role after the "second call" on September 10, 1946, celebrated the mass in the convent chapel. Sisters were gathered together from all the Calcutta houses. In the evening, the Sisters presented a cantata dramatizing in song and dance, the steps in the life of a Missionary of Charity—the call, the acceptance of the call, the work of messengers of love, and the movement out into the world.

There was also a showing for the Sisters of Malcolm Muggeridge's film, *Something Beautiful for God.* Mrs. Ann Blaikie had brought it to Calcutta so that the Sisters could see it for the first time.

At the mass on Sunday morning, October 5, in the Cathedral of Our Lady of the Rosary, Archbishop L. T. Picachy was joined by a number of priests as concelebrants. The archbishop began his homily saying, "When Mother Teresa and her Sisters were preparing for the Silver Jubilee celebration, they decided that it should consist of a common act of thanksgiving and prayer. As far as possible, all external manifestation should be done away with. It is an occasion of spiritual rejoicing, which began last Sunday just a hundred yards from here at the Armenian church . . . Naturally our first thanks goes to God."

The archbishop made it a point to thank all those who were not in the limelight, the Brothers, all the chaplains of the Sisters, holy men who guided them and sustained them through the daily Eucharist, and all the other Brothers, Sisters, and priests working in the archdiocese of Calcutta.

Archbishop Picachy ended his homily with the words, "In the name of the Calcutta archdiocese, at this Eucharistic service which is the center of our lives, we could do no better than gather round the altar and say, 'Thank you, God, for everything you have done for the Missionaries of Charity and also, we say thank you to all of you for the great help you have given to our Sisters.' "

"Then came the great day, long awaited, October 7," wrote a Sister. The Sisters from all over Calcutta gathered in the Motherhouse on Lower Circular Road for a mass at six-thirty in the morning. Around Mother Teresa were most of the first women to join her twenty-five years earlier, Sisters Agnes, Dorothy, Margaret Mary, Bernard, Florence, Clare, and Francesca. Of the original twelve, counting Mother Teresa, two young women, the fourth and the ninth to join the group, left as novices.

Missing from the Jubilee were Sister Gertrude in Yemen and Sister Laetitia in Papua New Guinea. To them went a message telling them how close they were to the hearts of all the Sisters. The mass was concelebrated by Archbishop Picachy together with the priests who had served as chaplains to the sisters. They included Fr. Edward Le Joly, spiritual adviser to the Sisters and a spiritual writer of note, and Fr. Celeste Van Exem, both of the Society of Jesus. Father Julien Henry, who did not relish public ceremonies, was not present. Serving the mass was the layman who had first given shelter to Mother Teresa on Creek Lane in Calcutta, Michael Gomes. His wife was in the front row, as was his daughter Mabel, who had accompanied Mother Teresa on some of her earliest forays into the streets of Calcutta. Mabel brought her three children.

Brother Andrew was present, as well as a large number of Brothers. Also, in the front row were what the Sisters called "the most precious gift for us," some of the old patients of Mother Teresa, people who had survived after being rescued from the streets twenty-five years before.

The hymns sung by the Sisters in the Calcutta Jubilee mass were the same as those sung by the Sisters in sixty-one houses all over India and in twenty-seven houses in eight countries beyond India's borders. The hymns had been mimeographed and sent out to emphasize the spiritual unity of all Missionaries of Charity.

During the Jubilee week Mother Teresa found time, with a few of the first Missionaries of Charity, to steal away for a visit to 14 Creek Lane, the Gomes house where the Society took its beginnings.

The Sisters did not fail to note that when their Silver Jubilee celebrations were over, Calcutta was still celebrating. It was the time of the *puja* holiday for Durga. Durga, meaning the Inaccessible, is another name for the black goddess, Kali, beside whose temple at the Home for the Dying, the Sisters had worked every day of the Jubilee week.

There were messages of prayer and congratulations from all over the world, including from Cardinal Villot for Pope Paul VI. There were also Jubilee celebrations all over the world. Mother Teresa's letter addressed to "My dearest Sisters, Brothers, our Poor, our Co-Workers, all those who have shared in our work all over the world," had helped Sisters and Co-Workers keep to her spirit.

> For the 25 years we have spent together in God's service, giving wholehearted, free service to Christ in His distressing disguise, during which we have lived, worked, prayed together, let us together say:
>
> Thank you, Jesus, for choosing us to be your Missionaries of Charity;

Thank you, Jesus, for loving us with a deep and personal love;
Thank you, Jesus, for trusting us with Your Body and Blood;
Thank you, Jesus, for the privilege of serving the Poor;
Thank you, Jesus, for everything, especially for being Jesus to each one and loving us as the Father loves You.

It has been pointed out that the surest grounding for an appreciation of other paths to God is a deep commitment to the highest teachings of one's own religion. A person humbly striving for an experience of God would not deny the possibility of that experience to those on other pathways to that experience. This was surely true of Mother Teresa whose devotion to prayer involved the trust that it is the one Spirit at work in those who pray. It was through her that the religious rites of vast millions of the human family, at a meeting place of East and West, were turned in October 1975, to a single direction, toward the Infinite.

In Rome, the Silver Jubilee was marked by a mass celebrated in the chapel in Tor Fiscale. A bishop and two priests from the neighboring parishes celebrated the mass for the people of the *baracche* and the Co-Workers.

In Tabora, Tanzania, there was a morning mass for the Sisters in the compound and, at 4:30 in the afternoon, a mass which filled the Tabora Cathedral. Twelve African and European priests assisted at it. Most of the old people and children were brought from the compound to take part in the cathedral service. A priest from the White Fathers gave a sermon in which he described how the Missionaries of Charity had begun, with Mother Teresa coming to a great city with only five rupees. When he described how the Sisters depend only on the providence of God, and how they have over eleven hundred Sisters working all over the world, just like the ones in Tabora, the people burst into clapping and began to sing and dance for joy.

In Lima, the Jubilee mass was celebrated in the renovated church at the side of the "dirty pink" convent, on the far side from the jam-packed "thieves market." The auxiliary bishop of Lima and fifteen priests concelebrated a mass for the Sisters, their needy family in the Home of Peace, and the local people. Father Richard Mulroy gave the homily, echoing Mother Teresa in saying that the poor are the body of the suffering Christ. He wrote that the overflowing crowd in the church showed how the Sisters had endeared themselves to the people of Lima.

In New York City, St. Patrick's Cathedral was the scene of a mass celebrated by Terence Cardinal Cooke. He was flanked by two bishops and six priests. Bishop Patrick Ahern gave the homily in which he was helped by a simple-minded little man sitting next to me. When Bishop Ahern said from the pulpit, "Jesus loves each and every one," the little man said loudly, "of us." When he said, "Jesus calls to each and every one," he again helped with a loud "of us." At other times, he interjected "Amen."

Sister Andrea read one of the Scripture readings and Sister Mridula led the responsorial psalm. There were four carrying the gifts in the offertory procession, two Missionaries of Charity and two Co-Workers, Mrs. Helen Sartan and Sister Jacqueline, from the black congregation in Harlem. The little man left his seat when the others did. A priest hurriedly took the covering from the chalice and gave it to him, so he became the fifth member of the offertory procession. He walked proudly up and handed over the cloth and then walked solemnly back to his seat with Sister Jacqueline. He felt a part of the celebration. He was surely one of the least in the family of God and was given his due dignity. Someone said he reminded her of the tale of Our Lady's Juggler, who had only one gift to give to the Blessed Virgin, his juggling, and was found in church juggling joyously. After the mass, the cardinal asked the Sisters and Co-Workers to join him at the Lady Chapel behind the altar so that he could greet and thank them personally. Sister Andrea added the Indian touch by placing a *mala,* a wreath of red and white flowers, around the cardinal's neck.

In a converted chicken coop on the outskirts of Amman, Jordan, two American Co-Workers joined with the Missionaries of Charity in celebrating the Silver Jubilee. Dr. Anita Figueredo Doyle and her husband, William Doyle, of San Diego, California, wrote from Amman. "The Sisters' chapel is a converted chicken coop without electricity, and there we had the joy of joining in a mass of celebration for the twenty-fifth anniversary of the founding of the Missionaries of Charity. The bishop of San Diego, in company with the bishop of Jordan, said mass by the light of a lantern."

Scarcely a week after the conclusion of the Jubilee, Mother Teresa left Calcutta for New York to take part in a Spiritual Summit Conference called by the Temple of Understanding in connection with the thirtieth anniversary of the United Nations. The Temple of Understanding, a nongovernmental interfaith organization wished to find channels that would permit spiritual resources to be brought to bear on world problems, operating under the theme of "One is the spirit of man." Mother Teresa's presence was arranged by Mrs. Sarala Birla of the powerful Birla family of Calcutta.

The trip gave Mother Teresa the opportunity to be in Rome on October 20, when a more formal celebration of the Silver Jubilee took place. In the Basilica of Saint John Lateran, Cardinal Poletti, with sixty priests, concelebrated a mass of thanksgiving in the presence of a congregation that included many Co-Workers and the poor of Rome.

On Friday, October 24, Mother Teresa was on the dais of a hall adjoining the United Nations headquarters in New York. Before this appearance, she had traveled to the University of North Carolina in Wilmington to receive the Albert Schweitzer Prize in the humanities. There she was compared to Schweitzer whose concept of "reverence for life" led him to devote his life to healing the poor in the African jungle. His work was recognized by awarding him the Nobel Peace Prize in 1952. As her companion, I had to arrange a schedule that allowed her to be at the UN in time for the morning program which climaxed the week-long interfaith parley. Beside Mother Teresa on the dais were the Lord Abbot Kosho Ohtani, a representative of Buddhism; Rabbi Robert Gordis, speaking for Judaism; Dr. Seyyed Houssein Nasr, speaking for Islam; and Srimati Gayatri Devi, for Hinduism. Mother Teresa was the Christian speaker.

The opening meditation by Sri Chinmoy, a leader of the United Nations meditation group, turned out to be a time devoted to utter silence. The Secretary-General of the United Nations, Kurt Waldheim, then greeted the speakers and guests. The program carried a quotation from the monk Thomas Merton, "My dear brothers, we are already one, but we imagine we are not. What we have to be is what we already are." Merton had made the statement at the Spiritual Summit Conference held in Calcutta in 1968. It took place at the Birla Academy, since the Birla family supported the movement. Merton had written to me at that time that he wanted to meet Mother Teresa, but she was not in Calcutta. He went on to Bangkok and to his death, termed an "electric crucifixion." His death occurred due to the faulty wiring of a standing electric fan which fell on him.

Mother Teresa spoke on God's love, the heart of the message brought by Jesus. She asked the participants—Jews, Christians, Muslims, Hindus, and Buddhists—to serve the poor and suffering as "brothers and sisters in the same family, created by the same loving God."

The religion editor of the New York *Times,* Kenneth A. Briggs, in an article entitled "Spiritual Parley Hears Living Saint," commented: "The years of toil have left Mother Teresa stooped, but with discernible loss of verve. Her brown eyes sparkle and she speaks with resolve. Her approach remains her trademark: person-to-person contact, giving the desperate and the deprived a feeling of dignity."

The next stop for Mother Teresa was the residence of the apostolic delegate in Washington, D.C., where Archbishop Jean Jadot welcomed her. Mother Teresa was the guest of the delegation on October 25, to attend a gathering that was a sequel to the International Women's Year Conference in Mexico. Three women, representing the aims of Peace,

Development, and Equality, were invited to be present. Mother Teresa's identification with peace was underlined in her choice as the woman of Peace. Barbara Ward, representing Development, could not attend, but Margaret Mead, renowned as anthropologist and writer, was present as representative of Equality. On meeting Mother Teresa, Margaret Mead bent over and, taking Mother Teresa's hand in hers, kissed it.

"This is the woman who is doing all the great work. I wanted so much to meet you," she said with a warm smile. All three women contributed messages to the commemorative program, Mother Teresa's consisting chiefly of the Peace Prayer attributed to St. Francis of Assisi.

As happened when Mother Teresa's appearance was announced in an area, a series of events was clustered around it. It was only possible for Mother Teresa to reach each destination on time because Frank and Vi Collins, Co-Workers from Calcutta but now residents of Washington, drove her in their car and took part in the events. On Sunday morning, after breakfast at the embassy of India, Mother Teresa was driven to the Shrine of the Immaculate Conception on the grounds of the Catholic University of America. Her appearance to deliver the homily at noonday mass had been announced, and the shrine was thronged, even the aisles packed with people. Patrick Cardinal O'Boyle led her into the sanctuary where her small figure could scarcely be seen among the altar-full of concelebrating priests. O'Boyle, who had known her for fifteen years, spoke briefly about Mother Teresa's witness to the sacredness of human life in presenting her to the congregation. At the reception held in the basement of the shrine, long lines of people came to greet her or shake her hand.

Mother Teresa's next appearance was also related to the International Women's Year, this time a discussion of "Women's Role in Reconciliation and Renewal." It was held at the College of Notre Dame of Maryland, conducted by the School Sisters of Notre Dame. Before setting out for the college, located in Baltimore, Mother Teresa met with Dr. Elisabeth Kubler-Ross, who had flown to Washington especially for the meeting. The Home for the Dying at Kali's temple had captured the imagination of Dr. Kubler-Ross, whose experiences with dying patients was recounted in a bestselling book, *Death and Dying*. Both women talked about their lives with those marked for death and of the importance of personal loving human care for them. The experience of Dr. Kubler-Ross with the regimented impersonality of modern hospitals had inspired her to give strong impetus to the hospice movement for the care of the dying.

Emmitsburg, the shrine of the American saint, Elizabeth Ann Seton, was not far from Baltimore, and there the Sisters of Charity were waiting for Mother Teresa. There was a mass at the shrine and then the Sisters showed Mother Teresa the saint's original school, her simple home, and her burial place. St. Elizabeth Ann Seton, a widow with several children and a convert to the Catholic Church, had founded an American branch of the Sisters of Charity in 1813.

Hundreds of seminarians were lined up on the steps as we drove up to Mount St. Mary's Seminary, also in Emmitsburg. As Mother Teresa emerged from the car, there was long and loud applause. Mother Teresa had time only for a short talk, but one that breathed her exalted view of the priest as minister of the Eucharist and inspirer of holiness. Only then could the Collins family drive us to the train to return to New York City.

Again, as we crossed the Willis Avenue Bridge connecting Manhattan with the South Bronx, we confronted the gutted buildings betokening so many broken, gutted lives. Sister Andrea and the Sisters were busy with their shut-ins, the paralyzed and dying in hospitals, the prisoners' families in trouble, and the children.

One family from Haiti could find no other shelter, so the Sisters set up a temporary home for them on the second floor of the convent building. The family had six children and the mother was pregnant with the seventh. One afternoon, a bright-eyed Hispanic girl of seven or eight caught sight of Mother Teresa among the Sisters and said to me, "That's Mother Teresa. I remember her." I asked her how she recognized her and she replied, "By the stripes on her face." As the newspaperman had noted, years of toil had bent a straight back, but it had also added deep gulleys to the face of one who suffered with the suffering. At the little girl's descriptive term, some words of Scripture flashed through my mind, that it is "by His stripes that we are healed." Was it outrageous to think that though the "stripes" meant different things, there was a sense in which many had been healed through Mother Teresa's stripes?

The gulleys on Mother Teresa's face were pictured for millions around the world to see when, at the end of 1975, her face appeared on the cover of *Time* magazine. The painting, executed from a photograph, unsparingly depicted the ravages of time and toil on the countenance of a woman of sixty-five years. The cover in letters more than an inch high read, LIVING SAINTS, and in bold print: "Messengers of Love and Hope."

Though some seventeen examples of modern sanctity were cited, among them two friends of Mother Teresa's, Dorothy Day and Jean Vanier, most of the cover story dwelt on Mother Teresa, exploring the implications of modern saintliness. The article offered one definition of saintliness that had evoked remarkable agreement, namely, a person "through whom the light of God shines." It went on to say that many saw that light in Mother Teresa.

The article pointed out that the saint in contemporary terms is seen as a person of unremitting and heroic virtue and of courage that serves as a model for others. It mentioned a man and a woman who might be said to incarnate these qualities, both from India, Mahatma Gandhi and Mother Teresa.

17

Darshan

There is a concept in India that the very sight of a holy person, the *darshan*, brings a sort of blessing. To get even a glimpse of Gandhi, hundreds of thousands would stand for hours in furnace heat, even though his small figure might be no more than a speck across an expanse of packed bodies.

The concept of *darshan* exists without a name in western societies. It is far removed from the curiosity that attracts crowds to public figures or the hysteria that draws the young to musical stars. It was called forth on continent after continent by the presence of a pope. It was also called forth by the presence of Mother Teresa and seemed to express a radical hunger for the holy in a secularized world. Her face on the cover of *Time* magazine, coupled with the words LIVING SAINTS, drew even greater numbers of people than had been drawn by the book and film of Malcolm Muggeridge. Giant halls and stadiums were filled with people wanting to be in the presence of Mother Teresa. What was memorable was not simply the crowds who pressed in on her, but the fact that no matter how enormous the throng, or how exhausted she might be by appearances before them, she always summoned up enough energy to see the individual person and to give that person undivided loving attention.

The hunger for the sight of holiness seemed ready to devour Mother Teresa at the International Eucharistic Congress in Philadelphia from the first to the eighth of August 1976. Close to a million people took part in the week-long event centered on the gift and covenant of the body and blood of Christ with His followers. The crowd ran after her, sometimes only to gaze on her, often detaining her to ask for prayers or begging her to hear their hurts. They reached out to touch her sari even when they did not speak to her. Mother Teresa responded to all. She could scarcely move from place to place and her small body was almost crushed by the press of people. Finally, the congress organizers, without consulting her, assigned a squad of eight uniformed guards to protect her and clear her path. Two men in blue walked before her and two after her as a human shield. Four more were ready to take their places when a tour of duty was done. Mother Teresa was called upon to address group after group and to take part in many moving ceremonies. She had little time to adjourn to a small room alongside the large auditorium to take a hurried lunch. Even there, people slipped by the door guard. Mother Teresa would forget about eating to hear their needs. One woman stood for many.

She brought a small baby to Mother Teresa and asked her to pray that the child would not die.

"She is only ten weeks old," she explained, "and she will have to have a heart operation."

A friend of the mother's related that the baby had been diagnosed as having Down's syndrome and would have to be taken care of for her whole life if she survived.

Yet the mother was saying, "I want my baby to live. I want this child. Pray, Mother, that Shannon will live."

Tears were streaming down the mother's face as Mother Teresa put her hand gently on the child's head. The baby's eyes were closed in the pale little face and the hand hung limply. Mother Teresa's presence seemed to comfort the woman and, as she spoke, the mother's tears stopped.

"God has given you this great gift of life. If He wants you to give the gift back to Him, give it willingly, with love." They talked quietly for some time. The mother later wrote that the child had died at the age of seven months and that the words of Mother Teresa had echoed in her mind as a source of strength.

The year of 1976 was a time when *darshan* played an especially prominent role in Mother Teresa's life; it was an airborne year that was an epiphany of the "flying trapeze" existence of a modern-day nun whose work had captured the communications media. Besides criss-crossing the United States, putting down in eleven states, she visited Canada and opened houses in two Central American countries, Guatemala and Mexico. She took part in a large youth gathering in France and a religious peace conference in Singapore, meanwhile spending quiet, hidden time with Sisters in the Western Hemisphere, Europe, and India.

The record of four months in the Western Hemisphere is a revealing one. It not only offers a picture of many other journeys undertaken by Mother Teresa, but it indicates how she always expressed the deepest reality of a faith that was brought by a person, the person of the Son of Man. Despite the rush of events and the crush of people surrounding her, she honored each person she met, giving the same earnest attention to a brokenhearted mother as she gave to Robert S. McNamara, head of the World Bank, or to the President of a country.

The year began with the opening, in January, of a new house in Bombay, the city's third center conducted by the Missionaries of Charity. It was called Asha Dan (Gift of Hope) and was to receive, like Nirmal Hriday in Calcutta, the abandoned sick and dying. The site and building were a gift of the Hindustan Lever Company. To the group assembled for the opening ceremony, Mother Teresa said, "Asha Dan is a gift of hope and love, not only for the poor and needy, but for you and me. While your gifts in cash and kind are welcome, I am more anxious that you come sometimes to this home and give those living here your presence. Smile at them, touch them, and make them feel that they are your brothers and sisters. Gandhi said, 'He who serves the poor, serves God.' "

Prime Minister Indira Gandhi stressed Mother Teresa's identification with Indian culture later the same year by presenting her with an honorary doctorate at Visva-Bharati University, whose curriculum stressed social reconstruction. It grew from Santiniketan (abode of peace), the school founded by Rabindranath Tagore. Mrs. Gandhi placed the sign of honor on Mother Teresa's forehead and around her shoulders the scarf of the university.

In February, Mother Teresa, reading of the earthquake that rent a wide expanse of the Guatemalan earth, killing many thousands and destroying towns and villages, took, what was for her, an unprecedented step. She decided to send a team of Sisters to help the distressed people without a prior invitation from the hierarchy of Guatemala. It could be said that she made up her mind to send them in anticipation of an invitation, since the bishops of the world were clamoring for teams of the Missionaries of Charity. She sent a cable to the cardinal of Guatemala City telling him that she was ready to send her Sisters with love to Guatemala from India. The cardinal responded with enthusiasm and gratitude.

Mother Teresa arrived in New York City in mid-April in time to spend Easter with Sr. Andrea and the Sisters in the South Bronx. Stopping in Rome on the way, she received from the Camaldolese Benedictine monks the use of a monastery on the Coelian Hill, the home and monastery of St. Gregory the Great. It was to serve homeless men of Rome. The monastery was to be the site of the International Chapter of the Co-Workers in 1982.

"I have seen all the houses in India," she told me. "We have nearly three hundred novices. Wonderful, isn't it?"

I supposed that outside Calcutta, where the Muggeridge film had not reached the people and where *Time* magazine was not found at local news stalls, the problem of *darshan* had not arisen. I already knew it was a phenomenon in Calcutta itself. Once in Dum Dum Airport, we passed a circle of people sitting on the floor in prayer. They might have been members of any sect or followers of any guru. When they caught sight of Mother Teresa, they hurriedly broke the circle to surround her and carry out the Indian custom of bending low to touch her feet. In Calcutta, she constantly lifted people up as they attempted to pay this homage and tried to forestall it by folding her hands together for the Indian greeting.

In Easter week of 1976, Mother Teresa's first destination was Chicago. Under the theme of "Forward in Faith Together," Catholic educators from all over the nation were gathered for the seventy-third annual convention of the National Catholic Educational Association. The Rev. John Myers, president of the association, had long been anxious to have Mother Teresa as a speaker.

In her reply to his invitation, Mother Teresa wrote, "You must really pray very fervently that I let Jesus use me to the full during the days I am in the U.S. For I am so small, so empty, so nothing—only Jesus can stoop so low as to use one such as me. Pray much for us and for our people."

It was around this invitation that Mother Teresa planned her visits to Guatemala and Mexico. Having accepted a call from the President of the National Council of Bishops to participate in the Eucharistic Congress in Philadelphia, she then agreed to participate in over a score of meetings from New England to Texas, from Texas to the Midwest and Northwest, and as far north as Vancouver, Canada.

The Catholic press termed her presence at the Chicago gathering "the highlight of the convention." Mother Teresa gave her message before two plenary sessions, one on the evening of April 21, and the other on the morning of April 27. More than six thousand participants were present in an immense hall in McCormick Place for each. There was "standing room only" at each session.

"I am grateful to God," she began at the first plenary session, "for everything you have done for us through Catholic Relief Services. The gratitude of our people I bring to you today. From the beginning of our work, the American people have been helping us through the CRS."

The period of Lent in the parochial schools of the nation was a time when youngsters put into action the ancient concept of the Lenten fast, "Let the fasting of the faithful be the banquet of the poor."

Teachers, aided by a Lenten calendar of charity, dramatized the sufferings of children beyond the borders of the United States. The combined donations of the children for the work of Catholic Relief Services often reached over a million dollars.

"The greatest gift God can give you is to form God in the minds of the children. Do it with care," she told the assembled educators.

"To teach is not only a profession. It is a faith—the faith that it is Jesus we are teaching.

"You must teach the value of life, which is God's life.

"Our sisters do not teach always as you teach; but they teach also, with their hands, the hands that serve people with love."

From a hall filled with priests holding the highest degrees in theology, and with laity, Sisters, and Brothers who had completed doctoral studies in many fields of knowledge, came the question, "Mother Teresa, will you talk of God's love for you?"

"If it was not for God's tender love, every moment of the day, we would be nothing," she said. "We are nothing from the point of view of the world. The humility of God is to use you and me for His great work. So that we will share in the great vocation of belonging to Jesus. Christ came to bring the Good News that the Father loves each one of us with a personal love."

She had a fund of stories to illustrate God's care for the work with its daily miracles, small and big.

"Divine providence has been so delicate, so thoughtful in such small things. A few weeks ago, a patient needed a special medicine that would have to be bought from England. A basketful of medicines was brought to us that day. On top of the basket was that medicine. Only the delicate love of the Father could do that."

She told them how the young Sisters bringing care and love to those cast off by society helped them to know that God's love existed. A leprosy patient, she recalled, sunk in despair, was given hope by the attention of the Sisters. He said, "Now I know I am somebody to somebody."

During her talk, Mother Teresa pointed out that leprosy patients are cast off even by their own families. She related how a government official once came to her. He told her, "I had everything, cars, servants. I did not even have to carry my own briefcase. The day I discovered I had leprosy, I went home to my wife. She told me that she loved me, but she said I had to leave home. If I stayed, my children would have to suffer. Our daughters would have no chance to marry."

It was for these that the Missionaries of Charity had started such little townships as Shanti Nagar (Town of Peace).

Every Sister at the convention seemed to want to grasp Mother Teresa's hand. It seemed to bring them joy and strength that the work of a Sister, a vowed woman like themselves, was being recognized by the world, particularly when the vowed life was being put in question. Teaching Sisters in particular were under stress, when many of their number had left their congregations, and when the wearing day-to-day task of teaching did not win the appreciation it had enjoyed in earlier generations.

In Chicago, Mother Teresa renewed her friendship with Sargent

Shriver, who addressed the final session of the convention. Shriver had just withdrawn from a campaign to win the nomination for the vice presidency of the United States. In his talk, he laughingly asked Mother Teresa if she had any advice about what he should undertake next.

Mother Teresa had a morning free before she left Chicago for Davenport, Iowa. Loyola University sent a car to bring her to a convocation called in her honor. Sister Mary Evelyn Jegen, S.S.N.D. who was associated with the college, had spent time in India and had met Mother Teresa. The entire community of Sisters and the student body had gathered to meet her and hear the citation of the honorary degree of humane letters conferred on her.

"Mother Teresa gives her life for her friends; and her friends are the sick, the injured, the dying, and the lonely of our imperfect world. She has brought help to the dearest and least of the brethren, hers, yours, and Christ's."

Our hostess in Davenport, Iowa, the next stop, was Sister Concetta, a short, vibrant member of the Sisters of the Sacred Heart, who showed Mother Teresa a dramatic form of witness. She, with two other members of her congregation, had cleaned and renovated the old frame house where we were staying. It had been previously condemned. The three Sisters shared the lives of the poorest families. Sister Concetta explained to Mother Teresa that the house was known as the Renewal Center and from it the three Sisters went out to serve the neighborhood. They visited the old and the sick and helped them to get public aid and hospitalization. They organized programs for children and took care of homes and children while mothers were giving birth to other children.

Father Marvin Mottet, director of social action for the diocese of Davenport, was responsible for the Davenport gathering. From speaking in the convention center of a great city, Mother Teresa now came to a high school gymnasium. It was packed with twenty-five hundred people who filled the bleacher seats almost to the ceiling. Before the meeting, Mother Teresa had joined hundreds of people in the school cafeteria in a "poverty meal," consisting of homemade soup and dark, homemade bread. Each person had paid six dollars for the meal, with all the funds going to Mother Teresa's poor.

"I am glad to be with you," she told them, "because I see that you also want to love until it hurts, the way Jesus did."

Bishop Gerald O'Keefe, bishop of Davenport, led seven children who gave Mother Teresa the entire amount saved during Lent. One little girl spoke up. It was quite clear that she was breaking ranks. She asked Mother if she was sure that all this money would really get to the poor. Mother

Teresa reassured the young skeptic. A lovely dark child was brought to Mother Teresa for her blessing. She was Katie Bindu McBride, Bangladeshi-American, from Sister Margaret Mary's Shishu Bhavan in Dacca.

Bishop O'Keefe presented Mother Teresa with the Pacem in Terris Award, an award voted by the Catholic Interracial Council and awarded earlier to Martin Luther King. The bishop told the audience, "I think that in my lifetime, we shall not have as great a personage with us as we have tonight."

In Boston the Sisters of the entire archdiocese were assembled to hear Mother Teresa in Hines Hall. Afterward, a happy gathering was arranged by a group of families who, with her help, had adopted orphan children from India. The sturdy boys and girls hugged Mother Teresa and gave her their new names as had Katie Bindu McBride. Back in New York again, she was received by her friend Terence Cardinal Cooke and talked at a meeting of the clergy of the archdiocese.

The next journey was to Scranton, Pennsylvania, to respond to an invitation of the Diocesan Council of Catholic Women. Ever since Mother Teresa's appearance at the Las Vegas convention of the National Council of Catholic Women in 1960, her work had been supported by the Diocesan Councils which were part of the national federation. The teaching Sisters of the diocese took advantage of her visit to ask her to be with them at an all-day gathering at the University of Scranton, a university conducted by the Jesuit fathers. Hanging on the wall was a large banner: "Do Something Beautiful for God."

"We are all working together," she told them, "to bring Christ to the university or high school or right down to the slums. We are doing it together. The work that you do is His gift to you. Today, talking about the poor is in fashion. Knowing, loving, and serving the poor is quite another matter. The little St. Thérèse said, 'In the heart of the Church, I will be love.' That is what we are, love in the heart of the church. The password of the early Christians was joy. Serve the Lord with joy."

The meeting of the Catholic women was opened to the people of Scranton and became an ecumenical event, attended by representatives of many faith groups. More and more, the meetings planned around Mother Teresa became prayer meetings. It was a way of responding to her incessant call for prayer. More and more, they became events that crossed all faith barriers.

Present were Rita Burke, president of the Diocesan Council of Catholic Women, William Byron, S.J., president of the university, and two robed prelates, Bishop Carroll McCormick, the Roman Catholic bishop, and Archimandrite Herman, head of the Russian Orthodox community of the

Orthodox Church in America. The local papers were filled with news of Mother Teresa's presence and the evening meeting at the John Long Center of the University of Scranton was filled to overflowing with over forty-five hundred people. The mayor of Scranton came to give Mother Teresa the key to the city and President William Byron presented her with the La Storta Medal for Human Service. She was greeted with a garland of flowers by the wife of an Indian national, a professor of physics at the university. The professor, himself a Hindu, compared her work with that of Buddha, Ashoka, and Gandhi. In asking Mother Teresa for her blessing, the professor said, "Once in several centuries, God chooses to send someone who may serve as the connecting link between Him and His children."

In Allentown, not far from Scranton, the children of all parochial schools were given a half-day holiday to come to hear Mother Teresa. Bishop Joseph McShea termed her visit "a historic event in the Catholic life of this community."

The place was the Church of St. Thomas More, a modern, round church with blazing stained glass windows forming the upper half of the walls. The children marched, two by two, class by class, school by school, in a line that extended almost as far as the eye could see. They were led by sisters from thirty-seven parishes. Mother Teresa's eyes glowed with pleasure as she saw the signs of a living church.

The pastor of St. Thomas More, Monsignor Robert Coll, was acquainted firsthand with the misery of Asia, including Calcutta. He had been the prime mover in a special collection, "Operation Rice Bowl," that soon englobed the parishes of the United States.

Each family had been given a cardboard model of a rice bowl in which the savings from Lenten sacrifices were placed. The millions of dollars were sent to Catholic Relief Services in addition to the annual collection on the fourth Sunday of Lent. The funds were used for self-help programs around the world, particularly in famine-stricken areas.

Mother Teresa gave her message of love and service to Jesus in need, first in one's own home, then in the neighborhood and town, and then in faraway places. She asked everyone, especially the children, to try to see Jesus even when he seemed to be disguised or disfigured by disease.

A woman approached Mother Teresa immediately after the meeting. Her gaze was of great intensity. "How can you see Jesus in everyone?" she asked. "I know this man who has done terrible things to my family, terrible things. If I could, I would pay him back. I hate him. I think I could kill him."

"That man," responded Mother, "is Jesus, too, only in the most distressing disguise."

The woman stopped, seeming unable to say anything more. She seemed to be trying to manage to smile. Finally, she blurted out, "Thank you," and moved quickly away.

After Allentown, Mother Teresa flew to Toronto for a return engagement at the youth forum in which she had participated in 1975 with Jean Vanier.

The Convocation Hall was filled with young people who squatted in the aisles and filled the balcony. A teenaged girl remarked afteward, "Just seeing her took away a lot of the doubts I might have had about the whole religious thing. She seems so very full of God and full of love."

Mother Teresa spent the first of May in Chicago with the Institute on Religious Life, an organization concerned with the preservation of traditional values in the church and in the vowed life. She had had many meetings with the Rev. John Hardon, S.J., to plan for the meeting. She talked on "The Joy of Belonging to Jesus as a Religious." Her audience was composed chiefly of Sisters, but with a number of priests and religious Brothers.

When a Sister read aloud the daily schedule of the Missionaries of Charity, Mother Teresa asked that one thing must be stresed, namely, that the Sisters did everything in community. They went to mass, they prayed, they worked, they took their meals, and they enjoyed their time of recreation in the evening as a community. "Everything together," was one of the messages she brought to communities of Sisters in the United States. This advice arose out of her experiences in visiting a number of convents, especially those of Sisters teaching in colleges and universities. Sisters who staffed colleges told her repeatedly there were so many professional meetings, so many calls on their time, that they rarely had time for the traditional community life.

"The Church," said Mother Teresa to the Institute on Religious Life, "has entrusted us with the great apostolate to bring Christ into the hearts of our people. We must give Jesus to them. But unless we have Jesus, we cannot give Him. That is why we need the Eucharist. It is true, our way of life is difficult. It has to be like that. It is not only the material poverty, but the poverty of being surrounded by suffering people, by death. Only the Eucharist, only Jesus, can give us the joy of doing the work with a smile. Our Sisters have done much to spread the Good News by their joy."

She went on, "A Hindu gentleman stood behind a young Sister who was washing a man just brought into the Home for the Dying. She did not see him. Then, after a time, the man came to me and he said, 'I came into this home empty, full of bitterness and hatred, godless. I am going out full of God. I saw the living love of God through the hands of that Sister, the way she was touching and caring for that man.' He did not say another word and he left."

Mother Teresa's Albanian concept of *besa* entered the talk when she reminded the Sisters of the need for complete fidelity to the "word of honor" they had given to God.

Mother Teresa took out the constitutions of the Missionaries of Charity and read to the members of the Institute a part devoted to joy:

> Joy is indeed the fruit of the Holy Spirit and a characteristic mark of the Kingdom of God, for God is joy.
> — in Bethlehem "Joy" said the Angel;
> — Christ wanted to share His joy with His Apostles "That my joy may be with you";
> — Joy was the password of the first Christians;
> — St. Paul often repeats, "Rejoice in the Lord always; again I say to you, rejoice."
> — in return for the great grace of Baptism the priest tells the newly baptized: "May you serve the Church joyfully . . ."

Mother Teresa related that many nuns she had met wanted to work in the slums, even to leave their work in the United States and come to Calcutta. She stated in the strongest terms that they should not desert their work, that they were needed where they were. If they left, she queried, who would bring Jesus into the classrooms, into the hospitals, and into the homes for the aged?

Sunday, May 2, Mother Teresa spent with the Franciscan fathers at their college in Steubenville, Ohio. She was to leave Chicago early Sunday morning, attend graduation ceremonies at the college, and be at her next destination, Omaha, Nebraska, by eight P.M. on Sunday evening. It began to seem as though Mother Teresa were spending as much time in the air as on the ground. She was presented with the Poverello Medal by the Rev. Michael Scanlan, president of the college, as a person "who exemplifies in our age, the Christlike spirit of charity which filled the life of St. Francis of Assisi."

At Omaha, Nebraska, the boys of the famous Boys Town founded by Father Flanagan awaited her. For several generations, Boys Town had accepted homeless boys, protectionless boys, runaways, and boys in all kinds of trouble. Its work was so dramatic that it became the subject of a Hollywood film, with Spencer Tracy playing Father Flanagan. After the talk, Mother Teresa was presented with a statue of a boy carrying another boy on his shoulder. Under it was the motto, "He ain't heavy, Father—he's my brother." Mother Teresa took the statue back to Calcutta for the

Missionaries of Charity Brothers who were rescuing street boys. She was often to refer to the motto, adding, "And this is for girls, for sisters, too."

One result of her visit was that Rev. Robert Hupp, the director of Boys Town, was put in touch with the Brothers in Calcutta. In July of that year, two young citizens of Boys Town, Shawn Ellis and Joseph Pearson, took off from Omaha for the long air journey to Calcutta. They lived with the Brothers and worked with boys from the streets for the steamy days of July and August. They even spent some time helping the Brothers at the Titagarh Leprosy Center. They admired the industry of the lepers who made sandals out of old tires. Sharing the simple diet of the Brothers, the boys reported that they dreamt of hamburgers. Joseph described how "french fries were dancing in my head in my dreams."

On May 10, Mother Teresa was to take the first leg of her trip to Guatemala and Mexico. For three days after her return to New York, she gave herself to a triduum, three days of prayer, with her Sisters.

Saturday afternoon, May 8, Mother Teresa spent with the Co-Workers who came together from the area around New York City and on Sunday went to Jamaica, Long Island, to St. John's University. At the graduation ceremony, the Vincentian fathers, who conduct the university, awarded her an honorary degree.

On May 10, we took the plane from New York for Oklahoma and Texas. Mother Teresa had committed herself to giving talks in Tulsa, Oklahoma, and in three Texan cities, Fort Worth, El Paso, and San Antonio. We also had to go to Houston to take the plane for Guatemala. So great are the distances in Texas, and so short the available time, that for part of the trip a private plane was put at Mother Teresa's disposal. A Texan pilot in a large cowboy hat flew her over the second largest state in the union. In each city, immense halls were rented for her appearances. These were in addition to the prayer services that filled local cathedrals and churches.

In Tulsa, Bishop Bernard Ganter had arranged for Mother Teresa and me to be given the hospitality of the Holy Family Sisters, a congregation of black religious. The superior, Sister Siena Maria, told us that her congregation had been founded in New Orleans. Another member of the congregation, Sister Augustine, was principal of the school attached to the Holy Family Convent.

A prayer service, to which members of other faith groups were invited, filled the cathedral, and the evening public meeting filled the Tulsa Assembly Center. A voluntary offering of twenty thousand dollars, a large amount from a relatively poor diocese, was given to Mother Teresa. She announced that she would put it to use for the work in Mexico.

This delighted Bishop Ganter since his father had been born in Mexico City and he had close ties with the people of Mexico.

Shortly after the visit to Tulsa, Bishop Ganter wrote me saying, "I want to share with you something that seemed providential. Two days after Mother Teresa was here, I received a call from a layman who was a virtual stranger, asking to see me the next day. He came to my office and presented me with a check for the diocese in the amount of twenty thousand dollars, the same amount the diocese had been able to collect for Mother. The Lord is not going to be outdone in generosity."

In Fort Worth, in front of the convention center auditorium was a massive sign in blazing lights, the kind that would normally advertise a film or a boxing match, MOTHER TERESA OF CALCUTTA—8 P.M. The meeting had been arranged by the Catholic Renewal Center of North Texas, a group of Catholic lay people as well as clerics and Sisters, working to keep Christian values alive in every aspect of life. A gift of twenty-five thousand dollars was given to Mother Teresa to help start the work in Guatemala and Mexico.

In El Paso, the civic center was filled, chiefly with young people, who made the hall ring with their singing in English and Spanish. The moving spirit behind the gathering was a young man in his twenties, Ruben Garcia, a leader in the diocesan youth group. He had been so determined to have Mother Teresa come to El Paso that when his written invitation brought no response, he took to the telephone. He tracked her by telephone from Calcutta to Madras and then to Bombay before he reached her. She then asked him to get in contact with me to include El Paso in her program.

The meeting included questions from the young people. Two questions seemed to mirror the concerns of many.

"Mother Teresa, when you began your work, did you have only some love? I mean, when you started, did you have less love, and did it grow as you helped the poor and dying?"

"Over the years," she responded, "we have seen the sufferings of our people and their greatness, and we have deepened our love."

"Have you seen miracles?" asked another. "And, if so, what is the greatest miracle you have seen in all your work?"

Mother Teresa replied, "There is a sort of miracle every day. There is not a day without some delicate attention of God, some sign of His love and care, like the time we ran out of food because of rains and flood. Just that time the schools closed in Calcutta and all the bread was given to us so that the people would not go hungry. For two days, our poor had bread and bread, until they could eat no more. The greatest miracle is that God can work through nothings, small things like us. He uses us to do His work."

In San Antonio, the municipal auditorium was the scene of an unforgettable public mass with a hundred and twenty priests and deacons. Monsignor Charles Grahmann, who had organized the event, had prepared for a large crowd. He was still surprised at seeing the vast auditorium filled with people. The hall resounded with enthusiastic choirs, one of them composed of Mexican-Americans with a mariachi band.

At every airport, the usual platoons of reporters were ready for Mother Teresa. They seemed to pose ever more searching questions to a person already dubbed a "living saint" in the media.

"Are you ever angry?" one reporter asked her. "Are you ever frustrated?"

"Yes," she replied, "I get angry sometimes. When I see waste, when the things that are wasted are what people need, things that could save them from dying. Frustrated? No, never."

A reporter asked her about a much-used photograph of Mother Teresa holding a Bengali child. Her expression is one of profound grief, possibly mingled with anger.

"Yes," she commented, "I was angry. The child was very sick and they were leaving him behind. That's why I look angry. I picked him up and we took him to Shishu Bhavan, our children's home in Calcutta. We did everything, but he died in two weeks."

"What makes you feel sad?" came from another reporter.

"Things like this. A woman came to us in Calcutta with a sick baby in her arms. We were going to do our best, and she gave me the little one. But the baby died right there in my arms. I saw that woman's face as she stood there, and I felt the way she did."

"What is your purpose in picking up dying people?"

"Each one is the homeless Christ, no?"

"Is Christ partial to the poor, Mother Teresa?"

"Christ is not partial. He is hungry for our love, and to give us the chance to put our love into a living action, He makes Himself the poor one, the hungry one, the naked one. He said it clearly, 'I was hungry and you fed Me; I was naked and you clothed Me. You did it to Me.' He also said, 'I am the living bread.' He is disguised in the broken body of the poor and in the living bread of the Eucharist."

When asked about the hardest part of the work, she said it was the publicity.

"If I don't go to heaven for anything else, I think I will go to heaven for this, for publicity."

"Do you feel that the Church, the churches, spend too much money on unnecessary things, on luxuries, while so many people are in want?"

Turning back the reply on the questioner, Mother Teresa said, "When you talk about the Church—we all are the Church. We must not judge others but ourselves. We must remember that we will be judged on what

Mrs. Ann Blaikie, head of the International Co-Workers, makes presentation to Pope John Paul II. *(Arturo Mari)*

Mother Teresa with Co-Worker Jacqueline de Decker, International Link with Sick and Suffering in Germany, 1976.

International Links for Relief Supplies from Holland, Mr. and Mrs. G. J. Colenbrander (Valentina Muggeridge), with Brazil's National Link, Francisco de Goes, and Britain's National Link, Mrs. Evelyn Armistead, at Rome Co-Worker meeting.

Patty and Warren Kump, International Co-Links/ Editors, International Association of Co-Workers of Mother Teresa.

Dr. B. C. Roy, Chief Minister of Bengal and a former campaigner with Gandhi. Dr. Roy was an early supporter of Mother Teresa.

Brother Andrew, General Servant of Missionaries of Charity Brothers (left of Mother) with Cardinal McIntyre, Mother Teresa, and Cardinal Manning.

The Los Angeles (California) community of Brothers at prayer in chapel. *(Al Antczak)*

Father Celeste Van Exem, Mother Teresa's spiritual guide, at age seventy-five.

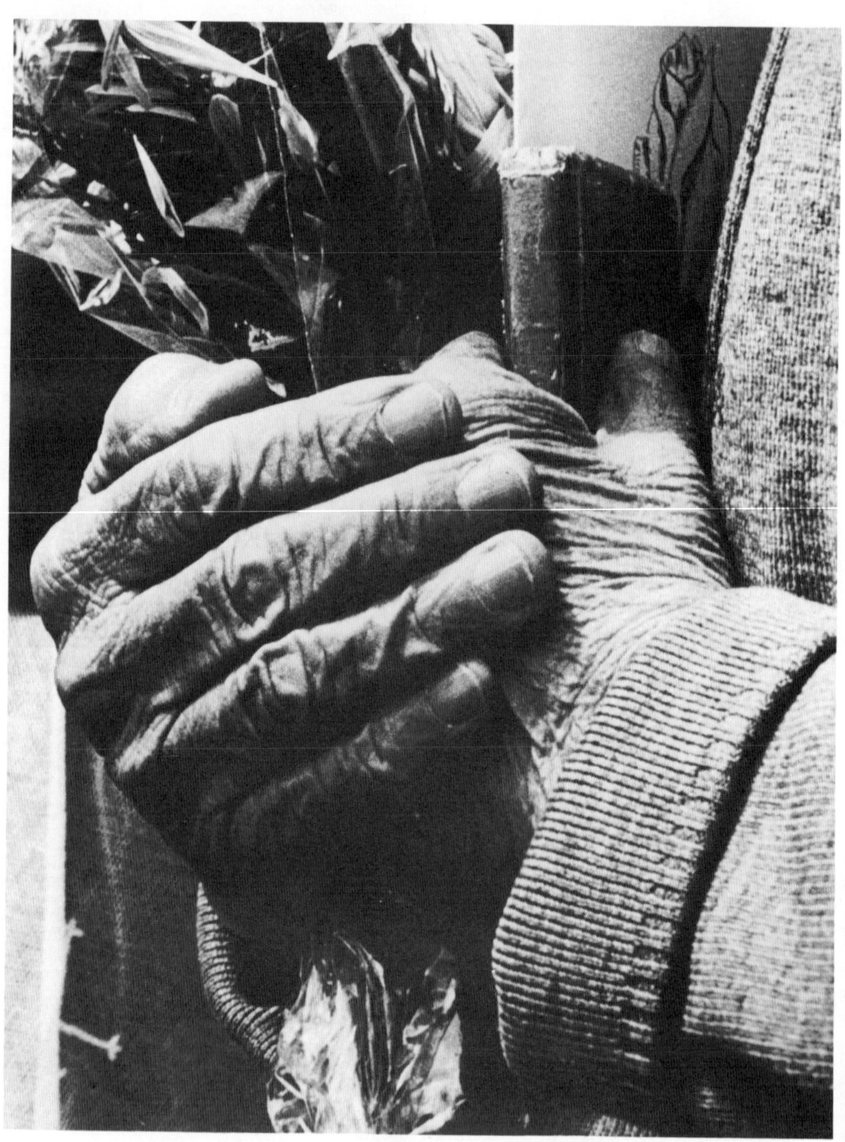

Hands.

we have done for the hungry Jesus, the homeless Jesus. That's what we must always remember."

"Mother Teresa, do you have any prophecies for the future?"

"Who am I to prophesy? I am nobody. I know only one thing. If people only had more love for each other, our life would be better. If more people realized that Jesus was in their neighbor, and they would help, things would be much better than they are."

Even in press conferences, people posed to her the perennial problem of a loving God and the sufferings of His creatures. "How can a merciful God," asked a newspaperman, "allow such suffering, children dying of hunger, people killed in earthquakes in Guatemala? What can you say to that?"

Mother Teresa spoke softly and meditatively.

"All that suffering—where would the world be without it? It is innocent suffering, and that is the same as the suffering of Jesus. He suffered for us and all the innocent suffering is joined to His in the redemption. It is coredemption. That is helping to save the world from worse things."

An earnest young woman queried, "Isn't it next to impossible to be a Christian in our society?"

"Yes," she replied. "It is hard. And we cannot do it without help, without prayer. We Catholics have the body of Christ. This gives us the strength we need. Jesus comes to us in the form of bread to show us His love for us, and He makes Himself the hungry one so that we can feed Him. He is always there, the hungry one, the homeless one, and the naked one."

As we traveled between cities, Mother Teresa's thoughts went back to the late Archbishop Perier of Calcutta and his advice not to say No, but Yes, to invitations to speak in public.

"The old 'His Grace' was right," she said. "People are hearing so much about bad things. I am carrying out his advice to go to them to tell them something about the good things. The Good News."

It seemed that Mother Teresa was the practitioner of a special apostolate, the airport sermon.

❧

Mother Teresa arrived at Aurora Airport in Guatemala on May 14, 1976. A meal of meat had been served aboard the plane, but as it was Friday, she refused it, preferring to keep the old Friday rule of abstinence from meat. Awaiting her was Bishop Richard Hamm, an American belonging to Maryknoll, the American overseas missionary society, and the papal nuncio. The nunciature building was undamaged, so Mother Teresa had her first meeting about her work in that setting.

Sitting in the shadow of large canvases of St. Francis Xavier and a few popes, she told Bishop Hamm, "I decided to send the Sisters from India to Guatemala with love. We will go where the people are poorest, wherever no one else is working. We will bring what the Sisters need."

"What about a convent?" the bishop asked.

"We live in the barracks in Rome. We can live in a prefabricated hut. We need only a dormitory, a refectory, and a kitchen. We can manage with that, but we must be near the people."

Bishop Hamm replied, "We are so much a part of the institutional Church that you present a problem, Mother Teresa. We have to approach things differently with you."

Mother Teresa wanted to know what was the worst area, where the people were suffering the most. Bishop Hamm described a place where four thousand people were squatting on government land.

"There was nothing there before the earthquake," he explained. "Now there are acres covered with tents and huts of lamina, wood, cardboard, anything. There is no light or water. Latrines have been put up."

"The area is called 'Quatro Febrero,'" the nuncio interjected. Bishop Hamm commented that he had not known that the area had been baptized—the name coming from the date of the earthquake.

That night we were given shelter in a part of a convent that had survived the earthquake. The next morning, Mother Teresa walked among acres of desolation. Three months after the tragedy, whole families were crouching in tents or under huts with roofs of corrugated metal. Whatever they had saved was with them—a few blankets, cooking pots, sometimes a garish lithograph of the Sacred Heart of Jesus or the Virgin Mary. Hordes of children dressed in jeans and T-shirts that clearly came in bales of relief clothing followed us. Many had lost brothers or sisters or mothers or fathers in the sudden, savage upturning of the earth. Two men were presented to Mother Teresa, one the president of the Committee of the Fourth of February, and the other, his vice president. He showed us that the tents and huts were in even rows and that every row was marked with a letter and a lot number. Learning that Mother Teresa was a Catholic nun, they brought her to a larger hut, set apart at the end of a row of huts.

"This is our chapel," they told us. "There will be mass here."

There was a table for an altar and behind it a brilliant hanging of yellow satin. On the altar were two vases with enormous plastic flowers, purple, pink, and blue. We continued to walk among the people, learning their hopes and expectations. They were sure that with all the aid arriving from overseas, there would soon be frame houses for all of them on the *periferias* of the city. The sounds of a hymn floated over the huts of the homeless and we made our way back to the chapel. A priest was beginning to celebrate mass and the hordes of children were sitting quietly on rows of benches. Again, they took up a hymn, the sound came toward us in waves, joined with waves of desolation that seemed to rise from men and women looking unutterably worn and from children whose lives had been shaken and distorted with tragic suddenness. After the mass, we met several local nuns from a teaching order who were working full time with the children of Quatro Febrero.

Mother Teresa was asking about a place to house the four Sisters already on their way. Near the convent where we were staying was the Church of the Holy Rosary which had withstood the earthquake. The priest took Mother Teresa through the church and showed her three small rooms behind the altar, two of which were storerooms and a third, which might have been a sacristy. The church was modern and the rooms clean.

Mother Teresa asked the priest if the rooms could be spared for the Missionaries of Charity. He was delighted and wanted to know what the Sisters would need. He was told that their needs consisted of a few chairs or benches, some beds, and a stove. In less than two hours the priest had gathered all the furniture and had delivered it in his car. He also brought an electrician who ran a line from the church proper to a small electric stove. The spare convent was ready.

The bishop was on hand the next morning when the four Sisters arrived at Aurora Airport. Mother Teresa had brought with her some silk roses presented to her in San Antonio. She gave one to each of the Sisters as a sign of greeting in a new land. The Sisters had brought cooking utensils from Calcutta as well as plates and cups and even bedding. They needed to buy little or nothing for their own needs in Guatemala City.

The Sisters also came with four thousand pounds of relief items. Airlines had given free air transport as well as free tickets to the Sisters. Bishop Hamm organized three cars to move everything to the convent. Sister Terremike, a Missionary of Charity of Philippine origin, would not be parted from two large packages. One turned out to be an Autoharp and the other a broom.

That evening, the Sisters opened cans of corned beef and made their first meal in Guatemala. They were given a few instructions on how to act if another quake, which was expected, were to occur. They were to have all keys handy and to carry a flashlight in case of the cutoff of electricity. If doors were jammed shut, they were to try to escape through a window. Mother Teresa smiled and said, "We all have to die sometime." There was indeed a tremor, but a slight one.

During the meal, there was much counting of overseas houses, some maintaining that Guatemala was the ninety-ninth house of the Missionaries of Charity outside of India. Other Sisters maintained it was the hundredth. Sister Terremike took out her Autoharp and all joined in a hymn. I left them in their tiny living space behind the altar and went to the partly destroyed convent nearby.

Mother Teresa wanted to see other areas of devastation to decide if the Sisters belonged outside of Guatemala City. We were driven into the highlands where village after village had been crushed as by an avenging army. We were able to drive through the main roads because bulldozers had been flown in from the United States to lift the rubble with giant mechanical claws.

In the town of San Pedro Sacatepéquez, we stood on rough, cleared ground in the marketplace. Of the actual market, only the back wall was still standing. Close to a thousand small homes had fallen, and the two churches were filled with the rubble of their towers and roofs. We were shown photographs of San Pedro, with rows of bodies wrapped in cloths and men and shawled women kneeling in prayer and agony. There was money in San Pedro because the year's harvest was exceptionally good, but blocked roads had prevented much of the fruits and vegetables and grains from reaching the markets. The people of San Pedro had set up makeshift stalls directly across from the destroyed market and were offering for sale not only such produce as onions, oranges, and bananas, but also religious pictures and medals.

A woman with a walnut-colored, deeply lined face came to talk to us. She told us that she was Cecilia Vasquez, *viuda* (a widow). She told us that she had lost her son, daughter-in-law, and little grandson in the earthquake. She was no more than four feet ten inches tall, and seemed to be pure Indian. Her skirt was a dark wraparound piece of handwoven material, with a blouse of intricate Indian designs. A necklace of coins hung around her neck, and in the center, a crucifix. She kept looking at Mother Teresa and I explained that she was a Catholic nun coming from India to help the sufferings of Guatemala. Then came what could only be described as communication by crucifix.

Cecilia Vasquez held up her crucifix in front of Mother Teresa's eyes. Mother Teresa took hold of the crucifix on her left shoulder and also held it up. Both crucifixes were about the same size. They placed them beside each other. Cecilia Vasquez then threw her arms around Mother Teresa, holding her as though her presence brought consolation in a place marked by sorrow.

Back in Guatemala City, we traveled around the outskirts, the *periferia* while Mother Teresa studied the possibilities. A poor area called Betania impressed her. There were poor families without number, clustered around a parish led by a spirited missionary priest from Holland. Homeless families were expected to be placed in the area. The very thought that Mother Teresa's Sisters might work in his parish sent him into a transport of joy. He was an outgoing man in his forties and as he walked around his parish, people greeted him warmly and children put loving hands into his. He had visions of a day-care center and of all the things the Sisters could do for his people. Mother Teresa's mind was made up. Her Sisters would settle in Betania and start with the small and humble works that the people needed.

Mother Teresa sent Sister Premila as superior for Guatemala. I was soon receiving letters from her. Sister Premila, originally a teacher, had invented creative projects in the Kidderpore dock area of Calcutta. The poorest women were enabled to earn money by the simplest work. Through obtaining supplies of all kinds of paper, including newspapers, Sister Premila had the women making usable paper bags to be sold to storekeepers. Women with more skills were sewing and embroidering articles that brought them an income.

In a few months she wrote that already the Hogar de Amor (Home of Love) had received its first nine patients, "two beautiful old men in their eighties, without families and four paralyzed men, one a victim of Parkinson's disease. In the day-care center we already have one hundred twelve children." Sister Premila must have mastered Spanish speedily, since she wrote that she was translating into that language the report of one of Mother Teresa's talks I had sent her.

Sister Premila's center in Kidderpore had united all the work under the title of Parivaraksha Kendra, the family care center. Within a year, her letter, on the cheapest paper, had the stamped address: "Misioneras de la Caridad, Centro Familiar, Galeras Colonia Betania, Zona 7, Guatemala." The work had extended to include not only a clinic, but a center where the women of the Colonia could learn and practice sewing and handicrafts. In time, a youth center for boys and girls was added to all the other programs. Help came from overseas, and local Co-Workers helped care for and feed over one hundred fifty children whose mothers found paid work. Sister Premila mentioned none of the difficulties she might have met in setting up so broad a service for a poor Colonia.

"God," she said, "is indeed overwhelmingly good to us. He answers our needs even before we have voiced them. It has been like that ever since we have come to this country. There is a miracle almost every day."

In Mexico City, a team of Sisters had already arrived and were housed in rented rooms in what had once been a Catholic boarding school. Their arrival came just short of half a century after the execution of Father Pro when the Catholic religion had been proscribed in the country. Sister Frederick and the Sisters had been canvassing the neighborhoods of a city of over fifteen million, a city growing daily from a high birthrate and relentless migration from rural areas. They were aided in their search by priests of the diocese. One priest offered the Sisters a stucco building that had served as a dispensary for the poor. It was a damp, one-story building with one large room with a window and several windowless, dungeonlike rooms. The Sisters were ready to take it. Sister Christauria, Sister Annunziata, Sister Medard, and Sister Joseph were ready for anything. But Mother Teresa refused it categorically. She told the Sisters that they would become ill from the dampness and unhappy from the lack of light. Her simple common sense changed the minds of the Sisters. They were supposed to live poorly and simply, but not to go to extremes in exposing themselves to tuberculosis and even emotional distress.

The Sisters went around the slum areas, visiting such places as Nezahualcóyotl. We found that the section of Neza visited by Mother Teresa in 1975, with its tiny square houses, was almost middle class compared with sections we now saw. There were acres upon acres of huts roofed over by pieces of corrugated material. Often the door was no more than a piece of board, or a discarded door, moved to the side during the daytime. The fumes of factories and buses settled in the thin air of a city over seven thousand feet above sea level. The miasmic fog threatened the poor with every type of respiratory disease.

The people were asked about their needs. Sister Frederick knew Spanish. One answer brought a light into Mother Teresa's eyes. The reply from some poor families was *la palabra de Dios.* What they needed was "the word of God."

The Sisters moved from the poor to the very poor and, finally, to the poorest of the poor—to those living on an enormous garbage dump situated on a deserted quarry. Mexico City threw off about ten thousand tons of refuse every day. Those sorting out this garbage had endless work. They kept pigs, goats, and chickens to add to their daily diet of beans and tortillas.

As in any refuse heap, their competitors in scavenging were large rats. In this area, the smog on some days was heavier than in other parts of the city since it mingled with the smoke of the fires that consumed useless garbage at night. The burning of old tires made the smoke particularly acrid. It was here, among "our people," that the Sisters felt they belonged.

When Mother Teresa went to see President Echeverría, she told him her decision. She forestalled any hesitancy he might have about bringing to greater public attention the plight of the city's poorest by asserting her admiration for the industry and dignity of the people who survived by performing that difficult work. She stressed the conviction that any honorable work could never be demeaning. The President fulfilled his promise to help the work by providing a van for transport and a plot of land for a center. The wife of the President, who had greeted Mother Teresa on her first visit to Los Pinos in 1975, was not in Mexico City. Mother Teresa was told that she was visiting her father who was critically ill. The father, a former general, had been one of the leaders in antichurch activity that had closed down churches, had forbidden religious observance, and made fugitive criminals of priests who persisted in their ministry.

Mother Teresa inquired if the aged man were receiving spiritual care. She was probably the only person who would dare broach such a subject with regard to the person in question. For Mother Teresa, for whom the primacy of the spiritual was the mainspring of life, it was the most important query to pose. Echeverría may have been taken aback, but he replied that the needs of the ailing man were taken care of.

Soon the Sisters were writing from Mexico, "Our people live right in the *basura,* the place where the city brings its garbage. They go through everything. They pick out things like bottles, broomsticks, and cans. There is a special truck that comes to buy them. Our people usually get ten to twenty pesos a day for their efforts. But when they have big families, and some of them have eight and ten children, it is not possible to buy enough food and clothing. On Sundays, the little church nearby is packed with people. They also come to join us in our Holy Hour."

The plot of land was not far from the garbage dump. It was in the Colonia, or district of Santa Fe, where a Franciscan friar from Spain, Vasco de Quivoga, worked in the sixteenth century for the Indian poor. His statue was in front of the colonial church.

A complex of buildings was built with the help of the Mexican President, a home for deserted and dying people, a clinic, a home for children, and a convent for the Missionaries of Charity. In the center of the complex was a garden where the children could play and the old people take the air. The children in the Sisters' care had been abandoned, many with handicaps, cleft palates, blindness, or deformed limbs. Some had bodies shrunken from hunger and were prey to respiratory diseases and dysentery. After a few months with the Sisters, they became normal active children.

A large band of Co-Workers had joined their efforts to those of the Sisters. They taught the children in the Home to read and write and expanded their teaching to adults who wanted literacy. The Co-Workers visited the neediest families with the Sisters and often drove pregnant mothers and sick people to hospitals. They were always on hand for feast days like Christmas and Mother's Day and found that one of their especially important services was to drive the Sisters to market to obtain food for their numerous charges. One destination to which Co-Workers and Sisters went regularly, namely the airline companies at Mexico's International Airport, provided free food. Old women, grounded for life by age and destitution, found themselves eating what to them were luxurious meals, meals prepared for travelers detined for far points on the world map. The gnarled hands of old men dealt with tiny sandwiches originally intended for snacks on short flights.

Mother Teresa accepted the invitation to be in Vancouver, Canada, May 31, 1976. In conjunction with Habitat, the United Nations conference on human settlements, there was a two-day Habitat Forum. The forum, planned by nongovernmental organizations allied with the United Nations, would deal with the subject "Improving the Quality of Life for the Handicapped in the World's Settlements."

Hanne Marstrand, coordinator of the forum, in inviting Mother Teresa's participation, urged her to come to Vancouver "because we feel you are the foremost spokesman in the world for the poor and handicapped." Mother Teresa was to deliver the opening statement. Also urging Mother Teresa's presence were Maurice Strong, a former director of the United Nations Environmental Program and Lady Barbara Ward. Both had been involved in an effort to win greater international recognition for Mother Teresa as will be recounted later.

Barbara Ward, the noted author and leader in causes of peace, justice, and environmental protection, had intimate knowledge of Mother Teresa's work but had never met her.

Between Mexico and Canada where she alighted on May 21, Mother Teresa was hurried by plane and car from place to place, meeting new groups of people, many of them young people just graduating from college.

Mother Teresa decided to cut down on her schedule and asked me to telephone Vancouver to request that her appearance be cancelled. The call was to Bishop James Carney of Vancouver who had sent an invitation to Mother Teresa on behalf of the diocese.

There was real alarm in the bishop's voice. "What can I do?" he asked. "I have rented our fifteen-thousand-seat Pacific Coliseum; I can't get the money back." Mother Teresa changed her mind and we so informed the relieved bishop.

Between public appearances, Mother Teresa made unpublicized visits to convents and Motherhouses. There she often found a situation revealing a new development in the American Catholic Church, and her heart was opened to the wrenching problems facing congregations of Sisters.

The bountiful flow of young women into religious congregations, a flow which had necessitated the building of large novitiates had tapered off after the end of the Second Vatican Council in 1965. Motherhouses had been left with large, well-appointed buildings, resounding emptily with fewer and fewer novices, until finally the buildings had to be put to other uses. Many of them had been built in the decade and a half following the end of the Second World War.

In a Motherhouse in New England, a mother superior showed Mother Teresa a beautiful, modern brick building, set in a lawn under the shade of great trees. The rapid growth of her religious community had come to a halt. There were two novices where once there had been forty or fifty. The pale face of the mother superior seemed set in a mask of strain and sadness.

Since it was the month of May, when colleges hold graduation ceremonies, four Catholic colleges took advantage of Mother Teresa's presence to award her honorary degrees, Immaculata College, Holy Cross College, Regis College, and Iona College. A seminary asked her to give a lecture to students for the priesthood.

At Immaculata College, Mother Claudia, Mother General of the Congregation of the Immaculate Heart of Mary pointed out to Mother Teresa that a special concern of the Sisters in the United States was the care of aging Sisters as the number of older Sisters grew while too often they were not replaced by the entrance of young candidates. She took Mother Teresa to Camilla Hall, on the grounds of the Motherhouse where the retired Sisters lived. So extensive were the grounds of the Motherhouse and college that the Pennsylvania town in which they were situated was called Immaculata. Mother Teresa spent a long time going from floor to floor to greet the over two hundred Sisters who had grown old in the service of the Lord and the human family. Some were confined to their beds, so frail that their skin seemed transparent and their hair like white silky halos.

Two Catholic colleges in Massachusetts presented honorary degrees to Mother Teresa, the Jesuit College of the Holy Cross in Worcester and Regis College for Women in Weston. At Regis, Mother Teresa was also the recipient of the Bicentennial Humanitarian Award presented on behalf of the International Cardiology Foundation by Dr. Paul Graham Toomey.

There was time for a drive to Walden Pond, near Concord, on the banks of which Henry Thoreau lived in his little cabin to meditate and write. As we stood gazing at the pond through a wire fence, I related to Mother Teresa the immense influence of Thoreau's works and, in particular, of his essay on "Civil Disobedience." This work had influenced the thinking and practice of Gandhi. I must have sounded reverentially enthusiastic, since she commented smilingly that Thoreau seemed to be one of my saints. She added that she was glad to learn about a man who had influenced Gandhi, "the father of our country."

Mother Teresa also agreed to talk to the graduating class of Cathedral College of the Immaculate Conception in Douglaston, Queens, New York. It was engaged in preparing priests for the dioceses of New York, Brooklyn, and Rockville Centre and was the largest college seminary in the United States. A photographic display on the work of the Missionaries of Charity was set up in the seminary. The seminarians were already helping the Missionaries of Charity in the South Bronx and were also serving retarded children in a large state institution. One of their special apostolates was cooperating with a telephone hot-line suicide prevention program in cooperation with a nearby state hospital for the insane.

The last engagement before leaving for Canada was at Iona College, where, after presenting the honorary degree, the college committed itself to cooperating with the New York Missionaries of Charity. Mother Teresa was well acquainted with the Brothers who conducted Iona College since they were the same congregation that had come from Ireland to Calcutta in 1849 for much the same reasons as the Sisters of Loreto. She recalled that the Brothers accepted at their Dum Dum orphanage the homeless boys sent by her Sisters.

To their school in Bow Bazaar went many boys from the poorest families who could receive an education only through scholarships. In the meantime, the congregation had become internationalized, changing their name from the Christian Brothers of Ireland to the Congregation of Christian Brothers.

"You have been given much," Mother Teresa told the seven hundred fifty graduates. "Now it is time to share your gifts." Brother John Driscoll, president of the college, promised that Iona College would give Mother Teresa a graduation gift, a program of cooperation with the Missionaries of Charity. When Sister Andrea was approached, she said that the greatest need was for skilled volunteers for a summer camp program soon to start in the South Bronx. Three Iona graduates volunteered, and Mr. Jack Rudin, a college trustee, provided a fund for their living expenses. Sister Andrea put them to work on the first day of the summer program. Noreen Dunne helped with the athletic and recreational program, including crafts and trips. Barbara Scully, a specialist in remedial reading and the media, was able to involve the young people in creative efforts which raised their reading skills. Patricia Donahue, whose training was in music and art, responded to the interests of the children and in addition to other musical programs was soon leading them in African chants.

At the end of the summer, Brother Driscoll commented with a smile, "We have here a Jewish real estate man working with Irish-American young people and Sisters from a Calcutta Motherhouse for the benefit of Puerto Rican and black children from the South Bronx." Iona College's commitment was made good as volunteers were provided annually in the coming years for the summer camp program. The cooperation between the Missionaries of Charity and the Congregation of Christian Brothers in Calcutta was duplicated in the slums of New York City.

In Vancouver, British Columbia, Mother Teresa found with delight that we were housed in the same convent as Barbara Ward. It was as though two souls had met. Both in their own ways were champions of all life as coming from God. Mother Teresa and Barbara Ward presented contrasts —Mother Teresa beginning to show her age at sixty-five, Barbara Ward slightly younger, enthusiastic but frail as a reed. They talked of the trials of the poor. Barbara Ward, after publishing many books on economic justice and on the protection of the planet, including *Spaceship Earth* and *The Home of Man,* had decided on a particular crusade. She still promoted people-oriented control of land use, but explained to Mother Teresa that her crusade was now for pure water. This concerned in a special way the health of the poor of the world. Waterborne diseases sapped the health of millions, and she wanted the United Nations, governments and nongovernmental agencies to mount a concerted effort so that people, especially the poor, would have access to pure drinking water by 1990. She estimated that clean water would eliminate at least thirty percent of the most desperate ills of the human race.

"Do you think that it is an adequate justification for the rest of my life?" Barbara Ward asked Mother Teresa. Mother assured her it was, and the fact that she was the person inspired to lead it was a special gift.

At lunch with Bishop James Carney, Barbara Ward talked of the peril to humankind and to the planet from all kinds of technology, especially nuclear, from deforestation to a host of other threats. Above all, she focused on the moral aspects, the unchecked human greed and the consumerism that was devouring people's lives.

"These days," she said thoughtfully, "when the earth is in peril, we must think what 'the Son of Man' means. He is 'Son of Man' and Son of God."

Mother Teresa stated in response, "People can feel close to Jesus because He is like them, 'Son of Man.' How could we do without Him Who gave us the bread of life?"

She turned to Barbara Ward, "Talking of bread of life, Barbara, you have not eaten anything."

Barbara Ward laughed it off, saying, "I am a Volkswagen. I go sixty miles to a gallon."

In point of fact, Barbara Ward had struggled against cancer for many years. Her throat was so constricted that she could consume only liquids and easily swallowed foods. Bishop Carney asked Mother Teresa, "Have you ever studied theology?"

"No," she replied, "just the gospels."

The bishop spoke meditatively. "I find that people who spend a great deal of time on theology don't seem to get any nearer to the truth or any nearer to Jesus."

Mother Teresa's Habitat Forum talk was in a rough hangar, part of a former army barracks, called the Jericho Barracks. Extra benches of unpainted wood had been installed and on the highest ones, young people in jeans and long, flowered dresses sat singing, their legs hanging free. In the first rows, below the rough-hewn podium, were special guests, mostly in wheelchairs, some with elephantine, useless legs, some with necks held in metal braces. Sitting on the benches was a group of persons who were deaf and dumb. Mother Teresa began with the prayer, "Lord, make us worthy to serve the poor around the world who live and die in poverty and hunger." As she spoke, a young girl with flying fingers translated the words into sign language.

"We are all handicapped in one way or another," said Mother Teresa. "Sometimes it can be seen on the outside; sometimes it is on the inside. You and I come together today not to plan any big thing, but to give to others until it hurts. The poo. and the needy enrich us."

Mother Teresa was in no hurry to leave the hangar. She shook hands with every person in a wheelchair and with the speechless people on the long benches. She gave special thanks to the young girl who had translated her talk into sign language. Then the rush of young people enveloped her. One carried a sign, "Mother Teresa, you have made your life a bread for others."

A large garbage can had been placed near the podium. Mother Teresa had asked for nothing, but it was filled with gifts. We found that the total was over four thousand dollars.

When the bishop came to take Mother Teresa by car to the Pacific Coliseum, he seemed a bit uneasy. Filling a great coliseum was not too easy and he told us that there had not been sufficient time to publicize the event. His uneasiness became evident as we arrived at the great hall to find the houselights dark. It was time for the meeting to begin, so the bishop led Mother Teresa directly to the auditorium and began to walk toward the stage. Suddenly the houselights were turned on and a blinding spotlight focused on the figure of Mother Teresa, already beginning to be noticeably stooped. A choir burst into song as she approached the stage. It was the hymn that the Sisters sang as Mother Teresa took leave of them, "Lord Jesus, of You will I sing as I journey," followed by, "Lord, make me a channel of Your peace; where there is hatred, let me sow love . . ." The coliseum was filled to capacity with people standing at the back. The bishop began to smile.

Mother Teresa spoke of the love of God that expresses itself in compassion for our brothers and sisters made in His image. She spoke of the Jesus Who is homeless, the Jesus Who is disfigured, the Jesus Who is unwanted. She talked of the poverty that she knew first—the man or woman dying on the street, the leprosy patient rotting without care. She talked about providing homes for leprosy patients outside of the city where they could live normal lives. Then she came to the poverty of the richer countries, the poverty that comes from hurt, from being rejected. This poverty is more difficult to serve because it is within, she said. Poverty from within produces more hurt. "Being unwanted is great suffering and great pain," she asserted. She talked of the great poverty of the Western nations who cannot afford to feed one more child and so "the child has to die."

A dignified dark-haired boy in traditional Indian costume came forward to present a gift, a hand-carved totem topped by an eagle head. He told her that he spoke for the Indian people and that his name was Dennis Matilpi. He explained that his tribal name was Eagle Bear. Dennis was a Kwakiutl Indian, the original inhabitants of Vancouver of whom only a remnant remained. A Sister who worked with the Indians called out, "We all love you, Mother Teresa," and the cry spread through the hall.

As we sat later with Barbara Ward at the convent, the conversation returned to the Son of Man. "When Jesus said 'Why have you forsaken me,'" Ward said to Mother Teresa, "He showed that He understood us in our humanity. He understood our aloneness. A God Who gave us freedom—what would we be if He did not give us Jesus to suffer with us and for us?"

Barbara Ward added, "I wonder if God did not doubt His decision when He saw what we did with our freedom."

Mother Teresa smiled, "We know that God could not have a doubt."

Barbara Ward asked Mother Teresa if she could be one of her Co-Workers and from then on they were in direct contact with each other. A few months after their meeting in Vancouver, she replied to a letter of Mother Teresa's, saying, "Thank you for making me a Co-Worker . . . We are getting great support for the idea of clean water by 1990. UNEP (United Nations Environmental Program), the World Bank, and the BBC are chasing me for a film on the needs of the poor in a less greedy and wasteful world. But I still have pleurisy (getting better) and no firm promises on the progress of the cancer treatment. So perhaps I am to work! Or perhaps I am to be ill! But, as you say, it is God's way whatever it is, and it is a wonderful privilege to feel that anything I can do can be united with your work and pushed forward by your prayers. So your loving letter made me very happy and I will try now to think of nothing but doing God's will in *whatever* form He presents it to me." It was signed, "Your loving child, Barbara."

Barbara Ward, who had once said that she would like to spend her last days with Mother Teresa in Calcutta, fought the malignancy until 1981, when she died in England. She remained close to the work of Mother Teresa and became a "Sick and Suffering Co-Worker," offering up her own sufferings for the poor and for the work of the Missionaries of Charity among them.

Mother Teresa made another effort to be excused from an engagement that she had previously scheduled. She appealed personally to John Cardinal Krol, the president of the National Conference of Catholic Bishops, to excuse her from appearing at the Eucharistic Congress. The cardinal said that he could not set her free from her promise. He stressed the importance of participation. As 1976 was the Bicentennial Year of the founding of the United States, the Catholic community decided, as a recognition of the event, to hold a Congress around the Eucharist, the central act of worship of the Church.

In acceding to be present, Mother Teresa offered an unusual gift to the United States. It was a gift in the spiritual order marking the Eucharistic Congress, namely, a new foundation of the Missionaries of Charity. It would be the first house of the Contemplative Missionaries of Charity where the Sisters would "live the word of God in Eucharistic adoration and contemplation." This was a step that Mother Teresa had long kept in her heart and there were Sisters who had longed for such a life. Sister Nirmala, who had led the team of Sisters to the New World in 1965, was the superior of the new house which was opened on June 25, 1976. Terence Cardinal Cooke rededicated a convent for the new foundation in the parish of St. Anthony of Padua in the troubled heart of the Bronx. The Sisters who formerly served the parish had vacated it a few years before. The parish school had been put to other uses. The church, a beautiful structure with stained glass windows honoring donors of earlier generations with German names, now served a reduced number of parishioners. Crime invaded the rectory. On more than one occasion the rectory had been entered at night by robbers and the pastor had been threatened with violence. One Sunday, the pastor and two laymen were bound and gagged after the midday mass and burglars made off with the Sunday collection.

The Missionaries of Charity were already known as "contemplatives in the world." The new foundation, however, would follow earlier contemplative congregations such as the Carmelites in having contemplative prayer consume most of the Sisters' lives. Though equally austere, the rule of life differed in some respects from that of the traditional contemplative communities. The Missionaries of Charity would not be enclosed in the manner of the Carmelites. Their lives would not be confined to their convent and convent garden with communication only through a grill in the parlor. The Sisters would leave the convent for mass in the adjoining parish and would open their chapel to those who wished to meditate. They would spend about two hours of the day visiting the sick in hospitals and shut-ins, or talking to people in their neighborhood about God. Laywomen might join the Sisters for days of shared prayer. The object of the contemplative life, often viewed as vertical, the union of the soul with God, had as its horizontal dimension the sharing of the God-life with human beings.

It was not long before the contemplatives' chapel was a place of tranquil peace. The decorations reflected both poverty and love of beauty. Logs discarded in nearby parks were topped by ivy and other plants so that the chapel ambience was one of quiet green. Sister Nirmala often took the Sisters to a nearby park for air. She told us that sometimes unemployed men came to them and asked for prayers, while in other cases angry young men shot barbed remarks in their direction. When the Sisters tried to start conversations with people in the park or on the streets, they found that the people were nonplussed.

As Sister Nirmala put it, "We were shown a better way," and illustrated it with the tale of Hassan.

On September 8, celebrating the day dedicated to the birthday of Mary, she walked with seven members of the community to Crotona Park, an oasis in the South Bronx. "Then we prayed together, and I sat down on a rock on a little hill. The other Sisters went off and prayed in different parts of the park. Suddenly a man in his twenties in a black suit appeared below me. He shouted, 'What did Jeremiah say?' When I did not reply, he repeated the question in a louder voice. I finally replied in a low voice, 'Jeremiah said many things. What did you have in mind?'

"He shouted, 'Jeremiah prophesied that God will work His anger. He will pour out His anger and blood will flow on the earth.'

"I began to quote from the New Testament about the Prince of Peace bringing peace to all mankind. 'I am preparing for war,' he said, 'I am an instrument of destruction.' He put out his two fingers as a sign of victory. I asked him his name. 'My name is Hassan,' he said. 'Hassan means good,' I told him. 'You cannot be an instrument of destruction with that name.'

"Hassan walked up the incline to where I was and took out a switchblade knife. He pointed the blade at me and without thinking, I lifted up the cross and held it up with the rosary.

" 'These are my only weapons,' I said. 'They mean love. They mean that the lion and the lamb can live together in peace.'

"I could not think of another thing to say, so I just remained silent as he threatened me with the knife. When the Sisters came back and began to gather round, he put his knife away. Before leaving, we prayed and sang Psalm 19. He joined in. Then he said, 'I will protect you in this park as if I am the guardian angel of the place.'

"We met Hassan many times after that, and he was always gentle in his greeting. I was grateful to him because he taught us that one way to proclaim the word is just to go out in a park or public place with the Sisters and start to pray or sing a Psalm. We don't need to approach the people then; they come to us."

Sister Nirmala, as the spiritual pioneer of the contemplative branch, helped open two more houses when aspirants for the contemplative life presented themselves. The second house was in Brooklyn, New York, and the third outside Washington, D.C., in a depressed community in Anacostia near a house of the active Sisters. Sister Nirmala was one of the first hundred young women to become a Missionary of Charity. We discovered that not only the first twelve Sisters remembered and referred to the order of their entry, but others like Sister Nirmala, number 76, Sister Priscilla, number 78, Sister Andrea, number 84, and Sister Shanti, number 99 did too.

"Mother Teresa has become the most magnetic figure at the Congress," said the New York *Times* on August 3, 1976. "Wherever she goes, crowds follow her, hoping to touch her clothing or hear her speak."

One of Mother Teresa's experiences at the forty-first Eucharistic Congress has already been described. The near-million pilgrims who streamed into Philadelphia were joined by many thousands from outside the borders of the United States. Other faith groups also participated, taking part in many ceremonies such as sharing unconsecrated bread and the washing of feet. It was clear that only a part of the immense throng could come close to Mother Teresa, but they could catch sight of her as she went from meeting to meeting.

For a week, *darshan* reigned supreme.

Just the sight of the poor woman who had touched the leper with compassion and lifted the forsaken dying from the gutters seemed to bring people close to Jesus, her Master. Many who did not attend the Congress experienced *darshan* at secondhand, if one can use such a term, by means of television. On the afternoon of August 1, an hour-long television interview with Mother Teresa conducted by Philip Scharper, a well-known editor and author, was broadcast throughout the nation.

"We give the dying tender love and care—everything possible that the rich get for their money, we give them for the love of God," she told the viewers. "If people in the United States do not answer the needs of other people . . . they will miss the touch of Christ in their lives. What is given them is given to share, not to keep."

The Congress addressed itself to the spiritual and physical hunger of humankind. At the opening general session on hunger, Mother Teresa seemed to stand for all the hungry of the world and the need to break bread with them. Over a table of round loaves, she recited a prayer, then broke the bread and shared it. Among those taking part were Dom Helder Camara, Archbishop of Olinda-Recife, Brazil, and the Rev. Pedro Arrupe, S.J., superior general of the world's Jesuits. A morsel of bread was eventually shared with as many as possible of the six thousand people crowded into the Civic Center auditorium. Father Arrupe made a practical suggestion to American Catholics, urging that they forgo a meal every week and give what they saved, averaging a dollar per person, to a fund for the hungry.

The Congress was the occasion for the first appearance together of Dom Helder Camara and Mother Teresa, both identified as voices of the world's poor and rejected.

One of the most dramatic moments of the Congress occurred in that session when Dom Helder interrupted his speech to say that he wanted to pause "to kiss the two hands of Mother Teresa." He walked to where she sat on the platform and, taking her hands in his own, he kissed them reverently. Then he gave her the traditional Latin *abrazo.* Mother Teresa, taken aback, cast her eyes down. The people packed into the auditorium responded with prolonged clapping. Many had tear-filled eyes.

Dom Helder talked of institutional violence and of the need to build new structures that would eliminate oppression and bring justice to the poor. He stressed the nonviolent methods of Martin Luther King. There were those who said, he pointed out, that building these structures was the only task and that helping the poor came second. "But in the meantime—in the meantime," he emphasized, looking toward Mother Teresa, "the hunger of the poor cries out for those who will feed and help them."

Mother Teresa told stories of the work in Calcutta and around the world. Sometimes a pithy statement would bind the stories together. "You cannot give what you do not live." Sometimes she seemed to put into a sentence the very meaning of the Eucharistic Congress, "Jesus has come to break the living bread with you."

A mass for Freedom and Justice was celebrated that evening in the Veterans' Stadium. The main celebrant was a cardinal from Poland, Cardinal Karol Wojtyla of Kracow, who presided with four hundred concelebrants at a huge altar constructed on the field.

There was little pomp at the Congress. An evening procession came closest to it, with a large float holding an oversized model of the monstrance utilized in holding the holy host. Kneeling behind it were cardinals Krol and James Robert Knox representing the Holy See. Catholic bishops from every corner of the world followed the float and behind them a procession of nearly 500,000 pilgrims. Mother Teresa, flanked by Sister Anastasia Hearne and myself, joined the throng. As night descended, the marchers lit candles and filled the air with hymns.

One evening, before a prayer service, there was a foot-washing ceremony in which Mother Teresa washed the feet of a participant from the Mennonite community, one of the "historic peace churches." He told me afterward how deeply he had been moved.

In preparation for the Eucharistic Congress, there had been a series of meetings in which representatives of various Christian faith groups discussed the significance, in their respective traditions, of the "Table of the Lord." I had been a participant in these meetings. At the Congress itself, three hundred theologians and leaders of religious groups held sessions on the Eucharistic meal. Mother Teresa joined them, her main contribution being to ask the theologians to pray together. She had carried copies of Cardinal Newman's prayer to the Congress and she distributed them. The theologians joined her in praying, "Lord, help me to spread Thy fragrance everywhere I go. Flood my soul with Thy spirit and life. Penetrate and possess my whole being so utterly that all my life may only be radiance of Thine . . ."

Afterward, one of the theologians commented to the group that the faith of Mother Teresa was a faith they all could emulate. She seemed to incarnate the words of a Lutheran theologian, "The Eucharist loved is the Eucharist lived."

The four uniformed guards who formed a human shield around Mother Teresa caused a near commotion one afternoon. Mother Teresa sat in the back of a hall to hear Bishop Carroll Dozier talk on women in the Church. The guards sat quietly nearby. Suddenly the door opened and the four guards rose to leave as four others walked in. Their heavy boots echoed throughout the hall. It was time for the changing of the guard. Bishop Dozier paused in consternation.

"Is there a fire?" he asked in alarm.

The presence of the security guards was explained and the speech continued. Mother Teresa looked down. I was convinced that those days must have been among the most trying days of her whole life.

There were Eucharistic liturgies morning, noon, and evening, all with the kiss of peace or some other sign of reconciliation. An afternoon liturgy in the open air which Mother Teresa made a special point to attend was that attended by members of twenty-one American Indian tribes. Many were in Indian dress and exhibited the various facial types of the different tribes. There were special prayers for peace with God's creation phrased in the imagery of Indian traditions.

There was an evening Eucharist especially for young people, and Mother Teresa was asked at the last moment to give a talk at its close. She was informed that in preparation for the Congress, large numbers of young people across the country, and in some overseas nations, had for a year concentrated on works of mercy for the sick, the needy, and the lonely. The program was known as SIGN (Service in God's Name). "To help another in God's name"—the motto of the young people—"is to give a sign of His Kingdom and to proclaim the message of love brought by Jesus."

Accepting the last-minute call was simple for Mother Teresa, her preparation being the sign of the cross made with her thumb on her lips. With spotlights from various angles beaming on her small figure, she began, "Jesus said to the people of His time, 'If you want to be My disciples, take up your cross and come follow Me.' "

Some of us were surprised at the choice of theme and her development of it. She went on to talk of the passion of Christ and of the stations of the cross by which Jesus made His way to the place of crucifixion.

"Today, in young people of the world, Jesus lives His passion, in the suffering, in the hungry, the handicapped young people—in that child who eats a piece of bread crumb by crumb, because when that piece of bread is finished, there will be no more and hunger will come again.

"That is a station of the cross.

"Are you there with that child?

"And those thousands who die not only for a piece of bread, but for a little bit of love, of recognition. That is a station of the cross. Are you there?

"And young people, when they fall, as Jesus fell again and again for us, are we there as Simon Cyrene to pick them up, to pick up the cross?

"The people in the parks, the alcoholics, the homeless, they are looking at you. Do not be those who look and do not see.

"Look and see.

"We can begin the stations of the cross step by step with joy. Jesus made Himself the bread of life for us.

"We have Jesus in the bread of life to give us the strength."

Immediately after the Eucharistic liturgy, a priest remarked that her talk was perfect for the occasion. Young people thanked her. They were grateful that she talked of suffering and the cross because of Eileen Potts. Eileen had been prayed for by name during the prayer of the faithful and the young people knew why. Mother Teresa said she did not know who Eileen Potts was.

The priest looked surprised and explained that Eileen, a twenty-year-old girl, was the leader of the SIGN program and of youth participation in the Congress. Before its opening, her friends on the committee were stunned to learn that she had just been struck down by leukemia. At that moment, she was in a hospital near Philadelphia.

Mother Teresa turned to us. "I do not know what made me talk like that about the cross. It suddenly came to me. We must go and visit that girl."

On August 5, Dorothy Day came from New York to stay at the same convent as Mother Teresa. Dorothy Day and Mother Teresa were to speak at a general session on the morning of August 6, on "Woman and the Eucharist."

Dorothy Day was already seventy-nine years of age and tired easily. She told us that she was uneasy about her talk because it contained a criticism of the Congress organizers. For the first time, she had a prepared talk to give, instead of her usual extemporaneous presentation. She showed us the typed copy.

Dorothy Day, in a cotton dress of blue check with kerchief tied around her white hair, told the audience of eight thousand, "Our Creator gave us life and the Eucharist to sustain life. But we have given the world instruments of death of inconceivable magnitude." She voiced her criticism clearly in lamenting the fact that the organizers of the Congress had not remembered that August 6 was the anniversary of the atomic bombing of Hiroshima. They had planned no penitential service but instead had scheduled a mass for the military on this day. The audience interrupted her speech to give her an ovation.

"Women," she said, "are born to nourish, not to destroy life." She asked them to do penance for the sins of war and destruction. When Dorothy Day, tall and frail, gathered the papers of her prepared speech and left the podium, she was never to return to a podium. It was her last public speech.

The prolonged outburst of applause that greeted Dorothy Day was renewed at the appearance of Mother Teresa. She began by reminding her hearers that Mary, the Mother of the Church, could say of Jesus, "This is my body," and that it was by surrendering herself that she became the Mother of God. When His followers deserted Jesus, she went on, it was Mary who stayed with Him. She remained when He was spat upon, treated like a leper, disowned by all and crucified.

"Do we remain with our people when they are disowned, thrown out, when they suffer? Do we give them our understanding love?" she asked. "Do we have the eyes of compassion of Mary? Do we understand their pain? Do we recognize their suffering?

"The beginning of Christianity," she continued, "is the giving. God so loved us that He gave His own Son. Jesus took bread, the simplest of foods, and He made that bread into His body. He made Himself the living bread to satisfy our hunger for God."

I was asked to close the meeting on the theme of reconciliation. The Eucharist can be seen in this light, as a foretaste of the heavenly banquet in which people are reconciled to God and to each other. I asked the assembled women to see that Dorothy Day and Mother Teresa were writing a theology of peace in carrying out Jesus' commands to feed, clothe, and shelter Him despite the attitudes or actions of societies or nations. The meeting ended with eight thousand persons, chiefly women, standing in silent prayer for those who had died at Hiroshima, and for all the victims of violence in all wars, as well as for military personnel who in good conscience carry out orders in warfare.

Mother Teresa slipped away from Philadelphia on August 7, the day before the close of the Congress. She asked to be taken straight to the hospital where Eileen Potts was confined, in Cherry Hill, New Jersey. The beautiful young girl was overwhelmed with joy to have a quiet time with Mother Teresa. During a remission of the disease, Eileen Potts returned to the University of Scranton, but death took her in a few years. She is memorialized in the Eileen Potts Student Room at the university.

Mother Teresa was counting the hours until she could be back with her Sisters in the Bronx. Sister Andrea had been able to bring some of the Sisters from the South Bronx to Philadelphia to take part in Congress masses and gatherings, but that was the only contact the Sisters had had with her. In her generosity, Mother Teresa had promised to visit St. Joseph's, a poor parish in Camden, New Jersey, on her return journey to New York City. The visit to the hospital delayed her schedule, and when she arrived at St. Joseph's, she found that the people who had filled the church a few hours earlier were still there, ready to welcome her. The mass began, and at the offertory, a patriarch of ninety years of age, an immigrant from Italy, brought her a large loaf of bread that he had baked himself. Her visit to the people of St. Joseph's was so memorable that it was memorialized in a calendar with a different picture of Mother Teresa for every month of the year.

That evening, after a week of publicity that would help her into heaven, if nothing else could, as she kept saying, Mother Teresa arrived in the South Bronx. She put the loaf of bread into the hands of Sister Andrea and slipped into the convent.

In a few days, the Sisters were at Kennedy Airport, singing a hymn to Mother Teresa as she left for Rome and a retreat with the Sisters there. It seemed to those of us who traveled with her, that only these retreats and the hours of recollection in the morning and evening could give her the spiritual as well as emotional strength to carry on. From the retreat, she traveled with Sister Frederick to Lippstadt, Germany, for the second meeting of the International Co-Workers.

At her next stop, the Burgundian village of Taizé, she was welcomed by the prior of the Ecumenical Center, Brother Roger Schutz. Brother Roger, a Protestant, had been given the blessing of Pope John XXIII to conduct a program looking toward the reconciliation of all Christians. Young people streamed into the village of Taizé to experience and pray for peace between the different communions. After she had attended mass in the parish church, Mother Teresa joined Brother Roger in the Chapel of Reconciliation for the evening office. Close to three thousand young people had come to Taizé and they overflowed the chapel. At the end of the evening office, the young people raised powerful voices in the prayer of the Mother of God, "My soul magnifies the Lord," the Magnificat, to the accompaniment of trumpets.

Before leaving, Mother Teresa joined with Brother Roger in composing a prayer, "The Prayer of the Poor."

> Oh God,
> Father of each human being,
> You ask each of us to carry love
> To the places where the poor are humiliated,
> Joy to the places where the Church is brought low,
> Reconciliation to the places where men are divided,
> Father against son,
> Mother against daughter,
> Husband against wife,
> The believer against those who find it impossible to believe,
> The Christian against his unloved brother Christian.
> You open the way for us,
> So that the wounded Body of Jesus Christ, Your Church,
> May become the leaven of Communion
> For the Poor of the earth,
> And the whole human family.

On November 25, 1976, Mother Teresa was in Singapore, speaking at a historic assembly of three hundred representatives of over ten different world religions from seventeen Asian nations. The meeting was organized by the Asian branch of the World Conference on Religion and Peace. We had met one of the leaders of the conference, Dr. Mehervan Singh, a white turbaned Sikh of immense dignity at an airport in Canada after the Habitat Forum. Dr. Singh immediately asked Mother Teresa to take part in the conference and his invitation was made formally by Archbishop Angelo Fernandez of Delhi, India, cochairman of the conference. To the Buddhists, Confucianists, Jains, Muslims, Shintoists, Sikhs, Hindus, Zoroastrians, Jews, and different groups of Christians, she repeated her prescription of love and offered it as the means to overcome evil, "We do not need guns and bombs. We need love and compassion to overcome the world and to overcome evil . . . All the works of love are works of peace."

On her return to Calcutta, Mother Teresa received a visit from Brother Roger Schutz. They prepared a joint appeal which began,

> We are, both of us, challenged by the suffering of the modern world. Confronted with all that wounds humanity, we find the division between Christians unbearable. Are we ready to set aside our separations, freeing ourselves from our fear of one another.

In the three years after 1976, Mother Teresa criss-crossed the globe, her journeyings in response to calls from the hierarchy in remote corners of the earth where few Sisters ventured, or from those dealing with vast urban slums. For many of the world's great cities, despite the presence of social agencies and religious congregations, the resources to meet new and tragic needs were nowhere in sight.

On February 11, 1977, Mother Teresa arrived in Manila, the Philippines, and took five Sisters to Tondo, a sprawling slum with thousands of shanties reminiscent of Calcutta. The Sisters were met not only by people needing everything they might be able to provide, but by five young women anxious to join them as aspirants in the Society. By the end of the year, there were nine aspirants, and Mother Teresa decided to open a novitiate in Manila, with Sister Andrea, who had started the work in the South Bronx, as mistress of novices.

In March of the same year, Mother Teresa took a team of Sisters to Kerema in Papua New Guinea. Among them was Sister Laetitia, one of the original twelve Sisters who had gained experience with the aborigines of Australia. As usual, their work was "right on the ground." Two teams of Sisters had already adapted to the life of simple people in Hanubada and Tokarara. Working chiefly with women and children, the Sisters described how a favorite food, *mumu,* was cooked in the ground with hot bricks.

All in all, seven houses were opened outside of India in 1977. Mother Teresa placed the Sisters in London's East End, Port-au-Prince in Haiti, Rotterdam in Holland, Dire Dawa in Ethiopia, and a second house in Peru. Three new houses were begun in India. In each place, the Sisters plunged into whatever need was most urgent. In Dire Dawa, for example, they began to care for three hundred seriously malnourished children in an intensive care center. From Ethiopia, she made a hurried trip at the request of the papal nuncio of Addis Ababa to talk to the Ladies of Charity of Los Angeles, California. Brother Andrew shared the platform with her.

A cyclone and giant tidal wave brought Mother Teresa back to India to the ravaged state of Andhra Pradesh where as many as twenty-five thousand people perished. She and the Sisters joined the relief efforts for the survivors.

A Sister wrote: "Hundreds of corpses had to be buried. Mother went down on her knees and prayed as flames consumed the bodies of cyclone victims at Mandapakala Village." Mother Teresa became ill and wrote me, "I had an attack of malaria. That was the gift to me from Andhra Pradesh."

On November 1, 1977, which in the Catholic Church is the feast of All Saints, Mother Teresa decided to mark the twenty-fifth anniversary of

Nirmal Hriday, the Home for the Dying. The actual opening date had been August 22, 1952.

Many citizens of Calcutta, as well as clubs and business firms, joined giving their time and gifts so that the one hundred fifty people then in the home could have a special festive meal, the women new saris, the men, new garments, and all the pallets, bright new blue and green sheets.

Twenty-five new foundations of the Missionaries of Charity were opened in 1978, sixteen of them in India, including two in Andhra Pradesh, one in Amritsar in the Punjab, and nine outside India.

One of the places where Mother Teresa took her Sisters in 1979 had been for years a crucible of violence, Beirut. There, in East Beirut, the Sisters cared for children and families bereft by war and fear of killings and destruction. When violence was almost at its height, three years later, she was back with them, braving whatever might come from bombs or snipers.

In March of that year, two missionaries who had both left Yugoslavia to work in Bengal, one to enter the Loreto Sisters, the other to enter the Jesuit order, returned to that country. On the seventeenth of March, at the invitation of the archbishop of Zagreb, Franjo Kuharic, both Mother Teresa and her long-time priest Co-Worker, Father Michael Gabric, stood before a gathering of Catholics. The archbishop told Mother Teresa that he himself was a Co-Worker and that the Co-Workers had been founded there in 1976 when that border region had celebrated thirteen centuries of Christianity. From September 1976 to March 1978, the number of Co-Workers had grown to thirteen thousand. In communities of prayer and works of mercy, the Co-Workers had spread to every corner of Yugoslavia.

Mother Teresa and Father Gabric then visited Split, Karlovac, and Rijeka to tell of their experiences in a far-off land and incidentally to learn what had occurred in Yugoslavia during their long absence. They also visited Mother Teresa's birthplace, Skopje. The two gave their message of love in a town that was the site of the assassination of Archduke Francis Ferdinand of Austria. It was that act that unleashed the violence which left ten million dead and twenty million wounded in the First World War. The town was Sarajevo.

In May of that year, the Holy Father, Pope Paul VI, sent a special message of blessing to the Missionaries of Charity:

> Remember always, beloved daughters in Christ, the value of your religious consecration. Through your consecration to the Lord Jesus, you respond to His love and discover the needs of His brothers and sisters throughout the world . . .

September brought what the Sisters termed a "deluge" to Calcutta. Mother Teresa and the Sisters had to find ways to reach the centers all over the city. "No trams, no buses, only the poor, courageous 'rickshaw-wallas' struggling through to be able to earn something," wrote a Sister. It was a repetition of those days of 1970 described in Chapter 13, "The Mango Showers of Calcutta." The days in Nirmal Hriday presented special problems. "The Sisters in Nirmal Hriday had their beautiful days of sharing life with the patients. Soaking wet, they could not remain like that. So as to be able to do God's work, they found anything to change into, spare blouses, shirts, and whatnot."

The only conveyance that could move large amounts of provisions in the main streets was the big van given the Sisters by Pope Paul VI. When the white limousine was raffled off, the pope made a second, more practical gift of a large van.

The United Nations declared 1979 the "International Year of the Child," and Mother Teresa and the Sisters made the annual Calcutta Children's Party a larger and more joyful event than ever before. A circus donated its best performers and they put on their acts on January 11 for thirteen thousand children who filled the Netaji Subhas Stadium. There were comics, military bands, folk dances, and trained dogs. Free transport to the stadium was made available by tramcars, school buses, and every type of vehicle. Calcutta outdid itself in helping the Sisters provide a package of food for each child. The Governor of West Bengal and the Chief Minister were there with Mother Teresa. A Sister wrote, "Mother herself spoke very lovingly and tenderly to the children and brought this Big Day for our children to a happy end."

The twenty-five houses opened by Mother Teresa in 1978 were exceeded by one in 1979. Of the twenty-six new houses, thirteen were in India and thirteen in ten countries around the world. The convent opened in Zagreb was described by Ann Blaikie as "the smallest convent in the world." The thirty-six overseas houses opened by the Sisters from the beginning of 1977 to the end of 1979, spanned the globe, ranging from Haiti to Ethiopia, from Peru to Kenya, from Germany to Rwanda, and from Brazil to Yugoslavia. Mother Teresa, whose travels within India had long been facilitated by passes on rail and airlines, found her overseas travels made easier at national borders by two things. An Indian passport, issued by a nonaligned nation, gave entry to all continents and was above restraints often imposed by Cold War problems. In addition, she had been issued a diplomatic passport by the Vatican.

Mother Teresa could not be present at all the openings. She sent the teams of Sisters with a plea to the hierarchy and Co-Workers, "I give you my Sisters. Take care of them and help them to keep their poverty, because our poverty is our dowry. Don't let my Sisters lose their love of poverty."

In the summer months of 1979 Mother Teresa came herself to open the two new houses in the United States, one in St. Louis, Missouri, and the other in Detroit, Michigan. The house in a Detroit slum needed much cleaning to be habitable. Sister Manju, the superior, described how the opening was achieved in record time.

"Mother was with us for three days and what a privilege it was having her with us. She worked from morning until night in the heat, constantly being interviewed by people. For us, it was the first time any of us opened a new house. We hope never to forget our beloved Mother and her example of prayer, thoughtfulness, goodness, and love in action."

The number of foundations reached 158 by the end of 1979.

It was on October 16, 1979, that the news reached Calcutta, news that blazed around the world, that a nun had been awarded the Nobel Prize for Peace. When Mother Teresa got the news, she slipped into the chapel to pray and thank God for His gift to the poor.

"I am unworthy," was her first response. "Thank God for His gift to the poor."

One by one, the Sisters at the Motherhouse slipped after her into the chapel, barefoot and noiseless. After a while they sang together a hymn of praise and thanksgiving.

Crowds descended on the Motherhouse on Lower Circular Road, well-wishers from every station in life, including many of the poor and, again, the platoons of journalists and cameramen. Caught off guard, Mother Teresa said, "Last night it was like vultures had descended." Then she caught herself and her Franciscan side of love for all creation asserted itself: "But, even vultures can be beautiful." The Associated Press carried her words around the world, "Quickly, people are coming to realize that sharing, sharing and the works of love are really works of peace."

For the Sisters an even deeper joy came in November when the chapter general of the Society met, bringing Sisters delegated from all parts of the world. Mother Teresa was elected to be superior general for the fourth term of six years, and she accepted, as one of the Sisters remarked, "to remain Mother of us all."

Another joy came to Mother Teresa and the Sisters to crown the International Year of the Child. The building to the left of Shishu Bhavan, long prayed for as an addition to the overcrowded children's center, was handed over to Mother Teresa.

As Mother Teresa prepared to leave for Oslo for the Nobel ceremonies, she wrote to the Sisters of the congregation:

"On the eighth [of December] I will be at Oslo, Norway, God willing. As the Nobel Peace Prize Committee have sent me two more tickets, besides the one for me, and above all, as a mark of love and gratitude to all our Sisters of the first group for having the courage to join when there was nothing, the joy of having nothing and yet possessing Jesus to the full, and because they loved Jesus they loved the Poor, I will be taking Sr. M. Agnes and Sr. M. Gertrude with me to Oslo."

After Oslo, Mother Teresa became all the more an object of *darshan* even though outside of India the phenomenon still remained without a name.

18

Come and See

"Come and See," two verbs that became a noun, was an expression brought to the Missionaries of Charity by Brother Andrew, head of the Missionaries of Charity Brothers. As explained in the constitutions of the Brothers, "a period of introduction to the life and novitiate will be called the time of 'Come and See', on the pattern of Jesus calling His first followers. It may last from three to twelve months depending on the candidates' grasp of the life and spirit of the Society."

The young men were soon called the "Come-and-Sees," and they were introduced to visitors as "our Come-and-Sees" to distinguish them from the Brothers who had taken vows. Mother Teresa took over the term for young women who wanted an experience of the Sisters' life before making a formal decision to enter it. This might be no more than a few weeks, after which the young "Come-and-See" would leave or become an aspirant and then a postulant. As explained in the constitutions of the Brothers, the period of postulancy, literally of petitioning, is not obligatory for religious societies of men.

Although the aims of the Missionaries of Charity Brothers were those of the Missionaries of Charity, to give loving service, to feed, heal, and shelter the poorest and most rejected as the very person of the Christ, the special gifts of Brother Andrew, and the different possibilities open to men, made for some distinctions between the original Society and its male branch. While pursuing identical goals, the branch founded by Mother Teresa and the one founded by the Reverend Ian Travers-Ball, who took the name of Brother Andrew, developed separate and clearly marked identities.

An experience related by Brother Andrew gives an insight into the distinctive temperament of the founder of the male branch. It was recounted in a letter shared with friends at Christmas 1971 and revealed, in addition to the literary gifts of the writer, the freedom of a man to stay up all night in a railway station. One could not imagine a Sister—or Mother Teresa—staying up all night alone in a railway station, even to pray.

Such letters, mimeographed on cheap paper, were sent at intervals to a circle of friends and supporters of the Society. The general monthly letter for the members of the Society was limited strictly to the Brothers.

"In November, I made my annual retreat," he wrote, "and I spent a night of prayer—a sort of vigil—in the Howrah Railway Station, a main station of Calcutta. So much happened, but I would like to share a glimpse of a little family who came to sleep after the trains stopped around midnight. There was a mother and four children, from about eleven years to five. The mother was a funny little thing in a thin white cotton sari on a winter's night, and she had her hair closely cropped for a woman. She had a few tins or mugs, a few bits of cloth, and some pieces of bread. They were beggars. The station was their home.

"The children, three girls and the youngest, a boy, were full of life and at that hour of night, they all sat down on the station floor with so many other families and lone people sleeping all around, and they had their 'evening' meal of dry bread—perhaps the leftovers from some vender sold cheaply at the end of the day to meet a beggar's purse. But it was not a sad meal. They talked and laughed and joked so much, it would be hard in fact to find a happier family gathering. And when the meal was over, they went to a public hydrant and washed their tins and mouths and drank water. Then they spread out their rags to sleep on and a bit of sheet to cover themselves.

"And then it was that the little boy did something wonderful. He danced a little dance. He skipped and jumped and laughed and sang. Such a dance, at such an hour, in such utter deprivation.

"I had my vigil, more than enough for any man's meditation. And the words of the old song became real:

> Dance, then wherever you may be,
> I am the Lord of the Dance, said He,
> And I'll lead you all wherever you may be,
> And I'll lead you all in the Dance, said He."

In his own special way, Brother Andrew had the vision of a poet, a poet of the poor. Mother Teresa was surely a poet of the poor, artlessly and unselfconsciously, and that is probably why she suggested that he lead the male branch, and why he accepted. The poetic vision in both cases was bathed with the light of the Incarnation.

Brother Andrew's meditation continued, "In the bewilderment that I feel in the face of the hunger of my sisters and brothers by the millions, I approached the mystery of Christmas, of that dark, homeless night long ago, when a poor couple brought their poor Child into the darkness of night. And that Child became the Light that enlightens every man.

"That same poor Child born again this Christmas in Asia or Africa or South America is still the light that bursts in on the darkness of our world and our cold hearts."

When Brother Andrew came through the rain to meet Dorothy Day in Calcutta back in 1970, he had told us laughingly that Mother Teresa "after buttonholing priests to start a Brothers' branch, finally kidnapped me from the Jesuits."

He described the formation of the Brothers in more formal terms in a page of explanations supplied to prospective "Come-and-Sees."

"Some years after Mother Teresa had so wonderfully established the work of her Sisters among the poorest of the poor in Calcutta, she was inspired by the need for a group of men who would work in the same spirit. And so, on March 25, 1963, a start was made with the Brothers' congregation."

It was on that day that Archbishop Albert D'Souza of Calcutta blessed the small beginning of the new branch. The group consisted of a priest and twelve young men anxious to vow their lives to working among the poor. They lived on the first floor of Shishu Bhavan, the Children's Home, on Lower Circular Road. The young men began their studies which were accompanied by a sharing in the life of poverty and a daily reaching out to the poor.

Also on March 25, 1963, an Australian was ordained a Jesuit priest at the center of Australian Jesuits in Hazaribagh, in Bihar, northeast India. This was Ian Travers-Ball, S.J. As he entered the third year of his priesthood, known as the tertianship, he received permission for a month-long "experiment" of living with the Brothers founded by Mother Teresa in Calcutta. The purpose was to get some more ideas on how he could serve the poor as a Jesuit. He arrived in Calcutta on December 1, 1965, and joined the group in Shishu Bhavan. He soon knew at firsthand the realities of the work, not only of the small band of Brothers, but of Mother Teresa and the Sisters.

The priests originally charged with the direction of the Society of Brothers had left to do parish work after finding that their ideas did not coincide with those of Mother Teresa. In the interim, the spiritual preparation of the Brothers was being carried on by Father Julien Henry of Sacred Heart Church on Lower Circular Road not far from Shishu Bhavan and by Mother Teresa herself when she could fit it into her schedule. This was an emergency situation. The Church does not permit a woman to be the head of a male congregation. Father Travers-Ball was deeply moved by the work of the Brothers and by their poverty and simplicity. He was impressed by the Brothers' need for a priest to be with them full time to help in their religious formation.

At the end of the month, Mother Teresa came to him and invited him to stay to become the director of the male branch of the Missionaries of Charity. Father Travers-Ball agreed if his Jesuit superiors would also accede to the plan.

After Christmas 1965, he returned to Hazaribagh and the question was referred to the superior general of the Society of Jesus in Rome. On January 22, 1966, he received a reply from the superior general agreeing to his release from the society with three options. The choice he made would decide his future as a religious.

The first option was that he could remain a Jesuit and continue the work of his society, a work emphasizing teaching and the programs of the Poona Catholic Enquiry Center. The Center had published two of his booklets, "What Do You Think of Christ?" dealing with the life of Christ for non-Christians, and "A Catholic Speaks to Protestants and Orthodox." His articles had also appeared in leading newspapers and periodicals.

As a second course, he could maintain his ties with the Jesuit order while giving whatever help might be needed by the infant male branch of Mother Teresa's order.

A third option was to make a complete break with the Jesuit order and join the male branch of the Missionaries of Charity. This would call for him to become responsible for its organization and for the training of the men who would enter it.

As he had related to Dorothy Day, his awakening to the concreteness of the command to love and to the social mission of the Church was given impetus by the Catholic Worker movement. His own yearning to bring the rejected into a sense of community through Houses of Hospitality and to give love to those suffering and dying for lack of love and care, impelled him to say "Yes" to the invitation of Mother Teresa.

He chose the third option.

Leaving his first call, as Mother Teresa had done, for a second call that bound him to the poor of the world, Ian Travers-Ball, S.J., became the male founder of the Missionaries of Charity Brothers and chose the title of General Servant.

He was thirty-eight years of age, exactly the same age as Mother Teresa had been when she embarked upon her second call.

Ian Travers-Ball was born on August 27, 1928, sharing the baptismal feast day of Mother Teresa, August 27, 1910, one day after her birth. By a strange chance or providence, he came into the world in the same year that Mother Teresa "left the world" to become a Sister of Loreto. The place was Hawthorn, a suburb of Melbourne, Australia. His family was comfortably middle class and his father involved with the insurance business. He grew up in Kew, another suburb of Melbourne, and was enrolled at the age of seven in Xavier College, a Jesuit school described as prestigious. There he remained for ten years, matriculating in 1945, at the age of seventeen. In July 1951, he heard a talk by a Jesuit, Father H. Lalor, S.J., on the urgency of the mission of the Church in the world. He talked with the priest who, it developed, had a pivotal influence on his life. The young man did some work in the insurance business, but as he put it, he wanted to do something more useful with his life than "hanging around racecourses and insurance companies." He pursued his hopes and longings in discussions with Father Lalor. Despite the disapproval of his father, he decided he would be a priest. Father Lalor helped Ian Travers-Ball to enter the Jesuit novitiate at Loyola College in Watsonia, Melbourne, on February 1, 1952.

His decision to work in India meant that he would pursue his seminary studies in India, the country to which he would give his life. Similarly, Mother Teresa had spent her novitiate days in India.

The young seminarian left Melbourne by ship and arrived in Bombay on December 17, 1954, just a quarter of a century after the arrival of Mother Teresa. This was almost the last moment for unrestricted missionary entry into India. His first journey was to Ranchi, in Bihar, to study Hindi. The long preparation period of the Society of Jesus, longer than that of any religious congregation, accounted for the fact that it was 1963 before he was ordained.

After Father Ian Travers-Ball's momentous "Yes" to the second call, the Brothers began searching for a headquarters of their own. They found the three-story house at 7 Mansatala Row, Kidderpore, Calcutta, visited by Dorothy Day and myself. There Brother Andrew became proficient in Bengali; he was already fluent in Hindi. This simple house, purchased by Mother Teresa, remained their headquarters as the Brothers grew in numbers and carried their work around the world.

The first works of the Brothers arose out of the Sisters' network of mercy already in being for a decade and a half. The young men were able to expand the works of mercy in ways foreseen and prayed for by Mother Teresa. While Mother Teresa and the Sisters brought food to the homeless who continually crept into every corner of Sealdah Station, the Brothers rescued and gave shelter to young boys with no home or protection but the station walls. They carried the same work into Howrah Station across the

Hooghly River. It was the greatest blessing when the Brothers took as their special charge the men's ward at the Home for the Dying.

When they began to work outside India, the Brothers opened houses in many areas where the Sisters were not working. Brother Andrew chose to work on the West Coast of the United States, in Los Angeles. There, the Brothers settled near the acres of misery known as "Skid Row," a gathering place of the homeless, the alcoholics, derelicts, the mentally disabled, and those simply broken on the wheel of life. They arrived in a time of special terror, since someone referred to as the "Skid Row slasher" was stalking the area slitting the throats of derelicts.

While Mother Teresa, after visiting Saigon and Phnom Penh in 1973, decided against stationing young women in areas ravaged by hostilities, Brother Andrew sent teams of Brothers to both cities.

In an early tentative year, Brother Andrew described the seventeen Brothers as "a fragile group," and he continued to emphasize their simplicity and weakness as the years went by. In September 1970, at the visit of Dorothy Day, there were seventy-seven Brothers and, by the end of the year, the community had grown to eighty-six members. In the Home for Boys in Kidderpore, there were just over seventy boys, most of them attending school and the older ones engaged in learning various trades. It was often necessary to find schools in which the boys could study in their own tongue since not all came from Bengali-speaking families.

Already by 1969 young men from England were coming to Calcutta to volunteer with the Brothers for a few months at a time, or for the vacation period, as British students had done with the Missionaries of Charity in Rome. These were not "Come-and-Sees," since their plan was to return home after their period of volunteering.

Groups of "Come-and-Sees" came regularly; however, but at first, only from the provinces of India. One volunteer from England related how he got up and rolled up his sleeping mat with the Brothers at 4:30 A.M. and took his shower with a bucket of water. After joining them for meditation and mass, he shared their breakfast of tea, *chappaties*, and condensed milk. He took part in rescuing homeless boys from Howrah Station, giving them food and a good scrub so that they looked human again, and seeing that they started in one of the slum schools run by the Brothers.

The young volunteer found it hardest to assist the Brothers when they went to Dhappa to give injections and dress leprous ulcers. The almost limbless torsos, the caved-in faces, and the lepers' tendency to burn and mutilate their feelingless limbs scarred his mind. There was also an occasional rat, he noted, that contributed to the loss of fingers and toes. In the Home for the Dying, working with the Brothers in the hall for men, he told of a man of forty, who looked seventy, brought in with a gangrenous leg. "A rag was wrapped around it," he wrote, "and we had to take him outside because of the stench. When we washed it down, the water started the blood flowing over the green flesh; bone and muscle dropped off. The foot was no more than a skeleton and you could see right through the leg up to the knee. A crow came down and picked up a bone that had fallen from the foot—they were hungry, too."

The Brothers, he recounted, ate for lunch and dinner the same food they distributed to the poor, bulgur wheat, a parboiled wheat, or rice and curry. After returning to Mansatala Row at 6 P.M., there was religious formation until 6:30 P.M., when there was dinner. During the meal there was silence, and a lesson was read.

From 6:30 P.M. until 7:30 P.M., he joined in the Brothers' recreation. This was the time, he said, when "Everyone goes mad, laughs, and generally has a good time. It is so obviously a day's release in an hour, as the Brothers are so preoccupied with their work at all other times."

The first "Come-and-See" from the United States appeared in Mansatala Row in May 1968. He was a rangy man, well over six feet tall, who walked like a cowboy, the son of the wide spaces of Colorado. In point of fact, he was already a vowed Brother in the Cistercians, one of the most austere orders of the Catholic Church. One day, the refectory reading at his monastery was an article on Mother Teresa in the magazine published by the Missionary Society of St. Columban in Ireland. Moved to the depths of his being, the Brother, already forty years of age, wrote to Mother Teresa to find out if there were a group of men engaged in the same response to suffering. She replied, informing him that the congregation of Brothers had been founded.

Brother Nicholas Prinster, the Cistercian Brother, received the permission of his abbot to reply to Brother Andrew, who accepted him. He received a leave of absence from the Cistercians to test his vocation on the streets of Calcutta. In May 1968, he took leave of the monks of the Abbey of the Holy Trinity in the desert of Utah, a few hours from Salt Lake City, to fly to Calcutta. The monastery he was leaving behind was a foundation formed in 1947 from the Abbey of Gethsemani, in Kentucky, which Thomas Merton had entered in 1941. In the years immediately after the Second World War, young American Catholics, who had been part of the worldwide carnage, filled monasteries and seminaries to overflowing, and the Abbey of the Holy Trinity had no lack of vocations.

Brother Nicholas threw himself into the schedule of the Brothers and shared their life without difficulty. He found he was the same age as Brother Andrew. Soon, however, a debilitating fever began to incapacitate him. As soon as he recovered from one bout, he was struck down again. No matter what treatment he received, the sickness returned. It was clear to

Brother Andrew and to him that the second vocation was not for him. In 1968, he returned to the Abbey of the Holy Trinity. The tie between the Brothers in Calcutta and the Cistercian monks was to last and bear much fruit. There was little doubt that Brother Nicholas served the Missionaries of Charity Brothers more effectively from his monastic cell than he could have in Calcutta's streets and *bustees.*

Whenever young Americans wrote to Brother Andrew about joining the congregation, he referred them to Brother Nicholas. One by one, they came to the Abbey in the desert, where they found time to reflect and pray and learn from Brother Nicholas the details of life as lived by the Brothers in Calcutta. In the procession of young men were Michael Gielenfeld from Iowa, Gary Richardson from Arizona, and Jeremy Hollinger from Maryland. All three passed through the Abbey of contemplatives to become contemplatives in the world as Missionaries of Charity. All three went through the vortex of war in Vietnam and were the ones to open the Brothers' house in Los Angeles. Brother Jeremy, whose interest in the Missionaries of Charity had been awakened by Malcolm Muggeridge's book, became the Local Servant in Los Angeles. He went on to become the Regional Servant for North and South America and at thirty years of age, vicar general of the Brothers under Brother Andrew.

Brother Nicholas opened the monastery to the Co-Workers, as will be described in Chapter 19, and served the Co-Workers in important ways. About his experiences in Calcutta, he said, "If only I had been ten years younger, I might have been able to survive there. But the time spent with Brother Andrew stays with me, his superabundant energy, his faith that is beyond conviction, but urges and drives him on. To me, Brother Andrew's outstanding trait is his fortitude, or what we Americans call 'guts.' He does not seem to be afraid of anything, especially not afraid to fail. This trait certainly includes a complete lack of human respect, either of the praise or ridicule of the world. Much of this trait is natural to him, but one can see in it, too, the marks of his training as a Jesuit. This fortitude is in every sense a gift of the Spirit and springs from his inner conviction; faith in and love of God. It seems to be that he and Mother Teresa differ in that she is more like St. Thérèse of Lisieux, filled with the charismatic vision of the love of God, while Brother Andrew keeps stressing that he is a very human person, or to use a term that he uses all the time about himself, 'earthy.' "

Brother Andrew himself found spiritual nourishment at the Abbey of the Holy Trinity and he went there to share in the prayer life of the monks whenever he came to the United States.

At year's end of 1970, Brother Andrew, despite the horrors which daily assailed the Brothers, described some of the joys.

"The joys of work with the suffering poor," he said, "are many and deep. There is the joy of seeing people relieved of at least a little of their suffering, of the sick cured, of families finding employment for a breadwinner, of children of the streets finding a home and responding as loved and loving human beings, of alcoholics and drug addicts overcoming their difficulties. There was a man and his five-year-old son huddled in a railway station platform, homeless, sick unto death, the mother already dead. They are picked up in a daze of lifelessness and brought to the home. The father dies in a few days without a word. The boy stops coughing, comes to life, and begins to laugh and play with new little brothers who have similarly been touched by love. There is the joy in seeing a little one-legged boy from the railway station playing happily in the room with me. Now he finds shelter, a home, food, and a little love.

"For us here," he continued, "seeing these things directly, it is much easier, for such sights and experiences are a great encouragement and happiness. I think that the faith and love of those from afar who share in the work is much greater, for they do not have the consolation of seeing the light in young eyes, or hearing the laughter and singing."

As the Sisters sent out small teams of women to open houses first in Calcutta and then throughout India, the Brothers proceeded to expand their work also. A home for homeless and handicapped boys was founded in Dum Dum where the youngsters received training in radio repair work. In Howrah, across the Hooghly River, the Brothers took on the work for the dying. They called the home Nabo Jivan (New Life) and at the start they had room for twenty-five men. One of the aged men said, "We thank God for the Brothers who became our sons in our old age to help us—as we had no one on this earth." Then, said the Brother, "The old man started weeping and praising God."

A fourth home was opened on Pipe Road near the headquarters on Mansatala Row. Homeless boys were not only cared for, but enrolled in different schools according to their language. After a fifth center was opened on Picnic Gardens Road (the relics of genteel British custom die hard) the Brothers made a leap out of the city.

They acquired a coconut farm, situated about fifteen miles from Calcutta at Hooghly Point in 24-Parganas. Brother Andrew wrote me that he was taking a leaf out of Dorothy Day's book in opening the farm, since each Catholic Worker Hospitality House aimed to have its own farm. Nurpur Farm served several purposes, including the sheltering of mentally disabled persons and of boys and men who were tubercular. Ponds were stocked with fish and retarded boys and men helped with the simple farming tasks. Those threatened by tuberculosis often recovered away from the dust of Calcutta's streets. The population of Nurpur Farm grew to two hundred persons, with twenty-five Brothers and "Come-and-Sees" aiding them. When the Brothers took their work into India's villages, their centers resembled the ashrams of Indian monks. The villagers accepted their presence, as well as their help. Some of the centers were in tribal areas and the Brothers, after mastering English, had to learn the local tribal tongues, Santali, Ho-Munda, or Pahari. The villagers, at the margins of Indian life, were eager teachers.

After helping the Sisters at Titagarh Leprosy Center, later rededicated as the Gandhiji Prem Nivas (Gandhi Abode of Love), the Brothers took over the entire work. Brother-doctors and medical aides served the close to three hundred patients needing full care. About the same number were rehabilitated and continued to make *charpoys.* In addition, they were trained to make sandals out of used automobile tires and eventually to weave bed sheets and the blue-bordered saris worn by the Sisters. The Gandhiji Prem Nivas gave care to over twenty thousand outpatients.

After branching out from Bengal into Bihar, the neighboring state, into Kerala in southwest India, and Bombay, across the subcontinent, Brother Andrew looked toward East Asia. There were already eleven houses in India, and Brothers with sufficient maturity were ready to continue the training of the "Come-and-Sees" and the young Brothers in Mansatala Row.

Brother Andrew explained that his four-month stay in Australia during 1972 had proved to him that he could give more responsibility to the Indian Brothers.

His choice was Vietnam. He wrote, "I left India at the end of February (1973) in fear and trembling . . . I was instantly welcomed by the Jesuit community in Saigon."

Saigon was a city packed with soldiers, with displaced Vietnamese, and all the activities that go along with the presence of armies. He decided to bring a team of Indian Brothers to find out what small work of mercy they could offer to the very least of the people in the crowded city. He wrote me on April 30 from Saigon.

"I have got something started here in a small way. It is something of a House of Hospitality. A few widows with their children, a few girls who have lived with GI's and who are in a pretty bad state. We are in a rented house and will need a place to ourselves before we go much further."

He was among those he called "the little, wounded, and overlooked people."

Brother Andrew was in touch with Catholic Relief Services which conducted a relief program for war victims in Vietnam, and he was eventually able to obtain food and other supplies. He commented on his Hospitality House, "There seems great value in a community that doesn't set out to 'do' anything, but to strive for a spirit or atmosphere in which people can love and grow and be what God wants them to be. If this happens, then it is enough. Already here it is wonderful to see the hope that the few children and the people in the house seem to have found. The mustard seed is the heart of the gospel."

These words were written while Vietnam was enduring the third decade of what the Vietnamese referred to as "the everlasting war."

In October 1973, Brother Andrew flew to the United States and gave a few talks on his work. For one of these talks in Washington, D.C., he shared the platform with Dorothy Day and publicly acknowledged her influence on him and the spiritual debt he owed her. It was the annual assembly of Pax Christi, the American branch of the International Catholic Movement for Peace. He related how people had come to the House of Hospitality:

"One day a rickshaw drew up and out of it came a young woman with three little children, two girls and a boy. She was homeless. She told me that her husband had been killed in a car accident on the streets of Saigon by an Australian civilian. Without resources, she fell into the easy trap of prostitution. When she turned away from that life, she begged help from her family. For a while they helped, but when they failed her, she was helpless. Someone knew about our house."

He continued: "We took her in. Her name was My Le. She was thirty-four years of age, and each of her children had a different father. One was half-American. She was determined to raise her children and was a careful and devoted mother. My Le became the heart of our House of Hospitality, and as the numbers grew until our family reached over sixty persons, she helped make it a real community. After a while, that little community needed our presence less and less. We found shelter and some material help for them and they worked to make life easier for each other. A blind old woman would hold the smallest children on her lap to calm them and put them to sleep. A sick person would never be left alone. We had quarrels and problems, but we had reconciliations, too.

"We knew what our people had suffered and we felt that they were teaching us, that they were enriching us. I felt grateful to them. The mystery of suffering is deep, but one thing it does is to bring us together. It is the poor and their sufferings that bring us together. They will help save the world."

He told us that the people of the streets spoke the lingo of the American soldiers. If he asked a young woman to cook a meal or care for a newcomer, she would reply with a soldierly, "No sweat, Father, no sweat."

Brother Andrew ended his talk by stating that the Pax Christi conference had demonstrated to him in a way he had not been able to see before that the works of mercy were works of peace. He had been feeling guilty because he was not contributing to peace, but now he felt his own work was a work of peace.

A third talk was given before the same group addressed by Mother Teresa in 1960 in Las Vegas, the National Council of Catholic Women. The meeting was held in New Orleans. The women wasted no time in organizing help for the house in Saigon by immediately taking up a collection among the thousands of participants. Brother Andrew's work became one of the programs aided by the "Works of Peace" program. When the Brothers moved into Phnom Penh, the help was extended to Cambodia.

Before returning to India and Vietnam, Brother Andrew had the opportunity to see the most desolate section of Los Angeles. The occasion was a gathering of the Ladies of Charity of that city. This time he shared the platform with Mother Teresa who had made a hurried trip for the meeting.

On his return to Vietnam, Brother Andrew was able to add the American Brothers and a Dutch Brother, trained as a nurse, to the team in Saigon. In February 1974, a call came from Cambodia. Could the Brothers help with the refugees around Phnom Penh?

"And so," Brother Andrew related, "we are making a small start in that beautiful but troubled land. It is terrible to see what is happening there, to see from a helicopter an endless line of families with their few belongings on a buffalo cart moving on, crossing streams like a scene from *The Ten Commandments*. Terrible to lie in bed at night and hear the rockets and feel everything beneath you tremble. Terrible to drive thirty miles along Highway Four out of Phnom Penh and see not a village or a building that is not in ruins. Terrible to realize that it is not just the buildings of the village that are destroyed, but the whole village with its life and structures. Terrible to see people flung into refugee camps or strung out along the roadside or riverside by the clash of political theories which they probably do not grasp and none of which are worth the cost these people are paying.

"At any rate, it is a much simpler thing to be able to offer an old Cambodian grandmother some rice and dried fish for herself and her daughter's orphaned children, who have only her left to care for them. I don't think we can be too simple in our love—for it is the little things in the lives of us all—be we homeless in Cambodia or refugees in Cambodia, or well-provided for in New York or Sydney—that are really the big things for us."

Settled in Phnom Penh among the refugees from war, bombing, and shelling, the Brothers took in the helpless old and the helpless young. Many were street children who had lost or been separated from their families. When the first house was filled to overflowing, a second house was opened.

In Saigon the number of the homeless guests grew, necessitating a second and then a third house.

Early in January 1975, Brother Andrew wrote me, ". . . The houses in Saigon are really beautiful in the way the people are growing. What has been done and is being done in Cambodia is wonderful. Let us pray that if God wants, we shall be able to continue in both countries. Things look so bad everywhere, but we do have God's promise to be with us always."

And from a short note I received just before Easter of 1975:

"Just back from Phnom Penh. I've never seen the like. Rockets, fear of rockets, fear of bloodbath, danger, risk in evacuation, risk in staying . . . . It is awful to be keeping the young Brothers there at this late point. But they mean so much to the people. The striking thing about them right now is the tremendous spirit of joy they have.

"The offensive has really burst here, too, in a very big way. May the Passion of Indochina be a way to a glorious Resurrection for these people."

Brother Andrew made a decision. He asked all the Brothers to leave Phnom Penh. They returned to Mansatala Row, all except one. Brother Brian Walsh, a twenty-three-year-old American member of the community, told Brother Andrew that he would stay with the Cambodian people whom he had grown to love. Brother Andrew did everything in his power to have the young man come to Saigon so that his evacuation could be arranged. Before they took off from Phnom Penh, Brothers Michael and George considered taking him with them by force. But Brother Brian had slipped away and was thought to be with a group of French Benedictine monks.

The occupation of Phnom Penh by the Khmer Rouge was followed by the change of regime in Saigon. During April, before the soldiers of North Vietnam occupied Saigon, Brother Andrew had seen to the evacuation of all the Brothers. As General Servant, he could freely make the choice of staying or being evacuated. He chose to stay—alone.

While Brother Andrew made the decision to stay, hundreds of thousands of Vietnamese civilians and soldiers fought for the privilege of leaving their country, of becoming refugees. From points along the long shoreline, they took off into the South China Sea in every type of craft, from frail coastal fishing boats to cargo boats whose only cargo became the packed bodies of human beings. Thousands of displaced Vietnamese clogged the roads to Saigon. Planes could not take off from the airport as desperate human beings filled the runways. The American Embassy was surrounded by people begging for a place on the helicopters that were taking off from the roof to ferry people to the carrier ships of the U.S. Seventh Fleet. The last sad scene of the Embassy showed men, women, and children trying to scale the Embassy wall. Their bleeding hands were dislodged by rifle butts from the barbed wire that topped the wall. One of the last television scenes showed a middle-aged man and woman who had failed in their attempt to lift themselves over the wall and were impaled on the barbed wire. The flight of the "boat people" went on for years, and no one knew how many perished in futile attempts to escape, drowning in the open sea or attacked by pirates.

Brother Andrew stayed with the people, going from one House of Hospitality to the other to see that their needs were met. He still had some funds at his disposal, but day by day they dwindled. Foreigners like himself had to present themselves to the authorities regularly, who consulted the lists of those scheduled for evacuation. Armed men came to see him to check his papers and covered him with guns while they examined his passport and papers. It was a harrowing experience each time it happened.

The first building sheltering the aged, the widows, and the children was taken over by the new authorities. There were no other shelters for the people and no plans had been made for their future. Then the second building and finally the third was taken over. Brother Andrew was an oddity as he walked the streets. When he met people who had worked for the Americans as drivers or clerks, they avoided him after gazing into his eyes. All people formerly employed by the Americans had to carry the papers announcing that damning fact. They could not find work and faced hunger for themselves and their families. There were cases where whole families committed suicide by eating poison together.

Each day a different list of the foreigners to be deported was posted and finally Brother Andrew's name appeared. Twenty-five hours before he was to report to Tan Son Nhut Airport, his passport had to be surrendered. It was returned to him as he boarded the plane.

While awaiting evacuation on August 19, 1975, he wrote, "Twilight in the coconut trees on my last night in Vietnam. I remembered Jesus' last night (I so different) but I can make the same prayer that the Spirit may come and be with these people. I feel the enormity of the final separation but I can't grasp it. I looked out into the night and said farewell to all in Saigon, in Vietnam, to the people so dispersed—and asked God to be with them, to give them life. And I thanked God."

He was to say later, "I shall never be the same again, and I know that I shall have an ache in my heart for these people till the day I die."

The days between the end of April and August when Brother Andrew was alone in Saigon, were days of pain and prayer for the Brothers. They received an occasional letter from him and his assistant superior, Brother Ferdinand, wrote me whenever he received word. The letters often took two or three weeks to reach Calcutta from Saigon. The male congregation had taken shape and had a chain of command. The constitutions, ninety-nine pages of spiritual and practical advice, served as their guide until Brother Andrew's return in August 1975.

According to the constitutions, Brother Andrew, the general superior, or General Servant, was supported by a council of four members, a general secretary, a general procurator, and a master of novices. The superior of each house was called a Local Servant. Every six years, a general chapter was called for the election, by secret ballot, of the General Servant and the councillors. The aims of the Society were couched in terms similar to those of the Sisters. After referring to the twofold love of God and man, the constitutions state, "The special aim of the Society is to live this life of love by dedicating oneself to the service of the poorest of the poor in slums, on the streets, and wherever they are found. Leprosy patients, destitute beggars, the abandoned, homeless boys, young men in the slums, the unemployed, and those uprooted by war and disaster will always be the special object of the Brothers' concern."

The constitutions were separate and distinct from those of the Sisters. The Brothers made the study of the constitutions an integral part of their spiritual life.

In June 1975, Brother Ferdinand wrote, "The second of June was the day of great thanksgiving for us when there were seventeen Brothers making their first profession and five making their final profession. Mother Teresa was with us and many friends. We missed Brother Andrew on that great day. On 9th June, we started a new house in Gaya in Bihar State."

As Indians, the Brothers were aware that they were entering a region sacred to Buddhist and Hindu pilgrims and near the spot, Bodh Gaya, where the Buddha received his enlightenment.

On June 21, Brother Ferdinand wrote me, "By the advice of our general superior, Brother Andrew, and the decision of our general council, we are sending four of our Brothers to make an attempt to start to work in a simple way for the poor and needy people of Los Angeles.

"Of course, the work will not be exactly like in India, but I feel that we could do some work for the needy people in the USA, too. Among the four Brothers, three are from the USA and one is from Holland."

The four arrived in Los Angeles in July 1975 and were helped by a priest of the diocese, also active in Mother Teresa's Co-Workers, to find a house in a poor neighborhood. The priest, Father Don Kribs, was himself immersed in work for the poor. A towering six and a half feet tall and with warm light in his blue eyes, Father Don Kribs had easily won the respect and confidence of the homeless men in the St. Vincent's Shelter which he headed.

In October of the same year, in the course of some lectures, I was in Los Angeles and met the four young men. They occupied a tiny frame house in a section called the *barrio* where their neighbors were Mexican-Americans.

The house was so small that it had only half a number, its address being 157½ Edgeware Road. Beside it was a minuscule plot of land where a couple of small trees were fighting their way into the sunlight.

"I am Brother Jeremy," said a young man who looked no more than twenty years of age. "This is Brother Michael and this is Brother Gary. They were both in Phnom Penh. This is Brother Anton, our Dutch Brother, who was with me in Saigon. And this is Dennis, our 'Come-and-See.' "

When, at a later date, I was to ask about Dennis, Brother Jeremy replied, "Dennis left. We also have our 'Come-and-Gos.' "

The team of Brothers was full of excitement, since Brother Andrew was due in Los Angeles in two days. In the meantime, they continued their work. They took me to visit a few of the SRO hotels. There were about seventy of these single room occupancy hotels that covered block after block of skid row. They resembled nothing more than warehouses for unwanted throwaway members of the human community, social lepers.

Wondering about the origin of the expression "skid row," we could only assume that it was related to the expression "on the skids." This term had a sense of fatality about it, of people sliding into utter failure, of losing whatever chance they had of work, success, or even of self-reliance.

One hotel in particular remained in my memory. It was not the worst, and the lobby, paved with small black and white tiles like in a bathroom, was freshly swabbed. One sign stated: "No Cooking In Rooms." Another sign at the desk announced, "No Visitors Allowed," the reference being obvious. Exception was made for the Brothers who went regularly to the rooms of the men least able to care for themselves, whether because of age, or because they were sodden with drink or drugs. Brother Jeremy would leave me to go to a room, often no more than a cubicle, and clean a man doused in his own filth, supplying him with clean underwear and secondhand clothes. The Brothers, I learned, gained the confidence of men who had decided that no one could be trusted, who were estranged from their own families or had possibly been cast out by them.

A section of the Brothers' Constitution stated, "The Brothers shall frequently visit the houses of the poor in the slums, going from house to house in search of the sick, destitute and dying. They must be ready to wash and clean them, to clean the house, and do whatever is necessary, no matter how humble. They must always be watchful to help those near death to die in the love of the Lord."

Even when they needed medical attention, the men had to be coaxed outside. One of the centers of help was the clinic attached to the Catholic Worker Hospitality Kitchen. We went there at mealtime, when over five hundred men were served a hot meal by a large group of volunteers. It was a place of happy bustle, with members of the Catholic Worker community greeting many of the men by name. There was continuous banter about how smart a man looked in his new clothes (new to him but chosen from the Catholic Worker secondhand clothes rack) or about how many days a man had stayed "off the stuff." The work of the Brothers was not deterred by the stalking murderer who had already claimed the lives of ten derelicts. It was well into the following year before the killer, a drifter himself, was caught and convicted.

In their little house on Edgeware Road, the Brothers found strength and peace in a little room set aside for prayer. The chapel was absolutely bare of furniture, except for a large free-standing crucifix taller than a man and outlined against a white wall. There they prayed, kneeling or squatting on the floor. I sat on the floor with them for some blessed moments of silence under the overpowering shadow of the enormous cross. Then they recited the rosary, a very calming prayer after the difficult day. It was here that the Brothers meditated after getting up at five-thirty in the morning. There was no altar in the little chapel, since the Brothers went down the hill to the seven-thirty mass at the Mission Church of the Holy Rosary at its base.

"The Eucharist," said the constitutions, "is the center of the Society's religious and community life."

After climbing the hill to take their breakfast, the Brothers then set out for the SRO hotels, for visits to needy families in the *barrio* or to the market for food supplies. Besides buying basic foods, the Brothers went regularly to a large city market to collect supplies of vegetables in danger of spoilage. These they were beginning to share with the families of the *barrio*.

Brother Andrew arrived at the Los Angeles Airport to be greeted by a small welcoming committee, the Brothers, two friends, Grace and Lloyd Telvis, and myself.

His thin face seemed even thinner and more elongated. His blue-gray eyes were more compelling and ringed with dark circles.

Back at Edgeware Road, there was talk of the last days spent by Brother Andrew in Saigon and of Brother Brian Walsh who had stayed behind out of identification with the people of Cambodia. The exodus from Cambodia had been by way of the border with Thailand, and one of the evacuees reported seeing a young American being led away by a soldier at the point of a gun.

Brother Michael had an extra task in addition to the regular schedule of the Brothers; he was called upon to translate for the first Cambodian refugees, mostly children, who had arrived in California. The tragedy that the Brothers had left behind in Phnom Penh pursued them to Los Angeles. The children who crossed the Thai border carried tales of such horror that the world refused at first to give them credence. Their parents and grandparents had been done to death in a massive program of liquidation. In the "murderous Utopia" inflicted on Cambodia, the refugee-packed city of Phnom Penh had been evacuated in twenty-four hours. Even hospitals were evacuated, with patients dying by the roadside. The people were to be resettled on the land and become food producers, but no advance plans had been worked out. Those unlikely to become workers, like doctors and teachers and people who showed their "social origins" by wearing spectacles, were summarily executed by order of a small cadre of ideologues. Most reports agreed that as many as two million people perished.

Brother Michael and Brother Gary had no news of the men, women, and children who had been given refuge in their houses in Phnom Penh.

Brother Brian was presumed dead since no word was received from or about him after his presumed arrest. Possibly a similar fate overtook the residents of the houses in Phnom Penh, driven out of the city to unknown destinations that might have meant their death. The decimated nation was now referred to as Kampuchea.

Brother Andrew concentrated on the work of the Brothers in Los Angeles, rather than dwelling too much on the loss of five of their houses and the fate of people they loved and served half a world away. After visiting the Catholic Worker Hospitality Kitchen, he remarked, "Our Brothers have the freedom of Dorothy Day and Mother Teresa to give personal services to people—services that they could only get from those who believe in poverty and hospitality."

Brother Andrew had written to the mother of Brother Brian, as had Brother Michael and Brother Gary. She shared the copies of his last letters in which he tried to explain his decision to remain in Phnom Penh. On March 7, 1975, he had written to his parents and four brothers and sisters:

"Death," he wrote, "doesn't seem to be made into such a big thing here as in the West. A number of children here have died and it is accepted like every other aspect of life. I can honestly say that in the saving truth of Christ's message that the death of a person's soul through resisting God's spirit is so much worse than the death of these children.

"I hope you're at peace. Even if this is wrong, staying on here, I know that God can make it up to you a hundred times over. I don't believe that though, that I'm doing anything wrong. But rather I have a lot of peace that I know belongs to you as much as it does to me. As two good parents, I don't know what else you could want for me. We must think of the words that there is no greater love than to lay down one's life for one's friends. I have been given God's peace and joy and I know that it is for you also."

Brother Andrew remained with the Brothers in Los Angeles through Christmas 1975. On November 26, he wrote me, "It was so lovely that you were with us to share everything of those first days together in Los Angeles. As Mother says, 'God is so delicately kind.' "

In the letter he sent to the Brothers and friends that Christmas, he referred to the last days in Saigon:

"When we were finally dispersed, a woman, who had done so much in the building up of our Houses of Hospitality, remarked amid all the tears, 'Now we are being separated. But one day we shall all be together again.' And she pointed to the heavens. In the meantime, there is only tears and Jesus to hold us together. And that is the story of so many refugee families divided by continents . . .

"In India our leprosy work grows in many ways. We have more houses for dying and handicapped people; there are more homeless children with us, more child-feeding programs and little slum schools. And the miracle of the loaves and fishes continues in providing for all these people through so many of you who, I'm sure, share our feeling of being so weak and inadequate in our love. *It is the miracle of God's love working through our weakness.* There is no other explanation. This is our secret . . . I am ready to believe that we are all being used in a sort of new Franciscan movement where the Spirit of God is at work in His world of people, coming into the world in smallness and meekness to bring His saving love and life just like that first Christmas. And there is the pain of birth and the anguish of the cross which we all feel in our various lives. But the end is life, the joyful life of Easter."

Mother Teresa once remarked regarding Brother Andrew, "We are so different, but both of us have the same mind." Regarding the congregations, Brother Andrew commented, "Canonically, the Sisters and Brothers are two congregations. We have our own constitutions; we operate separately but we do have the same spirit."

In the main, the two congregations worked separately and harmoniously, though some differences did arise. In particular, there was disagreement and a temporary rift, over a contemplative branch of the Brothers. Mother Teresa, as a born leader, took steps to establish a Brothers' contemplative branch without the prior acquiescence of Brother Andrew. When he refused absolutely to go along with such a step, the contemplative branch was severed from the Brothers. The new branch was put under the direct supervision of a Roman prelate. The contemplative Brothers, called "The Brothers of the Word," opened their first house in a Roman slum under Brother Sebastian, a priest-brother from India.

Behind an exterior of utmost gentleness, Brother Andrew could exhibit rocklike firmness whenever it was required. His utter dependence on the providence of God matched that of Mother Teresa, but he was willing to take seemingly wild risks, such as that of remaining alone in Vietnam after the evacuation of his Brothers.

Despite his deep seriousness, his face would often light up with insouciant humor. When someone did not measure up to an exacting standard, he would remark, "Everyone can be a 'bad actor' for three minutes out of every day." Only he used a more salty term.

He began to delegate authority earlier than Mother Teresa. This might have been possible because the spirit of the Missionaries of Charity had been so deeply imbedded in the Calcutta houses under Mother Teresa's tutelage of the Sisters. The Brothers caught that spirit as they took up the work in the Home for the Dying, the leper centers, and the slum schools.

Brother Andrew's emotions were nearer the surface than those of Mother Teresa. I was with him once in New York when he came upon a strange Cambodian-type cross made by refugees in Phnom Penh. They had made thousands of such crosses from scraps of wood and tin expertly tooled. His eyes filled with tears and he stopped dead, covering his face with his hands. Brother Andrew was more vulnerable than Mother Teresa and more open in admitting to vulnerability. This encouraged the Brothers to share their own vulnerability. He was also more analytical and talked about neuroses and described some of the work of the Brothers as being concerned not only with Alcoholics Anonymous but with "Neurotics Anonymous."

While his face in repose was that of an ascetic, a type withdrawn from the world, conversation evoked lively, responsive expressions. His smile was a benediction and was frequent. His talks were without rhetoric, given in his pleasant voice with its Australian accent that was clipped and clear. Before an audience, he used no oratorical gestures, but spoke directly and earnestly, his entire concentration focused on the message for which he was the channel. There was an understatement in his speeches and actions that made them even more effective than if he had injected himself to a greater degree or had been more emphatic.

Perhaps the greatest insight into the mind and heart of Brother Andrew comes from his stamp on the constitutions of the Society of which he was the founder.

The first words of the document state, "The general aim of the Society comes from the lips of Christ our Lord Himself: 'I give you a new commandment: Love one another as I have loved you so you are to love one another. If there is love among you, then all will know that you are my disciples . . .' "

While the Sisters had one habit only, worn in Yemen or on the sidewalks of New York, the Brothers might vary their dress. Their constitutions state: "The dress of the Brothers is to be poor and simple. They shall wear the clothes of poor people of the place. The more universal to the various groups of the local population the better. The dress is to be poor, but always clean and neat. In India it will be a shirt and trousers . . . The sign of their profession and dedication to Christ is a simple crucifix worn over the heart."

The constitutions stipulate that after the period of "Come and See," the Brother becomes a novice. After two years of novitiate training in the Scriptures, in Christian theology and spirituality, coupled with participation in the work for the poor, the Brothers make their first profession of vows: poverty, chastity, obedience, and devoting oneself to work among the poor. The vows are for one year only. After the novitiate the vows continue to be taken each year for one year.

Following five years of annual vows, the Brothers make profession of vows for a lifetime. In January 1980 I received an invitation to the final profession of vows in Los Angeles by Brothers Michael, Gary, and Jeremy. For the rest of their lives, they would aim to incorporate the words of their constitutions into the very fabric of their existence:

"The Brothers' poverty comes from the life and example of Christ Himself Who was rich, yet for our sake, became poor, so that through His poverty we might become rich.

"Chastity 'for the sake of the kingdom of heaven' which the Brother professes should be counted as an outstanding gift of grace. It frees the heart of man in a very special way so that it may be more inflamed with love for God and all men.

"The supreme inspiration for our obedience is Christ our Lord Who repaired the damage caused by the disobedience of Adam by His own sacrifice of obedience."

There is much stress on the importance of community life and the constitutions remind the Brothers that they are never more truly Christian or more truly Brothers than when they are assembled around the altar to share the same divine meal.

Even though there are several priests in the Society, all are called by the same name, "Brother." No young man is accepted for the Society if his aim is to become a priest, although a Brother may go on to become a priest under certain circumstances. The priest-Brothers were in the main, those who, like Brother Andrew, were ordained prior to joining the Brothers.

Regarding work for the poor, the constitutions echoed Mother Teresa's telling phrase regarding the disguise of divinity: "Let each Brother see Jesus Christ in the person of the poor; the more repugnant the work or the person, the greater also must be his faith, love, and cheerful devotion in ministering to our Lord in the distressing disguise."

The Missionaries of Charity Brothers became international in membership as well as in extent. The Los Angeles house soon had Brothers from Australia and Ireland as well as from the United States and India. When they began their work in Hong Kong in 1977, the team comprised two Indian Brothers, a Swiss Brother, a Chinese Brother, and a French Brother.

During 1978, teams of Brothers went to Japan, Taiwan, Korea, and Guatemala. People wondered what the Brothers would be doing in a developed country like Japan. They settled in an area of Tokyo with alcoholics. In the ensuing years, the Brothers moved to Macao, the Philippines, El Salvador, Dominican Republic, Haiti, Brazil, and Madagascar. In 1982, the Brothers finally came to Europe, opening a house in Paris for street people who escaped from other categories of social service.

Brother Andrew, while rejoicing at the growth, commented, "Growth and expansion are a mixed blessing. They take away our smallness. They demand more complicated administration. They can take away somewhat from being a family. Such things are so precious that we can afford to remain a little scattered, a little disorganized, a little bit free to be what God wants us to be, without demanding too much uniformity. That asks a lot of us. We have to be free, free to love, to love especially the smallest and seemingly most insignificant members of the human family."

The Society was eventually divided into eight regions, with two Indian regions for thirty-two houses. There were Regional Servants for East Asia, Africa, Central America, South America, and the United States. There were eight houses in the Western Hemisphere: three in California, two in Guatemala, and one house each in El Salvador, the Dominican Republic, and Haiti. During 1983, the Brothers opened a new house every month of the year. The novitiate in Mansatala Row proved too small and a second center for novices was opened in Howrah. Because of the many young people coming from southern India, a novitiate was founded there in Vijayawada. Besides the novitiate in Los Angeles, novitiate houses were opened in Peru, Guatemala, the Dominican Republic, and Brazil for the Western Hemisphere; and in Madagascar for Africa and in South Korea for East Asia. The number of young Korean candidates was so great that there were soon twenty-five Korean Brothers ready to take over the work of four houses in South Korea. The Brothers' habit of sleeping on mats made their life-style acceptable in places like South Korea and the poorest slums of Asia and the Western Hemisphere. The mats also made the furnishing of a new novitiate a simple affair.

The Brothers who were trained overseas did not spend time in Calcutta but went on to make their final profession of vows wherever they were stationed. They were less identified with Calcutta than the Sisters who customarily returned to the Motherhouse for the crucial sixth year before taking lifetime vows. Also, Brother Andrew had arrived in India after the period when it was possible to opt for Indian citizenship and thus retained his Australian citizenship.

As the Brothers had dared enter areas of violence in Vietnam and Cambodia, they decided to plant themselves in a center of violence in the Western Hemisphere, El Salvador. A Brother wrote, "Last month Brother Andrew visited us and celebrated mass in our little house. How we felt the presence of God! We shall continue our work, trying to be instruments of peace no matter what violence is breaking around us or in the world at large."

One of the works of the Brothers in El Salvador was visiting the sick in poor families and giving or finding medical aid. They also learned how to build *champas* for people made homeless by the continuing violence in the countryside. The *champa,* a one-room home made of mud, bamboo, and tin, was the next step to being shelterless, but it was an important step for destitute and desperate families.

One day a Brother disappeared. It was soon discovered that he had been kidnapped and was being held as a hostage. The Brothers went to Archbishop Oscar Romero to ask for help. Through the archbishop's intervention the Brother was released. Three months later in March 1980, Archbishop Romero, the Archbishop of San Salvador, was assassinated with a bullet to the heart as he was celebrating mass.

The Brothers were not deterred when they found little welcome and some criticism. In a slum of one of Brazil's great cities, a group of foreign missionary priests told them simply to move on, "We don't want you. All you do is give the people a wash and something to eat—and nothing changes for the poor." The Brothers in a short time were conducting a shelter for homeless and troubled boys wanted by no one—except perhaps by the police.

The Brothers followed the Sisters into Guatemala, working first in a village, but trekking into a slum of Guatemala City when the villagers abandoned their homes to escape the violence. On a visit to Guatemala, Brother Andrew celebrated mass for Sisters and Brothers in the little chapel of the Sisters. He was to leave for El Salvador on the following day. "In front of them," he related, "I was struck by the seeming insignificance of the little group in the midst of all the violence, killing, and civil war. They are so small and weak and young. They have no power. They care for the old, the sick babies, the mothers, the disabled and helpless, the hungry. And they are so full of joy. The light of God shines in their eyes.

"It seems that God calls them to this and other violent places to be a little center of love, peace, joy, and prayer. There is no hope here of a solution from arms or politics or ideologies of the right or of the left. These

Sisters and Brothers are so weak, so small. They only have God—His love and His power.

"In Calcutta, amid all the problems and the continuing poverty there, this year has seen welcome changes in several young men whom we found fourteen or fifteen years ago homeless and abandoned on the streets or railway stations begging. They were with us over the years as they grew up. Now they are married. They are settled and starting their own little families with hope and courage and love.

"It is important to see the flowers sometimes."

Among the flowers was the growth of the Society. After twenty years of existence, at the end of 1983, there were 401 members of the society, 302 who had made their profession of vows and 99 novices. In addition there were over a hundred "Come-and-Sees" spending periods of time in houses across the world. The Brothers included men of twenty-five nationalities, working in fifty-one houses in India and overseas. Mother Teresa's second branch, the Brothers, exhibited a healthy and steady growth, even in comparison with the phenomenal growth of the Sisters.

The comparable figures for the Sisters, after twenty years of existence in 1970, were 585 members of the Society, 332 having made profession of vows. They represented thirteen nationalities in all. Besides the sixty centers in Calcutta, the Sisters worked in forty houses in thirty cities of India and in twelve houses in ten overseas countries. In 1982 the growth of the work of the Brothers gained momentum, with a new house being opened every month for the twenty-five months ending in August 1984. By the end of that year, the number of houses came to seventy.

Brother Andrew repeatedly surveyed the tragic enormity of human problems and the response of love that seemed madness to the many without faith in a Creator. Yet in his experience he saw flowers continually growing from the love that reached the rejected and dehumanized who had received too little love.

In this he was at one with Mother Teresa who persisted in sharing experiences that carried "the good news," examples of love in action among the poor of the world who are nameless and unknown to history. To her, holy priests were the key to holiness among the Christian community. Brother Andrew was a striver for this holiness and was willing to suffer for it.

His attitude recalled to me the meditations of a Jesuit priest who recorded them in prison while awaiting execution. The words of Alfred Delp came to light after his death for opposing Nazism. Delp asserted that the burden of the priest is now not only the "outside" man who has no belief in God, but the "inside" man who does not believe in himself because he has given and received too little love.

Brother Andrew contrasted what faced him daily and what he called "our funny little Missionaries of Charity thing that grows, expands, is full of life, as it exists in such weakness, fragility, and folly." Then he posed a question, "What is God saying to us in all this?"

"It seems to me," he said, giving voice to his conviction in an answer to his question, "Have faith in the Lord of History. For there is nothing else that is certain or solid. Everything may collapse, and one may find oneself trapped in some fallen or falling city with all escapes gone. Yet in a strange way, that would be grace-filled—the chance to make up at the end for all one's failures to identify with people, for using all the privileges one has, through nationality, prestige, resources to fall back on. Then one would be finally poor—and free. Then one could give one's life and die in peace and love."

19

The Shared Vision

"As I climbed the steps of the Writers' Buildings leading to my office, I was thinking of Mother Teresa who devotes her life to the service of the poor."

These were the words of Dr. B. C. Roy, Chief Minister of Bengal on his eightieth birthday which Calcutta celebrated as a holiday by closing Bengal's government offices. Almost from the beginning of her work, Mother Teresa had counted on the support of Dr. Roy, and on July 1, 1961, he was still finding ways to help her. In an interview on the front page of the *Calcutta Statesman,* he told how one of his tasks before leaving for a trip to Europe was to arrange for the customs authorities to waive the duties on a shipment of sewing machines for Mother Teresa.

"Dr. Roy," reported the *Calcutta Statesman* "felt that Mother Teresa was doing magnificent work. She served those who were most miserable and found no place in hospitals, and among them were lepers and cholera patients."

Roy himself needed help for many health and welfare projects and his approach sounded much like that of Mother Teresa.

"I believe in God," he told the reporters. "A good cause never suffers for want of money. Money will come from unexpected sources."

Dr. Roy was one of the many inspired by the work of Mother Teresa from its earliest days. It was a source of joy for Mother Teresa when almost from the beginning, people from all branches of society, various castes, and many religious groups came forward as volunteers. Many came on their own to Shishu Bhavan or to the Home for the Dying. At times they came as members of a group, like the students, including Rama Coomaraswamy, introduced to the work by Father Robert Antoine. Some brought funds and gifts of food and clothing and then left; some stayed to perform any number of tasks, from shaving and cutting the toenails of helpless men in Kalighat, to holding and feeding an infant in Shishu Bhavan, struggling for its life. Mother Teresa encouraged the women volunteers to cradle in their arms abandoned infants and children even though they seemed marked for death. The child in its last hours, she said, would have the experience of being loved.

There was no organizational link binding those who gathered around Mother Teresa and the various works of the Missionaries of Charity in the scourged city.

One day, a woman met Mother Teresa whose life was to be from then on intertwined with hers. She was to help Mother Teresa in forming an association that took roots in countries around the globe. United in this association, men, women, young people, and even children, took as an integral part of their lives the binding up of the wounds of those hurt by life. In awarding to Mother Teresa the Templeton Prize for Progress in Religion, the committee made special mention of the growth of a lay group devoted to the free service of the poor in the same spirit as that of the Missionaries of Charity. As time went on, the association flourished and worked in places where there were no groups of Sisters.

The association was the Co-Workers of Mother Teresa. She gave her time and energy to training the Co-Workers, for being a Co-Worker, she used to say, was a way of life just as was being a Missionary of Charity.

The woman concerned with its founding was Ann Blaikie. She was in Calcutta as the wife of John Blaikie, a businessman, and participated in the life of the British business colony domiciled there. She described how she came to cooperate with Mother Teresa.

"In June 1954, I was busy as a voluntary worker in The Good Companions, a shop selling the handicrafts of needy groups, especially women, throughout India. I was following the customary life of my friends. As we were all voluntary workers, we were able to send goodly amounts of funds to those who had crafted the items. The goods were of the highest quality; the needlework was exquisite, night dresses, lingerie, lampshades. There were also carved bookends and many other items.

"That June I was seven months pregnant; the temperature was 115 degrees and it was getting difficult to pull out the heavy drawers to sell the goods. I could not go in on a regular basis, so I gave in my notice.

"I returned home and sat on the verandah and thought, 'What shall I do now?' We had servants and an easy life—an Ayah for the other two children. Then the thought came to me: find Mother Teresa and do something with her."

Ann Blaikie knew that Mother Teresa rescued babies from dustbins and taught children in the slums and ran a big Christmas party, but she did not know how to get in touch with her. She finally got the address of the

Mother and Child Clinic in Kidderpore and, on July 26, 1954, she went there with a friend, Mrs. Margaret McKenzie, to meet Mother Teresa. She dates the founding of the Co-Workers from that July day.

Ann Blaikie told Mother Teresa that she and her friends could make over children's toys for the Christmas party. Mother Teresa said that would be good but she would rather have dresses, shirts, and pants for the poor children.

"Mother Teresa," Ann Blaikie related, "bundled Margaret and me into the van and we drove with her to the next stop, the Home for the Dying. Margaret was also pregnant. Right from the start, Mother Teresa took charge. We told her we would follow her suggestion. Margaret is an artist and she designed tinfoil angels which were made by our friends and sold for quite a sum of money. Mother Teresa and I went to the bazaar and bought practical clothes. We repaired and remade numbers of toys as well.

"After Christmas, Mother Teresa came to our group to thank us. We were, I fear, quite smug that we had done so well. After words of thanks, she said, 'Now I would like you to start gathering new clothes for the children for Diwali, and for the Muslim festival.' I could see in my mind's eye the Hindu festival of Diwali that lit up Calcutta around October—and also the time of the Muslim festival. I realized we had a year's work ahead of us. So, we were 'hooked.' "

As Ann Blaikie and other Co-Workers were to realize, they were not "hooked" simply to become "Lady Bountifuls" giving an occasional thought to the poor, but bound to a new awareness of the needs of the community around them. They were not simply to give of their surpluses, but of their time, their energy, their necessities, their resources of talent, and they were to reach out to the poorest of the poor from whom they might shrink in revulsion. In Calcutta, this meant the poor lepers.

"That is how the Co-Workers actually got started," Ann Blaikie related. "And my daughter was born that August. She reminds me that if she had not come into the world at that time, the Co-Workers might not have taken their start with me."

The women who gathered for help to the needy, including those served by Mother Teresa, called themselves the Marian Society, the name deriving from the fact that they started work in a year designated as the Marian Year. During that year, Catholics were to intensify their devotion to the Mother of Jesus through prayer and the practice of virtues. Ann Blaikie and the group soon became deeply involved with Mother Teresa's work for lepers, helping to organize Flag Days with a bold slogan that resurrected a taboo only to demolish it, namely, "Touch the Leper with Your Compassion." On Flag Days, which began in 1956, volunteers stood at street-corners ringing bells to remind Calcuttans of the needs of lepers. Posters were everywhere. The six words of the theme were inscribed in a circle around a hand holding a bell—reminiscent of the bell with which lepers used to warn people of their coming.

This activity became known throughout Calcutta and soon had the support of non-Catholics as well as Catholics, of Indians and Anglo-Indians, and members of the consular staffs of the United States and other countries.

While visiting the Calcutta and Howrah leper stations with Mother Teresa in 1958, I knew that her desire was a permanent leper dispensary and a refuge for them. Ann Blaikie accompanied Mother Teresa to the opening of such a center in March 1959 in Titagarh. Close to 250 lepers attended the function and a work was begun simply and humbly that was to expand to reach many thousands of afflicted people. The Titagarh center was the one Mother Teresa chose to rededicate sixteen years later during the Silver Jubilee of the Society, as the Gandhiji Prem Nivas Center.

Besides giving their time to the lepers, to the children and the dying, the volunteers took on other tasks. One of these was giving the young Sisters from all over India English lessons, as English was the language of the congregation. Men joined in the work. In addition to helping in the men's ward at Kalighat, those who had the use of cars chauffeured the Sisters, when necessary, and picked up the sick poor in emergency situations.

Frank Collins of the American consulate gave his free time to driving Mother Teresa, the Sisters, and the needy. Mother Teresa considered him her "right-hand man" for urgent transportation needs. His wife, Violet Collins, was given a unique task. Interest in the work of Mother Teresa was evinced by officials from the Philippines and a confidential report on the overall work was requested. Violet Collins took on the task. She put aside all other concerns to produce a detailed account of Mother Teresa and the development of her work. This was dispatched to the Philippines. The result was announced in 1962. Mother Teresa had been chosen to receive one of the Magsaysay Awards. She was judged one of the worthiest women of Asia because of her work for international understanding. The prizes, made possible by a grant from the Rockefeller Brothers Fund, were made in honor of Ramon Magsaysay, the Philippine President killed in an airplane crash. Mother Teresa had to fly to Manila to receive the prize, her first trip outside of India since the 1960 visit to the United States. From Hong Kong, she wrote me, "Here I am alone. How I would love you to be here. But you can't have all the good things."

In Manila, she found that the monetary gift accompanying the award was the equivalent of 50,000 rupees. It was just sufficient to carry out an urgent plan, the opening of a children's home in Agra. Mother Teresa wrote to Frank and Violet Collins, "After God, I owe the Magsaysay

Award to you both, especially Mrs. Collins who has taken all the trouble and given so much of your precious time. 'Thank you' does not really express what I want to say," she continued, but promised to pray for them and for their family.

I came to know the American members of the Marian Society in Calcutta in 1958 and attended a meeting at the home of Mrs. Muriel Hansen, member of a prominent black Catholic family of New York City. Her husband was in the American foreign service, as was Mrs. Katherine Bracken, who threw herself into the work of the Sisters. Mother Teresa wrote me, "Mrs. Bracken has transformed Shishu Bhavan and comes to Kalighat for real hard work every Sunday." Mrs. Bracken took on a personal project to mark the birthday of the Missionaries of Charity on October 7—the supplying of ice cream for all Sisters at the Motherhouse. After her retirement from the foreign service, she arranged for an annual delivery of ice cream, increased each year according to the Sisters; the stipulation was that it be consumed by them, and not sent to Shishu Bhavan.

Also active in Calcutta, besides the women in the Marian Society, were people of professional skills, like Dr. Sen, who gave his retirement years to the leprosy work, and a Jewish dentist who gave free service to the poor. Mother Teresa wrote me about a businessman who came forward to meet an urgent need.

"A Hindu gentleman, Mr. Guha," she wrote, "when he heard that we had trouble with the water, put in a tube well in the convent. So, you see, God is spoiling us."

Those with great skills and abundant resources were joined by people of little skills and almost no resources, who felt part of a great work of mercy in doing "small things with great love."

One day a week, Ann Blaikie took Mother on her rounds.

"I took her to the bazaars in the poorest quarter of Calcutta," she recounted, "to Mother and Child Clinics, to leprosy centers, and to the Home for the Dying. We went to the Bengal Ministry of Health when we were coordinating the leprosy appeal throughout Calcutta. I remember the reply of a young Indian medical assistant after Mother Teresa had thanked him for his work. 'But, Mother,' he said, 'we are all a little better for knowing you.'

"One day, when we were together in downtown Calcutta, a young man came up to her. He bent down and touched her feet. Mother Teresa raised him up and he launched into a rush of words. He seemed very happy. What he told her was that he was getting married that day. He had been brought to the Home for the Dying as a beggar close to death. Nursed back to life, he was set up by the Sisters in the business of shining shoes. He was now a self-respecting citizen about to marry and set up a little home. Mother Teresa's joy was wonderful to see. This was the epitome of all she had set out to do, to give a beggar back his life and dignity.

"Mother Teresa had no telephone in those days. One day I sent a message that I couldn't come for her because I had a fever. Her remark was, 'I also had a fever, but it is better to burn in this world than in the next.' "

❧

After spending the years from 1950 to 1960 in Calcutta, the Blaikie family returned to England to settle in Surrey. Ann Blaikie found that others of Mother Teresa's helpers from Calcutta were living nearby. Mother Teresa put Ann Blaikie in touch with a young man, John Southworth, who had helped her leprosy work through the Order of Charity. A Mother Teresa Committee was formed with Southworth as Chairman and Ann Blaikie as Vice-Chairman. The wives of businessmen, who had returned to England from Calcutta, formed the nucleus of the group. An impetus was given to the work by Mother Teresa's visit to London in November 1960 when, as related in Chapter 10, she made her first television appearance. Soon Ann Blaikie became Chairman of the committee and went on to lead the association as it became international.

Ann Simons Blaikie began life in a sedate Anglican parsonage in Kent. Her father, an erudite rector, who read the Scriptures in Hebrew and Greek, was steeped in scriptural and theological studies. Ann Simons led a sheltered life as a child, playing with a limited group of children from families close to the established church. Through a college friend, she met a young Englishman of Scotch-Irish forebears. He was studying law, was a Catholic, and a graduate of the famous Ampleforth School run by the Benedictine order. After war service in China and India, John Blaikie returned to England where he and Ann renewed their friendship. He began work in Shanghai and Ann joined him there, their marriage taking place in 1947.

Ann Simons Blaikie entered the Catholic Church and the three children born to the couple, a son and two daughters, were baptized into the same faith. The bond between Ann Blaikie and Mother Teresa became even stronger after the death of John Blaikie in 1974, after which the Association of Co-Workers absorbed her life.

Those of us who were close to Mother Teresa knew that she wanted a lay association to work in the same spirit as the Society she had founded. It took a little while to realize where her ideas were taking her—and us. The association was first thought by people like Patricia Kump, the first Chairman for the United States, to be a sort of auxiliary to the Missionaries of Charity. Finally, Mother Teresa made it clear; she wanted no auxiliary dedicated to collecting funds and supplies. What she had in mind was a spiritual family which would be united in a vision of "the other," especially the suffering shunned and rejected, as the repository of the divine. There were precedents for a lay association linked with a congregation and partaking of its particular dimension of spirituality. The Third Order of St. Francis allowed lay people to follow the spiritual path of St. Francis. The sixteenth rule of the Third Order reflected the peacemaking spirit of St. Francis. At a time when local princes could conscript men bound by the feudal oath to fight in their endless conflicts, Francis freed his Third Order followers from the feudal oath. The men who entered the Third Order were not to bear arms. "They are not to take up lethal weapons or bear them about against anybody," were the words of the rule, a rule which profoundly altered feudal society. The monastic order of Benedictines, dating back to the sixth century, also had its lay association, the Third Order of St. Benedict. Lay people learned from the Benedictine Rule the virtues of hospitality and of work as prayer. The Third Order of St. Francis and the Third Order of St. Benedict served successive generations of Catholics, giving them in a changing world the spiritual sustenance derived from great spiritual traditions.

The association envisioned by Mother Teresa was to be affiliated with the Missionaries of Charity and since Mother Teresa was head of a recognized society within the Catholic Church, she presented its rules to the head of the Church, Pope Paul VI.

Sister Anand wrote, "On March 23, 1969, Mother Teresa visited our Sisters in the small convent on the edge of Rome. She drew up with Mr. and Mrs. John Blaikie and Fräulein Josepha Gosselke the regulations for the International Association of the Co-Workers of Mother Teresa. On the twenty-sixth of March, the three of them had the great honor of handing the regulations to the Holy Father. The Holy Father blessed those who were present, the order of the Missionaries of Charity and the Co-Workers in all the world."

The Co-Workers of Mother Teresa were recognized and the regulations became the constitutions. Mrs. Ann Blaikie was named as Chairman in the constitution after Mother Teresa and Sister Frederick. Her title was soon changed to International Link. Jacqueline de Decker was named as the Link with Sick and Suffering Co-Workers.

There was a significant difference between the Co-Workers and the Third Order of St. Benedict of Nursia or of St. Francis of Assisi. The two older organizations were designed for members of the Catholic Church. The Co-Workers of Mother Teresa were to cut across all religious barriers. The first paragraph stated: "The International Association of Co-Workers of Mother Teresa consists of men, women, young people, and children of all religions and denominations throughout the world, who seek to love God in their fellowmen, through wholehearted service to the poorest of the poor of all castes and creeds, and who wish to unite themselves in a spirit of prayer and sacrifice with the work of Mother Teresa and the Missionaries of Charity."

Without publicity, without the expenditure of funds, an international association that had been growing was now brought into formal life. Perhaps the word formal might be misleading, since what Mother Teresa wanted was the spirit of the family and she later was to call the Co-Workers "a most disorganized organization." With the use of poor means, the sharing of mimeographed newsletters describing the work of the Sisters, Brothers, and Co-Workers, the association flourished. Ann Blaikie, catching the inspiration of Mother Teresa, found Co-Workers who gave their time to the preparation of the International Newsletter, to collating reports, typing them, copying them on a mimeograph machine, and mailing them. Copies were sent not only to groups of Co-Workers as soon as they were set up, but to every house of the Sisters and Brothers. Every year a report of the growth of the Sisters and Brothers was an annual feature of the newsletter. Ann Blaikie received the statistics and figures on the Sisters and Brothers from Calcutta. A list of addresses was carefully kept up to date.

There were no dues. Meetings were to be held without the serving of food so that they could be held in the homes of the poor. Only water could be served. Sharing and prayer were to mark the gatherings of the Co-Workers. "Sharing" referred to experiences of compassion and a deeper reflection on them, so that, in Mother Teresa's words, "Co-Workers could be enriched by each other."

The bedrock of the Association was prayer and the constitution carried the text of two prayers which the Co-Workers were asked to pray daily in union with the Missionaries of Charity, a prayer which begged for the grace to merit serving the poor, seen as "the ambassadors of God."

The first was a short prayer of Pope Paul VI:

Make us worthy, Lord,
To serve our fellowmen
Throughout the world
Who live and die in poverty
  and hunger.
Give them, through our hands,
This day their daily bread;
And by our understanding love,
Give peace and joy.

The second was the prayer attributed to St. Francis, long called a simple prayer, and recited by millions throughout the world. Whether or not it came from the "Little Poor Man" himself seems hardly relevant, since it breathes his spirit:

> Lord, make me an instrument
> of your peace,
> That where there is hatred,
> I may bring love;
> that where there is wrong, I may bring
> the spirit of forgiveness,
> that where there is discord, I may
> bring harmony;
> that where there is error, I may
> bring truth;
> that where there is doubt,
> I may bring faith;
> that where there is despair, I
> may bring hope;
> that where there are shadows,
> I may bring light;
> that where there is sadness, joy.
>
> Lord, grant that I may seek
> rather to comfort,
> than to be comforted;
> To understand than to be
> understood;
> To love than to be loved,
> For it is by forgetting self
> That one finds;
> It is by dying that one awakens
> to eternal life.

These prayers were printed by the various national groups in different languages around the world, French, German, Spanish, Swedish, Hungarian, Korean, Chinese, Bengali, Hindi, Malayalam, and the other languages of India.

The constitution stated that "The Co-Workers of Mother Teresa recognize that all the goods of the world—including gifts of mind and body, advantages of birth and education—are the free gifts of God, and that no one has the right to a superfluity of wealth while others are dying of starvation and suffering from every kind of want. They seek to right this grave injustice by the exercise of *voluntary poverty* and the *sacrifice of luxuries* in their way of life."

Besides the daily prayers, the Co-Workers were urged to pray together and to hold a Day of Prayer and Thanksgiving, along with the Sisters and Brothers, on October 7, the anniversary of the founding of the Society.

The other lay person named in the Co-Worker constitution, Jacqueline de Decker, embodied a special strand of Mother Teresa's life and was present at the Nobel ceremonies in Oslo. She was able to make her way about only with the aid of canes and an encasement of rigid steel braces around her body. She was listed as the Link with those described in the constitution as: "The Sick and those unable to join in activities may become a close Co-Worker of an individual Sister or Brother by offering their prayers and sufferings for each Sister and Brother."

When I accompanied Mother Teresa to the home of Jacqueline de Decker in Antwerp, we found ourselves in a home of culture with books, wall tapestries, and an array of family photographs. Jacqueline de Decker's face was of striking beauty, with large gray eyes of unusual clarity and skin of transparent whiteness. Jacqueline took out a prized possession, a box holding letters received from Mother Teresa and dating back to 1950. I realized that the two women were twin spirits. Jacqueline had nourished the same dream as Mother Teresa, that of working among India's poor as one of them, sharing their dress and poverty. It was evident that the home she had been prepared to abandon was one of comfort, even affluence.

"From the age of seventeen," she related, "I wanted to be a missionary. I met a Jesuit father who wished to form a team of skilled lay people to start a school for social and medical training in India."

Eight young Belgian Catholics were ready for the venture, a venture wrecked by the Second World War. Trained as a nurse, with a degree in sociology from the Catholic University of Louvain, Jacqueline became a wartime nurse. She served the sick and wounded of the occupied city of Antwerp and kept on serving through the heavy bombardments of 1944 after the city's recapture by the Allied forces. Of the prewar group of eight, some died, others entered the convent or married. Only Jacqueline persisted. On the last day of December 1946, she boarded a ship for India. As she did, a telegram was handed to her announcing the sudden death of the priest committed to the project.

In Madras, Bishop Mathias, who had initiated the program, suggested that she learn the local language and she began the study of Tamil.

India was on the road to freedom and the Gandhian program of village uplift was already in action in the area. Jacqueline took up work in a village dispensary in Gokulam near Madras. The bishop had left for the United States to gather funds for the original project. Jacqueline was left with the limited funds she brought with her. She gave her services free and managed to live, as she put it, on a quarter of an American dollar a day. She slept on the floor and began to dress in the sari, identifying with Indian culture.

"I was happy to be poor," she said of those days. It was the sari that actually brought about her meeting with Mother Teresa. A Jesuit priest in Madras told her in 1948 of another sari-wearer, a nun in Calcutta who had put aside her traditional habit to work with the poor. This nun he told her, was staying just then with the American Medical Mission Sisters in Patna.

"I went to Patna," she related, "and there I met Mother Teresa for the first time. It was in the chapel. She was there after the tiring day's work, alone, wrapped in prayer. When we came to know each other, we talked a lot. We worked together. She told me she wanted to remain a nun and hoped to have companions. But she left it to the Lord.

"I told her that before starting to work with her, I had to go back to Belgium to take care of a pain in the back. In Belgium I began to get paralyzed in one arm, then the eye, then the leg. The doctors decided that they would have to graft a spinal vertebra."

Jacqueline had been convinced that her vocation to use her gifts in India was of the Spirit. She faced with anguish the realization that she was to live out her days far from India and to undergo repeated surgery to stave off paralysis. Eventually, the operations on her spine numbered twenty.

"I wrote to Mother Teresa," she related, "and straightway the answer was, 'May I ask you to offer everything for me and the work?' This was in 1950. Later, she asked me to find one sick and suffering person for each young woman who came to join her in the work."

Jacqueline de Decker showed me letters that lit up her life because they allowed her a share in the work she longed to do. Mother Teresa wrote to her in October 1952 from 14 Creek Lane, from the upper room where the first candidates joined her.

"Why not become spiritually bound to our Society which you love so dearly. While we work in the slums, you share in the merit, the prayers, and the work with your sufferings and prayers. The work is tremendous and I need workers, it is true, but I need souls like yours to pray and suffer for the work."

Calling Jacqueline her sister, Mother Teresa told her that she would be a true Missionary of Charity, "in body in Belgium but in soul in India." Mother Teresa reminded her, "Our Lord must love you much to give you so great a part in His suffering. Be brave and cheerful and offer much for me—that I may bring many souls to God"—and in another letter, "You are a burning light which is being consumed for souls."

Jacqueline de Decker agreed to become spiritually bound with the Society and to find other handicapped people who would offer up their sufferings for a Missionary of Charity. In January 1953, Mother Teresa sent her the names of the first twenty-seven novices to be linked with sick and suffering persons. They were all linked with the crippled and other incurably ill people whom Jacqueline came to know in her own travail. So began a program which united two great mysteries, the mystery of the redemptive power of innocent suffering and the mystery of what has been called the "communion of saints." This communion is seen as transcending all physical barriers in the spiritual union of all human beings of good will, human beings desiring to unite their wills with that of the Creator.

"I am very happy," Mother Teresa wrote to a Suffering Co-Worker, "that you are willing to join the suffering members of the Missionaries of Charity . . . . Your sufferings and prayers will be the chalice in which we working members will pour in the love of souls. Therefore, you are just as important and necessary for the fulfillment of our aim . . . . In reality, you can do much more on your bed of pain than I running on my feet, but you and I together can do all things in Him who strengthens me . . ."

As the Co-Workers grew, Sick and Suffering members from various countries were put in touch with her and she supplied them with the names of Sisters and Brothers. All her letters were written by hand, as was the letter she wrote to me for the newsletter of the International Co-Workers.

"There are now 2,600 Sick and Suffering persons linked with the Missionaries of Charity. France still has the largest number, with 310 individual Sick and Suffering and about 250 more who live in homes for the aged and are aged religious Sisters. There are Sick and Suffering persons in twenty-six other countries. During the past year, Brazil, Yugoslavia, and Switzerland joined the program." As the work grew, a Link for the Sick and Suffering was named in each country to coordinate the work with Jacqueline de Decker.

Despite frequent pain and the difficulty of moving about, Jacqueline traveled to various countries in Europe to further the program and spent laborious hours listing the linked Sick and Suffering and the Missionaries of Charity and writing her own letters to console those who confided in her. She called her work "a great chain of love, prayers, suffering, and apostolate around the world" and often quoted Mother Teresa that "Suffering itself may be nothing but suffering shared with Christ's passion is a wonderful gift."

Letters from the Sisters brought new awareness into the lives of Suffering Co-Workers.

A Sister Link wrote from India to her Suffering lay Link, "Really, you are a special gift given to me by our good Lord. I am working among leprosy patients. They suffer because of the loss of their hands, legs, or eyesight—and eventually the healthy people look down on them. But when we talk to them, and smile at them, their eyes are shining out of happiness. When they come to us, their flesh is often eaten by sores or insects, but after some weeks of care, their wounds become dry and they say with a big smile, 'Thank you, Sister.' "

Mother Teresa carried the message of fruitful suffering to every place she visited. One evening, after a talk at St. Olaf's Church in Minneapolis, Minnesota, there was time for questioning. A woman in a wheelchair, whose body was in continuous, uncontrolled motion, raised her right arm. Through waving unremittingly, it became clear that she wanted to ask a question. Formed with great effort, the question was finally grasped through her distorted speech.

"What can people like me do?"

"You can do the most," replied Mother Teresa without hesitation. "You are the ones who live with Jesus on the cross every day. You pray the work with us and help give us the strength to work."

After the meeting, the woman whose name was Dorothy Wojciak was wheeled into the vestry of St. Olaf's Church for a talk with Mother Teresa. We were told that this victim of cerebral palsy, whose body by pragmatic standards was "useless," was a woman of brilliant mind. She made herself understood to Mother Teresa despite impaired speech and the incessant movement of her head which seemed to be maneuvered back and forth by relentless strings. Mother Teresa spent time recounting how the Sisters and Brothers rely on the prayers of people like her in their daily work among the dying, the leprosy patients, the unwanted.

"You can really do the most," she repeated. I do not think I ever saw a face so suffused with joy as was Dorothy Wojciak's during that talk. She agreed to carry out the work with the Sick and Suffering Co-Workers in the Minneapolis area with the National Chairman, Patty Kump, who lived near her. They became close friends.

Dorothy Wojciak was brought in her wheelchair to the meetings of the Minneapolis-St. Paul Co-Workers and was for the Co-Worker family a spiritual light.

"We can never obtain complete happiness on earth," she said, "for happiness is found only in heaven. And we cannot obtain it if we give in to our despair. We are fortunate to have a share in Christ's cross."

She suggested a prayer: "Give us this day the grace to live now as you intend, dear God; to smile even when our burdens seem heavy and our hearts seem broken. Let us be charitable and humble in humiliation and in our inconveniences. Above all, O Merciful Lord, let us suffer without regret, for in your will, and in our gracious acceptance of that same holy will lives our eternal destiny. Thanks be to God." She died the year following her meeting with Mother Teresa—at the age of forty-three.

Mother Teresa, with her genius for the concrete, had clothed a mysterious and transcendent concept, that of the redemptive power of innocent suffering, in a personalized and concrete program of participation in a worldwide work of mercy. There was no "useless body" for the Sick and Suffering program or for anyone who grasped its meaning.

Her letters to the Sick and Suffering Co-Workers revealed their importance to her and to the work. "How happy I am to have you all," she wrote. "Often when the work is very hard, I think of you—and tell God—look at my suffering children, and for their love, bless this work. And it works immediately. So, you see, you are our treasure house—the powerhouse of the Missionaries of Charity." She called them "the faithful branch," sharing in the Passion of Christ.

As each Sister or Brother was to see the Sick and Suffering Co-Worker as a "second self," so Mother Teresa saw Jacqueline de Decker as a "second self." When Jacqueline's seasons of pain were at their most extreme, she offered them with greater intensity for Mother Teresa, who began to sense the times of trial of her "second self."

Many ordinary people grasped Mother Teresa's insistence on the crucial role of innocent suffering, willingly accepted and offered for others, as it applied to their daily lives. It gave meaning to lives of pain and, as she assured them, helped those who confronted the pain of others in their day-to-day work. Innocent suffering, she said in so many ways, was redemptive for humanity at large, as was the vicarious suffering of Jesus. In an age when monstrous suffering was inflicted on the innocent, people seemed willing to pay attention to a woman whose entire life was an argument against the "uselessness" of suffering. Many who grasped Mother Teresa's outlook might not have realized that the man who led India into freedom shared it. Gandhi saw innocent suffering not only in its personal light, but as the heart of his nonviolent movement to replace colonial shackles with self-rule. He called it *satyagraha,* (truth force), and his followers *satyagrahi,* practitioners of "truth force." "*Satyagraha,*" said Gandhi, "is the argument of suffering . . . . Success is the certain result of suffering voluntarily undergone."

As Gandhi saw it, love for the opponent, shown by accepting rather than inflicting suffering, was the true path to an eventual change of heart by the oppressor. The Satyagrahi need not feel powerless, said Gandhi, because "the living God of Truth and Love is with the Satyagrahi." In seeing the transcendent and mysterious power of innocent suffering, Mother Teresa and Gandhi met.

"God bless you for your lovely letter. I just enjoyed every line of it and I told the Sisters about you and your wonderful husband Warren and of your dear little ones, and so you are all in our big family now."

This was Mother Teresa's first letter to Patricia Burke Kump early in 1960. The 1958 article in *Jubilee* magazine about Mother Teresa and the work in Calcutta had moved Mrs. Kump so that she wrote to Mother Teresa and expressed her deep desire to be associated with her work in a personal way. She and her husband had enclosed a donation for the work.

"Your gift is very precious to me because of the love that makes this gift," Mother Teresa wrote. "Yes, I will pray for you and you must also pray for me that I may help my 119 Sisters to come closer to the heart of Jesus. So let us both now keep close to Jesus and from His heart ask the one grace for each—that we become holy according to His Heart."

As with Ann Blaikie, the association with Mother Teresa changed and enriched the future life of a young mother. Patricia Burke, a young woman of dark Irish beauty was an airline stewardess when she met Warren Kump, a young medical student. When Patty, as she preferred to call herself, and Warren were married, they looked forward to children. Their commitment to each other was complete and their marriage was one of deep happiness. They discovered that their marriage would be childless and decided to share their happiness as adoptive parents. A baby girl became theirs and, in just over a year, a baby boy. In the three following years, another baby girl and a baby boy were welcomed into their home, the simple but well-run home of a struggling young doctor.

"It was a time of great wonder for me," Patty explained, "having children of our own. But it was a time of weariness, too, trying to keep house and take care of the little ones. The pictures in *Jubilee* of a woman wearying herself for the poor and suffering of a great city stayed with me. I could not get it out of my mind. Her spiritual outlook captured me completely."

By the end of the year, Patty's enthusiasm for Mother Teresa's life and work spread to their close friends. In January 1961, a small group had formed, young doctors and their wives, all eager to become members of Mother Teresa's "big family." In a letter of May 1961, Mother Teresa told them, "I would like you to call yourselves the Co-Workers of Mother Teresa. I want you to share in our work to the full."

Just as she had spiritually prepared the leaders of the Co-Workers who had started in Calcutta and then later returned to England, she impressed the spirit of the organization on the young woman involved with the first green shoots of the movement in the United States.

By the middle of 1961, there were three small groups meeting in the Minneapolis area, praying together and finding ways to help those around them.

"How proud I feel of you and Warren and our little groups of Co-Workers there with you. Please God, there will be many more such groups. Make many all over the city, over the U.S., over the world, but keep them, like yours, in small groups. Your material help is great, but your holiness of life is a much greater help to me. Often, very often, I think of you all and when I am in difficulty offer to God your prayers and sacrifices and for certain help comes. I am sure you will keep Warren's birthday this month beautifully. I wish I could be a bird to come across to you and then come back to India."

A letter of September 1963 said, "I am so happy that you are my Co-Workers and that you are growing in fervor and sanctity . . . From now on, I will try to send extracts of the First Friday lessons I write to my Sisters."

As the story of the nun on the streets of Calcutta was becoming known throughout the United States and people spontaneously sent donations to Calcutta, Mother Teresa would send a packet of her replies to Patty Kump for forwarding. This gave rise to correspondence with other Americans who were eager to become Co-Workers. With the four children, Theresa, named for Mother Teresa, Lee, Mary, and John, in school, Patty Kump planned her time to keep the growing correspondence up to date. Groups began to be formed in New York, Chicago, New Orleans, and in smaller communities across the continent. Mother Teresa addressed a letter through Patty Kump for all the groups.

> My dear Co-Workers,
>
> Be true Co-Workers of Christ. Radiate and live His life. Be an angel of comfort to the sick, a friend to the little ones, and love each other as God loves each one of you with a special, most intense love. Be kind to each other in your homes. Be kind to those who surround you. I prefer that you make mistakes in kindness rather than that you work miracles in unkindness. Often just for one word, one look, one quick action, and darkness fills the heart of the one we love.

After the constitution of the International Co-Workers was adopted, Mother Teresa asked Patty Kump to be the chairman for the American branch which was formally constituted in New York City on December 8, 1971.

Monsignor J. Richard Feiten, a priest Co-Worker, celebrated mass for a little group of twelve people from various parts of the United States. Feiten, a leader of Catholic Charities in Minnesota, had seen Mother Teresa's work in Calcutta on a trip organized by supporters of Catholic Relief Services. Patty Kump wrote to Mother Teresa about the event and the first Co-Worker newsletter carried Mother Teresa's reply.

"I fully approve of the Co-Workers of Mother Teresa in America which was formed in New York on the eighth of December 1971, with Mrs. Warren Kump as Chairman, Mrs. Lavern Sykora as Secretary, Monsignor J. Richard Feiten as Treasurer, Dr. Warren Kump and Eileen Egan as Consultants and Mrs. Rama Coomaraswamy as Legal Consultant."

"Let us from the beginning try to live the spirit of the Missionaries of

Charity which is one of total surrender to God, loving and trusting each other, and cheerfulness with all."

Bernadette Coomaraswamy was not the only former resident of Calcutta in the early Co-Workers. The regional chairmen for Washington, D.C., were Mr. and Mrs. Frank Collins.

Monsignor Feiten of Winona, Minnesota, felt that his burden as treasurer would be light, since in the newsletter, he informed all those who wished to help Mother Teresa's work to forward their gifts to Catholic Relief Services since the work of the Missionaries of Charity was part of its overall aid program for India. However, the donations soon began to mount up to the proportions of a blizzard. In a year the Co-Workers were incorporated as a legal entity, so that donations could be sent directly to the treasurer. Patty Kump's Co-Worker family grew to the demands of the task. A Co-Worker with the speed of wind on her electric typewriter, Mrs. Robert Hattery, became assistant treasurer and volunteered to help Monsignor Feiten in keeping records and sending letters of gratitude. Diane Hattery, a graduate of the University of Indiana and a former teacher, was the mother of two children. Her husband, a friend of Warren Kump's, was also in the medical profession. Diane organized her home life so that she could spend six and sometimes more hours a day replying to donors. Every donated penny went to the work of the Missionaries of Charity.

Diane and her husband were converts to the Catholic Church. Searching for a spiritual home, they felt they had to make a decision when Angela, their first child, was born. They were drawn to the Catholic Church and wanted the child to be baptized in it. They studied the faith and took instruction in it. When it came time for the baptism of their child, both mother and father were also baptized.

Year in and year out with the loving zest of a Co-Worker, Diane pounded out letters of thanks for gifts that permitted Mother Teresa to expand the efforts of the Missionaries of Charity on behalf of the suffering and neglected members of the human family. The gifts were spontaneous, arising from film showings, from continued sales of *Something Beautiful for God* in paperback, from the talks and travels of Mother Teresa, from her recorded talks made available by the Co-Workers, and from the unflagging attention of the media, including her appearance on the cover of *Time* magazine. The generosity of the American people increased each year, until for several years the donations exceeded a million dollars annually. Monsignor Richard Feiten and Diane Hattery diligently assumed an immense burden, giving in Minnesota "wholehearted free service" that in turn helped the Missionaries of Charity to give "wholehearted free service" in the neediest corners of the globe.

The volunteer service of the American Co-Workers was not unique, nor was the generosity of the American people. In Germany, contributions built up over the years until they often reached a total of a million and a half dollars annually. Under the chairmanship of Josepha Gosselke and the Co-Worker treasurer, a team of Co-Worker volunteers recorded and transmitted every gift, from the tiniest mite to large donations. Free service in acknowledging and transmitting funds was given by Co-Workers in England, Ireland, Holland, Belgium, France, Denmark, Sweden, Italy, Australia, and other countries as Co-Worker branches were set up.

As Missionaries of Charity opened houses in such countries as the United States, Mother Teresa asked that all gifts be sent directly to the Sisters. She wanted the direct contact between donors and Sisters. In the United States, the Missionaries of Charity could by then offer the donors the tax deductability allowed for charitable donations. Gifts continued to come in and the Sisters in New York took on the task of acknowledging, recording, and transmitting them. The same changeover took place in Germany, where Sister Anand, already mentioned as of German origin, had become superior and in every country where there were teams of Missionaries of Charity.

Mother Teresa became ever more explicit about forbidding the Co-Workers to solicit or collect money for the work.

"I don't want the Co-Workers to become a business," she insisted, "but to remain a work of love. I want you to have that complete confidence that God won't let us down. Take Him at His word and seek first the kingdom of God, and all else will be added on. Joy, peace, and unity are more important than money. If God wants me to do something, He gives me the money."

Around the world, the stream of gifts continued to flow in, from the small gifts of those who "gave until it hurt," to larger gifts from those who felt the hurt less, but still might have forfeited a luxury or pleasure. Through the gifts, bonds were forged between the Missionaries of Charity and those whose participation in the work consisted in supplying vitally necessary funds.

Co-Workers in the various countries held a national meeting once a year. Whenever possible, Mother Teresa found time to meet with her Co-Worker family. Because of the great distances, the American Co-Workers held their national meeting only every two years. Mother Teresa was able to attend most of them. She was present at the first national meeting, one that, perhaps because of its location, helped cement the Co-Workers spiritually in a powerful way.

It lasted for three memorable days of October 1972 in the lonely setting of an abbey of Cistercian monks, or Trappists, the legendary men of silence and austerity within the body of the Catholic Church. Each monk carried the initials O.C.S.O. after his name, Order of Cistercians of the Strict Observance. They did not impose their strict observance of a meatless diet on the guests. The Abbey of the Holy Trinity was located in two thousand acres of a desertlike expanse in Utah in the Great American West.

The invitation had come from Abbot Emmanuel through the efforts of Brother Nicholas, another fruitful effect of his stay in Calcutta. The twelve founding members of the American Co-Workers were among the eighteen who responded to the invitation. They came from every part of the nation. Patty Kump and Msgr. Richard Feiten came from Minnesota and Mrs. Maurine Patterson from Wisconsin. From the inner city of Detroit came Fr. Edward Farrell, pastor and spiritual writer. From the West Coast came Fr. Don Kribs, and from the South, the city of New Orleans, Sr. Mary John, a Benedictine Sister. Mrs. Del Prinster journeyed from Colorado and Frank and Vi Collins from Washington, D.C. From the East Coast came Bernadette Coomaraswamy from Connecticut and myself from New York City. For many, the retreat-meeting represented their vacation.

At the Salt Lake City Airport, we found Brother Nicholas awaiting us. We were taken in vans past Temple Square, with its golden angel shining from a pinnacle over the Church of Jesus Christ of Latter-day Saints, known as Mormons. Then the journey led through the wide-open expanse of the American West.

We knew the Abbey was poor, but we somehow were expecting some conventional sign of a religious establishment, a chapel tower or a tall spire piercing the blue air. What we came upon was of unimaginable simplicity, a collection of large Quonset huts left over after the Second World War and shored up by patient carpentry and cement blocks. This was the Abbey that in 1971 had sent its savings of twenty thousand dollars to Mother Teresa for work among refugees and for those who returned destitute to Bangladesh after their hapless sojourn in Calcutta's Salt Lake.

Priests and male Co-Workers shared the monastery with the monks, while the women were given hospitality in a simple frame house at the entrance to the monastery grounds.

A daughter abbey to Gethsemani Abbey where Thomas Merton had written *Seven Story Mountain,* about his conversion and calling to the Cistercian life, the Abbey of the Holy Trinity now had thirty-six monks.

When we joined the monastic mass at dawn, we found ourselves in one of the converted Quonset huts, its spacious arch totally white except for darts of blue, yellow, orange, and green from a window made of jagged pieces of stained glass. We seemed enveloped in an unearthly radiance, of which the monks, in their white robes, were a part.

Mother Teresa had accepted with good reason to come to an abbey in a remote desertlike expanse to meet with Co-Workers who were to lead the movement in the coming years. All of them, though committed to Jesus, were caught up in an activist life and were part of a society in which rampant consumerism subtly but inexorably entered the spirit. Here, hidden in the vast expanse of Utah, were monks who had broken utterly and irrevocably with the values of this society and were living their lives in daily, hourly communion with eternal values. We all brought our worries and our questions about our own lives, our futures, the future of the Co-Workers. Churning inside us were unanswered questions, unresolved problems. It was as though we had come to hear that unforgettable command given to the churning waters of Galilee, "Peace, be still!" There, if anywhere, we could ponder the reality that "God is the friend of silence."

Mother Teresa told us, "If we really love Jesus in the poor, then our first connection must be with Him. Only after that can we really see Him in the poor."

She told us in many ways and with many examples that as Co-Workers, we must "be" before we can "do." She told us of a priest who came to her and told her he wanted to be rid of the rigidities of the priesthood. The priestly life kept him from really serving the poor, he said. So, he gave up his priesthood and went to the poor.

"What has he to give the poor now?" she asked. "Only himself. As a priest, he could bring them Jesus." Mother Teresa told of one of the Brothers who came to her and told her that his vocation was to serve the lepers. His love was for them and he longed to spend himself for them. He did not want to be assigned to any other work.

" 'Your vocation, Brother,' " she told him flatly and unequivocally, " 'is not to serve the lepers. It is to belong to Jesus. He has chosen you for Himself; the work is the means to put your love for Christ in action, but your vocation is to belong to Jesus.' He changed completely. Now it doesn't matter whether he is cooking or washing or cleaning the streets or taking care of the lepers. It is 'I belong to Jesus and that is all that matters.' "

The lessons were not lost on the Co-Workers. The examples of firebrands for social justice who continually "gave of themselves" until they ended up emotionally "burnt-out cases" had shaken many of us.

"Let God use you without consulting you," was a maxim Mother Teresa gave us and it became the theme of many Co-Worker gatherings. It was her way of phrasing the traditional spiritual advice of "resignation to the will of God," a timeworn phrase that had lost much of its resonance.

"Let the Lord catch you," she would say. "Let yourself be caught by Him and then let Him dispose of you utterly.

"Love to pray and pray frequently during the day," was something we could hardly forget. Prayer in common was also crucially important. She told us how the Sisters grew closer to each other in community through a

Mother Teresa with Sister Frederick at Basilica of St. Clare, Assisi, May 1982. *(Ann Petrie)*

London—Prince Philip and Dr. Eugene Carson Blake at the presentation of the Templeton Prize for Progress in Religion to Mother Teresa, the award's first recipient, 1973.

Mother Teresa receives her first honorary degree—from Catholic University, Washington, D.C.

Receiving the Kennedy International Award for "Outstanding Service to Mankind," Washington, D.C., 1971. *(Religious News Service)*

Mother Teresa with Prime Minister Indira Gandhi, 1980. The honorary doctorate from Visva-Bharati University was awarded to Mother Teresa by the Prime Minister who bestowed upon her the Indian mark of honor. *(Religious News Service)*

The Missionaries of Charity observe Twenty-fifth Jubilee of founding, with unprecedented prayerful observation by eighteen religious congregations in India, 1975. *(Sunil Kumar Dutt/Camera Press)*

Holy Hour added to their prayer life. Co-Workers, through Holy Hours held each month wherever possible, would bring them closer in spirit to each other.

"We are enriched by the presence of each other in God," Mother Teresa told us, "and we can carry that love when we go to others."

We joined the monks in their common prayer and felt the atmosphere filled with praise and closeness to God.

One evening, the Abbot asked Mother Teresa to enter the cloister to talk to the monks. I had some confused idea that she would be sharing with them some esoteric ideas about infused contemplation not applicable to lay people. When a tape recording of her talk was shared with us, it was clear that her message of spirituality was for all, though the path chosen might be different. She talked of the "oneness with Christ" which was the heart of the lives of the monks as it was of the Missionaries of Charity. The same Jesus who could "neither deceive nor be deceived" was the suffering one the Sisters touched every day.

Here were men of great gifts, who by the standards of the world, of a sensate culture at that, were living wasted lives. Yet it was evident that they were finding happiness and peace without any of the things the world considered basic to fulfillment: possessions, recognition, physical love, even freedom of movement and association. This life they freely chose in the pursuit of holiness.

All of them, in solidarity with all the laborers of the world, worked in either the dairy farm or the poultry houses or took care of their colonies of bees. They earned their living by their labor, selling milk, whole wheat bread from their own grain, and honey.

Lay people were called to the same holiness as these vowed men by different paths. "Holiness," Mother Teresa kept reminding us, "is not the luxury of the few; it is the simple duty of all.

"Here in America," she warned us, "you can easily be suffocated by things. And once you have them you must give time to taking care of them. Then you have no time for each other or for the poor. You must give freely to the poor what the rich get for their money."

She was bringing the Co-Workers back to the simplicity of the gospel and helping to join them to Christ so that in Him, each would become a "new creation." She was reasserting the gospel message that nothing matters but the formation of this new creature—who is not transformed by his world, no matter how sensate or alluring. Mother Teresa's emphasis on prayer in common and Holy Hours was a way of including the simplest person in the path to holiness. Worship and contemplation were to undergird the activities of the Co-Workers. In this Abbey, a place sheared of all distractions and superfluities, Co-Workers were being schooled in the need for constant awareness of the presence of God, for the experience of God in our lives. Many who were already reaching out to the poor and unwanted around them would continue doing so but with a new spirit. Others would search with a keener spiritual eye for needs they could meet and wounds they could staunch—always beginning with those in their own families. After meeting the monks of Holy Trinity Abbey, it was possible to see the correspondence between the lives of the Cistercians and the lives of the Missionaries of Charity. The poverty of the Cistercians had always been a planned poverty. In *The Waters of Siloe* Thomas Merton described the founding of Gethsemani Abbey when each monk brought from France to America two blankets, just as the Sisters had brought their bedrolls and the Brothers brought their floor mats. On the ship, during the long voyage to the United States, the planned poverty of the Cistercians proved to be bearable. In a section of the steerage, forty monks baked fresh loaves of bread and made cauldrons of soup. The other passengers, who had not planned for the austere life were reduced to hardtack when supplies gave out. Their austerity was not of choice. The monks then shared their fare with the weakest of the voyagers, the mothers with children and the sick. The poverty of the Sisters, like that of the Cistercians, is a planned poverty that allows them to go to the weakest.

Abbot Emmanuel gave Mother Teresa a four-foot high crucifix as a gift from the Abbey, carefully wrapped in cloth. The Abbot carried it aboard the plane and Mother Teresa placed it beside her on the seat. The steward suggested that as there were empty seats in the first-class section, she could put the crucifix on one of them. Mother Teresa carried it forward and carefully tied the safety belt around it. She then returned to economy class, echoing with a delighted smile what she had been saying in the Abbey, "That's right. We must put Jesus in first class."

The American branch of the Co-Workers came together every two years for meetings similar to that held in the Cistercian Abbey in Utah. They met in such places as the Tau Franciscan Center in Winona, Minnesota, and once, in 1978, they again made their way to the Abbey of the Holy Trinity in the Utah desert. The discussions and messages were preserved through the efforts of Msgr. Richard Feiten who recorded the meetings from beginning to end on tape. Cassettes were made available to the Co-Workers to meditate on at their leisure. A further useful service was performed by a founding member of the American Co-Workers, Mrs. Maurine Patterson, who gathered short sayings of Mother Teresa for publication in the Co-Worker newsletter.

After "Let God use you without consulting you," she cited these sayings of Mother Teresa:

Being a Co-Worker is not doing; it is being.
It is a way of life, not a name.
"Love me as I have loved you."
We are using the name of Mother Teresa, but we are actually Co-Workers of Jesus.
A Co-Worker is one who loves. People will know us by our love.
It is not so much what we do, but how much love we put into it.
To be a Co-Worker is to belong to Jesus.
We must bring more of Jesus, more of the love of Jesus to the people we meet.
We must proclaim Christ by the way we talk, by the way we walk, the way we laugh, by our life, so that everyone will know we belong to Him.
Proclaiming is not preaching; it is being.
Everyone has something to give.
Holiness is the acceptance of the will of God.
Pray the work. Pray while you work. Offer it up.
Above all, do everything with joy.
Bring prayer back into family life.
We must act so that people can look and see God in us.
What is important is giving freely what has been given freely without taking pleasure in the giving.
May the Lord keep you in His heart because it is the only place we can be together.

For many years, priest Co-Workers joined lay Co-Workers in the programs of the Co-Workers, often leading Holy Hours and local retreats for local Co-Worker groups. As with Ann Blaikie, Jacqueline de Decker, and Patty Kump, they soon found their lives tightly intertwined with Mother Teresa and her work. Fr. Don Kribs cooperated with the Brothers in Los Angeles, particularly in their beginning years. Fr. Edward Farrell, whose spiritual books, including *Prayer Is a Hunger,* reached large numbers of readers, directed that his earnings be turned over to Mother Teresa.

Besides giving his time and energies to the task of Co-Worker treasurer at a time when donations descended like a benevolent storm, Father Patrick Tobin, a Co-Worker priest, pastor, St. Joseph's Cathedral, St. Joseph, Missouri, drew into his Co-Worker group a happy union of black and white parishioners. Father Tobin was asked if he would give the Sisters in the South Bronx their annual retreat. He took his vacation to give the week-long spiritual exercise. Then Mother Teresa asked if he would be available to give retreats to groups of Sisters in other countries. Tobin gave up his vacations to give a retreat to the Sisters in La Parada in Lima, Peru;

and then to the Sisters in Caracas, Venezuela. Next came London, Rome, and New Delhi, and in later years, in Beirut, Cairo, and Gaza.

In 1980 he led an eight-day retreat in Calcutta for twenty-eight superiors who came to the Motherhouse from all over India. After the Calcutta retreats, he traveled the one hundred fifty miles to Shanti Nagar to give a retreat to the Sisters of the leper center. "Concelebrating mass with a leper priest gives a person an insight into the life of people who share a common special cross," Father Tobin remarked.

When asked about his reaction to giving retreats to the Missionaries of Charity, Patrick Tobin remarked, "To me, it's not giving a retreat to the Sisters but making a retreat with them. Their love and dedication, their devotion and spirit, their commitment to the Lord is an ongoing inspiration."

Priests in many countries were key figures in the Co-Worker movement. In Japan, Father André Bogaert led the Co-Workers. Father Christian Daleau of France faced the problem of a name for the Co-Workers. The term "*collaborateur,*" which would have been a natural choice, was ruled out, poisoned by its political tainting during the Second World War. Instead, the Co-Workers were united under the title, *Les Amis de Mère Teresa* (The Friends of Mother Teresa). On occasion, these Co-Workers referred to themselves as *cooperateurs* or cooperators. The Friends of Mother Teresa published an illustrated quarterly magazine carrying the powerfully poetic contributions of Father Daleau as well as reports of religious developments of special concern to France and news of the Missionaries of Charity.

In France, another priest, Father Georges Gorrée, was considered to be a "second self," as Jacqueline de Decker was, as well as other Co-Workers Mother Teresa considered close to her. She asked him to carry out a new program.

"In September 1974," he recounted, "when passing through France, Mother Teresa expressed the wish to see each of her congregation's houses "spiritually adopted" by one or more contemplative communities. She asked me to undertake the responsibility for promoting such a link.

"In just one year, about four hundred convents in Germany, England, Belgium, Canada, Spain, France, Italy, and Luxembourg, have enthusiastically accepted this spiritual twinning. All the Missionaries of Charity had four or five convents sustaining them by their prayers. This is marvelous! unique! Many of the Missionaries of Charity have written to me to say how happy they are at the thought of their contemplative Sisters offering their prayers and sacrifices for them, in union with Christ, to obtain the graces necessary to make their apostolic work fruitful."

When Father Gorrée died, his work lived on and increased. Mother Teresa gave the task of uniting the contemplative monasteries with the

Sisters and Brothers to Sister Nirmala, now herself superior of a contemplative house of the Missionaries of Charity. The twinning of religious houses spread to such countries as Poland, where Carmelite Sisters expressed immense gratitude for the insight into work in the farthest reaches of the globe. The program also included Anglican contemplative convents.

Sister Nirmala received from the prioress of a Carmelite monastery in the United States a letter that illuminated events at the beginning of the Missionaries of Charity. It also revealed the loving concern of Loreto for their Sister Teresa who had left them to answer a second call.

"This may be of interest to you, and even to Mother Teresa," wrote the prioress. "Years ago, while Mother Teresa was in Calcutta, awaiting the decision of Rome, Mother Canisia of Loreto wrote to one of our Sisters asking for prayers for the project. Ever since that day in the 1940s, we have been praying for Mother Teresa and for her work, following with loving apostolic interest each new development that providence permitted us to hear about. We were linked with your order since the time there were four members, all unknown to any of you, but hopefully supporting all of you. This we will continue to do, putting special emphasis on the Missionaries of Charity in Silchar."

In country after country, Mother Teresa heard of the numbers of priests separating themselves from the ministry by formal laicization, or by simply taking leave of the ministry. For someone with her concept of *besa,* the breaking of a pledged word was appallingly beyond her ken. She became aware of the dwindling number of priestly vocations to fill the depleted ranks. When some priests suggested that a group of Priest Co-Workers be formed, her reply was to wait on God and to pray. Mother Teresa had infinite reverence for priests and the priesthood. After a year, the question arose again and the project was presented to Pope John Paul II on November 1, 1980. The Holy Father read the petition and listened with great attention to Mother Teresa's proposal. Then he said, "Mother Teresa, allow me to be the first priest to be accepted into this community of Co-Workers of Mother Teresa."

The Holy Father asked that the draft of the statutes be studied by the Congregation for the Clergy, and from that office came a warm letter of approbation on June 26, 1981.

In the case where a priest had a role as a National or Regional Link in the Co-Workers, he was to surrender the post to a married couple. In appointing married couples, Mother Teresa was following the lead of Pope John Paul II in emphasizing the capital importance of the family.

Fr. Joseph Langford, a young American priest of the Congregation of Oblates of the Blessed Virgin, who was familiar with the work of the

Missionaries of Charity in New York City and Rome, was asked by Mother Teresa to head the Priest Co-Workers as an international movement of priestly renewal.

Two new branches of Mother Teresa's family were born in 1984, one, the Medical Co-Workers, affiliated with the International Co-Workers. Dr. Francesco Di Raimondo, head physician of the Lazzaro Spallanzana Hospital for Infectious Diseases in Rome agreed to head the new branch which aimed to unite medical personnel around the world who practiced their profession in the spirit of Mother Teresa and the Missionaries of Charity. Already, doctors who had volunteered in centers served by the Missionaries of Charity, many traveling long distances to donate their services in such places as Calcutta and Haiti, were developing a sense of community among themselves. The new group, however, was not simply for those who volunteered with the Missionaries of Charity, but for doctors in their own practice, who, in the words of Dr. Raimondo, wished to develop "a different manner of seeing, of touching, of speaking to the sick, a manner which gives confidence and hope to all, even when the sickness is serious and death inevitable."

The other branch was separate from the Co-Workers, the movement of the Carriers of God's Love. It arose in response to requests from women, mostly young women, who wanted to go a step further than the Co-Workers in spirituality and commitment. They wished to live a life similar to that of the Missionaries of Charity but without actually becoming Sisters. Some Christian women were prevented by circumstances from entering the Society; women of other religious groups wanted to emulate the life of simplicity, purity, and service exemplified by the Sisters. On one occasion, a group of Hindu young women approached Mother Teresa in Calcutta to ask if they could model their lives on those of the Sisters and have Mother Teresa as their guide. Mother Teresa referred them to their own spiritual guides. Those who chose to be part of the movement of the Carriers of God's Love would have recourse to recognized leaders of their own spiritual paths and to the riches of their own traditions. The word "God" was used to imply, by whatever name, the spiritual force guiding the life of each individual.

The concept that would unite the Carriers of God's Love across spiritualities and cultures would be the merciful compassion for the lowliest and the least that undergirds all religions and spiritual paths, a concept illumined by the life of Mother Teresa.

Over the years, the Co-Workers around the globe were made aware of the ever-growing family founded by Mother Teresa through the newsletter of the International Co-Workers prepared by Ann Blaikie with the help of the local Co-Workers. When the editorship of the newsletter fell to me as Co-Link in 1980, I realized the enormity of the task she had assumed for so long with unflagging energy. The network was so vast, and the works of mercy of the Sisters, the Brothers, and the Co-Workers so incredibly varied, that to sift them gave one a sense of the beautiful things for God and His creatures being carried out somewhere at every moment.

Of the many letters that poured in one of the loveliest came from Skopje, Yugoslavia, the birthplace of Mother Teresa. In 1980 Mother Teresa brought a team of Sisters to the town of her girlhood. Accompanying her team, Mother Teresa remarked, "You gave one person. I bring back four."

Sr. Joselette, the superior, who had worked in New York, wrote, "We are four Sisters, two Indians, one Maltese, and one Albanian. Our convent is small, just three rooms. We go about everywhere on bicycles. For many material-minded people, we are crazy and funny young ladies. It does not disturb us, since we are crazy for the One who was crazy enough to do many more things for us. Only may our craziness spread His glory."

A visitor to Skopje shortly after the arrival of the Sisters gave her opinion that it was precisely in that town that the Sisters received a markedly cool reception. Mother Teresa, who had earlier returned to her home place was welcomed with festivities by church leaders and by the city fathers, proud of a world-famous daughter. The Sisters were placed in a poor sector where the people hardly knew of such festivities and did not know what to make of the strangely clad young women, three of them foreigners, who sped by them on bicycles. Sister Joselette was revealing the distant attitude of the public by admitting that the citizens of Skopje considered them a bit demented. Her description of the work showed why the neediest soon gave them the warmest of welcomes.

"Among the people we visit and care for," she wrote, "are the very old people, the blind, the lame, the crippled, and the poor. There are very few Catholics and we visit all groups, including the Gypsies. We go around doing what we can as a sign of God's love. There is so much to say about our people. They are so lovable. Our old people are so beautiful. Many consider us as their daughters and when we delay, they ask, 'Where are you, my daughters? Have you forgotten your Mama?' We have an old blind woman who takes care of a grandson. She says, 'If it were not for the Sisters, I would never see tomatoes and peppers and all those fresh vegetables and fruits.' "

If Mother Teresa had wanted to show her Sisters where her life had begun, she would have had no success. There was not a stone left standing of her girlhood home, nor of Sacred Heart Church. After the 1963 earthquake, the area was built over. Only a statue of the Sacred Heart had been saved from the debris. She found no trace of her father's grave in the cemetery which also suffered from the earthquake.

In Singapore, Co-Workers made regular visits to the Cheshire home for the handicapped, some to help with physiotherapy, some to talk with the residents and share their lives.

In Australia, Ann Blaikie joined Co-Workers to attend an Easter mass with the aborigines.

"One of the Sisters," she recalled, "had set some of the responses to aboriginal music. We had an aboriginal band and after the service, a dozen young girls in long dresses with white flowers in their hair danced a beautiful Resurrection dance before the altar. All morning small children came to the Sisters' door with hibiscus flowers and were rewarded with Easter eggs."

In Japan, Mother Teresa met with the Co-Workers, who had been organized there under Father Bogaert long before the arrival of the first Missionaries of Charity in the spring of 1981. She had walked through the Sanya district of Tokyo, a gathering place for alcoholics. She encouraged the Co-Workers to a difficult task with these words, "You will say that they are drunkards. But, my brother there, my sister here, for that person Jesus died on the cross. For that person, Jesus was crucified. Even we passed by. If it was Calcutta, I would have picked him up, police or no police . . . But here I don't know your rules, so I could not. But my heart was beating fast with hurt . . . Here in Japan, maybe you don't have people hungry for bread or for rice. But there are hungry, lonely people."

In Haiti, the closest approximation to Calcutta in the Western Hemisphere, a team of twenty-five students, led by Monsignor Richard Feiten, helped to construct a building that would house a clinic and a school. With him the team consisted of an engineer, a dentist, a university professor, and a medical doctor. A second team, composed completely of adults, came shortly afterward to add a second story to the building. They found Haitian Co-Workers organized and active with the Sisters and their community. In line with the effort to have every Co-Worker, even the aged or handicapped, play a part, a blind Co-Worker became the leader of the choir in the local church.

When Mother Teresa asked that the Co-Worker leaflet, with the prayers and the Co-Worker Way of Life be uniform for all countries, it was a simple matter to send it to any country where someone could be found to put it into the local language. The prayers and accounts of Mother Teresa reached the Albanian population of Yugoslavia through a Catholic publication *Drita* (Light), printed in Skopje in the Albanian tongue.

A new prayer was added to the two prayers regularly recited by the Co-

Workers. This was a prayer composed by the English convert and cardinal, John Henry Newman. Though originally it was addressed to Jesus, Mother Teresa obtained permission to change it so that it could be said by those with faith in a divine principle. Mother Teresa was always aware of Co-Workers who were not Christian, especially in India where numerous Hindus and Parsis were an intimate part of the work of the Missionaries of Charity. While the founding members of the Co-Workers were Catholic, it soon became an ecumenical organization. In the United States, Lutherans, Methodists, and others took part, and even became leaders, in Co-Worker activity. The situation developed similarly in England and on the European continent.

"Shine through me," said Newman's prayer,

> and be so in me that every soul I come in contact with may feel Thy presence in my soul.
>
> Let them look up and see no longer me—but only Thee, O Lord!
>
> Stay with me and then I shall begin to shine as Thou dost—so to shine as to be a Light to others.
>
> The Light, O Lord, will be all from Thee;
>
> None of it will be mine.
>
> It will be thou shining through me.

After responsibility for the international newsletter had crossed the Atlantic from England, it remained in the United States. Patty and Warren Kump, who had been named International Links, became the editors. Mimeographed by donated labor on cheap paper, also donated, the newsletter was sent to every house of the Missionaries of Charity, Sisters, and Brothers, and to the National Links in forty countries of the world. In many countries, the English text was recopied for distribution and in others, translated into the local language for sharing with regional and local Links.

A plain hall of the ancient Camaldolese Benedictine Monastery of San Gregorio on the Coelian Hill of Rome was the scene of the Third International Chapter of the Co-Workers of Mother Teresa. In mid-May 1982, sixty-five men and women came from thirty countries in Europe, Africa, Australia, and North and South America to meet as a family. All received hospitality in the homes of Italian Co-Workers through the efforts of Italy's National Links, Giacomo and Virginia Cuppari.

The meeting place was one that breathed history. The monastery and church of San Gregorio honored Pope St. Gregory who from this spot dispatched a band of monks to evangelize England. They had set out nearly fourteen hundred years earlier, carrying with them precious gospel texts, holy books, and sacred vessels. In the ancient chapel of San Andrea was an incredible relic, the very marble table, the "table of the poor," from which St. Gregory, and his mother, St. Sylvia, had personally fed the hungry of sacked and gutted Rome. In the monastery itself, Mother Teresa's Sisters conducted a shelter for the aged and homeless. Their convent consisted of outbuildings that had been converted from chicken coops.

Mother Teresa was the heart of the three-day international gathering as she had been at the two earlier meetings, one held in London in 1973 after the Templeton Prize for Progress in Religion, and the second in 1976 in Lippstadt, Germany, the home city of Germany's National Link, Josepha Gosselke. The Lippstadt meeting was attended by National Links from eleven European countries and Canada. It was decided to hold an International Chapter every six years, following the pattern of the Sisters and Brothers. At Lippstadt it was formally decided to change from using the term "Chairman" to the word "Link."

"I would rather like to use 'Link'—like a branch, a joining. I would like the fifteenth chapter of St. John (on the vine and the branches) to become our life," Mother Teresa said, reverting to one of her favorite quotations from Scripture. She wrote to all Co-Worker Links:

> Let us become a true and faithful branch on the vine. Jesus, by accepting Him in our lives as it pleases Him to come:
> as the Truth—to be told;
> as the Life—to be lived;
> as the Light—to be lighted;
> as the Love—to be loved;
> as the Way—to be walked;
> as the Joy—to be given;
> as the Peace—to be spread;
> as the Sacrifice—to be offered in our families and with our close neighbors as well as our faraway neighbors.

Around Mother Teresa in Rome were her earliest Co-Workers, Ann Blaikie, who led the meetings with a firm hand, Jacqueline de Decker, Violet Collins, who had lost her husband Frank, Patty Kump, and Bridget Eacott, International Link Secretary. Among the National Links were Thelma Harpley of Australia, Frau Michaela Scheichl of Austria, Micheline Gultens of Belgium, Prof. Francisco Goes of Brazil, Mrs. Gerry Moen and the Reverend Frank West, S.J., of Canada, Mrs. Grete Lauritzen of Denmark, Abbé Christian Daleau and Michel and Marie Louise Lorphelin of France, Carla Wiedeking of Germany, Michael and Evelyn Armistead and David Jarret of England, Mary Walsh and Co-Worker archivist Alice Grattan-Esmonde of Ireland, Fr. André Bogaert and Mr. Harukatsu Toshizawa of Japan, and Joseph and Colette Probst of Luxembourg.

From Malta came four Links, the National Link, Rose Crech being accompanied by Vittorio Filletti, representing the recently founded Youth Co-Workers. The Joint International Youth Links were also from Malta, Tony and Lillian Miceli Ferrugia. From Mauritius came Jacques and Gilberte Ducasse.

Gerrit Jan Colenbrander and his wife Valentine, daughter of Malcom Muggeridge, were the National Links for the Netherlands, soon to be named International Links for relief supplies. With them was the Dutch Vice-Link, Mrs. Maud Franken Spee. Alan and Pat Lovelady were the Links for New Zealand, Mrs. Eli Werner for Norway, Antoine and Marie Victor for Singapore, Mrs. Pilar Santos for Spain, Dagny Arbman for Sweden, Eugen Vogt for Switzerland, and Mrs. Marija Krile for Yugoslavia.

Representatives came from countries where the Co-Workers were being organized, Mrs. Birgit Ranken from Finland, Mr. Torfi Olafsson from Iceland, Evelyn Lebona from Lesotho, Margaret Cullin from South Africa, and Mrs. Funia Negri from Zimbabwe. The representative from Hungary did not wish her name listed publicly.

In welcoming the Co-Worker family, Mother Teresa said, "My gratitude to the Co-Workers is a prayer that you may each grow in the likeness of Christ and be carriers of God's love. You should be a living example of God's presence in the world . . . God loves the world through you."

Though the Co-Workers took time to discuss their constitution and to share their experiences, they spent much time praying together, singing hymns, and meditating. Though there was not inter Communion, the non-Catholics attended mass in historic San Gregorio.

Mother Teresa insisted on the special witness of the Co-Workers:

"Just as God sent His Son to proclaim the Good News that God loves us and that God loved the world so much, He also gave the Co-Workers and the Missionaries of Charity to the world. I believe this. I am very sure of this, and I want you to believe and live up to it. To allow God to love through you, be His love, His compassion, His joy, His everything."

She reminded Co-Workers of the two words which heralded the coming of Jesus, "Fear not."

"There will be suffering, and more and more people are suffering, I am sure, in every country. There is that terrible fear of nuclear war, that terrible, terrible fear . . . But such a terrible fear is not for you. We will pray. We will pray. Prayer cannot fail, and not only pray, but put that prayer into a loving action, and do something for somebody. This is what I have been longing to say to you. You are so much a part of my very life. Though we live far apart, nobody can separate us."

Referring to her request that Co-Workers do no fund-raising, she informed them that since fund-raising had been discontinued, donations to the work had increased. Dependence on the providence of God for the work with the poor was the clear and only course.

Mother Teresa related the story of the rich man in India who wanted to bank an immense amount of money, "lakhs of rupees," in her words, for the Sisters, so that they would not find themselves someday without support or funds for the work. (A lakh is 100,000 rupees.) The sum he offered was over half a million dollars.

"The condition was," Mother Teresa explained, "that this money should not be touched. It should be a security for the work. So, I wrote back and said that rather than offend God, I would offend him a little bit, though I was grateful for his thoughtfulness. I could not accept the money because all these years, God has taken care of us and the security of this money would take away the very life of the work. I could not have money in the bank while people were starving.

"It shocked him," she went on, "it shook him. Before he died, he sent the money, so much for the lepers, so much for the Home for the Dying, so much for food, and so on. He gave it all."

She added, "We must have the courage to say 'No' sometimes."

Then Mother Teresa said something we had not heard before, a reference to the time when she would no longer be alive. "I do not want money to make difficulties when we are no longer here—when we are dead."

To a person who had had the courage to ask her what might happen to the Missionaries of Charity and the Co-Workers when she died, she replied, "Let Mother Teresa die first."

Trust in the future, as with everything else, was part of her trust in the profound, inscrutable designs of providence. The only fund-raising in which Co-Workers could participate would be among themselves for local needs, a party or outing for shut-ins or the aged, or the printing of prayer cards or guidelines, given out gratis.

The "new branch on the vine," the Priest Co-Workers, was described when Father Joseph Langford, head of the movement, was introduced to the Co-Workers. He related that the new group was "taking a leaf from the book of Jacqueline's (de Decker) life," the role of Jesus in His passion.

"Mother Teresa," he related, "said that she would like to envision the Priest Co-Workers as the spiritual heart of the Co-Workers as a family."

He talked of becoming aware, as a priest, "of the Calcutta of my own parish, the Calcutta that is everywhere, to find the hungry hearts, the thirsting souls of the people in my streets." Though the new movement was no more than a tiny mustard seed, priests from over a score of countries were already members. Mother Teresa added that the movement of Priest Co-Workers was already known to bishops who had received the constitution. Priest Co-Workers were not to be a part of the organizational activities of the Co-Workers.

The two presences of Jesus as illuminated by the work of Mother Teresa, the Eucharist and the body of the poor, were united in the title chosen by the movement, Corpus Christi (Body of Christ).

We heard from European Co-Workers who arranged for the shipment of millions of antileprosy tablets and from the Co-Worker from Lesotho whose group had adopted a leper settlement. In Maseru, Lesotho, Evelyn Lebono led a group that as a joint project served the Botsabelo leper settlement. Beside Basotho members, the group included Zimbabweans, Sri Lankans, Indians, Taiwanese, Irish, and British residents, whose faith communities ranged from Catholic, Angelican, and Evangelical to Hindu and Buddhist.

The National Link from Hungary talked of her joy at being in Rome after receiving an exit visa at the last moment. The Co-Workers, she related, met informally as individuals, generally after church. The work with the blind, the shut-ins and multihandicapped children was well organized, but in a hidden way. Sometimes a Co-Worker went alone on visitations, sometimes with one or two others. The association was not publicized. From Poland came a moving letter from university students in Warsaw who had opened a shelter for homeless and alcoholic men in which they served as volunteers.

Gerrit Jan Colenbrander told of his hesitancy in taking on the daunting task of coordinating gifts-in-kind from Europe to India and other countries. Mother Teresa had encouraged him and Valentine to start small. They had gradually gained the courage to handle the large variety of donations and supervise shipments. Micheline Gultens of Brussels told of the work of her husband, Willie Gultens, in the procurement of medical and other supplies through Brussels for the Sisters' houses, especially those in the Middle East. After extensive discussion of the Co-Worker constitutions and guidelines, a new subject was introduced, the bond between the Co-Workers and the Sisters and Brothers. It developed that in some places, as someone put it, "they do not always treasure each other."

Young Sisters were unaware of the Co-Worker role and, in moving from less developed to more developed societies, might need to adjust to the scope of volunteer activity. I was asked to frame a statement on this relationship and to word it in such a way that it would reach beyond Catholic Co-Workers to those many Co-Workers of other faiths.

The third International Chapter was formally ended on Monday, May 17, at midday when the group met Mother Teresa at the Bronze Door near the Colonnade on St. Peter's Square. Mother Teresa had returned from a lightning trip to Bari in southern Italy. We made our way through a series of stairs and waited in the Consistory Hall of the Apostolic Palace for the arrival of the Holy Father. It was a fifteen-minute wait. Mother Teresa looked unusually weary and shortly after she sat down, her head sank on her breast and she was asleep. Once she raised her head, but again it sank gently downward.

The Pope had returned late the night before from a taxing trip to Portugal in which another attempt had been made on his life. His eyes seemed almost closed with tiredness. As Mother Teresa rose to present the Co-Workers to the Holy Father, I wondered if they were not the two most tired people in the Eternal City. Pope John Paul II praised the work of the Co-Workers on behalf of the members of the human family "who have been set aside." He added that "it is only by putting on love that new life can be shared with them." He talked informally with the Co-Workers and accepted the annual report issue of the international newsletter. Among those at the audience were a number of children adopted from India, including the daughter of Virginia and Giacomo Cuppari. Through Mother Teresa, these little ones, rescued from Calcutta's streets, were now sons and daughters of Italian families.

Maud Franken Spee from Holland commented that she had not felt the three-day gathering was a meeting, but rather a spiritual experience which reminded her, in a small way, of Pentecost.

Mother Teresa invited Co-Workers, both Italian and those who remained in Rome after the International Chapter, to attend a ceremony that had occurred scores of times, first in Calcutta, then in cities around the world, the reception of Sisters into the Missionaries of Charity. Called the rite of perpetual profession, it took place on May 24, 1982, in the large and crowded church of St. Barnabas. The profession was in the setting of an afternoon mass concelebrated by thirty-six priests from many of Rome's parishes, as well as foreign priests resident in Rome. The chief celebrant was Silvio Cardinal Oddio. Among the priests was Msgr. Joseph Harnett of Catholic Relief Services who had played a part in having the Sisters enter Yemen and who regularly celebrated mass in their convent at Tor Fiscale. The twelve Sisters making their lifetime profession of vows were led to the altar by Sister Kathleen. She was an American who had been a member of the team in the South Bronx. A graduate of Syracuse University in New York State, Sister Kathleen had been one of many young Americans who had looked for an answer to the spiritual poverty of the life around her. She found it in the Missionaries of Charity. Her year of intense preparation in Calcutta was behind her, and her life commitment had been made.

The cardinal asked the Sisters to respond publicly to their resolve to undertake the life of the Missionaries of Charity.

The central act of the profession ceremony revealed Mother Teresa in her spiritual authority as the Mother Foundress of a new religious family and as its Mother General.

Each Sister-candidate came forward to present herself to Mother Teresa at the altar. She stated solemnly, "For the honor and glory of God and moved by a burning desire to quench the infinite thirst of Jesus on the cross for love of souls, by consecrating myself wholly to Him in total surrender, loving trust and cheerfulness, here and now, in the hands of Mother Teresa, I, (and here the candidate gave her name) vow for life chastity, poverty, obedience, and wholehearted and free service to the poorest of the poor, according to the constitutions of the Missionaries of Charity. I give myself with my whole heart to this religious family, so that by the grace of the Holy Spirit and the help of the Immaculate Heart of Mary, cause of our joy and Queen of the world, I may be led to the perfect love of God and my neighbor and make the Church fully present to the world of today."

Mother Teresa replied, as I had seen her respond at other ceremonies of final profession.

"By the authority entrusted in me, I accept your vows, in the name of the Church for the community of the Missionaries of Charity. I commend you earnestly to God that you may fulfill your dedication which is united with this Eucharistic sacrifice."

Each newly professed Sister signed the formula of profession and placed it on the altar. The main celebrant of the mass then blessed the newly professed Sisters. "The poor are waiting for you," he told them, "and you have to show that you are reflecting the God of love."

After the profession ceremony, there was a welcoming ceremony at the convent, in which the superior said, "We confirm that you are now one with us as members of this religious community of the Missionaries of Charity, sharing all things in common with us for the future, fulfilling loyally this ministry entrusted to you by the Church to be carried out in her name."

The Sisters of the community, to manifest their assent, said in unison, "Amen."

After their reception by the community, the Sisters invited friends, and Co-Workers, including priests and lay people, to join them for a simple reception in the convent garden. There, under a leafy canopy, the Sisters, mostly young women from India, brought to Western eyes a mode of celebration native to India. The Sisters in their saris danced about, each holding a light, a candle in a small glass receptacle. The lights seemed to dance as the saried figures dipped and swayed with grace. Dusk was descending as the dance of lights was concluded. It occurred to me that the message of Jesus had too often come from Rome in a Western guise with religious Sisters garbed not only in Western dress, but in a dress that spoke of medieval Christianity, or of the age in which a particular congregation had been born. It also occurred to me how simply Mother Teresa and her Sisters expressed respect for Eastern culture, in this dance, echoing the Psalm sung at the professions, "The Lord is my light."

No matter how many Sisters were professed as Missionaries of Charity, there were more of the world's poor waiting for them than they could reach.

One task remained to be done to complete the work of the Rome International Chapter, namely the framing of a general statement reflecting the relationship between the Missionaries of Charity and the Co-Workers. The title chosen was "The Shared Vision."

The first draft was sent to Mother Teresa and Ann Blaikie. The final draft represented amendments by Sister Frederick, assistant Mother General, and Sister Nirmala, head of the first house of the contemplative Sisters. After asserting that the aim of the Co-Workers was to share the vision of Mother Teresa and the Missionaries of Charity, the statement explained, "This vision is shared by 'radiating God's love' in their lives, by becoming 'carriers of God's love' to all the members of the human family they may meet, and by giving wholehearted and free service to the poorest of the poor. Co-Workers are of all religions and denominations."

There was a definition of a Co-Worker: "A Co-Worker is one who chooses a way of life that calls for seeing the presence of God in every human being. Seeing God in everyone, starting with those closest to the Co-Worker, often calls for a transformation of life, and this transformation brings its fruits. People become ready to share themselves and their possessions with the lonely, the ill, the bereaved, the poor, the unwanted, and unloved. They learn the immeasurable power of suffering willingly accepted, of forgiveness freely given, and are strengthened by being part of a worldwide company of those who bear witness to the presence of God in every member of the family of man."

In returning the final version to us, Mother Teresa wrote, "Let us all be one heart, full of love." "One heart" *(Ek Dil)* was the term she used to express the unity of the Sisters, and we were included in it. The expression was a reminder that living the life of the Co-Worker meant a change of heart. The Co-Workers, an international web-work of human beings, were committed to this change of heart and to expressing it in their varied cultures. They were attempting to internalize a vision of "the other" as a being of ultimate value, worthy not only of cool respect, but of loving service. Mother Teresa's "vision of the street," a vision of every human being, including every poor and rejected human creature, as a repository of the divine, was being shared by more and more people of every race, culture, and belief.

20

Works of Mercy—Works of Peace

When word of the awarding of the 1979 Nobel Peace Prize to Mother Teresa came to Bengal, its Chief Minister, Jyoti Basu, a Communist, held a reception in her honor. "You have been the mother of Bengal," said Basu, "and now you are the mother of the world."

On that same day, a tiny abandoned infant was brought to the Children's Home, Shishu Bhavan. She was named Shanti (Peace) in honor of the award, and she survived.

"Joy Swept Calcutta" was the headline in the *Calcutta Statesman.* It was over six decades since a Nobel Prize had come to the province. In 1913, the Nobel Prize for Literature had come to a member of one of Calcutta's great families, Rabindranath Tagore. The 1979 Award was the first time that the Peace Prize had come to an Indian. "We claim you as our own," said Dr. D. N. Banerjee, reading from a citation of the Corporation of Calcutta, after referring to Mother Teresa's origin outside India. The citation was read at a gathering held for Mother Teresa on the premises of the Calcutta Corporation shortly before she left for Oslo. It was the Calcutta Corporation which had supported Mother Teresa's work by opening the Pilgrims' Hostel at Kali's temple for the dying people she rescued from the gutter. In responding to the citation, Mother Teresa thanked the Corporation for its continuous sharing of the work with the Missionaries of Charity. She recalled that her relationship with the Corporation dated back to 1952 when the Hostel, which she named Nirmal Hriday, had been placed at her disposal. "Since 1952," she said, "we have picked up over thirty-eight thousand human beings; of these, eighteen thousand have died with us in peace and dignity at Nirmal Hriday."

Besides the receptions by the city of Calcutta and the province of Bengal, the Government of India held its own reception at which Prime Minister Charon Singh stated, "It will take either a Shakespeare or a Milton to record her services to India. Indeed, her services to humanity as a whole are beyond compare."

The Minister for External Affairs of India, Shyam Mishra, described Mother Teresa's help to the suffering as the reflection "of a mission that finds its fulfillment in wiping out the tears from every eye as Mahatma Gandhi sought to do."

The anthem of praise, both within and outside India, at the choice for the 1979 Nobel Peace Prize was, in general, a harmonious one. The cover of the weekly magazine *Sunday*, carried a color photograph of Mother Teresa with the one word "Mother," in bright blue letters to match the blue bands of her sari. Inside was a lengthy article by the Calcutta newspaperman and writer, Desmond Doig. A Bombay weekly also carried a color photograph on its cover with the headline, "Peace on Earth: Mother Teresa Goes to Oslo." In the same issue, in addition to a feature article, was a poem addressed to her as "Mother of Calcutta, Ma Teresa, Lady of Compassion." "Ma" (Mother) is a reminder of the way the goddess Kali is addressed, "Kali Ma" (Mother Kali). It asked Mother Teresa to pray for all, for those who passed by the poor and the poor themselves. "In the valley of our sorrow, in the city of Calcutta."

Mother Teresa's Gandhian efforts at Hindu-Muslim harmony were recalled by Shakti Prakash De who wrote to *Sunday* magazine: "Many will find it difficult to forget how Mother dashed to Jamshedpur earlier this year when the steel city was in the grip of a communal riot." De saw Mother Teresa as a mother not only to the poor, but to all. "It would not be an exaggeration to say," he wrote, "that she is a universal mother symbol." A writer from Bengal suggested that Mother Teresa and her Sisters adopt a village and carry out programs specifically focused on communal harmony. "They could help," he said, "usher in a new era of progress in communal relations in this country." What Gandhi and the wide network of Gandhian organizations were unable to achieve was expected of Mother Teresa and her teams of Sisters.

Letters to the press, both newspapers and magazines, came from every part of India, some filled with fulsome rhetoric. "Mother is not merely godly; she is a goddess herself. She is not simply divine, but the institutionalized divinity in the form of service," stated one correspondent. Reflecting the Hindu mode of thinking, the writer wondered if Mother Teresa were the reincarnation of Jesus. "She has done God proud," asserted another correspondent.

Dissent came from an extremist anti-Gandhian group in an article in its publication entitled "Nothing Noble about Nobel." "For when all is said and done," said the article, "she is a missionary. In serving the poor and the sick, her sole objective is to influence people in favour of Christianity and, if possible, to convert them. Missionaries are instruments of Western imperialist countries—and not innocent voices of God." Her work, continued the article, did not merit the description, *nishkama seva* (selfless service, or service without hope of reward). Other Indian publications immediately rose to the defense of Mother Teresa and assailed the prejudice of the extremists. They defended the work of the Missionaries of Charity as true *nishkama seva* and an example to all. A correspondent from Bangalore expressed a fear: "This spearheads the birth of another 'ism' in India—"Mother Teresa-ism."

England's Manchester *Guardian* concurred with the president of the Nobel Peace Prize Committee, who stated that out of fifty-six candidates, Mother Teresa was chosen because "the hallmark of her work has been respect for the individual human being, for his or her dignity and innate value."

The praise intended by the New York *Times* editorial in calling Mother Teresa a "secular saint" has already been mentioned. The same newspaper printed among its letters to the editor, a dissenting voice. The writer observed that it was his understanding that the Nobel Peace Prize was to be given to those persons who made positive contributions to the peace of the world: the 1979 recipient, in his view, had not made such a contribution but had merely helped distressed individuals.

The Washington *Post* saw Mother Teresa's contribution in a more positive light, asserting: "Most of the recipients of the Nobel Peace Prize over the years have been politicians and diplomats. But Mother Teresa, the nun who founded the Missionaries of Charity, has spent the last thirty-one years working with the destitute and dying in Calcutta. It is the example of personal devotion to these people, as individuals, that is compelling . . . . Occasionally, the Norwegian Nobel Committee uses the prize to remind the world that there is more than one kind of peace, and that politics is not the only way to pursue it."

A question touched on in an article in the *National Catholic Reporter* of Kansas City was the fact that the work of Mother Teresa's Sisters does not attack the structures that cause poverty. The author, Mary Bader Papa, pointed out that some hold that such work as Mother Teresa's "merely bandages the wounds of capitalism" and does little to change the conditions that make people poor in the first place. Papa made the distinction between the "revolutionary love" animating Mother Teresa and the "revolutionary anger" so often called for in changing structures. She commended the Nobel Committee for honoring "revolutionary love." It was noteworthy that while there was the simultaneous announcement of Nobel prizes in such fields as physics, economics, chemistry, and literature, awarded in Stockholm, Sweden, more attention was paid to the single Peace Prize awarded in Oslo.

The announcement of the Peace Award in 1979 came as a complete surprise to those concerned with the work of Mother Teresa. The hopes of a few had been raised in 1972, on learning that Lester B. Pearson of Canada, the 1957 recipient of the Peace Prize, had submitted Mother Teresa's name. Malcolm Muggeridge supplied Mother Teresa's writings and accounts of her work as documentation. Muggeridge was indefatigable in keeping communication alive with the Norwegian committee. He was faithful to his statement at the time of the publication of *Something Beautiful for God* in London in 1971 that Mother Teresa's writings would be useful when she was considered for a Nobel Prize.

In 1975, hopes rose wherever there were groups of Co-Workers or supporters. That year the nomination of Mother Teresa was sent to Oslo by the Right Honorable Shirley Williams, a member of the British Government, and was supported by Maurice Strong of Canada, the head of the UN Environmental Program. Word of the nomination reached the press and was widely reported not only in the secular press but in the Catholic press of the world. Many of us had naively helped generate letters of support to the Nobel Committee early in 1975. U.S. Senator Edward M. Kennedy sent a letter endorsing the nomination. We received copies of letters of endorsement from Robert S. McNamara, head of the World Bank, and from U.S. Senators Mark O. Hatfield, Hubert H. Humphrey, and Pete V. Domenici. The head of the U.S. National Council of the Churches of Christ wrote a strong letter, as did the leaders of Church Women United and the National Council of Catholic Women.

Letters of support came from Europe, from Africa and Australia, from such persons as the mayor of Addis Ababa and the head of the UN Disaster Relief Organization, Faruk N. Berkol, a native of Turkey. As 1975 was International Women's Year, it seemed the time to press Mother Teresa's cause. Many heads of relief agencies as well as parliamentarians and officials lent their support.

Letters of support came from India, in particular from representatives of the various religious communities. A prominent member of the Jain community wrote, "During my visit to Calcutta, amongst various humanitarian activites, Mother Teresa's concept to make a 'Home for the Dying' appealed to me most. Hers is a Catholic Institution, adjoining the famous Hindu Kali Temple, speaking of her compassion for suffering mankind. This Institution performs an ideal function, providing the last ceremony according to the religion of the dying person . . . When the civil population of Bangladesh suffered the cruelties of war, especially the innocent women, Mother Teresa saved the lives of many unborns by the slogan of 'Adoption and not Abortion.' She helped give dignity to many ill-treated women . . . I feel very strongly that Rev. Mother Teresa's devotional humanitarian activites should be appreciated and honoured by the august Institute of the Nobel Prize Committee."

In some countries the enthusiasm for the cause had been whipped up into a storm resulting in the fact that the Norwegian committee was inundated by letters from individuals. Someone jokingly remarked that half the nuns of Spain had taken pen in hand.

When Barbara Ward heard of such developments, she cautioned that "letters out of the blue from unknown enthusiasts" would not have the desired effect. In point of fact, they probably had the opposite effect, since the Nobel Committee might have felt that undue pressure was being put on them. The 1975 Award did not go to Mother Teresa, but to someone who indeed could merit the description of "secular saint," Andrei Sakharov. His willingness to court suffering for selfless service on behalf of human rights and persecuted people did not stem from a religious or transcendental motivation. His scientific achievements had in wartime contributed to the development of the Soviet Union's hydrogen bomb. Mother Teresa's friends and supporters considered the matter closed.

There was one exception. In 1977, Barbara Ward quietly resubmitted the nomination, sharing with the Nobel Committee later developments that might be helpful to them. One of the few who knew of this and who again endorsed the nomination was Robert S. McNamara. Barbara Ward stated: "One of the priorities which is beginning to be accepted by the World Bank and other agencies and seems likely to be incorporated in any formal definition of the New Economic Order is that help must first go to the poorest." She briefly described the thanksgiving services held in Calcutta by most of the world's major religions in the fall of 1975 to mark the Silver Jubilee of the Missionaries of Charity. Barbara Ward concluded: "In a world of still bitter sectarian divisions, Mother Teresa has at least found one of the possible routes of reconciliation." Again the Nobel Committee honored another candidate.

It was not possible to keep Mother Teresa unaware of these developments. When a friend expressed regret that the award had not come to her, Mother Teresa replied, "I had a good laugh over the Nobel Prize—It will come only when Jesus thinks it is time. We have all calculated to build two hundred houses for the lepers if it comes—so our people will have to do the praying."

It was thus a secret whose nomination had effectuated the Nobel Committee's announcement of October 16, 1979 of Mother Teresa as that year's recipient of the Peace Prize. It was not until December 10 at the ceremony in Oslo that the Nobel Committee gave a clear hint, though according to custom, it did not make public the nominator. The chairman quoted one man, the Presbyterian layman and international public servant, Robert S. McNamara. The citation indicated that the letter of nomination in 1979 was substantially the same as earlier letters of support. Robert McNamara sent me a copy of his 1975 letter to the Nobel Committee.

I would like to express my support for the nomination of Mother Teresa of Calcutta for the 1975 Nobel Peace Prize.

Many public personalities—government officials, diplomats, members of international communities, and others—advance the cause of peace, and deserve recognition. But I believe Mother Teresa merits the unique honor of the Nobel Peace Prize because she advances peace in the most fundamental way possible: by her extraordinary reaffirmation of the inviolability of human dignity.

She does this by serving the needs of the absolute poor—the poor who are so disadvantaged that they have nowhere else to turn. She serves them irrespective of their religion, their race, their nationality, or their political beliefs. She serves them simply because of their intrinsic worth as individual human beings.

Her work is not sentimental. It is realistic and effective. And it is expanding. A growing number of others around the world—in an international ecumenical association, the Co-Workers of Mother Teresa—are undertaking similar efforts under her inspiration.

But more important than the organizational structure of her work is the message it conveys: that genuine peace is not the mere absence of hostilities, but rather the tranquility that arises out of a social order in which individuals treat one another with justice and compassion. The long history of human conflict suggests that without greater recognition of that fact—a fact which Mother Teresa's concern for the absolute poor so strikingly illustrates—the prospects for world peace will remain perilously fragile.

It was undoubtedly such sentiments from the president of the World Bank, a man who dealt daily with the crises of the world's poorest nations and their peoples, that brought Mother Teresa to the podium of the Aula Magna of Oslo University on December 10, 1979. Her name then joined the roster of the bringers of peace of nearly eight decades: Albert Luthuli, the Zulu chief, who had offered nonviolent moral resistance to oppression in South Africa; Fridtjof Nansen, the Norwegian who had protected refugees after the First World War and Georges Pire, Dominican priest, who had brought works of compassion to refugees after the Second World War; Albert Schweitzer, whose "reverence for life" was expressed in service to suffering people in Africa; and Martin Luther King, Jr., who called on the teachings of Jesus and the example of Gandhi in breaking with an oppressive past.

The Year of the Child, 1979, seemed perhaps a more fitting year for Mother Teresa to be honored than the International Women's Year.

The Aula Magna of the University of Oslo was filled when the slightly stooped, little figure of Mother Teresa was led to the stage where the chairman of the Norwegian Nobel Committee, Professor John Sannes, awaited her. All stood at the entrance of King Olav V, Crown Prince Harald and Crown Princess Sonja. A symphony orchestra placed onstage played Grieg's "Gratitude," and multicolored bouquets of flowers shone under the brilliant lights. We heard from Professor Sannes a powerfully worded address in English which began, "Your Majesty, Your Royal Highnesses, Your Excellencies, Ladies and Gentlemen. The Norwegian Nobel Committee has awarded the Peace Prize for 1979 to Mother Teresa."

> The year 1979 has not been a year of peace: disputes and conflicts between nations, peoples, and ideologies have been conducted with all the accompanying extremes of inhumanity and cruelty. We have witnessed wars, the unrestrained use of violence; we have witnessed fanaticism hand in hand with cynicism; we have witnessed contempt for human life and dignity.
>
> We are faced with new and overwhelming floods of refugees. Not without reason the word genocide has been on many lips. In many countries completely innocent people have been the victims of acts of terror. In this year, moreover, we recalled the way in which an entire ethnic group was virtually exterminated in Europe only a generation ago. The Holocaust film series has shaken us, not only as an evil memory from our own not-too-distant past, but as we consider the world of 1979, not one of us can be certain that the like may not recur in the future.

Without belaboring the point, Sannes was pointing to a person who incarnated mercy in an age when millions fell victim to utter mercilessness.

"The Norwegian Nobel Committee has considered it right and appropriate, precisely in this year," he continued, "in their choice of Mother Teresa, to remind the world of the words spoken by Fridtjof Nansen: 'Love of one's neighbor is realistic policy.'

"As a description of Mother Teresa's life's work we might select the slogan that a previous Nobel Peace Prize Laureate, Albert Schweitzer, adopted as the leitmotif for his own work: 'Veneration for Life.' "

Sannes pointed out that Mother Teresa's work for the poor was performed without condescension and as a witness to the dignity of every person. He explained that her work was done in such a way as to build bridges across the great gulfs that separate parts of the human family.

He asserted, "In awarding Nobel's Prize for 1979 to Mother Teresa, the Committee has posed a focal question that we encounter along all these paths: Can any political, social, or intellectual feat of engineering, on the international or on the national plane, however effective and rational, however idealistic and principled its protagonists may be, give us anything but a house built on a foundation of sand, unless the spirit of Mother Teresa inspires the builders and takes its dwelling in their building?"

Sannes quoted an Indian journalist: " 'The Sisters, with their serene ways, their saris, their knowledge of local languages . . . have come to symbolize not only the best in Christian charity, but also the best in Indian culture and civilization from Buddha to Gandhi.' "

Sannes reviewed the growth of Mother Teresa's work and the motivation behind it of seeing Christ in every human person. Toward the conclusion of his address, he made a statement that indicated the Nobel Committee's understanding of something at the heart of Mother Teresa's witness: "Mother Teresa works in the world as she finds it, in the slums of Calcutta and other towns and cities. But she makes no distinction between poor and rich persons, between poor and rich countries. Politics have never been her concern, but economic, social, and political work with these same aims are in complete harmony with her own life's work." Reminding the international audience that help on the international level can only serve the cause of peace if it does not offend the self-respect of poor nations, he urged that such help from the rich countries be given in the spirit of Mother Teresa.

Sannes concluded: "There would be no better way of describing the intentions that have motivated the decision of the Norwegian Nobel Committee than the comment of the president of the World Bank, Robert S. McNamara, when he declared 'Mother Teresa deserves Nobel's Peace Prize because she promotes peace in the most fundamental manner, by her confirmation of the inviolability of human dignity.' "

The gold peace medal and diploma representing the prize and its gift of over $190,000 were placed in Mother Teresa's hands, and she was left alone in the spotlight before the microphones on the impressive rostrum. Her furrowed features were softened by a smile, and the bright red flush that suffused them was the only sign of strain. Her speech was undoubtedly the simplest Nobel response ever delivered in that academic hall. As already noted, she led the entire assemblage in reciting the peace prayer attributed to St. Francis of Assisi.

Even here, with the eyes of the world upon her, Mother Teresa spoke without a note,

> Let us all thank God on this beautiful occasion, for the joy of spreading peace, the joy of loving one another and the joy of recognizing that the poorest of the poor are our brothers and sisters.
>
> Let us thank God for the opportunity that we all have together today, for this gift of peace that reminds us that we have been created to live that peace, and Jesus became man to bring that Good News to the poor. He being God became man in all things like us except sin,

and He proclaimed very clearly that He had come to give the Good News. The news was peace to all men of good will, and this is something that we all want—the peace of heart. And God loved the world so much that He gave His son—it was a giving—it is as much as if to say it hurt God to give, because He loved the world so much that He gave his son, and He gave Him to Virgin Mary, and what did she do with Him?

That brought Mother Teresa close to her message of the defense of life. Some of us had been in touch with her about facts from the peace movement, including the numbers of cities with their populations targeted for indiscriminate destruction by stockpiles of the nuclear deterrent. She did not advert to these things. Her defense was of the very weakest human form, subject to legal destruction by the millions in many of the world's countries. She took up the subject in her inimitable way.

As soon as Jesus came into her life, Mary went in haste to give that Good News. As she came into the house of her cousin, the child—the unborn child—the child in the womb of Elizabeth, leapt with joy. It was that little unborn child that was the first messenger of peace. He recognized the Prince of Peace; he recognized that Christ had come to bring the Good News for you and for me.

It was near Christmas, and many Norwegian homes had a lighted Advent star in their windows. It was a country that had recently made abortion, paid for by the state, an easy option for any woman, thus joining many other countries in the developing as well as the developed world. The subject was one that was not welcome to the ears of many. After mentioning as enemies of peace the neglect of the old in institutions and the neglected young who succumb to drugs, she said,

We are talking of peace, but, I feel that the greatest destroyer of peace today is abortion. Because it is a direct war, a direct killing—direct murder by the mother herself. And we read in the Scripture, for God says very clearly: "Even if a mother could forget her child—I will not forget you—I have carved you in the palm of my hand" [she said, quoting Isaiah]. We are all carved in the palm of His hand, so close to Him. That unborn child has been carved in the hand of God. And that is what strikes me most, the beginning of that sentence, that even if a mother could forget, something impossible, but even if she could forget—I will not forget you.

And today, the greatest means—the greatest destroyer of peace is abortion. And we who are standing here—our parents wanted us. We would not be here if our parents would do that to us. Our children, we want them, we love them, but what of the millions. Many people are very, very concerned with the children of India, with the children of Africa, where quite a number die, maybe of malnutrition, of hunger and so on, but millions are dying deliberately by the will of the mother. And that is what is the greatest destroyer of peace today. Because if a mother can kill her own child—what is left but for me to kill you and you to kill me—there is nothing in between. And this I appeal in India, I appeal everywhere: Let us bring back the child, and this year being the child's year! What have we done for the child?

One of the petitions of the peace prayer of St. Francis was "Lord, grant that I may seek not so much to be loved, as to love." Mother Teresa, took the opportunity of uttering hard sayings in high places, not courting love and admiration, but testifying to her vision of the truth. She talked of alternatives to abortion, the alternatives that she and the Missionaries of Charity were carrying out in Calcutta. For many years, the Sisters had been fighting abortion by adoption, she explained, and she went on to discuss family planning by natural means, telling the audience,

> We are teaching our beggars, our leprosy patients, our slum dwellers, our people of the street, natural family planning. Our poor people understand, I think, that if our people can do like that, how much more can you and all the others do.

Mother Teresa then related some of her favorite examples of giving; that of the little boy, by then quite famous, who gave up sugar for three days when he heard that Mother Teresa had no sugar for her people, and that of the Hindu mother who shared the rice given her for her family with an equally hungry Muslim family. Perhaps her most moving story dealt with a woman picked up on a Calcutta street who was in so terrible a condition that Mother Teresa told the Sisters to take care of the others so that she could personally look after the woman.

> I did for her all that my love can do. I put her in bed, and there was such a beautiful smile on her face. She took hold of my hand, as she said one word only, "Thank you"—and she died.
>
> I could not help examining my conscience before her, and I asked what would I say if I was in her place. And my answer was very simple. I would have tried to draw a little attention to myself; I would have said, "I am hungry, that I am dying, I am cold, I am in pain," or something, but she gave me much more—she gave me her grateful love. And she died with a smile on her face.

Mother Teresa mentioned many times the greatness of the poor. She also contrasted the poverty she had found in the West with the poverty she served in Calcutta.

> Around the world, not only in the poor countries, I found the poverty of the West so much more difficult to remove. When I pick up a person from the street, hungry, I give him a plate of rice, a piece of bread. I have satisfied, I have removed that hunger. But a person that has been thrown out from society—that poverty is so hurtful, and so much, that I find it very difficult. Our Sisters are working amongst that kind of people in the West.

It was love that was the heart of her message.

> It is not enough to say I love God, but I do not love my neighbor. St. John says you are a liar if you say you love God and you do not love your neighbor. How can you love God whom you do not see, if you do not love your neighbor whom you see, whom you touch, with whom you live. And this is very important for us to realize that love, to be true, has to hurt. It hurt Jesus to love us, it hurt him.

At the informal reception that replaced the ceremonial banquet, someone asked Mother Teresa to see the Nobel medal. She could not remember where she had placed it and a few of us went looking for it. It was found among the coats deposited on a shelf at the entrance to the hall. Mother Teresa stood to greet everyone and took as her only repast a glass of water. Her mind was on love, repeating to the Norwegians, "I have received so much love since I came. I have simply been surrounded by love. I go back to India with love."

She did not depart, even at such gatherings from her usual refreshment, water. It was what she had taken at the reception held for her by the Indian Ambassador to Norway on her arrival on the eighth of December. The Ambassador, G. C. Swell, anticipating a large attendance, had arranged the reception in two sections. As Mother Teresa's plane was delayed, and the press held her at the airport, the early and later guests merged, and nearly a thousand guests filled every room and nook of the Embassy. Awaiting her were the Foreign Minister of Norway, the Chief Justice, members of the royal household, members of Parliament, other government dignitaries and ambassadors, including the Chinese Ambassador, and members of their families. Mother Teresa's warm smile, that seemed to erase the deep lines of age and weariness, lit up her face until the last guest had departed.

Mother Teresa had been taken from the plane to a press corps larger than any she had faced before, with about a hundred journalists from around the world, armed with countless cameras and microphones. The whole theme of her acceptance response to the Nobel Award came in response to a question as to why she had decided to come to Norway in person.

"I am myself unworthy of the prize. I do not want it personally. But by this award the Norwegian people have recognized the existence of the poor. It is on their behalf that I have come."

In reply to the question as to whether she was ever overwhelmed by the numbers of the needy, she answered simply, "No, one by one by one." She pointed out, as she often did, that picking up the first dying person was the decisive step.

The Norwegian paper, *Aftenposten,* commented: "How wonderful to see the world press for once spellbound by a true star, a star without false eyelashes and makeup, without jewels and fur coats, without theatrical gestures. Her joy is the thought of spending the Nobel Prize money for the good of the poorest and most miserable of the world's people." The same newspaper featured Mother Teresa in color photographs at every function: standing on the rostrum, being shepherded through crowds, kneeling in church, being greeted by young people holding high their torches. Before her arrival, a photographer had taken a picture of the celllike room in the St. Joseph's Institute where she would be housed. It was at St. Joseph's Institute that she had time to visi+ with her brother, Lazar Bojaxhiu, and her niece, Mrs. Agi Guttadauro, on the evening of her arrival. She told us some of the details of how the news of the prize had affected life in Calcutta.

"When I came home [to the Motherhouse] from Kalighat, I found photographers and television men in our little parlor. I have given strict orders that no one is to be brought in like that. I asked them what they were doing.

"They said, 'We have come all the way from Norway. You have been given the Nobel Peace Prize.' Then they took their pictures.

"The people began arriving, every type of person, the poor and the richer people. Then the telegrams began coming, from President Carter and Senator Kennedy. The one that came from President Reddy (of India) I remember. He said, 'You are following closely in the steps of the Prince of Peace.' The Sisters said there were more than five hundred telegrams. Every day more letters, sometimes eighty, sometimes more. Then we had our Chapter meeting. People understood I was on retreat. It lasted nine days, and it was wonderful. We settled so many things."

Lazar Bojaxhiu remarked, "Every time I see 'Mother' she becomes smaller—but every time I see her, she becomes better."

Sunday, December 9, was marked by morning services at St. Olaf's

Catholic Cathedral, an afternoon mass in the chapel of St. Joseph's Institute, and an evening ecumenical service at the Domkirche, the Lutheran Cathedral of Oslo. It was a service of intercession for the indigents of the world. Mother Teresa was always flanked by Sister Gertrude and Sister Agnes. At the crowded service at St. Olaf's, the children were all called up to the front and bundled into the first pews near the altar. A two year old, enveloped in a green and scarlet snowsuit, suddenly decided that a clear space between the children and the altar was perfect for somersaults and for standing on his head. There were marvelous moments as the little green-scarlet figure twirled before the altar and finished upside down.

To an informal gathering in the cathedral hall, Mother Teresa brought her message of love, starting always with the family. Ann Blaikie talked of the Co-Workers, explaining that if they spread God's love on earth and became channels of this love, then they were Co-Workers in spirit. At the afternoon liturgy in the chapel of St. Joseph's Institute, presided over by Bishop Nikola Prela of Skopje, Mother Teresa joined with the congregation, chiefly immigrants or guest workers from Yugoslavia, in the responses, "*Gospodine smiluj se, Kriste smiluj se.*" (Lord have mercy, Christ have mercy.) When called upon to speak to the congregation in Serbo-Croatian, she had to pause halfway through her talk. She smiled and asked for help with some words. The language of her schooldays was too infrequently used to allow for speedy recall. She took time to write a short message in Albanian, which she could still write but had forgotten how to speak. "My fellow-countrymen," she wrote, "the Albanians are always in my heart. I pray that God's peace may come into our hearts, our families, and the entire world. Please pray for our poor and also for me and my Sisters. I do pray for you." Instead of signing herself, "M. Teresa, M.C.," she signed it with her family name, "M. Teresa Bojaxhiu."

The beautiful and cavernous Lutheran Domkirche was filled for the service of intercession. Besides scriptural readings and hymns, there was a long litany of prayers for the poor, the suffering, and the victims of disaster in the whole world. The printed program was in Norwegian and English, but the congregation intoned, "Lord hear our prayer" in many tongues. The Lutheran bishop had invited John William Gran, the Catholic bishop of Oslo to preside with him at the altar, and joining with them were representatives of the Greek Orthodox Church, the Anglican Church, the Baptists, Methodists, and the Salvation Army.

The vice-chairman of the Nobel Committee, Egil Aarvik, delivered a sermon in which he stated: "If there is something that our divided world without peace needs, it is people who in the name of Christ will cross boundaries to lessen his neighbor's need, regardless of standing and reputation. 'Blessed are the merciful,' said Jesus.

"It is this care without boundaries, this understanding of the worth of man, this desire to heal the broken—it is this that after all lies at the bottom of all the peacemaking work, regardless of where it is done, and by whom. That is why it is so natural that Mother Teresa and what she stands for would be honored with this year's Peace Prize."

The glorious cathedral choir, in a gallery halfway up the height of the cathedral, sang the "Hallelujah Chorus" from Handel's *Messiah* in a burst of heavenly sound. Mother Teresa told the people of her gratitude for the gift that would provide homes for the homeless and for leper families. She said that she was especially grateful for "the gift of recognition of the poorest of the poor in the world."

The final hymn was Cardinal Newman's *Lead, Kindly Light*, "Keep Thou my feet; I do not ask to see the distant scene; one step enough for me."

The evening air was icy as we left the cathedral. A lighted torch was put into our hands and we found ourselves part of a procession through the streets of Oslo.

We were told that a similar procession had been held for Martin Luther King, Jr. The Nobel Award of the previous year, we were told, had been held under tight security. So fearful were the Norwegians of an attack by international terrorists on the life of Menachem Begin, Prime Minister of Israel, that the ceremonies had been moved from the university to an ancient Oslo fortress. Now all was open and jubilant. Thousands of torch carriers lit up the night, and thousands of young people raised their voices lustily in freedom songs that had leapt from the United States to people around the globe: "We shall overcome; deep in our hearts, we do believe, we shall overcome someday"; "Someone's cryin', Lord, Kumbaya (Come by here), Someone's prayin' Lord, Kumbaya, O Lord, Kumbaya."

The destination of the march was the Norwegian Mission Society where the Lutheran women's association had laid out a supper for five-hundred people in the mission hall. Before she entered the hall, Mother Teresa was prevailed upon to say a few words to those gathered, still holding their torches so high that the night was bright. As she entered the hall, a choir of a hundred young girls, holding candles like a band of Christmas angels, welcomed her with a hymn to Sancta Lucia. The girls presented Mother Teresa with a gift of about three-hundred dollars which they had collected through their own sacrifices. Someone came forward and put into her hands a ceramic Infant Jesus for the Christmas crib. Mother Teresa smiled delightedly, cradling it in her arms.

A sign of mission was pictured on the wall, a ship with a net, a reminder of Jesus' words, "Let down your nets." Standing near it, Mother Teresa spoke, "This understanding love I have received since I put foot in Norway —it is just what will bring peace to the world. I have no words to thank you. My gratitude is my prayer for you that we will all grow in holiness."

When Bishop Gran was called upon, he said, "Mother Teresa, we feel from you the radiation of love. This is because you are on fire and burn for others. It is good for us to be in the presence of someone who burns for others."

Mother Teresa followed custom by delivering the Nobel Lecture on the evening of December 11 in the same Aula Magna of the university. Again speaking extemporaneously, she covered the same ground as in the December 10 response.

Though pressed for television and newspaper interviews during every free hour, Mother Teresa stole away to spend several hours with her Co-Workers in a room at St. Joseph's Institute. Sitting in a circle, we joined her in prayer. Among the group were Ann Blaikie of England, Josepha Gosselke of Germany, Dagny Arbman of Sweden, Jacqueline de Decker of Belgium, Maud and Guus Franken Spee of the Netherlands, Tony and Lillian Miceli Ferrugia of Malta, Abbé Christian Daleau of France, and Mrs. Eli Werner of Norway.

Mrs. Werner explained that there was a People's Prize in addition to the Nobel Prize. This was a voluntary effort by the Norwegian people, a campaign that had begun well in advance of the Nobel presentation. With exquisite delicacy, the Norwegians had given the campaign leadership to the minuscule Catholic community of Norway, centered chiefly in Bergen.

"Headmaster Gyermund Hogh of St. Paul's School in Bergen is the chairman," Eli Werner explained, "and I am on the committee assisting him. I am also on the school staff."

The campaign had caught fire, she reported, and it was thought that the total would be close to that of the Nobel Prize money. What had impressed Mrs. Werner was the enthusiasm of the young people. They had appeared on radio and television; they had put on programs in their schools, and many had stood on streetcorners appealing on behalf of the world's needy.

Mother Teresa told the Co-Workers that she was doing less work than before, and we wondered how that could be with so many houses around the globe.

"I have divided up the work so much among the Sisters that they have asked me, 'Mother, what are *you* going to do?'

"I told them," she said laughing, "I will be loving you."

The division of the work into regions proceeded until there were soon nineteen regions with regional superiors in charge, both in India itself and outside. Someone asked her if it was actually her signature on the receipts sent out from Calcutta. She answered that she signed each one and he wondered why.

"It is like praying for me," Mother Teresa replied. "When I am writing 'God bless you,' I am praying. It is something I do for the people. They appreciate that." Another Co-Worker teasingly asked if they could ever expect to see Mother Teresa just loving the Sisters and quietly signing "God bless you," "God bless you," by the hour.

A long-distance telephone call for Mother Teresa was announced. It was from Washington, D.C., from Mrs. Violet Collins of the Co-Workers. It dealt with a burning issue in the United States; the capture and detention of American embassy personnel in Teheran who were shown in the press blindfolded and humiliated. A group of families of the American hostages held in Iran were meeting in Washington. Already the embassy personnel had been held captive many months. The families asked if Mother Teresa would personally intercede on their behalf and ask for their freedom. This was the first task that had fallen to Mother Teresa as the recipient of the Nobel Peace Prize. She had not been successful in two earlier peacemaking efforts; once to talk with Archbishop Lefebvre, leader of a dissident group within the Catholic Church, and another time with Rev. Ian Paisley, religious leader in Northern Ireland. She agreed to undertake the task and personally visit the Embassy of Iran as soon as she arrived in Rome.

In Rome, on the afternoon of December 13, Mother Teresa was received by a staff member of the Iranian Embassy. As she related it, "I went to the Embassy and told the man that I had been asked to see him about the American hostages. I told him, 'I know nothing. I have been too busy to read anything. I come to you as a mother would who longed for her children. People have appealed to me to do this. I am willing to go to Iran or to talk to Ayatollah on the telephone. Meantime, we will be praying.' The man said he would look into the matter."

Earlier that morning, Mother Teresa had attended mass celebrated by Pope John Paul II in his private chapel. He had said that her Sisters could accompany her, so she brought twenty-five of the professed Sisters and fifteen of the postulants. By squatting on the floor, there was room for all. Afterward the Holy Father spoke to them in the hall near the chapel, telling them to continue to give the Good News to the poor. "He is a real father," Mother Teresa remarked. "And he is humble and simple as a child."

The next day, Mother Teresa was able to do something she had longed to do, but for which, in all her visits to Rome she had never found the time. She went into the Roman catacombs.

Accompanied by a few Sisters, she paid a visit to the Catacomb of St. Priscilla. By tradition, it was the chapel where St. Peter had baptized new Christians. Before the mass, a Benedictine Sister took us around the dank, dimly lit passageways, showing us the ancient frescoes, and explaining their significance. She pointed to Susannah, the woman in the Hebrew Scriptures unjustly accused by the two elders as a figure of the early Church, also unjustly persecuted. Susannah was pictured with arms outstretched and palms upward in the attitude of prayer of the people of Israel. With her flashlight, the nun guide threw bright beams on tombs in the walls; some with inscriptions that this man, this woman, this child, had been martyred.

Asked by the priest-celebrant to say a few words at the end of the mass, Mother Teresa began: "Here we are in a place where people loved God so much that they were ready to die for that love; men, women, and even little children. We have just seen the grave of a martyred child. They had hope in the Resurrection.

"What went through my mind," she said gravely, "was the temptation to suicide by so many people today, young people. Let us pray that for them that they will realize that they are loved by God. Let us pray that they may learn to love and to overcome the temptation to take their lives."

Mother Teresa waited for a response from the Embassy of Iran. She had made an unequivocal offer. There was no response. They did not even give her the opportunity to communicate by telephone with the concerned authorities in Teheran. Meanwhile, in the United States, the headline in the New York *Times* read, "Mother Teresa, Receiving Nobel, Assails Abortion."

If Mother Teresa thought that the days of public ceremony were behind her as she left Oslo, she was mistaken. India was getting ready to honor her with its highest civilian award, the Bharat Ratna, the Jewel of India. To the strains of the Indian national anthem in the Rashtrapati Bhavan, the presidential palace in Delhi, she approached the President of India to be invested with the ultimate honor of her adopted country. She was the first naturalized Indian ever to receive it. President Neelam Sanjiva Reddy told the audience, "She embodies in herself compassion and love of humanity as few in history have done . . . . Her entire life has been a personification of service and compassion. These are the imperatives of human existence which are generally affirmed in words but denied in actions."

Immediately afterward, Prime Minister Indira Gandhi came forward to congratulate her. Though they had differences on the matter of family planning, sterilization, and abortion, Mother Teresa respected her. Mother Teresa not only stood her ground on natural family planning as the way to limit population growth but presented Mrs. Gandhi with a letter signed by thousands of nuns in India opposing sterilization (especially forced sterilization) and abortion. Indira Gandhi nevertheless said of her, "To meet her is to feel utterly humble, to sense the power of tenderness and the strength of love."

The strength of the love taught and practiced by Mother Teresa and the Missionaries of Charity could be seen in works of mercy, since mercy is only love under the aspect of need, love going out to meet the needs of the person loved. The works of mercy, feeding the hungry, clothing the naked, sheltering the shelterless, interrupted or reversed by every war, were being recognized as works of peace. The ultimate accolade of the Nobel Peace Prize to Mother Teresa awakened many to the realization that works of mercy might be the truest undergirding of peace, to be reversed only at humanity's peril.

It was during the Nobel ceremonies in Oslo that Mother Teresa made one of her most succinct statements about her own identity. It was elicited by the probing question of a journalist who, after pointing out that she was born in Yugoslavia and lived in India, while her Sisters worked all over the world, asked, "And you, Mother Teresa, how do you feel about yourself?"

"By blood and origin," she replied, "I am all Albanian. My citizenship is Indian. I am a Catholic nun. As to my calling, I belong to the whole world. As to my heart, I belong entirely to the heart of Jesus."

21

From the Same Hand—Honors and Barbs

Though honors came to Mother Teresa from around the world, the first recognition had come to her from her adopted country. The Padma Sri Award was given to her in September 1962, at a time when the Missionaries of Charity had only been in existence for twelve years. Mrs. Vijaya Lakshmi Pandit was present. The sister of Prime Minister Nehru described the event, pointing out that several other people receiving awards were greeted with only polite applause in Rashtrapati Bhavan, the presidential palace in Delhi.

"But when this little lady entered that magnificent hall," commented Mrs. Pandit, "with its painted ceiling and all the pomp and panoply that attend such functions—the military on parade and the guards on duty, all dressed in splendid colors, a band in attendance—she walked up just as she is every day. She received the award as she would have received a dying man or picked up a child, but the hall went mad. The stamping and the clapping and the cheering were absolutely spontaneous. I looked at the President (Dr. Sarvepalli Radhakrishnan), there were tears in his eyes."

Ten years later, in November 1972, the Government of India awarded Mother Teresa the Jawaharlal Nehru Award for International Understanding. The presenter was President V. V. Giri, who like Mother Teresa, had a connection with Ireland, having taken his law degree there and having participated in the 1916 Easter Rebellion. The citation said in part, "Someday perhaps mankind will devise satisfactory solutions for every human predicament. But as long as compassion counts for something in the human condition, the hopes of defeated men everywhere, despairing men at the end of their tether, will rest on a chosen few for whom the giving is all. One such messenger of mercy is Mother Teresa."

The authorities dispatched a helicopter to bring Mother Teresa to Santiniketan in 1976 to receive an honorary degree from the Visva-Bharati university in Bengal. Prime Minister Gandhi was shown on the front page of *The Times* of India conferring the degree—the Deshikottama—for contributions to suffering humanity. Mrs. Gandhi remarked, "She is so tiny to look at, but there is nothing small there."

Perhaps the least publicized Indian honor, but one deeply appreciated by Mother Teresa, was the invitation to lay the foundation stone of the Gandhi Bhavan, the Institute of Gandhian Thought and Peace Studies in Allahabad in 1976. The Institute, whose aim was to examine the relevance of Gandhian thought to contemporary society, published a commemorative booklet with a picture of Mother Teresa on its cover. It carried her message: "May God bless the beautiful work of spreading Gandhiji's work for love and peace. God bless you, M. Teresa, M.C." Indians saw Gandhi and Mother Teresa in the same light. An Indian told me, "Gandhi is a karma yogi, carrying his contemplation into action. Mother Teresa is a karma yogin." Mother Teresa's approach to artificial birth control was exactly that of Gandhi, one of whose followers, Rajkumari Amrit Kaur, as India's Minister of Health, undertook to make available to Indians of all classes, but particularly the rural families, the rhythm method of birth control.

When Mother Teresa reached her seventieth birthday in August 1980, her face appeared on millions of Indian postage stamps, an unheard-of honor for a nun and for someone born outside India. A special ceremony marked the issuance of the stamp, a ceremony televised and broadcast all over India. It took place in Loreto House, Calcutta.

Already mentioned were some of the honors that came to Mother Teresa from outside India; honors such as the Templeton Award in 1973 that brought significant monetary aid to keep alive the growing network of houses.

An honor came to Mother Teresa in Rome on January 6, 1971. This was the Pope John XXIII Peace Prize commemorating the Pope whose peace letter *Pacem in Terris* was addressed not only to his fellow-religionists, but to all humanity. The award carried with it the sum of twenty-five thousand dollars. This came from a fund set up by Pope John XXIII himself, utilizing a gift he had received from the Balzan family. "We will all make this year especially a year of peace," said Mother Teresa after accepting the prize from the hands of Pope Paul VI. "To this end we will try to speak more to God and with God and less to men and with men. Let us preach Christ's peace as He has done."

The award of the *Mater et Magistra* medal was also a reminder of Pope John XXIII and his second encyclical letter, "Mother and Teacher." It was given to Mother Teresa by the Third Order of St. Francis of the United States in 1974.

An award came in 1979 to Mother Teresa from the hands of the President of Italy, Sandro Pertini, in Rome's National Academy. It was the

Balzan International Prize awarded by the Balzan International Foundation provided for in the will of Angelina Balzan Danieli. Already, through Pope John XXIII, funds from the Balzan family had been channeled to her work. The prize was given to those who promoted initiatives of peace and humanitarianism and brotherhood among peoples, and brought to the work an amount equal to $325,000.

On December 10, 1981, in Rome, Mother Teresa voiced a theme that was to become familiar; namely, "Fear of the child." On the occasion of receiving an honorary doctorate of medicine from Rome's Catholic University of the Sacred Heart, she said, "Abortion is nothing but fear of the child—fear to have to feed one more child, to have to educate one more child, to have to love one more child. Therefore the child must die."

Mother Teresa reminded the assemblage, as she had done in Oslo, that the first to recognize Jesus the Messiah as an unborn child, was the unborn child in the womb of Elizabeth. "I ask the doctors, the people of this hospital, never to allow a mother to kill her child." Then she made a direct request.

"If there is no one who wants the child, I want it. In Primavalle, the Holy Father has given us a beautiful place, where every single child, every unwed mother, will be always most welcome."

The Primavalle building was Vatican property to which Pope Paul VI had personally given Mother Teresa the keys.

Honorary degrees had begun to come to Mother Teresa with the 1971 honorary doctorate of humane letters from the Catholic University of America in Washington, D.C. This was followed by an honorary doctorate from St. Francis Xavier University in Antigonish, Nova Scotia, Canada, in 1974, and another from Iona College, New Rochelle, New York in 1976. The first three were Catholic institutions, but these were followed by honors from non-Catholic universities including Temple University in Philadelphia, Pennsylvania, in 1979 and Harvard University in Cambridge, Massachusetts, in 1982.

Most unexpected, perhaps, of all the honorary degrees was the one conferred by England's Cambridge University, an institution dating from the early eleven hundreds. When the university public orator presented her to the university chancellor for the degree on June 10, 1977, he used the old language of the Catholic Church, "Reverendae Matris quam laetissimi praesentem intuemur si honorum cursum exquiras respondeat ipsa nullius momenti esse." (The Reverend Mother whom we are delighted to see among us would reply, if you inquired about her career, that it was of no importance.)

After briefly summarizing that career, the orator concluded with an echo of the words, "ancilla Domini," (handmaid of the Lord), used by the Virgin Mary in describing herself: "Praesento vobis, inter Domini ancillas haud minimam, Congregationis Caritatis fundatricem ac principem, Reverendam Matrem Teresam." (I present to you one who is not the least among the handmaids of the Lord, the Reverend Mother Teresa, founder and leader of the Congregation of the Missionaries of Charity.)

Cambridge University was a center of the theology of the Reformation after the separation of the Church of England from Rome, so it seemed rather surprising that the degree conferred on Mother Teresa was an honorary doctor of divinity. After the ceremony, Mother Teresa preached a sermon to a packed congregation at Great St. Mary's, the university church of Cambridge. Though she spoke as usual without notes, the speech was taken down and the text shows it to be one of the longest talks she ever delivered. Contained in it is the theology of the Eucharist; a theology on which the English Church differed with Rome following the break at the time of Henry VIII.

"Jesus gave himself totally," she said. "He died on the cross, but before He died, He made Himself the Bread of Life to satisfy our hunger for love for Him. He said, 'Unless you eat my flesh and drink my blood you cannot have eternal life.' " Then she drew the conclusion for the followers of Jesus: "And the greatness of that love of His made Him the hungry one, and He said, 'I was hungry and you fed me . . . and unless you feed Me, you cannot enter eternal life.' "

At Cambridge she was among old friends. Standing by her side was Ann Blaikie; the person who conferred the degree was Prince Philip, newly installed as chancellor of the university, who had also made the presentation of the Templeton Prize. At Great St. Mary's she was introduced by a Cambridge graduate whose proforma baptism and confirmation at seventeen were occasioned by his acceptance at an Anglican residential college, Malcolm Muggeridge.

The Discovery Medal was awarded to Mother Teresa in June 1981 at a special convocation at Marquette University, a Jesuit school in Milwaukee, Wisconsin. The medal memorialized the seventeenth-century French Jesuit, Père Jacques Marquette, who was not only a missionary to Indian tribes, but an explorer of the Mississippi River. Mother Teresa was asked at a press conference whether she had made any discoveries.

"I am too small to discover anything," she replied. Then she caught herself. "Yes, I suppose it is a discovery for some that the poorest of the poor, the rejected, the throwaways among us—they are Jesus in His disguise." She had passed her seventieth birthday at the time of the convocation and one of the questions dealt with the possibility of her retirement. It was an idea that had seemingly never occurred to her and she dismissed the query by associating herself with the great masses of poor people. "The poor cannot retire," she said.

When it became known that Mother Teresa was to be honored with an honorary doctorate of law by Harvard University in 1982, student groups went to work in the spring to prepare leaflets on her work and on her Co-Workers. She was not to be the commencement speaker, so the senior class invited her to be the speaker at the Class Day exercises on June 9, 1982. Over ten thousand people, including students and their families and friends in one of the largest groups ever to attend the exercises, heard her talk of love, prayer and sacrifice, of chastity, and the evil of abortion. She also spoke in a similar vein at the neighboring Radcliffe College.

The *Harvard Gazette* noted, "Standing five feet tall and clad in a sarilike white habit and sandals, Mother Teresa received two standing ovations from an audience not all of whom shared her views on chastity and abortion—but clearly respected the sincerity of her appeal." In the audience were a group of children who had been adopted from Shishu Bhavan in Calcutta by families in Boston. One of them, Sadhana Rebecca Mohr was pictured being hugged by Mother Teresa.

After the Class Day, the Boston City Council honored Mother Teresa with a resolution proclaiming June 9, 1982, as "Mother Teresa Day." On many occasions Mother Teresa was the recipient of the key to this or that city, once receiving the key to New York City from the hands of Mayor Edward Koch. The ritual was one that was strange to her. Once, after she had been told that she was the first citizen of a midwestern town, she spoke with a group of Co-Workers.

"Yesterday," she said, "I was the first citizen, and I said 'Thank you very much.' But I don't understand what it means. It makes no difference; it is coming from the same hand. And tomorrow, if people would say 'Crucify' —all right. It is the same loving hand. That acceptance for you and for me —it is what Jesus wants from us. To allow Him to use us without consulting us."

Mother Teresa was not speaking lightly with such words. She had made it clear again and again that all the honors and prizes were a matter of indifference to her as a person. "I am not the centerpiece on a prize-giving day," she asserted. "It is Christ using me as His instrument to unite up all the people present. This is what I see happening: people coming to meet each other because of their need for God. I feel that to bring all these people together to talk about God is really wonderful. A new hope for the world."

The day did not come when people said "Crucify" regarding Mother Teresa, but there were days when she met rejection, and judgments were harsh, with words sharp as knives. That day, in 1949, when completely alone on the streets of Calcutta, she was asked to take her meager meal on the back steps like a beggar, was the forerunner of other rejections.

The first rejection was a test of her conviction, but some later rejections dealt with those dear to her heart; the lepers. In one city of India, the news that she was to open a center for lepers in a certain neighborhood evoked protest and angry refusal. Mother Teresa found a way to serve the lepers anyhow. She brought in a mobile clinic and saw that they were served as they had been served in Calcutta by going directly to the groups of infected families.

In another city, however, Mother Teresa was not able to reach a solution. She acquired a piece of land for a Home for the Destitute Dying. It happened that in that locality, many families had built new homes and they organized the opposition to having the destitute in their midst. A wall was erected to block Mother Teresa and the Sisters from coming into the section. When supporters of Mother Teresa's work tried to remove the barrier there were beatings. On the day of Mother Teresa's arrival, she stood at the barrier and spoke to the people. Word had been spread that she would bring lepers into the neighborhood. She explained that this was untrue, but that she would be bringing the poor and homeless. The leaders of the opposition were obdurate. They told the press that dying people and cadavers around the corner from their homes would take away the peace of the neighborhood and the value of their properties. Mother Teresa made her entreaties on behalf of the rejected, but her way was still barred. She decided to leave that locality, saying, "I'm sorry for you people. Later on you will regret it. You have not rejected me, but you have rejected God's poor." She complied with the people's "Go back," and left. One could picture her shaking the dust of that locality from her sandals.

There were times when the Missionaries of Charity had to accept changes that moved them suddenly from continent to continent. This often required the rapid study of a new language. When Mother Teresa brought a team of Sisters to Belfast, Northern Ireland, she found that while they loved the people and were loved in return, there were other Sisters who could do the work. Already in place were the Sisters of Charity, who knew the long history of troubles in that anguished corner of the world. Their ties with the people were strong. Meantime, urgent appeals for the Missionaries of Charity were reaching Mother Teresa from such places as Gaza and Ethiopia. Mother Teresa decided that the Belfast Sisters should serve in the Middle East and Ethiopia, and, as always, the team accepted the change with grace.

The blows that cut Mother Teresa to the heart were the times when her professed Sisters left the Society. It did not happen very often, but it did happen. The number was not large, but it included two superiors, on whom she had placed great trust and responsibility. One separated herself from the Society during the 1970s and the other in the early 1980s. Both were outstanding Missionaries of Charity and had made significant contributions to the order. One had suffered grievously in health, while the second had immersed herself so thoroughly in the culture of the people she served that she could not face going elsewhere and learning another tongue. Mother Teresa never discussed her pain at the loss of these members of her spiritual family.

Mother Teresa never knowingly strayed from her decision to avoid politics. Once in a press interview she was caught off guard by adroit questioning with political implications. With regard to the emergency rule imposed on India during part of the 1970s, she commented, "People are happier. There are more jobs. There are no strikes." These comments made newspaper headlines.

From her experience with the poor and workless and a strike-ridden metropolis, there had been an improvement. In the Catholic as well as the secular press, there were strong demurrings on the basis of principle. Msgr. George G. Higgins, long a leader of social action in the American Catholic Church, devoted an entire newspaper column to the matter. The column, distributed throughout the United States, made the point that any approval of the repressive labor policy then in force was unfortunate, and that charity, even the heroic charity practiced by Mother Teresa, was no substitute for justice.

There were times when Mother Teresa's views were misrepresented through honest misunderstanding.

"Mother Teresa Approves of Women Priests" went around the world in a report by United Press International in 1984. Co-Workers and those who knew Mother Teresa were amazed. They knew that Mother Teresa had many times expressed herself in opposition to female priests. The news release was based on an interview with an Indian journalist. When he put the question to her, she had replied that if anyone had the right to the priesthood it was Our Lady. The pressman, a Hindu, understood her to say "our ladies," and attributed all the praise Mother Teresa had expressed for the mother of Jesus to women in general. Thus the story went out on the international wire. Mother Teresa, in denying her support for female priests, stated, "I stand by what the Holy Father has said." She added an explanation that had given rise to the confusion, "No one could have been a better priest than Our Lady, and she remained only the handmaiden of the Lord."

There were other times when Mother Teresa was the victim of outright misrepresentation by the press. Under a headline, "Buy Cheaper Clothes, Eat Less, Mother Teresa Urges Trudeau," Mother Teresa was reported as having chastised Canada's Prime Minister, Pierre Eliot Trudeau during the Habitat Conference in Vancouver, Canada. I was present at the press interview when she replied to a question as to how people could live closer to the poor. Speaking of love in action, she advised people to eat more simply and to choose a cheaper dress or suit than they could afford. They could thus make a sacrifice and be better able to share with others. Trudeau's name never entered the statement.

When Mother Teresa was writing letters aboard an Air Canada plane after the Habitat Conference, I told her of the news report and urged her to send a correction to the Prime Minister. I mailed him her letter, written as usual on cheap, lined copybook paper. A commentator on the Habitat Forum had objected to Mother Teresa's presence because, in his view, Mother Teresa made it too easy to "dump one's guilt" about poverty and homelessness by a donation without confronting the reality of the problems.

In a "Reluctant Demurrer on Mother Teresa" in *The Christian Century* magazine, the author pointed out that "the Albert Schweitzer torch of ministering to woebegone peoples in the backwaters of the world" had passed to Mother Teresa. He then asserted that Mother Teresa's pronouncements were devoid of prophetic criticism. The article appeared early in 1981 in the ecumenical journal. The author felt Mother Teresa could do more good by pointing an accusing finger at society and stating that this or that situation must be changed, or addressing the wreckage-makers rather than only dealing with the human wreckage. In a response to the author, Dr. Homer Jack, Secretary of the World Conference on Religion and Peace, wrote, "It is interesting that you opened your article discussing Albert Schweitzer. He also was severely criticized, in his lifetime and still today, but often for not doing what he never intended to do."

Dr. Jack's point needed to be made repeatedly when priests, ministers, religious leaders, and lay people faulted Mother Teresa for not addressing herself to changing structures, when she had never intended to do so. In many interviews she alluded to the matter of giving fish to the poor to eat in contrast to giving them a fishing rod so that they could feed themselves. Her reply was, "Our people, so many can't stand. They are hungry, or they are diseased and disabled. Still less are they able to hold the rod. What I do, I give them the fish to eat and when they are strong enough, we'll hand them over to you, and you give them the rod to catch the fish."

The arguments that had been used by the group of priests in Lima, Peru, in 1973 and 1974 that so disturbed the Missionaries of Charity as they rescued people from hunger, disease, and even death, surfaced over and over again. The works of mercy, according to this group of priests, were palliatives, permitting unjust structures to continue and thus blocking change. If Mother Teresa's work showed anything it was that aged-old problems, like the heritage of colonialism and the strictures of traditional societies, were not amenable to speedy change. In the meantime (and as Don Helder Camara pointed out, "in the meantime" is a crucial phrase), the human victims of such situations could not wait for the big structural solutions. It was precisely to the victimized or marginalized that Mother Teresa took her witness of revolutionary love.

In the United States, where nuns are perhaps more outspoken than in other parts of the world, the dissent of some from the ways of Mother Teresa raised a storm of controversy. In an article in July 1981 in a secular paper with a two-million circulation, a columnist quoted the negative sentiments of two nuns active in the New York area. One nun said that while Mother Teresa might be an "enormously holy and compassionate woman," she might be doing American nuns a disservice by being used by the media as a model for Sisters in the United States. It was her opinion that Mother Teresa personified a pre-Vatican II view of faith which did not address systemic evils such as defense spending. She feared the use of Mother Teresa as a safe model, who could be put on a pedestal. The message to women would be, "Be docile, do your womanly caring thing." This would limit women's contributions in a time when criticism and questioning were needed. Another Sister made the point in the same article that while Mother Teresa came from the same dimension of faith, she was living under an old tradition from which American nuns had been drawing away after Vatican II. She added that Mother Teresa's narrow focus might have arisen from her limited experience in America. The columnist himself went further. After insisting that Mother Teresa was doing a disservice to American nuns, he said that she actually owed them an apology.

Within ten days, at least twenty Catholic papers and magazines across the United States carried the comments of the two nuns. In response, there were editorials, articles, and letters to the editors for the ensuing months. Some nuns concurred and said so publicly, but most of the public discussion consisted of a defense of Mother Teresa. Bernard Casserly, in a front-page editorial in the *Catholic Bulletin*, the weekly newspaper of the Minneapolis-St. Paul diocese, took note of the criticism that Mother Teresa was used by the media to personify a pre-Vatican Two view of faith.

"The tradition Mother Teresa follows is not only pre-Vatican Two," he asserted, "it goes back some two thousand years—to the time of Jesus of Nazareth, who also fed the hungry, healed the sick, and brought comfort to the poor and wretched of the earth."

A priest-editor of another midwestern Catholic paper regretted that there was an element of "either-or" in the criticism of the two nuns. Abigail McCarthy, well-known as columnist and author, in the lay Catholic magazine *Commonweal* of September 25, 1981, brought clarification in an article entitled "Neither Paul Nor Cephas." She stated, "I suppose the simplest explanation for the great popularity of Mother Teresa is that, in a world of structures and technology in which no person seems to matter very much, she has affirmed the preciousness of each human life."

The discussion continued on television and in interviews with the two Sisters. In further explanation of her position, one Sister stated, "We are concerned that the media is capitalizing on the human hunger for heroes and heroines and male church leaders, desiring a model of docility to authority are upholding Mother Teresa as the only model for all Sisters."

Mother Teresa could hardly be held responsible for the role played by the media, nor for any inferences drawn by certain church leaders. She had repeatedly made it clear what media attention meant to her—a rare example when she admitted to a sacrifice on her part. "This celebrity has been forced on me," she said. "I use it for the love of Jesus. The press makes people aware of the poor, and that is worth any sacrifice on my part." Describing the need to face the press, she confessed, "For me it is more difficult than bathing a leper."

Mother Teresa found herself in the middle of an issue affecting American nuns when a letter by her regarding the vocation of religious Sisters reached the media in October 1983. Some questions were raised among the nuns of the United States, numbering just under 100,000, by an action of the Holy See. Archbishop John Quinn of San Francisco was appointed by Rome to head a Commission on Religious Life which was to make a study of American nuns. Learning of the study, Mother Teresa wrote a letter on the vocation of Sisters to American bishops. By that time, she had many American Sisters in the congregation and had Missionaries of Charity in eight American cities and one rural area.

"Though most unworthy to write to you," she wrote, "still I feel I need to turn to you, to beg you to help our religious Sisters in USA to turn to our Holy Father with childlike confidence and love."

> We, who have consecrated our lives to God—we all know that this consecration
> — binds us in a special way to the Church and
> — to His Vicar on Earth
> and through him to the clear will of God which is so beautifully expressed through
> — the teaching of the Holy Father
> — the written will of God, our constitutions—approved by the Church as our way of life.

"There has been much disturbance in the religious life of Sisters, all due to misguided advice and zeal."

Mother Teresa wondered if the ambition of lay and religious women to be equal to men, even in the priesthood, was taking away the peace and joy of oneness in Jesus and the Church. She went on to cite the words of St.

Thérèse of Lisieux that Sisters should be love in the heart of Mother Church and that that tender love creates peace.

A copy of Mother Teresa's letter was sent to each American bishop and was released to the press. Archbishop Quinn, head of the commission studying the Sisters' role, indicated that he would note Mother Teresa's letter at the next meeting of the American bishops.

While there was gratitude for the letter from some Sisters, there were critical and even harsh responses from others. One of the associations of American nuns published in its newsletter an extended criticism of Mother Teresa. It stressed that her Sisters, unlike many American nuns, did not make use of the tools of social analysis to change sinful social structures. Mother Teresa's approach was deemed authoritarian and patriarchal. The Sister-author also expressed resentment at the fact that when the Missionaries of Charity came into a city, the media singled them out for laudatory attention while the long-term programs of other Sisters in the area were ignored.

Mother Teresa and the Missionaries of Charity took no part in the charges and countercharges that resulted from critical articles and the matter died down. In May 1984, the whole controversy was rekindled when the *National Catholic Reporter* reprinted the Sisters' criticism under the title, "Mother, Why Are There Poor?"

In the ensuing months, the same arguments were aired, and Mother Teresa was defended by those who saw her doing precisely what she set out to do—which was not mounting a challenge to structures. I kept being reminded of Mother Teresa's often-repeated approach to persons, "One by one by one." Co-Workers caught the simplicity and concreteness of this approach to work. When results were slow in coming, her words would be repeated, *"Ek, Ek, Ek"* (One, One, One) in Hindi. Mother Teresa and the Sisters concentrated all their energy and blazing love on the human person and left other tasks and ministries to those answering different calls. One of the defenders of Mother Teresa in the controversy following the reprinting of "Mother, Why Are There Poor?" recalled the words of John Henry Newman when he was dealing with extremes in the church, "God will overrule us all."

India's officialdom, which had showered so many honors on Mother Teresa, sometimes made difficulties for the work of the Missionaries of Charity. One day in 1980, at the same time her face was appearing on postage stamps throughout the country, she learned that the Missionaries of Charity were among a group of foreign-aided welfare organizations prohibited from starting new welfare programs among the tribal peoples of West Bengal. Also included in the ban were CARE, OXFAM, and the Salvation Army. The Minister for Tribal Welfare justified the ban on the possibility of links between welfare organizations and separatist movements among the tribal peoples.

The *Calcutta Statesman* featured the story and quoted Mother Teresa, who stated that the Missionaries of Charity did not distinguish between tribals and nontribals. "All are our brothers and sisters," she said, and added, "If people need us, nothing will stop us."

West Bengal authorities hastened to correct the matter, stating that the Missionaries of Charity were not prohibited from starting new programs for the poor in the State's tribal areas.

A far more serious matter was a measure introduced into the Indian Parliament in 1978 under the title of the "Freedom of Religion Bill." Ostensibly aimed at prohibiting conversion by "inducement," it was focused on the tribal and *harijan* communities among whom Christianity had gained many adherents. Christian missionaries from outside India, earlier numbering over six thousand, but by then reduced to a few hundred, joined Indian Christian leaders in pointing out that "inducement" could be broadly interpreted. Even the promise of salvation could be termed inducement and therefore could be a criminal offense punishable by imprisonment. There were sporadic outbursts against many Christian groups, in which extremists went so far as to force tribal people into reverting to tribal religions and to burn down Christian houses of worship.

The measure evoked from Mother Teresa a statement that might stand as a justification for her life, much simpler, but much in the spirit of the *Apologia pro Vita Sua* offered by John Henry Cardinal Newman in explanation of his religious stand.

"There is no freedom if a person is not free to choose according to his or her conscience," Mother Teresa wrote on March 25, 1979 to Prime Minister Morarji Desai, the old co-worker of Gandhi. (This statement is included in its entirety in the Appendices.)

The criticism that was directed at Mother Teresa from many sources because of her stand against artificial methods of birth control did not move her to change her position. For her it was a principle. When an interviewer asked her if she thought the Church would change its position on contraceptives, she replied, "Tomorrow has not come. Yesterday has already gone. I live only for today."

As a solution, she pointed to natural methods of family planning. Sister Paulette was a pioneer in introducing natural family planning to the neediest families in Calcutta, and soon part of the Sisters' training consisted of courses in the field. National and international agencies concerned with population control began to show interest in natural methods after scientific proof of their accuracy became available.

Neither the well-publicized honors nor the barbs counted with Mother Teresa. What counted was the fact that little branches of the Missionaries of Charity were being planted where God's merciful love might seem distant. It was these foundations, carrying the message of a Creator's merciful love mediated through His creatures that hastened her steps and gladdened her heart—as did the stream of young women who made the new foundations possible. The foundations themselves, as Mother Teresa saw them, were also "from the same loving hand."

At the time of the Nobel Award, there were 158 houses. This number was increased by nineteen in the following year, 1980. Besides seven new houses in India, including one in Jammu-Kashmir, the Sisters, generally in teams of four or five, moved into Papua New Guinea, Nepal, Ethiopia, Belgium, France, Spain, Argentina, and Chile. The house in Papua New Guinea was in the heart of a village, Bereina, three hours by truck from Port Moresby. Three other teams of Sisters were already there, in Tokarara, Kerema, and Hanuabada. Two houses were added to the Missionary of Charity network in Italy, one in the United States, and one in Yugoslavia. One house in Yugoslavia was already in operation in Zagreb, while the second house involved a historic step, the return of Mother Teresa, with a team of Sisters, to her birthplace, Skopje. In Katmandu, Nepal, the Sisters served the dying at a shrine on the Baghmati River, a place where devout Hindus came to end their days.

During the year, there were the usual talks before rallies of people. One, in West Berlin June 1980, especially impressed Mother Teresa. "It was beautiful in Berlin," she told me. "They invited me to the Catholic Day because the young people asked for me. There were seventeen thousand young people there. The theme was "Christ's Love Is Stronger." Three of us talked on the same theme, the bishop of Berlin, another bishop, and me." One of the subjects she talked about was purity of heart, and she told the young people that even if they had made mistakes against purity, there was always forgiveness. She was told later, that after the talks, the confessionals were besieged by young people.

"No matter how much evil there is in the world, Christ's love is always stronger, no?" Mother Teresa's question simply asked for a corroboration from her hearer. It was at that meeting that Maria Schell, the actress, came forward to present Mother Teresa with a gift of $280,000, her earnings from television appearances.

Mother Teresa was back in West Berlin the following year, this time to take four Indian Sisters behind what is called the Iron Curtain. They quietly crossed the guarded entry point, referred to by the Americans as "Checkpoint Charlie," to settle in East Berlin. A request by the local bishop to have the Sisters work there had brought a positive reply. The Sisters settled into a simple apartment and began, as their work usually did, by visiting in the neighborhood and talking with those alone, ill, or in need of some help. It was one of the twenty-six houses opened during 1981, eighteen of them outside India. In Korea, a congregation of Sisters named for the Korean Martyrs welcomed the Missionaries of Charity. A Korean Sister wanted to know exactly what the Sisters from India would be doing in Seoul and where they would be staying.

"We don't know yet," said the Missionary of Charity.

"You have come all this way and you don't know where you will stay!" said the surprised Korean Sister. "How nice. It is just like what God said to Abraham, 'Leave for the place I will show you.' " Mother Teresa went by boat with four Sisters to Macao, off the China coast, and took two teams to Egypt.

When Mother Teresa returned to Australia to start another house, she was accorded a "citizen's welcome" in Sydney. James Cameron, a prominent Baptist layman and parliamentarian, termed Mother Teresa "the world's most outstanding human being." The Rev. Fred Niles, a well-known Protestant minister, had Mother Teresa join him on his call-in radio program. When a caller informed Mother Teresa that he was nervous since it was his first time on a call-in program, Mother Teresa reassured him with the words, "Me too."

In May 1981, Mother Teresa celebrated the fiftieth anniversary of her life as a nun. There was a mass at the Motherhouse in Calcutta on Lower Circular Road, with a bishop and priests concelebrating at the altar and with her Sisters and novices around her. On June 6, 1981, she was in New York City, and there was a mass of thanksgiving in the basement church of St. Rita in the South Bronx. Cardinal Cooke was the main celebrant, and twenty-five priests came together from throughout the whole city, among them Franciscans and Jesuits as well as diocesan clergy.

Around Mother Teresa, besides the Sisters, were her friends and Co-Workers and the local community of the South Bronx and Harlem, black and hispanic Americans. Behind the altar was an enormous banner with a heart at its center. Human figures etched in white, brown, red, and black clustered around the heart under, "Let's Do Something Beautiful for God." The shut-ins had been brought to the church by the Sisters and Co-Workers. Men and women in wheelchairs filled the first rows. One of them, Theoria English, a gifted woman suffering from muscle atrophy, read the Scripture lesson from her wheelchair. All were waiting for the words of Mother Teresa, who stood close to the shut-ins outside the altar rail.

"These fifty years have been fifty years of love," she told the people. "Together let us thank God for what He has done, not only through me, but through the Sisters, through the whole society, for the lepers, the dying, and the unwanted. We are all the body of Christ. Our faith in Him must prove itself in works. Today, I thank the archdiocese for inviting me to come here and I thank all of you for accepting us to work with you."

Afterward, Mother Teresa stood outside the church to greet the people who came to embrace her affectionately and brought her their children for a blessing.

As we walked to the convent, we passed the empty lots where two large tenement houses had stood. A series of fires and the invasion of drug dealers had emptied the apartments of solid, working-class families. As in many vacated tenements, the residents had fled before the invasion of society's dropouts, many of them tragically young. These groups were anxious to drive out the occupants so that they could sell the brass piping and household fixtures to support their costly drug habit. The New York City authorities had finally dispatched a team of wreckers to demolish the buildings. The wasteland extended from the convent to the basement church.

One day, early in 1979, a building contractor, who had just made a religious retreat at which the film *Something Beautiful for God* was shown, heard that the Missionaries of Charity in the South Bronx might need some help. He had heard something vague about removing bricks. When he presented himself to Sister Priscilla, he was told that, yes, there were some bricks to be removed. "But," said Sister Priscilla, "I want to make a garden here." To Stephen La Sala, the removal of the bricks and the leveling of the ground could be managed, since he had access to powerful machinery. But a garden?

La Sala was mulling over the seemingly insurmountable problem of covering the wasteland with topsoil when he had a conference with a fellow contractor in New Rochelle, just outside of New York City. The man had a problem; the disposal of truckloads of soil about to be displaced in digging the foundations for a large housing development. La Sala solved the problem by trucking the topsoil to the leveled ground. When the covering of earth was laid, Sister Priscilla contacted landscapers and in her gentle but persuasive way presented the opportunity to do "something beautiful for God" in the South Bronx. The garden grew rapidly, with a carpet of grass, rose bushes, miniature fruit trees on one side, and on the other, tomatoes, rhubarb, string beans, lettuce, and cabbages.

Before entering the convent, Mother Teresa paused before the little parklike garden. There were pathways of bricks and flat stones with borders of bright marigolds. People in the tenements on the far side of the block could gaze out of their windows on a green oasis and often see groups of youngsters studying there peacefully. From one of the tenements, homeless men, cared for by the Sisters in the Home of Peace, could see signs of hope amid blight. Stephen La Sala arranged for the lease of the garden space for a yearly rental of one dollar. He and his wife, Joan, became Regional Links in the Co-Workers and took part in the work of the Sisters.

It was ten years since Sister Andrea and the first team of Sisters had arrived in New York. In the convent of black Sisters—since integrated with white novices—the first team had joined Mother Teresa and Andrew Young, Martin Luther King's aide, in singing, "Lead, Kindly Light." Mother Teresa had told Young that she wanted to emphasize the beauty of the people to whom she was bringing the Missionaries of Charity. While the Sisters had been faithful in doing this, they were also bringing beauty into the people's lives.

After addressing a large rally in Frankfurt, Germany, on "Solidarity with the Third World," and talking before ten thousand assembled young people at a town on the Danube in the spring of 1982, Mother Teresa arrived in the United States for a speaking tour that took her across North America. Not long after the ending of the International Co-Workers' Chapter in mid-May in Rome, she arrived in New York City in time to begin a tour through the United States and Canada, one which called for over a dozen talks, more awards, and two honorary degrees. Some of her talks were in large stadiums, including those in Charleston, South Carolina, and Winnipeg and Toronto, Canada, the latter in a return engagement before Fr. Tom McKillop's youth corps and an assembly on global peace.

The honorary degree from Harvard University has already been mentioned. The honorary doctorate from the University of Alberta, in Edmonton, Alberta, Canada, was accompanied by a visit to the town of St. Paul. This was a town of about five thousand people in the northeastern part of the province of Alberta. It seemed as though every resident was present at the ceremony of the presentation of a gift by Bishop Raymond Roy. The gift was for the incredibly large amount of $925,000, not far from a million dollars, all collected by the people of this small town. They explained to Mother Teresa how it had come about. A group of St. Paul residents had attended the Habitat Conference in Vancouver in 1976. Their contact with Mother Teresa had so inspired them that they came back determined to help the work for lepers and the rejected. They called their group the Habitat Institute and they chose a novel method. With partially donated labor and construction materials, they built a house. They then counted on selling the house for about $50,000. What they had not counted on was that the house would be sold more than once with one buyer giving the entire amount to the Institute. When the story of the unique project was carried by the Canadian press, gifts poured in. The story must have traveled outside Canada, since donations came from many foreign countries. As the members of the Habitat Institute were not Co-Workers, they did not worry whether their project came under the ban on collecting funds.

Mother Teresa was also the beneficiary of another large gift as a result of another visit to Canada. When I accompanied her to the town of Sydney, Nova Scotia, in 1974, two Indian medical men came to greet her after her talk. One of them was Dr. M. M. Chauhan, a doctor who gave all his energies to his practice. When some years later, Dr. Chauhan a bachelor and a devout Hindu, died, he left his entire estate to the work of Mother Teresa. The legacy came to nearly $500,000.

The sixteen houses opened by Mother Teresa in 1982 spanned a dizzying swath around the earth's surface, from Gangtok, Sikkim, to Dublin, Ireland, to Jenkins, Kentucky, in the Appalachian area of rural America. Mother Teresa "walked by faith and not by sight," in the words of the Apostle Paul, in taking her Sisters where they would give absolutely free service to those in need. The Co-Workers, still aghast at Mother Teresa's ban on the solicitation and collection of funds, began to see that her faith was matched by providential help from unexpected sources. The ban, however, never prohibited each Co-Worker from "giving until it hurt." After Mother Teresa's talk in the Winnipeg Stadium, the archbishop, Adam Exner, asked her if she would bring a team of Sisters to work in a poor section of that city. The Canadian Co-Workers went to work and in two years had a center ready for the Sisters who arrived in July 1984.

Every house of the Missionaries of Charity had its special character as the Sisters shaped their programs to the needs of the people. Two houses founded in 1981 served as an epiphany of the diversity of those needs. On a number of visits to Ireland, during which Mother Teresa renewed her acquaintance with the Loreto Sisters in the Motherhouse at Rathfarnham, the question had arisen about a team of Sisters for the capital, Dublin. Co-Workers, including Youth Co-Workers, were active in Dublin and in every part of the Republic. When Mother Teresa agreed to send a team of Sisters, an enthusiastic group of Dublin Co-Workers, led by Mrs. Mary Walsh, the National Link, renovated a solid old building to serve as a center. Men and women, young and old, came to a poor section of the capital to put the place in working order.

"The house is in the parish of St. Teresa," said Mrs. Walsh, "the first parish in the world named for St. Thérèse of Lisieux, Mother Teresa's patron. It was established shortly after her canonization in 1925."

The Co-Workers had little need to explain the lifestyle of Catholic Sisters to the solidly Catholic population of a poor district and of a low-rent housing development. The availability of an arts and crafts center and a carpentry center for unemployed neighborhood youth brought excitement to a depressed area. People were being brought together, as students from the Dublin Botanical Gardens came in to clear the land around the center and help with the planting of flowers and vegetables.

The center of the Missionaries of Charity in Dublin was inaugurated on June 18, 1982, the day celebrated as the feast of the Sacred Heart. It was located not far from Rathfarnham, where a young Albanian girl, silent and shy, had entered the Loreto order fifty-four years earlier in the year 1928.

When Mother Teresa accepted the invitation of Bishop William A. Hughes to bring her Sisters to a rural part of his diocese of Covington, Kentucky, she knew she was plunging them into a different setting from any they had ever encountered. Here was rural impoverishment, the poverty of hardworking people with a proud culture. Catholics were hardly more than one percent of the population of thirty thousand in Letcher County in southeastern Kentucky. The Catholic parish of Jenkins, a town of eight hundred, where the Sisters came in May 1982 was jubilant. The mining community had been decided upon by Sister Priscilla after visiting the "hollows," the hills and valleys of Appalachia. The four Sisters, headed by Sister Fidelia who had come from the house in Detroit, went visiting among the people. Two by two, the Sisters knocked on doors in Jenkins and in the "hollows."

"We are Sisters, and we'll be living in Jenkins. We wanted to come so that we would know each other."

Always, the reception was courteous and hospitable, with families asking the Sisters to "Come right in and have a cup of coffee." The Sisters refused gently, not going into the rule that barred them from accepting food in the homes they visited.

Mother Teresa's visit to Jenkins in June 1982 was the occasion for many newspaper stories and pictures of the Catholic nun who had won the Nobel Prize for Peace. A lighted sign was placed on the main street, "Welcome Mother Teresa," to give honor to a renowned figure who was not only a Catholic Sister but one dressed in a strange Eastern wraparound. There was an outdoor prayer service attended by hundreds of local people and others who had traveled considerable distances. Mother Teresa was presented with a gift that symbolized, as nothing else could, the reality of the poor mining community, a statue of the Virgin Mary hacked out of coal. Mother Teresa responded with a delighted smile, saying that this was the very first time she had ever possessed so rare a representation of "Our Lady."

"I feel very happy and grateful to God," she told the people, "for giving us this beautiful joy of being with you, and I thank each one of you for accepting our Sisters with so much trust, so much confidence, and so much love."

What the people saw in Mother Teresa was something close and familiar to them, as an article pointed out. Her face, with its "deep creases and weathered skin" was the face of the Appalachian woman, worn by long years of hard work and poverty. The traditional suspicious attitudes toward Catholics in an almost wholly Protestant area seemed to have vanished as the people took Mother Teresa and the Sisters to their hearts. The families told of someone with black lung from years in the mines, or an aged person who would be glad of a visitor, or a mother of a family who "could do with some help." The Sisters' program of home visiting branched out during the summer months into camp programs for children.

Then came a "problem," or in Mother Teresa's terminology, a "gift." The people read why Mother Teresa had been given the Nobel Prize. It was for service to "the poorest of the poor."

"We ain't got the 'poorest of the poor' around here," the people of Letcher County explained. The proud Appalachian rural and mining folk, with access to the media, rejected such a classification of themselves out of hand. This rejection might serve as a clarifying gift for the future work of the Missionaries of Charity. The descriptive phrase "poorest of the poor" had had to be replaced in Tanzania with the phrase "our people." While "poorest of the poor" certainly applied to Calcutta, a city overwhelmed by a million refugees, and while it might be retained in the M.C. constitutions as an infallible guide for the Sisters to go to, and to stay with, those whom society had failed, the phrase might need to be replaced with another for people whose dignity meant everything to them.

At the start of the work in Calcutta, in a scourged society inundated by refugees, the phrase "poorest of the poor" was apt. In situations that were not dissimilar, when the Sisters came like "shorn lambs," sharing the poverty of the poor, they were welcomed unquestioningly. In developed societies, the Sisters would still be welcomed and honored for their poverty which was a chosen poverty. However, with access to the media, people whose poverty was something brought on by unemployment or by catastrophic illness, the description would be as unacceptable as it was in Appalachia. Without any change in their commitment the Missionaries of Charity could find a solution similar to that of Tanzania. In developed countries, people with an egalitarian tradition would resist the category of "poorest of the poor." From any but the Sisters, the phrase might seem condescending, but from them it was a reminder that all depend on the providence of God and all are beggars before Him. Daily, they prayed "to be worthy to serve the poor."

❧

An unusual photograph, appearing in *The Times* of London toward the end of 1982, brought joy to the heart of Mother Teresa. It showed an old man kneeling at an altar to receive the Eucharist. He was receiving it in the old way, directly in the mouth from the hands of the priest, rather than in the hand.

The seventy-nine-year-old man was Malcolm Muggeridge, who had just been received into the Catholic Church along with Kitty, his wife of fifty-four years. They attended mass in a small chapel surrounded by friends and by a group of mentally handicapped children from a nearby children's home. Malcolm Muggeridge had been followed by Mother Teresa's prayers ever since they had met, and in particular after he had come to Calcutta to make the film. Mother Teresa had been deeply impressed by his devotion at mass, which he attended at the Motherhouse with the Sisters. Muggeridge's devotion to Mother Teresa was intense. Once in 1974 when he was told that she had had a small stroke, he wrote me that the news had given him "a stab of fear and desolation." When he gave me news of the translations of *Something Beautiful for God* into more and more languages, he told me, "It's the one thing in my life that gives me more joy and pride than everything else put together and multiplied by a million."

Muggeridge related in an article in *The Times* of London how Mother Teresa's eagerness to see him a fellow Catholic tempted him to become one simply to please her. When she wondered how he could turn aside from the Eucharist, which was her strength, Muggeridge reminded her of Simone Weil who felt that God needed some outsiders in His service. These arguments did not impress Mother Teresa. "Nor did my grumbles," he wrote, "about dissident priests and prelates in her Church impress her. Jesus, she said, handpicked twelve disciples, one of whom proved to be a crook and the others ran away. Why, then, should we expect popes and such like to do better?

"Words cannot convey how beholden I am to her," he wrote. "She has given me a whole new vision of what being a Christian means: of the amazing power of love, and how in one dedicated soul it can burgeon to cover the whole world.

"In our spiritual lives, I suppose," Muggeridge continued, "some sort of subterranean process takes place whereby, after years of doubt and uncertainty, clarification and certainty suddenly emerge, and like the blind man whose sight Jesus restored, we say, 'One thing I know, that, whereas I was blind, now I see.' " He described becoming a Catholic as, "a sense of homecoming, of picking up the threads of a lost life, of responding to a bell that has long been ringing, of finding a place at a table that has long been vacant. Nor does this in any way involve separation from other fellow Christians. On the contrary, it brings one nearer them."

Choosing Sisters from five novitiates, in Calcutta, Rome, Manila, Tabora (Tanzania), and San Francisco, Mother Teresa took them to sixteen new houses in 1983, all but one outside of India. This was a time when the novitiates of many congregations were being closed down or were receiving diminished numbers of candidates. Having opened a house in East Berlin, the Sisters also started work in West Berlin. Among the destinations of the Sisters was a tiny dot in the Indian Ocean well north of Madagascar, the Seychelles. They also began their work in Hong Kong, the British colony marked for eventual return to the mainland Chinese government. They went to work among refugees in Honduras and among the isolated poor in Jérémie, Haiti. Two new houses were opened in the United States, one in Chicago's "inner city," and one in Little Rock, Arkansas, where shelter and care were provided for unwed mothers, both black and white.

The unity of spirit of these women, many of them young and more and more a mix of nationalities and cultures, was a cause for continuing wonder. Imbibing the spirit of Mother Teresa, they accepted everything as "coming from the same loving hand" and their dependence on that loving hand was total. When they arrived in the torn city of Belfast, with their bedrolls and a violin, they were given a tiny house whose former occupant, a priest, had been murdered. They cleared away the debris and made the house habitable, saying, "We have come from Calcutta to try to improve relations between the people in the whole of Belfast in whatever little way we can." When called away, they packed up and moved on.

By a strange coincidence, they arrived to start their work in seething Gaza (part of Israel) just after the priest, Fr. Hana Nimry, had been murdered. I knew the compound they took over, not far from the Gaza Strip with its four hundred thousand refugees. The first work of Sister Damien and the team was to clean the bloodstains from the floor of the house which then became their center. Sister Damien, whose five languages included Arabic as well as Hebrew, soon made friends with the children, the sick, and the aged. The young Sisters from afar, asking nothing and ready to help freely and lovingly, were accepted by all communities.

The lessons the Sisters learned at the caravanserai at Kali's temple, they carried with them wherever they served the dying in many such homes. Somehow, Varanasi, formerly Benares, in India remains in the memory. The people in the Home for the Dying were not simply the destitute of the area but the poorest of the pilgrims to what was to them the holiest of cities. To die there, near the holy Ganges, would release them from the cycle of rebirths. I saw Sister Lily and the other Sisters feed helpless old men, gently turning heads so that they could more easily swallow the food, and then cleaning away the saliva and food that escaped. This, I thought, they had to do every day, and the monotony of it all struck me. I remembered a short prayer of Mother Teresa, "Lord, give me this vision of faith, and my work will not become monotonous." A patriarchal figure, with brown, sunken cheeks like old leather and a beard like wisps of fine silk, was sitting up and chanting the *Mahabharata.* When two of the Sisters accompanied me on a boat along the Ganges at dusk, we had a view of the ghats, the rows of steps, and of the innumerable temples along the shore. We also saw small fires and curls of smoke, and we caught the whiff of sandalwood. At the burning ghat, several shrouded bodies were being put to the flames.

I wanted to know if the constant reminder of dying did not sometimes depress them.

A Sister replied, "We hardly think of it. We know why we came. These people are going home to God. Our first home was right above the Manikarnaka Ghat. We were closer to the cremation place."

Sister Valerie, from Malta, and five Missionaries of Charity, accepted another gift "from the loving hand" that many would want to refuse—the work among the garbage-pickers of Cairo, Egypt. After driving through the glutted city, we passed the chalklike hills of Mokattam, from which the pyramid stones had been quarried, and the City of the Dead where the living made homes among the tombs. We then made our way through the vast acreage of the city dumping ground. In one corner was the dispensary and welfare center of the Missionaries of Charity. Women sat in chairs holding infants who wheezed and had all the sicknesses one would expect from life lived among refuse. These were people whose whole life was surrounded by refuse—and whose livelihood depended upon it. They were part of an army of over ten thousand garbage collectors, men, women, and children, who gathered the refuse in donkey carts, and having deposited it in the dumping ground, picked over it for salable or usable objects. The people were almost without exception Christian. They kept pigs around their huts, pigs who also kept alive by rooting in the garbage. Into these huts the Sisters went to help heal the sick. We came upon a young woman sitting in front of a hut, feeding a baby at her breast. She was squatting on the ground and carefully sorting out objects that she hoped to sell. The women met regularly at the center where the Sisters gave lessons in hygiene, in sewing and in other crafts, along with supplies of soap.

There was no doubt that the pattern of life, marked by prayer and by the daily Eucharist, gave the Sisters the spiritual and emotional strength to face up to work that seemed almost unbearable. The sense of community, so nurtured by Mother Teresa, was of immeasurable importance, as was the study of the constitutions. The shared experiences through *Ek Dil* united the Sisters in their far-flung missions. In addition, a crucial force binding the Sisters in spirit was the monthly letter of Mother Teresa. The letters were written from every country she visited, not a few written on planes en route to a new foundation. She sent news of the different houses she visited, of joys, of the honors that came to the work, of the deaths of Sisters, and always spiritual counsel and quotations from her spiritual readings.

Mother Teresa's first letters were to the houses in India.

"My own dearest Sisters,

As the Society is growing, it is but natural that a deep desire grows in my heart to be with you wherever you are—love, help, and guide you to become Saints. Since this is not possible, I shall try every First Friday to be with you through my letters."

It was a fairly long letter, containing the question, "Am I convinced of Christ's love for me and mine for Him? This conviction is like a sunlight which makes the sap of life rise and the buds of sanctity bloom. This conviction is the rock on which sanctity is built."

Urging the Sisters to grow in "knowing Jesus, loving Jesus, serving Jesus," she tells them, "If we do this the conviction will grow—and as the conviction will grow—we become a 'Professional' in holiness."

Her concluding sentence asks for a response.

"Let me know if you want me to write you on something else."

In August 1961, Mother Teresa's letter announced a milestone in the Society. She told the Sisters that on October 7, 1961, "We shall have our first elections for the Chapter General." She suggested a daily prayer for enlightenment: "Come, O Blessed Spirit of Knowledge and Light, and grant that I may perceive the Will of the Father; show me the nothingness of earthly things, that I may realize their vanity and use them only for Thy glory and my own salvation, looking ever beyond them to Thee and Thy eternal rewards." Eleven years after the recognition of the Society, Mother Teresa was elected its Mother General.

"Be happy" Mother Teresa encouraged the Sisters, "and make it a special point to become God's sign of happiness in your community . . . we have to be the 'sign of God' of that true poverty of Christ. Therefore, we must radiate the joy of being poor, but do not speak about it. Do not tell people of the hard life—just be happy with Christ."

When one of the Sisters died, she wrote, "Pray for Sr. Mary Cecilia—who went home to Jesus to hear Him, 'I was hungry, and you gave me to eat; I was thirsty, and you gave me to drink; I was a stranger and you took me in; naked and you clothed me; I was in prison and you came to me.' "

"Our life has all the more need of humility since it is so much in the public eye," she warned them in one letter.

Mother Teresa wrote much on prayer. "During this Lent, let us improve our spirit of prayer and recollection. Let us free our minds from all that is not Jesus. If you find it difficult to pray, ask Him again and again, 'Jesus come into my heart, pray with me, pray in me—that I may learn from Thee how to pray.' "

Mother Teresa shared her own experiences. In a letter headed, "Air India—Across the Ocean," she wrote, "My dearest Children, Once again I am crossing the ocean to prepare the way for you in search of God's poor—in search of the hungry Christ, the homeless Christ, the sick Christ. God's ways are very wonderful. As a very small child I had longed to go to Africa and work for Jesus, but for some reason I did not join the convent in Africa, and now, today, I go as a M.C. to fulfill the desire of God in my heart. I go with different hopes, with different love because of you, who will fulfill that hope and put that love into action for the poor of Africa."

Her ever-repeated insistence was on the need to become holy.

"The first step to becoming," she wrote, "is to will it. St. Thomas says, 'Sanctity consists in nothing else than a firm resolve—the heroic act of a soul abandoning herself to God.' By an upright will we love God, we choose God, we run toward God, we reach Him, we possess Him. 'O good, good will which transforms me into the image of God and makes me like to Him,' so St. Augustine says. My progress in holiness depends on God and myself—on God's grace and my will."

22

Brother Francis and Mother Teresa

Of all the figures in the annals of Christianity to whom Mother Teresa was likened, Brother Francis, the Poor Man of Assisi, was the one most frequently mentioned. In the springtime of the year that marked the eight hundredth anniversary of the birth of St. Francis, the Friars Minor of St. Francis and the Commune, the town government of Assisi, invited Mother Teresa to take part in a Pilgrimage of Love.

A Franciscan priest, Fr. Giulio Mancini, in the traditional brown robe and ropelike girdle, presented himself at San Gregorio in Rome to take Mother Teresa and Sister Frederick by car to the "seraphic city" in the Umbrian hills. It was May 22, 1982, shortly after the International Co-Worker Chapter, and I was invited to accompany them.

It was one instance when I had practiced the absolute dependence on God that marked Mother Teresa. Though I longed to visit Assisi, I wanted the visit to have the spirit of a pilgrimage and had refused earlier opportunities. To be part of a Pilgrimage of Love was a special boon. On the journey, Father Giulio stopped for coffee and asked if he could bring some for us. Mother Teresa and Sister Frederick declined but said they would take tea. The roadside stand did not serve tea. I remembered that something had moved me to pack teabags in my suitcase. Supplied with hot water, Mother Teresa, Sister Frederick, and I had Darjeeling tea sitting in the car in the sunlit Italian countryside. Mother Teresa was still wearing the old gray cardigan sweater, in her possession at least six years, and a secondhand gift to begin with. By now, successive darnings barely held it together.

As we entered Assisi, we could not miss posters announcing the coming of "Madre Teresa di Calcutta" on lampposts and at the corners of winding streets. The Pilgrimage of Love began with a visit to the Porziuncola (little portion), the tiny chapel restored by Francis. It was later enclosed within the walls of the basilica of St. Mary of the Angels. Mother Teresa knelt at the spot beloved of Francis, for it was there he received his special call to follow the gospel of Jesus in simplicity and trust. It was a call still being answered in the world by over forty thousand friars in different religious families and by hundreds of thousands of Sisters and lay followers.

When the friars asked Mother Teresa to write a message in their memorial book, she wrote, "Let us keep the joy of loving Jesus in our hearts and share this joy with all we meet and so become carriers of God's peace." In other settings, she wrote, "carriers of God's love," but in the land of Francis, she talked of peace.

After prayers at the tomb of St. Francis, Mother Teresa was taken to the Sala della Conciliazione (Conciliation Hall), where the mayor and officials of Assisi, as well as its citizens, awaited her. The children of Assisi came forward with a parchment scroll, hand lettered and illuminated with flowers, thanking her for the lesson that "the world can be renewed through the courage of love." The speech of the mayor revealed how the stamp of St. Francis was still on his city. The mayor reminded his hearers that the little city on the hill had been the scene of many initiatives for peace; one of them very recent. During the Falkland Islands war between England and Argentina, young Englishmen and Argentinians who refused to bear arms against each other were offered refuge in the seraphic city. The mayor pointed out that they would be received and protected in the same way as Jewish brothers and sisters had been saved from the Holocaust during the Second World War. He was referring to the Assisi underground which rescued Jews marked for deportation and death under Nazism. He ended his speech giving Mother Teresa the greeting of St. Francis, "May God give you peace," and asking for her prayers.

Hospitality for the night was at the hostel of the Poor Clares behind the church. It was conducted by Sisters known as externs, to distinguish them from the cloistered nuns. The cloister of the Poor Clares, originally called the Poor Ladies, was directly behind the church. Dinner was served by the extern Sisters in a parlor attached to the convent, with the bishop of Assisi and several friars as guests. After the meal, an iron grill was revealed in the wall connecting the parlor with the cloister. Mother Teresa was asked to speak to the Sisters, over thirty of them, invisible figures behind the bars. A Canadian Sister translated Mother Teresa's words. Then there was the sound of a camera clicking. One of the cloistered Sisters was taking Mother Teresa's picture. The bishop laughed to see the Poor Clares updating their mode of life.

When we stepped from the convent to the church, the Poor Clares participated in a prayer vigil from behind an enclosed gallery, unseen by the congregation, just as they would have done in the time of St. Clare.

Mother Teresa was placed inside the altar rail of the seven-hundred-year-old church of St. Clare and was to talk on "St. Francis and the Poor

Today." The prayer vigil arranged by the friars seemed to have attracted most of the population of Assisi. Those who could not fit into the church were gathered in the piazza outside in the spring air.

There were hymns and invocations for the poor of the world.

Mother Teresa began, "We read in the gospel that Jesus came into this world to give us the Good News. The Good News was that God loved the world so much. And Jesus told us to keep that Good News alive by loving one another."

Sister Frederick stood by Mother Teresa's side, translating her words into Italian. By now, Sister Frederick was the assistant to Mother Teresa and shared some of the tasks of the Mother General. "Good News" in the translation, came out as *"La Bella Notizia,"* (Beautiful News) and it seemed a fresh and lovely way of expressing it. Mother Teresa's presence was a fitting one in the church dedicated to St. Clare, the young woman to whom Francis himself gave the poor habit of a sackcloth tied with a cord.

Mother Teresa asked her hearers to look for the lonely, poor, and hungry of Assisi; hungry not simply for bread, but for love. "All of us, you and I and that poor man on the street, we have all been created to love and to be loved. None of us have been created not to be loved. That is why today there is that terrible, great poverty in the world; poverty of heart. It is so great because people have forgotten to love one another as God loves each one of us." She told her parablelike stories of the greatness of the poor. "The poor people, the hungry, the naked, the homeless are very wonderful people and we owe them great gratitude because they give us an opportunity to love God.

"Our Sisters take great care of leprosy patients and, as they were for St. Francis of Assisi, they are the most beloved people. They have a tender love. I have never heard them complain. At present the Sisters and Brothers take care of ninety-three thousand lepers."

She did not need to remind the people of Assisi that Francis, at his conversion to a new life, embraced a leper and from then on lost his disgust at the sight of the ulcerous wounds of leprosy.

Toward the end of the vigil, there was a thrust toward the altar and before Mother Teresa could move away, countless hands were stretched out through the altar rail to touch her feet. It was as though Francis himself had come among the people. Francis had made God so lovable, His creation so worthy of loving care, and the spiritual world so real that his appeal to followers was close to irresistible. Something similar could be said of Mother Teresa, and her appeal was powerfully in evidence that evening of May 22, 1982.

The Poor Clares, hidden in the gallery, made a transcript of Mother Teresa's talk and sent it as a gift to other convents of their order. They shared a copy with me.

After pointing to the example of St. Clare, the Sisters of Assisi wrote, "In our time another woman, who owes much to Francis of Assisi, is consumed by the fire of love. Her name is Mother Teresa of Calcutta and on the evening of May 22, we had the privilege of praying together with her in the context of the celebrations for the anniversary of our Seraphic Father. As a Franciscan Year gift, we should like to share her meditation with you." The letter ended by joining the name of Mother Teresa with the two great saints of Assisi. "May we, like Clare, Francis, and Mother Teresa, reveal, by the testimony of our lives, the love with which we are loved."

Just two weeks later, Mother Teresa was being feted in the city hall of a great city named for St. Francis—San Francisco, California. The city officials had arranged a ceremonial welcome since San Francisco was memorializing the man of Assisi. There was an evening service of Benediction in the Catholic Cathedral of St. Mary's—a service so packed with people that security guards and ushers were everywhere trying to keep order. Dale Vree, writing of the event in the *National Catholic Reporter*, remarked, "How odd that this founder of the Missionaries of Charity—an order given, not to preaching but to doing the Word—should be preaching! Women don't have an important role in the church, it is said, and here is (literally) a little old lady, not quite in tennis shoes but in sandals, preaching to ecclesiastics and magistrates. Why am I almost in tears?"

He answered his own query. "Maybe because she's one of those who indubitably earned a right to proclaim the gospel. And more. The gospel simplicity of the message is matched by the gospel simplicity of the messenger."

At the inevitable press conference, she turned the inevitable question of what it feels like to be called a "living saint" back on the questioner.

"I'm very happy if you can see Jesus in me, because I can see Jesus in you. Holiness is not just for a few people. It's for everyone, including you, sir.

The lives of people of the past, people of extraordinary achievement or great holiness, often arouse a wish that one could have known them personally. Those of us who knew Mother Teresa were grateful for the gift, and I felt that gratitude with special power at Assisi. The journey to Assisi brought me back to the first journey I had taken with her in response to her letter of 1960, on the occasion of her first trip to the United States. That journey, which broke an uninterrupted stay of thirty-one years in India, led to many succeeding journeys. On those journeys, and during the days in Calcutta, we discussed many issues. Sometimes we came down on opposite sides. When Mother Teresa stressed the absolute importance of obedience, I demurred. Could not too much be made of obedience in an age when unquestioning obedience was offered as excuse for the commission of horrendous crimes? Would it not be more in line with the times to emphasize the role of conscience, which soldiers were asked to abdicate during war, or even of resistance, as in early Christianity? Mother Teresa conceded to a point and explained that in the constitutions of the Missionaries of Charity there was the right of representation. A Sister did not have to give blind obedience. She could present her point of view and ask for an explanation if she had a conscientious difference with a superior.

Because of my experiences in war-ravaged areas, I raised the question of modern war and its morality. Back in 1958, Mother Teresa asked, "But when it is attacked, doesn't a country have the right to defend itself?" Her question was well taken and fitted in well with traditional just war teaching. It was the indiscriminate methods of modern warfare, hardly any of them defensive, that put the just war concept in question for many of us. It was not until 1965 that indiscriminate methods of warfare were banned by the world's Catholic bishops at the Second Vatican Council.

In those early years, I wondered why she had chosen the name "Missionaries of Charity" when the term "missionary" had a poor connotation in some places. When I asked her, she replied that the original meaning of the term "mission" referred to "being sent." "We are sent," she said and saw no need to question her choice. We had different views regarding newspapers, Mother Teresa at first taking the traditional view that Sisters, having left worldly things, did not need to keep up with worldly happenings. Later, she allowed the Sisters to read daily newspapers when they had time, if only to pray for the people whose travails filled their pages.

Over the years, Mother Teresa's concept of poverty changed to englobe the poverty that in Western countries defied social welfare systems, the poverty of loneliness and unwantedness. She sometimes referred to it as the "leprosy of the West." She pointed out, "For all kinds of diseases there are medicines and cures. But for being unwanted, except there are willing hands to serve and loving hands to love, there is no cure." This was why in the countries of Europe, as well as in the United States, a chief work of the Sisters was to visit and serve the lonely, the rejected, the aged, the shut-ins —those for whom no one else had time.

Fr. Celeste Van Exem, the spiritual director who knew Mother Teresa from the beginning, noted some changes in the spiritual order. In an interview in "Love Without Frontiers," published by the Friends of Mother Teresa in France, he stated that in the earliest houses, there was not the emphasis on daily contemplation, the adoration before the Eucharist in the chapel. It was only after the congregation had been in existence for a few years that there was to be fifteen minutes of daily adoration when the Sisters gathered in the chapel. In the nineteen seventies, it was decided that at the end of the day, there was to be a full hour of adoration. I remembered the time when the change was made. Mother Teresa remarked delightedly, "The Sisters tell me that it has not taken anything away from their work. They still do as much and it has given them greater strength."

Another growth on the part of Mother Teresa, according to Fr. Van Exem, related to the place of the Eucharist. "It was somewhat later that Mother Teresa made the Eucharist the center of all the spiritual life of the Society—to contemplate the same Christ in the Eucharist and in the suffering body of human beings."

To Fr. Van Exem, the outstanding trait of Mother Teresa was her absolute faith in God. Those of us who worked closely with her could only agree on this. Her mind could be at peace, because whatever came from the providence of God was what she accepted with all her heart and mind. The priest also stressed her fidelity to prayer. Not only did she pray and meditate alone, at break of day, but when a few of us were traveling with her, she involved us in prayer. We would recite the rosary, each person taking one of the mysteries. Once when Patty Kump was driving us across Minnesota, we joined in prayer for an unemployed man to find a job. After the prayer, Mother Teresa said, "Let us thank God for his job." She was taking the gospel literally, and I thought of the words of Jesus, "According to your faith, be it done to you." Mother Teresa took it for granted that, "Whatever you ask, believe you will receive and it will come to you." The man received the job.

To travel with Mother Teresa was to experience the presence of a person who was recollected. On one occasion, we were driven at breakneck speed through the heart of Chicago to catch a plane. Patty Kump and I caught our breath as we made swift turns in traffic, barely grazing a taxi and shooting forward like a rocket as soon as the light changed to green. Mother Teresa's countenance never changed; she sat calmly with her rosary beads in her hand. She never started a journey by car without a prayer, asking the protection of God and the intercession of Mary, "cause of our joy." She reminded us that as Mary was the cause of our joy in bringing Jesus to us, we should be the cause of her joy by bringing Jesus to others.

Mother Teresa was a very easy person to travel with. Like the early apostles, she ate whatever food was put before her. She did not require any special foods but did appreciate my finding bananas which seemed to help her digestion. Only once did I hear her ask for a particular food. A dinner served by the Franciscan Sisters at their retreat house in Washington, D.C., was interrupted when people arrived to whisk Mother Teresa away to a speaking engagement. When she came back three hours later, she turned to Sister Walburga with a tired smile and said, "I'll take some of that ice cream now." She seemed to appreciate cool, clean water most of all and when given a glass would bless herself before drinking it. One could not help thinking of Francis's canticle, "Praised be you, my Lord, for Sister Water, which is very useful and humble and precious and chaste."

Mother Teresa's humility was true to the origin of the word from the Latin *humus* (earth). It permeated the congregation, and the phrase "right on the ground" described the place of the Missionaries of Charity in service to the poor. She was always amazed at the attention she received and the fact that people flocked to hear her. When she took part in conferences, there was always a crush of people at her session even though other prominent persons were also on the program.

"I have been to so many meetings," she once remarked. "There were important and intelligent speeches. I said simple things, even stupid things, things like a child would say. But," she added, "people are longing for those things."

When we brought up to her a variety of matters, new movements, new books, she would say, almost apologetically, "I can't remember all those things. My mind is on two things, God and the Society." Once she said, "I have no imagination. I cannot imagine God the Father—so great. All I see is Jesus." Her humility made her one with the mystics who said the same thing in many ways. Asked about the future of the congregation after her death, she said simply, "Let me die first, then God will provide. He will find someone more helpless, more hopeless than I to do His work."

Mother Teresa's loving attention to each person who came to her, "one by one by one," as she put it, served to bring them courage. An older woman who came to bring her a gift of great value, a large gem that her late husband had given her, suddenly confessed to Mother Teresa, "I am full of fear. I am afraid of death. That is why I wanted to see you in person. You face dying people every day."

Mother Teresa took time with the woman. They found that both their fathers were named Nikola. Mother Teresa explained that some Jain friends of hers, gem dealers, would turn the gift into cash and that she would put the money into a home for the destitute and dying in Bombay called Asha Dan.

" 'Asha Dan' means 'Gift of Hope,' " said Mother Teresa. "Through your gift, rejected people will be brought to a place where they will receive love and they will find hope." She pictured death as she always did, as a going home to a loving father.

People with almost unbearable sorrows came to Mother Teresa for a rekindling of hope. A distressed family brought their son to meet Mother Teresa in Minneapolis. The boy, in his early teens, had suffered an accident with fireworks, in which he was blinded and had lost both hands. The boy sat on a couch with Mother Teresa in the living room of Patty and Warren Kump. He told her that he had been in a tree as he and his friends were getting ready to set off powerful fireworks for the Fourth of July. The fireworks had exploded and he had fallen from the tree into flames which seared his eyes and caused the amputation of his hands. The two talked for some time, Mother Teresa reminding the mutilated boy that he was in a position to understand and have sympathy for the many people around the world who had also lost the sight of their eyes and the use of their hands. He could help them in a special way. The boy agreed with her and told her that he was thinking of what he could do. He had thought that perhaps he could be a counselor because he could understand people's sufferings.

Mother Teresa told him that would be wonderful work and that he would make a fine counselor. The boy's face broke into a smile. "Yes," he said, as the encouragement of someone as acquainted with tragedy as Mother Teresa had set a seal on his importance as a person. "I can be a good counselor," he said. It was almost as though he went on his way rejoicing.

Mother Teresa's lightness of spirit reminded me of the woman mystic, Juliana of Norwich, who stated that the worst had already happened and had already been remedied—meaning the original sin and the remedy of Jesus in becoming man and dying for sin. Though there was the cross, there was always solace and joy in the Resurrection that was its inevitable sequel. Mother Teresa seemed to be saying with Juliana, "All shall be well, and all, all shall be well." One day, after my conversation had been filled with a litany of problems, some seemingly insoluble, she remarked, "Everything is a problem. Isn't there another word?" I confessed that I knew no other word that carried the same weight. "Why not use the word gift?" she suggested. With that began a shift in vocabulary.

One of the first times that the new vocabulary came into use was on the return to New York City from the Habitat Conference in Vancouver, British Columbia, Canada. She had tried without success to be excused from the conference and was extremely anxious to have time with the Sisters in New York. I was dismayed to learn that the trip had to be broken en route, with a four-hour delay. I was about to explain the "problem," when I caught myself and said, "Mother, I have to tell you about a gift. We have to wait four hours here and you won't arrive at the convent until very late."

Mother Teresa agreed that this was indeed a great "gift". She settled down in the airport to read and ponder Alan Paton's *Instrument of Thy Peace.* The book of meditations inspired by the peace prayer of St. Francis of Assisi was a favorite of hers and one she recommended to Co-Workers around the world.

From that time on, items that presented disappointments or difficulties would be introduced with, "We have a small gift here," or "Today we have an especially big gift." There were smiles, perhaps rueful smiles, at situations which had earlier been described by the dour word "problem."

When Mother Teresa found a group of Co-Workers dispirited, she would raise their spirits with a joke. One joke concerned a traveler whose car broke down at the edge of a lonely, barren region. The only refuge was a monastery and the only transport the monks could offer the man was a donkey. The traveler insisted on continuing his journey, so the monks explained that to manage the animal, the man must remember to say "Amen, Amen," when he wanted it to stop, but "Thank God, thank God" when he wanted it to go forward. All went well until a precipice loomed before him, and the nervous man remembered just in time to shout "Amen, Amen." The donkey stopped at the very edge of the precipice. The relieved man said, "Thank God, thank God," and over they plunged. We burst out laughing because in a way it was a joke on Mother Teresa herself, who was saying "Thank God" everywhere and at all times.

She did not take herself too seriously and never stood on her dignity. She would squat unself-consciously on the carpeted area at an airport terminal to have a chance to talk to the Sisters as they sat around her. When she began using the Indian trains to visit the first houses of the Sisters, she would swing herself into the capacious luggage rack for a few hours' sleep. That was before she was given a free pass on the Indian railway. It was probably the rail pass that prodded her into suggesting to Indian Air Lines that they take her on as a stewardess. She could serve meals and do the necessary work in return for free travel throughout India to visit the Sisters. She did not get the job, but instead was, in 1973, given a free pass on Indian Air Lines.

She often gave people unexpected advice. When a group of Americans, many in the teaching profession, visited the work in Calcutta, they asked her for some advice to take home to their families.

"Smile at your wives," she told them. "Smile at your husbands."

Thinking perhaps that the advice was simplistic, coming from an unmarried person, one of them asked, "Are you married?"

"Yes," she replied to their surprise, "and I find it very hard sometimes to smile at Jesus. He can be very demanding." The concept of spiritual marriage, perhaps coming from the Church as the bride of Christ has been carried over into seeing the vowed Sister in a similar light though some may find it a strained metaphor.

Even her talks about the wounds and sorrows of the world did not send people away steeped in gloom. She found ways to lift people's hearts, sometimes by recounting a humorous incident. She told of trying to help a very drunk woman on a London street, when the woman turned to her saying, "Mother Teresa, didn't Jesus turn the water into wine for us to enjoy it?"

For Mother Teresa, things "came down right" again and again, an example, already recounted, being the last-minute call to visit with the President of Mexico as she was about to leave the country. This was always associated with her pilgrimage to the tomb of Fr. Augustin Pro. A consoling instance of things "coming down right" concerned a memorial service for my own brother, Brother John Mark Egan, a member of the Congregation of Christian Brothers who had known Mother Teresa from his visits to India. Mother Teresa was with the Sisters in New York shortly after his death early in 1978—a sudden and untimely death on the eve of his departure for India and Australia to give a series of Christian lectures and meet with other communities of Brothers. The students and faculty of Iona College, where Brother John Mark had founded the Pastoral Counseling Institute, were planning a memorial service for him. They asked Mother Teresa to name a day when she could be present and told her they would plan the service around that date. She told them her free day was on a Thursday, which turned out to be April 25. The planning committee was happily surprised at the providential date, which turned out to be the feast of St. Mark, the patron of Brother John Mark whose name he had chosen in religion, and the one hundredth day after his heart had suddenly failed. Speaking during the mass to a large group of students, Mother Teresa stressed the irreplaceable task of the teacher in bringing Jesus into the lives of young people. As a teaching order, the Brothers needed to keep open their schools. In India, she pointed out, it was to the Brothers that she sent many of the poorest boys for schooling.

Following the mass, at which Brother Sebastian, an Indian priest-Brother soon to head the Brothers of the Word, was one of the celebrants, there was a distribution of Brother John Mark's possessions. Mother Teresa received a statue of the Virgin and Child from his room. She wrote me later that the statue was on her desk at the Motherhouse in Calcutta.

After the death of her own brother Lazar in 1981, she wrote, "One person who must have been longing for him to join the family was, I am sure, my mother. Her only son, whom she loved more than her life, is at last with her. He died a beautiful death—it was really going home to God." In another letter she wrote, "Yes, our brothers, yours and mine, they must have met in heaven. I would love to know what they said to each other about you and me."

Of all Mother Teresa's qualities, the one most overpoweringly impressive to those close to her was, paradoxically, her emptiness. Mother Teresa asked her Sisters to be "clear as glass," and she led the way. It was as though she had no needs of her own, but rather was an empty reed through which the Spirit blew. There might have been a time when she had discernible personal needs, but as the years went by, these were no longer in evidence. She could be seen at the point of exhaustion, with red-rimmed eyes and her voice rasping because of a soreness in her throat, but still ready to grant an interview or listen to someone's troubles without impatience.

People seemed to think, if they thought about it at all, that she was barely human, indefatigable. Though she did not intrude her human needs on others, she was deeply human. Out of her boundless grief when she knew her mother's health was failing and it was certain that she and Age would never leave Albania, she wrote, "They are all His more than mine. You don't know what this sacrifice of not seeing my mother has obtained for my Sisters." Later, as "Nana Loke's" strength was failing, Mother Teresa wrote, "Her and my sacrifice will bring us closer to God."

When an interviewer asked if she would not have wanted children of her own, she answered, "Naturally, naturally. That is the sacrifice." She stated publicly that she needed to go to confession like anyone else and that she could make mistakes, even in the placement of Sisters. "I can make mistakes," she would say, "but God does not make mistakes." She did not exhibit many shortcomings; one that Co-Workers wondered about was the speed with which she reached decisions and her reluctance to make changes even when there were, from their point of view, negative effects. She sometimes reached a decision without hearing the two sides of a question. Strong and dedicated as she was, she had difficulty in comprehending and making allowances for human weaknesses, especially among those living vowed lives. She was taken aback when people asked her to prophesy about the future. She did not possess second sight and prophecy was not for her.

Indefatigable she certainly was. Those who traveled with her had to find ways to protect her since she did not protect herself; she simply spent herself in gladness. Her emptiness made it possible for her to respond to the almost impossible schedules she accepted and to overcome her initial fear of speaking before a "big public." Her emptiness offered no block or bar in her response to individuals. The indissoluble connection between that special emptiness and true holiness became clearer each time one was in her presence.

In a letter to a priest Co-Worker, she talked of being empty. "You have said 'YES' to Jesus—and He has taken you at your word. The word of God became man—poor; your word to God became Jesus—poor. And so this terrible emptiness you experience. God cannot fill what is full—He can fill only emptiness—deep poverty—and your 'YES' is the beginning of being or becoming empty. It is not how much we really 'have' to give—but how empty we are—so that we can receive fully in our life and let Him live His life in us."

The points at which Mother Teresa's life and work are close to that of Brother Francis, the poor man of Assisi, are many. Some of them can hardly be missed, in particular the poverty demanded by both congregations and their identification with the poor. Francis made the point of calling his followers the friars minor, as a distinction blazingly clear to the people of his time. Society was divided then into *minores,* the serfs and common people, and the *majores,* those of nobility, power, and land. Franciscan poverty was allied with simplicity of life and function. The early friars minor were mostly unordained and even unlettered, though later many became ordained clerics and moved from being mendicant friars, preaching in the town piazzas, to teaching in university aulas. The Missionaries of Charity, Sisters and Brothers, took no posts of any kind, remaining close to the poor "to give them for nothing what the rich can get through their money."

Mother Teresa's unfailing joy was also akin to that of Francis. She, like Francis, spent time with lepers and was closer than most of humankind to what Francis termed, "Our Sister, Bodily Death." Like the words of Francis, Mother Teresa's words were not depictions of doom but rather songs of hope and joy.

"For what else are servants of God," Francis asked, "but minstrels, whose work it is to lift up people's hearts and move them to spiritual gladness?" Mother Teresa told her Sisters and Co-Workers, "Let no one ever come to you without leaving better and happier. Be the living expression of God's kindness, kindness in your face, kindness in your eyes, kindness in your smile, kindness in your warm greeting."

Mother Teresa's closeness to the Eucharist was no less than that of Francis and included as well the priest, who is minister of the Eucharist. In his letter to the General Chapter of 1226, which he was too ill to attend, Francis wrote, "If the tomb wherein Jesus reposed for a few hours is the object of such veneration, then how worthy, virtuous and holy ought he to be who touches with his fingers, receives in his mouth and in his heart, and administers to others, Christ, no longer mortal, but eternally triumphant and glorious!" Mother Teresa's promotion of the Corpus Christi movement for priests was an expression of the same veneration for ministers of the Eucharist.

There is, however, another more concrete similarity, which became clear to me as I saw the work of the Missionaries of Charity around the world. Francis, while praying in the chapel of San Damiano heard the call to repair the house of God which was falling into ruins. Taking the words literally, he began by repairing San Damiano itself, abandoned and left to fall into ruins. He proceeded to rebuild other churches and chapels around Assisi. In one of the restored chapels, the Porziuncola, Francis heard the clear call to restore the Church to the simplicity and poverty of the gospel.

It was then that Bernard, Peter, Giles, and the others joined him to preach the word and live in gospel poverty. Their rule was given verbal approval by the Pope when a company of twelve, including Francis, presented it to him.

In the twentieth century, Mother Teresa's Sisters took part in the restoration of the Church in a not dissimilar way. They heralded a return to simplicity of life. Recognizing that there had been a time when the Church needed to display majesty and greatness, Mother Teresa said, "Today, people have found the emptiness of all that pomp and so they are coming down more to the ground." She added a warning that in coming down, there was danger that some were not finding their proper place.

Again and again, the Missionaries of Charity restored the vigor of merciful service to places where the work of other societies had faltered or diminished. In Macao, off the coast of China, the Missionaries of Charity took over an old Portuguese Franciscan monastery to house the blind and poor. In Dacca, Bangladesh, an ancient convent of the Poor Clares became a Shishu Bhavan for sick and orphaned children. In Tabora, Tanzania, the great work of the White Sisters had diminished, while the coming of the Missionaries of Charity had so invigorated the local church that a novitiate had to be opened for African girls. In Yemen, where the Missionaries of Charity were the first Christian presence after nearly a thousand years, the people saw their work and found it good. The director of health there asked the Sisters to add mental patients to those already in their care, including the lepers and the very poorest. His confidence was so great that he said, "Mother Teresa is my mother. She will agree to what I ask." She agreed and the Sisters took in mental patients in a wing added to their center.

Already recounted is the example of the South Bronx, where the Sisters brought renewal to a parish where a team ministry had scattered and worked with priests recruited from Spain. The contemplative branch of the Sisters found homes in convents in the South Bronx and Brooklyn from which teams of Sisters had vanished. In Harlem, St. Joseph's Convent, formerly housing school Sisters, was given to the Missionaries of Charity to become a home for homeless women, as well as battered women with their children. Wherever they went, the Sisters and Brothers carried out the mission of the Church by serving the weakest members of the human family. As the ranks of vowed Religious thinned out, particularly in the developed world, young men and women presented themselves at the doors of the novitiates of the Missionaries of Charity in India, the Philippines, Korea, Africa, Latin America, and the United States. In the United States, where rampant consumerism could command more material satisfactions than most regions of the globe, over 130 young American women and men were in the Missionaries of Charity by the end of 1984. As in the

Mother Teresa bids farewell to her brother, Lazar, at Rome airport.

With author and Dorothy Day at Maryhouse, New York City. *(Bill Barrett, O.F.M.)*

Candlelight procession during Eucharistic Congress, Philadelphia, 1976. *(Robert S. Halvey)*

Mother Teresa receiving the 1979 Nobel Peace Prize from Professor John Sannes. *(UPI/Bettmann Archive)*

The Mother Teresa stamp.

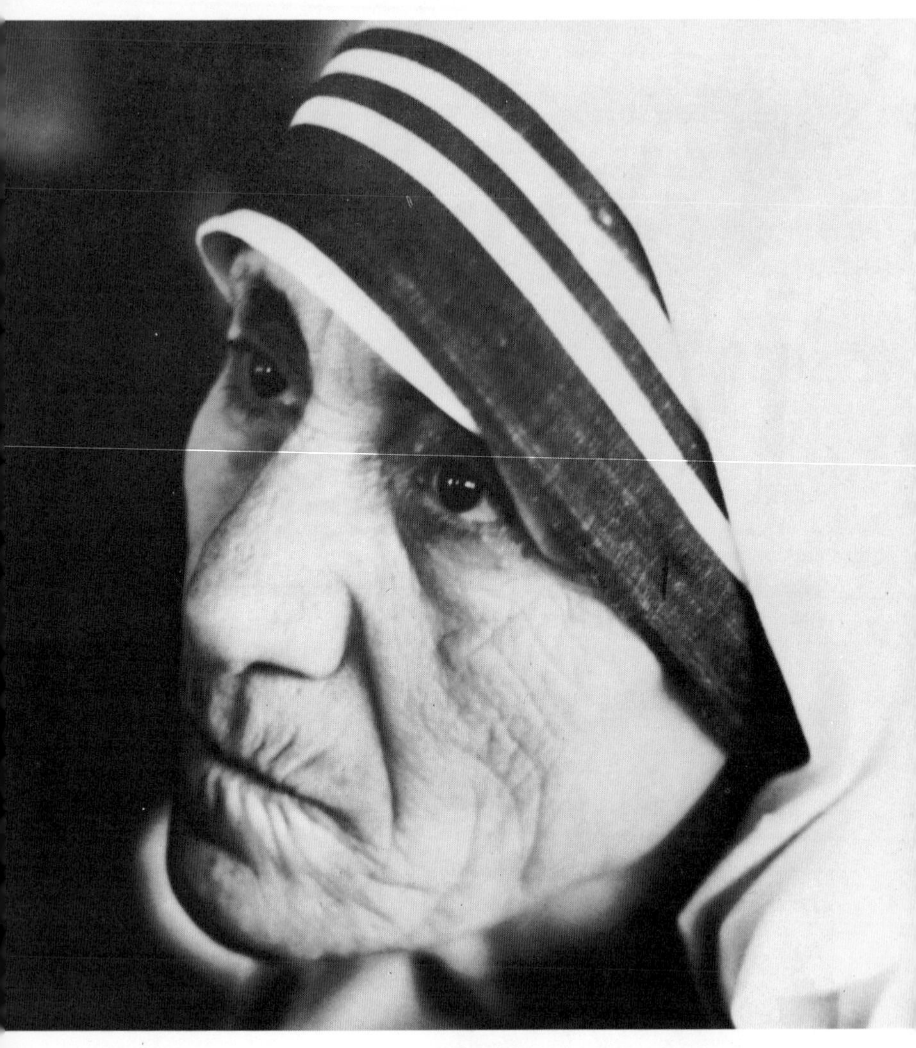

Such a vision of the street . . . *(Laurence Jankowski)*

time of Francis of Assisi, the Church was being strengthened from the ground up by those who freely chose to serve in evangelical poverty.

The habitual greeting of Brother Francis, "The Lord give you peace," was linked, as mentioned earlier, to positive contributions to peace. His own age was not the gentle age of innocence that one might infer from the lyrical paintings of Giotto and Cimabue, but one in which violence was a dreadful reality, not only in wars between cities but in the Crusades. Francis not only released the members of the Third Order from the obligation to bear arms, but intervened for peace during the Crusades, at one time moving many soldiers in the Crusaders' camp at St.-Jean-d'Acre in the Holy Land to abandon the profession of arms. During the bloodiest days of the Crusades, Francis with Brother Illuminato dared to enter the enemy lines to talk to the Sultan about Jesus. As the years went by, Mother Teresa became more and more a voice for peace and for reverence for life. She faced an attack on life that was hardly a general challenge in the time of Francis, namely abortion.

Before audiences in Australia, Japan, Europe, Latin America, and the United States, she gave her vision, described in the Nobel speech, of seeing Jesus in the unborn child—as John, another unborn child had done. Fr. Van Exem pointed out that these talks were certainly given at the call of the Holy See and were proof of that same obedience she had displayed at the foundation of her work.

"In Calcutta," she told large audiences concerned with the family, "every night we send word to all the clinics, to all the police stations, to all the hospitals: 'Please do not destroy the child. I will take the child.' So our house is always full; full of children. There is a joke in Calcutta: 'Mother Teresa is always talking about family planning and about abortion, but every day she has more and more children.' " She told of finding aborted, live babies, thrown away in a bucket and of saving some of them. She explained that in India, the adoption of the children from the children's home was a near miracle; something people had considered utterly impossible because of caste barriers. Yet families came and took as their own the little ones who might not have been allowed to be born.

"Our poor people say," Mother Teresa recounted, " 'you people who have a vow of chastity, you are the best people to teach us family planning.' . . . Today, when we hear of the terrible killings of the child, I wonder what has happened in our human hearts; something unnatural. Something has been lost, something has been broken."

Invited to Japan in April 1981 by the Rev. Anthony Zimmerman of the Japan Family Life Association, she stated that the country, though rich and beautiful, was poor in that it allowed so many abortions. She took as her companion Sister Paulette who led the work for natural family planning. After an address to the Tokyo International Conference on Reverence for Life, she participated in a seven-point Declaration on Reverence for Life which began, "The life of every human being is sacred as a creation of God and is of infinite value . . ."

Mother Teresa was invited to a breakfast meeting with members of the Japanese Diet. She consented to attend only when assured that various political groups had joined in the invitation. To 230 Diet members, she told of her gratitude for being among them and for being in their beautiful country. Begging them to help parents and unwed pregnant girls, she told them that the Missionaries of Charity would soon be in Tokyo and would have an "open door" for needy mothers and pregnant girls.

Two months after the Tokyo meeting, Mother Teresa was asked to participate in a symposium of the American Family Institute in Washington, D.C. The gathering, in the Dirksen Office Building, was attended by a number of U.S. congressmen and senators opposed to abortion and was addressed by experts on natural family planning, by economists, and by persons concerned with the breakdown of the American family.

In a setting with a strong political tinge, Mother Teresa stated, "I am not here to mix in politics, but to support life." Mother Teresa was introduced by former Senator James Buckley as a "heroine of our time."

"When the flux of history threatened to be changed by force," he said, "she shows the strength of personal power. Her road map comes from the pages of the New Testament. Mother Teresa sees not the face of ideology but the face of Christ. Moral truths may be out of fashion, but they still remain imbedded in our hearts."

After making the unobtrusive cross on her lips, Mother Teresa told the group, "Jesus became a child to teach us to love the child. In the eyes of the child, I see the spirit of life, of God.

"We must make sacrifices to protect life. But family life is broken. There is a hunger for more things. People need more cars, more machines. There is no time for family life. When Prime Minister Nehru came to open our Shishu Bhavan, our children's home in Delhi, he looked at the abandoned children we had taken in. He said, 'Take care of these children. One of them may be a Prime Minister one day.' Today, in some places, if you have an abortion, you don't have to pay. But if you give birth, you have to pay."

One of Mother Teresa's recurring themes was "fear of the child." It was a theme little appreciated by fervent champions of artificial methods of birth control, and even abortion, as the way to population control—and who saw population growth, particularly in the developing world, as a time bomb threatening to explode with devastating effects.

It was after the Symposium in Washington, D.C., that Mother Teresa was invited on June 4, 1981, to lunch at the White House with President and Mrs. Ronald Reagan. Accompanying her were Sister Priscilla and Mrs. Violet Collins, National Co-Worker Link. Mother Teresa revealed that she had told President Reagan that his suffering after the attempt on his life had brought him close to Jesus and to the poor who suffer so much. She asked him to think always of the poor. When President Reagan was asked about the conversation, he replied, "I listened."

In thanking the President for his hospitality, Mother Teresa sent him one of her little cards, "The presence of nuclear [arms] in the world has created fear and distrust among nations, as it is one more weapon to destroy human life—God's beautiful presence in the world. Just as abortion is used to kill the unborn child, this new weapon will become a means to eliminate the Poor of the World—our Brothers and Sisters whom Jesus has taught us to love, as He has loved each one of us. God bless you, M. Teresa, M.C."

"The image of God is on that unborn child," Mother Teresa kept repeating, but she was not simply the voice of the unborn. She was a voice for life on the planet, asking on different occasions if the trappings of war would be necessary if the image of God were seen in each person. Bombs and armies, in her vocabulary, were simply signs that love had been superseded, and that the human person was not seen in a true light. The fact that she was seen as a messenger of peace, and that she was carrying out a ministry of reconciliation became clearer, particularly after the Nobel Peace Prize. Her peace witness seemed particularly poignant in four places, two in the West, one in the Middle East, and one in the Far East. They were Corrymeela, in Northern Ireland, an Anglican church in the center of London, Nagasaki, Japan, and Beirut, Lebanon. She was present in those places in 1981 and 1982.

Mother Teresa's appearance at Corrymeela occurred in July 1981, eight years after a team of Missionaries of Charity, beloved of the people, had left Belfast. This time she brought no Sisters but was invited to talk on peace in a province that showed a bloodstained face to the world. Corrymeela, Hill of Harmony in Gaelic, was founded as a community of reconciliation by the Reverend Ray Davey, called by all a saintly man. A former Presbyterian chaplain at Queen's University in Belfast, his peace ministry owed much to his experience as a World War II prisoner in Germany when he had lived through the merciless bombing of Dresden which killed hundreds of thousands of civilians. A "Summerfest" at Corrymeela brought people together in prayer, discussion, and musical and other joy-bringing events. A large tent was erected on the Hill of Harmony that overlooked the sea fifty miles north of Belfast. The meeting brought

Mother Teresa into contact with bereaved people on both sides of the conflict in Northern Ireland, people mourning men, women, and children who had been cut down in nearly ten years of sporadic violence. She was in the midst of many people who had family members in prison. The violence, sparked by the 1972 Bloody Sunday when soldiers killed thirteen unarmed civil rights demonstrators, was a long-term effect of the unhealed wound of the partition of the island nation as it came into freedom from colonialism.

Mother Teresa's effect on her hearers at Corrymeela was described by two peacemakers: Mairead Corrigan, who had shared the Nobel Peace Price with Betty Williams in 1976 for their work in founding the Community of the Peace People, and Ciaran McKeown who had written the Declaration of the Peace Peopl.. Mairead's plunge into peacemaking came after a family tragedy. Three of her sister's children were killed in an accident related to the ongoing violence. Her sister, unable to recover from their loss, sank into despair and eventually cut her throat. Mairead wrote, "Mother Teresa said nothing I had not heard before or read from the gospels, but she brings the whole thing to life. In a gentle but at the same time extraordinarily demanding way, she challenges me to live out personally the Christian life. I think what makes Mother Teresa's words so effective is that she is living out her words in her life. When she tells you that she loves people and she is loved by God, one cannot for a moment doubt that fact. Standing on the hill outside the tent (as it was packed) with the gentle rain refreshing me, looking out over the sea, and listening to Mother Teresa saying, 'God loves you,' I felt a deep peace and, though tired, felt the desire to rededicate myself and redouble my efforts for peace."

Ciaran McKeown was also standing on the Hill of Harmony. He was the writer who in the Declaration of the Peace People stated, "We reject the use of the bomb and the bullet and all the techniques of violence."

He wrote me that he had come to Corrymeela as a small pilgrimage of thanksgiving to Mother Teresa, "for her unknown help to me in some of the darker moments of the Peace People experience . . . . Many's the late and lonely night, when exhaustion threatened to induce hopelessness in the struggle to suggest nonviolence for Northern Ireland, the thought of Mother Teresa's tireless exercise of love in vastly more intimidating circumstances provided energy and strength.

"I count July 8, 1981, a day of increasing rain and swirling mist, as the most beautiful day of my life . . . Though I am nervous of Mariology, yet when Mother Teresa spoke about the presence of Mary at the Crucifixion and asked people not to be bitter and to consider how 'entitled' to be bitter Mary was, Mary became a powerful and lovable example rather than an obscure and idealized abstraction. When Mother Teresa indicated that the loving presence of the forgiving God was available to everyone, free, one sensed the immediate truth of it, and that this was not the special preserve of persons like herself. The extraordinary effect was that, when she finished, she had left behind the desire, not so much to touch her hand, as happens with other 'charismatic' figures, but to speak immediately with the personal God who is so immediately present, and to see and hear God in the persons about, and in the very mist, then sweeping in from the sea."

"To speak immediately with the personal God," was what Mother Teresa was asking when she asked people to pray. McKeown's response was exactly what Mother Teresa was asking of all.

Immediately after Corrymeela, Mother Teresa flew to London, where she had been chosen from all the world's peacemakers, to give the first recitation of a peace prayer. It was composed by Satish Kumar, a follower of Gandhi living in London, and he hoped that people of all beliefs would join in reciting the words. He called it a peace mantra; a mantra, in the Hindu sense, being a repeated prayer that renews spiritual energy. To a packed congregation at St. James's Church in Piccadilly, in the heart of London, Mother Teresa recited the prayer:

"Lead me from death to life,
    from falsehood to truth;
Lead me from despair to hope,
    from fear to trust;
Lead me from hate to love,
    from war to peace;
Let peace fill our hearts, our world, our universe."

The prayer was recommended by Mother Teresa to all Co-Workers and printed in the International Co-Workers newsletter.

On one of her visits to Japan, Mother Teresa took a plane to Nagasaki, where the second nuclear bomb had been detonated on August 9, 1945. She wrote a peace prayer on the plane and on April 26, 1982, standing on ground zero, directly above which the bomb had exploded, she recited:

"Eternal Father,
In union with the suffering and passion of Christ which is being relived at every mass—we offer you the pain and suffering caused by the atomic bomb in this place to thousands of people, and we implore you, Eternal Father, to protect the whole world from the pain and suffering nuclear war would bring to the people of Japan and the whole world, already filled with so much fear and distrust and anxiety among the nations.
Eternal Father, have pity on us all."

In response to a question by a woman whose mother had died under the bomb, she said that all must pray "that no human hand will ever again do what has been done here."

A witness to peace that spoke through deeds even more loudly than words was made by Mother Teresa in Lebanon in August 1982. To reach her Sisters in Beirut, long a cauldron of violence, she took a plane from Rome to Athens and then another plane to Cyprus. From Cyprus, the only means of reaching Beirut was a seventeen-hour boat trip. She found the six Sisters safe in Mar Takla, in East Beirut. Accompanying Mother Teresa was Ann Petrie, a young American Co-Worker, who had earlier made a film on the work of the Sisters entitled *The World of Mother Teresa.* Ann Petrie related, "Mother Teresa arrived when the bombing and shelling were at their worst. Targets were no more than five miles from the Sisters' house. There were snipers everywhere. The devastation was horrifying."

John de Salis, head of the Red Cross delegation in Lebanon, told Mother Teresa of the plight of mentally ill children in an asylum of the upper floor of Dar al-Ajaza Islamia, a home for the aged. The home, located near a camp of Palestinian refugees, had been damaged by bombs. The needs of the children for food, water, and adequate shelter were tragically acute. Mother Teresa decided that all the children could be housed with her Sisters who had already opened a refuge for the homeless and destitute. The problem was that Dar al-Ajaza was situated across the Green Line, the no-man's land separating that predominantly Muslim sector from East Beirut, home of the Christian Lebanese. So tense had the feeling become between the residents of East and West Beirut, in particular after the great influx of Palestinian refugees, that the residents of Beirut found it safer to remain on their side of the Green Line, a street marked by militia-guarded checkpoints.

Mother Teresa insisted on crossing the line to evacuate the children. Against the advice even of church leaders, Mother Teresa traveled with four Red Cross vehicles into war-ravaged West Beirut to rescue the children. They found thirty-seven children, from seven to twenty-one, the most helpless examples of humanity. Among them were the deformed, the paralyzed, the severely mentally retarded, youngsters unaware of what was happening around them, but able to suffer hunger, thirst, and fear. "You don't need intelligence to experience fear," said Dr. Abdel Rahman Labban, chief medical officer.

Mother Teresa went among them, embracing them and giving a handshake to the older children. Among the Muslim children were some Palestinians. One by one, Mother Teresa, the International Red Cross, and hospital workers picked up the children and carried or led them to the vehicles. The convoy crossed the Green Line at an Israeli-controlled checkpoint and rushed the children to the Mar Takla convent. Two days later,

Mother Teresa crossed the Green Line again to evacuate another twenty-seven children.

One of the Red Cross officials commented, "What stunned everyone was her energy. She saw the problem, fell to her knees, and prayed for a few seconds, and then she was rattling off a list of supplies she needed . . . We didn't expect a saint to be so efficient."

Help came from all sides, and soon there were beds for all the children. People whose own resources had been reduced by the constant violence brought clothes, food, and supplies. Sister Gertrude was sent for from Yemen to help with medical assistance. John de Salis remarked, "Mother Teresa was the answer to prayer. The problem is that in wartime, most of the attention is focused on the casualties. But the blind, the deaf, the insane, and the spastics tend to be forgotten just when they need help the most. Mother Teresa understood that right away."

Mother Teresa realizing the precariousness of life in Beirut said, "All we can do is to give them tender, loving care. They are in God's hands."

When the press in Beirut wanted a statement from her, Mother Teresa avoided politics. Instead, to people reporting war and violence, she read the peace prayer of St. Francis. Some of her hearers may have realized that it was not far from Beirut, in St.-Jean-d'Acre, now 'Akko, that Brother Francis had come personally with his message of peace to Crusaders committed to violence.

Mother Teresa shared one impression which was carried in the international press. "I have never been in a war before, but I have seen famine and death. I was asking myself what do they feel when they do this. I don't understand it. They are all children of God. Why do they do it. I don't understand."

In a world where the expenditure of billions of dollars was justified for what was termed defense, Mother Teresa offered a different meaning for the word. "Today," she asserted, "nations put too much effort and money into defending their borders. If they could only defend defenseless people with food, shelter, and clothing, I think the world would be a happier place."

Not all the Sisters and Co-Workers shared the implications of Mother Teresa's peace witness. Some caught the vision, in particular Sister Nirmala and Patty Kump. Commenting on August 6, both the feast of the Transfiguration of Jesus before apostles Peter, James, and John, and the date of Hiroshima's destruction, she said, "That is the difference between the light that purifies and the light that destroys." In a letter to me she expressed the vision behind all her prayers, sacrifices, and journeyings, "If you only knew," she wrote, "how I long to light the fire of Love and Peace throughout the world. Pray for me that He may use me to the fullest."

At the beginning of June 1983, Sister Death came close to Mother Teresa and everything came to a full stop.

It happened in Rome while she was staying with the Sisters at San Gregorio on the Coelian Hill. She was two months short of her seventy-third birthday.

The little woman, who had rushed to the rescue of others, lay prone and helpless in Salvator Mundi Hospital on the Janiculum Hill, a hospital conducted by the Sisters of the Divine Savior. Sister Nirmala, superior of the Contemplative house in New York, was sent for. She related that at first Mother Teresa was not even allowed to raise her arms and had to be fed. In the beginning, Sister Nirmala and Sister Stella, the superior in Rome, were her only visitors outside of the hospital staff.

On May 27, Mother Teresa had met with the leaders of Caritas Internationalis at their Rome general assembly. Gathered for the assembly were representatives of such Catholic overseas aid agencies as Misereor of Germany and Catholic Relief Services of the United States. "As you are carriers of God's love," she told them, "people must be able to know your love for them. Not only words! I must say, nowadays, many more people are talking *to* the poor. They used to talk much *about* the poor . . . And teach the young people. They are yearning to do something. I cannot tell you all that the young people are doing when they come to Calcutta. A girl from Paris University came. On her face was worry. But after some weeks of working in the Home for the Dying, she came to me and said, 'I have found Jesus!' 'Where?' I asked her. And she said to me: 'I found Him in the Home for the Dying.' "

On May 30, Pope John Paul II remarked to Mother Teresa that she looked unusually tired. He urged her to have a medical checkup.

As Mother Teresa told me later, it was only a minor accident on June 2 that brought her to the attention of doctors. News of Mother Teresa's hospitalization was carried by the world press, and her doctor was approached by reporters. He informed them that part of her treatment was for poor blood circulation and that the painkillers he had prescribed, she had refused to take. "She wants to offer up her sufferings to God," he stated.

As her strength returned, Mother Teresa asked for pen and paper to write the fruit of her meditations. On June 19, she put on paper a sort of litany listing her answers to "Who is Jesus to me?" She began:

The Word made flesh.
The Bread of life.
The Victim offered for our sins on the cross.
The Sacrifice offered at the holy mass for the sins of the world and mine.

After describing Jesus in such terms as "The Way to be walked," "The Joy to be shared," and "The Peace to be given," and in her usual vocabulary of the naked, hungry, homeless, thirsty, sick, and lonely, Mother Teresa described Him in poignantly specific terms:

The Leper—to wash his wounds.
The Beggar—to give him a smile.
The Drunkard—to listen to Him.
The Mental—to protect Him.
The Little One—to embrace Him.
The Blind—to lead Him.
The Dumb—to speak for Him.
The Crippled—to walk with Him.
The Drug Addict—to befriend Him.
The Prostitute—to remove from danger and befriend her.
The Prisoner—to be visited.
The Old—to be served.

Mother Teresa concluded her meditation with the words:

To me, Jesus is my God.
Jesus is my Spouse.
Jesus is my Life.
Jesus is my only Love.
Jesus is my all in all.
Jesus is my everything.

Jesus I love with my whole heart, with my whole being. I have given Him all, even my sins, and He has espoused me to Himself in tenderness and love. Now and for life I am the spouse of my crucified Spouse. Amen.

The litany was shared with the Missionaries of Charity who in turn shared it with the Co-Workers.

Mother Teresa was not released from Salvator Mundi Hospital until July 4, and even then she was taken briefly to the Gemelli Hospital. There, with the help of the most sophisticated equipment she was given a final examination by a team of doctors. She was released to Sister Gertrude, the medical doctor who was at Oslo with her as her second daughter in the Society.

In less than seven weeks, Mother Teresa was again on her rounds, crossing the Atlantic to be with the Sisters in the United States. Her visit was unannounced, and she was spirited out of the airport without being glimpsed by the public. On a day of August heat, we sat in the tiny parlor of the convent in the South Bronx. It was behind the chapel, and all was quiet. The usual excitement of Mother Teresa's presence, with a constantly ringing doorbell and people asking to see her, "just for a minute," was absent.

The Sisters had hung a world map that took up most of one wall, with small markers for the places where Missionaries of Charity worked. There was also a cloth banner with Tagore's words, "Who but God visits the poor."

"I did not feel exhausted," Mother Teresa told me. "What happened was, I fell out of bed—not far, because it was a M.C. bed. I felt a pain in my side. I thought I ought to go to the hospital because something might be broken. They took X rays. The doctor said that there was no fracture, but there was something the matter with my heart.

"The doctor joked with me, 'I cannot say that Mother Teresa has a bad heart. But we must have more exams.' The doctors found it was the heart. The cardiologists wrote it all down, and I have to take medicine three times a day. They told me that if the fall had not made me come to the hospital, I would have had a heart attack. There was no reason for falling. See the wonderful ways of God! St. Peter must have said, 'Hold her back there. There are no slums in heaven.'

"Then I got letters and telegrams. I never realized that people loved the poor so much. A Hindu gentleman wrote from Kashmir—the Sisters are now in Jammu and Kashmir—and he said he was praying to goddess Kali for me. He prayed to Kali that she would take the bad part from me and give it to him and take the good healthy part from him and give it to me. To think of all those prayers. I received a card from Yemen from the President. President Singh of India telegraphed and a telegram came from President Reagan; he signed it from himself and Nancy.

"Jyoti Basu wrote that all the people were concerned. I can't tell you how many cards and telegrams and messages came from people I didn't know. I can't answer any of them. If I answered one, I would have to answer them all.

"The King and Queen of Belgium came to the hospital. People were coming, people I didn't know, offering to pay for everything. The doctors at Salvator Mundi would not take anything.

"All the Sisters were praying, and all the Co-Workers, and all the other people I don't know—what a great amount of prayers going to God. That was the wonderful thing; that's what the world needs.

"What a gift it was, to share in the passion of Christ. I said in the hospital that I missed the Eucharist, so they brought the Eucharist for adoration every day from nine to ten in the morning and three to four in the afternoon. A priest came to say mass every day in the room."

Once some photographers came as far as Mother Teresa's room, but were stopped before they could enter. Mother Teresa knew what was happening, and Sister Nirmala stated that her face became white and drawn. She was unable to take any strain.

Sister Nirmala, instead of returning to the Contemplative house, undertook Mother Teresa's visits to Haiti, Honduras, Santo Domingo, Guatemala, Panama, El Salvador, Miami, Florida, and San Francisco. She knew Spanish from her experience in Venezuela. In Honduras, a new foundation was being formed so that the Sisters could bring help to encampments of refugees from strife-ridden El Salvador. Ann Blaikie, who had gone to Rome, was told that if Mother Teresa obeyed instructions and took her medicine, she could live many years. Mother Teresa was ordered not even to lift anything, even babies.

"But you can still hug them, Mother," Ann Blaikie told her. While Mother Teresa was in Salvator Mundi, her friend James R. Cardinal Knox, the former nuncio to India, was taken ill and died in Rome.

Shortly after Mother Teresa left the hospital, she received a visit from Jozef Cardinal Glemp, the archbishop of Warsaw.

"The cardinal invited me to come to Warsaw. He wanted the Sisters there," Mother Teresa related. Sister Gertrude, to whose medical supervision she had been released, could not hold her down. She was soon on her way.

"I went to Poland and I spent three days there. They took me to Our Lady's Shrine at Jasna Gora. I will send four Sisters to Warsaw. On the way, I went to East Berlin, where our Sisters are working. The superior is Sister Sandia—they are all Indian. We can open another house on that side. It is in Karl-Marx-Stadt." I thought she had said Karl Marx Street, meaning a second house in Berlin. "No," she said, "it is in another city, named for Karl Marx." All I could say was "Incredible."

"It was incredible to me, too," Mother Teresa said.

On the August visit to New York, Mother Teresa saw no one but the Sisters, a few Co-Workers, and Cardinal Cooke who was near death from cancer. The Cardinal, she said, expressed his delight that the priests' movement, Corpus Christi, was to have its headquarters in New York.

"He gave us an empty convent for the movement. He trusts us blindly. What Jesus can do if we only let him. I am getting everything in writing. I don't know about the future. The priests' movement will be on its own. The Brothers are already on their own. We give them some help materially, but they are separate."

I was reminded of hints she had let fall at the meeting of the International Co-Workers in Rome in May 1982 and again at the American Co-Workers gathering in Minneapolis in June of the same year. She impressed on us the need to follow to the letter the rule of not collecting funds and of transferring all funds to the Sisters, so that all would be in order when she would not be with us.

Mother Teresa's face lit up with joy as she talked of the new novitiate in San Francisco.

"We have so many wonderful vocations, nineteen novices already in San Francisco. I just sent a French girl and a Yugoslav girl there. The novice mistress in charge of formation is Sister Assumpta from Ireland. I want to mix them up—all the nationalities—while they are novices. Then when they go on a mission, they are used to each other.

"Just this year, we had 143 applicants.

"We have four houses in Ethiopia now. Other missionaries were sent out, but they wanted us to stay. Catholic Relief Services was wonderful with the food for those poor people. We are now in Jijiga as well as Addis Ababa and Dire Dawa. The new house is in Kaffa. We must stay with the starving people.

"We opened a house in Khartoum in Sudan on August 16. I received a call to come to Sri Lanka." I was surprised at this, since Sri Lankan officials had earlier asked a team of Missionaries of Charity to leave. "We were invited to come to Assam. What terrible things happened there." She was referring to massacres of border-crossers from Bangladesh who were encroaching on tribal lands.

"All the terrible suffering, the unnecessary suffering. This is our opportunity to belong to Jesus. Today, there is no martyrdom. We have to live the faith right in front of them."

Then she paused and began a story about something that had happened to her not long before, a parablelike story that I felt sure she would tell in many places.

"A beautiful thing happened in Calcutta. Two young people came to see me; Hindu people. They gave me a very big amount of money. 'How did you get so much money?' I asked them. They answered me, 'We got married two days ago. Before our marriage, we decided we would not have a big wedding feast and we would not buy wedding clothes. We decided that we would give the money we saved to you to feed the people.' In a big Hindu family, a rich family, it's a scandal not to have special wedding clothes and not to have a wedding feast. 'Why did you do that?' I asked them. And they answered me, 'Mother, we love each other so much that we wanted to obtain a special blessing from God by making a sacrifice. We wanted to give each other this special gift.' Isn't that beautiful? Things like that are happening every day; really beautiful things. We must pull them out. We have to pull out the wonderful things that are happening in the world. Now we feed more than nine thousand people in Shishu Bhavan every day." I thought back to the steaming vats of food in the courtyard and the families who were kept alive by regular food.

Mother Teresa got up and we stood in front of the map of the world with its little markers all over India, and in Asia, Australia, the Middle East, Africa, Latin America, and North America.

"All those houses," she said, "two hundred and fifty-seven, I think. A hundred and twenty in India."

Mother Teresa put her hand on China and then her finger found Peking.

"That is where we must go, Peking." She used the old form rather than the later Beijing.

Gazing at the map, she said, "Look what God is doing with nothing. People must believe that it is all His, all His. We must allow God to use us, without adding or subtracting anything."

Her earlier statement came back to me, "I am more convinced of the work being His than I am convinced I am really alive."

In November 1983, less than six months after she was put on medications to help her weakened heart, Mother Teresa went to Hong Kong to visit the Sisters. A message came there that she was needed in Delhi. In the presidential palace where the Viceroy of His Imperial Majesty had ruled a subcontinent, Queen Elizabeth II, as part of a state visit, bestowed on Mother Teresa the Order of Merit, one of Britain's highest awards. The award seemed to complete a circle since it was given to a woman whose work had taken root at the breakup of the British Empire and who had asked for citizenship in a country just freed from the colonial yoke.

The year 1984 opened with Mother Teresa calling to her side in Calcutta the nineteen Sisters heading the nineteen regions of the Missionaries of Charity. Coming from Asia, Africa, Europe, and North and South America, the Sisters who with the six Councillors led the congregation under Mother Teresa, met for a spiritual retreat.

The opening of new houses continued. Some of us wondered if Mother Teresa would send someone else with the team for Poland, perhaps Sister Andrea, who spoke Polish. Mother Teresa went herself to Poland with four Sisters and on her return to Rome had to spend a few days in the hospital. In a few months, she was accompanying a team of Sisters to Assam, to remote Mokochung, center of the Naga tribal people. Much like native Americans, they fear for the survival of their culture and the retention of their tribal lands. She was given a tribal welcome with the ceremonial presentation of shawls before twelve thousand Nagas. When the Missionaries of Charity opened a house in Winnipeg, Manitoba, Canada, Mother

Teresa entrusted the task of accompanying the Sisters to Sister Priscilla, the regional superior for the area.

A longed-for event in the lives of the Sisters was the visit of Mother Teresa. Her visits brought joy to each house as she prayed with the Sisters, told them stories of other houses, and, above all, listened to what they had to say. Always joining in the daily work, Mother Teresa generally took the lowest task in the convent, that of cleaning the bathroom. During 1984, she visited the houses of the Sisters in India, traveling the expanse of the subcontinent, from Trivandrum in Kerala to Darjeeling in Bengal. She could no longer reserve to herself the task of visiting the Sisters outside of India and, in 1984, it was Sister Frederick, as Assistant to Mother Teresa, who went to see the Sisters in Haiti, Honduras, Venezuela, and Peru, as well as other countries in Central and South America. Besides serving as Mother Teresa's Assistant, Sister Frederick was one of the six Councillors guiding the Missionaries of Charity. Other Councillors were Sister Agnes, the first daughter of Mother Teresa; Sister Andrea who had opened the house in New York; Sister Shanti, who had started the work in Tabora, Tanzania; and Sister Damien, who had worked in Gaza; and Sister Joseph Michael, whose tasks at the Calcutta Motherhouse included dealing with the world's Co-Workers.

One call would evoke a response from Mother Teresa no matter where she found herself or what her condition of health, a call from the Holy Father. In April 1984, when a world rally of Catholic youth was held in Rome, she was there, addressing them in St. Peter's Square and again in the Colosseum. A photograph in *Osservatore Romano* showed her, tired and drawn, standing with Brother Roger of Taizé at the gathering in the Colosseum where so many of the early followers of Jesus had witnessed in blood. In October of the same year, she was again in Rome, this time to talk at a worldwide spiritual retreat for priests.

In the spacious audience hall where Pope John Paul II habitually addressed pilgrims, Mother Teresa spoke to 6,500 priests. Her words were simultaneously translated into several languages for priests from all the continents and representing all the races of humankind. There were priests from the developed world and priests serving the poorest and most isolated of peoples. To men charged with being the carriers of the word of Jesus and celebrators of the Eucharistic meal that He left His followers, the small woman stood for a life lived entirely for Jesus. At a time when fidelity to vows was being put in question, she was an example of the utmost in fidelity. Her fidelity to the pledged word stemmed not only from an irrevocable religious commitment, but from the bred-in-the-bones concept of *besa* from her Albanian culture. Fr. Joseph Langford, head of the Priest Co-Workers, related that as Mother Teresa talked of the holiness of the priest in today's world, he saw many priests moved to tears. "Be holy, like Jesus," she said simply.

It seemed somehow inevitable that Mother Teresa would become the inspirer and foundress of a congregation of priests, and it happened just after the Rome priests' retreat. Fr. Langford revealed to Mother Teresa that an idea had been germinating in his thinking for a number of years, namely the need for a congregation of priests linked to the spirituality and vision of Mother Teresa. A similar idea had been growing in Mother Teresa's mind and it had been part of her prayers. They went together to the Sacred Congregation for the Doctrine of the Faith and presented the proposition of a congregation to the secretary, Archbishop Jerome Hamer. It would be called the Missionary Fathers of Charity. The response from the Sacred Congregation was in the affirmative. Fr. Joseph Langford with three other priests were empowered to enter into a novitiate training at the center in the Bronx given to the Priest Co-Workers by the late Terence Cardinal Cooke. Cooke's successor, Archbishop John J. O'Connor, would be a sort of protector of the fledgling congregation, and Fr. Langford and his companions, after a two-year novitiate, would repeat their vows in the new congregation, as Mother Teresa had repeated her vows in the newly founded Missionaries of Charity. In her seventies, Mother Teresa was adding a new society to her spiritual family, a society that could be considered the spiritual summit.

"I don't think I will start anything more," said Mother Teresa in the New York convent at the end of October 1984. She was radiant after a flying visit to San Francisco where a group of eight young women had been received into the Missionaries of Charity.

"There were three Americans, two from Peru, two from India, and one from Costa Rica. A novitiate has opened in Warsaw for Eastern Europe. Wonderful, no?"

Within days after this conversation, Mother Teresa was at the cremation place on the banks of the Jumna River in New Delhi. Her friend, Prime Minister Indira Gandhi, killed by assassins' bullets on October 31, 1984, lay on a sandalwood pyre in the burning ghat called Shantivana, Enclave of Peace.

"May her soul live in peace forever," Mother Teresa prayed. The legacy of Mahatma Gandhi, who had been cremated nearby, lived on in the ecumenical service which included not only Vedic prayers, but the prayers of Muslim and Christian Indians.

Mother Teresa then turned immediately to works of peace, and she brought Missionaries of Charity to makeshift camps where Sikhs had taken refuge from the murder and pillage sparked by the assassination. Indira Gandhi was felled by Sikh members of her bodyguard in the wake of the military storming of the Golden Temple, holy place of Sikhism, five months earlier. Among the hundreds huddled in the camp were women whose husbands had been clubbed or slashed to death in bloody revenge. Hungry children who had been witness to the carnage were being fed mounds of rice on plantain leaves.

During the early days of November 1984, when communal violence set Indian murderously against Indian, Mother Teresa was repeating what she had done in Calcutta in the days of violence of August 1946. After the Day of the Great Killing on August 16, 1946, she had made a foray, alone, into streets strewn with corpses. As a vigorous woman of thirty-six, she had braved the dangers of a city in torment to feed the hungry. In 1984, a frail woman of seventy-four, she was still involved with the works of mercy which she called the works of peace, but she was no longer alone. With her were Sisters in white, blue-bordered saris who served as a sign of reconciliation—a sign which gave them entry into every scene of human need. "We must love one another," said Mother Teresa to a visitor to the refugee camp. "That is all Jesus came to tell us."

Mother Teresa looked frail and markedly more stooped. She did not refer to the state of her health, even after the illness of June 1983, but on occasion a word would drop indicating that her heart was failing. An American reporter, finding it hard to hear her above the bustle and street noises of Lower Circular Road, asked if they could not go upstairs where it would be quieter. Mother Teresa replied that the doctors had told her not to climb stairs unless it was absolutely necessary.

Though her heart might be failing physically, Mother Teresa's heart was overflowing with spiritual joy as the novitiates of the Society she founded were filled with a constant stream of young women from all the races that make up the human family. Each year, new teams of Sisters were ready to speed to the needy of the earth. The family of the Sisters came to 2,400 at the end of 1984. There were 270 houses at the end of the same year, including those in India. With the 70 houses of the Brothers, that meant that 340 houses had been planted among the poor of five continents in less than thirty-five years. As long as there were poor people, men, women, and children marked with the ineradicable stamp of the divine, Mother Teresa's Sisters and Brothers would find them. China, Nicaragua, Hungary,—and yet other countries—the Sisters and Brothers were knocking at the door and waiting to be admitted to go to the very least. A visa to enter Czechoslovakia surprised and delighted Mother Teresa.

Francis of Assisi has been called "Everybody's St. Francis" because his appeal reached far beyond his Church. His utter simplicity and poverty, together with his soaring love of all creation, and its Creator, have irresistibly drawn people to him over the centuries. He has inspired men and women to seek peace beyond all barriers of "enemy," and to protect not only each other's lives, but the life of the earth which is the Creator's gift to them. Countless representations of Brother Francis have appeared in art and literature and are still appearing. In the twentieth century he became the subject of widely distributed and popular films.

Mother Teresa's appeal also reached large segments of the human family. Again it was the poignant simplicity and the powerlessness of love that opened the gates of the human heart across great religious and cultural divides. People sent her letters from all over the world. So great was the blizzard of mail, especially after the Nobel Peace Prize, that it had to be set apart in a special section of the Calcutta Post Office, protected by a metal fence. Articles, books, and poetry have been inspired by her, and she has entered folk culture by being pictured in comic books and represented in stage reviews. When she was not the subject of news articles in the press, she was referred to innumerable times as a symbol of the poor. A writer called up the duality of India by juxtaposing two immediately recognizable symbols, "Mother Teresa and the Taj Mahal." Her recorded talks had wide distribution, as did short documentaries and slide film presentations. Millions of television viewers saw the repeated showings of Malcolm Muggeridge's film *Something Beautiful for God* and Ann Petrie's film *The World of Mother Teresa.* Both of these films concentrated on Calcutta, while a second film of Ann Petrie's documented the international scope of the work of Mother Teresa in twenty locations in ten countries. In this film, entitled *Mother Teresa,* Petrie stressed the spiritual sources of the work of the Missionaries of Charity.

Mother Teresa herself did not always realize how she belonged to everyone. Once, after an election in India, a Communist noted that she carried on her finger the indelible mark given to each voter. "Mother Teresa," he said, "You should not vote for any party. You belong to all of us."

In the matter of Brother Francis and Mother Teresa, there was another dimension, spiritual and immeasurable, their contribution to changed lives.

In one of her airport interviews, this one in Tulsa, Oklahoma, Mother Teresa explained, "When there is a call within a call, there is only one thing to do, to say 'Yes' to Jesus. That's all. If we belong to Him, He must be able to use us without consulting us. That's what Jesus did. When He called, I had only to say a simple 'Yes.' "

The picture of a woman of the twentieth century and the birth of a new religious family is strangely evocative of the story of the "Poverello" of seven centuries earlier. They both said "Yes" to a call to serve the human family in peace and love, a call which moved them to say "Yes" to life with such spectacular poetry and fire that countless hearts caught that fire.

As she was present to the agony of Calcutta, and that of India's other great cities, so Mother Teresa was present to the agony of Bhopal, a city four hundred miles south of Delhi, when a cloud of death enveloped a crowded slum on the night of December 3, 1984. The poisoned air, caused by a leak from a pesticide plant, seeped silently into the shantytown, killing many people as they slept. Over twenty-five hundred people died in a few days, and more than one hundred thousand suffered serious injuries to eyes and lungs. The Missionaries of Charity, who had long been working in Bhopal, escaped being among the victims because the death-bringing gas was blown by the wind in a different direction.

Even while the dead were being cremated or buried, Mother Teresa rushed to Bhopal with teams of Missionaries of Charity to work with the Sisters already on the scene. There were plans to be made for the helpless aged and, especially, for orphans and sick children. Many of the children were blinded, perhaps permanently, by the toxic fog of one of history's worst industrial accidents. "We have come to love and care for those who most need it in this terrible tragedy," said Mother Teresa, as she went from center to center, from hospital to hospital, visiting the afflicted people.

Epilogue: Sign and Countersign

One small woman, leaning over a spittle-covered, cadaverous man, trying with passionate care to fan the ebbing spark of life and thus show love to a "throwaway" human being seemed an important symbol in the Calcutta of 1955. Mother Teresa, in rescuing men and women and even children from the streets of an obscenely crowded, refugee-filled city so that they would not die untended like dogs in the gutter, was making a statement about the human condition. The caravanserai at the temple of Kali seemed a strange but perhaps providential place to make that statement.

Europe, where I had been involved with refugees and the effects of war's destruction, had been making a different statement. For well over five years during the Second World War, the continent had been made a charnel house, not only by the most destructive war of all the ages, but by the deliberate murder of human beings in camps designed for death. Over eleven million persons, men, women, and children, had perished in these camps, called "annihilation camps," expressing the mad conviction that some human creatures had the power to render into nothing other fellow human creatures. More than half of those who died had been Jews, who as a people had been condemned, torn from their homes, forced into cattle cars, gassed, and their bodies thrust into ovens for the burning. The word "Holocaust" was taken from the Hebrew Scriptures to describe a crime unprecedented in human history, holocaust being the wholly burnt offering of an animal victim in a sacrifice. The word "genocide" was added to the lexicon to describe the destruction of a people who have been termed "martyrs of the Decalogue."

Even before coming to postwar Europe, I had worked in a refugee camp, sequestered in northern Mexico, for people freed from Siberian exile. They were Poles, mostly simple farming people, deported from eastern Poland during the Hitler-Stalin pact that initiated the Second World War. In the camp were three hundred orphans who had seen their parents die in far-off wastes and in some cases had buried them. These survivors of a vast empire of slave labor camps, called the Gulag, were reminders that tyrants decreed millions of deaths by ice as well as by fire.

As I saw Mother Teresa and the Missionaries of Charity in the Home for the Dying, the thoughts of war's indiscriminate slaughter flooded my mind, the bombings of such cities as Coventry, Hamburg, and Dresden, and the testing of one type of atomic bomb on Hiroshima and of another on Nagasaki. The thought crossed my mind that around Mother Teresa in the Calcutta of 1950 the streets themselves had become death camps, not by intent, but by the magnitude of the tragedy with which colonialism ended. Death-dealing by intent had become a way of life in wartime Germany. The helpless people Mother Teresa brought from the streets and cared for would have been marked for death as "useless eaters" in an economy where all energies were mobilized for the works of war. Some were saved when church leaders cried aloud against this practice, and their flocks saved the blind, the insane, the paralyzed, and the old, only by keeping them out of the hands of the authorities and sharing their sparse rations with them. As the head of the Red Cross had observed in Beirut, the helpless and handicapped tend to be forgotten in wartime. In "Fortress Europe," under military tyranny, the handicapped who came under the care of the state authorities were candidates for destruction.

As time went on, Auschwitz, where the lifeless bodies of murdered Jews, Poles, and Gypsies were consigned to the pyres, and Hiroshima and Nagasaki, where the cities themselves became funeral pyres, rose up as signs of an age.

Mother Teresa was a countersign.

The Nobel Peace Prize Committee had recognized this in pointing to her witness to life in a time of genocide, of "the unrestrained use of violence," and of "contempt for human life and dignity."

Mother Teresa's witness ran counter to every policy that showed contempt for human life and the use of violence to end it.

In Beirut, she had said, looking out over war's destruction of human beings and their means of survival, "I don't understand it. They are all children of God." When asked about capital punishment, she had also said, "I don't understand it." She could not understand how any human being could dare take life since all life is a gift of God.

To Mother Teresa, the protection of life, starting with the child in the womb, englobed all members of the one human family, children of one Father.

To Mother Teresa, the protection of human life was a seamless garment.

It seemed inexplicable to many that Mother Teresa would talk of protecting life in the womb when life on the planet was threatened by the explosive power of 1.6 million Hiroshima bombs stockpiled by the two superpowers. While many stressed the dangers of overpopulation, others pointed out that the nuclear stockpiles represented the equivalent of two Hiroshima-type bombs for every day of every year from the birth of Jesus to the nineteen eighties, with explosive power to spare. As a countersign, Mother Teresa was talking a counterlanguage, the language of a moral vision, that saw all human beings as sacred and all creation as coming forth from the hand of a Creator. The language of absolute, eternal values was shocking in an age marked by relativism, pragmatism, and progressive desacralization.

"For me," Mother Teresa asserted, "life is the most beautiful gift of God to mankind, therefore people and nations who destroy life by abortion and euthanasia are the poorest—for they have not got food for one more child, home for one old person. So they must add one more cruel murder into this world." Her guileless statement was uttered in a year when five hundred billion dollars of the world's resources went into military expenditures.

In a letter, Barbara Ward, commenting on Mother Teresa's insistence on opposing abortion, said, "Mother Teresa seems to me almost the only human being with a clear right to speak on abortion. How weary I am of those who claim to be prolife but do not seem to care if the child dies of starvation at six months or six years." A strong statement, but one that was grounded in Mother Teresa's practical concern for the quality of life after the unborn child enters a world so often unfriendly to its needs and growth. Many promoters of abortion saw Mother Teresa's protection of life, even of the unborn, as obscurantist, to say the least. There were countless people, however, who responded to her message precisely because it emphasized the infinite value of life itself, and therefore of every human life. Mother Teresa's work grew in an age of massive assaults on human rights, when some innocent people disappeared into detention cells, others into custody in mental asylums, others into torture sessions, and still others to be numbered among the "disappeared," never again to be seen alive. Her work spread over five continents in a time which for some brought unexampled affluence but for others meant depersonalization, when the integrity of the person could be lost in the slums of bloated cities, in the repetitive sameness of factory work, or in the anonymous hopelessness of no work at all. Her works of mercy grew while nameless refugees by the millions were thrust across borders in Asia, the Middle East, Africa, and Central America, or escaped in frail craft to be swallowed up in Asian seas.

Human beings wanted to know if they mattered in the scheme of things. They seemed to want to hear it from someone who needed nothing from them, no party affiliation, no adherence on a road to power, nothing at all. They heard it from a poor and powerless woman who had plumbed the very depths of human agony and who traveled about the world with a tiny cloth bag containing her two saris, writing letters on the rough, lined copybook of the poorest school child. They heard something that answered to a radical hunger in the human heart to be assured that they were not mere meaningless links in the chain of history, not simply "naked apes." They listened when they heard that despite massive evidence of human cruelty, there was a force of love that was stronger, and that they could be a part of it. Mother Teresa's presence made them aware of the stream of love that the Creator poured over all his creation and of their place in it. Thomas Merton, the Cistercian monk, put it in a few words, "To say that I am made in the image of God is to say that love is the reason for my existence, for God is love." Mother Teresa left people with hopeful reminders, and people began to carry them on small cards: "Love is a fruit in season at all times, and within the reach of every hand. Anyone may gather it and no limit is set."

Mother Teresa faced ever larger groups as she reminded them that they came forth from the hand of a God who loved them dearly, no matter to what segment of the human family they belonged. She brought them the Good News of their infinite value, a value that often contradicted the messages the world was giving them. She became the symbol not only of a loving God, but of a living God. "God is," she kept telling people from every platform open to her. When Inter-Church Features, an association of nine American and Canadian church publications, selected six women in 1982 as "living Christian heroes worthy of recognition," Mother Teresa was one of them, joined, among others, by Dorothy Day and Barbara Ward. *Good Housekeeping,* a widely circulated American magazine concerned with women's interests, conducted a poll for the "Most Admired Woman." For two years in succession, 1981 and 1982, Mother Teresa was voted into first place.

Because she stressed her own response to a first and then a second call, Mother Teresa was asked about the role of a call in the lives of ordinary human beings. "All of us have been called," she said on various occasions. "The fact that you have been given a gift may constitute a call." She asked that people find ways to use their particular gifts not simply for self-advancement but for the good of others, especially the suffering. No one was useless, not even the person lying helpless on a bed or bound to a wheelchair or the leper who had lost the use of hands or feet. Mother Teresa sometimes sent notes on a piece of paper with a rough drawing of hands that someone had made for her. Underneath was the biblical assurance, "I have carved you in the palm of my hand." Her utter dependence on providence recalled the promise of Jesus that "All the hairs of your head are numbered." As a countersign to heart-stopping cruelty and dehumanization, Mother Teresa was saying to each person, "You are unique, irreplaceable, and beloved."

There were many, as mentioned earlier, who felt that Mother Teresa, intimately acquainted with the agony of the poorest of the poor, should be striving to change structures that cause or permit such horrifying deprivation. They seemed to expect from her some anger at the rich who could live with ostentatious superfluities while near or far neighbors were perishing for lack of basic needs. Yet, in the teachings of Jesus, there is no warrant for rage. Mother Teresa remarked, "There must be a reason why some people can afford to live well. But I tell you, this provokes avarice, and there comes the sin. Richness is given by God, and it is our duty to divide it with those less favored."

To an interviewer who asked her if the day would ever come when the ocean of poverty would dry up, she replied, "When all recognize that our suffering neighbor is God himself, and when you draw the consequences from that fact. On that day, there will be no more poverty, and we—the Missionaries of Charity—will have no work to do."

Mother Teresa was giving voice to the most ancient Christian tradition regarding the conquest of poverty. A fourth-century saint, Gregory of Nazianzen, said in a sermon "On the Love of the Poor," "Brothers and friends, let us not misuse God's gifts to us, or we shall be forced to hear God say: 'Be ashamed, you who keep to yourselves what belongs to others.' Imitate rather God's fairhandedness, and no one will be poor."

Mother Teresa was resurrecting for her Co-Workers and for all who would listen the basic Christian doctrine on the ownership of property. This calls for the resources that people possess over and above their needs to be shared with those who lack necessities. This might be taken even further when people would be moved to part with their resources, including time and talents, at a personal sacrifice. This has never called for a cold equality in the distribution of goods or income, since the needs of different people in different works and services are vastly divergent. However, though the example of ostentatious living by some followers of Jesus have captured attention, there have always been the examples of simple living, hardly more than sustenance existence, by millions of families. It is these who from their meager means supported the construction of the great monuments of faith and the parishes, schools, and shrines which dot the earth. It is they who have given their sons and daughters to the mission fields and kept alive the mission centers where their children worked in poverty, chastity, and obedience. This continuing reality is too often taken for granted.

Gandhi put the notion of property in a few pithy words, saying, "There is enough for everyone's need but not for everyone's greed."

When the Missionaries of Charity began their work in Latin and Central America, going from Venezuela to Peru, then to Argentina, Bolivia, Brazil, Colombia, Panama, and Honduras, Mother Teresa was confronted often with questions about liberation theology. Developed in Latin America, this approach proposed that the struggle to change structures involved the political as well as the spiritual dimension. Mother Teresa had to explain repeatedly that her work was outside politics. Basic to liberation thinking was the "option for the poor," and that option Mother Teresa had taken in a spectacular way by choosing to share the poverty of the poor. The Sisters and Brothers had surely made their own the experience of the world's poorest and had gained insight into their spiritual and material deprivation.

"To know the problem of poverty intellectually," Mother Teresa commented, "is not to understand it. It is not by reading, talking, walking in the slums . . . that we come to understand it and to discover what it has of bad and good. We have to dive into it, live it, share it." Linking everything with the servanthood of Jesus, who took on human agony "and carried it into the darkest night," she went on, "Only by being one with us has He redeemed us. We are allowed to do the same; all the desolation of the poor people, not only their material poverty, but their spiritual destitution must be redeemed."

In answer to a question about justified revolution Mother Teresa replied to a Brazilian journalist that she was in favor of revolution. She went on to say about herself what had already been said of her, that she was a revolutionary, working for a revolution of love. Certainly the Missionaries of Charity were part of this revolution and were moving many to join it, so that the poor and rich could come closer to each other through love. Mother Teresa had the true understanding of revolution, that it must result in a change of relationships, whether between rich and poor, or between powerful and powerless.

She was a countersign in a time when people called for great solutions, solutions starting at the top when power had been seized and rapid changes could be decreed and direst penalties for noncompliance imposed. Mother Teresa gave no overall answers to world economic or political problems. Her solution started at the very bottom. It dealt with the very deepest level of being and was thus the most basic revolution of all. It called for changes within the human heart from which would issue changed relationships with fellow human beings. Out of such changed relationships could come the new structures so needed in oppressive societies described by a leader in liberation thinking, Fr. Gustavo

Gutierrez, as marked by "premature and unjust death." Mother Teresa pointed to the new life possible through changed relationships.

The work of the Sisters and Brothers in their tiny communities offered an insight into what life was supposed to be like "after the revolution"—after the abolition of inequality, competitiveness, and acquisitiveness. Mother Teresa was like a finger pointing to efforts to reach numberless people who had fallen outside structures or had been failed by them. Her experiences pointed to structures that do not yet exist and that others may build, to structures that do not marginalize, that do not ignore, that do not polarize and do not produce refugees. Such structures can only be the fruit of revolutionary love. The Washington *Post* had reminded people at the time of the Nobel Award that there is more than one kind of peace. Mother Teresa was sowing social peace. The editorial also pointed out that politics is not the sole way to pursue peace. Politics involves the exercise of power or the taking of it. Mother Teresa had chosen a more fundamental way to peace. One thought of an old saying, "There is no way to peace; peace is the way."

The fellowship of the table, the community of shared bread, is a concept that binds the human family. The shared meal provides an experience of intimacy and trust, of close personal contact. Jesus in His humanity shared the fellowship of the table with the people of His time, many of them outcasts, known sinners, even tax collectors for the hated occupiers. When He instituted the Eucharistic banquet, Jesus became not only the giver of life to His followers, but the strength to sustain that life. The bread and wine, the body and blood of the resurrected Lord, provided sustenance in time and hope of resurrection beyond time. Mother Teresa reiterated at all times and in all places that it was the Eucharistic banquet, the daily thanksgiving feast, that sustained her and the Sisters and Brothers in their day-in-day-out support of the forlorn members of the human family. The Eucharistic meal also served as a foreshadowing of the messianic feast when humankind would share in the divine fellowship in the reign of God.

Jesus told His followers that in giving a feast they were not to invite relatives or wealthy neighbors who could return the invitation and repay the hospitality. They were to call to their table "the poor, the maimed, and the blind" who could make no recompense. Repayment would be the work of the Lord "at the resurrection of the just."

Mother Teresa responded to poverty and injustice by setting a table around the world for the excluded, the poor, the hungry, the maimed, the blind, the diseased, and the humiliated, for those whose very lives depended on the compassion of others—but who could make no recompense. For those who had seen and experienced the world at its worst, this table provided a glimpse of hope, a glimpse, in fact, of the reign of God.

Those who felt that Mother Teresa's work was like a finger pointing also to peace were aware that her first prescription for peace was simply prayer. The call for prayer made her a countersign for activists brought to near-despair by their fear for the fate of the earth.

A sidelight, humorous but telling, occurred when Mother Teresa crossed into Gaza. Asked at the checkpoint if she was carrying any weapons, she replied, "Oh yes—my prayer books."

Prayer can be seen as the action that is furthest from war.

Prayer speaks the language of powerlessness, since to commend a cause to the Creator is to admit one's creaturehood. Prayer issues from a habit of mind that reserves some actions to the Creator alone. "Vengeance is mine," says the Lord. Prayer helps human beings refrain from actions that are evil in the sight of God. Prayer speaks the language of patience, whose root meaning is suffering.

War expresses man's power, his domination over his kind. Even when the cause is considered just, war gives some human creatures the power to inflict the ultimate penalty on other human creatures. They take away what they cannot give back. War calls for speedy, visible results at whatever cost in destruction.

Mother Teresa urged all people to admit their creaturehood in prayer, repeating on every possible occasion, "Some call Him Ishwar, some call Him Allah, some simply God, but we all have to acknowledge that it is He who made us for greater things; to love and to be loved. What matters is that we love. We cannot love without prayer, and so whatever religion we are, we must pray together." She rejoiced in Calcutta in October 1975 and probably spent some of her happiest days when all the religious groups joined in prayers of thanksgiving for the Silver Jubilee of the Missionaries of Charity. Such an unprecedented outpouring of thanksgiving might have been expected after deliverance from the evils of war or plague, but was unique in thanking the Creator for a work of peace.

Mother Teresa's vision was that as more and more of humanity joined in prayer, they would also join in love since they would be open to the spirit of God which is love. Though she spoke in Christian terms, she advised all not to condemn or judge other people regarding their paths to God. "God has His own ways and means to work in the hearts of men, and we do not know how close they are to Him . . . If the individual thinks and believes that this is the only way to God for her or him, this is the way God comes into their life."

Peace, as Pope John XXIII said in "Pacem in Terris," is a gift of God, and Mother Teresa's first action for peace was to unite as many members of the human family as possible in asking for this greatest of gifts.

God-drenched souls like Mother Teresa or Gandhi did not address themselves to humanists, who might have seemed far from them. Even though prayer did not figure in the humanist prescription for peace, the vision of a humanist like Albert Camus approached that of Mother Teresa and Gandhi in its ethic of compassion. In his address upon receiving the Nobel Prize for literature, Camus talked of the task of the writer in bringing to light the travail of the "subjects of history," the victims who are voiceless and powerless. He used his gift for them by "taking up the word" on their behalf as Mother Teresa had taken up the word and the works of mercy. The ethic of Camus was not far from that of Mother Teresa in its championing of the approach of personal action. "Some say," said Camus, "that hope lies in a nation; others in a man. I believe, rather, that it is awakened, revived, nourished by millions of solitary individuals, whose deeds and works every day negate frontiers and the crudest implications of history. As a result, there shines forth fleetingly the ever-threatened truth that each and every person, on the foundations of his own sufferings and joys, builds for all."

The expression "builds for all" reflected in its widest sense a scriptural concept lived out by Mother Teresa—that we are all "members of one another."

In an age of peril to humanity, members of all Christian communities were urged to work for peace. Members of the Catholic community were told by their spiritual leaders that work for peace was not an option but a task central to the life of faith. Many seemed to ignore the responsibility enjoined on them by "Pacem in Terris" of Pope John XXIII, by the pastoral letter of the world's bishops at the Second Vatican Council, and by peace pastoral letters issued by bishops in France, Japan, Germany, the Netherlands, Ireland, and the United States. Countless humanists, on the other hand, were outstanding in putting their energies at the service of peace, tirelessly and even sacrificially. Their dedication to peace was a reminder of the biblical parable of the two sons, the younger who defied his father, but later carried out the father's command, and the older who agreed to do his father's bidding, but did nothing. Humanists, in their works of peace, recalled the younger son. While Mother Teresa was giving the prescription for peace on the basis of a humanity coming from the hand of a common Father, humanists were working for peace on the basis of a common humanity.

Mother Teresa's other prescriptions for peace, coming from the Sermon on the Mount of Jesus, were a countersign to numberless Christians. Among these prescriptions were the teaching of reconciliation before bringing a gift to the altar, the command against harboring anger, and the command to love the enemy. Some Christians went so far as to claim that the teachings of the Sermon on the Mount were not for the many but for the few, though in St. Luke's gospel, it is clear that Jesus preached the sermon to the multitudes. Some Christian citizens believed in good conscience that its teachings could be suspended, held in abeyance, at the behest of their governments in times of conflict. Judgment cannot be passed on the consciences of others, but there are tenable options that call for differing responses.

Mother Teresa was a voice for forgiveness and reconciliation, saying, "In his passion, Jesus taught us to forgive out of love, how to forget out of humility. So let us examine our hearts and see if there is any unforgiven hurt—any unforgotten bitterness." She described the way to remove anger by allowing the Holy Spirit to enter the human spirit. "The Spirit pours love, peace, joy into our hearts proportionately to our emptying ourselves of self-indulgence, vanity, anger, and ambition, and to our willingness to shoulder the cross of Christ." Shouldering that cross meant sharing the pain and desolation of Jesus' passion—the passion being the price of peacemaking, of reconciling human creatures to their Creator.

More than anyone in the twentieth century, it was Gandhi who made the hard sayings of the Sermon on the Mount known to millions the world over. He wrote, "When I read in the Sermon on the Mount such passages as 'Love your enemies and pray for them that persecute you, that ye may be sons of your Father which is in heaven,' I was overjoyed." He found that it deepened what he found in his beloved "Song of God," the *Bhagavad Gita,* and in a poem he had learned as a child in his home in Gujarat. He gave the sense of the poem: "If a man gives you a drink of water and you give him a drink in return, that is nothing. Real beauty consists in doing good against evil."

"To me," said Gandhi, "the ideas which underlie the Gujarati hymn and the Sermon on the Mount should revolutionize the whole life." To the amazement of the world, Gandhi put flesh on these revolutionary concepts in a nonviolent movement against an occupier whom he could have called "enemy." The fact that he was able to move others to such loving nonviolence in the struggle for justice awakened a world trapped in the mystique of violence. In returning good for evil in the struggle for justice, Gandhi pointed to the first Christians as antecedents. They also had been willing to accept rather than inflict suffering. Gandhi's way seemed irrational to many who lacked his profound faith. The tragedy of India was that as colonialism was a condition of violence, imposed by some on unwilling others, it left a sword behind at its leaving, the sword of partition.

Mother Teresa was one with Gandhi and St. Francis of Assisi in refusing to see anyone as "enemy." She would follow the simple guidance of the

Scriptures in treating anyone who might be termed "enemy," namely by feeding him if he were hungry and giving him to drink if he were thirsty.

"Let us not use bombs and guns to overcome the world," she said. "Let us use love and compassion. Let us preach the peace of Christ as He did. He went about doing good." She went to the heart of the matter when she posed that challenging question, "If everyone could see the image of God in his neighbor, do you think we should still need tanks and generals?"

Once, in my presence, when she was being interviewed by the religion editor of an international magazine, she expressed her conviction on the sacredness of life, even of the unborn. The writer wanted to know if she thought the taking of life was ever justified, in war, for example. She shook her head silently. She could not give assent to the taking of human life.

"But," said the interviewer, "your Church teaches that there can be a just war." Mother Teresa continued to shake her head, indicating the negative. "I can't understand it." The man pursued the subject. "Catholics have to believe that teaching."

Mother Teresa looked at the interviewer and, with a vehemence rare to her, put a question to him, "Then I am not a Catholic?" I imagined St. Francis of Assisi responding in the same way. It was only on being prodded that Mother Teresa became explicit regarding concepts that were implicit in every aspect of her life. Like millions of Christians she would have been hard put to name the conditions of the "just war." The just war age began in the fourth century when St. Augustine grafted just war conditions onto Christian thinking, deriving them from Roman philosophy. These conditions have permitted Christians to obey their rulers in taking up arms in most of the conflicts of history.

In Beirut, Mother Teresa experienced at firsthand how modern weaponry cannot distinguish between combatants and noncombatants, and how the works of mercy are mercilessly reversed.

The Sermon on the Mount opens with the eight Beatitudes, one of which Mother Teresa has made particularly her own, "Happy are the merciful, for they shall obtain mercy." She is seen as the very incarnation of the Beatitude. Her telling phrase, "Jesus in a distressing disguise," was her explanation of how she could deal with, and love, those found repulsive by most people.

In the social organization for destruction called war, the enemy is dehumanized, even diabolized. Could not Mother Teresa's insistence on the stamp of the divine in every human creature be supremely relevant to an age which prepares for conflict by first diabolizing the opponent? Could it not be crucially necessary at a time when the evils of a governmental system are ascribed to its citizens so that they cease to be seen as children of God? Could not Mother Teresa be like a finger pointing to the most impenetrable disguise of all, the divinity disguised in the "enemy?"

Might not the destiny of a nuclear-fragile world be changed if greater numbers of Christians penetrated this disguise, so potentially lethal, and refused to accept that the stamp of the divine could ever be eradicated, or that the people of an opposing nation could be anything but the children of God?

Only by refusing commands to reverse the works of mercy could Christians begin to serve as the reconciling community for mankind. The fear that pervades mankind would be lessened as greater numbers of Christians signified their unwillingness to accept the concept of "enemy" or to take part in the works of war. By breaking through the disguise of "enemy," the Christian would see that the person on whom he is called upon to inflict starvation, thirst, nakedness, homelessness, and all manner of suffering is Jesus.

At a time when there is no dearth of just causes, but also no dearth of fearful means of warfare, many are reminded of the rainbow sign which ended the Deluge—the sign that the Creator would not again disturb the operation of nature so as to destroy the earth. Man himself now has found the power to threaten humankind and its earthly home.

Mother Teresa has made people pause by reminding them by her life and by her words to be mindful always of the parable of the Last Judgment, when Jesus would reveal that it was He who was the very least of humankind. How often she repeated the message of Jesus, 'I am the hungry one, I am the naked one, the thirsty, homeless, suffering one.' Reminded of this parable, many Christians have come to realize that by neglecting or by taking part in the reversal of the works of mercy, they might be faced with an accusing Christ who could say, 'I was the hungry one, the thirsty one, the naked one, the suffering one brought low by your mercilessness.' There is an element of surprise in the parable, a surprise caused precisely by the failure to recognize Jesus in the person of the very least.

Mother Teresa's vision of the street, which drove her out among those rotting with disease and wracked with pain, came from the light of the Incarnation. It came from an awareness of the inbreaking of the divine in human history. Seeing every human being bathed in this light, she found joy in serving each person as a repository of the divine. This vision, expressed on the streets of Calcutta, brought mercy to streets which hardly understood her vision. In the nuclear age, such a vision is needed on all the streets of the world which might be engulfed in pitiless, indiscriminate destruction. Mother Teresa incarnated a message of life that ran counter to the laws of many nations and to the arms stockpiles targeted on this or that segment of the human family.

Kali, in her temple beside the Home for the Dying, stood as a reminder of an ancient belief that the world was to be purified by fire. This belief, arising from a different tradition, has been taking hold in the West among many groups of Christians. Mother Teresa, with her message of unconditional love, was a countersign. The poor woman, aging and wrinkled, her worn-out body wrapped in the cheapest of coverings, offered the hope that the world was not condemned, that a world created out of love, and redeemed by love, might also be purified by love.

APPENDICES

APPENDIX A

A Matter of Conscience

An Open Letter of Mother Teresa of Calcutta to Mr. Morarji Desai, Prime Minister of India, and the Members of the Indian Parliament, Regarding the Freedom of Religion Bill 1978.

Dear Mr. Desai and Members of our Parliament,

After much prayer and sacrifices I write to you asking you to face God in prayer, before you take the step which will destroy the joy and the freedom of our people.

Our people—as you know better than I—are God-fearing people. In whatever way you approach them, the presence of God—the fear of God is there. Today all over the country everybody feels insecure because the very life of conscience is being touched.

Religion is not something that you and I can touch. Religion is the worship of God, therefore, a matter of conscience. I alone must decide for myself and you for yourself what we choose. For me this is my very life, my joy, and the greatest gift of God in His love for me. He could have given me no greater gift.

I love my people very much, more than myself, and so naturally I would wish to give them the joy of possessing this treasure, but it is not mine to give, nor can I force it on anyone. So also no man, no law, no Government has the right to prevent me nor force me nor anyone, if I choose to embrace the religion that gives me peace, joy, love.

I was told that Gandhiji had said: "If the Christians would live their lives according to the teaching of Jesus Christ there would be no Hindus left in India." You cannot give what you do not have.

This new move that is being brought before the Parliament under the cover of freedom of religion is false. There is no freedom if a person is not free to choose according to his or her conscience. Our people in Arunachal are so disturbed. All these years our people have lived together in peace. Now religion is used as a deadly weapon to destroy the love they had for each other, just because some are Christians, some Hindus, some Tribals. Are you not afraid of God?

You call Him ISHWAR, some call Him ALLAH, some simply GOD, but we all have to acknowledge that it is HE who made us for greater things: to love and to be loved. Who are we to prevent our people to find this God who made them—who loves them—to whom they have to return?

You took over your sacred duty in the name of God—acknowledging God's supreme right over our country and her people. It was so beautiful. But now I am afraid for you. I am afraid for our people. Abortion being allowed has brought so much hatred, for if a mother can murder her own child, what is left for others to kill each other. You do not know what abortion has done and is doing to our people. There is so much immorality, so many broken homes, so much mental disturbance because of the murder of the innocent unborn child, in the conscience of the mother. You don't know how much evil is spread everywhere.

Mr. Desai, you are so close to meeting God face-to-face. I wonder what answer you will give for allowing the destruction of the life of the innocent unborn child and destroying the freedom to serve God, according to one's choice and belief. At the hour of death, I believe we will be judged according to the words of Jesus who has said:

> I was hungry, you gave Me food,
> I was thirsty, you gave Me to drink,
> I was homeless, you took Me in,
> I was naked, you clothed Me,
> I was sick, you took care of Me,
> I was in prison, you visited Me.
>
> Truly I say to you, for as long as you did it to those the least of my brothers, you did it to Me.

Gandhiji has also said: "He who serves the poor, serves God."

I spend hours and hours in serving the sick and the dying, the unwanted, the unloved, the lepers, the mental—because I love God and I believe His word: "You did it to Me." This is the only reason and the joy of my life: to love and serve Him in the distressing disguise of the poor, the unwanted, the hungry, the thirsty, the naked, the homeless, and naturally, in doing so, I proclaim His love and compassion for each one of my suffering brothers and sisters.

Mr. Desai and Members of Parliament, in the name of God, do not destroy the freedom our country and people have had, to serve and love God according to their conscience and belief. Do not belittle our Hindu religion saying that our Hindu poor people give up their religion for "a plate of rice." To my knowledge, I have not seen this being done though thousands have died in our hands beautifully in peace with God.

I remember I picked up a destitute from the street who was nearly eaten up with maggots. He said gratefully: "I have lived like an animal in the street—but I am going to die like an angel, loved and cared for." And he died a beautiful death, loved and cared for and in peace with God. I have always made it my rule to cooperate wholeheartedly with the central and state governments in all undertakings which are for the good of our people. You will be glad to know that we are cooperating very earnestly in helping in family limitations through morally sound means. In Calcutta alone we have 102 centers where families are taught self-control out of love. Here we promote the moral, legal, and scientific method of natural family planning. From 1971 to 1978 we have helped 11,701 Hindu families, 5,568 Muslims and 4,341 Christian families. Through this natural and beautiful method there have been 61,397 less babies born.

Turning to another sad point I wish to inform you that I have been trying to get into Arunachal Pradesh for some time now, but so far I have not succeeded and yet Ramakrishna Mission members are entering freely. We are in 87 places in India. Why are we not with our poor in Arunachal?

I pray and I beg you that you order a day of prayer throughout the country. The Catholics of our country have called an all-India day of fast, prayer, and sacrifice on Friday 6th April to maintain peace and communal harmony and to ensure that India lives up to its noble tradition of religious freedom. I request you to propose a similar day of intercession for all communities of our country—that we may obtain peace, unity, and love; that we become one heart full of love and so become the sunshine of God's love, the hope of eternal happiness, and the burning flame of God's love and compassion in our families, our country, and in the world.

God bless you,
M. Teresa M.C.

The Happiest Day

A long-held desire of Mother Teresa's was finally realized on January 20, 1985, when she arrived in Peking.

"The Chinese Government could not have been kinder," she related to me. "They helped me in every way during the three days that I was there. I went to mass in Peking at the Cathedral of the Immaculate Conception. It was said by an old priest—he was seventy-eight. He said a beautiful Latin mass. There were many people at the mass, early in the morning.

"The government people arranged for me to discuss things with the son of the leader of China. He was in a wheelchair."

The crippled man was Deng Pufang, son of Deng Xiaoping, China's premier and most powerful leader. As deputy director of China's Welfare Fund for the Handicapped, Deng Pufang had concerns similar to those of Mother Teresa. He had a broken back as a result of being thrown out of a window by Red Guards during the Cultural Revolution.

Deng Pufang praised Mother Teresa's "tremendous work for poor people." He had become a spokesperson for China's handicapped people, estimated to number 20 million, and he outlined his government's efforts on their behalf. He was probably not prepared for the direction the discussion took. According to reports of the interview, Deng stated, "Although we start from a different standpoint, we're doing the same work."

Through the interpreter, Mother Teresa responded, "It is the same standpoint. Out of love for God in action."

"Regardless of social system, we are doing the same thing for the same purpose. I myself am an atheist," Deng countered.

Mother Teresa, however, was insistent.

"The same loving hand has created you and me," she asserted. "What you do is your love for God in action. You put that desire into action and that is love."

A photograph of the interview shows Mother Teresa and Deng Pufang smiling amiably. Deng informed Mother Teresa that there were sixteen hundred state workshop-factories for the handicapped and arranged for her to visit one of them near Peking. After viewing the work of over two hundred workers, many of them blind, she wrote "God bless you all" in the visitors' book and promised prayers for the blind foreman. When she asked him to reciprocate, Wang Jingsheng responded, "We owe everything to the Communist Party."

After seeing one of the collectives run by the handicapped, Mother Teresa pointed out that though the Chinese Government had an extensive welfare program, her Sisters could provide "tender love and care" for the most needy. She was hopeful that, with the help of Bishop Michael Fu Tienshan of the National Association of Patriotic Catholics, an invitation would reach her so that Missionaries of Charity could work somewhere in the great expanse of China.

The bishop told her, "You are a good daughter of God and have done a lot of good in helping the poor and disabled, It is good work." In spite of the fact that the Patriotic Church had to break its ties to the Vatican in 1949 after the Communists took power, its sacraments were considered valid when performed by validly ordained priests. Mother Teresa received the Eucharist from the Chinese clergy during her stay. Though belief in God is discouraged by official Chinese policy, religious practices are permitted.

No invitation resulted from Mother Teresa's visit, but a team of Sisters would be ready to respond with lightning speed. Very possibly, young women of Chinese origin, of whom there were many in the Missionaries of Charity, would be members of the team.

When she was asked later, "Mother Teresa, what is a Communist to you?" her reply was, "A child of God, my brother, my sister."

"Ethiopia is like an open Calvary," Mother Teresa said on a visit during 1985 to a land where drought and war brought mass dying and desolation. She had been visiting eight teams of Sisters, most of them in the refugee centers where the starving gathered for relief food. At Alamata she saw, despite all efforts, four children die before her eyes. She conferred with government agencies and the staff of Catholic Relief Services about an intensification of feeding and medical programs. To the Ethiopian Government Relief Commission, Mother Teresa presented an unexpected proposal: the conversion of the palace of the former Emperor Haile Selassie into a home for those near death from starvation. The authorities promised to consider it. She met with Bob Geldof, the Dublin-born singer who led musicians in "Live Aid," the immensely successful famine relief campaign. Geldof related how impressed he was by Mother Teresa's way of approaching government officials. He saw her ask for, and receive, an empty building, not the palace, for an orphanage.

"Having the moral power and having nothing to gain by it," was what particularly impressed Geldof. "It's the whole thing, I realized when I saw Mother Teresa work in Ethiopia," he recounted. "She is the epitome of moral good."

When the famine emergency had abated, 7 million people threatened with death by starvation were saved; another million had perished.

When Mother Teresa attended the International Eucharistic Congress in Nairobi, Kenya, in mid-August 1985, she became a magnet figure as she had been at the Philadelphia Congress nine years earlier. She had a refuge, since she could steal away to a poor corner of the capital among the orphans and destitute cared for by her Sisters.

When she spoke to thousands of persons in the Nyayo Stadium on "Feeding the Starving," Margaret Cullis, a lay Co-Worker, reported there was weeping in the audience. Mother Teresa called on all present to accept pain and suffering, and thus help afflicted people accept and make an offering of their own suffering. Those called upon to suffer, she told them, can see themselves as the chosen ones. On the following day, Mother Teresa was the speaker at the Kenyatta International Conference Center, bringing the message of merciful love and the dignity of suffering to the throng assembled in Nairobi from the African continent and from around the globe.

Returning to Calcutta, Mother Teresa marked her seventy-fifth birthday on August 26, passing it quietly with her Sisters in prayer and in the daily immersion in the lives of the poorest of the poor of the great city, the slum schools, the children's home, the medical clinics and service to the lepers in the *bustees*, and the work in the Home for the Dying.

Mother Teresa was preparing for the General Chapter of the Missionaries of Charity, a gathering held every six years. On September 22, 1985, she brought to her side at the Motherhouse on Lower Circular Road sixty-eight Sisters from around the globe. With her were Sisters serving as Regional Superiors of fifteen regions and delegates elected from each of these regions. In Calcutta were six Councillors who served in the city and helped Mother Teresa conduct the affairs of the congregation. A retreat in the stark chapel of the Motherhouse, before the crucifix and the words I THIRST, preceded the General Chapter.

Probably no gathering of women anywhere in the world had more intimate acquaintance with the wounds and sufferings of the human family than these Missionaries of Charity. On October 7, there was an election for the Superior General of the Missionaries of Charity. Mother Teresa was elected as Superior General of the congregation she had founded on that date thirty-five years earlier; Sister Agnes was elected Assistant General. The other Councillors were Sister Priscilla, Sister Shanti, Sister Camillus, Sister Dorothy, and Sister Andrea. All had worked in Calcutta during the first twenty years of the congregation. They had known the agonies of those rescued from the street who could cry out with Job, "My flesh is clothed with worms and scabs and my skin cracks and festers." They had learned, as had Mother Teresa, another poverty, the poverty of the West, where, in more affluent settings, people were withering away from loneliness and perishing from humiliation and rejection.

"There is not only hunger for food," Mother Teresa kept repeating; "I see a big hunger for love. That is the greatest hunger, to be loved."

Mother Teresa and the Councillors would guide the Missionaries of Charity for the coming six years, until 1991. Around the world, young women were filling the six novitiates in Manila, Tabora (Tanzania), San Francisco, Warsaw, and Rome, as well as Calcutta. Sister Andrea, in charge of the Calcutta novitiate, was also in touch with the novitiate overseas.

Just before the opening of the General Chapter, on September 20, the priest with whom Mother Teresa had made her 1946 retreat after her time of discernment on the train to Darjeeling died. Fr. Pierre Fallon was honored by impressive memorials, not only by the Catholics of Calcutta, but by large numbers of Bengalis grateful for his devotion to Bengali culture. Fiery Fr. Robert Antoine, his fellow champion of Bengali language and culture, had preceded him in death, receiving one of the largest public funerals ever accorded a Christian minister in Calcutta. Only Fr. Celeste Van Exem, close to Mother Teresa in age, was still alive.

Mother Teresa, a documentary by Ann and Jeanette Petrie on the work of the Missionaries of Charity, had its premiere in the General Assembly Hall of the United Nations. The occasion was "A Salute to Mother Teresa," and the date, October 26, 1985, was the final day of the Fortieth Anniversary Week of the United Nations. The UN Secretary-General, Xavier Pérez de Cuellar, introduced the small, stooped figure of Mother Teresa, saying, "This is a hall of words. A few days ago, we had on this rostrum the most powerful men in the world. Now we have the privilege to have the most powerful woman in the world. She is peace in the world."

Mother Teresa stood at the same green marble podium from which over sixty prime ministers, presidents, foreign ministers, a sultan, a chancellor, and some members of royalty had spoken. She asked for prayer.

Noting that 1986 had been designated as the World Year of Peace, Mother Teresa began, "Let us say together the prayer for peace. Works of love are works of peace." The peace prayer of St. Francis of Assisi had been distributed to all in the packed chamber.

"If we have the joy of seeing God in each other," she continued, "we will love one another. That is why no color, no religion, no nationality should come between us, for we are all children of the same loving hand of God—created for greater things, to love and be loved. We all want peace. We are frightened of nuclear war; we are frightened of this terrible new disease, but we are not frightened to kill an innocent child, the little unborn child who has been created for the same purpose."

Mother Teresa's defense of the unborn drew questions from reporters during her visit, questions concerning the defense of life in general. Asked about the nuclear arms race, she responded, "I don't know much about that, but I know that anything that destroys life is evil." To a reporter who raised the question of the just war she commented, "War is killing human beings. How could this be just? How could war be just?" Mother Teresa made a rare public appeal on behalf of life when she sent a wire from Rome, early in 1986, to the governor of South Carolina. She asked that a young man whose crime of murder was committed when he was under eighteen years of age be saved from the electric chair. Her appeal failed to halt the execution.

❧

The "terrible new disease" referred to by Mother Teresa at the United Nations was called AIDS (acquired immune deficiency syndrome). It recalled the work at the Home for the Dying in Kalighat.

"I never expected that I would open a Kalighat in New York," Mother Teresa remarked to me. "When I heard that people were dying of this disease, I knew we must do something. We care for the dying in Kalighat and that must be our work in New York, too. I found that the dying are mostly young men, and that some of them are dying in prison. I told Cardinal O'Connor that our Sisters would do the work."

Victims of AIDS, chiefly homosexual men, drug users infected by contaminated needles, and hemophiliacs and hospital patients transfused with infected blood, have been feared and shunned. The disease, descending like a plague on such cities as New York and San Francisco, aroused the same dread as had leprosy in earlier ages.

On Christmas Eve, 1985, we saw Mother Teresa help a small man up the steps into a hospice in New York's Greenwich Village. He had come to die. The hospice was called "Gift of Love" and was run by four Missionaries of Charity. It was for patients in the final stages of AIDS, the affliction whose inexorable course toward death could not be halted by any medical means.

The opening of an AIDS hospice was a triumph for Mother Teresa, since plans to open such a center in other localities had been rebuffed by residents.

The little man, Ramon Galvan, enjoyed the attention he received as Mother Teresa settled him in the lounge. He was agreeted by the mayor of New York City, Edward Koch, Cardinal John O'Connor, and a group of dignitaries. He was the first of many prisoners with AIDS furloughed to the care of the Missionaries of Charity. Already over 150 victims of the disease had died behind prison walls.

Mother Teresa explained why she wanted the opening to be on Christmas Eve. "Then Jesus was born, so I wanted to help them to be born again in joy and love and peace. We are hoping that they will be able to live and die in peace by getting tender love and care, because each one of them is Jesus in a distressing disguise." The words "distressing disguise" took me back three decades to the Home for the Dying in Calcutta.

Ramon chatted happily with the guests, including Fr. Joseph Langford, just professed in St. Patrick's Cathedral as the first of two Missionary Fathers of Charity. When someone suggested that perhaps Ramon was too tired to talk, he said with a bright smile, "Oh, I love to talk."

"I made a mistake with the drugs," the little man explained, but he seemed at ease and at home.

Sister Dolores, the superior of the hospice, gave the patients the same sensitive, tender care she had given when she worked at Kalighat. There was a tragic difference in that while more than half of the patients in Calcutta survived to take up life anew, the sentence on those entering the hospice was irrevocable. It was not long before Ramon Galvan died, passing his last days in St. Clare's Hospital, which supported the hospice with expert medical services. The patients regularly released to the Missionaries of Charity knew gentle, loving care before death took them. When returned temporarily for hospital care, the patients asked to be allowed to "go home" to the hospice.

The opening of the AIDS hospice seemed to open many hearts.

"So many people have come forward," Mother Teresa told me. "It is beautiful. I have letters from people who are ready to give a house for the work. People are asking me to open a house in San Francisco. I hear that there are babies and little children who have the disease. I want to open a home for them."

Mother Teresa was back in Kalighat, Calcutta, in February 1986. By her side was a visitor to India who had initiated his stay by quoting Gandhi: "Conquer hate by love, untruth by truth, violence by suffering." The visitor, Pope John Paul II, went with Mother Teresa from pallet to pallet. He bent down to feed some of the weakest patients. He greeted each of the more than one hundred patients in the men's and women's wards, taking their heads between his hands or placing his arm around their shoulders. Conversations were translated. "Come to visit us again," said an old lady. In the little morgue, Pope John Paul blessed the bodies of four who died before friendly hands could save them, three men and a boy.

The photograph of the spiritual father of some 650 million Catholics leaning over the wasted body of a forsaken man, feeding and consoling him, went around the world. It was the ultimate validation of a work that proclaimed that mercy, as love under the aspect of need, was the heart of the Christian message. Mother Teresa, in translating into daily action the vision of mercy that spoke of the sacred, inviolable dignity of every least member of the human family, had a most powerful ally.

"I have had many happy days, but this," said Mother Teresa, "is the happiest day of my life."

In the Silence of the Heart God Speaks—Mother Teresa on Prayer

INTERVIEWER: "Mother Teresa, you love people whom others regard as human debris. What is your secret?"

MOTHER TERESA: "My secret is quite simple. I pray."

It was the apostles who asked Jesus: "Jesus, teach us how to pray"—because they saw Him so often pray and they knew that He was talking to His Father. What those hours of prayer must have been—we know only from that continual love of Jesus for His Father, "My Father!" And He taught His disciples a very simple way of talking to God Himself.

Before Jesus came God was great in His majesty, great in His creation. And then when Jesus came He became one of us, because His Father loved the world so much that He gave His Son. And Jesus loved His Father and He wanted us to learn to pray by loving one another as the Father has loved Him.

"I love you," He kept on saying, "as the Father loved you, love Him." And His love was the cross, His love was the bread of life. And He wants us to pray with a clean heart, with a simple heart, with a humble heart. "Unless you become little children you cannot learn to pray, you cannot enter heaven, you cannot see God." To become a little child means to be one with the Father, to love the Father, to be at peace with the Father, our Father.

Prayer is nothing but that being in the family, being one with the Father in the Son to the Holy Spirit. The love of the Father for His Son—the Holy Spirit. And the love, our love for the Father, through Jesus, His Son, filled with the Holy Spirit, is our union with God, and the fruit of that union with God, the fruit of that prayer—what we call prayer. We have given that name but actually prayer is nothing but that oneness with Christ.

As St. Paul has said, "I live no longer I, but Christ lives in me." Christ prays in me, Christ works in me, Christ thinks of me, Christ looks through my eyes, Christ speaks through my words, Christ works with my hands, Christ walks with my feet, Christ loves with my heart. As St. Paul's prayer was, "I belong to Christ and nothing will separate me from the love of Christ." It was that oneness: oneness with God, oneness with the Master in the Holy Spirit.

And if we really want to pray we must first learn to listen, for in the silence of the heart God speaks. And to be able to hear that silence, to be able to hear God we need a clean heart; for a clean heart can see God, can hear God, can listen to God; and then only from the fullness of our heart can we speak to God. But we cannot speak unless we have listened, unless we have made that connection with God in the silence of our heart.

And so prayer is not meant to be a torture, not meant to make us feel uneasy, is not meant to trouble us. It is something to look forward to, to talk to my Father, to talk to Jesus, the one to whom I belong: body, soul, mind, heart.

And when times come when we can't pray, it is very simple: if Jesus is in my heart let him pray, let me allow Him to pray in me, to talk to His Father in the silence of my heart. Since I cannot speak—He will speak; since I cannot pray—He will pray. That's why often we should say: "Jesus in my heart, I believe in your faithful love for me, I love you." And often we should be in that unity with Him and allow Him, and when we have nothing to give—let us give Him that nothingness. When we cannot pray —let us give that inability to Him. There is one more reason to let Him pray in us to the Father. Let us ask Him to pray in us, for no one knows the Father better than He. No one can pray better than Jesus. And if my heart is pure, if in my heart Jesus is alive, if my heart is a tabernacle of the living God to sanctify in grace: Jesus and I are one. He prays in me, He thinks in me, He works with me and through me, He uses my tongue to speak, He uses my brain to think, He uses my hands to touch Him in the broken body.

And for us who have the precious gift of Holy Communion every day, that contact with Christ is our prayer; that love for Christ, that joy in His presence, that surrender to His love for Christ, that joy in His presence, that surrender to His love is our prayer. For prayer is nothing but that complete surrender, complete oneness with Christ.

And this is what makes us contemplatives in the heart of the world; for we are twenty-four hours then in His presence: in the hungry, in the naked, in the homeless, in the unwanted, unloved, uncared; for Jesus said: Whatever you do to the least of my brethren, you do it to me."

Therefore doing it to Him, we are praying the work; for in doing it with Him, doing it for Him, doing it to Him we are loving Him; and in loving

Him we come more and more into that oneness with Him and we allow Him to live His life in us. And this living of Christ in us is holiness.

Excerpted from talk
of June 8, 1980
Berlin

APPENDIX B

Missionaries of Charity Worldwide—SISTERS

(Foundations Outside India)

1965 Cocorote, Venezuela

1968 Rome, Italy (Vicolo Tor Fiscale)
Tabora, Tanzania

1969 Bourke, Australia
Melbourne, Australia

1970 Catia La Mar, Venezuela
Amman, Jordan
Marin, Venezuela
Southhall, London, England

1971 London W.9, England
Bronx, New York, USA

1972 Khulna, Bangladesh
Dacca, Bangladesh
Mauritius
Belfast, Northern Ireland

1973 Gaza, Israel
Katherine, Australia
Hodeida, Yemen Arab Republic
Lima, Peru
Addis Ababa, Ethiopia

1974 Hanuabada, Papua New Guinea
Palermo, Sicily, Italy
Tokarara, Papua New Guinea
Ta'izz, Yemen Arab Republic
Mausaid, Bangladesh

1975 Naples, Italy
Ciudad Guayana, Venezuela

1976 Sanaa, Yemen Arab Republic
Rome, Italy (Pza San Gregorio al Cielo)
Mexico City, Mexico
Guatemala City, Guatemala
Bronx, New York, USA (Contemplative)
Dar es Salaam, Tanzania

1977 Kerema, Papua New Guinea
Binondo Manila, Philippines
Tabora, Tanzania (Novitiate)
London E.1, England
Haiti, West Indies
Rotterdam, Netherlands
Dire Dawa, Ethiopia

1978 Sylhet, Bangladesh
Metro-Manila, Philippines
Caracas, Venezuela
Zarate, Argentina
Liverpool, England
Dodoma, Tabora, Tanzania
El Dorado, Panama

1979 Beirut, Lebanon
Reggio Calabria, Italy
Essen, West Germany
Zagreb, Yugoslavia
Corato (Bari), Italy
St. Louis, Missouri, USA
Detroit, Michigan, USA
Toluca, Mexico
Salvador-Bahia, Brazil
Chimbote, Peru
Nairobi, Kenya
Sanfil, Haiti
Kigali, Rwanda
Ragusa, Italy

1980 Tezgaon, Bangladesh
Ghent, Belgium
Bereina, Papua New Guinea
Katmandu, Nepal

Refugee Camp, Jijiga, Ethiopia
Ghent, Belgium
Marseilles, France
Skopje, Yugoslavia
Madrid, Spain
Esquina, Argentina
Miami, Florida, USA
Santiago, Chile
Via Casalina, Rome, Italy
Primavalle, Rome, Italy

1981 Washington, D.C., USA
Newark, New Jersey, USA
Harlem, New York City, USA
Santo Domingo, Dominican Republic
Las Matas, Dominican Republic
Jacmel, Haiti
La Paz, Bolivia
Cucuta, Colombia
Batuco, Chile
East Berlin, Germany
Cairo, Egypt
Alexandria, Egypt
Belabo, Cameroon
Jijiga, Ethiopia
Tokyo, Japan
Seoul, South Korea
Macao
Queanbeyan, Australia

1982 Gangtok, Sikkim
Setubal, Portugal
Florence, Italy
Barcelona, Spain
Dublin, Ireland
Queanbeyan, Australia
Jenkins, Kentucky (Appalachia), USA
San Francisco, California, USA
Tampico, Mexico
Rio de Janeiro, Brazil
Kaffa, Ethiopia
Giteranyi, Burundi

1983 Barisol, Bangladesh
Kowloon, Hong Kong
Jérémie, Haiti
West Berlin, West Germany
Ǩogali, Rwanda
Chicago, Illinois, USA
Livingston, Scotland
Davao City, Philippines
Calbayog, Philippines
Darwin, Australia
Tegucigalpa, Honduras
Port Victoria, Seychelles
Little Rock, Arkansas, USA
Bujumbura, Burundi

1984 Mokochung, Assam
Warsaw, Poland
Karl-Marx-Stadt, East Germany
Winnipeg, Manitoba, Canada
Colombo, Sri Lanka
Norristown, Pennsylvania, USA

Damascus, Syria; Lahore, Pakistan; Glasgow, Scotland; and Singapore were among the houses opened by the Missionaries of Charity during 1985 and 1986. The number of houses, including those in India, rose to 330.

Missionaries of Charity Worldwide—BROTHERS

(Foundations Outside India)

1975 Los Angeles, California, USA

1976 Los Angeles, California, USA

1977 Hong Kong
Seoul, South Korea
Santa Ana, California, USA
Los Angeles, California, USA

1978 Taiwan
Tokyo, Japan
Las Escobas, Guatemala

1979	Macao San Salvador, El Salvador
1980	Guatemala City, Guatemala Santiago, Dominican Republic Pusan, South Korea
1981	Paris, France Manila, Philippines Port-au-Prince, Haiti Kwangju, South Korea São Paulo, Brazil
1982	Antananarivo, Madagascar
1983	Lima, Peru Stockholm, Sweden Inchon, South Korea
1984	Bogota, Colombia Addis Ababa, Ethiopia Kenya Mexico City, Mexico La Paz, Bolivia Tabora, Tanzania Houston, Texas, USA Philadelphia, Pennsylvania, USA Manchester, England
1985	Helsinki, Finland Noto, Sicily Taejon, Korea El Quiche, Guatemala Tegucigalpa, Honduras Addis Ababa, Ethiopia Nairobi, Kenya Dodoma, Tanzania Port Louis, Mauritius Surigao, Philippines Antsirabe, Madagascar Singapore

APPENDIX C

International Association of Co-Workers of Mother Teresa

Mother Teresa M.C.

Missionaries of Charity, 54A Lower Circular Road, Calcutta 700016, India

Brother Andrew M.C.

Missionaries of Charity Brothers, 7 Mansatala Row, Kidderpore, Calcutta 700023, India

M.C. CORRESPONDENTS:

Co-Workers' General

Sr. M. Joseph Michael M.C., Missionaries of Charity, 90 Park Street, Calcutta 700017, India

Vocations—SISTERS

Sr. M. Cabrini M.C., 54A Lower Circular Road, Calcutta 700016, India
In USA—Missionaries of Charity, 335 East 145th Street, Bronx, New York 10451

—BROTHERS

Brother Andrew M.C. (address above)
In USA—Missionaries of Charity Brothers, 1600 Ingraham Street, Los Angeles, California 90017

Adoptions

Sr. Margaret Mary M.C., 78 Lower Circular Road, Calcutta 700016, India

CO-WORKERS:

International Link

Mrs. Ann Blaikie, Stone Cottage, Wonersh, Near Guildford, Surrey, GU5 0PE, England

Link with Contemplative Orders

Sr. Nirmala M.C., Missionaries of Charity, 34 Aberdeen Street, Brooklyn, New York, 11207

International Co-Links (Editors)	Dr. Warren and Mrs. Patty Kump, 4243 Glenwood Avenue, Minneapolis, Minnesota 55422
Link with Sick and Suffering	Mlle. Jacqueline de Decker, Karmel Ooms. St. 14, 2018 Antwerp, Belgium
Medical Co-Workers	Francesco De Raimondo, M.D. Via Giovanni Antonelli 21 00197 Rome, Italy
Links for Relief Supplies	Mr. Gerrit Jan and Mrs. Val Colenbrander, 10 Noltheniusstraat, 3533, SH Utrecht, Netherlands
Links with Youth	Mr. Tony and Mrs. Lillian Miceli Ferrugia, Villa Elena, Ta X'biex, Malta
National Link—USA	Mrs. Vi Collins, 5106 Battery Lane, Bethesda, Maryland 20814
Missionaries of Charity, Fathers	Rev. Joseph Langford, 75 West 168th Street, Bronx, New York 10452

For addresses of National Links around the world contact Mrs. Ann Blaikie (address on previous page)

APPENDIX D

MISSIONARIES OF CHARITY—U.S.A.

SISTERS

1971 South Bronx, New York/335 East 145th Street 10451

1976 Bronx, New York/1070 Union Street (Contemplatives)

1979 Miami, Florida/727 N.W. 17th 33136
Detroit, Michigan/4835 Lincoln Street 48208
St. Louis, Missouri/3817 Maffit Street 63113

1980 East Bronx, New York/338 East 146th Street 10451

1981 Newark, New Jersey/168 Sussex Street 07103
Harlem, New York/406 127th Street 10027
Washington, D.C./3310 Wheeler Road S.E. 20052
Washington, D.C./1244 V Street S.E. 20020 (Contemplatives)

1982 San Francisco, California/312 29th Street 94131 (Novitiate)
Jenkins, Kentucky/P.O. Box 883 41537
Brooklyn, New York/34 Aberdeen Street 11207 (Contemplatives)

1983 Little Rock, Arkansas/1014 South Oak Street 72204
Chicago, Illinois/115 North Oakley 60612

1984 Norristown, Pennsylvania 630 De Kalb Street 19401
1985 Baton Rouge, Louisiana/St. Agnes Church, 349 East Boulevard 70802
New York, New York/657 Washington Street 10014
1986 Chicago, Illinois/1629 S. Allport (Contemplative)

BROTHERS

1975 Los Angeles, California/144 North Edgeware Road 90026

1977 Los Angeles, California/1600 Ingraham 90017
Santa Ana, California/1921 West Washington Avenue 92706

Index